Mixed Sources
Product group from well-managed
forests and other controlled sources
www.fsc.org Cert no. SA-COC-1565
© 1996 Forest Stewardship Council
FSC

Designed by Consider. www
Printed and bound in Great

SPOTLIGHT

MANAGING PARTNER
Ben Seale

EDITOR
Kate Poynton

DESIGN & EDITION LAYOUT
Kathy Norrish

ADVERTISING SALES
Frances Mordue 020 7440 5061

ACCOUNTS
Claire Adams – Chief Financial Officer
Nas Fokeerchand – Head of Accounts
Amelia Barnham Tanya Doganci Laura Ruocco

CASTING
Joe Bates – Head of Rooms & Studios
Nicholas Peel Sara Sehdev Liam Simpson Kittie Story

CLIENT RELATIONS
Pippa Harrison – Head of Client Relations
Emma Dyson Gary Andrews

CUSTOMER RELATIONS
Laura Albery – Head of Customer Relations
Sally Barnham
Elaine Compton Faye Maitland Joan Queva Elinor Samuels

DATA PROCESSING
Joanna MacLeod – Head of Data Processing
Amanda Lawrence Emma Lear Sharon Mulcahy Caroline Taylor

DIGITAL DEVELOPMENT
Gary Broughton – Head of Digital

EDITORIAL
Cindy Lemmer
Angela Cottrell (Editor, Case Studies & Information Pages) Martin Pavey

HR
Marylin Peach – Head of HR & Facilities
Luke Turvey

IT
Jay Johnston – Chief Technical Officer
Dylan Beattie – Head of IT
Dave Clements Christina Kassimatis Adrian Wardle Dan Woodhead

IT SYSTEMS
Paul Goldsmith – Operations Manager
Nicola Fahy Craig Osborne

MARKETING & SALES
Laura Albery – Head of Marketing & Sales
Kelly Taylor Kate Tozer

PRODUCTION
Neill Kennedy
Louise Fairweather Hannah Frankel Nick Goldfinch David McCarthy

C →

Contents

Contents

N

O

P

R

S

T

U

A →

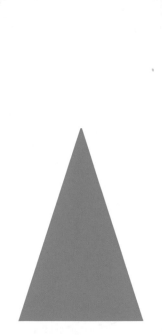

PMA

For information regarding membership of the Personal Managers' Association please contact:

T 0845 6027191
E info@thepma.com
W www.thepma.com

CPMA

For information regarding membership of the Co-operative Personal Management Association please contact The Secretary:

T 07876 641582
E cpmauk@yahoo.co.uk
W www.cpma.coop

Members of the above organisations are clearly marked as such in the appropriate listings.

Accountants, Insurance & Law

Why might I need this section?

This section contains listings for a number of companies and services which exist to help performers with the day-to-day administration of their working lives. Performers need to manage their business affairs personally, in ways that those in 'normal' jobs do not. For example, unlike most employees, a performer does not have an accounts department to work out their tax and national insurance, or an HR department to take care of contracts or health insurance on their behalf. On top of which, performers can often be away on tour or on set for many months and unable to attend to these matters themselves.

Areas covered in this section include:

Accountants and other financial services

Dedicated companies exist which can help you to manage key financial issues, including national insurance, taxation, benefits, savings and pensions. Specialist mortgage companies also exist for performers and other self-employed workers within the entertainment industry. Specific information about accountancy services is also provided in this section's case study. If you are a member of Equity, the main actors' union in the UK, you can also ask them for free financial advice. An Equity pension scheme exists into which the BBC, ITV, PACT, TV companies and West End theatre producers will pay when you have a main part with one of them. Similar schemes also exist for dancers and other performers.

Insurance

Performers may often need specialist insurance for specific jobs, as well as the standard life and health insurance policies held by most people. A number of specialist insurers are listed in this section. Equity also offers a specialist backstage/ accident and public liability insurance policy to all of its members.

Legal

There may be times in a performer's career when he/she needs specialist legal advice or representation. This could be because of a performer's high profile, complicated contractual details, or international employment issues. Legal advisors and solicitors are listed in this section.

In addition, as part of their membership, Equity performers can also obtain free legal advice regarding professional engagements or personal injury claims.

How should I use these listings?

As when looking to hire any company or individual, contact a number of different companies and carefully compare the services they offer. Ask others in the industry for recommendations. If you are an Equity member, don't forget to check first that the service isn't already available free of charge, as part of your annual membership. For information about joining Equity, visit www.equity.org.uk or see their case study in the 'Unions' section.

Accountants, Insurance & Law

Martin Greene Ravden (MGR) Chartered Accountants are an accounting, tax and business consulting firm. They advise clients across a wide range of industries and are well-known as one of the leading specialists in the media, sport and entertainment industries.

To throw or not to throw, that's the first question...

A well-known actor recently lost a tax case because his argument could not be validated. He was claiming for a variety of expenses: all valid, but some were "technically challenging". Had he kept adequate evidence of all the expenses claimed, he may have had a better result. The moral of the story is obtain receipts for expenses, keep them tidy and make them available.

Appoint an accountant?

Actors, artistes and sportspeople are generally not equipped to handle their taxes and record-keeping: you have better things to do. You should consider engaging a suitably qualified and experienced accountant to take charge.

You should get two or three recommendations from people you trust and chat things through with them before choosing the person you feel comfortable with. The worst thing a performer can do is hire a relative who is a respected accountant but specialises in, say, haulage. He may act as "interferer" to another accountant who is more familiar with the entertainment industry, or even worse risks misadvising his client.

With embryonic artistes, many accountants will agree a "sweetheart deal" for an initial period, perhaps a year or two, before charging a commercial rate.

Performing outside the UK

This is a much specialised area in which the writer is very experienced. It's too big a subject to deal with here except for the "Golden Rule:" if tax is deducted from performances outside the UK, always obtain a certificate for the tax deducted.

Media client expenses

The entertainment industry demands that performers outlay a wide range of media-specific expenses, which an accountant who does not specialise in media may not be aware of. To be tax-deductible, expenses must be "wholly and exclusively" laid out or expended for the purpose of a trade, profession or vocation. If expenses are part business and part personal, only the business proportion is deductible, e.g. telephone and motor expenses. Certain expenses are specifically disallowed by tax law, e.g. business entertaining.

Below are some examples of expenses which are tax-deductible, either wholly or partly, some of which you may not even be aware you can claim for:

- Accountancy fees
- Advertising, publicity and promotion
- Agent's commission
- Bank and credit card charges and interest for business overdrafts and loans
- Books, e-books, magazines, subscriptions and research materials (e.g. Spotlight, The Stage, Equity)
- CDs, DVDs, online subscriptions and downloads
- Cosmetic and dental consultations
- Editing costs and fees
- Exchange rate costs on foreign advances, royalties and earnings
- Foreign tax credits
- Gym membership and personal trainer fees
- Hair, make up and grooming
- HP interest on assets
- Legal fees for contractual work and debt collection
- Licences and permission fees
- Motoring running costs
- Parking, congestion charge and tolls
- Printing, postage and stationery
- Professional conference and training fees (including vocal or music lessons)
- Research costs
- Secretarial or production assistance
- Clothing and dry cleaning (location shoots or stage)
- Telephone, fax and internet
- Theatre, concert and cinema tickets, DVD rental and online streaming costs
- Travel for business purposes (e.g. fares, accommodation, car hire, taxis)
- TV licence, hire, satellite and cable costs

Depreciation allowances (called capital allowances) can be claimed on:

- Computer hardware and software including website design and set-up
- Landline and mobile telephones, iPads, tablets, android and smartphones
- Motor cars
- Office furniture and equipment (e.g. desk, chair, filing cabinets and shelving)
- TV, DVD, home cinema and music equipment

This list is not exhaustive, but may start to indicate how useful an accountant's guidance can be, and hopefully also demonstrates that you should never throw your receipts away.

ACCOUNTS ACTION LTD   T 020 7437 0301
Arts & Media Accountancy
Suite 247, Linen Hall
162-168 Regent Street, London W1B 5TB
E richard@accountsaction.net

ALEXANDER JAMES & CO   T 020 8398 4447
Contact: Andrew Nicholson
Admirals Quarters, Portsmouth Road
Thames Ditton, Surrey KT7 0XA
F 020 8398 9989
E actors@alexanderjames.co.uk
W www.alexanderjames.co.uk

BAMBRIDGE ACCOUNTANTS   T 020 7409 5244
34 South Molton Street, London W1K 5RG
E alistair@bambridgeaccountants.co.uk
W www.bambridgeaccountants.co.uk

BLACKMORE, Lawrence   T 020 7240 1817
Production Accountant
Suite 5, 26 Charing Cross Road, London WC2H 0DG
E laurieblackmore@aol.com

BLAKE LAPTHORN   T 020 7405 2000
Solicitors
Watchmaker Court, 33 St John's Lane
London EC1M 4DB
F 020 7814 9421
E info@bllaw.co.uk
W www.bllaw.co.uk

BLINKHORNS   T 020 7636 3702
27 Mortimer Street, London W1T 3BL
E info@blinkhorns.co.uk
W www.blinkhorns.co.uk

BOWKER ORFORD   T 020 7636 6391
Chartered Accountants
15-19 Cavendish Place, London W1G 0DD
F 020 7580 3909
E mail@bowkerorford.com
W www.bowkerorford.com

BREBNERS   T 020 7734 2244
Chartered Accountants
180 Wardour Street, London W1F 8LB
F 020 7287 5315
E partners@brebners.com
W www.brebners.com

BRECKMAN & COMPANY LTD   T 020 7499 2292
Chartered Certified Accountants
49 South Molton Street, London W1K 5LH
E info@breckmanandcompany.co.uk
W www.breckmanandcompany.co.uk

BRECKMAN & COMPANY LTD   T 01273 929350
Chartered Certified Accountants
95 Ditchling Road, Brighton BN1 4ST
F info@breckmanandcompany.co.uk
W www.breckmanandcompany.co.uk

CARNE, Charlie & CO   T 020 8742 2001
Chartered Accountants
49 Windmill Road, London W4 1RN
E info@charliecarne.com

CARR, Mark & CO LTD   T 020 7717 8474
Chartered Accountants
Garrick House, 26-27 Southampton Street
Covent Garden, London WC2E 7RS
T 01273 778802
E mark@markcarr.co.uk
W www.markcarr.co.uk

CHARTERED ACCOUNTANTS

Will Advise on Tax, Self Assessment, Accounts, Finance, Limited Companies etc **First meeting Free**

H And S Accountants LTD. Argo House, Kilburn Park Road, London NW6 5LF

T: 020 3174 1905 **F:** 020 7788 2984 **E:** hstaxplan@gmail.com

CBW (CARTER BACKER WINTER LLP) T 020 7309 3800
Business Advisers. Chartered Accountants
Enterprise House
21 Buckle Street, London E1 8NN
F 020 7309 3801
E info@cbw.co.uk
W www.cbw.co.uk

CENTRE STAGE CHARTERED ACCOUNTANTS T 0161 655 2000
Twitter: @CentreStageAcc
Hampton House
Oldham Road
Manchester M24 1GT
E accounts@centrestage-accountants.com
W www.centrestage-accountants.com

CITY ACCOUNTANTS & TAX ADVISORS T 01733 777782
24 Broadway Gardens
Peterborough PE1 4DU
T 07976 244746
E info@cityaccountants.org.uk

COLLINS & COMPANY T 020 8427 1888
Chartered Accountants
2nd Floor, 116 College Road
Harrow, Middlesex HA1 1BQ
F 020 8863 0068
E hq@collins116.com

COUNT AND SEE LTD T 020 8767 7882
Tax, Accountancy & Book-keeping Services
219 Macmillan Way, London SW17 6AW
E info@countandsee.com
W www.countandsee.com

DUB & CO T 020 7284 8686
7 Torriano Mews, London NW5 2RZ
F 020 7284 8687
E office@dub.co.uk
W www.dub.co.uk

La Playa Media, Arts & Entertainment
Insurance with Intelligence®

• **Specialist Insurance for the Performing Arts**
• **Media & Production Companies**

Business interruption | Property | Personal accident
Office/equipment | Liabilities | Cast & crew
Travel/touring | Cancellation | Errors & omissions
Directors & officers

T: +44 (0)1223 200655
www.laplayainsurance.com
tracey.mccreath@laplayainsurance.com

playa

EQUITY INSURANCE SERVICES T 01245 357854
131-133 New London Road
Chelmsford, Essex CM2 0QZ
F 01245 491641
E enquiries@equity-ins-services.com
W www.equity-ins-services.com

FILMANDBUSINESSLAW LLP T 020 7129 1449
*Contact: Julia de Cadenet. Boutique Transatlantic Legal
Brokerage with offices in London, Paris & California.
Industry Specialists in American Work Visas, Contracts,
Copyright, Co-productions, Artist Representation,
Intellectual Property & Business Formations. Discounts
for Spotlight & Equity Members*
T 07798 695112
E info@filmandbusinesslaw.com
W www.filmandbusinesslaw.com

FINDLAY, Richard T 0131 226 3253
Entertainment Lawyer. Biz Consultant
1 Darnaway Street
Edinburgh EH3 6DW
T 07850 327725
E richardmfindlay@me.com

FISHER BERGER & ASSOCIATES T 020 8732 5500
Chartered Accountants
Devonshire House
582 Honeypot Lane
Stanmore HA7 1JS
F 020 8732 5501
E nik@fisherberger.com

FISHER BERGER & ASSOCIATES T 020 8732 5500
Chartered Accountants
Simia Wall, Sir Robert Peel House
178 Bishopsgate
London EC2M 4NJ
F 020 8732 5501
E nik@fisherberger.com

FORD, Jonathan & CO T 0151 426 4512
Chartered Accountants
The Coach House
31 View Road
Rainhill, Merseyside L35 0LF
E info@jonathanford.co.uk
W www.jonathanford.co.uk

GALLAGHER ENTERTAINMENT T 01753 785859
Insurance Brokers
Pinewood Studios, Pinewood Road
Iver, Bucks SL0 0NH
W www.ajg.co.uk

H & S ACCOUNTANTS LTD T 020 3174 1905
Chartered Accountants
Argo House, Kilburn Park Road
London NW6 5LF
F 020 7788 2984
E hstaxplan@gmail.com
W www.dsummers.co.uk

HARDWICKE T 020 7691 0056
Contact: Mark Engelman (Barrister). Media Law
Hardwicke Building
Lincoln's Inn
London WC2A 3SB
T 07720 294667
E mark.engelman@hardwicke.co.uk
W www .hardwicke.co.uk

HARVEY MEAD & CO LTD T 01892 891572
Accountants
The Old Winery, Lamberhurst Vineyard
Lamberhurst, Kent TN3 8ER
F 01892 891892
E info@harveymead.co.uk

HILL DICKINSON LLP T 0151 600 8000
1 St Paul's Square
Old Hall Street, Liverpool L3 9SJ
E mediateam@hilldickinson.com
W www.hilldickinson.com

HOOD, Karl LLP T 07916 971998
28A Kings Road
Kingston, Surrey KT2 5HS
E karl@karlhoodtax.co.uk
W www.karlhoodtax.co.uk

HW LEE ASSOCIATES LLP T 020 7025 4600
New Derwent House
69-73 Theobalds Road
London WC1X 8TA
F 020 7025 4666
E enquiries@hw-lee.com
W www.hw-lee.com

JENKINS, Andrew LTD T 01799 531358
Accountancy Services. Book-keeping. Payroll
The Old House, High Street
Little Chesterford, Saffron Walden, Essex CB10 1TS
T 07977 425518
E andrew@andrewjenkinsltd.com
W www.andrewjenkinsltd.com

**LACHMAN SMITH
ACCOUNTANTS** T 020 8731 1700
16B North End Road
Golders Green, London NW11 7PH
F 020 8731 1701
E accounts@lachmansmith.co.uk
W www.lachmansmith.co.uk

**LA PLAYA MEDIA &
PRODUCTION** T 01223 200673
Insurance
The Stables, Manor Farm
Milton Road, Impington, Cambridge CB24 9NG
E tracey.mccreath@laplayainsurance.com
W www.laplayainsurance.com

**LARK INSURANCE
BROKING GROUP** T 020 7543 2800
Ibex House, 42-47 Minories, London EC3N 1DY
F 020 7543 2801
E mailbox@larkinsurance.co.uk
W www.larkinsurance.co.uk

MGM ACCOUNTANCY LTD T 020 7379 9202
3rd Floor, 20 Bedford Street, London WC2E 9HP
E admin@mgmaccountancy.co.uk
W www.mgmaccountancy.co.uk

MGR LLP   T 020 7625 4545
Chartered Accountants. Business Administration. Touring
55 Loudoun Road, St John's Wood, London NW8 0DL
F 020 7625 5265
E info@mgr.co.uk
W www.mgr.co.uk

MHA MACINTYRE HUDSON   T 020 7429 4100
Media & Entertainment Accountants
New Bridge Street House
30-34 New Bridge Street, London EC4V 6BJ
F 020 7248 8939
E entertainment@mhllp.co.uk
W www.macintyrehudson.co.uk

**MONEYWISE
INVESTMENTS PLC**   T 020 8552 5521
Insurance Brokers
440-442 Romford Road, London E7 8DF
E aadatia@moneywiseplc.co.uk
W www.moneywiseplc.co.uk

NYMAN LIBSON PAUL   T 020 7433 2400
Chartered Accountants
Regina House, 124 Finchley Road, London NW3 5JS
F 020 7433 2401
E entertainment@nlpca.co.uk
W www.nlpca.co.uk

O'DRISCOLL, G. & CO   T 01621 893888
2 Catchpole Lane, Great Totham
Maldon, Essex CM9 8PY
T 07780 662544
E info@godriscoll.co.uk
W www.godriscoll.co.uk

PLANISPHERES   T/F 020 7602 2038
Business & Legal Affairs
Sinclair House, 2 Sinclair Gardens, London W14 0AT
E info@planispheres.com
W www.planispheres.com

**REES ASTLEY INSURANCE
BROKERS LTD**   T 01686 626019
Mostyn House, Market Street
Newtown, Powys SY16 2PQ
F 01686 628457
E performingarts@reesastley.co.uk
W www.insurance4performingarts.co.uk

**SLOANE & CO CHARTERED
CERTIFIED ACCOUNTANTS**   T 020 7221 3292
36-38 Westbourne Grove
Newton Road, London W2 5SH
F 020 7229 4810
E mail@sloane.co.uk
W www.sloane.co.uk

THEATACCOUNTS LLP   T 01905 823177
Twitter: @theataccounts
The Oakley
Kidderminster Road
Droitwich Spa
Worcestershire WR9 9AY
F 01905 799856
E info@theataccounts.co.uk
W www.theataccounts.co.uk

**TOWERGATE PROFESSIONAL
RISKS**   T 0113 391 9521
Public Liability Insurance
Towergate House
5 Airport West
Lancaster Way, Yeadon, Leeds LS19 7ZA
F 0113 391 9556
E performingarts@towergate.co.uk
W www.performingartsinsurance.co.uk

USMAN ACCOUNTANCY   T 020 7436 8229
26 York Street, London W1U 6PZ
T 07809 448969
E info@usmanaccountancy.co.uk
W www.usmanaccountancy.co.uk

W & P LONGREACH   T 020 7929 4747
Specialist Insurance Brokers
20 St Dunstans Hill
London EC3R 8PP
F 020 7929 4884
W www.wandp-longreach.com

**WISE & CO CHARTERED
ACCOUNTANTS**   T 01252 711244
Contact: Stephen Morgan
Wey Court West, Union Road
Farnham, Surrey GU9 7PT
E smo@wiseandco.co.uk
W www.wiseandco.co.uk

**WISE & CO CHARTERED
ACCOUNTANTS**   T 01753 656770
Contact: Colin Essex
Room 245, Pinewood Studios
Iver Heath, Bucks SL0 0NH
E ces@wiseandco.co.uk
W www.wiseandco.co.uk

WMT LLP   T 01727 838255
Tax Specialists
Torrington House, 47 Holywell Hill
St Albans, Hertfordshire AL1 1HD
F 01727 861052
E info@wmtllp.com
W www.wmtllp.com

> Treating people with respect will gain one acceptance and improve business.
>
> Tao Zhu Gong, 500BC

Brebners offers much more than accountancy services and business advice. We offer trust, reliability and a truly personal service.

Whether you are just starting out or are more established, our committed and specialist team offers a full range of services to help your business succeed.

Please call Michael Burton or Mal Falora on 020 7734 2244 for a free and confidential discussion.

BREBNERS
CHARTERED ACCOUNTANTS
& BUSINESS ADVISERS

THE QUADRANGLE 180 WARDOUR STREET LONDON W1F 8LB TEL: 020 7734 2244
EMAIL: PARTNERS@BREBNERS.COM WEB: WWW.BREBNERS.COM

Tax and accounting a hassle?
We love it.

Want to succeed with financial matters or simplify them?
We care and we have the experience to help.

Contact us for a free initial consultation

Colin Essex
Room 245 **Pinewood Studios** Iver Heath Bucks SL0 0NH
t: 01753 656770 e: ces@wiseandco.co.uk

Stephen Morgan and Treena Turner
Wey Court West Union Road Farnham Surrey GU9 7PT
t: 01252 711244 e: smo@wiseandco.co.uk

www.wiseandco.co.uk

Accounting for the future...

WISE & CO
Chartered Accountants & Business Advisers

Agents & Personal Managers

Who are agents and personal managers?

There are hundreds of agents and personal managers in the UK, representing thousands of actors and artists. It is their job to promote their clients to casting opportunities and negotiate contracts on their behalf. In return they take commission ranging from 10-15%. Larger agencies can have hundreds of clients on their books; smaller ones may only have a handful. Agents usually try to represent a good range of artists (age, gender, type) to fill the diverse role types required by casting directors. A personal manager is someone who manages an artist's career on a more one-on-one basis.

What is a co-operative agency?

Co-operative agencies are staffed by actors themselves, who take turns to handle the administrative side of the agency and promote themselves to casting opportunities as a team. If you want more control over your career and can handle the pressures and responsibility that an agent takes away from you, then you might consider joining a co-operative agency. However it is very important that you think carefully about what you are signing up for.

You will be responsible for the careers of others as well as yourself, so you must first of all be able to conduct yourself well when speaking to casting professionals. You will also have to commit some of your time to administrative jobs. You must be prepared to deal with finances and forms – all the boring paperwork you usually hand over to your agent! You must also be aware that the other actors in the agency will want to interview you and, if you are successful, to give you a trial period working with them. The Co-operative Personal Management Association (CPMA) offers advice about joining a co-operative agency on their website www.cpma.coop

Why do I need an agent?

A good agent will have contacts and authority in the entertainment industry that you, as an individual actor, would find more difficult to acquire. Agents, if you want them to, can also deal with matters such as Equity and Spotlight membership renewal. They can offer you advice on which headshot would be best to send out to casting directors, what to include or exclude in your CV as you build on your skills and experience, what a particular casting director might expect when you are invited to an audition, and so on.

How should I use these listings?

If you are an actor getting started in the industry, or looking to change your agent, the following listings will supply you with up-to-date contact details for many of the UK's leading agencies. Every company listed is done so by written request to us. Members of the Personal Managers' Association (PMA) and the Co-operative Personal Management Association (CMPA) have indicated their membership status under their name.

Some agencies have also chosen to list other information such as relevant contact names, their preferred method of contact from new applicants, whether or not they are happy to receive showreels and/or voicereels with a prospective client's CV and headshot, the number of performers represented by the agency, the number of agents working for the company, and/or a description of the performance areas they cover. Use this information to narrow down your search for a suitable agent.

How do I choose a new agent?

When writing to agencies, try to research the different companies instead of just sending a 'blanket' letter to every single one. This way you can target your approaches to the most suitable agencies and avoid wasting their time (and yours). As well as using the listing information provided here, look at agency websites and ask around for personal recommendations.

Unfortunately Spotlight is not able to offer personalised advice on choosing an agent, nor is it in a position to handle any financial or contractual queries or complaints, but we have prepared some useful career advice on our website: www.spotlight.com/artists/advice. Click on our Frequently Asked Questions page for general guidance regarding agents, or you may wish to try consulting our list of Independent Advisory Services, if you want one-to-one tailored advice. You can also contact The Agents' Association www.agents-uk.com or The Personal Managers' Association (PMA) www.thepma.com

If you are a member of Equity then you can contact their legal and welfare department with general information about issues including commissions, fees and contracts. However, Equity is not able to recommend specific agencies or agents.

How do I approach agencies?

Once you have made a list of suitable agencies, consult the listings again. Some agencies have indicated their preferred method of initial contact, whether by post, e-mail or telephone. Do not e-mail them, for example, if they have stated that they wish to receive your headshot, CV and covering letter by post. If they have not given a preference, you should send your CV by post as this is the traditional method of contacting agents. You should **always** include a stamped-addressed envelope (SAE) big enough to contain your 10 x 8 photo and with sufficient postage. This will increase your chances of getting a reply. Write your name and telephone number on the back of your headshot in case it gets separated from your CV.

Remember that agents receive hundreds of letters and e-mails each week, so try to keep your communication concise, and be professional at all times. We also recommend that your covering letter has some kind of focus: perhaps you can tell them about your next showcase, or where they can see you currently appearing on stage. This should always be addressed to an individual, not "To whom it may concern" or "Dear Sir or Madam". Some agents have indicated a specific contact to whom you can direct correspondence in their listing, otherwise check the agency's website or give them a call and find out who you should address your letter or e-mail to.

Some agents have indicated that they are happy to receive a showreel and/or voicereel with your CV, but it would be best to exclude these from your correspondence if they are not mentioned. Point out in your covering letter that one is available and the agent can contact you if they want to find out more.

Should I pay an agent to join their books? Or sign a contract?

Equity (the actors' trade union) does not recommend that artists pay an agent to join their client list. Before signing a contract, you should be very clear about the terms and commitments involved. For advice on both of these issues, or if you experience any problems with a current agent, we recommend that you contact Equity www.equity.org.uk. They also produce the booklet *You and your Agent* which is free to all Equity members and available from their website's members' area.

How do I become an agent?

Budding agents will need to get experience of working in an agent's office; usually this is done by working as an assistant. It can be extremely hard work, and you will be expected to give up a lot of your evenings to attend productions. There are two organisations you may find it useful to contact: The Agents' Association www.agents-uk.com and the Personal Managers' Association www.thepma.com

Agents & Personal Managers

Niki Winterson has been an agent for eleven years. She is a member of the PMA. She created and ran the drama department as an Associate at Global Artists before moving the list to Wintersons at 59 St Martin's Lane. She handles classical actors and a smaller list of directors, choreographers, designers and casting directors. Wintersons recently expanded again to include a list of dancers with a solid technical training, headed by Rebecca Barrett.

Choosing an agent is the single most important decision a creative can make. Big agencies can be powerful but impersonal. Boutique agents such as myself build a select list of actors with the aim of them working at the highest levels of the industry. Building a client's career so they get the exposure they deserve is the most painstaking part of my work. For actors, this means introducing them to the right casting directors. Casting directors are among the most important and often the least appreciated people in the business. As any working actor will attest, jobs breed jobs. And a good agent will get you jobs, not just jobs which pay your rent but which bring your skills and your work to a wider audience – including the casting directors, directors and producers who might employ you.

But there's no way an agent can risk her reputation by putting every actor up for every job they could possibly do. A good casting director has not simply an encyclopaedic memory for every actor they have ever met or seen, but a deep and detailed understanding of the piece they are working on. They know exactly the kind of actor they need for a particular project, but will only consider someone if they've seen them work or trust their agent implicitly. It's my job to interface between the two sets of needs – the casting director's and my client's. This means making only the very best suggestions in order to remain trustworthy.

Unfortunately, there are now so many people trying to enter the industry that a lot of really good people never get an agent at all. An agent will only approach an actor she has real respect for – it would be pointless representing any actor you didn't believe in. PMA members have an agreement not to 'poach' each other's clients. So if you want to change agents you're going to have to research and approach one yourself. Remember that a good agent plays the long game – they'll even advise you against doing work which may be lucrative in the short-term but which could harm your long-term prospects.

As well as passion an agent needs vision. She needs to be able to see what work the actor has done, but, even more importantly, to be able to imagine what work the actor might do, given the chance – and then make sure they get that chance. You should never be afraid to ask your agent about your pay. Organisation is important. Efficiency is important. If an office looks chaotic then the agent may well be too. The website should be well-designed and easy to use. One of my major concerns is to make sure my clients are properly represented in emerging media. To do this my office must stay ahead of the game.

This is a business of egos and a good agent manages egos without feeling the need to assert her own – unless she wishes to. Communication skills are essential. Agents are in constant contact with other creatives. A central location helps me – it's obviously an advantage to be able to work late in the office until 7.20pm and be in my seat to watch a show for 7.30pm. We work long hours, from 10am to 6pm in the office and then frequently out in the evening introducing clients to contacts, meeting directors or attending industry events. Then there are the clients who work internationally and who have contractual questions or issues that can only be resolved in a personal call – at night because of the time differences. But it's essential – personal contact is everything. There are actually a relatively small number of key players in this industry and part of my job is to know them all.

And it's also a tough business. At its best the rewards are glorious but there can be down sides – it's financially unstable and emotionally wearing on the actor. My job is to get my people into that wonderful creative position while at the same time administrating the job to their maximum artistic and financial advantage. It's a two-way thing based on trust and respect. I like all of my actors. I talk to my actors all the time.

**To find out more about Wintersons contact Rebecca Barrett:
59 St Martin's Lane
London WC2N 4JS
T 020 7836 7849
E niki@nikiwinterson.com
W www.nikiwinterson.com**

The Short & Dwarf Actors Agency

Specialising in:
Prosthetics, Full Costume,
Motion Capture and Child Stunts.

www.ohsosmall.com

E: lisa@ohsosmallproductions.com
Telephone: +44 (0) 7787 788673

Supplying actors, models, extras and voices for the
entertainment and advertising industries.
T: 01664 569 738   E: beth@aardvarkcasting.com
SNIFFING OUT TALENT ACROSS THE UK

www.aardvarkcasting.com

**1984 PERSONAL
MANAGEMENT LTD**   T 020 7251 8046
*CPMA Member. Contact: David Meyer. By Post. Accepts
Showreels. 25 Performers*
Suite 508, Davina House, 137 Goswell Road
London EC1V 7ET
F 020 7250 3031
E info@1984pm.com   W www.1984pm.com

**21ST CENTURY ACTORS
MANAGEMENT LTD**   T 020 7278 3438
*CPMA Member. Contact: By e-mail. Commercials. Film.
Stage. Television*
206 Panther House
38 Mount Pleasant, London WC1X 0AN
E mail@21stcenturyactors.co.uk
W www.21stcenturyactors.org

2MA LTD   T 023 8074 1354
Sports. Stunts
Spring Vale, Tutland Road
North Baddesley, Hants SO52 9FL
F 023 8074 1355
E mo.matthews@2ma.co.uk   W www.2ma.co.uk

**A & B PERSONAL
MANAGEMENT LTD**   T 020 7794 3255
Personal Manager. Contact: By e-mail
PO Box 64671, London NW3 9LH
E billellis@aandb.co.uk

A & J ARTISTS LTD   T 020 8342 0542
242A The Ridgeway, Botany Bay, Enfield EN2 8AP
T 020 8367 7139
E jo@ajmanagement.co.uk
W www.ajmanagement.co.uk

**A-LIST LOOKALIKES &
ENTERTAINMENTS LTD**   T 0113 253 0563
Top Floor, Crank Mills
New Bank Street, Morley, Leeds LS27 8NT
E info@alistlookalikes.co.uk
W www.alistlookalikes.co.uk

A GENT THE   T 07779 595194
16 Globe Row, Dafen, Llanelli SA14 8PA
E mark@theagent.biz
W www.theagent.biz

AARDVARK CASTING   T 020 8667 9812
15 Deans Close, Croydon, London CR0 5PU
T 07587 006176
E london@aardvarkcasting.com
W www.aardvarkcasting.com

ABA (ABACUS ADULTS)   T 01306 877144
The Studio, 4 Bailey Road
Westcott, Dorking, Surrey RH4 3QS
F 01306 877813
E aba@abacusagency.co.uk
W www.abacusaba.com

ABAKPORO, Chris
Based in London
E info@christheagent.com   W www.christheagent.com

**ACCESS ARTISTE
MANAGEMENT LTD**   T 020 7866 5444
Contact: Sarah Bryan. By Post/e-mail. Accepts Showreels
71-75 Shelton Street, Covent Garden
London WC2H 9JQ
E mail@access-uk.com
W www.access-uk.com

Arab Actors – Voices – Presenters

Recent Clients:

BBC: "Andrew Marr's History of the World"

David Hare's "WALL"

The Edge • ORTV Int • PITV • DK "Borgen"

Arabic Cultural Expertise

Mobile: 07748 737374
info@genuinearabcasting.com
www.genuinearabcasting.com

GENUINE ARAB CASTING

Represents authentic stage, screen &
radio actors from across the
Arabic Speaking World

Matt Anker photographer
07835 241835

www.mattanker.com London based

student discounts

ACROBAT PRODUCTIONS   T 01923 518989
Advisors. Artists
2 The Grove, Whippendell
Chipperfield, Kings Langley, Herts WD4 9JF
E roger@acrobatproductions.com
W www.acrobatproductions.com

ACT IN AMERICA LTD   T 020 7129 1449
Personal Manager. Contact: Julia de Cadenet. Artist
Representation. Co-productions. Transatlantic Visa
Solutions. Offices in London, Paris & California
17 Cavendish Square, London W1G 0PH
T 07798 695112
E info@actinamerica.com
W www.actinamerica.com

ACTOR-MUSICIANS @ ACCESS   T 020 7866 5444
Personal Manager. Contact: Sarah Bryan. By Post/e-mail.
Specialises in Actor-Musicians
c/o Access Artiste Management Ltd
71-75 Shelton Street
Covent Garden, London WC2H 9JQ
E mail@access-uk.com
W www.access-uk.com

ACTORS AGENCY   T 0131 228 4040
1 Glen Street, Tollcross, Edinburgh EH3 9JD
F 0131 228 4645
E info@stivenchristie.co.uk
W www.stivenchristie.co.uk

**ACTORS AGENCY OF
SWEDEN THE**   T 00 46 8 56305400
Contact: Stina Cars Westrell (Agent),
Josefin Fridman (Assistant)
Gamla Brogatan 44, 111 20 Stockholm, Sweden
E info@actorsagency.se
W www.actorsagency.se

ACTORS ALLIANCE   T/F 020 7407 6028
CPMA Member. Contact: By Post. Commercials.
Corporate. Film. Stage. Stills. Television
Disney Place House, 14 Marshalsea Road
London SE1 1HL
E actors@actorsalliance.co.uk
W www.actorsalliance.co.uk

ACTORS' CREATIVE TEAM   T 020 7278 3388
CPMA Member
Panther House, 38 Mount Pleasant, London WC1X 0AN
F 020 7833 5086
E office@actorscreativeteam.co.uk
W www.actorscreativeteam.co.uk

ACTORS DIRECT LTD   T 0161 277 9360
Number 5, 651 Rochdale Road, Manchester M9 5SH
T 07427 616549
E info@actorsdirect.org.uk   W www.actorsdirect.org.uk

ACTORS FILE THE   T 020 7278 0087
Personal Manager. Co-operative. CPMA Member.
Contact: By Post/e-mail
Spitfire Studios, 63-71 Collier Street, London N1 9BE
E theactorsfile@btconnect.com
W www.theactorsfile.co.uk

ACTORS' GROUP THE (TAG)   T/F 0161 834 4466
Personal Manager. CPMA Member
21-31 Oldham Street, Manchester M1 1JG
E enquiries@theactorsgroup.co.uk
W www.theactorsgroup.co.uk

ACTORS IN SCANDINAVIA   T 00 358 4 00540640
Jääkärinkatu 10, 00150 Helsinki, Finland
E laura@actorsinscandinavia.com
W www.actorsinscandinavia.com

ACTORS INTERNATIONAL LTD   T 020 7025 8777
18 Soho Square, London W1D 3QL
F 020 7900 6800
E mail@actorsinternational.co.uk

ACTOR'S TEMPLE THE   T 020 3004 4537
13 Warren Street, London W1T 5LG
T 07771 734670
E info@actorstemple.com
W www.actorstemple.com

ACTORS WORLD CASTING   T 07960 332846
13 Briarbank Road, London W13 0HH
T 07870 594388
E katherine@actors-world-production.com
W www.actors-world-production.com

ACTORUM LTD   T 020 7636 6978
Personal Manager
9 Bourlet Close, London W1W 7BP
F 020 7636 6975
E info@actorum.com
W www.actorum.com

**ADA
(ACTORS DIRECT ASSOCIATES)**   T 07951 477015
2 Hawthorn Way, Sawtry
Huntingdon, Cambridgeshire PE28 5QB
E casting@actorsdirectassociates.net
W www.actorsdirectassociates.net

AFA ASSOCIATES   T 020 7682 3677
Unit 101, Business Design Centre
52 Upper Street, London N1 0QH
E afa-associates@hotmail.com

AFFINITY MANAGEMENT   T 01342 715275
The Coach House
Down Park, Turners Hill Road
Crawley Down, West Sussex RH10 4HQ
E jstephens@affinitymanagement.co.uk

BILLY MARSH DRAMA LIMITED
Personal Management

Representing Actors in Theatre, Film, Television, Commercials

Linda Kremer | Billy Marsh Drama Limited

20 Garrick Street London WC2E 9BT

Tel: 020 3178 4748   Fax: 020 3178 5488   Email: info@billymarshdrama.co.uk

AGENCY LTD THE　　　　T 00 353 1 6618535
Contact: Teri Hayden, Karl Hayden
9 Upper Fitzwilliam Street, Dublin 2, Ireland
F 00 353 1 6766615
E admin1@tagency.ie
W www.the-agency.ie

AGENCY OAKROYD　　　　T 07840 784337
Oakroyd, 89 Wheatley Lane
Ben Rhydding
Ilkley, Yorkshire LS29 8PP
E paula@agencyoakroyd.com
W www.agencyoakroyd.com

AHA
See HOWARD, Amanda ASSOCIATES LTD

AIM (ASSOCIATED INTERNATIONAL MANAGEMENT)　　　　T 020 7831 9709
PMA Member
Fairfax House, Fulwood Place, London WC1V 6HU
F 020 7242 0810
E info@aimagents.com
W www.aimagents.com

AIRCRAFT CIRCUS ENTERTAINMENT (ACE) AGENCY　　　　T 07946 472329
Circus Artists only
7A Melish House, Harrington Way, London SE18 5NR
E lucy@aircraftcircus.com　　**W** www.aircraftcircus.com

ALEXANDER PERSONAL MANAGEMENT LTD
See APM ASSOCIATES

Rhys Rusbatch

Ingrid Lacey

ROBERT WORKMAN Superb casting photographs
Tel: 020 7385 5442   www.robertworkman.demon.co.uk

**ALL TALENT -
THE SONIA SCOTT AGENCY**   T 0141 418 1074
*Contact: Sonia Scott Mackay. By Post/e-mail/Telephone.
Accepts Showreels/Voicereels. 2 Agents represent 40
Performers. Film. Modelling. Television. Voice Overs.
Walk-on & Supporting Artists*
Unit 325, 95 Morrison Street, Glasgow G5 8BE
T 07971 337074
E enquiries@alltalentuk.co.uk   W www.alltalentuk.co.uk

**ALLISTON & FOSTER
ARTIST MANAGEMENT**   T 020 3390 4321
Suite 3, 3rd Floor, 207 Regent Street, London W1B 3HH
E contact@allistonandfoster.com
W www.allistonandfoster.com

ALLSORTS AGENCY   T 020 8989 0500
Suite 3, Marlborough Business Centre
96 George Lane, London E18 1AD
F 020 8989 5600
E bookings@allsortsagency.com
W www.allsortsagency.com

**ALLSORTS DRAMA
FOR CHILDREN**   T/F 020 8969 3249
In association with LESLIE, Sasha MANAGEMENT
34 Crediton Road, London NW10 3DU
E sasha@allsortsdrama.com

ALLSTARS CASTING   T 0151 707 2100
66 Hope Street, Liverpool L1 9BZ
T 07739 359737
E sylvie@allstarscasting.co.uk
W www.allstarscasting.co.uk

ALPHA ACTORS   T 020 7241 0077
Co-operative. CPMA Member
Studio B4, 3 Bradbury Street, London N16 8JN
F 020 7241 2410
E alpha@alphaactors.com
W www.alphaactors.com

ALPHABET MANAGEMENT   T 020 7252 4343
Personal Manager. Adult & Child Actors
Daisy Business Park, 19-35 Sylvan Grove
London SE15 1PD
E lisa@alphabetmanagement.co.uk
W www.alphab etmanagement.co.uk

**ALRAUN, Anita
REPRESENTATION**   T 01253 343784
PMA Member. Contact: By Post only (SAE)
1A Queensway, Blackpool, Lancashire FY4 2DG
T 07946 630986
E anita@cjagency.demon.co.uk

**ALTARAS, Jonathan
ASSOCIATES LTD**   T 020 7836 8722
PMA Member
11 Garrick Street
Covent Garden, London WC2E 9AR
F 020 7836 6066
E info@jaalondon.com

ALW ASSOCIATES   T 020 7388 7018
Contact: Carol Paul
1 Grafton Chambers, Grafton Place, London NW1 1LN
E alw_carolpaul@talktalk.net

**AM PERSONAL
MANAGEMENT LTD**   T 020 7244 1159
*Contact: Amanda McAllister. Film, Stage & Television
Technical Personnel only*
4 Archel Road, London W14 9QH
E amanda@ampmgt.com
W www.ampmgt.com

**AMAZON ARTISTS
MANAGEMENT**   T/F 020 8350 4909
27 Inderwick Road, Crouch End, London N8 9LB
T 07957 358767
E amazonartists@gmail.com

**AMBER PERSONAL
MANAGEMENT LTD**   T 0161 228 0236
PMA Member
Room A, 2nd Floor, Planetree House
21-31 Oldham Street, Manchester M1 1JG
E info@amberltd.co.uk
W www.amberltd.co.uk

**AMBER PERSONAL
MANAGEMENT LTD**   T 020 7734 7887
PMA Member
London
E info@amberltd.co.uk
W www.amberltd.co.uk

AMC MANAGEMENT   T 01438 714652
Contact: Anna McCorquodale, Tricia Howell
31 Parkside, Welwyn, Herts AL6 9DQ
F 01438 718669
E anna@amcmanagement.co.uk
W www.amcmanagement.co.uk

AMCK MANAGEMENT LTD   T 020 7524 7788
125 Westbourne Studios, 242 Acklam Road
Notting Hill, London W10 5JJ
F 020 7524 7789
E info@amck.tv
W www.amck.tv

AMERICAN AGENCY THE   T 020 7485 8883
*Contact: By Post/e-mail. 3 Agents represent 81
Performers. Commercials. Corporate. Film. Musicals.
Stage. Television. Voice Overs (American)*
14 Bonny Street, London NW1 9PG
E americanagency@btconnect.com
W www.americanagency.tv

AMG ARTISTS   T 07889 241283
*Contact: Kyra Morrison. Film Actors, Directors, Producers,
Visual Artists & Writers*
E info@amgcom.eu
W www.amgcom.eu

**ANA
(ACTORS NETWORK AGENCY)**   T 020 7735 0999
Personal Manager. Co-operative. CPMA Member
55 Lambeth Walk, London SE11 6DX
F 020 7735 8177
E info@ana-actors.co.uk   W www.ana-actors.co.uk

**ANDERSON SAUNDERS
ASSOCIATES**   T 020 8806 6361
Kemp House, 152-160 City Road, London EC1V 2NX
E belanderson@talktalk.net

JOHN CLARK
London's leading headshot photographer

Karen Bryson: Shameless

Denise Welch

John Fitzpatrick

Zoe Lucker

Jonny Hynes

John Wark

Stephanie Tripp

Justin Pierre

07702 627 237
Book online at www.johnclarkphotography.com

ANDREA CASTING   T 07774 660253
Actors. Crew. Dancers. Musicians. Presenters.
Voice Overs
The Business Centre, 1-5 Peniel Green Road
Llansamlet, Swansea, Glamorgan SA7 9AP
E info@andreacasting.com   W www.andreacasting.com

ANDREWS, Amanda AGENCY   T/F 01782 393889
30 Caverswall Road, Blythe Bridge
Stoke-on-Trent, Staffordshire ST11 9BG
T 07711 379770
E amanda.andrews.agency@tesco.net
W www.amandaandrewsagency.org.uk

ANGEL, Susan &
FRANCIS, Kevin LTD   T 020 7439 3086
PMA Member
1st Floor, 12 D'Arblay Street, London W1F 8DU
F 020 7437 1712
E agents@angelandfrancis.co.uk
W www.angelandfrancis.co.uk

ANTONY, Christopher
ASSOCIATES   T 020 8994 9952
Studio F5, Grove Park Studios
188-192 Sutton Court Road, London W4 3HR
E info@christopherantony.co.uk
W www.christopherantony.co.uk

APM ASSOCIATES   T 020 8953 7377
PMA Member. Contact: Linda French. By Post/e-mail.
Accepts Showreels/Voicereels. 3 Agents represent 80
Performers
Elstree Studios, Shenley Road
Borehamwood WD6 1JG
F 020 8953 7385
E apm@apmassociates.net
W www.apmassociates.net

ARAENA/COLLECTIVE   T/F 020 8428 0037
10 Bramshaw Gardens, South Oxhey, Herts WD19 6XP
E info@collectivedance.co.uk

A.R.C. ENTERTAINMENTS   T 01740 631292
Contact: By e-mail. 1 Agent represents
800 Active Performers
10 Church Lane, Redmarshall
Stockton on Tees, Cleveland TS21 1EP
E arcents@btinternet.com   W www.arcents.co.uk

ARCADIA ASSOCIATES   T/F 020 7937 0264
18B Vicarage Gate, London W8 4AA
E info.arcadia@btopenworld.com

ARENA
ENTERTAINMENT (UK) LTD   T 0113 239 2222
Regent's Court, 39 Harrogate Road, Leeds LS7 3PD
F 0113 239 2016
E info@arenaentertainments.co.uk
W www.arenaentertainments.co.uk

ARENA PERSONAL
MANAGEMENT LTD   T/F 020 7278 1661
Co-operative
Room 11, East Block, Panther House
38 Mount Pleasant, London WC1X 0AN
E arenapmltd@aol.com   W www.arenapmltd.co.uk

A R G
(ARTISTS RIGHTS GROUP LTD)   T 020 7436 6400
PMA Member
4 Great Portland Street
London W1W 8PA
F 020 7436 6700
E argall@argtalent.com

ARGYLE ASSOCIATES   T 07905 293319
Personal Manager. Contact: Richard Argyle. By Post (SAE)
43 Clappers Lane, Fulking
West Sussex BN5 9ND
E argyle.associates@me.com

ARROWSMITH, Martin   T 0845 0540255
Contact: By Post. Accepts Showreels. 1 Agent represents
10 Performers. Children. Commercials. Film. Stage.
Television
Lower Ground Floor, Rama Actors Studio
1 Kayes Walk, Nottingham NG1 1PY
F 0115 948 3696
E office@martinarrowsmith.co.uk
W www.martinarrowsmith.co.uk

ARTEMIS STUDIOS LTD   T 01344 429403
30 Charles Square, Bracknell
Berkshire RG12 1AY
E agency@artemis-studios.co.uk
W www.agency.artemis-studios.co.uk

ARTIST MANAGEMENT UK LTD   T 0151 523 6222
PO Box 96, Liverpool L9 8WY
T 07948 793552
E chris@artistmanagementuk.com
W www.artistmanagementuk.com

ARUN, Jonathan   T 020 7840 0123
Personal Manager. PMA Member. Contact:
Jonathan Arun, Jeff Guerrera, Amy O'Neill
2.06 Clerkenwell Workshops, 31 Clerkenwell Close
London EC1R 0AT
E info@jonathanarun.com
W www.jonathanarun.com

ASH PRODUCTIONS LIVE LTD   T 020 8670 2302
Personal Manager. Education & Training.
Theatre Production
45 Dassett Road, West Norwood
London SE27 0UF
E office@ashproductionslive.com
W www.ashproductionsliveltd.com

ASHCROFT MANAGEMENT
TALENT AGENCY LTD   T 01422 399439
Elsie Whiteley Innovation Centre
Hopwood Lane, Halifax HX1 5ER
E ashcroftmanagement@gmail.com
W www.ashcroftmanagement.co.uk

ASQUITH & HORNER   T 020 8466 5580
Joined with Elspeth Cochrane Personal Management.
Personal Manager. Contact: By Telephone/Post (SAE)/
e-mail
The Studio, 14 College Road
Bromley, Kent BR1 3NS
T 07770 482144
E asquith@dircon.co.uk

ASSOCIATED ARTS T 020 8856 4958
Designers. Directors. Lighting & Sound Designers
8 Shrewsbury Lane, London SE18 3JF
F 020 8856 8189
E karen@associated-arts.co.uk
W www.associated-arts.co.uk

ASSOCIATED SPEAKERS T 020 8848 9048
Lecturers & Celebrity Speakers
24A Park Road, Hayes
Middlesex UB4 8JN

ASTON MANAGEMENT T 07974 793342
Aston Farm House, Remenham Lane
Henley on Thames, Oxon RG9 3DE
E agent@astonmgt.com
W www.astonmgt.com

ASTRAL ACTORS
MANAGEMENT T 020 8728 2782
22 Parc Starling, Johnstown
Carmarthen SA31 3HX
T 01267 616162
E liz@astralactors.com
W www.astralactors.com

AVALON MANAGEMENT
GROUP LTD T 020 7598 8000
4A Exmoor Street, London W10 6BD
F 020 7598 7300
E enquiries@avalonuk.com
W www.avalonuk.com

AVENUE ARTISTES LTD T 023 8076 0930
PO Box 1573, Southampton SO16 3XS
E info@avenueartistes.com
W www.avenueartistes.com

AVIEL TALENT
MANAGEMENT INC T 001 514 288 8885
1117 St Catherine Street West, Suite 718, Montreal
Quebec, Canada H3B 1H9
F 001 514 288 0768
E aviel@canadafilm.com

AWA - ANDREA WILDER AGENCY T 07919 202401
23 Cambrian Drive, Colwyn Bay
Conwy LL28 4SL
F 07092 249314
E andreawilder@fastmail.fm
W www.awagency.co.uk

AXM (ACTORS EXCHANGE
MANAGEMENT) T 020 7837 3304
Co-operative. CPMA Member
308 Panther House, 38 Mount Pleasant
London WC1X 0AN
F 020 7837 7215
E info@axmgt.com
W www.axmgt.com

BACK DOOR MANAGEMENT LTD T 01753 785175
PMA Member
Pinewood Studios, Pinewood Road
Iver Heath, Buckinghamshire SL0 0NH
E info@back-door.co.uk
W www.back-door.co.uk

B A M ASSOCIATES T 01934 852942
Benets, Dolberrow
Churchill, Bristol BS25 5NT
E casting@ebam.tv
W www.ebam.tv

BANANAFISH MANAGEMENT T 0151 708 5509
The Arts Village, 20-26 Henry Street
Liverpool L1 5BS
T 07974 206622
E info@bananafish.co.uk
W www.bananafish.co.uk

BARKER, Gavin
ASSOCIATES LTD T 020 7499 4777
PMA Member. Contact: Gavin Barker, Michelle Burke
2d Wimpole Street, London W1G 0EB
F 020 7499 3777
E katie@gavinbarkerassociates.co.uk
W www.gavinbarkerassociates.co.uk

BARR, Becca MANAGEMENT T 020 3137 2980
Dorland House, 5th Floor
14-16 Regent Street, London SW1Y 4PH
E info@beccabarrmanagement.co.uk
W www.beccabarrmanagement.co.uk

BEDFORD, Eamonn AGENCY T 020 7395 7528
4th Floor, 80-81 St Martin's Lane
London WC2N 4AA
E info@eamonnbedford.com
W www.eamonnbedford.com

BELFAST TALENT AGENCY T 028 9024 3324
The Crescent Arts Centre, 2-4 University Road
Belfast, Antrim BT7 1NH
E info@belfasttalent.com
W www.belfasttalentagency.com

BELFIELD & WARD T 020 3416 5290
PMA Member
26-28 Neal Street, Covent Garden
London WC2H 9QQ
F 020 3292 9382
E office@belfieldandward.com

BELFRAGE, Julian
ASSOCIATES T 020 7287 8544
PMA Member
3rd Floor, 9 Argyll Street
London W1F 7TG
F 020 7287 8832

BELL, Olivia MANAGEMENT T 020 7439 3270
*PMA Member. Contact: By Post. 6 Agents represent
100 Performers. Commercials. Film. Musicals. Stage.
Television*
193 Wardour Street, London W1F 8ZF
E info@olivia-bell.co.uk
W www.olivia-bell.co.uk

BENJAMIN MANAGEMENT LTD T 020 7766 5223
Cameo House, 11 Bear Street
London WC2H 7AS
E agent@benjaminmanagement.co.uk

BENNETT DARLING
MANAGEMENT T 020 7183 6029
3rd Floor, 207 Regent Street
London W1B 3HH
E info@bdartists.co.uk
W www.bdartists.co.uk

BERLIN ASSOCIATES T 020 7836 1112
PMA Member. Dramatists & Technicians only
7 Tyers Gate, London SE1 3HX
F 020 7632 5296
E agents@berlinassociates.com
W www.berlinassociates.com

BETTS, Jorg ASSOCIATES T 020 7903 5300
PMA Member
Gainsborough House, 81 Oxford Street
London W1D 2EU
F 020 7903 5301
E agents@jorgbetts.com

BILLBOARD
PERSONAL MANAGEMENT T 020 7735 9956
45 Lothrop Street, London W10 4JB
T 07791 970773
E billboardpm@btconnect.com
W www.billboardpm.com

NICK BRIMBLE

CATHERINE SHAKESPEARE LANE

PHOTOGRAPHER

020 7226 7694   **www.csl-art.co.uk**

BILLY MARSH DRAMA LTD
See MARSH, Billy DRAMA LTD

BIRD AGENCY　　T 020 8269 6862
Personal Performance Manager
The Centre, 27 Station Road
Sidcup, Kent DA15 7EB
T 07889 723995
E birdagency@birdcollege.co.uk
W www.birdcollege.co.uk

BIZZY ADULTS AGENCY　　T 0845 5200402
Bizzy Studios, 10-12 Pickford Lane
Bexleyheath, Kent DA7 4QW
F 0845 5200401
E bookings@bizzyadults.com
W www.bizzyadults.com

**BLACKBURN SACHS
ASSOCIATES**　　T 020 7292 7555
Argyll House, All Saints Passage
London SW18 1EP
F 020 7292 7576
E presenters@blackburnsachsassociates.com
W www.blackburnsachsassociates.com

BLOND, Rebecca ASSOCIATES　　T 020 7351 4100
PMA Member
69A Kings Road, London SW3 4NX
F 020 7351 4600
E info@rebeccablond.com

BLOOMFIELDS MANAGEMENT　　T 020 7659 2001
PMA Member
77 Oxford Street, London W1D 2ES
F 020 7659 2101
E emma@bloomfieldsmanagement.com
W www.bloomfieldsmanagement.com

BLUE STAR ASSOCIATES　　T 020 7836 6220
Apartment 8 Shaldon Mansions
132 Charing Cross Road, London WC2H 0LA
T 020 7836 4128
E bluestar.london.2000@gmail.com

BMA ACTORS & PRESENTERS　　T 01442 878878
*Personal Manager. Contact: Alex Haddad. By e-mail. 1200
Performers. Children. Commercials. Corporate. Dancers.
Film. Modelling. Presenters. Singers. Television. Walk-on &
Supporting Artists*
346 High Street, Marlow House
Berkhamsted, Hertfordshire HP4 1HT
F 01442 879879
E info@bmamodels.com
W www.bmamodels.com

BODENS AGENCY　　T 020 8447 0909
*Personal Manager. Contact: Adam Boden,
Katie McCutcheon, Sarah Holder. By Post/e-mail/
Telephone. 3 Agents represent 400 Performers.
Children. Commercials. Film. Television.
Walk-on & Supporting Artists*
Bodens Studios & Agency
99 East Barnet Road
New Barnet, Herts EN4 8RF
T 07545 696888
E info@bodens.co.uk
W www.bodens.co.uk/clients

BODY LONDON　　T 020 3441 9878
Studio 1, Fairbanks Studios 2
65-69 Lots Road, Chelsea, London SW10 0RN
E info@bodylondon.com
W www.bodylondon.com

BODYWORK AGENCY　　T 07792 851972
25-29 Glisson Road, Cambridge CB1 2HA
F 01223 568231
E agency@bodyworkds.co.uk

BOSS CASTING　　T 0161 237 0100
Fourways House, 57 Hilton Street
Manchester M1 2EJ
F 0161 236 1237
E cath@bosscasting.co.uk
W www.bosscasting.co.uk

**BOSS CREATIVE
ENTERTAINMENT**　　T 020 8299 0478
PMA Member
Office 1, 6 Lordship Lane
Zenoria Street, London SE22 8HN
E enquiries@bosscreativeentertainment.com
W www.bosscreativeentertainment.com

**BOSS CREATIVE
MANAGEMENT**　　T 0161 237 0100
Fourways House, 57 Hilton Street, Manchester M1 2EJ
F 0161 236 1237
E info@bossmodels.co.uk
W www.bossmodelmanagement.co.uk

BOSS LIFESTYLE　　T 0161 237 0100
Fourways House, 57 Hilton Street
Manchester M1 2EJ
F 0161 236 1237
E info@bossmodels.co.uk
W www.bossmodelmanagement.co.uk

BOSS MODEL MANAGEMENT　　T 0161 237 0100
Fourways House, 57 Hilton Street
Manchester M1 2EJ
F 0161 236 1237
E info@bossmodels.co.uk
W www.bossmodelmanagement.co.uk

**BOX ARTIST
MANAGEMENT - BAM**　　T 020 7713 7313
Choreographers. Musicals. Commercial Dancers
The Attic, The Old Finsbury Town Hall
Rosebery Avenue, London EC1R 4RP
E hello@boxartistmanagement.com
W www.boxartistmanagement.com

BOYCE, Sandra MANAGEMENT　　T 020 7923 0606
PMA Member
125 Dynevor Road, London N16 0DA
F 020 7241 2313
E info@sandraboyce.com
W www.sandraboyce.com

**BRAIDMAN, Michelle
ASSOCIATES LTD**　　T 020 7237 3523
PMA Member
2 Futura House, 169 Grange Road
London SE1 3BN
F 020 7231 4634
E info@braidman.com
W www.braidman.com

**BRAITHWAITE'S
THEATRICAL AGENCY**　　T 020 8954 5638
8 Brookshill Avenue, Harrow Weald
Middlesex HA3 6RZ

**BREAK A LEG
MANAGEMENT LTD**　　T 020 7359 3594
Units 2/3 The Precinct, Packington Square
London N1 7UP
F 020 7359 3660
E agency@breakalegman.com
W www.breakalegman.com

**BRIDGES: THE ACTORS'
AGENCY**　　T 0131 226 6433
St George's West, 58 Shandwick Place
Edinburgh EH2 4RT
E admin@bridgesactorsagency.com
W www.bridgesactorsagency.com

Peter Simpkin PHOTOGRAPHY

020 8364 2634
07973 224 084
petersimpkin@aol.com
www.petersimpkin.co.uk

Ed Coleman

Evanna Lynch

BROADCASTING AGENCY LTD T 020 3131 0128
Unit 106A Netil House, 1 Westgate Street
London E8 3RL
E info@broadcastingagency.co.uk
W www.broadcastingagency.co.uk

BROOD T 020 8699 1757
PMA Member. Contact: By e-mail.
1 Agent represents 40 Performers
High Street Buildings
134 Kirkdale
London SE26 4BB
F 020 8699 8787
E broodmanagement@aol.com
W www.broodmanagement.com

BROOK, Dolly AGENCY T 01371 875767
PO Box 5436, Dunmow CM6 1WW
F 01371 875996
E dollybrookcasting@btinternet.com

BROOK, Jeremy LTD T 020 7434 0398
37 Berwick Street, London W1F 8RS
F 020 7287 8016
E info@jeremybrookltd.co.uk
W www.jeremybrookltd.co.uk

BROOK, Valerie AGENCY T 0161 486 1631
10 Sandringham Road, Cheadle Hulme
Cheshire SK8 5NH
T 07973 434953
E colinbrook@freenetname.co.uk

Ricky Whittle

Antonia Clarke

Charlie Clements

BRANDON BISHOP

t: 020 7275 7468   m: 07931 383 830

www.brandonbishopphotography.com

PETE BARTLETT
PHOTOGRAPHY

petebartlettheadshots.co.uk
info@petebartlett.com
07971 653994

Noel Samuels   Lara Honnor   Paul Herwig

BROWN, SIMCOCKS & ANDREWS   T 020 7953 7484
PMA Member
504 The Chandlery
50 Westminster Bridge Road
London SE1 7QY
F 020 7953 7494
E info@bsaagency.co.uk
W www.brownsimcocksandandrews.co.uk

BRUNO KELLY LTD   T 020 7183 7331
3rd Floor, 207 Regent Street
London W1B 3HH
F 020 7183 7332
E info@brunokelly.com
W www.brunokelly.com

BRUNSKILL MANAGEMENT LTD   T 020 7581 3388
Personal Manager. PMA Member.
Contact: Aude Powell. By Post only. Accepts Showreels/
Voicereels. Commercials. Corporate. Film. Musicals.
Radio. Stage. Television. Voice Overs
Suite 8A, 169 Queen's Gate
London SW7 5HE
F 020 7589 9460
E contact@brunskill.com

BRUNSKILL MANAGEMENT LTD   T 01768 881430
Personal Manager. PMA Member.
Contact: Aude Powell. By Post only. Accepts Showreels/
Voicereels. Commercials. Corporate. Film. Musicals.
Radio. Stage. Television. Voice Overs
The Courtyard, Edenhall
Penrith, Cumbria CA11 8ST
F 01768 881850
E aude@brunskill.com

BSA LTD
See HARRISON, Penny BSA LTD

BSA MANAGEMENT   T 0845 0035301
Personal Manager. Actors & Presenters. Commercials.
Film. Television
Crusader House, 2nd Floor
145-157 St John Street, London EC1V 4PY
E agent@bsamanagement.co.uk
W www.bsamanagement.co.uk

BUCHANAN, Bronia ASSOCIATES LTD   T 020 7395 1400
PMA Member
1st Floor, 23 Tavistock Street
London WC2E 7NX
F 020 7379 5560
E info@buchanan-associates.co.uk
W www.buchanan-associates.co.uk

BURNETT CROWTHER LTD   T 020 7437 8008
PMA Member. Contact: Barry Burnett, Lizanne Crowther
3 Clifford Street, London W1S 2LF
F 020 7287 3239
E associates@bcltd.org
W www.bcltd.org

BURNINGHAM ASSOCIATES   T 07807 176287
Personal Manager. Actors. Directors. Playwrights
4 Victoria Road, Twickenham
Middlesex TW1 3HW
E info@burnassoc.org
W www.burnassoc.co.uk

BUTTERCUP AGENCY   T 0843 2899063
20 Station Road, Claygate, Esher, Surrey KT10 9DH
E info@buttercupagency.co.uk
W www.buttercupagency.co.uk

BWH AGENCY LTD THE   T 020 7734 0657
PMA Member
5th Floor, 35 Soho Square, London W1D 3QX
F 020 7734 1278
E info@thebwhagency.co.uk
W www.thebwhagency.co.uk

BYRAM, Paul ASSOCIATES   T 020 3137 3385
13 Embassy Court, 24 Inglis Road
London W5 3RL
F 020 3468 7450
E admin@paulbyram.com
W www.paulbyram.com

BYRON'S MANAGEMENT   T 020 7242 8096
Contact: By Post/e-mail. Accepts Showreels.
Commercials. Film. Musicals. Stage. Television
180 Drury Lane, London WC2B 5QF
E byronsmanagement@aol.com
W www.byronsmanagement.co.uk

C.A. ARTISTES MANAGEMENT   T 020 8834 1608
26-28 Hammersmith Grove, London W6 7BA
E casting@caartistes.com
W www.caartistes.com

CAMBELL JEFFREY MANAGEMENT   T 01323 730526
Set, Costume & Lighting Designers
Flat 2, 4 Jevington Gardens
Eastbourne BN21 4HN
E cambell@theatricaldesigners.co.uk

CAMPBELL, Alison MODEL & PROMOTION AGENCY   T 028 9080 9809
381 Beersbridge Road, Belfast BT5 5DT
F 028 9080 9808
E info@alisoncampbellmodels.com
W www.alisoncampbellmodels.com

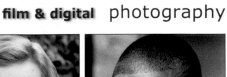

claire grogan
film & digital photography

Annette Badland	Tiffany Graves	Duane Henry

Ben Richards	Abi Hardingham	Natalie Viccars

Elliot James Langridge	Maria Crocker	Martin Freeman

 Claire Grogan Photography | facebook

020 7272 1845   07932 635381   claire@clairegrogan.co.uk www.clairegrogan.co.uk

CAPITAL VOICES   T 01372 466228
Contact: Anne Skates. Film. Session Singers. Stage.
Studio. Television
PO Box 364, Esher, Surrey KT10 9XZ
F 01372 466229
E capvox@aol.com
W www.capitalvoices.com

CAREY, Roger ASSOCIATES   T 01932 582890
Personal Manager. PMA Member
Suite 909, The Old House, Shepperton Film Studios
Studios Road, Shepperton, Middlesex TW17 0QD
F 01932 569602
E info@rogercarey.f2s.com
W www.rogercareyassociates.com

CAREY DODD ASSOCIATES   T 020 7692 1877
78 York Street, London W1H 1DP
T 020 7504 1087
E agents@careydoddassociates.com
W www.careydoddassociates.com

CARNEY, Jessica ASSOCIATES   T 020 7434 4143
Personal Manager. PMA Member
4th Floor, 23 Golden Square
London W1F 9JP
F 020 7434 4173
E info@jcarneyassociates.co.uk
W www.jessicacarneyassociates.co.uk

CAROUSEL EVENTS   T 0844 2250465
Entertainment for Corporate & Private Events
Incentive House, 23 Castle Street
High Wycombe, Bucks HP13 6RU
F 01494 511501
E info@carouselevents.co.uk
W www.carouselevents.co.uk

CARR, Norrie AGENCY   T 020 7253 1771
Holborn Studios, 49 Eagle Wharf Road
London N1 7ED
F 020 7253 1772
E info@norriecarr.com
W www.norriecarr.com

CASA MANAGEMENT   T 0161 612 0082
Alison House, 5 Highfield Road
Mellor, Stockport, Cheshire SK6 5AL
E casamgmt@aol.com
W www.casamanagement.co.uk

CASAROTTO MARSH LTD   T 020 7287 4450
Film Technicians
Waverley House, 7-12 Noel Street
London W1F 8GQ
F 020 7287 9128
E info@casarotto.co.uk
W www.casarotto.co.uk

CASCADE ARTISTS LTD   T 020 7437 3175
Contact: By e-mail. Accepts Showreels. 3 Agents
represent 30 Performers. Commercials. Corporate. Film.
Stage. Television
Studio Soho, Royalty Mews (entrance by Quo Vadis)
22 Dean Street, London W1D 3RA
E info@cascadeartists.com
W www.cascadeartists.com

CASTAWAY ACTORS
AGENCY   T 00 353 1 6719264
30-31 Wicklow Street, Dublin 2, Ireland
F 00 353 1 6719133
E castaway@clubi.ie
W www.irish-actors.com

CASTCALL   T 01582 456213
Casting & Consultancy Service
106 Wilsden Avenue, Luton LU1 5HR
E casting@castcall.co.uk
W www.castcall.co.uk

CASTING DEPARTMENT THE   T 020 8582 5523
277 Chiswick Village, London W4 3DF
T 07931 491938
E jillscastingdpt@aol.com
W www.thecastingdept.co.uk

CAVAT AGENCY   T 020 7018 0536
2nd Floor, 56 Bloomsbury Street
London WC1B 3QT
E enquiries@cavatagency.co.uk
W www.cavatagency.co.uk

C B A INTERNATIONAL   T 00 33 2 32671981
Contact: Cindy Brace
c/o C.M.S. Experts Associés
149 Boulevard Malesherbes, 75017 Paris, France
E c_b_a@club-internet.fr
W www.cindy-brace.com

CBL MANAGEMENT   T 01273 321245
Artistes. Creatives
20 Hollingbury Rise, Brighton
East Sussex BN1 7HJ
T 07956 890307
E enquiries@cblmanagement.co.uk
W www.cblmanagement.co.uk

C C A MANAGEMENT   T 020 7630 6303
Personal Manager. PMA Member. Contact: By Post.
Actors. Technicians
Garden Level, 32 Charlwood Street
London SW1V 2DY
F 020 7630 7376
E actors@ccamanagement.co.uk
W www.ccamanagementinfo.com

CCM   T 020 7278 0507
CPMA Member
Panther House, 38 Mount Pleasant, London WC1X 0AN
E casting@ccmactors.com
W www.ccmactors.co.uk

CDA   T 020 7373 3323
Personal Manager. PMA Member. Contact: By Post/
e-mail. Accepts Showreels. Film. Stage. Television
125 Gloucester Road, London SW7 4TE
F 020 7373 1110
E cda@cdalondon.com
W www.cdalondon.com

CELEBRITY GROUP THE   T 0871 2501234
12 Connaught Square, London W2 2BE
E info@celebrity.co.uk
W www.celebrity.co.uk

CENTER STAGE AGENCY T 00 353 1 4533599
Personal Manager. Contact: By e-mail. Accepts
Showreels. Commercials. Film. Presenters. Stage.
Television. Voice Overs
7 Rutledge Terrace
South Circular Road, Dublin 8, Ireland
E geraldinecenterstage@eircom.net
W www.centerstageagency.com

CENTRAL LINE T 0115 941 2937
Personal Manager. Co-operative. CPMA Member.
Contact: By Post
11 East Circus Street, Nottingham NG1 5AF
E centralline@btconnect.com
W www.the-central-line.co.uk

CHAMBERS MANAGEMENT T 020 7796 3588
Comedians. Comic Actors
39-41 Parker Street, London WC2B 5PQ
F 020 7831 8598
E hannah@chambersmgt.com
W www.chambersmgt.com

CHAMPION TALENT T 020 8761 5395
10 Birkbeck Place, London SE21 8JU
E info@championtalent.co.uk
W www.championtalent.co.uk

CHARLESWORTH,
Peter & ASSOCIATES T 020 7792 4600
67 Holland Park Mews, London W11 3SS
F 020 7792 1893
E info@petercharlesworth.co.uk

CHATTO & LINNIT LTD T 020 7352 7722
123A Kings Road, London SW3 4PL
F 020 7352 3450
E info@chattolinnit.com

CHP ARTIST MANAGEMENT T 01844 345630
Meadowcroft Barn, Crowbrook Road, Askett
Princes Risborough, Buckinghamshire HP27 9LS
T 07976 560580
E charlotte@chproductions.org.uk
W www.chproductions.org.uk

CHRYSTEL ARTS AGENCY T 01494 773336
6 Eunice Grove, Chesham, Bucks HP5 1RL
T 07799 605489
E chrystelarts@waitrose.com   .

CINEL GABRAN MANAGEMENT T 029 2066 6600
Personal Manager. PMA Member. Contact: By Post.
Accepts Showreels. 60 Performers. Commercials.
Corporate. Film. Musicals. Presenters. Radio. Stage.
Television. Voice Overs
PO Box 5163, Cardiff CF5 9BJ
E info@cinelgabran.co.uk   W www.cinelgabran.co.uk

CINEL GABRAN MANAGEMENT T 0845 4300060
Personal Manager. PMA Member. Contact: By Post.
Accepts Showreels. 60 Performers. Commercials.
Corporate. Film. Musicals. Presenters. Radio. Stage.
Television. Voice Overs
Adventure House, Newholm
Whitby, North Yorkshire YO21 3QL
E mail@cinelgabran.co.uk   W www.cinelgabran.co.uk

CIRCUIT PERSONAL
MANAGEMENT LTD T 01782 285388
Co-operative. Contact: By Post/e-mail. Accepts
Showreels. Commercials. Corporate. Film. Stage.
Television
Suite 71 S.E.C., Bedford Street, Shelton
Stoke-on-Trent, Staffs ST1 4PZ
F 01782 206821
E mail@circuitpm.co.uk   W www.circuitpm.co.uk

CITY ACTORS' MANAGEMENT T 020 7793 9888
CPMA Member
Oval House, 52-54 Kennington Oval, London SE11 5SW
E info@cityactors.co.uk
W www.cityactors.co.uk

CLARKE & JONES LTD T 020 8438 0185
28 Fordwych Court, Shoot Up Hill, London NW2 3PH
F 0870 1313391
E mail@clarkeandjones.plus.com

CLASS - CARLINE LUNDON
ASSOCIATES T 07853 248957
25 Falkner Square, Liverpool L8 7NZ
E clundon@googlemail.com

CLAYMAN, Tony
PROMOTIONS LTD T 020 7368 3336
Vicarage House
58-60 Kensington Church Street, London W8 4DB
F 020 7368 3338
E tony@tonyclayman.com
W www.tonyclayman.com

CLAYPOLE MANAGEMENT T 0845 6501777
PO Box 123, DL3 7WA
E info@claypolemanagement.co.uk
W www.claypolemanagement.co.uk

CLIC AGENCY T 01248 354420
7 Ffordd Seion, Bangor, Gwynedd LL57 1BS
E clic@btinternet.com
W www.clicagency.co.uk

COCHRANE, Elspeth PERSONAL
MANAGEMENT
See ASQUITH & HORNER

COLE KITCHENN
PERSONAL MANAGEMENT LTD T 020 7427 5681
PMA Member
ROAR House, 46 Charlotte Street, London W1T 2GS
F 020 7353 9639
E info@colekitchenn.com
W www.colekitchenn.com

COLLINS, Shane ASSOCIATES T 020 7826 8560
PMA Member
45 Beech Street, London EC2Y 8AD
F 0870 4601983
E info@shanecollins.co.uk
W www.shanecollins.co.uk

COLLIS MANAGEMENT LTD T 020 8767 0196
PMA Member
182 Trevelyan Road, London SW17 9LW
T 07850 435303
E marilyn@collismanagement.co.uk

COMEDY CLUB LTD THE T 0845 4595656
2nd Floor, 28-31 Moulsham Street
Chelmsford, Essex CM2 0HX
F 01245 255507
E info@thecomedyclub.co.uk
W www.thecomedyclub.co.uk

COMIC VOICE MANAGEMENT T 0845 4595656
Comedians
2nd Floor, 28-31 Moulsham Street
Chelmsford, Essex CM2 0HX
F 01245 255507
E info@thecomedyclub.co.uk
W www.comicvoice.com

COMMERCIAL AGENCY THE
See TCA (THE COMMERCIAL AGENCY)

COMMERCIALS@BBA T 020 7395 1402
Commercials. Corporate
1st Floor, 23 Tavistock Street
London WC2E 7NX
E commercials@buchanan-associates.co.uk
W www.commercialsatbba.co.uk

CONTI, Italia AGENCY LTD T 020 7608 7500
PMA Member. Contact: By Post/Telephone
Italia Conti House, 23 Goswell Road
London EC1M 7AJ
F 020 7253 1430
E agency@italiaconti.co.uk

**CONWAY VAN GELDER
GRANT LTD** T 020 7287 0077
Personal Manager. PMA Member
3rd Floor, 8-12 Broadwick Street
London W1F 8HW
E info@conwayvg.co.uk

paulcable
photography & design

www.paulcable.com
info@paulcable.com
07958 932 764

COOKE, Howard ASSOCIATES T 020 7591 0144
*PMA Member. Contact: Howard Cooke. By Post. 2 Agents
represent 50 Performers. Commercials. Film. Stage.
Television*
19 Coulson Street, Chelsea
London SW3 3NA
F 020 7591 0155

**COOPER, Tommy
MAGICAL AGENCY** T 07860 290437
Comedy. Magicians
21 Streatham Court, Ashley Cross
Poole, Dorset BH14 0EX
E info@clivegreenaway.com
W www.tommycooperremembered.co.uk

**COOPER & CHAND
TALENT MANAGEMENT** T 020 8450 3901
69 Teignmouth Road, London NW2 4EA
T 07723 324828
E agents@cooperandchand.com
W www.cooperandchand.com

CORNER, Clive ASSOCIATES T 01305 860267
*Contact: Duncan Stratton. By Post. Accepts Showreels.
2 Agents represent 40 Performers. Commercials. Film.
Musicals. Stage. Television*
'The Belenes', 60 Wakeham
Portland DT5 1HN
E cornerassociates@btconnect.com

**CORNISH, Caroline
MANAGEMENT LTD** T 020 8743 7337
Technicians only
12 Shinfield Street, London W12 0HN
T 07725 555711
E carolinecornish@me.com
W www.carolinecornish.co.uk

CORONA MANAGEMENT T 020 8941 2659
Unit B
The Kingsway Business Park, Oldfield Road
Hampton, London TW12 2HD
E info@coronatheatreschool.com
W www.coronatheatreschool.com

**COULSON, Lou
ASSOCIATES LTD** T 020 7734 9633
PMA Member
1st Floor, 37 Berwick Street
London W1F 8RS
F 020 7439 7569
E info@loucoulson.co.uk

**COULTER MANAGEMENT
AGENCY LTD** T 0141 357 6666
PMA Member. Contact: Anne Coulter
PO Box 2830, Glasgow G61 9BQ
E coultermanagement@ntlworld.com
W www.coultermanagement.com

**COVENT GARDEN
MANAGEMENT** T 020 7392 7324
Cida, 7-15 Greatorex Street
London E1 5NF
T 07713 480964
E info@coventgardenmanagement.com
W www.coventgardenmanagement.com

CPA MANAGEMENT T 01708 766444
The Studios, 219B North Street
Romford, Essex RM1 4QA
E info@cpamanagement.co.uk
W www.cpastudios.co.uk

CRAWFORDS T 020 8947 9999
PO Box 56662, London W13 3BH
E cr@wfords.com
W www.crawfords.tv

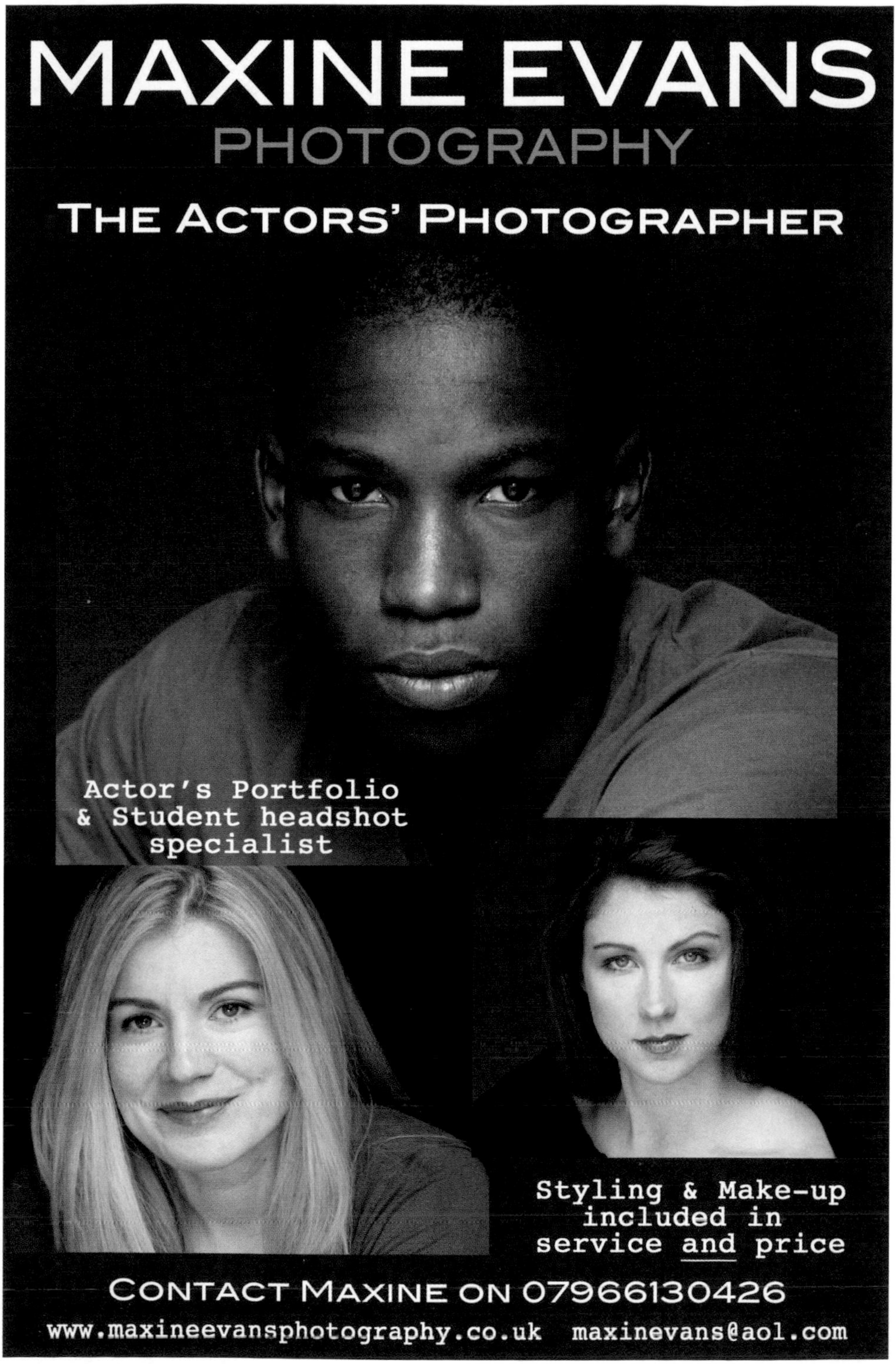

www.kmcagencies.co.uk e: casting@kmcagencies.co.uk

Full Production & Casting Team available for Shows & Events.
Dancers, Choreographers, Actors & Singers for TV, Film, Theatre, Commercial & Cruise Work.
Specialising in Musical Theatre and Actors Personal Management Service.

| PO Box 12248 | Great Ancoats Street | Manchester M4 5AB | t 0161 237 3009 | f 0161 237 9812 |
| Garden Studios | 71-75 Shelton Street | London WC2H 9JQ | t 0845 034 0772 | |

**CREATIVE ARTISTS
MANAGEMENT (CAM)** T 020 7292 0600
PMA Member. Contact: By e-mail only
4th Floor, 111 Shoreditch High Street
London E1 6JN
E reception@cam.co.uk
W www.cam.co.uk

CREATIVE BLAST AGENCY T 020 8123 6386
The Training Centre, Radford Way
Billericay, Essex CM12 0DX
T 07545 009830
E info@cbagency.co.uk
W www.cbagency.co.uk

**CREATIVE MEDIA
MANAGEMENT** T 020 8584 5363
*PMA Member. No Actors. Film, Television & Stage
Technical Personnel only*
Ealing Studios, Ealing Green
London W5 5EP
F 020 8566 5554
E enquiries@creativemediamanagement.com
W www.creativemediamanagement.com

CRESCENT MANAGEMENT T 020 8987 0191
*Personal Manager. Co-operative. CPMA Member.
Contact: By Post. Accepts Showreels*
10 Barley Mow Passage, Chiswick
London W4 4PH
F 020 8987 0207
E mail@crescentmanagement.co.uk
W www.crescentmanagement.co.uk

CROI8 ACTORS AGENCY T 00 353 85 1420683
Galway, Co. Galway, Ireland
E croiactorsagency@yahoo.co.uk
W www.croiproductions.webs.com

CRUICKSHANK CAZENOVE LTD T 020 7735 2933
*PMA Member. Contact: Harriet Cruickshank. By Post.
1 Agent. Choreographers, Designers & Directors only*
97 Old South Lambeth Road
London SW8 1XU
F 020 7582 6405
E harriet@ccagents.co.uk

CS MANAGEMENT T 020 8886 4264
The Croft, 7 Cannon Road
Southgate, London N14 7HE
F 020 8886 7555
E carole@csmanagementuk.com
W www.csmanagementuk.com

C.S.A. T 020 7499 7534
4th Floor, 45 Maddox Street
London W1S 2PE
F 020 7499 7535
E csa@shepherdmanagement.co.uk

CURTIS BROWN GROUP LTD T 020 7393 4400
PMA Member
Haymarket House, 28-29 Haymarket
London SW1Y 4SP
F 020 7393 4401
E actorsagents@curtisbrown.co.uk
W www.curtisbrown.co.uk

CV ACTOR MANAGEMENT T 07989 811999
The Studio, 1st Floor, RAFA Wings Club
37 Ruthin Road, Wrexham LL13 7TU
E cvactormanagement@yahoo.co.uk
W www.cvactormanagement.co.uk

CWC T 0113 244 5277
Top Floor, 67 St Pauls Street
Leeds LS1 2TE
F 0113 245 9665
E info@cwc-uk.net
W www.cwc-uk.net

DAA MANAGEMENT T 020 7255 6123
PMA Member. Formerly Debi Allen Associates
Welbeck House, 66-67 Wells Street
London W1T 3PY
F 020 7255 6128
E info@daamanagement.co.uk
W www.daamanagement.co.uk

DALY, David ASSOCIATES T 020 7384 1036
Contact: David Daly, Louisa Miles
586A King's Road, London SW6 2DX
F 020 7610 9512
E agent@daviddaly.co.uk
W www.daviddaly.co.uk

**DALY, David ASSOCIATES
(MANCHESTER)** T 01565 631999
Contact: Mary Ramsay
16 King Street, Knutsford
Cheshire WA16 6DL
F 01565 755334
E north@daviddaly.co.uk
W www.daviddaly.co.uk

DALZELL & BERESFORD LTD T 020 7341 9411
26 Astwood Mews, London SW7 4DE
F 020 7341 9412
E mail@dbltd.co.uk
W www.dalzellandberesford.co.uk

DANCERS T 020 7637 1487
Trading as FEATURES
1 Charlotte Street, London W1T 1RD
E info@features.co.uk
W www.features.co.uk

DANCERS INC T 020 7557 6654
9-13 Grape Street, Covent Garden
London WC2H 8ED
F 020 7557 6656
E dancersinc@international-collective.com
W www.dancersinc.co.uk

**DAVID ARTISTES MANAGEMENT
AGENCY LTD THE** T 020 8834 1615
26-28 Hammersmith Grove, London W6 7BA
E casting@davidagency.co.uk
W www.davidagency.co.uk

DAVIS, Chris MANAGEMENT LTD T 020 7240 2116
PMA Member
2nd Floor, 80-81 St Martin's Lane
London WC2N 4AA
E tadams@cdm-ltd.com
W www.cdm-ltd.com

Steve Lawton

NATURAL LIGHT · COLOUR · BLACK & WHITE · DIGITAL & FILM

WWW.STEVELAWTON.COM · 07973 307487 · STUDENT RATES

Dev Patel · Chloe Farnworth · Marc Baylis · Danielle Hope · Robert Kazinsky · Lara Goodison · Douglas Booth · Merissa Porter · Tony Discipline

DAVIS, Chris
MANAGEMENT LTD   T 01584 819005
PMA Member
Tenbury House, 36 Teme Street
Tenbury Wells, Worcestershire WR15 8AA
F 01584 819076
E tadams@cdm-ltd.com
W www.cdm-ltd.com

DAVIS, Lena,
BISHOP, John ASSOCIATES   T 01604 891487
Personal Manager. Contact: By Post. 2 Agents
Cotton's Farmhouse
Whiston Road
Cogenhoe, Northants NN7 1NL
E admin@cottonsfarmhouse.org

DAVIS-PRIOR ASSOCIATES   T 020 7635 7083
Unit 2, The Wheelwright Building
125 Pomeroy Street, London SE14 5BT
E info@davis-prior.co.uk
W www.davis-prior.co.uk

DENMARK STREET
MANAGEMENT   T 020 7700 5200
Personal Manager. Co-operative. CPMA Member.
Applications via Website
Suite 4, Clarendon Buildings
25 Horsell Road, Highbury N5 1XL
E mail@denmarkstreet.net
W www.denmarkstreet.net

DEREK'S HANDS AGENCY   T 020 8834 1609
Hand & Foot Modelling
26-28 Hammersmith Grove
London W6 7BA
E casting@derekshands.com
W www.derekshands.com

DEVINE ARTIST MANAGEMENT   T 0844 8844578
145-157 St John Street, London EC1V 4PW
E mail@devinemanagement.co.uk
W www.devinemanagement.co.uk

de WOLFE, Felix   T 020 7242 5066
Personal Manager. PMA Member. Contact: By Post.
Accepts Showreels. 3 Agents. Film. Musicals. Radio.
Stage. Television
Kingsway House, 103 Kingsway
London WC2B 6QX
F 020 7242 8119
E info@felixdewolfe.com
W www.felixdewolfe.com

DHM LTD
(DICK HORSEY MANAGEMENT)   T 01923 710614
Personal Manager. Contact: By Post/e-mail/Telephone.
Accepts Showreels/Voicereels. 2 Agents represent 40
Performers. Corporate. Musicals. Stage. Television
Suite 1, Cottingham House, Chorleywood Road
Rickmansworth, Herts WD3 4EP
T 07850 112211
E roger@dhmlimited.co.uk
W www.dhmlimited.co.uk

DIAMOND MANAGEMENT   T 020 7631 0400
PMA Member
31 Percy Street, London W1T 2DD
F 020 7631 0500
E agents@diman.co.uk

DIESTENFELD, Lily   T 07957 968214
Personal Manager. Over 50+ ages. No Unsolicited Post/
e-mails/Calls from Actors
28B Alexandra Grove
London N12 8HG
E lilyd@talk21.com

DIRECT PERSONAL
MANAGEMENT   T/F 020 8694 1788
Co-operative. CPMA Member. Contact: Daphne Franks.
By Post/e-mail. Commercials. Corporate. Film. Stage.
Television
St John's House, 16 St John's Vale
London SE8 4EN
E daphne.franks@directpm.co.uk
W www.directpm.co.uk

DIRECT PERSONAL
MANAGEMENT   T/F 0113 266 4036
Co-operative. CPMA Member. Contact: Daphne Franks.
By Post/e-mail. Commercials. Corporate. Film. Stage.
Television
Park House, 62 Lidgett Lane, Leeds LS8 1PL
E daphne.franks@directpm.co.uk
W www.directpm.co.uk

DOE, John MANAGEMENT   T 020 7871 2969
Kemp House, 152-160 City Road
London EC1V 2NX
T 07957 114175
E casting@johndoemgt.com
W www.johndoemgt.com

DOE, John MANAGEMENT   T 0161 241 7786
83 Ducie Street, Manchester M1 2JQ
T 07957 114175
E casting@johndoemgt.com
W www.johndoemgt.com

DOUBLE ACT
CELEBRITY LOOK ALIKES   T 020 8381 0151
PO Box 25574, London NW7 3GB
F 020 8201 1795
E info@double-act.co.uk
W www.double-act.co.uk

DOUBLEFVOICES   T 01580 830071
Singers
1 Hunters Lodge, Bodiam, East Sussex TN32 5UE
T 07976 927764
E rob@doublefvoices.com

DOWNES PRESENTERS AGENCY   T 07973 601332
55 Montgomery Road, South Darenth
Kent DA4 9BH
E downes@presentersagency.com
W www.presentersagency.com

DP MANAGEMENT   T 07837 138892
Contact: Danny Pellerini. By Post. Accepts Showreels/
Voicereels. 1 Agent represents 60 Performers
Argyle House, 29-31 Euston Road
London NW1 2SD
E danny@dpmanagement.org
W www.dpmanagement.org

DQ MANAGEMENT   T 01273 721221
27 Ravenswood Park, Northwood
Middlesex HA6 3PR
T 07713 984633
E dq.management1@gmail.com
W www.dqmanagement.com

DRAGON PERSONAL
MANAGEMENT   T 029 2075 4491
20 Nantfawr Road, Cyncoed, Cardiff CF23 6JR
T 020 7183 5362
E casting@dragon-pm.com
W www.dragon-pm.com

DRAKE, Simon MANAGEMENT   T 020 7183 8995
9 Golden Square, London W1F 9HZ
F 020 7183 9013
E admin@simondrakemanagement.co.uk
W www.simondrakemanagement.co.uk

IAN HOSKIN PHOTOGRAPHY 07773902071 www.ianhoskin.co.uk
Headshots and Portraiture. Student Discount. London and Devon. info@ianhoskin.co.uk

DS PERSONAL MANAGEMENT T 020 8743 7777
St Martin's Theatre, West Street, London WC2H 9NZ
E ds@denisesilvey.com

DYSON, Louise at
VisABLE PEOPLE T 01905 776631
Contact: Louise Dyson. Artists with Disabilities
T 07930 345152
E louise@visablepeople.com
W www.visablepeople.com

EARLE, Kenneth
PERSONAL MANAGEMENT T 020 7274 1219
214 Brixton Road, London SW9 6AP
F 020 7274 9529
E kennethearle@agents-uk.com
W www.kennethearlepersonalmanagement.com

EARNSHAW, Susi
MANAGEMENT T 020 8441 5010
Personal Manager
The Bull Theatre, 68 High Street, Barnet, Herts EN5 5SJ
E casting@susiearnshaw.co.uk
W www.susiearnshawmanagement.com

ECLECTIC ARTISTS T 001 323 798 5102
1714 North McCadden Place, Suite 2419
Hollywood, Los Angeles, CA 90028, USA
F 001 323 315 4263 E kat@nextstoplax.com

EDEN, Shelly
ASSOCIATES LTD T/F 020 8558 3536
The Old Factory, Minus One House
Lyttelton Road, London E10 5NQ
E shellyeden@aol.com

KAREN SCOTT PHOTOGRAPHY

07958 975 950

www.karenscottphotography.com
info@karenscottphotography.com

student rates

NEED AMERICAN ACTORS?

The North American Actors Association is *the* source for genuine professional American and Canadian actors, based in the UK without permit restrictions. Get in touch today!

e: admin@naaa.org.uk w: www.naaa.org.uk

EJA ASSOCIATES　　　　T 020 7564 2688
Incorporating Simply Singers International
PO Box 63617, London SW9 1AN
T 07891 632946
E ejaassociates@aol.com

EKA ACTOR MANAGEMENT　　T 01925 761088
Contact: Amy Musker (Senior Casting Agent). Accepts Showreels. Commercials. Corporate. Film. Television. Voice Overs
The Warehouse Studios, Glaziers Lane
Culcheth, Warrington, Cheshire WA3 4AQ
T 01925 761210
E castings@eka-agency.com
W www.eka-agency.com

ELITE TALENT LTD　　　　T 07787 342221
54 Crosslee Road, Blackley
Manchester M9 6TA
E paul@elite-talent.net
W www.elitetalent.co.uk

ELLIOTT AGENCY LTD THE　　T 01273 454111
10 High Street, Shoreham-by-Sea BN43 5DA
E elliottagency@btconnect.com
W www.elliottagency.co.uk

ELLIS, Bill LTD
See A & B PERSONAL MANAGEMENT LTD

ELLITE MANAGEMENT　　　T 0845 6525361
Contact: By Post/e-mail. Accepts Showreels. 3 Agents represent 40 Performers. Dancers
'The Dancer', 8 Peterson Road
Wakefield WF1 4EB
T 07957 631510
E enquiries@ellitemanagement.co.uk
W www.elliteproductions.co.uk

EMPTAGE HALLETT　　　　T 020 7436 0425
PMA Member
14 Rathbone Place, London W1T 1HT
F 020 7580 2748
E mail@emptagehallett.co.uk

EMPTAGE HALLETT　　　　T 029 2034 4205
PMA Member
2nd Floor, 3-5 The Balcony
Castle Arcade, Cardiff CF10 1BU
F 029 2034 4206
E cardiff@emptagehallett.co.uk

ENCORE UK CASTING　　　T 01626 211040
PO Box 251, Newton Abbot
Devon TQ12 1AL
F 01626 202989
E hannah@encorecasting.co.uk
W www.encorecasting.co.uk

ENGERS, Emma ASSOCIATES LTD　　　T 020 7278 9980
56 Russell Court, Woburn Place
London WC1H 0LW
T 07790 011920
E emma@emmaengersassociates.com
W www.emmaengersassociates.com

ENGLISH, Doreen '95　　　T/F 01243 825968
Contact: By Post/Telephone
4 Selsey Avenue, Aldwick, Bognor Regis
West Sussex PO21 2QZ

EPSTEIN, June ASSOCIATES　　T 020 7328 0864
Contact: By Post/e-mail
Flat 1, 62 Compayne Gardens
London NW6 3RY
F 020 7328 0684
E juneepstein@googlemail.com

ESSANAY　　　　　　　T 020 8998 0007
Personal Manager. PMA Member. Contact: By Post
PO Box 56662, London W13 3BH
E info@essanay.co.uk

ESTALL, Jane AGENCY THE　　T 07703 550006
37 Madeira Drive, Hastings
East Sussex TN34 2NH
E thejaneestallagency@gmail.com

ETHNICS ARTISTE AGENCY　　T 020 8523 4242
86 Elphinstone Road, Walthamstow
London E17 5EX
F 020 8523 4523
E info@ethnicsaa.co.uk

EUROKIDS CASTING AGENCY　　T 01925 761088
Contact: Amy Musker (Senior Casting Agent). Accepts Showreels. Children & Teenagers. Commercials. Film. Television. Walk-ons, Supporting Artists & Extras
The Warehouse Studios, Glaziers Lane
Culcheth, Warrington
Cheshire WA3 4AQ
T 01925 761210
E castings@eka-agency.com
W www.eka-agency.com

EVANS, Jacque MANAGEMENT LTD　　T 020 8699 1202
Top Floor Suite, 14 Holmesley Road
London SE23 1PJ
F 020 8699 5192
W www.jacqueevansltd.com

EVANS, Stephanie ASSOCIATES　　　T/F 0870 6092629
Rivington House, 82 Great Eastern Street
London EC2A 3JF
T 07855 460341
E steph@stephanie-evans.com
W www.stephanie-evans.com

EVANS, Stephanie ASSOCIATES　　　T/F 01269 870944
6 Bryn Tirion, Pontyberem
Llanelli, Carmarthenshire SA15 5BX
T 07855 460341
E steph@stephanie-evans.com
W www.stephanie-evans.com

EVANS & REISS　　　　T 020 8871 0788
104 Fawe Park Road
London SW15 2EA
E janita@evansandreiss.co.uk

Headshots With Personality
Make You Stand Out From The Crowd

Nick Gregan - Premier Headshots
for TV, Stage & Film for 20 Years

www.nickgregan.com   t: 020 85333003   m: 07774 421878
info@nickgregan.com

NIC KNIGHT MANAGEMENT *in association with* **THE ANNA SCHER THEATRE**

23 Buckler Court
Eden Grove
London N7 8EF
T: +44 (0) 203 093 5422
E: enquiries@nicknightmanagement.com
www.nicknightmanagement.com

Specialist Representation • Film
Television • Theatre • Commercials
Over 40 Years
drama training
experience (AST)
www.annaschertheatre.com

**EVOLUTION TALENT
MANAGEMENT**   T 020 7749 9187
64 Great Western Street, London EC2A 3QR
E info@evomngt.com
W www.evolutionmngt.com

EXCESS ALL AREAS   T/F 020 7737 5300
*Contact: Paul L. Martin (Director). Cabaret, Circus &
Variety Entertainment*
1st & 2nd Floors, 20 Stansfield Road
Stockwell, London SW9 9RZ
E info@excessallareas.co.uk
W www.excessallareas.co.uk

**EXPERTS MANAGEMENT
SERVICES LTD**   T 01625 858556
Trading as Jane Hughes Management
PO Box 200, Stockport, Cheshire SK12 1GW
T 07766 130604
E gill@jhm.co.uk

**EXPRESSIONS
CASTING AGENCY**   T 01623 424334
3 Newgate Lane, Mansfield
Nottingham NG18 2LB
E expressions-uk@btconnect.com
W www.expressionsperformingarts.co.uk

EYE AGENT MANAGEMENT
E info@christheagent.com
W www.christheagent.com

EYE CASTING THE   T 020 7377 7500
1st Floor, 92 Commercial Street
Off Puma Court, London E1 6LZ
E bayo@theeyecasting.com
W www.theeyecasting.com

FARINO, Paola   T 020 7207 0858
Actors
109 St Georges Road, London SE1 6HY
E info@paolafarino.co.uk
W www.paolafarino.co.uk

**FARNES, Norma
MANAGEMENT**   T 020 7727 1544
9 Orme Court, London W2 4RL
F 020 7792 2110

FBI AGENCY   T 07050 222747
PO Box 250, Leeds LS1 2AZ
T 07515 567309
E casting@fbi-agency.co.uk
W www.fbi-agency.co.uk

FD MANAGEMENT   T 07730 800679
Sandhill, Sandhill Lane
Crawley Down Village RH10 4LE
E vivienwilde@mac.com

**FEA MANAGEMENT
(FERRIS ENTERTAINMENT)**   T 0845 4724725
London. Belfast. Cardiff. Los Angeles
Number 8, 132 Charing Cross Road
London WC2H 0LA
E info@ferrisentertainment.com
W www.ferrisentertainment.com

FEAST MANAGEMENT LTD   T 020 7354 5216
PMA Member
1st Floor, 34 Upper Street, London N1 0PN
F 020 7354 8995
E office@feastmanagement.co.uk

**FEATURED & BACKGROUND
CASTING LTD (FAB)**   T 01628 522688
Contact: Lois Ward, Suzanne Johns
13A Waldeck House, Waldeck Road
Maidenhead, Berkshire SL6 8BR
T 07808 781167
E info@fabcastingagency.com
W www.fabcastingagency.com

FEATURES   T 020 7637 1487
1 Charlotte Street, London W1T 1RD
E info@features.co.uk
W www.features.co.uk

FIELD, Alan ASSOCIATES   T 020 8441 1137
*Personal Manager. Contact: By e-mail. Celebrities.
Composers. Musicals. Presenters. Singers*
3 The Spinney, Bakers Hill
Hadley Common, Herts EN5 5QJ
T 07836 555300
E alan@alanfield.com

FILM CAST CORNWALL & SW   T 01326 311419
T 07811 253756
E enquiries@filmcastcornwall.co.uk
W www.filmcastcornwall.co.uk

FILM RIGHTS LTD   T 020 7316 1837
Personal Manager. Contact: By Post
Suite 306, Belsize Business Centre
258 Belsize Road, London NW6 4BT
F 020 7624 3629

FINCH & PARTNERS   T 020 7851 7140
Top Floor, 35 Heddon Street, London W1B 4BR
F 020 7287 6420
E reception@finchandpartners.com
W www.finchandpartners.com

**FIRST & FOREMOST
ENTERTAINMENT LTD**   T 07505 565635
*Contact: Chris Neilson. By Post/e-mail. Accepts
Showreels. 2 Agents represent 100 Performers.
Entertainment Agency & Corporate Entertainment.
Corporate, Musical, Speciality & Variety Acts*
90 Longridge Avenue, Brighton, East Sussex BN2 8RB
E info@firstandforemostentertainment.com
W www.firstandforemostentertainment.com

FIRST CALL MANAGEMENT   T 00 353 1 6798401
29-30 Dame Street, Dublin 2, Ireland
F 00 353 1 6798353
E fcmeleanor@gmail.com

**FITZGERALD, Sheridan
MANAGEMENT**   T 0845 5390504
*PMA Member. Contact: Edward Romfourt. By Post only
(SAE). No Phone Calls/e-mails*
16 Pond Lane, Brandon
Suffolk IP27 0LA
W www.sheridanfitzgerald.com

anna hull photography

t: 07778 399 419
e: info@annahullphotography.com
www.annahullphotography.com

FK ASSOCIATES　　　　　T 020 7431 2848
Suite 18, 58 Chetwynd Road
London NW5 1DJ
T 07961 192124
E admin@fkassoc.com

FLAIR TALENT　　　　　T 020 7287 0407
15 Poland Street, London W1F 8QE
E bookings@flairtalent.com
W www.flairtalent.com

FLETCHER ASSOCIATES　　T 020 8361 8061
Personal Manager. Contact: Francine Fletcher. Corporate
Speakers. Experts for Radio & Television. Stage
Studio One, 25 Parkway
London N20 0XN
F 020 8361 8866
W www.fletcherassociates.net

FLETCHER JACOB　　　　T 020 3603 7340
Artist Management
162-168 Regent Street, London W1B 5TD
F 020 7038 3707
E info@fletcherjacob.co.uk
W www.fletcherjacob.co.uk

FLP MANAGEMENT　　　　T 020 7371 0300
136-144 New Kings Road, Fulham
London SW6 4LZ
F 020 7371 8707
E info@flpmanagement.co.uk
W www.flpmanagement.co.uk

FOCUS TALENT　　　　　T 020 3240 1064
Personal Manager. Representing Actors in Feature Films,
Television, Stage & Commercials. Existing Clients only
81 Sutherland Avenue
London W9 2HG
T 07532 158818
E info@focustalent.co.uk
W www.focustalent.co.uk

FOLEY, Kerry
MANAGEMENT LTD　　　T 07747 864001
Communications House, 26 York Street
London W1U 6PZ
E contact@kfmltd.com
W www.kerryfoleymanagement.com

FOSTER, Sharon
MANAGEMENT　　　　　T 0121 443 4865
15A Hollybank Road, Birmingham B13 0RF
E mail@sharonfoster.co.uk
W www.sharonfoster.co.uk

FOX, Clare ASSOCIATES　　T/F 020 7328 7494
Set, Lighting & Sound Designers
9 Plympton Road, London NW6 7EH
E cimfox@yahoo.com
W www.clarefox.co.uk

FOX, Julie ASSOCIATES　　T/F 01628 777853
Personal Manager. Contact: Julie Fox. By e-mail only.
Accepts Showreels/Voicereels. 2 Agents represent 50
Performers
E agent@juliefoxassociates.co.uk
W www.juliefoxassociates.co.uk

FRENCH, Linda
See APM ASSOCIATES

FRESH AGENTS LTD　　　T 01273 711777
Suite 5, Saks House
19 Ship Street, Brighton BN1 1AD
T 0845 4080998
E info@freshagents.co.uk
W www.freshagents.co.uk

FRESH PARTNERS LTD　　T 020 7198 8478
1 Hardwick's Square, Wandsworth
London SW18 4AW
E hello@fresh-partners.com
W www.fresh-partners.com

FRONTLINE ACTORS
AGENCY DUBLIN　　　　T 00 353 1 6359882
30-31 Wicklow Street
Dublin 2, Ireland
E frontlineactors@eircom.net
W www.frontlineactors.com

FUNKY BEETROOT
CELEBRITY MANAGEMENT LTD　T 01227 751549
Personal Manager. Actors. Television Celebrities
PO Box 143, Faversham
Kent ME13 9LP
F 01227 752300
E info@funky-beetroot.com
W www.funky-beetroot.com

FUNNY SIDE ARTIST
MANAGEMENT THE　　　T 0844 4780404
Comedy
Number 1, 63 Mount Ephraim
Tunbridge Wells, Kent TN4 8BG
E contact@thefunnysideagency.com
W www.thefunnysideagency.com

GADBURY
PERSONAL MANAGEMENT　T 01942 635556
5 Bolton Road, Atherton
Manchester M46 9JQ
T 07791 737306
E vicky@gadbury-casting.co.uk
W www.gadburycasting.co.uk

GAELFORCE 10 MANAGEMENT　T 0845 6031266
14 Bowmont Gardens, Downahill
Glasgow G12 9LR
T 07778 296002
E info@gaelforce10.com
W www.gaelforce10.com

GAGAN, Hilary ASSOCIATES　T 020 7404 8794
Personal Manager. PMA Member
187 Drury Lane, London WC2B 5QD
F 020 7430 1869
E hilary@hgassoc.co.uk

GALLOWAYS　　　　　　T 020 7636 7770
PMA Member
16 Percy Street, London W1T 1DT
F 020 7636 7761
E info@gallowaysagency.com
W www.gallowaysagency.com

GANNON, Kay   T 07892 816283
Central Chambers, 93 Hope Street
Glasgow G2 6LD
F 0141 221 8622
E kay@revolutiontalentmanagement.com
W www.revolutiontalentmanagement.com

GARDNER HERRITY LTD   T 020 7388 0088
PMA Member. Contact: Andy Herrity, Nicky James
24 Conway Street, London W1T 6BG
F 020 7388 0688
E info@gardnerherrity.co.uk
W www.gardnerherrity.co.uk

GARRICKS   T 020 7738 1600
PMA Member
Angel House, 76 Mallinson Road
London SW11 1BN
E info@garricks.net

GAY, Noel   T 020 7836 3941
PMA Member
19 Denmark Street, London WC2H 8NA
F 020 7287 1816
E info@noelgay.com
W www.noelgay.com

GDA MANAGEMENT   T 01322 278879
Contact: By e-mail only. No Post
Suite 793, Kemp House
152 City Road
London EC1V 2NX
T 07974 680439
E info@gdamanagment.co.uk

GENUINE ARAB CASTING   T 07748 737374
Contact: By e-mail. Accepts Showreels/Voicereels.
Commercials. Corporate. Film. Television.
Voice Overs
78 York Street
London W1H 1DP
E info@genuinearabcasting.com
W www.genuinearabcasting.com

GENUINE CASTING   T 07748 737374
Contact: By e-mail. Accepts Showreels/Voicereels.
Commercials. Corporate. Film. Television.
Voice Overs
78 York Street
London W1H 1DP
E info@genuinecasting.com
W www.genuinecasting.com

Alistair McGowan

Rachel Weisz

GFI MANAGEMENT　T 020 8943 1120
Personal Manager
Green Gables, 47 North Lane
Teddington, Middlesex TW11 0HU
T 07540 881007
E agency@goforitcentre.com
W www.gfimanagement.co.uk

GIELGUD MANAGEMENT　T 01444 447020
PMA Member
The Old Cinema, 1st Floor, 59-61 The Broadway
Haywards Heath, West Sussex RH16 3AS
F 01444 447030
E info@gielgudmanagement.co.uk
W www.gielgudmanagement.co.uk

GILBERT & PAYNE　T 020 7734 7505
Room 236, 2nd Floor, Linen Hall
162-168 Regent Street, London W1B 5TB
F 020 7494 3787
E ee@gilbertandpayne.com

GILLMAN, Geraldine
ASSOCIATES　T 07799 791586
Malcolm House, Malcolm Primary School, Malcolm Road
Penge, London SE20 8RH
E geraldi.gillma@btconnect.com

GLASS, Eric LTD　T 020 7229 9500
25 Ladbroke Crescent, Notting Hill
London W11 1PS
F 020 7229 6220
E eglassltd@aol.com

GLOBAL7　T/F 020 7281 7679
PO Box 56232, London N4 4XP
T 07956 956652
E global7castings@gmail.com
W www.global7casting.com

GLOBAL ARTISTS　T 020 7839 4888
PMA Member. Contact: By Post/e-mail. Accepts
Showreels/Voicereels. 5 Agents
23 Haymarket, London SW1Y 4DG
F 020 7839 4555
E info@globalartists.co.uk
W www.globalartists.co.uk

GLYN MANAGEMENT　T 01449 737695
The Old School House, Brettenham, Ipswich IP7 7QP
F 01449 736117
E glyn.management@tesco.net

GMM (GREGG MILLARD
MANAGEMENT)　T 07710 562774
38 Barton House, Sable Street
London N1 2AF
E greggmillard.gmm@gmail.com

GO ENTERTAINMENTS LTD　T 01260 276627
Circus Artistes. Chinese State Circus. Cirque Surreal.
Bolshoi Circus "Spirit of The Horse"
Dane Mill, Broadhurst Lane
Congleton, Cheshire CW12 1LA
F 01260 270777
E info@arts-exchange.com
W www.arts-exchange.com

GOLD ARTISTES
TALENT MANAGEMENT　T 020 7873 2356
2 Alric Avenue, London NW10 8RB
E goldartistes@live.co.uk
W www.goldartistes.com

GOLDMANS MANAGEMENT　T 01323 472391
E casting@goldmansmanagement.co.uk
W www.goldmansmanagement.co.uk

GORDON & FRENCH　T 020 7734 4818
PMA Member. Contact: By Post
12-13 Poland Street, London W1F 8QB
F 020 7734 4832
E mail@gordonandfrench.net

GRAHAM, David PERSONAL
MANAGEMENT (DGPM)　T/F 020 7241 6752
The Studio, 107A Middleton Road, London E8 4LN
E info@dgpmtheagency.com

GRANT, James MEDIA　T 020 8742 4950
94 Strand On The Green, Chiswick, London W4 3NN
F 020 8742 4951
E enquiries@jamesgrant.co.uk
W www.jamesgrant.co.uk

GRANTHAM-HAZELDINE LTD　T 020 7038 3737
PMA Member
Suite 315, The Linen Hall
162-168 Regent Street, London W1B 5TD
F 020 7038 3739
E agents@granthamhazeldine.com

GRAY, Darren MANAGEMENT　T 023 9269 9973
Specialising in representing/promoting Australian Artists
2 Marston Lane, Portsmouth, Hampshire PO3 5TW
F 023 9267 7227
E darren.gray1@virgin.net
W www.darrengraymanagement.co.uk

GREEN, Jay ASSOCIATES　T 07972 585320
Personal Manager. Contact: By e-mail
Suite 569, Kemp House
152 City Road, London EC1V 2NX
T 07973 233632
E jga@jaygreenassociates.com
W www.jaygreenassociates.com

SHEILA BURNETT

P H O T O G R A P H Y

Simon Pegg

Imelda Staunton

Patsy Palmer

Ewan McGregor

020 7289 3058

www.sheilaburnett-headshots.com

Student Rates

GREEN & UNDERWOOD T 020 8998 0007
In association with ESSANAY. Personal Manager.
Contact: By Post
PO Box 56662, London W13 3BH
E ny@greenandunderwood.com

GRESHAM, Carl GROUP T 01274 735880
PO Box 3, Bradford
West Yorkshire BD1 4QN
F 01274 827161
E gresh@carlgresham.co.uk
W www.carlgresham.com

GRIFFIN, Sandra
MANAGEMENT LTD T 020 8891 5676
6 Ryde Place,
Richmond Road
East Twickenham, Middlesex TW1 2EH
F 020 8744 1812
E office@sandragriffin.com
W www.sandragriffin.com

GROUNDLINGS
THEATRE COMPANY T 023 9273 7370
42 Kent Street, Portsmouth
Hampshire PO1 3BT
E richard@groundlings.co.uk
W www.groundlings.co.uk

GROVES, Rob
PERSONAL MANAGEMENT T 020 3174 0501
Contact: By e-mail
4th Floor, 33 Glasshouse Street
London W1B 5DG
F 07092 873538
E rob@robgroves.co.uk
W www.robgroves.co.uk

GUBBAY, Louise ASSOCIATES T 01959 573080
Marstdean, Westmore Road
Tatsfield, Kent TN16 2AX
E louise@louisegubbay.com
W www.louisegubbay.com

GUBBAY, Louise
ASSOCIATES (LA) T 01959 573080
15021 Ventura Boulevard, Suite 343
Sherman Oaks, CA 91403, USA
T 001 323 522 5545
E louise@louisegubbay.com
W www.louisegubbay.com

GURNETT, J. PERSONAL
MANAGEMENT LTD T 020 7440 1850
12 Newburgh Street, London W1F 7RP
F 020 7287 9642
E mail@jgpm.co.uk
W www.jgpm.co.uk

HALL JAMES
PERSONAL MANAGEMENT T 020 8429 8111
PO Box 604, Pinner
Middlesex HA5 9GH
E agents@halljames.co.uk
W www.halljames.co.uk

HALLY, Yvette
MANAGEMENT T 00 353 1 4933685
121 Grange Road, Rathfarnham
Dublin 14, Ireland
F 00 353 1 4933076
E yhmgt@eircom.net

HAMBLETON, Patrick
MANAGEMENT T 020 7226 0947
Top Floor, 136 Englefield Road
London N1 3LQ
T 020 7993 5412
E info@phm.uk.com

HAMILTON HODELL LTD T 020 7636 1221
PMA Member
5th Floor, 66-68 Margaret Street
London W1W 8SR
F 020 7636 1226
E info@hamiltonhodell.co.uk
W www.hamiltonhodell.co.uk

HARLEQUIN ARTISTES T 0191 385 8834
Personal Manager
14 Beatrice Terrace, Shiney Row
Durham DH4 4QW
E paul@harlequinartistes.co.uk
W www.harlequinartistes.co.uk

HARRIS AGENCY LTD THE T 01923 211644
71 The Avenue, Watford
Herts WD17 4NU
E theharrisagency@btconnect.com

HARRISON, Penny BSA LTD T 020 8672 0136
Trinity Lodge, 25 Trinity Crescent
London SW17 7AG
E harrisonbsa@aol.com

HARVEY VOICES T 020 7952 4361
58 Woodlands Road, London N9 8RT
W www.harveyvoices.co.uk

HAT MANAGEMENT T 07902 579235
Contact: Laurence James
15 Dargle Road, Sale
Cheshire M33 7FN
E hatactors@hotmail.co.uk

HATTON McEWAN T 020 7253 4770
Personal Manager. PMA Member.
Contact: Stephen Hatton, Aileen McEwan,
James Penford. By Post
Unit 3, Chocolate Studios
7 Shepherdess Place, London N1 7LJ
F 020 7251 9081
E mail@hattonmcewan.com
W www.hattonmcewan.com

H C A
See COOKE, Howard ASSOCIATES

HEADNOD TALENT AGENCY T/F 020 3222 0035
RichMix 1st Floor West, 35-47 Bethnal Green Road
London E1 6LA
E info@headnodagency.com
W www.headnodagency.com

HENRIETTA RABBIT CHILDREN'S
ENTERTAINMENT AGENCY T 0333 000 4567
Children's Entertainers. Balloonologists. Close-up
Magicians. Clowns. Face Painters. Jugglers. Punch &
Judy. Stiltwalkers
The Warren, 12 Eden Close
York YO24 2RD
E info@henriettarabbit.co.uk
W www.henriettarabbit.co.uk

HICKS, Jeremy
ASSOCIATES LTD T 020 7734 7957
Personal Manager. Contact: By Post/e-mail. Accepts
Showreels. 2 Agents represent 25 Performers. Chefs.
Comedians. Presenters. Writers
3 Richmond Buildings, London W1D 3HE
F 020 7734 6302
E info@jeremyhicks.com
W www.jeremyhicks.com

HILTON, Elinor ASSOCIATES T 020 7240 2555
1 Goodwin's Court, London WC2H 4LL
T 07894 062820
E info@elinorhilton.com
W www.elinorhilton.com

Sean Gleeson

Natalie Barrett

HIRED HANDS   **T** 020 7267 9212
12 Cressy Road
London NW3 2LY
E hiredhandsagency@aol.com
W www.hiredhandsmodels.com

HOBBART & HOBBART   **T** 07595 260208
24 Kelvedon Road
London SW6 5BS
E braathen@hobbart.no
W www.hobbart.co.uk

HOBBS, Liz GROUP LTD   **T** 0870 0702702
65 London Road, Newark
Notts NG24 1RZ
F 01636 703343
E casting@lizhobbsgroup.com
W www.lizhobbsgroup.com

**HOLLAND, Dympna
ASSOCIATES**   **T** 01753 647551
Casualty Cottage, Kiln Lane, Hedgerley, Bucks SL2 3UT
T 07841 162354
E dympna@dympnaholland.com

**HOLLOWOOD, Jane
ASSOCIATES LTD**   **T** 0161 237 9141
Apartment 17, 113 Newton Street, Manchester M1 1AE
T 020 8291 5702
E janehollowood@btconnect.com
W www.janehollowood.co.uk

**HOLMES, Kim SHOWBUSINESS
ENTERTAINMENT AGENCY LTD**   **T** 0115 930 5088
8 Charles Close, Ilkeston, Derbyshire DE7 5AF
F 0115 944 0390
E kimholmesshowbiz@hotmail.co.uk

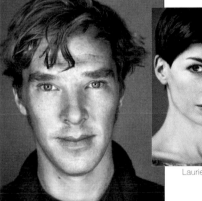

Benedict Cumberbatch

Laurie Hagen

Eddie Redmayne

Victoria Atkin

HOPE, Sally ASSOCIATES   **T** 020 7613 5353
PMA Member
108 Leonard Street, London EC2A 4XS
F 020 7613 4848
E casting@sallyhope.biz
W www.sallyhope.biz

**HOWARD, Amanda
ASSOCIATES LTD   **T** 020 7287 9277
PMA Member. Contact: By Post
21 Berwick Street, London W1F 0PZ
F 020 7287 7785
E mail@amandahowardassociates.co.uk
W www.amandahowardassociates.co.uk

HOWELL, Philippa
See PHPM
(PHILIPPA HOWELL PERSONAL MANAGEMENT)

**HOXTON STREET
MANAGEMENT**   **T** 020 7503 5131
Hoxton Hall, 130 Hoxton Street
London N1 6SH
E agents@hoxtonstreetmanagement.com
W www.hoxtonstreetmanagement.com

HR CREATIVE ARTISTS   **T** 020 3286 8830
Contact: By e-mail only
18 Soho Square, London W1D 3QL
E agent@hrca.eu
W www.hrca.eu

**HUDSON, Nancy
ASSOCIATES LTD   **T** 020 7499 5548
50 South Molton Street
Mayfair
London W1K 5SB
E agents@nancyhudsonassociates.com
W www.nancyhudsonassociates.com

HUNTER, Bernard LTD   **T** 020 8876 5927
Contact: Shirley Crowther
13 Spencer Gardens
London SW14 7AH
F 020 8392 9334
E shirleyannecrowther@gmail.com

HUNWICK HUGHES LTD   **T** 0131 271 5900
Personal Manager
Hudson House
8 Albany Street
Edinburgh EH1 3QB
E maryam@hunwickhughes.com
W www.hunwickhughes.com

I-MAGE CASTINGS   **T** 020 7725 7003
Regent House Business Centre
Suite 22, 24-25 Nutford Place
Marble Arch, London W1H 5YN
F 020 7725 7004
E jane@i-mage.uk.com
W www.i-mage.uk.com

**I.A.G.
(IDENTITY AGENCY GROUP)**   **T** 020 7470 8711
PMA Member. Black Actors
71-75 Shelton Street, Covent Garden
London WC2H 9JQ
E casting@identityagencygroup.com
W www.identityagencygroup.com

ICON ACTORS MANAGEMENT   **T** 0161 273 3344
Tanzaro House
Ardwick Green North
Manchester M12 6FZ
F 0161 273 4567
E info@iconactors.net
W www.iconactors.net

 **AM LONDON**

ACTORS HEADSHOTS

SIMON PEGG

JULIA SAWALHA

CHRIS DALEY

JOHN BARROWMAN

MATHEW HORNE

PETER SERAFINOWICZ

CATHERINE TATE

JAMES SUTTON

MODEL, DANCER & PERFORMER PORTFOLIOS

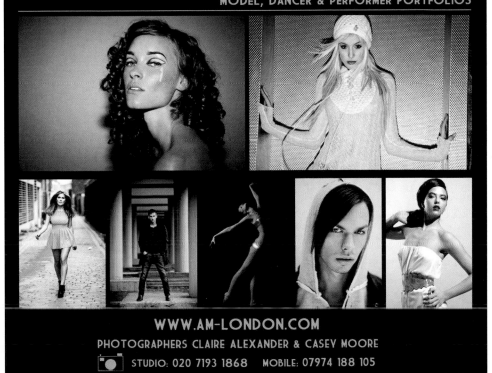

WWW.AM-LONDON.COM

PHOTOGRAPHERS CLAIRE ALEXANDER & CASEY MOORE

STUDIO: 020 7193 1868   MOBILE: 07974 188 105

I.M.L.   T/F 020 7587 1080
Personal Manager. CPMA Member. Contact: By Post.
Accepts Showreels. 35+ Performers. Commercials.
Corporate. Film. Stage. Television
The White House
52-54 Kennington Oval, London SE11 5SW
E info@iml.org.uk
W www.iml.org.uk

IMPACT INTERNATIONAL
MANAGEMENT   T 07941 269849
Personal Manager. Contact: Colin Charles. By e-mail.
Accepts Showreels/Voicereels. 1 Agent represents 10
Performers. Cruises. Musicals. Speciality Acts & Events
310 Cascades Tower
4 Westferry Road, London E14 8JL
E colin.charles310@gmail.com
W www.impact-london.co.uk

IMPACT MEDIA MANAGEMENT   T 020 7287 1923
83-84 Berwick Street, London W1F 8TS
E info@impactmediamanagement.com
W www.impactmediamanagement.com

IMPERIAL PERSONAL
MANAGEMENT LTD   T 0113 244 3222
102 Kirkstall Road, Leeds, West Yorkshire LS3 1JA
T 07890 387758
E katie@ipmcasting.com
W www.ipmcasting.com

IMPERIUM MANAGEMENT   T 020 8351 3152
179 Muswell Hill Broadway, London N10 3RS
E info@imperium-management.com
W www.imperium-management.com

IN GOOD COMPANY   T 00 353 1 2542252
Personal Manager. Contact: By e-mail. Accepts
Showreels/Voicereels. 2 Agents represent 50 Performers.
Commercials. Film. Stage. Television
The Glass House, 11 Coke Lane
Smithfield, Dublin 7, Ireland
T 00 353 86 4073358
E info@ingoodcompany.ie
W www.ingoodcompany.ie

IN HOUSE AGENCY   T 07921 843508
12 Cliffe House, Blackwall Lane, London SE10 0RB
F 020 8588 5444
E info@inhouseagency.co.uk
W www.inhouseagency.co.uk

I.N.C ARTIST MANAGEMENT   T 020 7557 6651
9-13 Grape Street, Covent Garden, London WC2H 8ED
F 020 7557 6656
E sarah@international-collective.com
W www.incartistmanagement.com

INDEPENDENT TALENT
GROUP LTD   T 020 7636 6565
PMA Member. Formerly ICM, London
Oxford House, 76 Oxford Street
London W1D 1BS
F 020 7323 0101
W www.independenttalent.com

INDEPENDENT THEATRE
WORKSHOP THE   T 00 353 1 2600831
8 Terminus Mills, Clonskeogh
Dublin 6, Ireland
E office@itwstudios.ie
W www.itwstudios.ie

INSPIRATION MANAGEMENT   T 020 7704 0440
Co-operative. CPMA Member. Est 1986
Unit 1, Highbury Business Centre
71-85 Canonbury Road, London N1 2DG
E mail@inspirationmanagement.org.uk
W www.inspirationmanagement.org.uk

INSPIRE ACADEMY   T 0115 988 1800
The Attic Studio, 3rd Floor
46-48 Carrington Street
Nottingham NG1 7FG
E admin@inspireacademy.co.uk
W www.inspireacademy.co.uk

INTER-CITY CASTING   T/F 01942 321969
Personal Manager. Contact: By e-mail. Accepts
Showreels. 2 Agents represent 60 Performers
27 Wigan Lane, Wigan
Greater Manchester WN1 1XR
E intercitycasting@btconnect.com

INTERNATIONAL MODEL
MANAGEMENT LTD   T 020 7610 9111
Incorporating Yvonne Paul Management
Elysium Gate, Unit 15
126-128 New Kings Road
London SW6 4LZ
F 020 7736 2221
E info@immmodels.com
W www.immmodels.com

INTERNATIONAL MODELS
& TALENT AGENCY   T 001 310 760 1082
Contact: Margaret Guiraud
Admin: IMTAgency, PO Box 4475
West Hills, CA 91308, USA
E int.talent@gmail.com

IRISH ACTORS LONDON   T 020 7125 0539
2 Bloemfontein Road, London W12 7BX
E irishactorslondon@gmail.com
W www.irishactorslondon.co.uk

JAA
See ALTARAS, Jonathan ASSOCIATES LTD

JABBERWOCKY AGENCY   T 01580 714306
Contact: Christina Yates. By e-mail. 4 Agents represent
135 Performers. Children. Teenagers
Glassenbury Hill Farm
Glassenbury Road
Cranbrook, Kent TN17 2QF
F 01580 714346
E info@jabberwockyagency.com
W www.yt93.co.uk

JAFFREY MANAGEMENT LTD   T 01708 732350
Personal Manager. Contact: Kim Barry. By Post/e-mail.
Accepts Showreels/Voicereels (SAE). 60 Performers.
Commercials. Film. Stage. Television
74 Western Road, Romford
Essex RM1 3LP
E mail@jaffreyactors.co.uk
W www.jaffreymanagement.com

JAM2000 AGENCY   T 01895 624755
The Windmill Studio Centre
106A Pembroke Road
Ruislip, Middlesex HA4 8NW
E info@jam2000.co.uk
W www.jam2000.co.uk

JAM AGENCY   T 020 7269 7923
Holborn Hall, 193-197 High Holborn
London WC1V 7BD
F 020 7831 7267
E info@jamagency.co.uk

JAMES, Susan
See SJ MANAGEMENT

JAMESON, Joy LTD   T/F 020 7359 2581
Personal Manager
PO Box 68182, London N1P 2BN
E joy@jote.freeuk.com

katie vandyck
headshots
www.excellentheadshots.co.uk

JB ASSOCIATES　　　　　**T** 0161 237 1808
Personal Manager. Contact: John Basham. By Post/
e-mail. Accepts Showreels/Voicereels. 2 Agents represent
60 Performers. Commercials. Radio. Stage. Television
PO Box 173, Manchester M19 0AR
F 0161 249 3666
E info@j-b-a.net　　　　　**W** www.j-b-a.net

JEFFREY & WHITE
MANAGEMENT LTD　　　　　**T** 01462 433752
Personal Manager. PMA Member
2 Ladygrove Court, Hitchwood Lane
Preston, Hitchin, Hertfordshire SG4 7SA
E info@jeffreyandwhite.co.uk
W www.jeffreyandwhite.co.uk

JERMIN, Mark MANAGEMENT　　**T** 01792 458855
Contact: By Post/e-mail. Accepts Showreels. 5 Agents
8 Heathfield, Swansea SA1 6EJ
E info@markjermin.co.uk
W www.markjermin.co.uk

J.M. MANAGEMENT　　　　**T** 020 8908 0502
Personal representation to a small number of Actors/
Actresses in film work
20 Pembroke Road, North Wembley
Middlesex HA9 7PD

JOHNSON WHITELEY LTD　　**T** 020 7348 0163
12 Argyll Mansions, Hammersmith Road
London W14 8QG
F 020 7348 0164
E johnsonwhiteley@btconnnect.com

JOHNSTON & MATHERS
ASSOCIATES LTD　　　　**T/F** 020 8449 4968
PO Box 3167, Barnet EN5 2WA
E johnstonmathers@aol.com
W www.johnstonandmathers.com

JOYCE, Michael
MANAGEMENT　　　　　**T** 020 3178 7190
3rd Floor, 33 Glasshouse Street
London W1B 5DG
T 07903 324405
E info@michaeljoyce.tv
W www.michaeljoycemanagement.com

JPA MANAGEMENT　　　　**T** 01494 520978
PMA Member
30 Daws Hill Lane, High Wycombe
Bucks HP11 1PW
F 01494 510479
E agent@jpamanagement.co.uk
W www.jpamanagement.co.uk

K TALENT ARTIST MANAGEMENT   **T** 020 7430 0882
Personal Manager. Contact: By Post/e-mail. Accepts Showreels/Voicereels. 4 Agents represent approx 130 Adult Performers. Children. Commercials. Dancers. Film. Musicals. Singers. Stage. Television
187 Drury Lane, Covent Garden
London WC2B 5QD
E mail@ktalent.co.uk
W www.ktalent.co.uk

KAL MANAGEMENT   **T** 020 8783 0039
Contact: By Post
95 Gloucester Road, Hampton, Middlesex TW12 2UW
F 020 8979 6487
E kaplan222@aol.com
W www.kaplan-kaye.co.uk

KANAL, Roberta AGENCY   **T** 020 8894 2277
82 Constance Road, Twickenham, Middlesex TW2 7JA
T/F 020 8894 7952
E roberta.kanal@dsl.pipex.com

KEDDIE SCOTT ASSOCIATES LTD   **T** 020 7836 6802
Personal Manager. PMA Member. Contact: By Post/ e-mail. Accepts Showreels. 6 Agents & 1 Assistant represent 200 Performers. Commercials. Corporate. Film. Musicals. Radio. Singers. Stage. Television
Studio 1, 17 Shorts Gardens
Covent Garden, London WC2H 9AT
F 020 7147 1326
E london@keddiescott.com
W www.keddiescott.com

KSA - NORTH   **T** 07792 022490
PMA Member
c/o Head Office, 17 Shorts Gardens
Covent Garden, London WC2H 9AT
T 07708 202374
E north@keddiescott.com
W www.keddiescott.com

KSA - SCOTLAND   **T** 07973 235355
Personal Manager. PMA Member. Contact: Paul Michael. By Post/e-mail. Accepts Showreels/Voicereels. 1 Agent represents 45 Performers. Film. Musicals. Stage. Television
c/o Head Office, 17 Shorts Gardens
Covent Garden, London WC2H 9AT
F 020 7147 1326
E scotland@keddiescott.com
W www.keddiescott.com

KSA - WALES   **T** 07917 272298
PMA Member
Studio 1, 17 Shorts Gardens
Covent Garden, London WC2H 9AT
E wales@keddiescott.com
W www.keddiescott.com

KELLY, Robert ASSOCIATES (RKA)   **T** 020 7240 0859
PMA Member
11 Garrick Street, London WC2E 9AR
E rob@robertkellyassociates.com
W www.robertkellyassociates.com

KENIS, Steve & CO   **T** 020 7434 9055
PMA Member
Royalty House, 72-74 Dean Street, London W1D 3SG
F 020 7287 6328
E sk@sknco.com

KEW PERSONAL MANAGEMENT T 020 8871 3697
PO Box 679, Surrey RH1 9BT
E info@kewpersonalmanagement.com
W www.kewpersonalmanagement.com

KEYLOCK MANAGEMENT   **T** 01494 563142
Contact: By e-mail. 2 Agents represent 55 Performers. Commercials. Film. Stage. Television
5 North Dean Cottages, Speen Road
North Dean, Bucks HP14 4NN
T 07712 579502
E agent@keylockmanagement.com
W www.keylockmanagement.com

KHANDO ENTERTAINMENT   **T** 020 3463 8492
1 Marlborough Court, London W1F 7EE
E info@khandoentertainment.com
W www.khandoentertainment.com

KING, Adrian ASSOCIATES   **T** 020 7435 4600
PMA Member. Contact: Adrian King. By Post/e-mail. Accepts Showreels
33 Marlborough Mansions, Cannon Hill
London NW6 1JS
F 020 7435 4100
E akassocs@aol.com

K.L.A. ENTERTAINMENTS   **T** 01245 250893
Contact: Andrew Wallis
Flat 5 Bridge House, 141 Upper Bridge Road
Chelmsford, Essex CM2 0AL
T 07854 536817
E anddenton2002@hotmail.com
W www.klaentertainments.co.uk

KMC AGENCIES   **T** 0161 237 3009
Personal Manager. Actors. Commercials. Corporate. Dancers. Musicals
PO Box 122, 48 Great Ancoats Street
Manchester M4 5AB
F 0161 237 9812
E casting@kmcagencies.co.uk

KMC AGENCIES   **T** 0845 0340772
Personal Manager. Actors. Commercials. Corporate. Dancers. Musicals
Garden Studios, 71-75 Shelton Street
Covent Garden, London WC2H 9JQ
E london@kmcagencies.co.uk

KNIGHT, Nic MANAGEMENT   **T** 020 3093 5422
23 Buckler Court
Eden Grove, London N7 8EF
E enquiries@nicknightmanagement.com
W www.nicknightmanagement.com

KNIGHT, Ray CASTING   **T** 020 7722 1551
Elstree Studios, Room 38
John Maxwell Building
Shenley Road, Boreham Wood, Herts WD6 1JG
E casting@rayknight.co.uk
W www.rayknight.co.uk

KNIGHT AYTON MANAGEMENT   **T** 020 7831 4400
35 Great James Street, London WC1N 3HB
F 020 7831 4455
E info@knightayton.co.uk
W www.knightayton.co.uk

KORT, Richard MANAGEMENT LTD   **T** 01636 636686
Moat Farm, Norwell Woodhouse
Newark, Notts NG23 6NG
F 01636 636719
E richardkort@playhouseproductionsltd.co.uk
W www.richardkort.co.uk

KREATE   **T** 020 7401 9007
Unit 232, Great Guildford Business Square
30 Great Guildford Street, London SE1 0HS
F 020 7401 9008
E hello@kreate.co.uk

KREMER ASSOCIATES
See MARSH, Billy DRAMA LTD

KSA - NORTH
See KEDDIE SCOTT ASSOCIATES

KSA - SCOTLAND
See KEDDIE SCOTT ASSOCIATES LTD

KSA - WALES
See KEDDIE SCOTT ASSOCIATES LTD

KW PROMOTIONS LTD   **T** 07835 316639
9 College Road
Alsager, Stoke-on-Trent ST7 2SS
E dkeeno1@hotmail.com
W www.kwpromotions.co.uk

L.A. MANAGEMENT   **T** 020 7183 6211
10 Fairoak Close
Kenley, Surrey CR8 5LJ
T 07507 276211
E info@lamanagement.biz
W www.lamanagement.biz

LADA MANAGEMENT   **T** 020 3384 5815
Personal Manager. Contact: Richard Boschetto.
By Post/e-mail. Accepts Showreels/Voicereels. 2 Agents
represent 40 Performers. Film. Musicals. Stage. Television
23 Austin Friars, London EC2N 2QP
F 020 3384 5816
E info@ladamanagement.com
W www.ladamanagement.com

LADA MANAGEMENT   T 01522 837243
*Personal Manager. Contact: Richard Boschetto. By Post/
e-mail. Accepts Showreels/Voicereels. 2 Agents represent
40 Performers. Film. Musicals. Stage. Television*
Sparkhouse Studios, Rope Walk, Lincoln LN6 7DQ
F 01522 837201
E info@ladamanagement.com
W www.ladamanagement.com

LADIDA   T 020 7462 0790
*Contact: By Post. Accepts Showreels. 4 Agents represent
100 Performers. Commercials. Creatives. Film. Musicals.
Radio. Stage. Television. Writers*
17 Percy Street, London W1T 1DU
E m@ladidagroup.com
W www.ladidagroup.com

LAINE, Betty MANAGEMENT   T/F 01372 721815
The Studios, East Street
Epsom, Surrey KT17 1HH
E enquiries@betty-laine-management.co.uk

LAINE MANAGEMENT LTD   T 0161 789 7775
Laine House, 131 Victoria Road
Hope, Salford M6 8LF
F 0161 787 7572
E sam@lainemanagement.co.uk
W www.lainemanagement.co.uk

LANGFORD ASSOCIATES LTD   T 020 8878 7148
*Personal Manager. Contact: Barry Langford. By Post/
e-mail. Commercials. Film. Stage. Television*
17 Westfields Avenue, Barnes
London SW13 0AT
F 020 8878 7078
E barry.langford@btconnect.com
W www.langfordassociates.com

LAWRENCE, Tonicha AGENCY   T/F 0113 289 3433
*Now trading as TLA Boutique Management.
Incorporating Young Boutique*
T 07766 415996
E tonichalawrence@gmail.com
W www.tlaboutiquemanagement.com

LAWRENCE-AGENCY   T 07883 250470
21-23 Glendale Gardens, Leigh on Sea, Essex SS9 2PA
E info@lawrence-agency.co.uk
W www.lawrence-agency.co.uk

**LE BARS, Tessa
MANAGEMENT**   T/F 01689 837084
Existing Clients only
54 Birchwood Road, Petts Wood
Kent BR5 1NZ
T 07860 287255
E tessa.lebars@ntlworld.com
W www.galtonandsimpson.com

LEE, Wendy MANAGEMENT   T 020 7703 5187
E wendy-lee@btconnect.com

LEHRER, Jane ASSOCIATES   T 020 7435 9118
*Personal Manager. PMA Member.
Contact: By Post/e-mail. 2 Agents*
PO Box 66334, London NW6 9QT
F 020 7435 9117
E jane@janelehrer.co.uk
W www.janelehrer.co.uk

LEIGH, Mike ASSOCIATES   T 020 7017 8757
11-12 Great Sutton Street, London EC1V 0BX
F 020 7486 5886
W www.mikeleighassoc.com

LEIGH MANAGEMENT   T 020 8951 4449
14 St David's Drive, Edgware
Middlesex HA8 6JH
E leighmanagement@aol.com

**LESLIE, Sasha
MANAGEMENT**   T/F 020 8969 3249
In association with ALLSORTS DRAMA FOR CHILDREN
34 Crediton Road
London NW10 3DU
E sasha@allsortsdrama.com

**LIGHT AGENCY &
PRODUCTIONS LTD**   T 020 7228 6558
Actors. Dancers
12 Molasses Row
Plantation Wharf
Battersea, London SW11 3UX
E agency@lightproductions.tv
W www.lightproductions.tv

**LIME ACTORS AGENCY
& MANAGEMENT LTD**   T 0161 236 0827
Contact: Georgina Andrew. By Post. Accepts Showreels
Nemesis House, 1 Oxford Court
Bishopsgate, Manchester M2 3WQ
F 0161 228 6727
E georgina@limemanagement.co.uk
W www.limemanagement.tv

LINKSIDE AGENCY
*Contact: By Post/e-mail. 2 Agents represent 40
Performers. Dancers. Musicals. Singers.
Stage. Television*
Southbank House
Black Prince Road, London SE1 7SJ
E info@linksideagency.com

LINTON MANAGEMENT   T 0161 761 2020
3 The Rock, Bury BL9 0JP
F 0161 761 1999
E carol@linton.tv

LINTON MANAGEMENT   T 020 7785 7275
27-31 Clerkenwell Close
London EC1R 0AT
F 020 7785 7276
E london@linton.tv

LONDON THEATRICAL   T 020 8748 1478
Contact: Paul Pearson
18 Leamore Street, London W6 0JZ
E agent@londontheatrical.com
W www.londontheatrical.com

LONG, Eva AGENTS   T 07736 700849
*Contact: By Post/e-mail. 2 Agents represent
30 Performers. Commercials. Corporate. Film. Musicals.
Radio. Singers. Stage. Television. Voice Overs*
Norwood House
9 Redwell Road
Wellingborough NN8 5AZ
F 01604 811921
E evalongagents@yahoo.co.uk
W www.evalongagents.co.uk

LONGRUN ARTISTES   T 020 8316 6662
*Contact: Gina Long. By Post.
Accepts Showreels/Voicereels. 3 Agents represent 100
Performers. Commercials. Corporate. Dancers. Film.
Musicals. Singers. Stage. Television*
3 Chelsworth Drive
London SE18 2RB
E gina@longrunartistes.co.uk
W www.longrunartistes.co.uk

LOOKALIKES   T 020 7281 8029
Contact: Susan Scott
106 Tollington Park
London N4 3RB
E susan@lookalikes.info
W www.lookalikes.info

Rebekah Thawley   Hadley Fraser   Damien Swaby

robin savage photography

www.robinsavage.co.uk

e: contact@robinsavage.co.uk   t: 07901 927597

LOOKS AGENCY   **T** 020 8341 4477
Contact: By Post/e-mail/Telephone. 200 Performers.
Commercials. Corporate. Modelling. Presenters. Walk-on
& Supporting Artists
PO Box 42783, London N2 0UF   **F** 020 8442 9190
E lookslondonltd@btconnect.com
W www.lookslondon.com

LOTHERINGTON, Michelle
PERSONAL MANAGEMENT   **T** 07785 293806
Contact: Michelle Lotherington. By e-mail.
Choreographers. Composers. Designers. Directors.
Lighting & Sound Designers. Music Technology. Musical
Directors. Orchestrators
23 Tell Grove, London SE22 8RH
E michelle@michellelotherington.com
W www.michellelotherington.com

LOVETT LOGAN ASSOCIATES   **T** 0131 478 7878
Formerly PLA. PMA Member
2 York Place, Edinburgh EH1 3EP
F 0131 478 7070
E edinburgh@lovettlogan.com
W www.lovettlogan.com

LOVETT LOGAN ASSOCIATES   **T** 020 7495 6400
Formerly PLA. PMA Member
40 Margaret Street, London W1G 0JH
F 020 7495 6411
E london@lovettlogan.com
W www.lovettlogan.com

LSW PROMOTIONS   **T/F** 020 7793 9755
PO Box 31855, London SE17 3XP
E londonswo@hotmail.com

LUXFACTOR GROUP (UK) THE T 0845 3700589
Personal Manager. Contact: Michael D. Finch. By e-mail.
1 Agent represents 20+ Performers. Creatives.
Presenters. Television. Walk-on & Supporting Artists
Fleet Place, 12 Nelson Drive
Petersfield, Hampshire GU31 4SJ
T 05603 680843
E info@luxfactor.co.uk
W www.luxfactor.co.uk

LYNE, Dennis AGENCY T 020 7272 5020
PMA Member
503 Holloway Road, London N19 4DD
E info@dennislyne.com
W www.dennislyne.com

MA9 MODEL MANAGEMENT T 020 7096 1191
New Bond House, 124 New Bond Street
London W1S 1DX
E info@ma9models.com
W www.ma9models.com

**MACFARLANE CHARD
ASSOCIATES LTD** T 020 7636 7750
PMA Member
33 Percy Street, London W1T 2DF
F 020 7636 7751
E enquiries@macfarlane-chard.co.uk
W www.macfarlane-chard.co.uk

**MACFARLANE CHARD
ASSOCIATES IRELAND** T 00 353 1 6638646
7 Adelaide Street, Dun Laoghaire
Co Dublin, Ireland
F 00 353 1 6638649
E derick@macfarlane-chard.ie

**MACFARLANE DOYLE
ASSOCIATES** T 020 3600 3470
90 Long Acre, Covent Garden, London WC2E 9RZ
E ross.macfarlane@btinternet.com
W www.macfarlanedoyle.com

**MACLEAN, Rose
MANAGEMENT** T 020 7636 2030
9 Coptic Street, London WC1A 1NH
E mgt@rosemaclean.com

**MACNAUGHTON LORD
REPRESENTATION** T 020 7499 1411
PMA Member. Choreographers. Composers. Designers.
Directors. Lighting Designers. Lyricists. Musical Directors.
Sound Designers. Video Designers. Writers
44 South Molton Street, London W1K 5RT
F 020 7493 2444
E info@mlrep.com
W www.mlrep.com

MAIDA VALE SINGERS T 020 7266 1358
Contact: Christopher Dee. Singers for Recordings, Stage,
Film, Radio & Television
7B Lanhill Road, Maida Vale
London W9 2BP
T 07889 153145
E maidavalesingers@cdtenor.freeserve.co.uk
W www.maidavalesingers.co.uk

MAITLAND MANAGEMENT T 07535 651639
Personal Manager. Contact: Anne Skates
3rd Floor, 183 Eversholt Street
London NW1 1AY
E maitmus@aol.com
W www.maitlandmanagement.com

MAMBAB AGENCY T 020 7587 5225
Contact: Nichola D. Hartwell
PO Box 51261, Kennington
London SE11 4SW
T 07868 120709
E contacts@mrandmissblackandbeautiful.com
W www.mrandmissblackandbeautiful.com

MANAGEMENT 2000 T/F 01352 771231
Contact: Jackey Gerling. By Post. Accepts Showreels.
1 Agent represents 40 Performers. Commercials. Film.
Radio. Stage. Television
11 Well Street, Treuddyn
Flintshire CH7 4NH
E jackey@management-2000.co.uk
W www.management-2000.co.uk

MANS, Johnny PRODUCTIONS T 01992 470907
Incorporating Encore Magazine
PO Box 196, Hoddesdon
Herts EN10 7WG
T 07974 755997
E johnnymansagent@aol.com
W www.johnnymansproductions.co.uk

MANTLE MANAGEMENT T 01273 454111
32 Westbourne Place, Hove
East Sussex BN3 4GN
E info@mantlemanagement.co.uk
W www.mantlemanagement.co.uk

**MARCUS & McCRIMMON
MANAGEMENT** T 020 7323 0546
Personal Manager. Contact: By Post/e-mail. Accepts
Showreels. 2 Agents represent 100 Performers.
Commercials. Film. Musicals. Stage. Television
Winston House, 3 Bedford Square
London WC1B 3RA
E info@marcusandmccrimmon.com
W www.marcusandmccrimmon.com

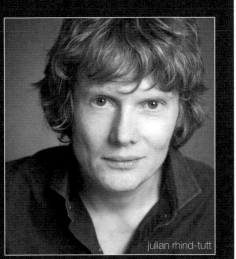

jackladenburg photography

hattie morahan

julian rhind-tutt

07932 053 743
www.jackladenburg.co.uk
info@jackladenburg.co.uk

MARKHAM AGENCY THE   T 020 7836 4111
Personal Manager. PMA Member.
Contact: John Markham. By Post/e-mail. Accepts
Showreels/Voicereels
405 Strand, London WC2R 0NE
F 020 7836 4222
E info@themarkhamagency.com
W www.themarkhamagency.com

MARKHAM, FROGGATT & IRWIN T 020 7636 4412
Personal Manager. PMA Member. Contact: By e-mail
4 Windmill Street, London W1T 2HZ
E admin@markhamfroggattirwin.com
W www.markhamfroggattirwin.com

MARLOWES AGENCY   T 07964 589148
HMS President, Victoria Embankment
Blackfriars, London EC4Y 0HJ
T 020 7103 7227
E miles@marlowes.eu   W www.marlowes.eu

MARLOWES AGENCY:
TV, THEATRE & DANCE   T 020 7193 4484
HMS President, Victoria Embankment
Blackfriars, London EC4Y 0HJ
E mitch@marlowes.eu   W www.marlowes.eu

MARMALADE MANAGEMENT   T 01628 483808
Jam Theatre Studios
Archway Court
45A West Street, Marlow, Buckinghamshire SL7 2LS
E info@marmalademanagement.co.uk
W www.marmalademanagement.co.uk

MARSH, Billy ASSOCIATES LTD T 020 7383 9979
PMA Member
4th Floor, 158-160 North Gower Street
London NW1 2ND
F 020 7388 2296
E talent@billymarsh.co.uk
W www.billymarsh.co.uk

MARSH, Billy DRAMA LTD   T 020 3178 4748
Actors. Actresses
20 Garrick Street, London WC2E 9BT
F 020 3178 5488
E info@billymarshdrama.co.uk

MARSHALL, Ronnie
AGENCY THE   T/F 020 8368 4958
66 Ollerton Road, London N11 2LA
E theronniemarshallagency@gmail.com
W www.theronniemarshallagency.com

MARSHALL, Scott PARTNERS LTD T 020 7637 4623
PMA Member. Contact: Amanda Evans, Suzy Kenway, Manon Palmer
2nd Floor, 15 Little Portland Street, London W1W 8BW
F 020 7636 9728
E smpm@scottmarshall.co.uk
W www.scottmarshall.co.uk

MARTIN, Carol PERSONAL MANAGEMENT T 020 8348 0847
19 Highgate West Hill, London N6 6NP
E carolmartin@talktalk.net

MAY, John T 020 8962 1606
46 Golborne Road, London W10 5PR
E may505@btinternet.com

MAYER, Cassie LTD T 020 7350 0880
PMA Member
5 Old Garden House, The Lanterns
Bridge Lane, London SW11 3AD
F 020 7350 0890
E info@cassiemayerltd.co.uk

MBA / MAHONEY BANNON ASSOCIATES T 01273 685970
Incorporating John Mahoney Management
Concorde House, 18 Margaret Street, Brighton BN2 1TS
E info@mbagency.co.uk
W www.mbagency.co.uk

McDONAGH, Melanie MANAGEMENT (ACADEMY OF PERFORMING ARTS & CASTING AGENCY) T 07909 831409
14 Apple Tree Way, Oswaldtwistle
Accrington, Lancashire BB5 0FB
T 01254 392560
E mcdonaghmgt@aol.com
W www.mcdonaghmanagement.co.uk

McKINNEY MACARTNEY MANAGEMENT LTD T 020 8995 4747
Technicians
Gable House
18-24 Turnham Green Terrace, London W4 1QP
E mail@mckinneymacartney.com
W www.mckinneymacartney.com

McLEAN, Bill PERSONAL MANAGEMENT T 020 8789 8191
Personal Manager. Contact: By Post
23B Deodar Road, London SW15 2NP

McLEAN-WILLIAMS MANAGEMENT T 020 7223 8683
PMA Member
Gainsborough House, 81 Oxford Street
London W1D 2EU
F 020 7228 2386
E info@mclean-williams.com
W www.mclean-williams.com

McLEOD AGENCY LTD THE T 01482 565444
1st Floor, 6 The Square
Hessle, East Yorkshire HU13 0AA
E info@mcleodagency.co.uk
W www.mcleodagency.co.uk

McMAHON MANAGEMENT T 020 8752 0172
17 Thistlefield Close, Bexley, Kent DA5 3GJ
E mcmahonmanagement@hotmail.co.uk
W www.mdm-ltd.co.uk

McREDDIE, Ken ASSOCIATES LTD T 020 7439 1456
Personal Manager. PMA Member. Contact: By Post only
101 Finsbury Pavement, London EC2A 1RS
F 020 7734 6530
E email@kenmcreddie.com W www.kenmcreddie.com

MEDIA CELEBRITY SERVICES LTD T 07946 531011
47 Dean Street, London W1D 5BE
T 07809 831340
E info@mcsagency.co.uk
W www.mediacelebrityservices.co.uk

MEDIA LEGAL T 01732 460592
Existing Clients only
Town House, 5 Mill Pond Close
Sevenoaks, Kent TN14 5AW

METROPOLITAN MANAGEMENT T 020 7193 5978
24 Beehive Lane, Basildon SS14 2LG
E info@metropolitan-management.co.uk
W www.metropolitan-management.co.uk

MGA MANAGEMENT T 0131 466 9392
The MGA Company, 207 Balgreen Road
Edinburgh EH11 2RZ
E info@themgacompany.com
W www.themgacompany.com

MILAEON T 01923 711358
Now known as Thomas Gerrard Casting Agent
Actors & Performers. Commercials. Film. Stage. Television
Based in Rickmansworth, Herts
E thomas@thomasgerrard.co.uk
W www.thomasgerrard.co.uk

MILBURN BROWNING ASSOCIATES T 020 3582 9370
The Old Truman Brewery, 91 Brick Lane, London E1 6QL
F 020 3582 9377
E info@milburnbrowning.com

MIME THE GAP T 07970 685982
Mime Artistes. Physical Comedy Specialists
29 Elizabeth Avenue, Staines, Middlesex TW18 1JW
E richard@mimethegap.com
W www.mimethegap.com

MISKIN THEATRE AGENCY THE T 01322 629422
The Miskin Theatre, Oakfield Lane
Dartford, Kent DA1 2JT
T 07709 429354
E miskintheatreagency@yahoo.co.uk

MITCHELL MAAS McLENNAN T 020 8301 8745
MPA Offices, 29 Thomas Street
Woolwich, London SE18 6HU
T 07540 995802
E agency@mmm2000.co.uk
W www.mmm2000.co.uk

MLR
See MACNAUGHTON LORD REPRESENTATION

MONDI ASSOCIATES LTD T 07817 133349
Personal Manager. PMA Member. Contact: Michelle Sykes.
By Post/e-mail. Accepts Showreels/Voicereels.
1 Agent represents 60 Performers. Children. Commercials.
Corporate. Dancers. Film. Musicals. Presenters. Radio.
Singers. Stage. Television. Voice Overs
Unit 3 O, Cooper House, 2 Michael Road
London SW6 2AD
E info@mondiassociates.com
W www.mondiassociates.com

MONTAGU ASSOCIATES LTD T 020 7263 3883
Ground Floor, 13 Hanley Road, London N4 3DU
E tom@montagus.org

MOORE, Jakki MANAGEMENT T 01229 776389
Halecote, St Lukes Road, Haverigg, Cumbria LA18 4HB
T 07967 612784
E jakki@jakkimoore.com

MORELLO CHERRY ACTORS AGENCY T 020 7993 5538
E info@mcaa.co.uk W www.mcaa.co.uk

MORGAN, Lee MANAGEMENT   T 020 7841 2802
88 Kingsway, Holborn
London WC2B 6AA
F 020 7841 1001
E lee@leemorgan.biz
W www.leemorgan.biz

MORGAN & GOODMAN   T 020 7437 1383
20 Hanover Square
London W1S 1JY
E tanya.greep@googlemail.com

MOUTHPIECE MANAGEMENT   T 01527 850149
18 New Road, Studley
Warwickshire B80 7LY
T 07900 240904
E karin@mouthpiecemanagement.co.uk
W www.mouthpiecemanagement.co.uk

MPC ENTERTAINMENT   T 020 7624 1184
Contact: By e-mail/Telephone
MPC House
15-16 Maple Mews
Maida Vale, London NW6 5UZ
F 020 7624 4220
E mpc@mpce.com
W www.mpce.com

MR MANAGEMENT   T 020 7886 0760
PMA Member
19 Bolsover Street
London W1W 5NA
E info@mrmanagement.net
W www.mrmanagement.net

MRS JORDAN ASSOCIATES   T 020 3151 0710
PMA Member. Contact: By e-mail only. 3 Agents represent
50 Performers. Commercials. Creatives. Film. Stage.
Television
Communications House, 26 York Street
London W1U 6PZ
T 0161 401 0710
E info@mrsjordan.co.uk
W www.mrsjordan.co.uk

MUGSHOTS AGENCY   T 07880 896911
E becky@mugshots.co.uk

MURPHY, Elaine ASSOCIATES   T 020 8989 4122
Suite 1, 50 High Street
London E11 2RJ
F 020 8989 1400
E elaine@elainemurphy.co.uk

MUSIC INTERNATIONAL   T 020 7359 5183
13 Ardilaun Road, London N5 2QR
F 020 7226 9792
E neil@musicint.co.uk
W www.musicint.co.uk

MV MANAGEMENT   T 020 8889 8231
Co-operative Agency for Graduates of Mountview
Academy of Theatre Arts
Ralph Richardson Memorial Studios
Kingfisher Place
Clarendon Road, London N22 6XF
F 020 8829 1050
E theagency@mountview.org.uk
W www.mvmanagement.org.uk

**MVW TALENT AGENCY
IRELAND**   **T** 00 353 87 2480348
Film. Modelling. Musicals. Stage. Television. Voice Overs
23 Burrow Manor, Calverstown
Kilcullen, Kildare, Ireland
F 00 353 45 485464
E mvwtalent@hotmail.com
W www.talentedkidsireland.com

MYERS MANAGEMENT   **T/F** 020 8204 8941
63 Fairfields Crescent, London NW9 0PR
E judy_hepburn@hotmail.com

**NARROW ROAD
COMPANY THE**   **T** 020 7379 9598
PMA Member
3rd Floor, 76 Neal Street
Covent Garden, London WC2H 9PL
F 020 7379 9777
E richardireson@narrowroad.co.uk

**NARROW ROAD
COMPANY THE**   **T/F** 0161 833 1605
PMA Member
2nd Floor, Grampian House,
144 Deansgate, Manchester M3 3EE
E manchester@narrowroad.co.uk

NEALON, Steve ASSOCIATES   **T** 020 3149 2902
PMA Member
2nd Floor, International House
1-6 Yarmouth Place, Mayfair, London W!J 7BU
E admin@stevenealonassociates.co.uk
W www.stevenealonassociates.co.uk

**NELSON BROWNE
MANAGEMENT LTD**   **T** 020 7970 6010
PMA Member
40 Bowling Green Lane, London EC1R 0NE
T 07796 891388
E enquiries@nelsonbrowne.com
W www.nelsonbrowne.com

NEVS AGENCY   **T** 020 7352 4886
Regal House, 198 King's Road, London SW3 5XP
F 020 7352 6068
E getamodel@nevs.co.uk
W www.nevs.co.uk

NEW CASEY AGENCY   **T** 01923 823182
129 Northwood Way, Northwood HA6 1RF

NEW FACES LTD   **T** 020 7439 6900
*Personal Manager. Contact: Val Horton, Kayleigh Mann.
By Post/e-mail. Accepts Showreels. 3 Agents represent
50 Performers. Children. Commercials. Film. Stage.
Television*
3rd Floor, The Linen Hall
162-168 Regent Street, London W1B 5TD
F 020 7287 5481
E info@newfacestalent.co.uk
W www.newfacestalent.co.uk

NFD AGENCY   **T/F** 01977 681949
The Studio, 21 Low Street
South Milford LS25 5AR
E info@northernfilmanddrama.com
W www.northernfilmanddrama.com

NIC KNIGHT MANAGEMENT
See KNIGHT, Nic MANAGEMENT

**NICHOLSON, Jackie
ASSOCIATES**   **T** 020 7580 4422
Personal Manager. Contact: Marvin Giles (Agent). By Post
Suite 44, 2nd Floor, Morley House
320 Regent Street, London W1B 3BD
F 020 7580 4489
E jnalondon@aol.com

N M MANAGEMENT   **T** 020 8853 4337
16 St Alfege Passage, Greenwich
London SE10 9JS
E nmmanagement@hotmail.com

NMP MANAGEMENT   **T** 01372 361004
*Personal Manager. Contact: By e-mail. 2 Agents represent
10 Performers. Comedians. Corporate. Presenters.
Television*
8 Blenheim Court, Brookway
Leatherhead, Surrey KT22 7NA
F 01372 374417
E management@nmp.co.uk
W www.nmpmanagement.co.uk

NOLAN & KAY MANAGEMENT   **T** 01444 401595
Studio 35 Truggers, Handcross
Haywards Heath, West Sussex RH17 6DQ
T 07966 382766
E info@nolanandkay.co.uk
W www.nolanandkay.co.uk

**NORTH OF WATFORD
ACTORS AGENCY**   **T** 01422 845361
CPMA Member
The Creative Quarter, The Town Hall
St Georges Street
Hebden Bridge, West Yorks HX7 7BY
T 020 3601 3372
E info@northofwatford.com
W www.northofwatford.com

**NORTH WEST ACTORS -
NIGEL ADAMS**   **T/F** 0161 724 6625
*Personal Manager. Contact: Nigel Adams. By Post.
Accepts Showreels/Voicereels. Commercials. Film. Radio.
Stage. Television*
36 Lord Street, Radcliffe
Manchester M26 3BA
E nigel.adams@northwestactors.co.uk
W www.northwestactors.co.uk

**NORTHERN LIGHTS
MANAGEMENT LTD**   **T** 01422 382203
Dean Clough Mills, West Yorks HX3 5AX
F 01422 330101
E northern.lights@virgin.net

NORTHONE MANAGEMENT   **T** 020 7359 9666
CPMA Member
The Biscuit Factory
Unit B202.6, Tower Bridge Business Complex
100 Clements Road, London SE16 4DG
E actors@northone.co.uk
W www.northone.co.uk

NS ARTISTES MANAGEMENT   **T** 0121 684 5607
10 Claverdon House, Holly Bank Road
Billesley, Birmingham B13 0QY
T 07870 969577
E nsmanagement@fsmail.net
W www.nsartistes.co.uk

**NSM (NATASHA STEVENSON
MANAGEMENT LTD)**   **T** 020 7720 3355
*Personal Manager. PMA Member. Contact: By e-mail/
Telephone. 2 Agents. Commercials. Film. Stage. Television*
Studio 7C, Clapham North Arts Centre
Voltaire Road, London SW4 6DH
F 020 7720 5565
E inbox@natashastevenson.co.uk
W www.natashastevenson.co.uk

NUMBER ONE MODEL AGENCY   **T** 01675 443900
The Barn, Pasture Farm
Coventry Road, Solihull B92 0HH
E info@numberonemodelagency.co.uk
W www.numberonemodelagency.co.uk

NYLAND MANAGEMENT   T 01663 745629
93 Kinder Road, Hayfield, High Peak SK22 2LE
E casting@nylandmanagement.com
W www.nylandmanagement.com

**OBJECTIVE TALENT
MANAGEMENT**   T/F 020 7202 2300
3rd Floor, Riverside Building, County Hall
Westminster Bridge Road, London SE1 7PB
E russell@objectivetalentmanagement.com
W www.objectivetalentmanagement.com

OFF THE KERB PRODUCTIONS   T 020 7437 0607
3rd Floor, Hammer House
113-117 Wardour Street, London W1F 0UN
F 020 7437 0647
E info@offthekerb.co.uk   W www.offthekerb.co.uk

**OH SO SMALL
PRODUCTIONS LTD**   T 07787 788673
*Short & Dwarf Actors Agency. Contact: Lisa Osmond.
By e-mail/Telephone. Prosthetics. Full Costume. Motion
Capture. Child Stunts. Commercials. Corporate. Film.
Stage. Television*
6 High Street, Penarth, Cardiff CF64 1EY
F 029 2041 1244
E lisa@ohsosmallproductions.com
W www.ohsosmall.com

OI OI AGENCY   T 01753 852326
*Actors, Actresses, Children & Young Performers, Dancers
& Models. Commercials. Film. Stage. Television*
Enquiries: 29B Battersea Rise, London SW11 1HG
F 01753 655622
E info@oioi.org.uk   W www.oioi.org.uk

John Colclough Advisory

Practical independent guidance for actors and actresses

t: 020 8873 1763   e: info@johncolclough.com   www.johncolclough.com

---

OPERA & CONCERT ARTISTS   T 020 7328 3097
Musicals. Opera
75 Aberdare Gardens, London NW6 3AN
F 020 7372 3537
E enquiries@opera-and-concert-artists.co.uk

ORDINARY PEOPLE   T 020 7267 7007
Actors. Modelling
16 Camden Road, London NW1 9DP
F 020 7267 5677
E info@ordinarypeople.co.uk
W www.ordinarypeople.co.uk

OREN ACTORS MANAGEMENT   T 0845 4591420
CPMA Member
Chapter Arts Centre, Market Road, Cardiff CF5 1QE
E info@orenactorsmanagement.co.uk
W www.orenactorsmanagement.co.uk

**ORIENTAL CASTING
AGENCY LTD**   T 020 8660 0101
*Contact: By e-mail/Telephone. Accepts Showreels/
Voicereels. 1 Agent represents 200+ Performers.
Afro/Asian Artists*
22 Wontford Road, Purley, Surrey CR8 4BL
E billiejames@btconnect.com
W www.orientalcasting.com

ORR MANAGEMENT AGENCY   T 01204 579842
1st Floor, 147-149 Market Street
Farnworth, Greater Manchester BL4 8EX
E barbara@orrmanagement.co.uk
W www.orrmanagement.co.uk

**OTTO PERSONAL
MANAGEMENT LTD**   T 0114 327 1013
Personal Manager. CPMA Member
Hagglers Corner, 586 Queens Road, Sheffield S2 4DU
E admin@ottopm.co.uk
W www.ottopm.co.uk

PADBURY, David ASSOCIATES   T 020 8883 1277
44 Summerlee Avenue, Finchley, London N2 9QP
E info@davidpadburyassociates.com

PAN ARTISTS AGENCY LTD   T 0800 6349147
Cornerways, 34 Woodhouse Lane
Sale, Cheshire M33 4JX
T 0161 969 7419
E panartists@btconnect.com
W www.panartists.co.uk

**PARADIGM ARTIST
MANAGEMENT**   T 01554 776836
49 St Josephs Court, Llanelli, Carmarthenshire SA15 1NR
T 07747 612157
E paradigmartistmgmt@live.co.uk
W www.paradigm-artist-management.co.uk

**PARAMOUNT INTERNATIONAL
MANAGEMENT**   T 020 8429 3179
30 Performers. International Comedians
Talbot House, 204-226 Imperial Drive
Harrow, Middlesex HA2 7HH
F 020 8868 6475
E mail@ukcomedy.com   W www.ukcomedy.com

PARKER, Cherry MANAGEMENT (RSM)
See RSM (CHERRY PARKER MANAGEMENT)

PARSONS, Cary MANAGEMENT   T 01926 735375
Set, Costume & Lighting Designers & Directors
118 Plymouth Place, Leamington Spa
Warwickshire CV31 1HW
E carylparsons@gmail.com
W www.caryparsons.co.uk

PAYNE MANAGEMENT   T 020 7193 1156 (London)
Contact: Natalie Payne
Suite 513, Piccadilly House
49 Piccadilly, Manchester M1 2AP
T 0161 212 1633 (Manchester)
E agent@paynemanagement.co.uk
W www.paynemanagement.co.uk

P B J MANAGEMENT LTD   T 020 7287 1112
*Personal Manager. PMA Member. Contact: Janette
Linden. By e-mail. Accepts Showreels. 11 Agents
represent 115 Performers. Comedians. Commercials.
Corporate. Presenters. Radio. Stage. Television.
Voice Overs. Walk-on & Supporting Artists. Writers*
22 Rathbone Street, London W1T 1LA
F 020 7287 1191
E general@pbjmanagement.co.uk
W www.pbjmanagement.co.uk

**PC THEATRICAL, MODEL &
CASTING AGENCY**   T 020 8381 2229
Large Database of Twins
10 Strathmore Gardens, Edgware, Middlesex HA8 5HJ
F 020 8933 3418
E twinagy@aol.com
W www.twinagency.com

PELHAM ASSOCIATES   T 01273 323010
Personal Manager. PMA Member. Contact: Peter Cleall
The Media Centre, 9-12 Middle Street, Brighton BN1 1AL
E agent@pelhamassociates.co.uk
W www.pelhamassociates.co.uk

PEMBERTON ASSOCIATES LTD   T 020 7224 9036
*Contact: Barbara Pemberton. By Post/e-mail. Showreels
on request. 5 Agents represent 130 Performers. Film.
Musicals. Radio. Stage. Television. Voice Overs*
51 Upper Berkeley Street, London W1H 7QW
E general@pembertonassociates.com
W www.pembertonassociates.com

PEOPLEMATTER.TV   T 020 7415 7070
40 Bowling Green Lane
Clerkenwell, London EC1R 0NE
F 020 7415 7074
E tony@peoplematter.tv
W www.peoplematter.tv

PEPPERPOT PROMOTIONS   T 020 7405 9108
Bands
Suite 20B, 20-22 Orde Hall Street
London WC1N 3JW
E chris@pepperpot.co.uk

**PERFORMANCE ACTORS
AGENCY**   T 020 7251 5716
Co-operative. CPMA Member
137 Goswell Road, London EC1V 7ET
F 020 7251 3974
E info@performanceactors.co.uk
W www.performanceactors.co.uk

**PERFORMERS LEAGUE
AGENCY LTD THE** T 07946 781116
Studio 55
55 Openshaw Road, London SE2 0TB
E johnson@tpla.co.uk
W www.tpla.co.uk

PERFORMING ARTS T 020 7255 1362
Personal Manager. PMA Member. Contact:
By Post/e-mail. 2 Agents represent 30 Performers.
Creative Team Members only
6 Windmill Street, London W1T 2JB
F 020 7631 4631
E info@performing-arts.co.uk
W www.performing-arts.co.uk

PERRYMENT, Mandy T 020 8941 7907
In association with CAREY, Roger ASSOCIATES
T 07790 605191
E mail@mandyperryment.com
W www.actorsmanagement.co.uk/mandyperrymentartists.html

PERSONAL APPEARANCES T/F 020 8343 7748
20 North Mount, 1147-1161 High Road
Whetstone N20 0PH
E patsy@personalappearances.biz
W www.personalappearances.biz

PHD ARTISTS T/F 020 7241 6601
Contact: Paul Harris® on behalf of Pineapple Agency
24 Montana Gardens
Sutton, Surrey SM1 4FP
E office@phdartists.com
W www.phdartists.com

PHILLIPS, Frances T 020 8953 0303
Personal Manager. PMA Member.
Contact: Frances Zealander. By e-mail.
2 Agents represent 50 Performers
89 Robeson Way
Borehamwood, Hertfordshire WD6 5RY
T 07957 334328
E frances@francesphillips.co.uk
W www.francesphillips.co.uk

**PHPM (PHILIPPA HOWELL
PERSONAL MANAGEMENT)** T 020 7836 2837
405 The Strand, London WC2R 0NE
T 07790 969024
E philippa@phpm.co.uk
W www.phpm.co.uk

**PHPM (PHILIPPA HOWELL
PERSONAL MANAGEMENT)** T 020 7836 2837
184 Bradway Road, Sheffield S17 4QX
T 07790 969024
E philippa@phpm.co.uk
W www.phpm.co.uk

PICCADILLY MANAGEMENT T 0161 953 4057
Personal Manager
23 New Mount Street
Manchester M4 4DE
F 0161 953 4001
E info@piccadillymanagement.com
W www.piccadillymanagement.com

PINEAPPLE AGENCY T 020 7241 6601
Montgomery House
159-161 Balls Pond Road
London N1 4BG
F 020 7241 3006
E pineapple.agency@btconnect.com
W www.pineappleagency.com

PLA
See LOVETT LOGAN ASSOCIATES

**PLATER, Janet
MANAGEMENT LTD** T 0191 221 2490
Contact: Janet Plater. By Post/e-mail. Commercials. Film.
Radio. Stage. Television
D Floor, Milburn House
Dean Street, Newcastle upon Tyne NE1 1LF
E magpie@tynebridge.demon.co.uk
W www.janetplatermanagement.co.uk

PLATINUM ARTISTS T 020 3006 2242
78 York Street, Marylebone, London W1H 1DP
E mail@platinumartists.co.uk
W www.platinumartists.co.uk

POLLY'S AGENCY T 020 8994 7714
The Bridge, 367 Chiswick High Road
London W4 4AG
E polly@pollysagency.co.uk
W www.pollysagency.co.uk

**POLLYANNA
MANAGEMENT LTD** T/F 020 8530 6722
1 Knighten Street, Wapping
London E1W 1PH
E aliceharwood@talktalk.net
W www.pollyannatheatre.org

POOLE, Gordon AGENCY LTD T 01275 463222
The Limes, Brockley
Bristol BS48 3BB
F 01275 462252
E agents@gordonpoole.com
W www.gordonpoole.com

PORTABLE COMEDY CLUB THE T 07767 696969
Fairfield House, Crouch End, London N8 1PV
E theportablecomedyclub@gmx.com
W www.theportablecomedyclub.co.uk

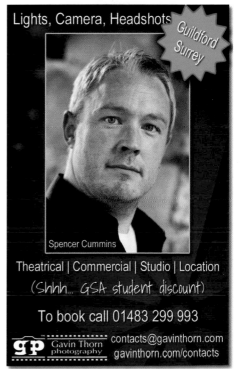

POT-KETTLE-BLACK GROUP THE　　T 07540 370430
3 Belton Road, Sidcup
Kent DA14 4AB
E info@thepkbgroup.co.uk
W www.thepkbgroup.co.uk

POWER MODEL MANAGEMENT CASTING AGENCY　　T 01603 777190
PO Box 1198, Salhouse
Norwich NR13 6WD
E info@powermodel.co.uk
W www.powermodel.co.uk

POWER PROMOTIONS　　T/F 0151 230 0070
PO Box 61, Liverpool L13 0EF
E tom2@powerpromotions.co.uk
W www.powerpromotions.com

PREGNANT PAUSE AGENCY　　T 020 8979 8874
Pregnant Models, Dancers, Actresses
11 Matham Road
East Molesey KT8 0SX
E sandy@pregnantpause.co.uk
W www.pregnantpause.co.uk

PRESTON, Morwenna MANAGEMENT　　T/F 020 8835 8147
49 Leithcote Gardens
London SW16 2UX
E info@morwennapreston.com
W www.morwennapreston.com

PRICE GARDNER MANAGEMENT　　T 020 7610 2111
PO Box 59908, London SW16 5QH
F 020 7381 3288
E info@pricegardner.co.uk
W www.pricegardner.co.uk

PRINCIPAL ARTISTES　　T 020 7224 3414
Personal Manager. Contact: By Post
Suite 1, 57 Buckingham Gate
London SW1E 6AJ

PROSPECTS ASSOCIATIONS　　T 020 8555 3628
*Sessions. Singers. Voice Overs for Commercials,
Film & Television*
28 Magpie Close, Forest Gate
London E7 9DE
E wasegun@yahoo.co.uk

PURE ACTORS AGENCY & MANAGEMENT LTD　　T 0161 832 5727
4th Floor, 20-22 High Street
Manchester M4 1QB
E enquiries@pure-management.co.uk
W www.pure-management.co.uk

PV MEDIA LTD　　T 01905 616100
County House, St Mary's Street
Worcester WR1 1HB
E md@pva.co.uk

QTALENT　　T 020 7430 5400
3rd Floor, 161 Drury Lane
Covent Garden, London WC2B 5PN
E reception@qtalent.co.uk
W www.qtalent.co.uk

RAFFLES, Tim ENTERTAINMENTS　　T/F 023 8046 5843
*Personal Manager. 2 Agents represent 9 Performers.
Corporate. Cruise Work. Singers. Television*
Victoria House
29 Swaythling Road
West End, Southampton SO30 3AG
E info@timrafflesentertainments.co.uk
W www.timrafflesentertainments.co.uk

RAGE MODELS　　T 020 7262 0515
Tigris House, 256 Edgware Road
London W2 1DS
F 020 7402 0507
E ragemodels@ugly.org
W www.ugly.org

RAPID TALENT LTD　　T 020 7734 5775
*Personal Manager. Contact: Jason Nicholls, Jason
Warren. By e-mail/Telephone. 3 Agents represent 300
Performers. Commercials. Film. Television. Walk-on &
Supporting Artists*
5 Vancouver Road, Eastbourne
East Sussex BN23 5BF
T 07980 899156
E enquiries@rapidtalent.co.uk
W www.rapidtalent.co.uk

RARE TALENT ACTORS MANAGEMENT　　T 0161 273 4004
Tanzaro House, Ardwick Green North
Manchester M12 6FZ
F 0161 273 4567
E info@raretalentactors.com
W www.raretalentactors.com

RAVENSCOURT MANAGEMENT
See CORONA MANAGEMENT

RAY KNIGHT CASTING
See KNIGHT, Ray CASTING

RAZZAMATAZZ MANAGEMENT　　T 01342 301617
*Personal Manager. Contact: Jill Shirley. By e-mail/
Telephone. 1 Agent represents 10 Clients. Children.
Dancers. Presenters. Singers*
204 Holtye Road, East Grinstead
West Sussex RH19 3ES
T 07836 268292
E razzamatazzmanagement@btconnect.com

RbA MANAGEMENT LTD　　T 0151 708 7273
*Personal Manager. CPMA Member. Contact: By
Post/e-mail. Accepts Showreels/Voicereels. Approx 25
Performers*
37-45 Windsor Street
Liverpool L8 1XE
E info@rbamanagement.co.uk
W www.rbamanagement.co.uk

RBM ACTORS　　T 020 7630 7733
3rd Floor, 168 Victoria Street
London SW1E 5LB
F 020 7630 6549
E info@rbmactors.com
W www.rbmactors.com

RDDC MANAGEMENT AGENCY　　T 01706 211161
52 Bridleway, Waterfoot
Rossendale, Lancashire BB4 9DS
T 07811 239780
E info@rddc.co.uk
W www.rddc.co.uk

RE-PM (RAIF EYLES PERSONAL MANAGEMENT)　　T 020 8953 1481
Film. Stage. Television
8 Dacre Gardens, Borehamwood WD6 2JP
T 07794 971733
E info@re-pm.co.uk
W www.re-pm.co.uk

REACH TO THE SKY PERSONAL MANAGEMENT　　T 0843 2892503
Actors. Artistes. Entertainers. Musicians
Maxet House, Liverpool Road
Luton, Beds LU1 1RS
E info@reachtothesky.com
W www.reachtothesky.com

REACTORS AGENCY   T 00 353 1 8786833
Contact: By Post/e-mail. Accepts Showreels.
Co-operative of 24 Performers
1 Eden Quay, Dublin 1, Ireland
F 00 353 1 8783182
E info@reactors.ie
W www.reactors.ie

RED CANYON MANAGEMENT   T 07931 381696
T 07939 365578
E info@redcanyon.co.uk
W www.redcanyon.co.uk

RED DOOR MANAGEMENT   T 0161 850 9989
The Greenhouse, Broadway
Media City UK, Manchester M50 2EQ
E mail@the-reddoor.co.uk
W www.the-reddoor.co.uk

RED HOT ENTERTAINMENT   T 01279 850618
Contact: Nicky Raby. By e-mail. Accepts Showreels/
Voicereels. 4 Agents represent 45 Performers.
Commercials. Disabled. Film. Musicals. Stage. Television
The Studio @ The Haven
Carter Lane
Henham, Hertfordshire CM22 6AQ
F 01279 850625
E info@redhotentertainment.biz
W www.redhotentertainment.biz

REDDIN, Joan   T 01494 882729
Personal Manager. Contact: By Post
Hazel Cottage
Frogg's Island
Wheeler End Common, Bucks HP14 3NL
E joan@joanreddin.com

REDROOFS ASSOCIATES   T 01628 674092
26 Bath Road, Maidenhead
Berkshire SL6 4JT
T 07531 355835 (Holiday Times)
E agency@redroofs.co.uk
W www.redroofs.co.uk

**REGAN RIMMER
MANAGEMENT**   T 020 7189 8323
Contact: Debbie Rimmer
25 Floral Street, Covent Garden, London WC2E 9DS
E reganrimmer@btconnect.com

**REGAN RIMMER
MANAGEMENT**   T 029 2047 3993
Contact: Leigh-Ann Regan
53 Mount Stuart Square, Cardiff CF10 5LR
F 029 2047 3938
E regan-rimmer@btconnect.com

REGENCY AGENCY   T 0113 255 8980
25 Carr Road, Calverley, Leeds LS28 5NE

**REPRESENTATION
UPSON EDWARDS**   T 01782 827222
Voice Coaches only
23 Victoria Park Road, Tunstall
Stoke-on-Trent, Staffs ST6 6DX
F 01782 728004
E sarah.upson@voicecoach.tv
W www.voicecoach.tv

REYNOLDS, Sandra AGENCY   T 020 7387 5858
*8 Agents represent 150 Performers. Film. Stage. Stills.
Television*
Amadeus House, 27B Floral Street
London WC2E 9DP
F 020 7387 5848
E info@sandrareynolds.co.uk
W www.sandrareynolds.co.uk

**REYNOLDS, Sandra
AGENCY (EAST ANGLIA)**   T 01603 623842
*8 Agents represent 150 Performers. Film. Stage. Stills.
Television*
Bacon House, 35 St Georges Street
Norwich NR3 1DA
F 01603 219825
E info@sandrareynolds.co.uk
W www.sandrareynolds.co.uk

RICHARD STONE PARTNERSHIP THE
See STONE, Richard PARTNERSHIP THE

**RICHARDS, Lisa
AGENCY THE**   T 00 353 1 6375000
108 Upper Leeson Street, Dublin 4
Ireland F 00 353 1 6671256
E info@lisarichards.ie
W www.lisarichards.ie

**RICHARDS, Lisa
AGENCY THE**   T 020 7287 1441
1st Floor, 33 Old Compton Street
London W1D 5JU
E office@lisarichards.co.uk
W www.lisarichards.co.uk

**RICHARDS, Stella
MANAGEMENT**   T 020 7736 7786
Contact: Stella Richards, Julia Lintott. Existing Clients only
42 Hazlebury Road, London SW6 2ND
E stellagent@aol.com
W www.stellarichards.com

RICHMOND SHARPE AGENCY   T 0161 858 0049
Merricourt, Windmill Lane
Appleton, Warrington, Cheshire WA4 5JP
E info@richmondsharpe.com
W www.richmondsharpe.com

**RIDGEWAY STUDIOS
MANAGEMENT**   T 01992 633775
Office: 106 Hawkshead Road
Potters Bar
Hertfordshire EN6 1NG
E info@ridgewaystudios.co.uk

RIGHTS HOUSE THE   T 020 3291 2929
PMA Member
Drury House, 34-43 Russell Street
London WC2B 5HA
E all@therightshouse.com
W www.therightshouse.com

**RISQUE MODEL
MANAGEMENT LTD**   T 0870 2283890
Rivington House
82 Great Eastern Street
London EC2A 3JF
E info@risquemodel.co.uk
W www.risquemodel.co.uk

ROAR GLOBAL   T 020 7462 9060
ROAR House, 46 Charlotte Street
London W1T 2GS
F 020 7462 9061
E info@roarglobal.com
W www.roarglobal.com

**ROBERTS, Nicola
MANAGEMENT**   T 01737 270500
9 Blackthorn Close
Reigate RH2 7NG
E info@nicolarobertsmanagement.com
W www.nicolarobertsmanagement.com

**ROGUES & VAGABONDS
MANAGEMENT LTD**   T 020 7254 8130
Personal Manager. CPMA Member
The Print House, 18 Ashwin Street
London E8 3DL
F 020 7249 8564
E rogues@vagabondsmanagement.com
W www.vagabondsmanagement.com

ROLE MODELS   T 020 7284 4337
12 Cressy Road, London NW3 2LY
E info@rolemodelsagency.com
W www.rolemodelsagency.com

**RONAN, Lynda PERSONAL
MANAGEMENT**   T 020 7183 0017
Hunters House
1 Redcliffe Road
London SW10 9NR
E lynda@lyndaronan.com
W www.lyndaronan.com

ROOM 3 AGENCY   T 0845 5678333
The Old Chapel, 14 Fairview Drive
Redland, Bristol BS6 6PH
F 0845 5679333
E kate@room3agency.com
W www.room3agency.com

ROSEBERY MANAGEMENT LTD   T 020 7684 0187
*CPMA Member. Contact: Lead Agent. By Post.
Accepts Showreels. 1 Agent represents 35 Performers.
Commercials. Film. Musicals. Stage. Television.
Voice Overs*
Hoxton Hall, 130 Hoxton Street
London N1 6SH
E admin@roseberymanagement.com
W www.roseberymanagement.com

ROSS BROWN ASSOCIATES   T 07860 558033
Personal Manager
F 020 8398 4111
E sandy@rossbrown.eu

ROSSMORE MANAGEMENT   T 020 7258 1953
PMA Member
10 Wyndham Place, London W1H 2PU
F 020 7258 0124
E agents@rossmoremanagement.com
W www.rossmoremanagement.com

ROUGH HANDS AGENCY THE   T 01992 578835
29 James Street, Epping, Essex CM16 6RR
T 07932 573228
E roughhandsagency@yahoo.co.uk

ROWE ASSOCIATES   T/F 01992 308519
33 Percy Street, London W1T 2DF
T 07887 898220
E agents@growe.co.uk
W www.growe.co.uk

ROYCE MANAGEMENT   T 020 8650 1096
121 Merlin Grove, Beckenham BR3 3HS
E office@roycemanagement.co.uk
W www.roycemanagement.co.uk

RPM2   T 0845 3625456
Studio House, Delamare Road
Cheshunt, Herts EN8 9SH
T 07795 606087
E rhino-rpm2@hotmail.com
W www.rhino2-rpm.com

RSM (CHERRY PARKER MANAGEMENT)   T 01702 522647
Contact: Cherry Parker
15 The Fairway, SS9 4QN
T 07976 547066
E info@rsm.uk.net   W www.rsm.uk.net

RUDEYE DANCE AGENCY   T 020 7014 3023
73 St John Street, London EC1M 4NJ
E info@rudeye.com
W www.rudeye.com

SAINOU   T 020 7734 6441
PMA Member
10-11 Lower John Street, London W1F 9EB
F 020 7734 1312
E office@sainou.com
W www.sainou.com

SANDERS, Loesje LTD   T 01394 385260
PMA Member. Contact: Loesje Sanders, Jo Probitts.
By Post. Choreographers. Designers. Directors.
Lighting Designers
Pound Square, 1 North Hill
Woodbridge, Suffolk IP12 1HH
F 01394 388734
E loesje@loesjesanders.org.uk
W www.loesjesanders.com

SARABAND ASSOCIATES   T 020 7609 7282
Contact: Sara Randall, Bryn Newton
39-41 North Road, London N7 9DP
E brynnewton@btconnect.com

SAROSI, Amanda ASSOCIATES   T 020 7993 6008
1 Holmbury View, London E5 9EG
F 020 7096 2141
E amanda@asassociates.biz

SASHAZE TALENT AGENCY   T 07968 762942
2 Gleannan Close, Omagh, Co. Tyrone BT79 7YA
E info@sashaze.com
W www.sashaze.com

Thornton Agency Artistes Representation
For People 5ft and Under
APT. 8 COURT ROYAL, ERIDGE ROAD, TUNBRIDGE WELLS, KENT TN4 8HT
01892 523 161   j.b.collins@btinternet.com

SCA MANAGEMENT T 01932 503285
Contact: By Post
Abbey Business Centre
Wellington Way
Brooklands Business Park
Weybridge KT13 0TT
T 01932 268375
E agency@sca-management.co.uk
W www.sca-management.co.uk

SCHNABL, Peter T 01666 502133
The Barn House
Cutwell, Tetbury
Gloucestershire GL8 8EB
F 01666 502998
E peter.schnabl@virgin.net

SCHWARTZ, Marie Claude -
AGENCE CINETEA T 00 33 1 42781717
9 Rue des Trois Bornes
75011 Paris, France
E cinetea@orange.fr
W www.cinetea.fr

SCOTT MARSHALL PARTNERS LTD
See MARSHALL, Scott PARTNERS LTD

SCOTT, Russell MANAGEMENT &
PRODUCTIONS LTD T 0844 5676896
Specialises in Finding, Developing & Giving Opportunities
to Emerging Professional Talent in Musical Theatre
E enquiry@russellscottmanagement.com
W www.russellscottmanagement.com

SCOTT, Tim T 020 7828 3824
PO Box 61776, London SW1V 3UX
E timscott@btinternet.com

SCOTT-NIVEN ASSOCIATES T 020 7884 0375
Lower Ground Floor Office
205 Victoria Rise
Clapham, London SW4 0PF
E theteam@scott-nivenassociates.com
W www.scott-nivenassociates.com

SCOTT-PAUL YOUNG
ENTERTAINMENTS LTD T/F 01753 693250
Artists Representation & Promotions
SPY Record Company, Northern Lights House
110 Blandford Road North, Langley
Nr Windsor, Berks SL3 7TA
E castingdirect@spy-ents.com
W www.spy-artistsworld.com

SCRIMGEOUR, Donald
ARTISTS AGENT T 020 8444 6248
Choreographers. Principal Dancers. Producers
49 Springcroft Avenue, London N2 9JH
F 020 8883 9751
E vwest@dircon.co.uk
W www.donaldscrimgeour.com

SECOND SKIN AGENCY T/F 01494 730166
Foxgrove House, School Lane
Seer Green, Beaconsfield, Bucks HP9 2QJ
E jenny@secondskinagency.com
W www.secondskinagency.com

SEDGWICK, Dawn
MANAGEMENT T 020 7240 0404
3 Goodwins Court, Covent Garden
London WC2N 4LL
F 020 7240 0415
W www.dawnsedgwickmanagement.com

SELECT MANAGEMENT T 07700 059089
PO Box 748, London NW4 1TT
T 07956 131494
E mail@selectmanagement.info
W www.selectmanagement.info

SEVEN CASTING AGENCY T 0161 850 1057
Personal Manager. Children. Modelling. Television
Manchester Office: 4th Floor, 59 Piccadilly
Manchester M1 2AQ
T 07730 130484
E guy@7casting.co.uk
W www.7casting.co.uk

SEVEN CASTING AGENCY T 01785 212266
Personal Manager
Staffordshire Office: Suite 3, Tudor House
9 Eastgate Street, Stafford ST16 2NQ
T 07730 130484
E guy@7casting.co.uk
W www.7casting.co.uk

SHAPER, Susan MANAGEMENT T 020 7585 1023
5 Dovedale Gardens
465 Battersea Park Road
London SW11 4LR
F 020 7350 1802
E info@susanshapermanagement.com

SHARKEY & TRIGG LTD T 020 7287 1923
46 Lexington Street, London W1F 0LP
E info@sharkeyandtrigg.com
W www.sharkeyandtrigg.com

SHELDRAKE, Peter AGENCY T 020 8876 9572
Contact: By e-mail. 1 Agent represents 35 Performers.
Commercials. Film. Musicals. Stage. Television
139 Lower Richmond Road
London SW14 7HX
T 07758 063663
E psagent@btinternet.com
W www.petersheldrakeagency.co.uk

SHEPHERD MANAGEMENT LTD T 020 7495 7813
4th Floor, 45 Maddox Street
London W1S 2PE
F 020 7499 7535
E info@shepherdmanagement.co.uk
W www.shepherdmanagement.co.uk

SHEPPERD-FOX T 07957 624601
Contact: Jane Shepperd, Sarah Fox, James Davies
(Agents)
5 Martyr Road, Guildford, Surrey GU1 4LF
E info@shepperd-fox.co.uk
W www.shepperd-fox.co.uk

SHOWSTOPPERS! T 01376 518486
Events Management & Entertainment
42 Foxglove Close, Witham
Essex CM8 2XW
E mail@showstoppers-group.com
W www.showstoppers-group.com

SHOWTIME CASTINGS T 020 7068 6816
112 Milligan Street, Docklands, London E14 8AS
T 07908 008364
E gemma@showtimecastings.com
W www.showtimecastings.com

SIMON & HOW ASSOCIATES T 020 7739 8820
12-18 Hoxton Street, London N1 6NG
E info@simon-how.com
W www.simon-how.com

**SIMPSON FOX
ASSOCIATES LTD** T 020 7434 9167
PMA Member. Set, Costume & Lighting Designers.
Directors. Choreographers
6 Beauchamp Place, London SW3 1NG
E david.bingham@simpson-fox.com

SINGER, Sandra ASSOCIATES T 01702 331616
Personal Manager. Contact: By e-mail. 2 Agents represent
60 Performers. Adults. Children. Choreographers.
Commercials. Feature Film. Musicals. Television
21 Cotswold Road, Westcliff-on-Sea
Essex SS0 8AA
E sandrasingeruk@aol.com
W www.sandrasinger.com

STAGEWORKS®
WORLDWIDE PRODUCTIONS

agency

SKATING
ICE DANCERS
FREE SKATERS
PAIR SKATERS
ADAGIO SKATERS
COMEDY SKATERS

DANCERS
ACTORS
SINGERS
MODELS

CIRCUS ARTISTS
SPECIALITY ACTS
MAGICIANS
ILLUSIONISTS
COSTUME CHARACTERS
STREET PERFORMERS

PROMOTIONAL PERSONNEL
HOSTS & HOSTESSES
GUEST SPEAKERS

SCRIPT WRITING

TECHNICAL STAGE MANAGEMENT

MUSIC PRODUCTION
PUBLISHING

MILLINERY AND COSTUMES

CHOREOGRAPHERS
DIRECTORS
PRODUCERS

00 44 **(0) 1253 342426**
00 44 **(0) 1253 336341**
info@stageworkswwp.com
stageworkswwp.com

SINGERS INC
T 020 7557 6650
9-13 Grape Street, Covent Garden, London WC2H 8ED
F 020 7557 6656
E chris@international-collective.com
W www.internationalcollective.com

SIRR, Peggy
See ORIENTAL CASTING AGENCY LTD

SJ MANAGEMENT
T 020 7371 0441
8 Bettridge Road, London SW6 3QD
E sj@susanjames.demon.co.uk

SMART MANAGEMENT
T 020 7837 8822
Contact: Mario Renzullo
PO Box 64377, London EC1P 1ND
E smart.management@virgin.net

SMEDLEY, Tom MANAGEMENT
T 07515 775220
53 Waterford Road, London SW6 2DT
E tom@tomsmedleymanagement.com
W www.tomsmedleymanagement.com

SMILE TALENT
T/F 01799 529333
2 Church Walk, Littlebury
Saffron Walden, Essex CB11 4TS
T/F 01799 618809
E info@smiletalent.com
W www.smiletalent.biz

SOPHIE'S PEOPLE
T 020 8812 4999
*Contact: Sophie Pyecroft. By Post/e-mail. Accepts
Showreels. 2 Agents represent 400 Performers.
Choreographers. Commercials. Corporate. Dancers.
Film. Television*
40 Mexfield Road, London SW15 2RQ
T 0870 7876446
E sophies.people@btinternet.com
W www.sophiespeople.com

S.O.S.
T 020 7735 5133
85 Bannerman House, Lawn Lane, London SW8 1UA
T 07740 359770
E info@sportsofseb.com
W www.sportsofseb.com

SPEAKERS CIRCUIT LTD THE
T 01892 750131
After Dinner Speakers
The Country Store, The Green
Frant, East Sussex TN3 9DA
T 01892 750921
E speakers-circuit@freenetname.co.uk

SPEAKERS CORNER
T 020 8365 3200
*Award Hosts, Comedians, Facilitators & Speakers for
Corporate Events*
207 High Road, London N2 8AN
F 020 8883 7213
E info@speakerscorner.co.uk
W www.speakerscorner.co.uk

SPLITTING IMAGES LOOKALIKES AGENCY
T 020 8809 2327
25 Clissold Court, Greenway Close, London N4 2EZ
E info@splitting-images.com
W www.splitting-images.com

SPORTS OF SEB LTD
T 020 7735 5133
85 Bannerman House, Lawn Lane, London SW8 1UA
T 07740 359770
E info@sportsofseb.com   **W** www.sportsofseb.com

SPORTS PROMOTIONS (UK) LTD
T 020 8771 4700
*Contact: By e-mail/Telephone. 300+ Performers.
Commercials. Dancers. Modelling. Presenters.
Sports Models. Stunts*
56 Church Road, Crystal Palace, London SE19 2EZ
F 020 8771 4704
E agent@sportspromotions.co.uk
W www.sportspromotions.co.uk

SPYKER, Paul MANAGEMENT
T 020 7462 0046
PO Box 48848, London WC1B 3WZ
F 020 7462 0047
E belinda@psmlondon.com

SRA PERSONAL MANAGEMENT
T 01932 863194
Lockhart Road, Cobham
Surrey KT11 2AX
E agency@susanrobertsacademy.co.uk

SSA MANAGEMENT
T 07904 817229
E info@ssamanagement.co.uk
W www.ssamanagement.co.uk

S.T. ARTS MANAGEMENT
T 0845 4082468
Contact: Tarquin Shaw-Young. Actors. Actresses
PO Box 127, Ross On Wye HR9 6WZ
F 0845 4082464
E tarquin@startsmanagement.co.uk
W www.startsmanagement.co.uk

ST JAMES'S MANAGEMENT
T 01621 772183
Personal Manager. Existing Clients only
7 Smyatts Close, Southminster, Essex CM0 7JT
E jlstjames@btconnect.com

STAGE CENTRE MANAGEMENT LTD
T 020 7607 0872
*Co-operative. CPMA Member. Contact: By e-mail/Post.
Commercials. Film. Musicals. Stage. Television*
41 North Road, London N7 9DP
E info@stagecentre.org.uk
W www.stagecentre.org.uk

STAGEWORKS ARTIST MANAGEMENT
T 020 7253 3118
Europa House, 13-17 Ironmonger Row
London EC1V 3QG

STAGEWORKS WORLDWIDE PRODUCTIONS
T 01253 342426
*Contact: By e-mail. Cirque Artistes. Corporate. Dancers.
Ice-Skaters. Musicals*
525 Ocean Boulevard, Blackpool FY4 1EZ
F 01253 343702
E kelly.willars@stageworkswwp.com
W www.stageworkswwp.com

STAR POWER PRODUCTIONS
T 07957 186947
Actors. Actresses. Dancers. Models. Rappers. Singers
23 Castalia Square, Docklands
London E14 3NG
E dannypage247@hotmail.co.uk
W www.starpowerproductions.co.uk

STENTORIAN
T 07808 353611
44 Broughton Grove, Skipton BD23 1TL
E stentorian@btinternet.com
W www.stentoriantowncryer.co.uk

STEVENSON, Natasha MANAGEMENT LTD
See NSM (NATASHA STEVENSON MANAGEMENT LTD)

STIRLING MANAGEMENT
T 01204 848333
*Contact: Glen Mortimer. By e-mail. Accepts Showreels.
3 Agents represent 70 Performers. Commercials. Film.
Presenters. Stage. Television*
490 Halliwell Road, Bolton
Greater Manchester BL1 8AN
E admin@stirlingmanagement.co.uk
W www.stirlingmanagement.co.uk

STIVEN CHRISTIE MANAGEMENT
T 0131 228 4040
Incorporating The Actors Agency of Edinburgh
1 Glen Street, Tollcross
Edinburgh EH3 9JD
F 0131 228 4645
E info@stivenchristie.co.uk
W www.stivenchristie.co.uk

Vanessa Valentine PHOTOGRAPHY
www.vanessavalentinephotography.com
t: 07904059541
Student rates available

Celia Imrie   Kate O'Flynn   Leon Ockenden   Rebecca Atkinson

STONE, Ian ASSOCIATES   T 020 8667 1627
Suite 262, Maddison House
226 High Street, Croydon CR9 1DF

**STONE, Richard
PARTNERSHIP THE**   T 020 7497 0849
PMA Member
Suite 3, De Walden Court
85 New Cavendish Street, London W1W 6XD
F 020 7497 0869
E all@thersp.com   W www.thersp.com

**STONEHOUSE, Katherine
MANAGEMENT**   T 020 8560 7709
*Contact: Katherine Stonehouse. By e-mail. 1 Agent
represents 35 Performers. Commercials. Film. Musicals.
Stage. Television*
PO Box 64412, London W5 9GU
E katherine@katherinestonehouse.co.uk
W www.katherinestonehouse.co.uk

STOPFORD AGENCY   T 020 8741 6158
Stage
56A Church Road, Barnes, London SW13 0DQ
E info@stopfordagency.com
W www.stopfordagency.com

STRAIGHT LINE MANAGEMENT   T 020 8393 4220
Division of Straight Line Productions
58 Castle Avenue, Epsom, Surrey KT17 2PH
F 020 8393 8079
E hilary@straightlinemanagement.co.uk

SUCCESS   T 020 7734 3356
Room 236, 2nd Floor, Linen Hall
162-168 Regent Street, London W1B 5TB
F 020 7494 3787
E ee@successagency.co.uk
W www.successagency.co.uk

**SUMMERS, Mark
MANAGEMENT**   T 020 7229 8413
1 Beaumont Avenue, West Kensington
London W14 9LP
E louise@marksummers.com
W www.marksummers.com

SUPERTED.COM   T 07956 511051
2 Chapel Place, Rivington Street, London EC2A 3DQ
E email@superted.com
W www.superted.com

TACT-AGENTS   T 00 31 6 24415744
Based in Amsterdam. Twitter: @tactagents
Palestrinastraat 10 hs
1071 LE Amsterdam, The Netherlands
E info@tactagents.nl
W www.tactagents.nl

TAKE2 CASTING AGENCY   T 00 353 87 2563403
28 Booch Park Road, Foxrock, Dublin 18, Ireland
E pamela@take2.ie
W www.take2.ie

TALENT4 MEDIA LTD   T 020 7183 4330
Studio LG16, Shepherds Building Central
Charecroft Way, London W14 0EH
F 020 7183 4331
E enquiries@talent4media.com
W www.talent4media.com

TALENT ARTISTS LTD   T 020 7923 1119
Contact: Jane Wynn Owen. No Unsolicited Enquiries
59 Sydner Road, London N16 7UF
F 020 7923 2009
E talent.artists@btconnect.com

TALENT SCOUT THE   T 01924 464049
19 Edge Road, Dewsbury WF12 0QA
E connect@thetalentscout.org
W www.thetalentscout.org

TALENTED ARTISTS LTD   T 020 7520 9412
Suite 17, Adam House
7-10 Adam Street, London WC2N 6AA
E info@talentedartistsltd.com
W www.talentedartistsltd.com

TAVISTOCK WOOD   T 020 7494 4767
PMA Member
45 Conduit Street, London W1S 2YN
F 020 7434 2017
E info@tavistockwood.com
W www.tavistockwood.com

**TCA
(THE COMMERCIAL AGENCY)**   T 020 7233 8100
12 Evelyn Mansions, Carlisle Place, London SW1P 1NH
F 020 7233 8110
E mail@thecommercialagency.co.uk
W www.thecommercialagency.co.uk

**TCG ARTIST
MANAGEMENT LTD**   T 020 7240 3600
*Contact: Kristin Tarry (Director/Agent), Johnny Muller
(Agent), Cal Griffiths (Assistant), Emma Davidson
(Assistant), Jackie Davis (Office Manager), Charlie Wale
(Legal/Contracts). By Post/e-mail. Accepts Showreels.
Commercials. Film. Musicals. Stage. Television*
14A Goodwin's Court, London WC2N 4LL
E info@tcgam.co.uk
W www.tcgam.co.uk

TDC AGENCY   T 01772 378337
Eden Street, Leyland, Preston, Lancaster PR25 2ET
E office@tdcagency.co.uk
W www.tdcagency.co.uk

TEAM PLAYERS   T 00 45 20494218
Carit Etlars Vej 3, Frederiksberg
Copenhagen DK-1814, Denmark
E info@teamplayers.dk
W www.teamplayers.dk

TENNYSON AGENCY THE   T 020 8543 5939
10 Cleveland Avenue, Merton Park, London SW20 9EW
E mail@tennysonagency.co.uk

THOMAS, Lisa MANAGEMENT   T 0845 9005511
Contact: By e-mail. 8 Agents represent 30+ Performers
Unit 10, 7 Wenlock Road, London N1 7SL
F 0845 9005522
E assistant@lisathomasmanagement.com
W www.lisathomasmanagement.com

THOMAS GERRARD CASTING AGENT
See MILAEON

**THOMPSON, David
ASSOCIATES**   T 020 8682 3083
7 St Peter's Close, London SW17 7UH
T 07889 191093
E montefioredt@aol.com

THOMSON, Mia ASSOCIATES   T 020 7307 5939
3rd Floor, 207 Regent Street, London W1B 3HH
F 020 7580 4729
E info@miathomsonassociates.co.uk
W www.miathomsonassociates.co.uk

**THORNTON AGENCY
ARTISTES REPRESENTATION**   T 01892 523161
For People 5 feet & under
Apt 8 Court Royal, Eridge Road
Tunbridge Wells, Kent TN4 8HT
E j.b.collins@btinternet.com

**THRELFALL, Katie
ASSOCIATES**   T 020 8543 4344
2A Gladstone Road, London SW19 1QT
F 020 8543 7545
E info@ktthrelfall.co.uk

**THRESH, Melody MANAGEMENT
ASSOCIATES LTD (MTM)**   T 0161 457 2110
Imperial Court, 2 Exchange Quay, Manchester M5 3EB
E melodythreshmtm@aol.com

TILDSLEY, Janice ASSOCIATES   T 020 8521 1888
PMA Member. Contact: Kathryn Kirton
47 Orford Road, London E17 9NJ
F 020 8521 1174
E kathryn@janicetildsleyassociates.co.uk
W www.janicetildsleyassociates.co.uk

**TINKER, Victoria
MANAGEMENT**   T/F 01403 210653
Non-acting. Technical
Birchenbridge House, Brighton Road
Mannings Heath, Horsham, West Sussex RH13 6HY

TOP TALENT AGENCY LTD   T 01727 855903
*Children & Adults. Commercials. Film. Photographic.
Stage. Television*
PO Box 860, St Albans
Herts AL1 9BR
F 01727 812666
E admin@toptalentagency.co.uk
W www.toptalentagency.co.uk

TOTAL VANITY   T 07710 780152
15 Walton Way, Aylesbury
Buckinghamshire HP21 7JJ
T 07739 381788
E richard.williams@totalvanity.com
W www.totalvanity.com

**TRENDS AGENCY &
MANAGEMENT LTD**   T 0871 2003343
*Contact: By e-mail. Commercials. Dancers. Musicals.
Singers. Stage*
Sullom Lodge, Sullom Side Lane
Garstang PR3 1GH
F 01253 407715
E info@squiresjohns.com
W www.squiresjohns.com

TROIKA   T 020 7336 7868
PMA Member
10A Christina Street, London EC2A 4PA
F 020 7490 7642
E info@troikatalent.com

TTA   T 01245 200555
59 Belvawney Close, Chelmsford
Essex CM1 4YR
E agents@tomorrowstalent.co.uk

TURNSTONE MANAGEMENT   T 0845 5576658
T 07866 211647
E mark_turner85@hotmail.com

TV MANAGEMENTS   T 01425 475544
Brink House, Avon Castle
Ringwood, Hants BH24 2BL
F 01425 480123
E etv@tvmanagements.co.uk

TWINS
See PC THEATRICAL, MODEL & CASTING AGENCY

TWO'S COMPANY   T 020 8299 4593
Existing Clients only. Directors. Stage. Writers
244 Upland Road, London SE22 0DN
E graham@2scompanytheatre.co.uk

UGLY MODELS   T 020 7402 5564
Tigris House, 256 Edgware Road, London W2 1DS
F 020 7402 0507
E info@ugly.org
W www.ugly.org

UNITED AGENTS LTD   T 020 3214 0800
Personal Manager. PMA Member
12-26 Lexington Street, London W1F 0LE
E info@unitedagents.co.uk
W www.unitedagents.co.uk

UPBEAT MANAGEMENT   T 020 8668 3332
Theatre Touring & Events. No Actors
Larg House, Woodcote Grove
Coulsdon, Surrey CR5 2QQ
E info@upbeat.co.uk
W www.upbeat.co.uk

UPSON EDWARDS
See REPRESENTATION UPSON EDWARDS

URBAN TALENT　T 0161 228 6866
Nemesis House, 1 Oxford Court
Bishopsgate, Manchester M2 3WQ
F 0161 228 6727
E liz@nmsmanagement.co.uk
W www.urbantalent.tv

UTOPIA MODEL MANAGEMENT　T 07771 884844
7 Ellerbeck, Manchester M28 7XN
F 0871 2180843
E kya@utopiamodels.co.uk

UVA MANAGEMENT LTD　T 01753 652233
*Contact: By e-mail. Commercials. Film. Presenters. Stage.
Television*
Pinewood Film Studios, Pinewood Road
Iver Heath, Buckinghamshire SL0 0NH
E berko@uvamanagement.com
W www.uvamanagement.com

VACCA, Roxane MANAGEMENT　T 020 7383 5971
61 Judd Street, London WC1H 9QT
E info@roxanevacca.co.uk

**VALLÉ THEATRICAL
AGENCY THE**　T 01992 622861
The Vallé Academy Studios, Wilton House
Delamare Road, Cheshunt, Herts EN8 9SG
F 01992 622868
E agency@valleacademy.co.uk
W www.valleacademy.co.uk

**VERBECK, Dean
PERSONAL MANAGEMENT**　T 01792 701570
c/o 26 Pine Crescent, Morriston
Swansea SA6 6AR
E info.dvpm@mail.com
W www.deanverbeck.co.uk

**VIDAL-HALL, Clare
MANAGEMENT**　T 020 8741 7647
*PMA Member. Choreographers. Composers. Designers.
Directors. Lighting Designers*
57 Carthew Road, London W6 0DU
F 020 8741 9459
E info@clarevidalhall.com
W www.clarevidalhall.com

VINE, Michael ASSOCIATES　T 020 8347 2580
Light Entertainment
1 Stormont Road, London N6 4NS
E stephen@michaelvineassociates.com

VISIONARY TALENT　T 020 3612 2458
19 Woodlands Heights, Vanbrugh Hill
London SE3 7EL
T 07827 446195
E info@visionarytalent.co.uk
W www.visionarytalent.co.uk

VJ MANAGEMENT　T 020 7237 8953
15 Jarman House, Hawkstone Road
Surrey Quays, London SE16 2PW
E vjh18@hotmail.co.uk

**VM TALENT LTD
(VIC MURRAY TALENT)**　T 020 7924 4453
PMA Member
185A/B Latchmere Road
London SW11 2JZ
E info@vmtalent.com
W www.vmtalent.com

VSA LTD　T 020 7240 2927
PMA Member. Contact: Andy Charles, Tod Weller
186 Shaftesbury Avenue
London WC2H 8JB
F 020 7240 2930
E info@vsaltd.com
W www.vsaltd.com

W ATHLETIC　T 020 7206 2301
Unit 309, 377-399 London Road
Camberley, Surrey GU15 3HL
E london@wathletic.com
W www.wathletic.com

WADE, Suzann　T 020 7486 0746
*Personal Manager. PMA Member. Contact: By Post only
(No Calls). Accepts Showreels. 2 Agents represent 19
Performers. Film. Musicals. Stage. Television*
9 Wimpole Mews, London W1G 8PG
F 020 7486 5664
E info@suzannwade.com
W www.suzannwade.com

WALK TALL MANAGEMENT　T/F 01474 561200
Contact: By e-mail. Accepts Showreels. 35 Performers
Britannia House, Lower Road
Ebbsfleet, Kent DA11 9BL
E annduke@lineone.net

**WARD, Mandy ARTIST
MANAGEMENT**　T 020 7434 3569
PMA Member
4th Floor, 74 Berwick Street
London W1F 8TE
E info@mwartistmanagement.com
W www.mandywardartistmanagement.com

WARD CASTING　T 020 7458 4474
Studio 5, 155 Commercial Street
London E1 6BJ
E casting@wardcasting.com
W www.wardcasting.com

WARING & McKENNA　T 020 7836 9222
PMA Member
44 Maiden Lane, Covent Garden
London WC2E 7LN
F 020 7836 9186
E dj@waringandmckenna.com
W www.waringandmckenna.com

**WELCH, Janet PERSONAL
MANAGEMENT**　T/F 01761 463238
Contact: By Post
Old Orchard, The Street
Ubley, Bristol BS40 6PJ
E info@janetwelchpm.co.uk

WEST CENTRAL MANAGEMENT T/F 020 7833 8134
CPMA Member. Co-operative of 21 Performers.
Contact: By Post/e-mail
Room 4, East Block, Panther House
38 Mount Pleasant, London WC1X 0AN
E mail@westcentralmanagement.co.uk
W www.westcentralmanagement.co.uk

WEST END MANAGEMENT T 0141 222 2333
Contact: Maureen Cairns, Allan Jones
2nd Floor
34 Argyle Arcade Chambers
Buchanan Street
Glasgow G2 8BD
E info@west-endmgt.com
W www.west-endmgt.com

WHATEVER ARTISTS MANAGEMENT LTD T 020 7372 4777
F24 Argo House, Kilburn Park Road
London NW6 5LF
F 020 7372 5111
E info@wamshow.biz
W www.wamshow.biz

WHITEHALL ARTISTS T/F 020 8785 3737
6 Embankment, Putney
London SW15 1LB
E whitehallfilms@gmail.com

WILDE MANAGEMENT T 07759 567639
11 Wilton Road, Chorlton
Manchester M21 9GS
T 07759 567640
E info@wildemanagement.co.uk
W www.wildemanagement.co.uk

WILKINSON, David ASSOCIATES T 020 7371 5188
Existing Clients only
115 Hazlebury Road, London SW6 2LX
F 020 7371 5161
E info@dwassociates.net

WILLIAMS BULLDOG MANAGEMENT LTD T 020 7585 1518
6 Vicentia Quay
Bridges Wharf
London SW11 3GY
T 07766 254877
E info@williamsbulldog.co.uk
W www.williamsbulldog.co.uk

WILLIAMSON & HOLMES T 020 7240 0407
51 St Martin's Lane, London WC2N 4EA
E info@williamsonandholmes.co.uk

WILLOW PERSONAL MANAGEMENT T 01733 240392
Specialist Agency for Short Actors (5 feet & under) & Tall Actors (7 feet & over)
151 Main Street, Yaxley
Peterborough, Cambs PE7 3LD
E office@willowmanagement.co.uk
W www.willowmanagement.co.uk

WILLS, Newton MANAGEMENT T 07989 398381
Personal Manager. Contact: By Post/e-mail. Accepts Showreels/Voicereels. 3 Agents represent 53 Performers. Commercials. Dancers. Film. Musicals. Singers. Stage. Television. Voice Overs
12 St Johns Road, Isleworth
Middlesex TW7 6NN
F 00 33 4 68218685
E newtoncttg@aol.com
W www.newtonwills.com

WINSLETT, Dave ASSOCIATES T 020 8668 0531
4 Zig Zag Road, Kenley
Surrey CR8 5EL
F 020 8668 9216
E info@davewinslett.com
W www.davewinslett.com

WINTERSONS T 020 7836 7849
PMA Member
59 St Martin's Lane
London WC2N 4JS
E info@nikiwinterson.com
W www.nikiwinterson.com

WIS CELTIC MANAGEMENT T 07966 302812
Welsh, Irish & Scottish Performers
86 Elphinstone Road
Walthamstow
London E17 5EX
F 020 8523 4523

WISE BUDDAH TALENT T 020 7307 1600
Contact: Chris North
74 Great Titchfield Street
London W1W 7QP
F 020 7307 1601
E chris.north@wisebuddah.com
W www.wisebuddah.com

WMG MANAGEMENT EUROPE LTD T 020 7009 6000
Sports Management Company
5th Floor, 33 Soho Square
London W1D 3QU
F 020 3230 1053
W www.wmgllc.com

WYMAN, Edward AGENCY T 029 2075 2351
Contact: Judith Gay. By Post/e-mail. Adults (16+ yrs). Books open Jan & July only. English & Welsh Language. Commercials. Corporate. Television. Voice Overs. Walk-on & Supporting Artists
23 White Acre Close
Thornhill
Cardiff CF14 9DG
E wymancasting@yahoo.co.uk
W www.wymancasting.co.uk

XL MANAGEMENT T 01926 810449
Edmund House, Rugby Road
Leamington Spa
Warwickshire CV32 6EL
F 01926 811420
E office@xlmanagement.co.uk
W www.xlmanagement.co.uk

YAT MANAGEMENT (YOUNG ACTORS THEATRE MANAGEMENT) T 020 7278 2101
70-72 Barnsbury Road
London N1 0ES
E agent@yati.org.uk
W www.yati.org.uk

YELLOW BALLOON PRODUCTIONS LTD T 01483 281500
Contact: Mike Smith
Freshwater House, Outdowns
Effingham, Surrey KT24 5QR
F 01483 281501
E yellowbal@aol.com

ZWICKLER, Marlene & ASSOCIATES T/F 0131 343 3030
1 Belgrave Crescent Lane, Edinburgh EH4 3AG
E info@mza-artists.com
W www.mza-artists.com

alphabetkidz

TV/Film, Commercial, Photographic, Theatre and Voiceovers

Naturally talented Artists with a multitude of different skills and talents for all your casting needs.
Our philosophy is Fun, Energy, Enthusiasm, Commitment, Equality and Diversity.

t: 020 7252 4343   f: 020 7252 4341
e: contact@alphabetkidz.co.uk
w: www.alphabetkidz.co.uk

BAFTA AWARD WINNING AGENCY alphabetmanagement | alphabetagency

---

A & J ARTISTS LTD   T 020 8342 0542
242A The Ridgeway, Botany Bay, Enfield EN2 8AP
T 020 8367 7139
E info@ajmanagement.co.uk
W www.ajmanagement.co.uk

ABACUS AGENCY   T 01306 877144
The Studio, 4 Bailey Road
Westcott, Dorking, Surrey RH4 3QS
F 01306 877813
E admin@abacusagency.co.uk
W www.abacusagency.co.uk

ACADEMY ARTS MANAGEMENT   T 01245 422595
6A The Green, Writtle, Chelmsford, Essex CM1 3DU
E info@academyarts.co.uk
W www.academyarts.co.uk

ACT 2 MANAGEMENT   T 07939 144355
Based in East London
105 Richmond Avenue, Highams Park, London E4 9RR
E management@act2drama.co.uk
W www.act2drama.co.uk

ACT OUT AGENCY   T/F 0161 429 7413
22 Greek Street, Stockport, Cheshire SK3 8AB
E ab22actout@aol.com
W www.abacademytheatreschool.webs.com

ALL EXPRESSIONS AGENCY   T 020 8898 3321
153 Waverley Avenue, Twickenham TW2 6DJ
E info@allexpressions.co.uk
W www.allexpressions.co.uk

**ALL THE ARTS CHILDREN'S
CASTING AGENCY**   T 020 8850 2384
PO Box 61687, London SE9 9RP
T 07908 618083
E jillian@allthearts.co.uk
W www.alltheartsagency.co.uk

ALLSORTS AGENCY   T 020 8989 0500
Suite 3 Marlborough Business Centre
96 George Lane, London E18 1AD
F 020 8989 5600
E bookings@allsortsagency.com
W www.allsortsagency.com

**ALLSORTS DRAMA
FOR CHILDREN**   T/F 020 8969 3249
In association with LESLIE, Sasha MANAGEMENT
34 Crediton Road, London NW10 3DU
E sasha@allsortsdrama.com

ALLSTARS CASTING   T 0151 707 2100
66 Hope Street, Liverpool L1 9BZ
T/F 07739 359737
E sylvie@allstarscasting.co.uk
W www.allstarscasting.co.uk

ALPHABET KIDZ   T 020 7252 4343
Also known as Alphabet Agency
Daisy Business Park, 19-35 Sylvan Grove
London SE15 1PD
F 020 7252 4341
E contact@alphabetkidz.co.uk
W www.alphabetkidz.co.uk

ANNA'S MANAGEMENT   T 020 8958 7636
*Formerly of Aladdin's Cave. Children. Teenagers.
Young Adults*
25 Tintagel Drive, Stanmore, Middlesex HA7 4SR
E annasmanage@aol.com
W www.annasmanagement.com

ARAENA/COLLECTIVE   T/F 020 8428 0037
10 Bramshaw Gardens, South Oxhey
Herts WD19 6XP
E info@collectivedance.co.uk

**A.R.K. AGENCY
(ALL ROUND KIDS)**   T 07900 998090
8 St Judes Close, Sutton Coldfield
Warwickshire B75 7SU
T 07976 755434
E allroundkids@hotmail.co.uk
W www.allroundkids.co.uk

ARNOULD KIDZ   T 020 8942 1879
1A Brook Gardens, Kingston upon Thames
Surrey KT2 7ET
T 07720 427828
E info@arnouldkidz.co.uk
W www.arnouldkidz.co.uk

Children's & Teenagers' Agents

How can my child become an actor?

If your child is interested in becoming an actor, they should try to get as much practical experience as possible. For example, joining the drama club at school, taking theatre studies as an option, reading as many plays as they can, and going to the theatre on a regular basis. They could also attend local youth theatres or drama groups. Some theatres offer evening or Saturday classes.

What are the chances of success?

As any agency or school will tell you, the entertainment industry is highly competitive and for every success story there are many children who will never be hired for paid acting work. Child artists and their parents should think very carefully before getting involved in the industry and be prepared for disappointments along the way.

What is the difference between stage schools and agencies?

Stage schools provide specialised training in acting, singing and dancing for the under 18s. They offer a variety of full and part-time courses. Please see the 'Drama Training, Schools & Coaches' section for listings. Children's and teenagers' agencies specialise in the representation of child artists, promoting them to casting opportunities and negotiating contracts on their behalf. In return they will take commission, usually ranging from 10-15%. Some larger stage schools also have agencies attached to them. A number of agents are listed in this section.

Why does my child need an agent?

While many parents feel they want to retain control over their child's career, they will not have the contacts and authority a good agent will have in the industry. Casting directors are more likely to look to an agent they know and trust to provide the most suitable children for a job than an independent, unrepresented child. This does not mean to say that a child will never get work without an agent to put them forward for work, but it will certainly be more difficult.

How should I use these listings?

This section lists up-to-date contact details for agencies specialising in the representation of children and teenagers. Every company listed is done so by written request to us. Always research agencies carefully before approaching them to make sure they are suitable for your child. Many have websites you can visit, or ask around for personal recommendations. You should make a short-list of the ones you think are most appropriate rather than sending a standard letter to hundreds of agencies. Please see the main 'Agents & Personal Managers' advice section for further guidance on choosing and approaching agents.

Can Spotlight offer me advice on choosing or changing my child's agent?

Unfortunately Spotlight is not able to advise performers on specific agents, nor is it in a position to handle any financial or contractual queries or complaints. For agent-related queries we suggest you contact The Agents' Association www.agents-uk.com or The Personal Managers' Association (PMA) www.thepma.com, or you could try one of the independent advisors on our website www.spotlight.com/artists/advice

Who can I contact for general advice?

Your local education authority should be able to help with most queries regarding your child's education, working hours, chaperones and general welfare if they are aged 16 or under. You could also try contacting an independent advisor for advice, or for legal guidance please see the 'Accountants, Insurance & Law' section for listings.

Can my child join Equity?

Since May 2012 children aged 10 or over can apply for full Equity membership. Please see www.equity.org.uk

Should I pay an agent to represent my child? Or sign a contract?

Equity does not recommend that you pay an agent an upfront fee to place your child on their client list. Before signing a contract, you should be very clear about the terms and commitments involved. For advice on both of these issues, or if you experience any problems with a current agent, we recommend that you contact Equity directly.

Why do child actors need licences?

Strict regulations apply to children working in the entertainment industry. These cover areas including the maximum number of performance hours per day/week, rest times, meal times and tutoring requirements. When any child under 16 performs in a professional capacity, the production company must obtain a Child Performance Licence from the child's local education authority.

Who are chaperones?

Child artists must also be accompanied by a chaperone at all times when they are working. Registered chaperones are generally used instead of parents as they have a better understanding of the employment regulations involved, and they have professional experience of dealing with production companies.

Listings for a number of child chaperones can be found in the 'Consultants' section, but please ensure that you research any company or individual before proceeding further. Registered chaperones will have been police checked and approved by their local education authority to act in loco parentis. Always contact your local education authority if you have any questions or concerns.

What is the Spotlight Children and Young Performers directory?

Children who are currently represented by an agent or attend a stage school can appear in the Spotlight Children and Young Performers directory. This is a casting directory, used by production teams to source child artists for TV, film, stage or commercial work. Each child pays an annual membership fee to have their photo featured in the printed directory along with others represented by the same agency or stage school, as well as receiving their own individual online CV on the Spotlight website, searchable by casting professionals. Please speak to your child's school or agency about joining Spotlight for ongoing promotion to hundreds of casting opportunities.

For further information about the directory visit www.spotlight.com/join

Children's & Teenagers' Agents

CASE STUDY

Each month Jemima Laing, mother of 13-year-old Spotlight member Felix Soper, charts the ups and occasional downs of being the parent of a child performer on Spotlight's news blog. Jemima is an ex-BBC, now freelance, journalist based in Plymouth.

So, you're basking in that first-night glow of parental pride following your little one's inaugural appearance on stage or screen: talent and a taste for performing have been established.

Chances are this moment has come courtesy of some serendipitous turn of events; a fluke meeting, an open casting, a friend of a friend heard someone, somewhere was looking for a kid just like yours and, bingo! they've only gone and got the part, but what next?

For many, the obvious answer is to try to get an agent, a good move for myriad reasons but crucially because they have access to casting directors and auditions you wouldn't otherwise get a sniff of.

As for the best way to go about it, Pandora's Box is nothing compared to this particular can of worms. Opinions on the most effective method are as diverse as anything you'll ever hear: it's as easy as it is hard and as simple as it is convoluted.

There's no mathematical formula to follow (if there were I suspect it would make Fermat's Last Theorem look like a walk in the park) so I'll just tell you how I did it – not right, not wrong, just my way.

You'll need three things: a computer, a copy of Contacts and time to consume as many films and watch as much telly as you can.

When a child popped up on screen whose performance impressed me I would note their name and, using various search engines, discover their agent.

A few agencies began to recur, I narrowed it down to three, checked their submission criteria and sent a decent-sized head and shoulder snapshot of my son and a simple covering letter outlining his relevant experience (which at that point amounted to a single role in a pantomime) and a little bit about his personality and interests and that was it.

We were contacted by two, met one and he was taken on.

But even while you're looking for an agent there is still plenty you can do to try to find opportunities for your child. Websites such as ScreenTerrier (screenterrier.blogspot.co.uk) and NotAPushyMum (www.notapushymum.com) are a great source of open audition information and also a good way of finding out which talented tyke snatched that plum part from under your offspring's nose.

Make the most of social media: many agencies are on Twitter and Facebook and announce via their walls and timelines when their books are open and their preferred method of application.

Once you've done it be sure to savour the thrill of securing a place in an agency for your child while you can because that search is a little like the gestation period: any initial elation at its completion is soon supplanted by the enormity of the task ahead.

What you have, in fact, been handed is a pass to the baffling world of auditions.

The contradictions are everywhere; it's a business of maddening competitiveness laced with unexpected support and kindness. There'll be stuff you'll slowly get to grips with and stuff you will never understand.

Your life will take on a distinctly Sisyphean tone as, time and again, you push that audition-shaped boulder tantalisingly close to the top of the casting hill only to see it roll right back down to the bottom, dumping you and your pint-sized performer unceremoniously on your backsides, back at square one with it all to do again.

You'll need to steel yourself, your child and your wallet.

TV and film auditions are usually in London (by usually I mean always) so, if you haven't been forward thinking enough to have laid your hat within the M25, treat yourself to a railcard, a comfy cushion and a Kindle. You will be spending a lot of time on trains.

If you can perfect the being-in-the-right-place-at-the-right-time thing while simultaneously ensuring your child looks like a mini version of any or all of IMDB's top 100 actors, so much the better.

Be prepared to spend large swathes of your time in a state of suspended anticipation, waiting for THAT call (they do actually come every now and then) which turns everyone's life on a sixpence.

And the final thing you'll need is luck, blinking great chunks of it.

Don't be under any illusion that this is some sedate perambulation you're embarking on, think of it more as a white knuckle rollercoaster trip with sufficient ups and downs to induce collywobbles in even the most iron of constitutions.

But it's certainly worth the ride and let me be the first to welcome you aboard, unless, of course, your child is a boy, playing age 12-15 with fair hair and blue eyes, in which case it's probably best if you get off now.

Please visit www.jemimalaing.co.uk to read more from Jemima, including past Spotlight pieces, or follow her on Twitter @jemimalaing.

ASHCROFT ACADEMY OF
DRAMATIC ART & AGENCY   T 0844 8005328
Malcolm Primary School, Malcolm Road
Penge, London SE20 8RH
T 07799 791586
E info@ashcroftacademy.com
W www.ashcroftacademy.com

AWA - ANDREA WILDER
AGENCY   T 07919 202401
23 Cambrian Drive, Colwyn Bay
Conwy LL28 4SL
F 07092 249314
E andreawilder@fastmail.fm
W www.awagency.co.uk

BABYSHAK AGENCY   T 0845 5200400
Bizzy Studios, 1st Floor Hall, 10-12 Pickford Lane
Bexleyheath, Kent DA7 4QW
F 0845 5200401
E clients@babyshak.com
W www.babyshak.com

BANANAFISH MANAGEMENT   T 0151 708 5509
The Arts Village, 20-26 Henry Street
Liverpool L1 5BS
T 07974 206622
E info@bananafish.co.uk
W www.bananafish.co.uk

BELFAST TALENT AGENCY   T 028 9024 3324
The Crescent Arts Centre
Belfast, Antrim BT7 1NH
E info@belfasttalent.com
W www.belfasttalentagency.com

BIG TALENT SCHOOL &
AGENCY THE   T 029 2132 0421
Contact: Shelley Barrett-Norton
53 Mount Stuart Square, Cardiff CF10 5LR
T 07886 020923
E info@thebigtalent.co.uk
W www.thebigtalent.co.uk

BIZZYKIDZ   T 0845 5200400
Bizzy Studios, 1st Floor Hall, 10-12 Pickford Lane
Bexleyheath, Kent DA7 4QW
F 0845 5200401
E bookings@bizzykidz.com
W www.bizzykidz.com

BODENS AGENCY   T 020 8447 0909
99 East Barnet Road
New Barnet, Herts EN4 8RF
E info@bodens.co.uk
W www.bodens.co.uk/clients

BONNIE & BETTY LTD   T 020 8301 8333
9-11 Gunnery Terrace, Royal Arsenal
London SE18 6SW
E agency@bonnieandbetty.com
W www.bonnieandbetty.com

BOSS JUNIORS   T 0161 237 0100
Fourways House, 57 Hilton Street
Manchester M1 2EJ
F 0161 236 1237
E info@bossmodels.co.uk
W www.bossmodelmanagement.co.uk

BOURNE, Michelle
CHILDREN'S MULTICULTURAL
ACADEMY & AGENCY   T 07852 932473
E info@michellebourneacademy.co.uk
W www.michellebourneacademy.co.uk

BRITISH MODEL KIDS   T 020 7193 5433
26-27 Southampton Street, Covent Garden
London WC2B 7RS
E info@britishmodelkids.co.uk
W www.britishmodelkids.co.uk

BRUCE & BROWN   T 020 7624 7333
17 Lonsdale Road, London NW6 6RA
F 020 7625 4047
E info@bruceandbrown.com
W www.bruceandbrown.com

BRUNO KELLY LTD   T 020 7183 7331
3rd Floor, 207 Regent Street
London W1B 3HH
F 020 7183 7332
E info@brunokelly.com
W www.brunokelly.com

BUTTERCUP AGENCY   T 0843 2899063
20 Station Road, Claygate
Esher, Surrey KT10 9DH
E info@buttercupagency.co.uk
W www.buttercupagency.co.uk

BYRON'S MANAGEMENT   T 020 7242 8096
Children & Adults
180 Drury Lane, London WC2B 5QF
E byronsmanagement@aol.com
W www.byronsmanagement.co.uk

**CAPITAL ARTS THEATRICAL
AGENCY**   T/F 020 8449 2342
Capital Arts Studio, Wyllyotts Centre
Darkes Lane, Potters Bar, Herts EN6 2HN
T 07885 232414
E capitalarts@btconnect.com
W www.capitalarts.org.uk

CARR, Norrie AGENCY   T 020 7253 1771
Babies, Children & Adults
Holborn Studios, 49 Eagle Wharf Road
London N1 7ED
F 020 7253 1772
E info@norriecarr.com
W www.norriecarr.com

**CAVAT SCHOOL OF
THEATRE ARTS & AGENCY**   T 020 8651 1099
16A Hook Hill, South Croydon
Surrey CR2 0LA
E enquiries@cavattheatrearts.co.uk
W www.cavattheatrearts.co.uk

CHILDSPLAY MODELS LLP   T 020 8659 9860
114 Avenue Road, Beckenham
Kent BR3 4SA
F 020 8778 2672
E info@childsplaymodels.co.uk
W www.childsplaymodels.co.uk

CHILLI KIDS   T 0333 666 2468
1 Badhan Court
Telford TF1 5QX
F 0333 666 2469
E info@chillikids.co.uk
W www.chillikids.co.uk

CHRYSTEL ARTS AGENCY   T 01494 773336
6 Eunice Grove, Chesham
Bucks HP5 1RL
T 07799 605489
E chrystelarts@waitrose.com

CONTI, Italia AGENCY LTD   T 020 7608 7500
Italia Conti House
23 Goswell Road
London EC1M 7AJ
F 020 7253 1430
E agency@italiaconti.co.uk

CORONA MANAGEMENT   T 020 8941 2659
Unit B, The Kingsway Business Park, Oldfield Road
Hampton, London TW12 2HD
E info@coronatheatreschool.com
W www.coronatheatreschool.com

CPA AGENCY   T 01708 766444
The Studios, 219B North Street
Romford, Essex RM1 4QA
E info@cpaagency.co.uk
W www.cpastudios.co.uk

**CREATIVE KIDZ THEATRICAL &
TALENT AGENCY**   T 07908 144802
9 Weavers Terrace, Fulham
London SW6 1QE
E info@creativekidzandco.co.uk

CS MANAGEMENT   T 020 8886 4264
Children & Young Adults
The Croft, 7 Cannon Road
Southgate, London N14 7HE
F 020 8886 7555
E carole@csmanagementuk.com
W www.csmanagementuk.com

D & B MANAGEMENT   T 020 8698 8880
Central Studios, 470 Bromley Road
Bromley, Kent BR1 4PQ
E bonnie@dandbmanagement.com
W www.dandbperformingarts.co.uk

DAISY & DUKES LTD   T 01707 377547
30 Great North Road, Stanborough
Herts AL8 7TJ
T 07739 380684
E info@daisyanddukes.com
W www.daisyanddukes.com

**DALE HAMMOND
ASSOCIATES (DHA)**   T 07790 176462
Pixmore Business Centre, Pixmore Avenue
Letchworth, Hertfordshire SG6 1JG
E info@dalehammondassociates.com
W www.dalehammondassociates.com

DANDG CASTING LTD
F 020 7687 1054
E info@dandgcasting.com
W www.dandgcasting.com

DD'S CASTING AGENCY   T 020 8502 6866
6 Acle Close, Hainault, Essex IG6 2GQ
T 07957 398501
E ddsagency@yahoo.co.uk
W www.ddtst.com

DEVINE ARTIST MANAGEMENT   T 0844 8844578
145-157 St John Street
London EC1V 4PW
E mail@devinemanagement.co.uk
W www.devinemanagement.co.uk

DRAGON DRAMA   T 07590 452436
Improvisational Drama for Children
347 Hanworth Road, Hampton TW12 3EJ
E askus@dragondrama.co.uk
W www.dragondrama.co.uk

**DRAMA STUDIO
EDINBURGH THE**   T 0131 453 3284
19 Belmont Road, Edinburgh EH14 5DZ
E info@thedramastudio.com
W www.thedramastudio.com

EARACHE KIDS (VOICE-OVERS) T 020 7287 2291
177 Wardour Street, London W1F 8WX
F 020 7287 2288
E julie@earachevoices.com
W www.earachevoices.com

**EARNSHAW, Susi
MANAGEMENT**   T 020 8441 5010
The Bull Theatre, 68 High Street
Barnet, Herts EN5 5SJ
E casting@susiearnshaw.co.uk
W www.susiearnshawmanagement.com

**EDUCATION IN STAGE &
THEATRE ARTS (E.S.T.A.)** T 020 8741 2843
16 British Grove, Chiswick, London W4 2NL
F 020 8746 3219
E estatheatreschool@googlemail.com
W www.estatheatreschool.com

**ELITE ACADEMY OF
PERFORMING ARTS** T 07976 971178
City Studios, 4 Sandford Street
Lichfield, Staffs WS13 6QA
E elitedancing@hotmail.com

ENGLISH, Doreen '95 T/F 01243 825968
Contact: Gerry Kinner
4 Selsey Avenue, Aldwick
Bognor Regis, West Sussex PO21 2QZ

**EUROKIDS CASTING &
MODEL AGENCY** T 01925 761088
Contact: Amy Musker (Senior Casting Agent). Accepts
Showreels. Children & Teenagers. Commercials. Film.
Television. Walk-ons, Supporting Artists & Extras
The Warehouse Studios, Glaziers Lane
Culcheth, Warrington, Cheshire WA3 4AQ
T 01925 761210
E castings@eka-agency.com
W www.eka-agency.com

**EXPRESSIONS
CASTING AGENCY** T 01623 424334
3 Newgate Lane, Mansfield, Nottingham NG18 2LB
E expressions-uk@btconnect.com
W www.expressionsperformingarts.co.uk

FBI AGENCY T 07050 222747
PO Box 250, Leeds LS1 2AZ
T 07515 567309
E casting@fbi-agency.co.uk
W www.fbi-agency.co.uk

**FEA MANAGEMENT
(FERRIS ENTERTAINMENT)** T 0845 4724725
London. Belfast. Cardiff. Los Angeles
Number 8, 132 Charing Cross Road, London WC2H 0LA
E info@ferrisentertainment.com
W www.ferrisentertainment.com

FILM CAST CORNWALL & SW T 01326 311419
T 07811 253756
E enquiries@filmcastcornwall.co.uk
W www.filmcastcornwall.co.uk

FIORENTINI, Anna AGENCY T 020 7682 3677
Islington Business Design Centre, Unit 101
52 Upper Street, London N1 0QH
T 07904 962779
E rhiannon@annafiorentini.com
W www.annafiorentini.com

**FOOTSTEPS THEATRE
SCHOOL CASTING AGENCY** T 07584 995309
1st Floor, Morrisons Enterprise 5
5 Lane Ends, Bradford BD10 8EW
E gwestman500@btinternet.com

**GENESIS THEATRE SCHOOL
& AGENCY** T 01536 460928
88 Hempland Close, Great Oakley
Corby, Northants NN18 8LT
E info@saracharles.com

GLOBAL7 T/F 020 7281 7679
PO Box 56232, London N4 4XP
T 07956 956652
E global7castings@gmail.com
W www.global7casting.com

**GO FOR IT
CHILDREN'S AGENCY** T 020 8943 1120
Green Gables, 47 North Lane
Teddington, Middlesex TW11 0HU
T 07540 881007
E agency@goforitcentre.com
W www.goforitagency.com

GOBSTOPPERS MANAGEMENT T 01442 269543
37 St Nicholas Mount, Hemel Hempstead
Herts HP1 2BB
T 07961 372319
E gobstoppersmanagement@hotmail.co.uk

GOLDMANS MANAGEMENT T 01323 472391
PO Box 23, Shipbourne Road
Tonbridge, Kent TN11 9NY
E casting@goldmansmanagement.co.uk
W www.goldmansmanagement.co.uk

GP ASSOCIATES   T 020 8886 2263
4 Gallus Close, Winchmore Hill
London N21 1JR
F 020 8882 9189
E info@gpassociates.co.uk
W www.greasepaintanonymous.co.uk

GROUNDLINGS MANAGEMENT   T 023 9273 7370
Groundlings Theatre, 42 Kent Street
Portsmouth, Hampshire PO1 3BT
E richard@groundlings.co.uk
W www.groundlings.co.uk

**HARLEQUIN STUDIOS
AGENCY FOR CHILDREN**   T 01273 581742
122A Phyllis Avenue, Peacehaven
East Sussex BN10 7RQ

HARRIS AGENCY LTD   T 01923 211644
71 The Avenue, Watford
Herts WD17 4NU
F 01923 211666
E theharrisagency@btconnect.com

HOBSONS KIDS   T 020 8995 3628
2 Dukes Gate, Chiswick, London W4 5DX
F 020 8996 5350
E gaynor@hobsons-international.com
W www.hobsons-international.com

**HOXTON STREET
MANAGEMENT**   T 020 7503 5131
Hoxton Hall, 130 Hoxton Street
London N1 6SH
E agents@hoxtonstreetmanagement.com
W www.hoxtonstreetmanagement.com

INTER-CITY KIDS   T/F 01942 321969
27 Wigan Lane, Wigan
Greater Manchester WN1 1XR
E intercitycasting@btconnect.com

JABBERWOCKY AGENCY   T 01580 714306
Glassenbury Hill Farm, Glassenbury Road
Cranbrook, Kent TN17 2QF
F 01580 714346
E info@jabberwockyagency.com
W www.yt93.co.uk

JERMIN, Mark MANAGEMENT   T 01792 458855
8 Heathfield, Swansea SA1 6EJ
E info@markjermin.co.uk
W www.markjermin.co.uk

JIGSAW ARTS MANAGEMENT   T 020 8447 4530
*Representing Children & Young People from Jigsaw
Performing Arts Schools*
64-66 High Street, Barnet
Herts EN5 5SJ
E enquiries@jigsaw-arts.co.uk
W www.jigsaw-arts.co.uk

**JOHNSTON & MATHERS
ASSOCIATES LTD**   T/F 020 8449 4968
PO Box 3167, Barnet
Herts EN5 2WA
E johnstonmathers@aol.com
W www.johnstonandmathers.com

K KIDS   T 020 7430 0882
0-16 yrs. Film. Stage
187 Drury Lane, Covent Garden
London WC2B 5QD
E mail@ktalent.co.uk
W www.ktalent.co.uk

**KELLY, Robert
ASSOCIATES (RKA)**   T 020 7240 0859
11 Garrick Street, London WC2E 9AR
E rob@robertkellyassociates.com
W www.robertkellyassociates.com

KIDS @ JFA THE   T 01628 771084
E agent@thekidsatjuliefoxassociates.co.uk
W www.thekidsatjuliefoxassociates.co.uk

KIDS LONDON   T 020 7924 9595
67 Dulwich Road, London SE24 0NJ
F 020 7501 8711
E info@kidslondonltd.com
W www.kidslondonltd.com

KIDS MANAGEMENT   T 01444 401595
Studio 35 Truggers, Handcross
Haywards Heath, West Sussex RH17 6DQ
T 07966 382766
E info@kidsmanagement.co.uk
W www.kidsmanagement.co.uk

KIDS PLUS   T 07799 791586
Malcolm House, Malcolm Primary School, Malcolm Road
Penge, London SE20 8RH
E geraldi.gillma@btconnect.com
W www.kidsplusagency.co.uk

KIDZ LTD   T 0871 2180884
348 Moorside Road, Swinton
Manchester M27 9PW
F 0871 2180843
E info@kidzltd.com
W www.kidzltd.com

**KIDZ ON THE HILL
PERFORMING ARTS SCHOOL**   T 07881 553480
PO Box 56951, Muswell Hill, London N10 2AS
E kidzonthehill@gmail.com
W www.kidzonthehill.co.uk

**KOOLKIDZ THEATRICAL
AGENCY LTD**   T 07976 904011
Based in West Cornwall
St Johns Hall, Alverton Street
Penzance, Cornwall TR18 2SP
T 07966 722053
E kool-kidz@sky.com
W www.koolkidztheatricalagency.co.uk

**KRACKERS KIDS
THEATRICAL AGENCY**   T/F 01708 502046
6-7 Electric Parade, Seven Kings Road
Ilford, Essex IG3 8BY
E krackerskids@hotmail.com
W www.krackerskids.co.uk

KYT AGENCY   T/F 01227 730177
Mulberry Croft, Mulberry Hill
Chilham CT4 8AJ
T 07967 580213
E richard@kentyouththeatre.co.uk
W www.kentyouththeatre.co.uk

L.A. MINI MANAGEMENT   T 07852 186411
Contact: Amanda Marsh
10 Fairoak Close, Kenley, Surrey CR8 5LJ
E amanda@lamanagement.biz
W www.lamanagement.biz

LAMONT CASTING AGENCY   T 07736 387543
2 Harewood Avenue, Ainsdale
Merseyside PR8 2PH
E diane@lamontcasting.co.uk
W www.lamontcasting.co.uk

**LESLIE, Sasha
MANAGEMENT**   T/F 020 8969 3249
In association with ALLSORTS DRAMA FOR CHILDREN
34 Crediton Road, London NW10 3DU
E sasha@allsortsdrama.com

LINTON MANAGEMENT   T 0161 761 2020
3 The Rock, Bury BL9 0JP
F 0161 761 1999
E carol@linton.tv

Mark Jermin
★★★ Management

8 Heathfield, Swansea SA1 6EJ
Phone: 01792 458855
Fax: 01792 458844
Email: info@markjermin.co.uk
www.markjermin.co.uk

❋ Children and young adults from all over the UK.

❋ Audition workshops and classes in London, Manchester, Bristol and Wales.

❋ Children with open performance licences, guaranteed to be licensed for any production and at very short notice.

LITTLE ADULTS ACADEMY & MODELLING AGENCY LTD   T 020 3130 0798
44 Broadway, Stratford
London E15 1XH
E info@littleadults.demon.co.uk
W www.littleadultsagency.co.uk

MARMALADE MANAGEMENT   T 01628 483808
Jam Theatre Studios, Archway Court
45A West Street, Marlow
Buckinghamshire SL7 2LS
E info@marmalademanagement.co.uk
W www.marmalademanagement.co.uk

McDONAGH, Melanie MANAGEMENT (ACADEMY OF PERFORMING ARTS & CASTING AGENCY)   T 07909 831409
14 Apple Tree Way, Oswaldtwistle
Accrington, Lancashire BB5 0FB
T 01254 392560
E mcdonaghmgt@aol.com
W www.mcdonaghmanagement.co.uk

MELODY'S THEATRICAL AGENCY   T 07583 295898
Melody House, Gillotts Corner
Henley-on-Thames, Oxon RG9 1QU
F 01491 411533
E info@melodysagency.co.uk
W www.jgdance.co.uk

MIM AGENCY   T 0871 2377963
Clayton House, 59 Piccadilly
Manchester M1 2AQ
E info@mimagency.co.uk
W www.mimagency.co.uk

MONDI ASSOCIATES LTD   T 07817 133349
Contact: Michelle Sykes
Unit 3 O, Cooper House
2 Michael Road
London SW6 2AD
E info@mondiassociates.com
W www.mondiassociates.com

NFD AGENCY   T/F 01977 681949
The Studio, 21 Low Street
South Milford LS25 5AR
E alyson@northernfilmanddrama.com
W www.northernfilmanddrama.com

O'FARRELL STAGE & THEATRE SCHOOL   T 020 7474 6466
Babies, Children, Teenagers & Young Adults
36 Shirley Street, Canning Town
London E16 1HU
T 07956 941497
E linda@ofarrells.wanadoo.co.uk

ORR MANAGEMENT AGENCY   T 01204 579842
Children, Teenagers & Adults
1st Floor, 147-149 Market Street
Farnworth, Greater Manchester BL4 8EX
T 07773 227784
E barbara@orrmanagement.co.uk
W www.orrmanagement.co.uk

PALMER, Jackie AGENCY   T 01494 520978
30 Daws Hill Lane, High Wycombe
Bucks HP11 1PW
F 01494 510479
E jackie.palmer@btinternet.com
W www.jackiepalmeragency.co.uk

PC THEATRICAL, MODEL & CASTING AGENCY   T 020 8381 2229
10 Strathmore Gardens, Edgware
Middlesex HA8 5HJ
F 020 8933 3418
E twinagy@aol.com
W www.twinagency.com

PD MANAGEMENT   T 020 3344 8496
17 The Heights, Frognal
London NW3 6XS
E pdmanagement1@gmail.com
W www.pdmanagement.org

PERFORMERS AGENCY LTD   T 01375 665716
Southend Road, Corringham
Essex SS17 8JT
F 01375 672353
E office@performersagency.biz
W www.performersagency.biz

PHA YOUTH   T 0161 273 4444
Tanzaro House
Ardwick Green North
Manchester M12 6FZ
F 0161 273 4567
E youth@pha-agency.co.uk
W www.pha-agency.co.uk

PLATFORM TALENT MANAGEMENT LTD   T 01276 23256
16 Shalbourne Rise, Camberley
Surrey GU15 2EJ
E casting@kidsagency.tv
W www.kidsagency.tv

POLLYANNA MANAGEMENT LTD   T/F 020 8530 6722
1 Knighten Street, Wapping
London E1W 1PH
E aliceharwood@talktalk.net
W www.pollyannatrainingtheatre.org

POWER MODEL MANAGEMENT CASTING AGENCY   T 01603 777190
PO Box 1198, Salhouse
Norwich NR13 6WD
E info@powermodel.co.uk
W www.powermodel.co.uk

PROKIDS MANAGEMENT   T 0151 336 8921
Based in the North West & London
32 Springcroft, Parkgate
Neston, Cheshire CH64 6SE
E mail@prokidsmanagement.co.uk
W www.prokidsmanagement.co.uk

PWASSOCIATES   T 01296 733258
7 Catherine Cottages, Calvert Road
Middle Claydon, Bucks MK18 2HA
E emma@pwacademy.com
W www.pwacademy.com

QK CREATIVE MANAGEMENT (QUIRKY KIDZ)   T 01494 415196
Custodia House
Queensmead Road
Loudwater, High Wycombe
Buckinghamshire HP10 9XA
E hello@quirkykidz.co.uk
W www.quirkykidz.co.uk

RAMA YOUNG ACTORS   T 0845 0540255
The Basement
Rama Actors Studio, 1 Kayes Walk
The Lace Market, Nottingham NG1 1PY
E office@ramayoungactors.co.uk
W www.ramayoungactors.co.uk

RASCALS MODEL AGENCY   T 020 8504 1111
77-79 Station Road, Chingford
London E4 7BU
E kids@rascals.co.uk
W www.rascals.co.uk

RAVENSCOURT MANAGEMENT
See CORONA MANAGEMENT

RDDC MANAGEMENT AGENCY   T 01706 211161
52 Bridleway
Waterfoot
Rossendale, Lancashire BB4 9DS
T 07811 239780
E info@rddc.co.uk
W www.rddc.co.uk

REACT KIDS AGENCY   T 01926 710001
83 Dudley Road, Kenilworth
Warwickshire CV8 1GR
T 07900 921779
E admin@reactkidsagency.co.uk
W www.reactkidsagency.co.uk

REBEL SCHOOL OF THEATRE ARTS & CASTING AGENCY LTD   T 07808 803637
Based in Leeds & Huddersfield
PO Box 169, Huddersfield HD8 1BE
E sue@rebelschool.co.uk
W www.rebelschool.co.uk

RECALL MANAGEMENT   T 07824 709745
35 Chase Cross Road, Romford
Essex RM5 3PJ
E info@recallmanagement.co.uk
W www.recallmanagement.co.uk

REDROOFS THEATRE SCHOOL AGENCY   T 01628 674092
26 Bath Road, Maidenhead
Berks SL6 4JT
T 07531 355835 (Holiday Times)
E sam@redroofs.co.uk
W www.redroofs.co.uk

RHODES AGENCY   T 01708 747013
5 Dymoke Road, Hornchurch
Essex RM11 1AA
F 01708 730431
E rhodesarts@hotmail.com

RIDGEWAY STUDIOS MANAGEMENT   T 01992 633775
Office: 106 Hawkshead Road
Potters Bar
Hertfordshire EN6 1NG
E info@ridgewaystudios.co.uk
W www.ridgewaystudios.co.uk

RISING STARS AGENCY   T 07947 345434
16 Llwyn Yr Eos Grove
Penyard, Merthyr Tydfil
Mid Glamorgan, Wales CF47 0GD
T 07894 164104
E risingstarsagency@yahoo.co.uk
W www.risingstarsagency.co.uk

RISING STARS PERFORMANCE AGENCY   T 07709 429354
53 Hurlingham Road, Bexleyheath
Kent DA7 5PE
T 07958 617976
E risingstars_agency@yahoo.co.uk

ROMY LEE MANAGEMENT   T 01704 551877
44 Wayfarers Arcade, Lord Street
Southport, Merseyside PR8 1NT
E info@romyleemanagement.co.uk
W www.romyleemanagement.co.uk

ROSS, David ACTING ACADEMY THE   T 07957 862317
8 Farrier Close, Sale, Cheshire M33 2ZL
E info@davidrossacting.com
W www.davidrossacting.com

SCALA KIDS CASTING   T 0113 250 6823
42 Rufford Avenue, Yeadon, Leeds LS19 7QR
F 0113 250 8806
E office@scalakids.com
W www.scalakids.com

SCALLYWAGS AGENCY LTD   T 020 7739 8820
12-18 Hoxton Street, London N1 6NG
F 020 7739 5753
E info@scallywags.co.uk
W www.scallywags.co.uk

SCHOOL CASTING   T 01325 463383
Liddiard Theatre, Polam Hall, Grange Road
Darlington, Durham DL1 5PA
F 01325 383539
E information@polamhall.com
W www.polamhall.com

SCREAM MANAGEMENT LTD   T 0161 850 1996
The Greenhouse, MediaCityUK
Salford, Manchester M50 2EQ
T 0161 850 1994
E info@screammanagement.com
W www.screammanagement.com

SELECT MANAGEMENT   T 07700 059089
PO Box 748, London NW4 1TT
T 07956 131494
E mail@selectmanagement.info
W www.selectmanagement.info

SEQUINS CASTING AGENCY   T 020 8360 6601
8 Summerhill Grove, Bush Hill Park
Enfield EN1 2HY
E sequinscastingagency@gmail.com

SEVEN CASTING AGENCY   T 0161 850 1057
Manchester Office: 4th Floor, 59 Piccadilly
Manchester M1 2AQ
T 07730 130485
E will@7casting.co.uk
W www.7casting.co.uk

SEVEN CASTING AGENCY   T 01785 212266
Staffordshire Office: Suite 3, Tudor House
9 Eastgate Street, Stafford ST16 2NQ
T 07730 130484
E will@7casting.co.uk
W www.7casting.co.uk

SHINE MANAGEMENT   T 07880 721689
Flat 10, Valentine House, Church Road
Guildford, Surrey GU1 4NG
E enquiries@shinemanagement.net
W www.shinemanagement.net

SINGER, Sandra ASSOCIATES   T 01702 331616
21 Cotswold Road, Westcliff-on-Sea, Essex SS0 8AA
E sandrasingeruk@aol.com
W www.sandrasinger.com

SMARTYPANTS AGENCY   T 01277 633772
San-Marie Studios, Southend Road, Billericay CM11 2PZ
F 01277 633998
E office@smartypantsagency.co.uk
W www.smartypantsagency.co.uk

SMITH, Elisabeth LTD   T 0845 8721331
8 Dawes Lane, Sarratt
Rickmansworth, Herts WD3 6BB
E models@elisabethsmith.co.uk
W www.elisabethsmith.co.uk

SNA / THRESHOLD THEATRE ARTS   T 020 3178 7196
3rd Floor, 33 Glasshouse Street
London W1B 5DG
E admin@thresholdtheatrearts.co.uk

SPEAKE, Barbara AGENCY   T 020 8743 6096
East Acton Lane
London W3 7EG
E speakekids2@aol.com
W www.barbaraspeake.com

SRA AGENCY   T 01932 863194
Lockhart Road, Cobham, Surrey KT11 2AX
E agency@susanrobertsacademy.co.uk

STAGE 84 YORKSHIRE SCHOOL OF PERFORMING ARTS   T 01274 569197
Old Bell Chapel, Town Lane
Idle, Bradford, West Yorks BD10 8PR
T 07785 244984
E valeriejackson@stage84.com

STAGE A MANAGEMENT LTD   T 07758 052325
Represents Centre Stage Academy Theatre School Students
6 Oak Tree Court, Midhurst
West Sussex GU29 9SE
T 07770 744282
E stageamanagement@gmail.com
W www.csa-theatreschool.co.uk

STAGE KIDS AGENCY   T 01707 328359
Children, Teenagers & Adults
1 Greenfield, Welwyn Garden City
Herts AL8 7HW
E stagekds@aol.com
W www.stagekids.co.uk

STAGECOACH AGENCY UK T 0845 4082468
PO Box 127, Ross-on-Wye HR9 6WZ
F 0845 4082464
E tarquin@stagecoachagency.co.uk
W www.stagecoachagency.co.uk

**STAGEWORKS PERFORMING
ARTS SCHOOL** T 07956 176166
The Stablehouse Barn, Remenham Hill
Henley on Thames, Oxon RG9 3HN
E emma_taylor@sky.com
W www.stageworks.org.uk

**STARDOM CASTING AGENCY &
THEATRE SCHOOL** T 07740 091019
16 Pinebury Drive, Bradford
West Yorkshire BD13 2TA
F 01274 818051
E liz.stardom@btinternet.com

STARMAKER T 0118 988 7959
17 Kendal Avenue, Shinfield
Reading, Berks RG2 9AR
F 0118 988 8708
E dave@starmakeruk.org
W www.starmakeruk.org

STARSTRUCK TALENT LTD T 01706 747334
In conjunction with Starstruck Theatre School
1 & 2 St Chads Court, School Lane
Rochdale OL16 1QU
E lisa@starstrucktalent.co.uk
W www.starstrucktalent.co.uk

**STEP ON STAGE
MANAGEMENT** T 020 8408 0633
5 Poulett Gardens, Twickenham
Middlesex TW1 4QS
T 07973 900196
E info@steponstagemanagement.co.uk
W www.steponstagemanagement.co.uk

STOMP! MANAGEMENT T 020 8446 9898
c/o Suite 6
Fiboard House
5 Oakleigh Gardens, London N20 9AB
E stompmanagement@aol.com
W www.stompmanagement.com

SWINDON YOUNG ACTORS T 07825 565161
Contact: Julia Dickinson, Mark Flitton
44 Redcliffe Street, Swindon
Wiltshire SN2 2BZ
T 07588 688681
E sya@gmx.co.uk
W www.swindonyoungactors.com

**TAKE2 CASTING AGENCY &
TALENT MANAGEMENT** T 00 353 87 2563403
28 Beech Park Road, Foxrock
Dublin 18, Ireland
E pamela@take2.ie
W www.take2.ie

**TALENTED KIDS PERFORMING
ARTS SCHOOL & AGENCY** T/F 00 353 45 485464
23 Burrow Manor, Calverstown
Kilcullen, Co. Kildare, Ireland
T 00 353 87 2480348
E talentedkids@hotmail.com
W www.talentedkidsireland.com

**TANWOOD
THEATRICAL AGENCY** T 07775 991700
Liberatus Studios, Isis Estate
Stratton Road, Swindon SN1 2PG
E tanwood@tiscali.co.uk
W www.tanwood.co.uk

TELEVISION WORKSHOP THE T 0115 845 0764
Nottingham Group
30 Main Street, Calverton
Notts NG14 6FQ
E ian@thetelevisionworkshop.co.uk

THIS IS YOUTH T 07956 838843
Teenagers & Young Adults
194B Addington Road, Selsdon
Croydon CR2 8LD
E hello@thisisyouth.com
W www.thisisyouth.com

TICKLEDOM AGENCY T 020 8341 7044
31 Rectory Gardens, London N8 7PJ
T 07947 139414
E agency@tickledomtheatreschool.com
W www.tickledomtheatreschool.com/agency.html

TIFFIN MANAGEMENT T 07712 816666
In association with MTPAS
High Street, Stony Stratford
Milton Keynes MK11 7AE
E agency@mtpas.co.uk
W www.tiffin-management.co.uk

TK MANAGEMENT T 07985 510038
Spires Meade, 4 Bridleways
Wendover, Bucks HP22 6DN
F 01296 623696
E tkpamanagement@aol.com

**TOMORROW'S TALENT
AGENCY** T 01245 200555
Contact: By e-mail only
Based in Chelmsford, Essex
E agents@tomorrowstalent.co.uk
W www.tomorrowstalent.co.uk

TOP TALENT AGENCY LTD T 01727 855903
*Representing Child Actors & Models from Babies to
Teenagers*
PO Box 860, St Albans
Herts AL1 9BR
F 01727 812666
E admin@toptalentagency.co.uk
W www.toptalentagency.co.uk

TRULY SCRUMPTIOUS LTD T 020 8888 4204
66 Bidwell Gardens, London N11 2AU
F 020 8888 4584
E bookings@trulyscrumptious.co.uk
W www.trulyscrumptious.co.uk

TUESDAYS CHILD T/F 01625 501765
Children, Teenagers & Adults
Oakfield House
Springwood Way
Macclesfield SK10 2XA
E info@tuesdayschildagency.co.uk
W www.tuesdayschildagency.co.uk

TURNSTONE MANAGEMENT T 0845 5576658
T 07866 211647
E mark_turner85@hotmail.com

TWINS
See PC THEATRICAL, MODEL & CASTING AGENCY

URBAN ANGELS T 0845 8387773
PO Box 45453, London SE26 6UZ
F 0845 8387774
E south@urbanangelsagency.com

URBAN ANGELS NORTH T 0845 5191990
Contact: Alysia Lewis
F 0845 8387774
E north@urbanangelsagency.com
W www.urbanangelsagency.com

VALLÉ THEATRICAL AGENCY THE T 01992 622861
The Vallé Academy Studios
Wilton House, Delamare Road
Cheshunt, Herts EN8 9SG
F 01992 622868
E agency@valleacademy.co.uk
W www.valleacademy.co.uk

VAN RENSBURG ARTIST MANAGEMENT T 07724 937331
Actors. Artists. Musicians
34 Campbell Road
Longniddry
East Lothian EH32 0NP
E michelle@vanartman.co.uk
W www.vanartman.co.uk

W-A-P-A AGENCY T 01422 351958
6-8 Akroyd Place
Halifax, West Yorkshire HX1 1YH
F 01422 360958
E enquiries@w-a-p-a.co.uk
W www.w-a-p-a.co.uk

WILDCATS KIDS MANAGEMENT T 07900 694156
PO Box 1198, Stamford
Lincolnshire PE2 2JE
E james@wildcats-uk.com
W http://agency.wildcatstheatreschool.co.uk

WILLIAMSON & HOLMES T 020 7240 0407
51 St Martin's Lane
London WC2N 4EA
E info@williamsonandholmes.co.uk

WINGS AGENCY T 01483 428998
The Chestnut Suite
Guardian House
Borough, Godalming, Surrey GU7 2AE
T 07745 443448
E wingsagency@gmail.com
W www.wingsmanagement.co.uk

WYSE AGENCY T 01223 832288
Hill House, 1 Hill Farm Road
Whittlesford, Cambs CB22 4NB
E frances.wyse@btinternet.com

YAT MANAGEMENT (YOUNG ACTORS THEATRE MANAGEMENT) T 020 7278 2101
70-72 Barnsbury Road
London N1 0ES
E agent@yati.org.uk
W www.yati.org.uk

YOUNG, Sylvia AGENCY T 020 7723 0037
Sylvia Young Theatre School
1 Nutford Place, London W1H 5YZ
T 07779 145732
E info@sylviayoungagency.com

YOUNG ACTORS COMPANY LTD THE T 01223 416474
3 Marshall Road, Cambridge CB1 7TY
T 07836 736352
E info@theyoungactorscompany.com
W www.theyoungactorscompany.com

YOUNGBLOOD THEATRE COMPANY T 020 7734 0657
35 Soho Square, London WC1D 3QX
E ybtc2000@aol.com

YOUNGSTARS THEATRE SCHOOL & AGENCY T 07966 176756
Contact: Coralyn Canfor-Dumas. 4-18 yrs
4 Haydon Dell
Bushey, Herts WD23 1DD
E youngstarsagency@gmail.com
W www.youngstarsagency.co.uk

ZADEK NOWELL MANAGEMENT T 07957 144948
398 Long Lane
London N2 8JX
T 07841 753728
E zadeknowell@gmail.com
W www.zadeknowell.com

ACORN ENTERTAINMENTS LTD T 01285 644622
PO Box 64, Cirencester, Glos GL7 5YD
F 01285 642291
E info@acornents.co.uk
W www.acornents.co.uk

**ARTIST PROMOTION
MANAGEMENT** T 020 7224 1992
5th Floor, Langham House
308 Regent Street, London W1B 3AT
F 020 7224 0111
E mail@harveygoldsmith.com
W www.harveygoldsmith.com

ASKONAS HOLT LTD T 020 7400 1700
Classical Music
Lincoln House, 300 High Holborn, London WC1V 7JH
F 020 7400 1799
E info@askonasholt.co.uk
W www.askonasholt.co.uk

AVALON PROMOTIONS LTD T 020 7598 7333
4A Exmoor Street, London W10 6BD
F 020 7598 7300
E enquiries@avalonuk.com
W www.avalonuk.com

**BLOCK, Derek
CONCERT PROMOTIONS** T 020 7724 2101
70-76 Bell Street, Marylebone, London NW1 6SP
F 020 7724 2102
E dbcp@derekblock.co.uk

FLYING MUSIC T 020 7221 7799
FM House, 110 Clarendon Road, London W11 2HR
F 020 7221 5016
E info@flyingmusic.co.uk
W www.flyingmusic.com

GUBBAY, Raymond LTD T 020 7025 3750
Dickens House, 15 Tooks Court, London EC4A 1LB
F 020 7025 3751
E info@raymondgubbay.co.uk
W www.raymondgubbay.co.uk

HOBBS, Liz GROUP LTD T 0870 0702702
65 London Road, Newark
Nottinghamshire NG24 1RZ
F 0870 3337009
E info@lizhobbsgroup.com
W www.lizhobbsgroup.com

HOCHHAUSER, Victor T 020 7794 0987
4 Oak Hill Way
London NW3 7LR
F 020 7431 2531
E admin@victorhochhauser.co.uk
W www.victorhochhauser.co.uk

IMG ARTS & ENTERTAINMENT T 020 8233 5300
McCormack House, Burlington Lane
London W4 2TH
F 020 8233 5301
E concerts@imgworld.com
W www.imgworld.com

**McINTYRE, Phil
ENTERTAINMENTS LTD** T 020 7291 9000
3rd Floor, 85 Newman Street
London W1T 3EU
F 020 7291 9001
E info@mcintyre-ents.com
W www.mcintyre-ents.com

**MEADOW, Jeremy &
ROSENTHAL, Suzanna** T 020 7436 2244
26 Goodge Street
London W1T 2QG
F 0870 7627882
E info@jeremymeadow.com
W www.jeremymeadow.com

RBM COMEDY T 020 7630 7733
3rd Floor, 168 Victoria Street
London SW1E 5LB
F 020 7630 6549
E info@rbmcomedy.com
W www.rbmcomedy.com

ACCELERATE　　T 07782 199181
374 Ley Street, Ilford IG1 4AE
T 07956 104086
E info@accelerate-productions.co.uk
W www.accelerate-productions.co.uk

AJK DANCE　　T 020 7831 9192
8B Lambs Conduit Passage
Holborn, London WC1R 4RH
E info@alexkordek.co.uk
W www.alexkordek.co.uk

BODYWORK AGENCY　　T 07792 851972
25-29 Glisson Road
Cambridge CB1 2HA
F 01223 568231
E agency@bodyworkds.co.uk

BOSS DANCE　　T 0161 237 0100
Fourways House, 57 Hilton Street
Manchester M1 2EJ
F 0161 236 1237
E info@bossdance.co.uk
W www.bosscasting.co.uk

**BOX ARTIST
MANAGEMENT - BAM**　　T 020 7713 7313
Choreographers. Musicals. Commercial Dancers
The Attic, The Old Finsbury Town Hall
Rosebery Avenue, London EC1R 4RP
E hello@boxartistmanagement.com
W www.boxartistmanagement.com

**CREATIVE KIDZ THEATRICAL
& TALENT AGENCY**　　T 07908 144802
9 Weavers Terrace, Fulham, London SW6 1QE
E info@creativekidzandco.co.uk

DANCERS　　T 020 7637 1487
Trading as FEATURES
1 Charlotte Street, London W1T 1RD
E info@features.co.uk
W www.features.co.uk

DANCERS@BBA　　T 020 7395 1405
1st Floor, 23 Tavistock Street
Covent Garden, London WC2E 7NX
F 020 7379 5560
E dancers@buchanan-associates.co.uk
W www.dancersatbba.co.uk

DANCERS INC　　T 020 7557 6654
9-13 Grape Street
Covent Garden, London WC2H 8ED
F 020 7557 6656
E dancersinc@international-collective.com
W www.dancersinc.co.uk

ELLITE MANAGEMENT　　T 0845 6525361
'The Dancer', 8 Peterson Road
Wakefield WF1 4EB
T 07957 631510
E enquiries@ellitemanagement.co.uk
W www.elliteproductions.co.uk

**EVENT MODEL
MANAGEMENT**　　T 020 3286 3135
Dancers. Models
Studio 230
405 Kings Road
Chelsea, London SW10 0BB
T 07581 223738
E info@eventmodel.co.uk
W www.eventmodelmanagement.co.uk

FEATURES　　T 020 7637 1487
1 Charlotte Street
London W1T 1RD
E info@features.co.uk
W www.features.co.uk

HEADNOD TALENT AGENCY　　T/F 020 3222 0035
RichMix 1st Floor West
35-47 Bethnal Green Road
London E1 6LA
E info@headnodagency.com
W www.headnodagency.com

INFINITE ENTERTAINMENT　　T 07803 847953
Entertainment & Speciality Acts for Events
Low Hills Lane, Oakes
Huddersfield
West Yorkshire HD3 3PQ
E entsyorkshire@yahoo.co.uk
W www.infiniteentertainment.co.uk

JK DANCE PRODUCTIONS　　T 0161 669 4401
T 020 7871 3055
E casting@jkdance.co.uk
W www.jkdance.co.uk

**KEW PERSONAL
MANAGEMENT**　　T 020 8871 3697
PO Box 679
Surrey RH1 9BT
E info@kewpersonalmanagement.com
W www.kewpersonalmanagement.com

Dance Agents

Why do I need a dance agent?

As with any other agent, a dance agent will submit their clients for jobs, negotiate contracts, handle paperwork and offer advice. In return for these services they will charge commission ranging from 10-15%. The agents listed in this section specialise in representing and promoting dancers. They will possess the relevant contacts in the industry that you need to get auditions and jobs.

How should I use these listings?

If you are a dancer getting started in the industry, looking to change your existing agent, or wishing to take on an additional agent that represents you for dance alongside your main acting agent, the following listings will supply you with up-to-date contact details for dance agencies. Every company listed is done so by written request to us. Please see the main 'Agents and Personal Managers' advice section for further guidance on choosing and approaching agents.

Should I pay an agent to join their books? Or sign a contract?

Equity (the actors' trade union) does not recommend that artists pay an agent to join their client list. Before signing a contract, you should be very clear about the terms and commitments involved. For advice on both of these issues, or if you experience any problems with a current agent, we recommend that you contact Equity www.equity.org.uk. They also produce the booklet *You and your Agent* which is free to all Equity members and available from their website's members' area.

What is Spotlight Dancers?

Spotlight Dancers is a specialist casting directory published annually by Spotlight. Members receive a page in the directory containing a headshot and body shot, agency contact details and selected credits as well as an online CV on the Spotlight website. These are used by dance employers throughout the UK to locate dancers and send out casting or audition information. Dancers who attend CDET (Council for Dance Education and Training) accredited schools receive a discount when applying in their graduating year. Dancers wishing to promote themselves for job opportunities in commercial theatre, musicals, opera, film, television, live music, video, corporate events and many other

areas of the industry should consider joining: visit www.spotlight.com/dancers for more information.

Should I join Spotlight's Actors/ Actresses directory or the Dancers directory?

Depending on your skills, training and experience, you may be eligible for both directories if you are interested in promoting yourself both as an actor and as a dancer. If you join both, you would receive an entry into each directory and two separate online CVs. You would also qualify for a 25% discount off the Dancers membership fee. If you only want to join one or the other, then you will need to consider which area of the industry you want to focus on in your career. Musical theatre experience can qualify you for either directory, depending on whether your training/ roles involved mainly dancing or acting. This is something you will need to think about, and something you should discuss with your agent if you sign with one.

Where can I find more information?

Please refer to our dance agent case study in this section and the information and advice pages in the 'Dance Companies' listings for further information about the dance industry.

CASE STUDY

Part of the Eyenncee Group, Dancers Inc. have cemented their presence within the industry with consistently high-profile assignments with world-renowned artists and leading brands. Dancers Inc. represents commercial dancers whilst their sister agency, I.N.C Artist Management, focuses on choreographers, creatives, musical theatre performers and actors.

The journey of a commercial dancer from graduation to establishing themselves within the industry requires a great deal of determination, stamina and endurance. There is no time frame to guarantee success, so dancers have to be remarkably well-adjusted to deal with daily rejection and be emotionally equipped to persevere with achieving their goals.

Here's our advice for creating and maintaining a successful career in commercial dance:

1. Research: Start working out 'who's who' in the industry and which choreographers and production companies book the most work for dancers. Obtain this information by looking into what attracts you the most. A favourite campaign for an artist? Find out who the choreographer is and which agency booked the dancers. This information can usually be found online. This is the same for large-scale events and TV shows. You will find that the same choreographer names and agencies will keep popping up and these will be the people to get your CV, photos and showreel to.

2. Representation: Make sure that whoever you sign with agent-wise does know who you are and what your statistics, skills and strengths are. It is very easy to send your CV into an organisation and then be added to their website without them really knowing anything about you. The result of this can mean being sent to castings and auditions that are not suitable for you, which wastes choreographers' and your time.

3. Marketing: Remember that you are your product. In the current age of social media and technology, creatives are becoming even better at promoting themselves so you must stay ahead of the game. Make sure your CV and photographs are current, well-presented, and up-to-date. Make sure that letters to agencies are typed, spell-checked and laid out in a professional manner. This is often your first contact with an agent and you cannot make a first impression twice. Don't be judged by poor marketing materials before anyone has even seen you dance or display your talent. Showreels are now also becoming popular and can illustrate your talents quickly. Guard against making showreels too long and look for quality material that shows you off rather than quantity that doesn't hold the viewer's attention. Make sure your best clips come near the beginning of the reel (0.00 – 0.45 seconds).

4. Castings and Auditions: If you are asked to come along to a dance call it is important to be prepared for anything. Bring heels (if you're female) that are suitable for dance, knee-pads, trainers and clothing that allows for free range of movement. Other specialist footwear like tap shoes should be brought if the brief requires. Often a choreographer may test your abilities in different styles of dance so make sure your clothing is adaptable. Please be well-groomed and well-dressed but try not to be too casting-specific. If you look too individual sometimes it's hard to visualise you as part of a troupe of dancers or someone who will not pull focus when dancing behind an artist. Whilst we would always encourage people to create their own style it should not be distracting or limiting.

5. Punctuality: The essential and first rule of being professional. Always leave yourself plenty of time to arrive at a destination and plan your route in advance. A bad reputation for being late is the easiest thing to obtain, yet the hardest thing to get rid of.

6. Professionalism: Your talent can speak for itself, but your reputation can carry you through your career happily or prevent future opportunities. Be polite and courteous to everyone you meet at castings. Many people don't realise that being rude to the person who takes your name at the door often filters back to the production team, and regardless of talent that person has demonstrated that they will not be a good company member. Avoid altercations with fellow artists and clients. Stay motivated on a job and always try to achieve what the creative team is asking of you. Direct any issues to your agent.

7. Health and Fitness: Make sure that you are always at your optimum health and fitness and work continually on your core strength and flexibility. For the stamina required in tough rehearsal and performance situations make sure you always stay hydrated and are working on a diet that directly supports your energy levels for prolonged amounts of time.

8. Insurance: At Dancers Inc. we insist that our artists have an up-to-date insurance policy that covers them for any eventuality, as injuries can occur at any time. We cannot stress enough how vital it is go into every job casting and assignment with adequate cover, such as Equity's scheme.

9. Communication: Make sure you keep in contact with your agent and update them regularly on your availability for work and changes to your address, hairstyle, measurements or new skills you may have been working on. We pride ourselves on being particularly approachable and are on call seven days a week.

To find out more about Dancers Inc. visit www.dancersinc.co.uk

KMC AGENCIES   T 0161 237 3009
PO Box 122, 48 Great Ancoats Street
Manchester M4 5AB
F 0161 237 9812
E casting@kmcagencies.co.uk
W www.kmcagencies.co.uk

KMC AGENCIES   T 0845 0340772
Garden Studios, 71-75 Shelton Street
Covent Garden, London WC2H 9JQ
E london@kmcagencies.co.uk
W www.kmcagencies.co.uk

LONGRUN ARTISTES   T 020 8316 6662
Contact: Gina Long
3 Chelsworth Drive, London SE18 2RB
E gina@longrunartistes.co.uk
W www.longrunartistes.co.uk

MARLOWES AGENCY:
TV, THEATRE & DANCE   T 020 7193 4484
HMS President, Victoria Embankment
Blackfriars, London EC4Y 0HJ
E mitch@marlowesagency.com
W www.marlowesagency.com

MITCHELL MAAS McLENNAN   T 020 8301 8745
MPA Offices, 29 Thomas Street
Woolwich, London SE18 6HU
T 07540 995802
E agency@mmm2000.co.uk
W www.mmm2000.co.uk

PINEAPPLE AGENCY   T 020 7241 6601
Montgomery House
159-161 Balls Pond Road, Islington, London N1 4BG
F 020 7241 3006
E pineapple.agency@btconnect.com
W www.pineappleagency.com

PIROUETTE DANCE AGENCY   T 07855 049862
Dancers. Singers. Speciality Acts
31 Russet House
Birch Close
Huntington, York YO31 9PN
E casting@pirouette-dance-agency.co.uk
W www.pirouette-dance-agency.co.uk

RAZZAMATAZZ
MANAGEMENT   T/F 01342 301617
204 Holtye Road, East Grinstead RH19 3ES
T 07836 268292
E razzamatazzmanagement@btconnect.com

RIVEN PRODUCTIONS LTD   T 07581 018549
Commercial Dance. Choreography Services
109 Park Road
Bearwood
Birmingham B67 5HR
E info@rivenproductions.com
W www.rivenproductions.com

RUDEYE DANCE AGENCY   T 020 7014 3023
73 St John Street, London EC1M 4NJ
E info@rudeye.com
W www.rudeye.com

SCRIMGEOUR, Donald
ARTISTS AGENT   T 020 8444 6248
49 Springcroft Avenue
London N2 9JH
F 020 8883 9751
E vwest@dircon.co.uk

SHOW TEAM
PRODUCTIONS THE   T 0845 4671010
Dancers & Choreographers
36 Vine Street, Brighton BN1 4AG
E info@theshowteam.co.uk
W www.theshowteam.co.uk

SINGER, Sandra ASSOCIATES   T 01702 331616
Dancers & Choreographers
21 Cotswold Road
Westcliff-on-Sea, Essex SS0 8AA
E sandrasingeruk@aol.com
W www.sandrasinger.com

S.O.S.   T 020 7735 5133
85 Bannerman House
Lawn Lane
London SW8 1UA
T 07740 359770
E info@sportsofseb.com
W www.sportsofseb.com

SUCCESS   T 020 7734 3356
Room 236, 2nd Floor
Linen Hall
162-168 Regent Street
London W1B 5TB
F 020 7494 3787
E ee@successagency.co.uk
W www.successagency.co.uk

SUMMERS, Mark
MANAGEMENT   T 020 7229 8413
1 Beaumont Avenue
West Kensington
London W14 9LP
E louise@marksummers.com
W www.marksummers.com

TASTE OF CAIRO   T 07801 413161
Bellydancers. UK & Europe
22 Gilda Crescent Road
Eccles
Manchester M30 9AG
E hello@tasteofcairo.com
W www.tasteofcairo.com

T W MANAGEMENT AGENCY   T 01253 749332
66-74 The Promenade
Blackpool
Lancashire FY1 1HB
E marie.cavney@twmanagementagency.co.uk
W www.twmanagementagency.co.uk

UNITED PRODUCTIONS   T/F 020 7498 6563
Choreographers, Dancers & Stylists
6 Shaftesbury Mews
Clapham
London SW4 9BP
T 07767 610908
E info@unitedproductions.biz
W www.unitedproductions.biz

W ATHLETIC   T 020 7206 2301
Unit 310, 377-399 London Road
Camberley, Surrey GU15 3HL
E london@wathletic.com
W www.wathletic.com

WARD CASTING   T 020 7458 4474
Studio 5, 155 Commercial Street
London E1 6BJ
E casting@wardcasting.com
W www.wardcasting.com

A & B PERSONAL MANAGEMENT LTD   T 020 7794 3255
PO Box 64671, London NW3 9LH
E billellis@aandb.co.uk

ABNER STEIN   T 020 7373 0456
10 Roland Gardens, London SW7 3PH
F 020 7370 6316
E accounts@abnerstein.co.uk

AGENCY (LONDON) LTD THE   T 020 7727 1346
PMA Member
24 Pottery Lane, Holland Park, London W11 4LZ
F 020 7727 9037
E info@theagency.co.uk
W www.theagency.co.uk

ASPER, Pauline MANAGEMENT   T/F 01424 870412
PMA Member
Jacobs Cottage, Reservoir Lane
Sedlescombe, East Sussex TN33 0PJ
E pauline.asper@virgin.net

BERLIN ASSOCIATES   T 020 7836 1112
PMA Member
7 Tyers Gate, London SE1 3HX
F 020 7632 5296
E agents@berlinassociates.com
W www.berlinassociates.com

BLAKE FRIEDMANN   T 020 7284 0408
Novels, Non-fiction & TV/Film Scripts
122 Arlington Road, London NW1 7HP
F 020 7284 0442
E info@blakefriedmann.co.uk
W www.blakefriedmann.co.uk

BRITTEN, Nigel MANAGEMENT   T 023 9263 1116
55 West Street, Chichester
West Sussex PO19 1RU
E office@nbmanagement.com

BRODIE, Alan REPRESENTATION LTD   T 020 7253 6226
PMA Member
Paddock Suite, The Courtyard
55 Charterhouse Street, London EC1M 6HA
F 020 7079 7990
E info@alanbrodie.com
W www.alanbrodie.com

CANN, Alexandra REPRESENTATION   T 020 7584 9047
Box 116, 4 Montpelier Street, London SW7 1EE
E alex@alexandracann.co.uk

CASAROTTO RAMSAY & ASSOCIATES LTD   T 020 7287 4450
PMA Member
Waverley House, 7-12 Noel Street
London W1F 8GQ
F 020 7287 9128
E info@casarotto.co.uk
W www.casarotto.co.uk

CLOWES, Jonathan LTD   T 020 7722 7674
PMA/Association of Authors' Agents Member
10 Iron Bridge House
Bridge Approach
London NW1 8BD
F 020 7722 7677
E admin@jonathanclowes.co.uk

COCHRANE, Elspeth PERSONAL MANAGEMENT
Existing Clients only. No New Applicants. See ASQUITH
& HORNER in Agents & Personal Managers section

CURTIS BROWN GROUP LTD   T 020 7393 4400
PMA Member
5th Floor, Haymarket House
28-29 Haymarket, London SW1Y 4SP
F 020 7393 4401
E cb@curtisbrown.co.uk
W www.curtisbrown.co.uk

DAISH, Judy ASSOCIATES LTD   T 020 8964 8811
PMA Member
2 St Charles Place, London W10 6EG
F 020 8964 8966
E judy@judydaish.com
W www.judydaish.com

DENCH ARNOLD AGENCY THE   T 020 7437 4551
PMA Member
10 Newburgh Street, London W1F 7RN
F 020 7439 1355
E contact@dencharnold.com
W www.dencharnold.com

de WOLFE, Felix   T 020 7242 5066
PMA Member
Kingsway House, 103 Kingsway
London WC2B 6QX
F 020 7242 8119
E info@felixdewolfe.com
W www.felixdewolfe.com

FARNES, Norma MANAGEMENT   T 020 7727 1544
9 Orme Court, London W2 4RL
F 020 7792 2110

FILLINGHAM, Janet ASSOCIATES   T 020 8748 5594
PMA Member
52 Lowther Road
London SW13 9NU
F 020 8748 7374
E info@janetfillingham.com
W www.janetfillingham.com

FILM RIGHTS LTD   T 020 7316 1837
Suite 306, Belsize Business Centre
258 Belsize Road, London NW6 4BT
F 020 7624 3629
E information@filmrights.ltd.uk
W www.filmrights.ltd.uk

FITCH, Laurence LTD T 020 7316 1837
Suite 306, Belsize Business Centre
258 Belsize Road, London NW6 4BT
F 020 7624 3629

FRENCH, Samuel LTD T 020 7387 9373
PMA Member
52 Fitzroy Street, Fitzrovia
London W1T 5JR
F 020 7387 2161
E theatre@samuelfrench-london.co.uk
W www.samuelfrench-london.co.uk

**FUTERMAN, ROSE &
ASSOCIATES** T 020 8255 7755
PMA Member. TV/Film, Showbiz & Music Biographies
91 St Leonards Road
London SW14 7BL
F 020 8286 4860
E guy@futermanrose.co.uk
W www.futermanrose.co.uk

**GILLIS, Pamela
MANAGEMENT** T 020 8340 7868
46 Sheldon Avenue
London N6 4JR
F 020 8341 5564

GLASS, Eric LTD T 020 7229 9500
25 Ladbroke Crescent
Notting Hill
London W11 1PS
F 020 7229 6220
E eglassltd@aol.com

HANCOCK, Roger LTD T 020 8341 7243
7 Broadbent Close, Highgate Village
London N6 5JW
E tim@rogerhancock.com

**HIGHAM, David
ASSOCIATES LTD** T 020 7434 5900
PMA Member
5-8 Lower John Street, Golden Square
London W1F 9HA
F 020 7437 1072
E dha@davidhigham.co.uk
W www.davidhigham.co.uk

**HOSKINS, Valerie
ASSOCIATES LTD** T 020 7637 4490
20 Charlotte Street
London W1T 2NA
F 020 7637 4493
E vha@vhassociates.co.uk

IMAGINE TALENT T 07876 685515
Top Floor, 40 Buckleigh Road
London SW16 5RZ
E christina@imaginetalent.co.uk
W www.imaginetalent.co.uk

**INDEPENDENT TALENT
GROUP LTD** T 020 7636 6565
PMA Member. Formerly ICM, London
Oxford House, 76 Oxford Street
London W1D 1BS
F 020 7323 0101
W www.independenttalent.com

JFL AGENCY LTD T 020 3137 8182
PMA Member
48 Charlotte Street, London W1T 2NS
E agents@jflagency.com
W www.jflagency.com

KASS, Michelle ASSOCIATES T 020 7439 1624
PMA Member
85 Charing Cross Road
London WC2H 0AA
F 020 7734 3394
E office@michellekass.co.uk

KENIS, Steve & CO T 020 7434 9055
PMA Member
Royalty House, 72-74 Dean Street
London W1D 3SG
F 020 7287 6328
E sk@sknco.com

**MACFARLANE CHARD
ASSOCIATES LTD** T 020 7636 7750
PMA Member
33 Percy Street
London W1T 2DF
F 020 7636 7751
E enquiries@macfarlane-chard.co.uk
W www.macfarlane-chard.co.uk

**MACNAUGHTON LORD
REPRESENTATION** T 020 7499 1411
PMA Member
44 South Molton Street
London W1K 5RT
E info@mlrep.com
W www.mlrep.com

MANN, Andrew LTD T 020 7609 6218
39-41 North Road
London N7 9DP
E info@andrewmann.co.uk
W www.andrewmann.co.uk

MANS, Johnny PRODUCTIONS T 01992 470907
Incorporating Encore Magazine
PO Box 196
Hoddesdon
Herts EN10 7WG
E johnnymansagent@aol.com
W www.johnnymansproductions.co.uk

MARJACQ SCRIPTS LTD T 020 7935 9499
Prose. Screenplays. No Stage Plays or Musicals
Submissions: Box 412
19-21 Crawford Street
London W1H 1PJ
F 020 7935 9115
E enquiries@marjacq.com
W www.marjacq.com

MARVIN, Blanche MBE T/F 020 7722 2313
Drama Critic for LTR
21A St Johns Wood High Street
London NW8 7NG
E blanchemarvin17@hotmail.com

**M.B.A. LITERARY & SCRIPT
AGENTS LTD** T 020 7387 2076
PMA Member
62 Grafton Way
London W1T 5DW
E submissions@mbalit.co.uk
W www.mbalit.co.uk

**McLEAN, Bill PERSONAL
MANAGEMENT** T 020 8789 8191
23B Deodar Road
London SW15 2NP

MLR
See MACNAUGHTON LORD REPRESENTATION

MORRIS, William
ENDEAVOR ENTERTAINMENT   T 020 7534 6800
PMA Member
Centre Point, 103 New Oxford Street
London WC1A 1DD
F 020 7534 6900
W www.wme.com

NARROW ROAD
COMPANY THE   T 020 7379 9598
PMA Member
3rd Floor, 76 Neal Street
Covent Garden
London WC2H 9PL
F 020 7379 9777
E richardireson@narrowroad.co.uk

PFD   T 020 7344 1000
PMA Member
Drury House, 34-43 Russell Street
London WC2B 5HA
F 020 7836 9539
E info@pfd.co.uk
W www.peterfraserdunlop.com

POLLINGER LTD   T 020 7404 0342
9 Staple Inn, Holborn
London WC1V 7QH
F 020 7242 5737
E info@pollingerltd.com
W www.pollingerltd.com

ROSICA COLIN LTD   T 020 7370 1080
1 Clareville Grove Mews, London SW7 5AH
F 020 7244 6441

SAYLE SCREEN LTD   T 020 7823 3883
PMA Member. Screenwriters & Directors for Film, Stage
& Television
11 Jubilee Place, London SW3 3TD
F 020 7823 3363

SEIFERT, Linda
MANAGEMENT LTD   T 020 3214 8293
PMA Member
48-56 Bayham Place, London NW1 0EU
E contact@lindaseifert.com
W www.lindaseifert.com

SHARLAND
ORGANISATION LTD   T 01933 626600
The Manor House, Manor Street
Raunds, Northants NN9 6JW
E tso@btconnect.com

SHEIL LAND ASSOCIATES LTD   T 020 7405 9351
PMA Member. Literary, Film & Stage
52 Doughty Street, London WC1N 2LS
F 020 7831 2127
E info@sheilland.co.uk

STEEL, Elaine   T 01273 739022
PMA Member. Writers' Agent
110 Gloucester Avenue
London NW1 8HX
F 01273 772400
E es@elainesteel.com

STEINBERG, Micheline
ASSOCIATES   T 020 7631 1310
PMA Member
104 Great Portland Street
London W1W 6PE
E info@steinplays.com
W www.steinplays.com

STEVENS, Rochelle & CO   T 020 7359 3900
PMA Member
2 Terretts Place, Upper Street
London N1 1QZ
F 020 7354 5729
E info@rochellestevens.com

SWA (THE SIMON WILLIAMSON
AGENCY)   T 020 7281 1449
Writers' Agent
155 Stroud Green Road, London N4 3PZ
E info@swagency.co.uk
W www.swagency.co.uk

TENNYSON AGENCY THE   T 020 8543 5939
10 Cleveland Avenue, Merton Park
London SW20 9EW
E submissions@tenagy.co.uk

TYRRELL, Julia MANAGEMENT   T 020 8374 0575
PMA Member
57 Greenham Road, London N10 1LN
F 020 8374 5580
E julia@jtmanagement.co.uk
W www.jtmanagement.co.uk

WARE, Cecily
LITERARY AGENTS   T 020 7359 3787
PMA Member
19C John Spencer Square, London N1 2LZ
F 020 7226 9828
E info@cecilyware.com
W www.cecilyware.com

WEINBERGER, Josef LTD   T 020 7580 2827
PMA Member
12-14 Mortimer Street, London W1T 3JJ
F 020 7436 9616
E generalinfo@jwmail.co.uk
W www.josef-weinberger.com

WESSON, Penny   T 020 7722 6607
PMA Member
26 King Henry's Road, London NW3 3RP
F 020 7483 2890
E penny@pennywesson.demon.co.uk

APM ASSOCIATES　　　　T 020 8953 7377
Contact: Linda French
Elstree Studios, Shenley Road
Borehamwood WD6 1JG
F 020 8953 7385
E apm@apmassociates.net
W www.apmassociates.net

**A R G (ARTISTS RIGHTS
GROUP LTD)**　　　　T 020 7436 6400
4 Great Portland Street
London W1W 8PA
F 020 7436 6700
E argall@argtalent.com

ARLINGTON ENTERPRISES LTD T 020 7580 0702
1-3 Charlotte Street, London W1T 1RD
F 020 7580 4994
E info@arlington-enterprises.co.uk
W www.arlingtonenterprises.co.uk

BARR, Becca MANAGEMENT　T 020 3137 2980
Dorland House, 5th Floor
14-16 Regent Street, London SW1Y 4PH
E becca@beccabarrmanagement.co.uk
W www.beccabarrmanagement.co.uk

**BLACKBURN
SACHS ASSOCIATES**　　　T 020 7292 7555
Argyll House, All Saints Passage
London SW18 1EP
E presenters@blackburnsachsassociates.com
W www.blackburnsachsassociates.com

CAMERON, Sara MANAGEMENT
See TAKE THREE MANAGEMENT

**CHASE PERSONAL
MANAGEMENT**　　　　T 07929 447745
2nd Floor, 3 Kew Road
Richmond, Surrey TW9 2NQ
T 07775 683955
E sue@chasemanagement.co.uk
W www.chasepersonalmanagement.co.uk

CHP ARTIST MANAGEMENT　T 01844 345630
Meadowcroft Barn
Crowbrook Road, Askett
Princes Risborough
Buckinghamshire HP27 9LS
T 07976 560580
E charlotte@chproductions.org.uk
W www.chproductions.org.uk

CINEL GABRAN MANAGEMENT T 029 2066 6600
PO Box 5163, Cardiff CF5 9BJ
E info@cinelgabran.co.uk
W www.cinelgabran.co.uk

CINEL GABRAN MANAGEMENT T 0845 4300060
Adventure House, Newholm
Whitby, North Yorkshire YO21 3QL
E mail@cinelgabran.co.uk
W www.cinelgabran.co.uk

CRAWFORDS　　　　T 020 8947 9999
PO Box 56662, London W13 3BH
E cr@wfords.com
W www.crawfords.tv

CURTIS BROWN GROUP LTD　T 020 7393 4460
Haymarket House, 28-29 Haymarket
London SW1Y 4SP
F 020 7393 4401
E presenters@curtisbrown.co.uk
W www.curtisbrown.co.uk

DAA MANAGEMENT　　　T 020 7255 6123
Formerly Debi Allen Associates
Welbeck House, 66-67 Wells Street
London W1T 3PY
F 020 7255 6128
E info@daamanagement.co.uk
W www.daamanagement.co.uk

DAVID ANTHONY PROMOTIONS T 01925 632496
PO Box 286, Warrington, Cheshire WA2 8GA
T 07836 752195
E dave@davewarwick.co.uk
W www.davewarwick.co.uk

DEVINE ARTIST MANAGEMENT T 0844 8844578
145-157 St John Street, London EC1V 4PW
E mail@devinemanagement.co.uk
W www.devinemanagement.co.uk

**DOWNES PRESENTERS
AGENCY**　　　　T 07973 601332
55 Montgomery Road, South Darenth, Kent DA4 9BH
E downes@presentersagency.com
W www.presentersagency.com

**EVANS, Jacque
MANAGEMENT LTD**　　　T 020 8699 1202
Top Floor Suite, 14 Holmesley Road, London SE23 1PJ
F 020 8699 5192
E jacque@jemltd.demon.co.uk

**EXCELLENT TALENT
COMPANY THE**　　　　T 0845 2100111
118-120 Great Titchfield Street, London W1W 6SS
F 020 7637 4091
E marie-claire@excellenttalent.com
W www.excellenttalent.com

**EXPERTS MANAGEMENT
SERVICES LTD**　　　　T 01625 858556
Trading as Jane Hughes Management
PO Box 200, Stockport, Cheshire SK12 1GW
T 07766 130604
E gill@jhm.co.uk

FBI AGENCY　　　　T 07050 222747
PO Box 250, Leeds LS1 2AZ
T 07515 567309
E casting@fbi-agency.co.uk
W www.fbi-agency.co.uk

FLETCHER ASSOCIATES　　T 020 8361 8061
Broadcasting Experts. Corporate Speakers. Journalists
Studio One, 25 Parkway, London N20 0XN
F 020 8361 8866
W www.fletcherassociates.net

**FORD-CRUSH, June
PERSONAL MANAGEMENT &
REPRESENTATION**　　　T 020 8742 7724
PO Box 57948, London W4 2UJ
T 07711 764160
E june@junefordcrush.com
W www.junefordcrush.com

GAY, Noel　　　　T 020 7836 3941
19 Denmark Street, London WC2H 8NA
F 020 7287 1816
E info@noelgay.com
W www.noelgay.com

GLOBAL7　　　　T/F 020 7281 7679
PO Box 56232, London N4 4XP
T 07956 956652
E global7castings@gmail.com
W www.global7casting.com

Presenters' Agents

How do I become a presenter?

There is no easy answer to this question. Some presenters start out as actors and move into presenting work, others may be 'experts' such as chefs, designers or sports people who are taken on in a presenting capacity. Others may have a background in stand-up comedy. All newsreaders are professional journalists with specialist training and experience. Often presenters work their way up through the production side of broadcasting, starting by working as a runner or researcher and then moving to appear in front of the camera. To get this kind of production work you could contact film and TV production companies, many of whom are listed in Contacts. A number of performing arts schools, colleges and academies also offer useful part-time training courses for presenters. See the 'Drama Training, Schools and Coaches' section for college/school listings.

Why do I need a presenting agent?

As with any other agent, a presenting agent will promote their clients to job opportunities, negotiate contracts on their behalf, handle paperwork and offer advice. In return for these services they take commission ranging from 10-15%. The following listings will supply you with up-to-date contact details for presenter agencies. They will possess the relevant contacts in the industry that you need to get auditions and jobs.

How should I use these listings?

Before you approach any agency looking for representation, do some research into their current client list and the areas in which they specialise. Many have websites you can visit. Once you have made a short-list of the ones you think are most appropriate, you should send them your CV with a covering letter and a good quality, recent photograph which is a genuine likeness of you. Showreels can also be a good way of showcasing your talents, but only send these if you have checked with the agency first. Enclosing a stamped-addressed envelope with sufficient postage (SAE) will also give you a better chance of a reply. Please see the main 'Agents and Personal Managers' advice section for further guidance on choosing and approaching agents.

Should I pay an agent to join their books? Or sign a contract?

Equity (the actors' trade union) does not recommend that artists pay an agent to join their client list. Before signing any contract, you should be very clear about the terms and commitments involved. For advice on both of these issues, or if you experience any problems with a current agent, we recommend that you contact Equity www.equity.org.uk. They also produce the booklet *You and your Agent* which is free to all Equity members and available from their website's members' area.

What is Spotlight Presenters?

Spotlight Presenters is a specialist casting directory published annually. It contains photographs and contact details for over five hundred professional TV and radio presenters and is a great way of promoting yourself for work. It is used by production companies, casting directors, TV and radio stations, advertising agencies and publicists to browse and locate talent for future productions. Membership is available to any presenter with proven professional broadcast experience. Just starting out in your presenting career? New presenters with limited broadcast experience or training can join the Spotlight Presenters directory in the 'Emerging Talent' pages. Please see www.spotlight.com/presenters to join or for more information.

Should I join the Spotlight Actors/Actresses directory or the Presenters directory?

Depending on your skills, training and experience, you may be eligible for both directories if you are interested in promoting yourself as an actor and as a presenter. You would receive an entry into each directory and two separate online CVs. You would also qualify for a 25% discount off the Presenters membership fee. You will however have to prove that you already have professional experience and/or relevant training in both areas.

Presenters' Agents

Peoplematter.TV represents and partners in business with specialist journalists and presenters. The company works to build on their client's broadcast exposure through commercial and business relationships. Tony Fitzpatrick, founder of the agency, has plenty of advice for anyone thinking of becoming a presenter...

Each year the 'marketplace' for presenters becomes ever more crowded. New and hopeful raw recruits enter the market at one end of the 'presenting spectrum' whilst older and well-established broadcasters and presenters are being squeezed out of their prime time roles by 'younger models'. So, every year the 'buyer's market' becomes more crowded, and the law of 'supply and demand' dictates that presenters can be asked to do more for less! And if that wasn't bad enough, the 'reality show' format has created unrealistic expectations amongst the public – suddenly anyone can become a broadcaster. It is unfortunate that many of these 'reality stars' have skewed our understanding of what it takes to be a 'Presenter'. They may be famous for their appearance on our screens for weeks on end – they may even get a temporary column in a magazine for a while. But that fame is fleeting and they in turn are replaced by a new reality star next season. There are so many 'ex-Big Brother' stars that you couldn't even get them together in one studio – let alone find TV jobs for them!

So – if you're still keen to join the 'broadcast jungle' read on!

The very best broadcasters know how they make a difference in the world. They can help change views and opinions. They can impart knowledge which can change the lives of viewers and readers. Imagine if your news item explained how somebody could save a life?

A broadcasting career should be just that – a career! A career where you learn your craft from others more qualified and in which you strive to be the best you can be. A career isn't part-time. It isn't something that will come easily and it will have a catalogue of setbacks that will make you wonder why you didn't take the accountancy course that your mum always wanted you to! But the rewards are great if you succeed.

The very best broadcasters know how they make a difference in the world. They can help change views and opinions. They can impart knowledge which can change the lives of viewers and readers. Imagine if your news item explained how somebody could save a life? Anne Diamond – the seasoned broadcaster and health campaigner – did just that when she used her journalist skills to launch a broadcast campaign to stop Cot Death, or SIDS (Sudden Infant Death Syndrome), in 1991. Since then there has been a dramatic reduction in the annual death rate of SIDS in Britain, measured in thousands of babies' lives, largely attributed to this campaign. When Michael Buerk and cameraman Mohammed Amin first brought the plight of millions of starving Ethiopians to British screens in 1984, the reports were watched in horror by singer Bob Geldof. He bullied and cajoled a host of pop stars into gathering to form Live Aid, and persuaded millions of people to part with their money to help the starving.

Without their broadcasts lives might never have changed for the better. That's why we called our company Peoplematter. There are many broadcasters – but very few who make a difference in people's lives! If you want to be one of the 'people who make a difference' here are our suggestions.

Remember – it will take more than good looks and an engaging smile to get you on that first rung of the ladder!

Be interested

If you're not, why should anybody else be? Unfortunately all agents receive a lot of unsolicited requests from aspiring presenters. As a specialist agency we only represent those specialists whose experience and journalistic talents truly make them 'people who matter'. But so often we receive requests from generalist presenters with no experience and no specialist talent. If they aren't interested in researching their own future agent – what hope do they think they will have in finding the right one? If you have a broadcast company in mind, research them and find out everything there is to know about them. Watch their channel. Read about them. Research the contacts you're hoping to pitch to. Know them well – and know why they should want you on their team. And, here's a word to the wise, in every letter received by an agent will include the words 'willing', 'keen', 'vibrant personality' and 'dedicated'! So you need to make yours stand out by using language that communicates your enthusiasm and commitment – by saying something real!

Be specialised!

Presenting to camera can be faked. Being passionate about your subject can't be! You may want to go on to be a generalist news reporter but unless you have perfected a specialist area, you'll never be able to learn a new one quickly. Having a specialism provides you with a way of learning and provides you with a passion! It is the passion that separates out presenters from auto cue readers. You can't fake passion! And interest and passion are nothing without the ability to…

Communicate your subject

You need to be able to make the most complex of subjects or issues understandable to your viewer. The best broadcasters are great journalists. Your goal is to distil a mass of information and find a simple way of telling your story which engages your audience and enriches their lives forever. Today's best broadcasters all started their careers in journalism. They learned their craft and honed it to be the best in their field.

Regard your agent as your business partner

If you aren't working, they aren't earning! As a business partner you should both be working to achieve the same ends, sharing your talents for each other's best benefit. Therefore, you should both communicate. You must jointly agree realistic expectations. How will either of you know if you've been successful if you haven't both agreed on joint objectives?

Be proactive

Your agent shouldn't be the only one in your business partnership who is working to make contacts. You must as well. Your agent should be using their industry contacts to ensure that your name is being promoted and you are being put up for suitable jobs, but you need to put yourself out there as well. Make sure you are looking out for work experience or industry opportunities. Every social occasion is a chance to meet people who will be contacts for the future. And any good journalist makes sure they keep their contacts organised. Every email address and telephone number logged now is a future opportunity for you. Also let your agent know of things that you hear about. They can't be everywhere, but you might be able to!

Be grown up if there are problems

And, if there are problems between you and your agent, then discuss your issues together. You should jointly decide whether to move forward together – or apart! If you're going to be in the industry for a long time (and hopefully you are) then you will find that it's a small world! Whatever you do today will definitely be remembered in ten years' time. Remembering that golden rule can save a great deal of embarrassment in years to come.

So what are the secrets of success as a presenter or broadcaster? Work hard to be the best at what you do. Treat everyone with respect. Take responsibility for your own career. And above all have fun. If you have the opportunity to change one person's life through your broadcasting career it will all have been worth it.

**To find out more visit
www.peoplematter.tv**

GLORIOUS MANAGEMENT   T 020 7704 6555
Lower Ground Floor, 79 Noel Road
London N1 8HE
E lisa@glorioustalent.co.uk
W www.gloriousmanagement.com

GRANT, James MEDIA   T 020 8742 4950
94 Strand On The Green, Chiswick, London W4 3NN
F 020 8742 4951
E enquiries@jamesgrant.co.uk
W www.jamesgrant.co.uk

GURNETT, J. PERSONAL
MANAGEMENT LTD   T 020 7440 1850
12 Newburgh Street, London W1F 7RP
F 020 7287 9642
E info@jgpm.co.uk
W www.jgpm.co.uk

HICKS, Jeremy
ASSOCIATES LTD   T 020 7734 7957
3 Richmond Buildings, London W1D 3HE
F 020 7734 6302
E info@jeremyhicks.com
W www.jeremyhicks.com

JLA (JEREMY LEE
ASSOCIATES LTD)   T 020 7907 2800
Supplies Celebrities & After Dinner Speakers
80 Great Portland Street, London W1W 7NW
F 020 7907 2801
E talk@jla.co.uk
W www.jla.co.uk

JOYCE, Michael MANAGEMENT   T 020 3178 7190
3rd Floor, 33 Glasshouse Street, London W1B 5DG
T 07854 251372
E info@michaeljoyce.tv
W www.michaeljoycemanagement.com

KBJ MANAGEMENT LTD   T 020 7054 5999
Television Presenters
22 Rathbone Street, London W1T 1LA
E general@kbjmanagement.co.uk
W www.kbjmgt.co.uk

KNIGHT, Hilary
MANAGEMENT LTD   T 01604 781818
Grange Farm, Church Lane
Old, Northamptonshire NN6 9QZ
E hilary@hkmanagement.co.uk
W www.hkmanagement.co.uk

KNIGHT AYTON MANAGEMENT   T 020 7831 4400
35 Great James Street, London WC1N 3HB
F 020 7831 4455
E info@knightayton.co.uk
W www.knightayton.co.uk

LEIGH, Mike ASSOCIATES   T 020 7017 8757
11-12 Great Sutton Street, London EC1V 0BX
F 020 7486 5886
W www.mikeleighassoc.com

LYTE, Seamus
MANAGEMENT LTD   T 07930 391401
Contact: By e-mail
E seamus@seamuslyte.com
W www.seamuslyte.com

MACFARLANE CHARD
ASSOCIATES LTD   T 020 7636 7750
33 Percy Street, London W1T 2DF
F 020 7636 7751
E enquiries@macfarlane-chard.co.uk
W www.macfarlane-chard.co.uk

MARKS PRODUCTIONS LTD   T 020 7486 2001
2 Gloucester Gate Mews, London NW1 4AD

MARSH, Billy ASSOCIATES LTD   T 020 7383 9979
4th Floor, 158-160 North Gower Street
London NW1 2ND
F 020 7388 2296
E talent@billymarsh.co.uk
W www.billymarsh.co.uk

McKENNA, Deborah LTD   T 020 8846 0966
Celebrity Chefs & Lifestyle Presenters only
64-66 Glentham Road, London SW13 9JJ
F 020 8846 0967
E info@deborahmckenna.com
W www.deborahmckenna.com

MEDIA PEOPLE
(THE CELEBRITY GROUP)   T 0871 2501234
12 Archery Close, Connaught Square
London W2 2BE
E info@celebrity.co.uk
W www.celebrity.co.uk

MILES, John ORGANISATION   T 01275 854675
Cadbury Camp Lane, Clapton-in-Gordano
Bristol BS20 7SB
F 01275 810186
E john@johnmiles.org.uk
W www.johnmilesorganisation.org.uk

MONDI ASSOCIATES LTD   T 07817 133349
Contact: Michelle Sykes
Unit 3 O, Cooper House, 2 Michael Road
London SW6 2AD
E info@mondiassociates.com
W www.mondiassociates.com

MOON, Kate MANAGEMENT LTD   T 01604 686100
PO Box 648, Draughton
Northampton NN6 9XT
E kate@katemoonmanagement.com
W www.katemoonmanagement.com

MPC ENTERTAINMENT   T 020 7624 1184
MPC House, 15-16 Maple Mews
London NW6 5UZ
F 020 7624 4220
E info@mpce.com
W www.mpce.com

MTC (UK) LTD   T 020 7935 8000
71 Gloucester Place, London W1U 8JW
F 020 7935 8066
E nicki@mtc-uk.com
W www.mtc-uk.com

NOEL, John MANAGEMENT   T 020 7428 8400
Block B, Imperial Works
Perren Street, London NW5 3ED
F 020 7428 8401
E john@johnnoel.com
W www.johnnoel.com

OFF THE KERB PRODUCTIONS   T 020 7437 0607
Comedy Presenters & Comedians
3rd Floor, Hammer House
113-117 Wardour Street, London W1F 0UN
F 020 7437 0647
E westend@offthekerb.co.uk
W www.offthekerb.co.uk

PANMEDIA UK LTD   T 020 8446 9662
18 Montrose Crescent, London N12 0ED
E enquiries@panmediauk.co.uk
W www.panmediauk.co.uk

PEOPLEMATTER.TV   T 020 7415 7070
Contact: Tony Fitzpatrick
40 Bowling Green Lane, Clerkenwell, London EC1R 0NE
F 020 7415 7074
E tony@peoplematter.tv
W www.peoplematter.tv

PFD   T 020 7344 1000
Presenters. Public Speakers
Drury House, 34-43 Russell Street, London WC2B 5HA
F 020 7836 9539
E info@pfd.co.uk
W www.pfd.co.uk

PVA MANAGEMENT LTD   T 01905 616100
County House, St Mary's Street, Worcester WR1 1HB
E md@pva.co.uk
W www.pva.co.uk

RARE TALENT ACTORS MANAGEMENT   T 0161 273 4444
Tanzaro House, Ardwick Green North
Manchester M12 6FZ
F 0161 273 4567
E info@raretalentactors.com
W www.raretalentactors.com

RAZZAMATAZZ MANAGEMENT   T/F 01342 301617
204 Holtye Road, East Grinstead
West Sussex RH19 3ES
T 07836 268292
E razzamatazzmanagement@btconnect.com

RED 24 MANAGEMENT   T 020 7559 3611
The Hospital Club, 3rd Floor
24 Endell Street, London WC2H 9HQ
E info@red24management.com
W www.red24management.com

RED CANYON MANAGEMENT   T 07931 381696
T 07939 365578
E info@redcanyon.co.uk
W www.redcanyon.co.uk

RPM2   T 0845 3625456
Studio House, Delamare Road
Cheshunt, Hertfordshire EN8 9SH
T 07795 606087
E rhino-rpm2@hotmail.com
W www.rhino2-rpm.com

SINGER, Sandra ASSOCIATES   T 01702 331616
21 Cotswold Road, Westcliff-on-Sea, Essex SS0 8AA
E sandrasingeruk@aol.com
W www.sandrasinger.com

SOMETHIN' ELSE   T 020 7250 5500
20-26 Brunswick Place, London N1 6DZ
F 020 7250 0937
E info@somethinelse.com
W www.somethinelse.com

TAKE THREE MANAGEMENT   T 020 7209 3777
110 Gloucester Avenue, Primrose Hill
London NW1 8HX
F 020 7209 3770
E sara@take3management.com
W www.take3management.co.uk

TALENT4 MEDIA LTD   T 020 7183 4330
Studio LG16, Shepherds Building Central
Charecroft Way, London W14 0EH
F 020 7183 4331
E enquiries@talent4media.com
W www.talent4media.com

TRIPLE A MEDIA   T/F 020 3370 4988
30 Great Portland Street, London W1W 8QU
E andy@tripleamedia.com
W www.tripleamedia.com

TROIKA   T 020 7336 7868
10A Christina Street, London EC2A 4PA
F 020 7490 7642
E info@troikatalent.com
W www.troikatalent.com

WANDER, Jo MANAGEMENT   T 020 7209 3777
110 Gloucester Avenue, Primrose Hill
London NW1 8HX
E jo@jowandermanagement.com
W www.jowandermanagement.com

WISE BUDDAH TALENT   T 020 7307 1600
74 Great Titchfield Street, London W1W 7QP
F 020 7307 1601
E talent@wisebuddah.com
W www.wisebuddah.com

ZWICKLER, Marlene & ASSOCIATES   T/F 0131 343 3030
1 Belgrave Crescent Lane, Edinburgh EH4 3AG
E info@mza-artists.com
W www.mza-artists.com

AD VOICE T 020 7323 2345
Oxford House, 76 Oxford Street
London W1D 1BS
F 020 7323 0101
E info@advoice.co.uk
W www.advoice.co.uk

ALPHABET AGENCY T 020 7252 4343
Also known as Alphabet Kidz. Children & Adults
Daisy Business Park, 19-35 Sylvan Grove
London SE15 1PD
E contact@alphabetkidz.co.uk
W www.thealphabetagency.co.uk

**AMERICAN AGENCY
VOICES THE** T 020 7485 8883
14 Bonny Street, London NW1 9PG
E americanagency@btconnect.com
W www.americanagency.tv

**ANOTHER TONGUE
VOICES LTD** T 020 7494 0300
The Basement, 10-11 D'Arblay Street
London W1F 8DS
F 020 7494 7080
E john@anothertongue.com
W www.anothertongue.com

ASQUITH & HORNER T 020 8466 5580
Contact: By Telephone/Post (SAE)/e-mail
The Studio, 14 College Road
Bromley, Kent BR1 3NS
T 07770 482144
E asquith@dircon.co.uk

**BRAIDMAN, Michelle
ASSOCIATES LTD** T 020 7237 3523
2 Futura House, 169 Grange Road
London SE1 3BN
F 020 7231 4634
E info@braidman.com

CALYPSO VOICES T 020 7734 6415
25-26 Poland Street, London W1F 8QN
F 020 7437 0410
E jane@calypsovoices.com
W www.calypsovoices.com

CASTAWAY T 020 7240 2345
Suite 3, 15 Broad Court
London WC2B 5QN
E info@castaway.org.uk
W www.castaway.org.uk

**CONWAY VAN GELDER
GRANT LTD** T 020 7287 1070
3rd Floor, 8-12 Broadwick Street, London W1F 8HW
F 020 7287 1940
E kate@conwayvg.co.uk
W www.conwayvangeldergrant.com

**CREATIVE KIDZ THEATRICAL
& TALENT AGENCY** T 07908 144802
9 Weavers Terrace, Fulham
London SW6 1QE
E info@creativekidzandco.co.uk

DAMN GOOD VOICES T 07702 228185
Chester House, Unit 1:04
1-3 Brixton Road, London SW9 6DE
T 07809 549887
E damngoodvoices@me.com
W www.damngoodvoices.com

DIAMOND MANAGEMENT T 020 7631 0400
31 Percy Street, London W1T 2DD
F 020 7631 0500
E cc@diman.co.uk

EARACHE VOICES T 020 7287 2291
177 Wardour Street, London W1F 8WX
F 020 7287 2288
E alex@earachevoices.com
W www.earachevoices.com

**EXCELLENT TALENT
COMPANY THE** T 0845 2100111
118-120 Great Titchfield Street, London W1W 6SS
F 020 7637 4091
E info@excellenttalent.com
W www.excellenttalent.com

**FERRIS ENTERTAINMENT
VOICES** T 0845 4724725
London. Belfast. Cardiff. Los Angeles
Number 8, 132 Charing Cross Road
London WC2H 0LA
E info@ferrisentertainment.com
W www.ferrisentertainment.com

FIRST VOICE AGENCY T 01494 678277
Foxgrove House, School Lane, Seer Green HP9 2QJ
F 01494 730166
E jenny@firstvoiceagency.com
W www.firstvoiceagency.com

FOREIGN LEGION T 020 8450 4451
1 Kendal Road, London NW10 1JH
E voices@foreignlegion.co.uk
W www.foreignlegion.co.uk

FOREIGN VERSIONS LTD T 0333 123 2001
Translation
E info@foreignversions.co.uk
W www.foreignversions.com

GAY, Noel VOICES T 020 7836 3941
19 Denmark Street, London WC2H 8NA
F 020 7287 1816
E info@noelgay.com
W www.noelgay.com

GLOBAL7 T/F 020 7281 7679
PO Box 56232, London N4 4XP
T 07956 956652
E global7castings@gmail.com
W www.global7casting.com

GORDON & FRENCH T 020 7734 4818
Contact: By Post
12-13 Poland Street, London W1F 8QB
F 020 7734 4832
E voices@gordonandfrench.net
W www.gordonandfrench.co.uk

Voice-Over Agents

How do I become a voice-over artist?

The voice-over business has opened up a lot more to newcomers in recent years; you don't have to be a celebrity already to be booked for a job. However, it is a competitive industry, and it is important to bear in mind that only a select few are able to earn a living from voice-over work. It is more likely that voice-over work could become a supplement to your regular income.

In order to get work you must have a great voice and be able to put it to good use. Being able to act does not necessarily mean that you will also be able to do voice-overs. Whether your particular voice will get you the job or not will ultimately depend on the client's personal choice, so your technical ability to do voice-over work initially comes second in this industry. Once the client has chosen you, however, then you must be able to consistently demonstrate that you can take direction well, you don't need numerous takes to get the job finished, you have a positive attitude and you don't complain if recording goes a little over schedule.

Before you get to this stage, however, you will need a professional-sounding voicereel and, in the majority of cases, an agent.

How do I produce a voicereel?

Please see the 'Promotional Services' section for advice on creating your voicereel.

Why do I need a voice-over agent?

As with any other agent, a voice-over agent will promote their clients to job opportunities, negotiate contracts on their behalf, handle paperwork and offer advice. In return for these services they take commission ranging from 10-15%. The agents listed in this section specialise in representing and promoting voice-over artists, mostly in the commercial and corporate sectors, but also areas such as radio and animation. They will possess the relevant contacts in the industry that you need to get auditions and jobs. In this industry in particular, time is money, and clients are often more likely to trust that an agent can provide someone who can get the job done in the least amount of takes but still sounds good in every project, rather than taking on an unknown newcomer.

How do I find work in radio?

Please see the 'Radio' section of Contacts for further information on this specific area of voice work.

How should I use these listings?

Whether you are completely new to the industry, looking to change your existing agent, or wishing to take on an additional agent to represent you for voice-overs alongside your main acting or presenting agent, the following listings will supply you with up-to-date contact details for voice-over agencies. Every company listed is done so by written request to us. Please see the main 'Agents and Personal Managers' advice section for further guidance on choosing and approaching agents.

Should I pay an agent to join their books? Or sign a contract?

Equity (the actors' trade union) does not recommend that artists pay an agent to join their client list. Before signing a contract, you should be very clear about the terms and commitments involved. For advice on both of these issues, or if you experience any problems with a current agent, we recommend that you contact Equity www.equity.org.uk. They also produce the booklet *You and your Agent* which is free to all Equity members and available from their website's members' area.

Voice-Over Agents

CASE STUDY

Damn Good Voices is a boutique voice-over agency that caters to a range of highly skilled voice-over artists rather than celebrity voices. They have strong connections with the commercial, gaming, corporate and documentary markets.

This article is about how we see the world of voice-overs and is designed to guide you in your search for the right agent. It's a highly competitive industry, so you must be serious about delivering the ultimate voice-over, be wiling to put in the hours and have a knack for delivering something special for clients.

There are two main types of voice-over agent – those that focus on celebrity talent and those that focus on a mix of highly skilled individuals with a lesser profile. The key thing is to not risk getting 'lost' within the mix of talent the agent already has on their books. Look for an agent who perhaps doesn't have a sound like yours.

We look for talent that can bring a script to life, are able to take direction well and, of course, stand out from the crowd as this business is highly competitive and only the great will survive! Trends in delivery styles change, trends in accents change and simply having a great voice is not enough. We need talent that guarantees to deliver the job as briefed in the least amount of takes, as time is money!

We expect our talent to make themselves as available as possible for auditions, demo recordings and last-minute sessions. Flexibility is a key part of the process as many sessions are turned around very quickly.

Our role is to market our talent to casting directors and producers of content, to increase your exposure and to negotiate contracts on your behalf. Warning: we receive around 10-20 submissions a week from a wide range of voices. It can take several days/weeks for agents to respond and engage with new voice submissions, as their focus will continue to be on bringing in work for talent currently on their books.

Pro: Voice-over work is very rewarding and can be over in a matter of hours, yet the fees can be relatively high for the amount of time spent on a job.

Con: The voice-over industry is highly competitive and only a small percentage earns a living from purely voice-over work. You should see voice-over work as a supplement to your regular income – please don't expect it to be your big earner.

Pro: Voice-over work opens up the opportunity to play a wider range of roles due to jobs being non-visual, thus offering you more castability as clients often don't care what you look like!

Con: Many companies will go all out to get voice-over talent for cheap – be very wary of these jobs as they will only decrease the long-term value of voice-over work.

Alongside recording new demos with our talent, preparing e-coms for our contacts and other tasks, here's how the team at Damn Good Voices might work on a typical day:

08:00   The boss is in going through the day's schedules and submitted briefs from casting directors and producers. He prepares information for the imminent arrival of the assistants.

10:00   The assistant agents arrive and sit down for the morning briefing (with a strong coffee).

10:15   The team deal with submitting voices for jobs that have come in overnight. All submissions are checked by a lead agent who ensures the right people are up for the right jobs. It's essential to us that we do not bombard producers or casting directors with the same voices time after time. This process continues through out the day.

10:30   Contact strategy – in between submitting voices and dealing with talent booked for sessions the team will have a clear strategy for making new contacts, catching up with current contacts and generally making sure we are 'front of mind' when agencies and casting directors are choosing voices.

13:00   Feeding time

14:00   Continue with the processes above and spend a little time catching up with one or two of the voices.

18:00   Home time for the assistant agents – although they do have smartphones and iPads in case anything comes up throughout the evening.

19:30   The boss gets to go home if he's lucky!

To find out more visit www.damngoodvoices.com

GREAT BRITISH VOICE COMPANY THE　　T 07504 076020
339 Norristhorpe Lane
Liversedge
West Yorkshire WF15 7AZ
E info@gbvcoltd.com
W www.gbvcoltd.com

HAMILTON HODELL LTD　　T 020 7636 1221
Contact: Louise Donald
5th Floor, 66-68 Margaret Street
London W1W 8SR
F 020 7636 1226
E louise@hamiltonhodell.co.uk
W www.hamiltonhodell.co.uk

HARVEY VOICES　　T 020 7952 4361
No unsolicited correspondence
58 Woodlands Road, London N9 8RT
E info@harveyvoices.co.uk
W www.harveyvoices.co.uk

HOBSONS SINGERS　　T 020 8995 3628
2 Dukes Gate, Chiswick
London W4 5DX
F 020 8996 5350
E singers@hobsons-international.com
W www.hobsons-international.com

HOBSONS VOICES　　T 020 8995 3628
2 Dukes Gate, Chiswick, London W4 5DX
F 020 8996 5350
E voices@hobsons-international.com
W www.hobsons-international.com

HOPE, Sally ASSOCIATES　　T 020 7613 5353
108 Leonard Street, London EC2A 4XS
F 020 7613 4848
E casting@sallyhope.biz
W www.sallyhope.biz

HOWARD, Amanda ASSOCIATES
See JONESES THE

iCAN TALK LTD　　T 01858 466749
Palm Tree Mews
39 Tymecrosse Gardens
Market Harborough, Leicestershire LE16 7US
E hello@icantalk.co.uk
W www.icantalk.co.uk

J H A VOICE　　T 020 7734 7597
3 Richmond Buildings, London W1D 3HE
F 020 7734 6302
E info@jeremyhicks.com
W www.jeremyhicks.com

JONESES THE　　T 020 7287 9666
21 Berwick Street, London W1F 0PZ
F 020 7287 7785
E mail@meetthejoneses.co.uk
W www.meetthejoneses.co.uk

JUST VOICES AGENCY THE　　T 020 7881 2567
140 Buckingham Palace Road
London SW1W 9SA
F 020 7881 2569
E info@justvoicesagency.com
W www.justvoicesagency.com

KIDZTALK LTD   T 01737 350808
Young Voices. Children. Teenagers. Twenties
F 01737 352456
E studio@kidztalk.com
W www.kidztalk.com

KMA VOICES   T 020 7439 1456
101 Finsbury Pavement, London EC2A 1RS
F 020 7734 6530
E email@kenmcreddie.com
W www.kenmcreddie.com/voices

LEHRER, Jane VOICES   T 020 7435 9118
PO Box 66334, London NW6 9QT
F 020 7435 9117
E voices@janelehrer.co.uk
W www.janelehrer.co.uk/voices.html

LIP SERVICE CASTING LTD   T 020 7734 3393
Twitter: @lipservicevoice
60-66 Wardour Street, London W1F 0TA
T 07956 892524
E bookings@lipservice.co.uk
W www.lipservice.co.uk

M2M VOICES   T 020 7631 1721
Specialises in Comedy
21 Foley Street, London W1W 6DR
E info@m2mvoices.com
W www.m2mvoices.com

MARKHAM, FROGGATT & IRWIN   T 020 7636 4412
4 Windmill Street, London W1T 2HZ
E tig@markhamfroggattirwin.com
W www.markhamfroggattirwin.com

MOON, Kate MANAGEMENT LTD   T 01604 686100
PO Box 648, Draughton
Northampton NN6 9XT
E kate@katemoonmanagement.co.uk
W www.katemoonmanagement.co.uk

MONSTER VOICE   T 020 7462 9950
14 Rathbone Place
London W1T 1HT
F 020 7580 2748

PEMBERTON VOICES   T 020 7224 9036
51 Upper Berkeley Street, London W1H 7QW
E fay@pembertonassociates.com
W www.pembertonvoices.com

QVOICE   T 020 7430 5405
3rd Floor, 161 Drury Lane
Covent Garden, London WC2B 5PN
E info@qvoice.co.uk
W www.qvoice.co.uk

RABBIT VOCAL MANAGEMENT LTD   T 020 7287 6466
94 Strand on the Green, London W4 3NN
F 020 7287 6566
E info@rabbitvocalmanagement.co.uk
W www.rabbitvocalmanagement.co.uk

RED 24 VOICES   T 020 7559 3611
The Hospital Club, 3rd Floor
24 Endell Street, London WC2H 9HQ
E paul@red24voices.com
W www.red24voices.com

RHUBARB VOICES   T 020 8742 8683
1st Floor, 1A Devonshire Road
London W4 2EU
F 020 8742 8693
E enquiries@rhubarbvoices.co.uk
W www.rhubarbvoices.co.uk

RPM2   T 07795 606087
Studio House
Delamare Road
Cheshunt, Hertfordshire EN8 9SH
T 0845 3625456
E rhino-rpm2@hotmail.com
W www.rhino2-rpm.com

SHINING MANAGEMENT LTD   T 020 7734 1981
81 Oxford Street
London W1D 2EU
E info@shiningvoices.com
W www.shiningvoices.com

SUGAR POD VOICES   T 020 8829 8969
Based in London
Studio 8C
Chocolate Factory 2, Coburg Road
Wood Green, London N22 6UJ
T 07967 673552
E info@sugarpodproductions.com
W www.sugarpodproductions.com

SVMK LTD   T 020 7434 0002
47 Dean Street, London W1D 5BE
E info@svmk.co.uk
W www.svmk.co.uk

TALKING HEADS   T 020 7292 7575
Argyll House
All Saints Passage
London SW18 1EP
E voices@talkingheadsvoices.com
W www.talkingheadsvoices.com

TERRY, Sue VOICES LTD   T 020 7434 2040
4th Floor, 35 Great Marlborough Street
London W1F 7JF
F 020 7434 2042
E sue@sueterryvoices.com
W www.sueterryvoices.com

TONGUE & GROOVE   T 0161 228 2469
PO Box 173, Manchester M19 0AR
F 0161 249 3666
E info@tongueandgroove.co.uk
W www.tongueandgroove.co.uk

UNITED VOICES   T 020 3214 0937
12-26 Lexington Street, London W1F 0LE
E voices@unitedagents.co.uk
W www.unitedvoices.tv

International Centre for Voice

Based at the Central School of Speech & Drama   Patrons: Cicely Berry CBE and Barbara Houseman

The ICV exists to serve the needs of professional users of voice and speech, including actors, singers, directors, voice coaches, musicians and teachers. We host workshops with world-renowned practitioners and enable members to develop their practice and research as part of a supportive network of people who are passionate about voice.

For further details please visit **www.icvoice.co.uk** or email **icv@cssd.ac.uk**

damngoodvoices

voiceover agency
www.damngoodvoices.com
+44 (0)7702 228185

THE UK'S NUMBER 1

CRYING OUT LOUD
PRODUCTIONS

voiceover demo production company
www.cryingoutloud.co.uk
+44 (0)7809 549887

VOCAL POINT   T 020 7419 0700
131 Great Titchfield Street
London W1W 5BB
E enquiries@vocalpoint.net
W www.vocalpoint.net

VOICE BANK LTD   T 0161 973 8879
PO Box 825, Altrincham
Cheshire WA15 5HH
T 07931 792670
E elinors@voicebankltd.co.uk
W www.voicebankltd.co.uk

VOICE SHOP   T 020 8742 7077
1st Floor, Thomas Place
1A Devonshire Road, London W4 2EU
F 020 8742 7011
E info@voice-shop.co.uk
W www.voice-shop.co.uk

VOICE SQUAD   T 020 8450 4451
1 Kendal Road, London NW10 1JH
E voices@voicesquad.com
W www.voicesquad.com

**VOICEBANK, THE IRISH
VOICE-OVER AGENCY**   T 00 353 1 6789800
62 Lower Baggot Street
Dublin 2, Ireland
E voicebank@voicebank.ie
W www.voicebank.ie

VOICECALL   T 020 7209 1064
67A Gondar Gardens
London NW6 1EP
T 07920 044615
E voices@voicecall-online.co.uk
W www.voicecall-online.co.uk

**VOICEOVER GALLERY
(LONDON) THE**   T 020 7987 0951
12 Cock Lane, London EC1A 9BU
E london@thevoiceovergallery.co.uk
W www.thevoiceovergallery.co.uk

**VOICEOVER GALLERY
(MANCHESTER) THE**   T 0161 881 8844
1st Floor, 1 Ridgefield
King Street, Manchester M2 6EG
E manchester@thevoiceovergallery.co.uk
W www.thevoiceovergallery.co.uk

VOICEOVERS.CO.UK   T 020 7099 2264
PO Box 326, Plymouth
Devon PL4 9YQ
F 020 3411 2699
E info@voiceovers.co.uk
W www.voiceovers.co.uk

**VSI - VOICE & SCRIPT
INTERNATIONAL**   T 020 7692 7700
Foreign Language Specialists
132 Cleveland Street, London W1T 6AB
F 020 7692 7711
E info@vsi.tv
W www.vsi.tv

WAM VOICES   T 020 7836 9222
The Voice Agency of Waring & McKenna
11-12 Dover Street, Mayfair
London W1S 4LJ
F 020 7836 9186
E info@wamvoices.com
W www.wamvoices.com

WOOTTON, Suzy VOICES   T 01604 765872
72 Towcester Road, Far Cotton
Northampton NN4 8LQ
E suzy@suzywoottonvoices.com
W www.suzywoottonvoices.com

WORDS-OUT   T 020 7183 0017
Hunters House, 1 Redcliffe Road
London SW10 9NR
E karin@words-out.com
W www.words-out.com

YAKETY YAK   T 020 7430 2600
7A Bloomsbury Square
London WC1A 2LP
F 020 7404 6109
E info@yaketyyak.co.uk
W www.yaketyyak.co.uk

---

fŏreignversions

Voice Overs
Translations
Script Adaptation
Foreign Copywriting
Studio Production

Contact:
Margaret Davies, Annie Geary
or Bérangère Capelle

On 0333 123 2001

Foreign Versions Ltd
e-mail: info@foreignversions.co.uk
www.foreignversions.com

2020 CASTING LTD   T 020 8746 2020
2020 Hopgood Street
London W12 7JU
F 020 8735 2727
E info@2020casting.com
W www.2020casting.com

ACADEMY EXTRAS   T 01204 417403
Film. Television. Based in the North West
490 Halliwell Road
Bolton, Lancs BL1 8AN
E admin@academyextras.tv
W www.academyextras.tv

AGENCY OAKROYD   T 07840 784337
Oakroyd, 89 Wheatley Lane
Ben Rhydding, Ilkley, Yorkshire LS29 8PP
E paula@agencyoakroyd.com
W www.agencyoakroyd.com

ALLSORTS AGENCY   T 020 8989 0500
Modelling
Suite 3, Marlborough Business Centre
96 George Lane, London E18 1AD
F 020 8989 5600
E bookings@allsortsagency.com
W www.allsortsagency.com

**ARTIST MANAGEMENT
UK LTD**   T 0151 523 6222
PO Box 96
Liverpool L9 8WY
E chris@artistmanagementuk.com
W www.artistmanagementuk.com

AVENUE ARTISTES LTD   T 023 8076 0930
PO Box 1573
Southampton SO16 3XS
E info@avenueartistes.com
W www.avenueartistes.com

**AWA -
ANDREA WILDER AGENCY**   T 07919 202401
23 Cambrian Drive, Colwyn Bay
Conwy LL28 4SL
F 07092 249314
E andreawilder@fastmail.fm
W www.awagency.co.uk

BENNETTON - CMP   T 01924 385400
The Casting Studio, 8-10 Teall Street
Wakefield, West Yorkshire WF1 1PT
T 07540 693657
E enquiries@bennetton-cmp.co.uk
W www.bennetton-cmp.co.uk

Walk-On & Supporting Artists' Agents

Who are Walk-on and Supporting Artists?

Sometimes known as 'extras', walk-on and supporting artists appear in the background of TV and film scenes in order to add a sense of realism, character or atmosphere. They do not have individual speaking roles, unless required to make background/ambient noise.

Working as a walk-on or supporting artist does not require any specific 'look', training or experience as such; however it does involve more effort than people think. Artists are often required to start very early in the morning (6am is not uncommon), and days can be long with lots of waiting around, sometimes in tough conditions on location. It is certainly not glamorous, nor is it a way to become a TV or film star!

Artists must be reliable and available at very short notice, which can make it difficult to juggle with other work or family commitments. Requirements vary from production to production and, as with mainstream acting work, there are no guarantees that you will get regular work, let alone be able to earn a living as a walk-on.

How should I use these listings?

If you are serious about working as a walk-on artist, you will need to register with an agency in order to be put forward for jobs. In return for finding you work, you can expect an agency to take between 10-15% in commission. The listings in this section contain contact details of many walk-on and supporting artist agencies. Some will specialise in certain areas, so make sure you research the different companies carefully to see if they are appropriate for you. Many have websites you can visit. It is also worth asking questions about how long an agency has existed, and about their recent production credits.

When approaching an agency for representation, you should send them your CV with a covering letter and a recent photograph which is a genuine, natural likeness of you. Enclosing a stamped-addressed envelope with sufficient postage (SAE) will give you a better chance of a reply.

Should I pay an agent to join their books? Or sign a contract?

Equity (the actors' trade union) does not generally recommend that artists pay an agent to join their client list. Before signing any contract, you should be clear about the terms and commitments involved. Always speak to Equity www.equity.org.uk or BECTU www.bectu.org.uk if you have any concerns or queries. Equity also produces the booklet *You and your Agent* which is free to all Equity members and available from their website's members' area.

Where can I find more information?

You may find it useful to contact the Film Artists Association, a subdivision of BECTU, who provide union representation for walk-on and supporting artists. You can read their case study in this section or for further details visit www.bectu.org.uk/get-involved/background-artistes

Walk-On & Supporting Artists' Agents

CASE STUDY

If you are working, or intend to work, as a background artiste, stand-in or a double, consider becoming a member of the Film Artistes Association. The FAA is a subdivision of BECTU, the independent trade union for those working in broadcasting, film, theatre, entertainment, leisure, interactive media and allied areas.

Central to BECTU's role in this dynamic and expanding sector is to give freelance members advice on agreed rates of pay and assist them when they need us. Some of our members are household names, and many more have won awards for their professional excellence — including Oscars, BAFTA awards and Royal Society awards. The FAA, which was formed in 1927, is a growing part of the union and represents background artistes, stand-ins and doubles who render such performances or services to set the atmosphere of scenes both on and off the camera.

Productions of course can be set in any period, country, or indeed planet and consequently background artistes are also expected to work with such clothing, make-up, wigs and hairstyles as the production dictates. This work is critical to the atmosphere of a scene and to the audience's suspension of disbelief. In a battle scene or horror film, for example, an artiste who does not die convincingly could completely change the audience's response from shock and revulsion to mirth, thus destroying the whole scene. This is why experienced background artistes provide an essential service to film-makers and independent producers. Whilst these workers may not be in the foreground of a particular shot, their skills are vital to the quality of the final work.

The FAA is not an agency and therefore doesn't find work for members. The current unlicensed agency market has led to the emergence, and sudden disappearance, of rogue agents who have cheated a number of background artistes in the past. So bear in mind that no reputable agency will put you or anyone else on their books without seeing you. After all you could be tall, dark and handsome according to your CV (and even your photo), but a good agency will ask

to see you to confirm this before accepting you on their books — and you can check them out too. Also beware of agencies trying to hide their location using PO Box numbers and premium rate telephone lines. Having acting experience and being confident, determined, reliable and punctual are all qualities a good agent will seek out.

If you work as a background artiste or you still think this is for you (and it's definitely not for everyone), you should join the FAA subdivision of BECTU. We negotiate and police the rates of pay within the film and TV sector. We offer individual legal assistance and help keep you out of trouble, or get you out when you're in it. We can also advise on the most reputable agencies to join: this valuable information is only free to members. BECTU is here to help you get the most out of the industry and avoid the worst: the latest pay increase we won for FAA members, at this time of national recession, is a whopping 5.2%.

If you're already a member, take a moment to check out our range of benefits and services on our website.

Having acting experience and being confident, determined, reliable and punctual are all qualities a good agent will seek out.

Finally, the entertainment industry is perceived as attractive because of the explosion of reality TV and the message that anyone can be a star. This is a very competitive industry, so don't believe that if an agent takes you on it will lead to instant success, fame and fortune. However, if it is a job you like and you are treated fairly it could be a most enjoyable way of earning money.

> **To find out more about BECTU visit www.bectu.org.uk or call 020 7346 0900**

BONNIE & BETTY LTD T 020 8301 8333
9-11 Gunnery Terrace, Royal Arsenal
London SE18 6SW
E agency@bonnieandbetty.com
W www.bonnieandbetty.com

BOSS CASTING T 0161 237 0100
Fourways House, 57 Hilton Street
Manchester M1 2EJ
F 0161 236 1237
E cath@bosscasting.co.uk
W www.bosscasting.co.uk

BROADCASTING AGENCY LTD T 020 3131 0128
Unit 106A Netil House
1 Westgate Street
London E8 3RL
E info@broadcastingagency.co.uk
W www.broadcastingagency.co.uk

BROOK, Dolly
CASTING AGENCY T 01371 875767
PO Box 5436, Dunmow CM6 1WW
F 01371 875996
E dollybrookcasting@btinternet.com

CAIRNS AGENCY THE T 0141 222 2333
Contact: Maureen Cairns, Allan Jones
2nd Floor, 34 Argyle Arcade Chambers
Buchanan Street, Glasgow G2 8BD
E info@thecairnsagency.com

CASTING COLLECTIVE LTD THE T 020 8962 0099
Olympic House
317-321 Latimer Road, London W10 6RA
F 020 8962 0333
E casting@castingcollective.co.uk
W www.castingcollective.co.uk

CASTING NETWORK LTD THE T 020 8391 2979
4 Vidler Close, Chessington
Surrey KT9 2GL
F 020 8391 5119
E info@thecastingnetwork.co.uk
W www.thecastingnetwork.co.uk

CELEX CASTING LTD T 01332 232445
Adults & Children
PO Box 7317, Derby DE1 0GS
T 07932 066021
E anne@celex.co.uk

CENTRAL CASTING LTD T 020 7722 1551
See also KNIGHT, Ray CASTING
Elstree Studios, Room 38, John Maxwell Building
Shenley Road, Boreham Wood, Herts WD6 1JG
E casting@rayknight.co.uk
W www.rayknight.co.uk

CREATIVE KIDZ THEATRICAL &
TALENT AGENCY T 07908 144802
9 Weavers Terrace, Fulham
London SW6 1QE
E info@creativekidzandco.co.uk

DARK ARTS T 01782 769213
Alternative & Tattooed Character Agency
2 Stamer Street, Stoke-on-Trent
Staffordshire ST4 1DX
T 07514 893326
E info@darkarts.org.uk
W www.darkarts.org.uk

DAVID AGENCY THE T 020 8834 1615
26-28 Hammersmith Grove, London W6 7BA
E casting@davidagency.co.uk
W www.davidagency.co.uk

DK MODEL MANAGEMENT T 0114 257 3480
4 Park Square, Thorncliffe Park
Chapeltown, Sheffield, South Yorkshire S35 2PH
F 0114 257 3482
E actors@dkmodels.net
W www.dkmodels.net

ELLIOTT AGENCY LTD THE T 01273 454111
10 High Street
Shoreham-by-Sea BN43 5DA
E elliottagency@btconnect.com
W www.elliottagency.co.uk

ETHNIKA CASTING T 0845 6031266
14 Bowmont Gardens, Glasgow G12 9LR
T 07778 296002
E ethnikacasting@yahoo.co.uk
W www.ethnikacasting.co.uk

**EUROKIDS & EKA
CASTING AGENCIES** T 01925 761088
*Contact: Amy Musker (Senior Casting Agent). Accepts
Showreels. Children, Teenagers & Adults up to 85 yrs.
Commercials. Film. Television. Walk-ons, Supporting
Artists & Extras*
The Warehouse Studios, Glaziers Lane
Culcheth, Warrington, Cheshire WA3 4AQ
T 01925 761210
E castings@eka-agency.com
W www.eka-agency.com

EXTRA PEOPLE LTD T 020 7734 7606
Based in London & Midlands
74 Berwick Street, London W1F 8TF
E team@extra-people.com
W www.extra-people.com

FACE MUSIC T 01209 820796
Musicians
Lambourne Farm, TR16 5HA
E facemusic@btinternet.com

FBI AGENCY T 07050 222747
PO Box 250, Leeds LS1 2AZ
T 07515 567309
E casting@fbi-agency.co.uk
W www.fbi-agency.co.uk

**FEATURED & BACKGROUND
CASTING LTD (FAB)** T 01628 522688
Contact: Lois Ward, Suzanne Johns
13A Waldeck House, Waldeck Road
Maidenhead, Berkshire SL6 8BR
T 07808 781169
E suzanne@fabcastingagency.com
W www.fabcastingagency.com

FILM CAST CORNWALL & SW T 01326 311419
T 07811 253756
E enquiries@filmcastcornwall.co.uk
W www.filmcastcornwall.co.uk

FRESH AGENTS LTD T 01273 711777
Actors. Extras. Modelling. Promotional
Suite 5, Saks House
19 Ship Street, Brighton BN1 1AD
T 0845 4080998
E info@freshagents.co.uk
W www.freshagents.co.uk

GOLD-CAST AGENCY T 07970 187801
PO Box 30, Treharris
Mid Glamorgan CF46 9AN
E enquiries@gold-castagency.co.uk
W www.gold-castagency.co.uk

GUYS & DOLLS CASTING T 020 8906 4144
Trafalgar House, Grenville Place
Mill Hill, London NW7 3SA
T 07890 774454
E info@guysanddollscasting.com
W www.guysanddollscasting.com

**HERRON, Alana
PERSONAL MANAGEMENT** T 07877 984636
51 Medrox Gardens, Glasgow G67 4AL
E alana@alanaherron.com
W www.alanaherron.com

ICON EXTRAS LTD T 020 7510 8453
Extras for Commercials, Film & Television
1602 Phoenix Heights West, 142 Byng Street
London E14 9AE
E iconextra@gmail.com
W www.iconextras.com

INDUSTRY CASTING T 0161 839 1551
Suite 5, Basil Chambers
65 High Street, Manchester M4 1FS
F 0161 839 1661
E lois@industrypeople.co.uk
W www.industrycasting.co.uk

IPM TALENT T 0113 244 3222
Contact: Stewart Ross
The Studio, 102 Kirkstall Road
Leeds, West Yorkshire LS3 1JA
E stewart@ipmcasting.com
W www.ipmcasting.com

JACLYN AGENCY T 01603 879303
61 Chapel Street, Cawston, Norfolk NR10 4BG
E info@jaclynagency.co.uk
W www.jaclynagency.co.uk

JPM EXTRAS T 0191 221 2491
A Division of Janet Plater Management Ltd
D Floor, Milburn House
Dean Street, Newcastle upon Tyne NE1 1LF
E extras@tynebridge.demon.co.uk
W www.janetplatermanagement.co.uk

KNIGHT, Ray CASTING T 020 7722 4111
Elstree Studios, Room 38, John Maxwell Building
Shenley Road, Boreham Wood, Herts WD6 1JG
E casting@rayknight.co.uk
W www.rayknight.co.uk

KREATE PROMOTIONS T 020 7401 9007
Unit 232, Great Guildford Business Square
30 Great Guildford Street
London SE1 0HS
F 020 7401 9008
E hello@kreate.co.uk
W www.kreate.co.uk

LEMON CASTING LTD   T 0161 205 2096
The Sharp Project, Thorpe Road
Newton Heath, Manchester M40 5BJ
T 07723 317489
E info@lemoncasting.co.uk

LINTON MANAGEMENT   T 0161 761 2020
3 The Rock, Bury BL9 0JP
F 0161 761 1999
E mail@linton.tv
W www.lintonmanagement.co.uk

MAD DOG CASTING LTD   T 020 7269 7910
2nd Floor, Holborn Hall
193-197 High Holborn
London WC1V 7BD
E info@maddogcasting.com
W www.maddogcasting.com

McDONAGH, Melanie MANAGEMENT
(ACADEMY OF PERFORMING ARTS &
CASTING AGENCY)   T 07909 831409
14 Apple Tree Way, Oswaldtwistle
Accrington, Lancashire BB5 0FB
T 01254 392560
E mcdonaghmgt@aol.com
W www.mcdonaghmanagement.co.uk

MIM AGENCY   T 0871 2377963
Clayton House, 59 Piccadilly
Manchester M1 2AQ
E info@mimagency.co.uk
W www.mimagency.co.uk

NEMESIS AGENCY LTD   T 0161 228 6404
Nemesis House
1 Oxford Court
Bishopsgate, Manchester M2 3WQ
F 0161 228 6727
E julie@nmsmanagement.co.uk
W www.nemesiscasting.co.uk

NIDGES CASTING AGENCY
See BOSS CASTING

ORIENTAL CASTING
AGENCY LTD   T 020 8660 0101
Contact: Billie James
22 Wontford Road, Purley
Surrey CR8 4BL
F 020 8674 9303
E billiejames@btconnect.com
W www.orientalcasting.com

PAN ARTISTS AGENCY LTD   T 0800 6349147
Cornerways, 34 Woodhouse Lane
Sale, Cheshire M33 4JX
T 07890 715115
E panartists@btconnect.com
W www.panartists.co.uk

PC THEATRICAL MODEL &
CASTING AGENCY   T 020 8381 2229
10 Strathmore Gardens
Edgware, Middlesex HA8 5HJ
F 020 8933 3418
E twinagy@aol.com
W www.twinagency.com

PERFORMERS LEAGUE
AGENCY LTD THE   T 07946 781116
Studio 55, 55 Openshaw Road
London SE2 0TB
E johnson@tpla.co.uk
W www.tpla.co.uk

PHA CASTING   T 0161 273 4444
Tanzaro House
Ardwick Green North
Manchester M12 6FZ
F 0161 273 4567
E info@pha-agency.co.uk
W www.pha-agency.co.uk

PHOENIX CASTING AGENCY   T 0117 973 1100
PO Box 387, Bristol BS99 3JZ
F 0117 973 4160
E info@phoenixagency.biz
W www.phoenixagency.biz

POLEASE   T 05600 650524
Specialist in Police & Military
1 Noake Road, Hucclecote
Gloucester GL3 3PE
T 07811 504079
E info@polease.co.uk
W www.polease.co.uk

POWER MODEL MANAGEMENT
CASTING AGENCY   T 01603 777190
PO Box 1198, Salhouse
Norwich NR13 6WD
E info@powermodel.co.uk
W www.powermodel.co.uk

RAPID TALENT LTD   T 020 7734 5775
5 Vancouver Road, Eastbourne
East Sussex BN23 5BF
T 07980 899156
E enquiries@rapidtalent.co.uk
W www.rapidtalent.co.uk

RAY'S NORTHERN
CASTING AGENCY   T/F 0161 643 6745
7 Wince Close, Alkrington
Middleton, Manchester M24 1UJ
E rayscasting@yahoo.co.uk

REGENCY AGENCY   T 0113 255 8980
25 Carr Road, Calverley
Leeds LS28 5NE

REVOLUTION TALENT
MANAGEMENT   T 07892 816283
Central Chambers, 93 Hope Street
Glasgow, G2 6LD
F 0141 221 8622
E enquiries@revolutiontalentmanagement.com
W www.revolutiontalentmanagement.com

SÉVA DHALIVAAL
07956 553879

REYNOLDS, Sandra AGENCY　T 020 7387 5858
Film. Stage. Stills. Television
Amadeus House, 27B Floral Street
London WC2E 9DP
F 020 7387 5848
E info@sandrareynolds.co.uk
W www.sandrareynolds.co.uk

**REYNOLDS, Sandra AGENCY
(EAST ANGLIA)**　T 01603 623842
Film. Stage. Stills. Television
Bacon House, 35 St Georges Street, Norwich NR3 1DA
F 01603 219825
E info@sandrareynolds.co.uk
W www.sandrareynolds.co.uk

RHODES AGENCY　T 01708 747013
5 Dymoke Road, Hornchurch, Essex RM11 1AA
F 01708 730431
E rhodesarts@hotmail.com

**SA19 - THE UNIFORMED
ARTISTE AGENCY**　T 020 8746 2523
2020 Hopgood Street
Shepherds Bush, London W12 7JU
F 020 8735 2727
E info@sa19.co.uk
W www.sa19.co.uk

**SAPPHIRES MODEL
MANAGEMENT LTD**　T 020 3603 9460
38 South Molton Street, London W1K 5RL
F 0870 9127563
E contact@sapphiresmodel.com
W www.sapphiresmodel.com

SCREAM MANAGEMENT LTD　T 0161 850 1996
The Greenhouse, Media City UK
Salford, Manchester M50 2EQ
T 0161 850 1995
E extras@screammanagement.com
W www.screammanagement.com

SCREENLITE AGENCY　T 01932 561388
Shepperton Studios, Studios Road
Shepperton, Middlesex TW17 0QD
T 01932 592271
E enquiries@screenliteagency.co.uk
W www.screenliteagency.co.uk

SEVEN CASTING AGENCY　T 0161 850 1057
Manchester Office: 4th Floor, 59 Piccadilly
Manchester M1 2AQ
T 07730 130485
E will@7casting.co.uk
W www.7casting.co.uk

SEVEN CASTING AGENCY　T 01785 212266
Staffordshire Office: Suite 3
Tudor House
9 Eastgate Street
Stafford ST16 2NQ
T 07730 130485
E will@7casting.co.uk
W www.7casting.co.uk

SHARMAN, Alan AGENCY　T 0121 212 0090
Office 6 Fournier House
8 Tenby Street
Jewellery Quarter, Birmingham B1 3AJ
E info@alansharmanagency.com
W www.alansharmanagency.com

SLICK CASTING LTD　T/F 020 8531 5061
Unit 23, Oaklands Avenue
London N9 7LN
T 07944 939462
E info@slickcasting.com
W www.slickcasting.com

SOLOMON ARTISTES　T 020 7748 4409
30 Clarence Street
Southend-on-Sea
Essex SS1 1BD
T 01702 437118
E info@solomon-artistes.co.uk
W www.solomon-artistes.co.uk

SPIRIT MODEL MANAGEMENT　T 01952 501145
Alternative & Commercial Agency
91 Stocking Park Road
Lightmoor Village
Telford, Shropshire TF4 3QZ
T 07896 978972
E info@spiritmodels.co.uk
W www.spiritmodels.co.uk

SPORTS PROMOTIONS (UK) LTD　T 020 8771 4700
56 Church Road, Crystal Palace
London SE19 2EZ
F 020 8771 4704
E agent@sportspromotions.co.uk
W www.sportspromotions.co.uk

STAV'S CASTING AGENCY　T 07539 810640
82 Station Crescent, Tottenham
Haringey, London N15 5BD
E stavros.louca@facebook.com
W www.stavscastingagency.com

**SUMMERS, Mark
MANAGEMENT**　T 020 7229 8413
1 Beaumont Avenue, West Kensington
London W14 9LP
E louise@marksummers.com
W www.marksummers.com

TUESDAYS CHILD LTD　T/F 01625 501765
Children & Adults
Oakfield House
Springwood Way
Macclesfield SK10 2XA
E info@tuesdayschildagency.co.uk
W www.tuesdayschildagency.co.uk

TURNSTONE MANAGEMENT　T 0845 5576658
T 07866 211647
E mark_turner85@hotmail.com

UNI-VERSAL EXTRAS　T 0845 0090344
Pinewood Studios
Pinewood Road
Iver Heath, Buckinghamshire SL0 0NH
E info@universalextras.co.uk
W www.universalextrascasting.co.uk

A1 ANIMALS   T/F 01753 621813
Farm, Domestic & Exotic Animals
64 Eton Wick Road
Eton Wick
Windsor, Berkshire SL4 6JL
T 07860 416545
E a1animals@btinternet.com
W www.a1animals.co.uk

A-Z ANIMALS LTD   T 01372 377111
The Bell House, Bell Lane
Fetcham, Surrey KT22 9ND
T 07836 721288
E info@a-zanimals.co.uk
W www.a-zanimals.co.uk

ACTION STUNT DOGS &
ANIMALS   T/F 01869 338546
3 The Chestnuts, Clifton
Deddington, Oxon OX15 0PE
E gill@stuntdogs.net

ALTERNATIVE ANIMALS   T 07956 564715
Contact: Trevor Smith. Animatronics. Taxidermy
28 Greaves Road, High Wycombe
Bucks HP13 7JU
F 01494 441385
E animalswork1@yahoo.co.uk
W www.animalswork.co.uk

ANIMAL ACTING   T 0161 655 3700
Animals. Horse-drawn Vehicles. Props. Stunts
7 Dovedale Court
Windermere Road
Middleton, Manchester M24 5QT
T 07831 800567
E information@animalacting.com
W www.animalacting.com

ANIMAL ACTORS   T 07710 348777
Animals. Birds. Reptiles
95 Ditchling Road, Brighton
Sussex BN1 4ST

ANIMAL AMBASSADORS   T/F 01635 200900
Old Forest
Hampstead Norreys Road
Hermitage, Berks RG18 9SA
T 07831 558594
E kayweston@tiscali.co.uk
W www.animalambassadors.co.uk

ANIMAL WELFARE
FILMING FEDERATION   T 07944 767068
Free Consultancy Service
56 Lance Way
High Wycombe
Bucks HP13 7BU
E animalswork1@yahoo.co.uk
W www.animalworld.org.uk

ANIMALS GALORE LTD   T 01342 842400
208 Smallfield Road
Horley, Surrey RH6 9LS
W www.animals-galore.co.uk

ANIMALS O KAY   T 01923 291277
16 Queen Street
Chipperfield
Kings Langley
Herts WD4 9BT
T 07831 305793
E kay@animalsokay.com
W www.animalsokay.com

ANIMALS WORK WITH
TREVOR SMITH   T 07956 564715
Contact: Trevor Smith
28 Greaves Road
High Wycombe, Bucks HP13 7JU
T 07770 666088
E animalswork1@yahoo.co.uk
W www.animalswork.co.uk

CELEBRITY REPTILES   T/F 020 8659 0877
11 Tramway Close
London SE20 7DF
E info@celebrityreptiles.co.uk
W www.celebrityreptiles.co.uk

CHEESEMAN, Virginia   T 01628 522632
21 Willow Close
Flackwell Heath
High Wycombe, Bucks HP10 9LH
T 07971 838724
E virginia@virginiacheeseman.co.uk
W www.virginiacheeseman.co.uk

COTSWOLD FARM PARK   T 01451 850307
Rare Breed Farm Animals
Guiting Power, Cheltenham
Gloucestershire GL54 5UG
F 01451 850423
E info@cotswoldfarmpark.co.uk

CREATURE FEATURE   T/F 01387 860648
Animal Agent
Gubhill Farm, Ae, Dumfries
Scotland DG1 1RL
T 07770 774866
E david@creaturefeature.co.uk
W www.creaturefeature.co.uk

DOLBADARN FILM HORSES   T/F 01286 870277
Dolbadarn Hotel
High Street, Llanberis
Gwynedd
North Wales LL55 4SU
T 07710 461341
E info@filmhorses.co.uk
W www.filmhorses.co.uk

DUDLEY, Yvonne
LRPS ARAD FISTD   T 020 8989 1528
Glamour Dogs & Stories for Films
55 Cambridge Park
Wanstead, London E11 2PR
T 07528 519591

FILM & TV HORSES   T/F 01753 864464
Crown Farm, Eton Wick Road, Eton, Windsor SL4 6PG
T 07831 629662
E filmhorses@yahoo.co.uk
W www.filmhorses.com

GET STUFFED   T 020 7226 1364
Taxidermy
105 Essex Road, London N1 2SL
T 07831 260062
E taxidermy@thegetstuffed.co.uk
W www.thegetstuffed.co.uk

GRAY, Robin COMMENTARIES   T 01420 23347
Equestrian Equipment. Horse Race Commentaries.
Voice Overs
Comptons, Isington
Alton, Hants GU34 4PL
T 07831 828424
E comptons1@hotmail.co.uk

HILTON HORSES   T 07958 292222
Contact: Samantha Jones
478 London Road, Ashford, Middlesex TW15 3AD
E samantha@hilton-horses.com
W www.hilton-horses.com

KNIGHTS OF ARKLEY THE   T/F 01269 861001
Glyn Sylen Farm, Five Roads, Llanelli SA15 5BJ
E penny@knightsofarkley.fsnet.co.uk
W www.knightsofarkley.com

KNIGHTS OF MIDDLE
ENGLAND THE   T 01926 400401
Horses & Riders for Film, Opera & Television
Warwick International School of Riding, Guys Cliffe
Coventry Road, Warwick CV34 5YD
E info@knightsofmiddleengland.co.uk
W www.knightsofmiddleengland.co.uk

MILLENNIUM BUGS   T 07770 666088
Live Insects
28 Greaves Road
High Wycombe, Bucks HP13 7JU
T 07956 566252
E animalswork1@yahoo.co.uk
W www.animalworld.org.uk

MINI PONY HIRE   T 07777 678687
E miniponyhire@hotmail.co.uk
W www.miniponyhire.com

MORTON, Geoff   T 01430 860185
Shire Horse & Equipment
Hasholme Carr Farm
Holme on Spalding Moor, York YO43 4BD
T 01430 860393

NOLTON STABLES   T 01437 710360
Nolton, Nr Newgale
Haverfordwest
Pembrokeshire SA62 3NW
F 01437 710967
E noltonstables@aol.com
W www.noltonstables.com

OTTERS   T 01285 760234
Contact: Daphne & Martin Neville. Tame Otters
Baker's Mill
Frampton Mansell
Stroud, Glos GL6 8JH
E martin_neville_bakers_mill@yahoo.co.uk

PROP FARM LTD   T 01909 723100
Contact: Pat Ward
Grange Farm
Elmton
Nr Creswell
North Derbyshire S80 4LX
F 01909 721465
E les@propfarm.co.uk

ROCKWOOD ANIMALS
ON FILM   T 029 2088 5420
Lewis Terrace, Llanbradach
Caerphilly CF83 3JZ
T 07973 930983
E martin@rockwoodanimals.com
W www.rockwoodanimals.com

SCHOOL OF NATIONAL
EQUITATION LTD   T 01509 852366
Contact: Sam Humphrey
Bunny Hill Top, Costock
Loughborough, Leicestershire LE12 6XN
T 07977 930083
E sam@bunnyhill.co.uk
W www.bunnyhill.co.uk

WHITE DOVES
COMPANY LTD THE   T 020 8508 1414
Provision of up to 300 Doves for Release
Suite 210 Sterling House
Langston Road
Loughton, Essex IG10 3TS
F 020 8502 2461
E thewhitedovecompany@yahoo.co.uk
W www.thewhitedovecompany.co.uk

WOLF SPECIALISTS THE   T 0118 971 3330
The UK Wolf Conservation Trust
UK Wolf Centre, Butlers Farm
Beenham, Berks RG7 5NT
E ukwct@ukwolf.org
W www.ukwolf.org

YORKSHIRE TERRIER   T 07963 818845
Based in Central London
17 Gardnor Road
London NW3 1HA
E woodlandcreature10@hotmail.com

ALDERSHOT: West End Centre   T 01252 408040
Queens Road, Aldershot
Hants GU11 3JD
BO 01252 330040
E westendcentre@hants.gov.uk
W www.westendcentre.co.uk

BILLERICAY:
Billericay Arts Association   T 01277 659286
The Fold, 72 Laindon Road, Billericay
Essex CM12 9LD
E baathefold@yahoo.co.uk
W www.baathefold.org.uk

BINGLEY: Bingley Arts Centre   T 01274 519814
Main Street, Bingley
West Yorkshire BD16 2LZ
E office@bingleyartscentre.co.uk

BIRMINGHAM:
Custard Factory   T 0121 224 7777
Gibb Street, Digbeth
Birmingham B9 4AA
F 0121 604 8888
E info@custardfactory.co.uk
W www.custardfactory.co.uk

BOSTON: Blackfriars
Theatre & Arts Centre   T 01205 363108
Contact: Mike Raymond
Spain Lane, Boston
Lincolnshire PE21 6HP
F 01205 358855
E director@blackfriarsartscentre.co.uk
W www.blackfriarsartscentre.co.uk

BRACKNELL:
South Hill Park Arts Centre   T 01344 484858
Contact: Ron McAllister (Chief Executive)
Ringmead, Bracknell
Berkshire RG12 7PA
BO 01344 484123
E admin@southhillpark.org.uk
W www.southhillpark.org.uk

BRENTFORD: Watermans   T 020 8232 1019
40 High Street, Brentford TW8 0DS
BO 020 8232 1010
E info@watermans.org.uk
W www.watermans.org.uk

BRIDGWATER:
Bridgwater Arts Centre   T 01278 422700
11-13 Castle Street, Bridgwater
Somerset TA6 3DD
E info@bridgwaterartscentre.co.uk
W www.bridgwaterartscentre.co.uk

BRISTOL: Arnolfini   T 0117 917 2300
16 Narrow Quay, Bristol BS1 4QA
F 0117 917 2303
E boxoffice@arnolfini.org.uk

BUILTH WELLS:
Wyeside Arts Centre   T 01982 553668
Castle Street, Builth Wells
Powys LD2 3BN
BO 01982 552555
E house@wyeside.co.uk
W www.wyeside.co.uk

BURY: The Met   T 0161 761 7107
Contact: David Agnew (Director)
Market Street, Bury
Lancs BL9 0BW
BO 0161 761 2216
E post@themet.biz
W www.themet.biz

CANNOCK:
Prince of Wales Centre   T 01543 466453
Contact: Richard Kay (General Manager)
Church Street, Cannock
Staffs WS11 1DE
BO 01543 578762
E princeofwales@cannockchasedc.gov.uk

CARDIFF: Chapter Arts Centre   T 029 2031 1050
Market Road, Canton
Cardiff CF5 1QE
BO 029 2030 4400
W www.chapter.org

CHIPPING NORTON:
The Theatre   T 01608 642349
Contact: John Terry (Director),
Ambereene Hitchcox (Head of Operations)
2 Spring Street, Chipping Norton
Oxon OX7 5NL
BO 01608 642350
E admin@chippingnortontheatre.com
W www.chippingnortontheatre.com

CHRISTCHURCH:
The Regent Centre   BO 01202 499199
Contact: Eliot Walker (Manager)
51 High Street, Christchurch
Dorset BH23 1AS
E info@regentcentre.co.uk
W www.regentcentre.co.uk

CIRENCESTER:
New Brewery Arts   T 01285 657181
Brewery Court, Cirencester
Glos GL7 1JH
F 01285 644060
E admin@newbreweryarts.org.uk
W www.newbreweryarts.org.uk

COLCHESTER:
Colchester Arts Centre   T 01206 500900
Contact: Anthony Roberts (Director)
Church Street, Colchester
Essex CO1 1NF
E info@colchesterartscentre.com
W www.colchesterartscentre.com

COVENTRY:
Warwick Arts Centre   T 024 7652 3734
Contact: Alan Rivett (Director)
University of Warwick, Coventry CV4 7AL
BO 024 7652 4524
E arts.centre@warwick.ac.uk
W www.warwickartscentre.co.uk

CUMBERNAULD:
Cumbernauld Theatre   T 01236 737235
Kildrum, Cumbernauld G67 2BN
BO 01236 732887
E info@cumbernauldtheatre.co.uk
W www.cumbernauldtheatre.co.uk

EDINBURGH:
Scottish Storytelling Centre   T 0131 556 9579
Contact: Dr Donald Smith (Director)
43-45 High Street, Edinburgh EH1 1SR
E reception@scottishstorytellingcentre.com
W www.scottishstorytellingcentre.co.uk

EPSOM: Playhouse   T 01372 742226
Contact: Elaine Teague
Ashley Avenue, Epsom
Surrey KT18 5AL
BO 01372 742555
E eteague@epsom-ewcll.gov.uk
W www.epsomplayhouse.co.uk

EXETER: Exeter Phoenix   T 01392 667060
Contact: Patrick Cunningham (Director)
Bradninch Place, Gandy Street
Exeter, Devon EX4 3LS
BO 01392 667080
E admin@exeterphoenix.org.uk
W www.exeterphoenix.org.uk

FAREHAM:
Ashcroft Arts Centre   T 01329 235161
Contact: Annabel Cook (Director/Programmer)
Osborn Road, Fareham
Hants PO16 7DX
BO 01329 223100
E ashcroft@hants.gov.uk
W www.ashcroft.org.uk

FROME: Merlin Theatre   T 01373 461360
Bath Road, Frome
Somerset BA11 2HG
BO 01373 465949
E admin@merlintheatre.co.uk
W www.merlintheatre.co.uk

GAINSBOROUGH:
Trinity Arts Centre   T 01427 676655
Trinity Street, Gainsborough
Lincolnshire DN21 2AL
E karen.whitfield@west-lindsey.gov.uk
W www.trinityarts.co.uk

GREAT TORRINGTON:
The Plough Arts Centre   T 01805 622552
9-11 Fore Street, Great Torrington
Devon EX38 8HQ
BO 01805 624624
E mail@theploughartscentre.org.uk
W www.theploughartscentre.org.uk

HAVANT: Spring Arts &
Heritage Centre   BO 023 9247 2700
Contact: Amanda O'Reilly (Director)
East Street, Havant
Hants PO9 1BS
E info@thespring.co.uk
W www.thespring.co.uk

HELMSLEY:
Helmsley Arts Centre   T 01439 772112
Contact: Umay Jones (Marketing Manager)
Meeting House Court, Helmsley
York YO62 5DW
BO 01439 771700
E marketinghelmsleyarts@yahoo.co.uk
W www.helmsleyarts.co.uk

HEMEL HEMPSTEAD:
Old Town Hall Theatre   T 01442 228095
Contact: Sara Railson (Art & Entertainment Manager)
High Street, Hemel Hempstead
Herts HP1 3AE
BO 01442 228091
E othadmin@dacorum.gov.uk
W www.oldtownhall.co.uk

HEXHAM: Queens Hall Arts   T 01434 652476
Contact: Geof Keys (Artistic Director)
Beaumont Street, Hexham
Northumberland NE46 3LS
BO 01434 652477
E boxoffice@queenshall.co.uk
W www.queenshall.co.uk

HORSHAM: The Capitol   T 01403 756080
North Street, Horsham
West Sussex RH12 1RG
F 01403 756092
W www.thecapitolhorsham.com

HUDDERSFIELD: Kirklees Communities &
Leisure Services   T 01484 222087
2nd Floor South
Civic Centre 1
Huddersfield HD1 2YU
E arts.creativity@kirklees.gov.uk
W www.kirklees.gov.uk

INVERNESS: Eden Court   T 01463 239841
Contact: Colin Marr (Director)
Bishop's Road, Inverness IV3 5SA
BO 01463 234234
E admin@eden-court.co.uk
W www.eden-court.co.uk

ISLE OF WIGHT: Quay Arts   T 01983 822490
Sea Street, Newport Harbour
Isle of Wight PO30 5BD
F 01983 526606
E info@quayarts.org
W www.quayarts.org

JERSEY: Jersey Arts Centre   T 01534 700400
Contact: Daniel Austin (Director)
Phillips Street, St Helier
Jersey JE2 4SW
BO 01534 700444
E enquiries@artscentre.je
W www.artscentre.je

KENDAL: Brewery Arts Centre   T 01539 722833
Contact: Richard Foster (Chief Executive)
Highgate, Kendal
Cumbria LA9 4HE
BO 01539 725133
E admin@breweryarts.co.uk
W www.breweryarts.co.uk

KING'S LYNN:
King's Lynn Arts Centre   T 01553 779095
29 King Street, King's Lynn
Norfolk PE30 1HA
BO 01553 764864
W www.kingslynnarts.co.uk

LEICESTER: Phoenix Square   T 0116 242 2803
Midland Street
Leicester LE1 1TG
BO 0116 242 2800
W www.phoenix.org.uk

LICHFIELD: Lichfield District
Arts Association   T 01543 262223
Contact: Chris Newcombe (Director)
Donegal House, Bore Street
Lichfield WS13 6LU
E info@lichfieldarts.org.uk
W www.lichfieldarts.org.uk

LISKEARD: Sterts Theatre   T 01579 362962
Upton Cross, Liskeard
Cornwall PL14 5AZ
T 01579 362382
E office2@stertsarts.org
W www.sterts.co.uk

LONDON: The Albany   T 020 8692 4446
Douglas Way, Deptford
London SE8 4AG
F 020 8469 2253
E boxoffice@thealbany.org.uk
W www.thealbany.org.uk

LONDON: The Amadeus   T 020 7286 1686
50 Shirland Road, Little Venice
London W9 2JA
E info@theamadeus.co.uk
W www.theamadeus.co.uk

LONDON: Artsdepot BO 020 8369 5454
5 Nether Street, Tally Ho Corner
North Finchley, London N12 0GA
E info@artsdepot.co.uk
W www.artsdepot.co.uk

LONDON: BAC T 020 7223 6557
Lavender Hill, Battersea
London SW11 5TN
BO 020 7223 2223
E mailbox@bac.org.uk
W www.bac.org.uk

LONDON: Chats Palace T 020 8533 0227
Contact: Sarah Wickens (Centre Director)
42-44 Brooksby's Walk, Hackney
London E9 6DF
E info@chatspalace.com
W www.chatspalace.com

LONDON: The Cockpit T 020 7258 2920
Gateforth Street, London NW8 8EH
BO 020 7258 2925
E mail@thecockpit.org.uk
W www.thecockpit.org.uk

LONDON:
The Hangar Arts Trust T 020 8317 8401
Unit 7A, Mellish House
Harrington Way, London SE18 5NR
E info@hangarartstrust.org
W www.hangarartstrust.org

LONDON:
Hoxton Hall Arts Centre T 020 7684 0060
Contact: Alice de Cent (Administrator)
130 Hoxton Street, London N1 6SH
E info@hoxtonhall.co.uk
W www.hoxtonhall.co.uk

LONDON: Institute of
Contemporary Arts T 020 7930 0493
Contact: Matt Williams (Curator).
No in-house productions or castings
The Mall, London SW1Y 5AH
BO 020 7930 3647
W www.ica.org.uk

LONDON:
Islington Arts Factory T 020 7607 0561
2 Parkhurst Road
London N7 0SF
E info@islingtonartsfactory.org
W www.islingtonartsfactory.org

LONDON: Jacksons Lane T 020 8340 5226
269A Archway Road
London N6 5AA
BO 020 8341 4421
E reception@jacksonslane.org.uk
W www.jacksonslane.org.uk

LONDON:
Menier Chocolate Factory T 020 7378 1712
Contact: David Babani (Artistic Director)
53 Southwark Street, London SE1 1RU
BO 020 7378 1713
E office@menierchocolatefactory.com
W www.menierchocolatefactory.com

LONDON: October Gallery T 020 7831 1618
Contact: Jo Walsh
24 Old Gloucester Street
London WC1N 3AL
F 020 7405 1851
E rentals@octobergallery.co.uk
W www.octobergallery.co.uk

LONDON: Oval House T 020 7582 0080
Contact: Rachel Briscoe & Rebecca Atkinson-Lord
(Directors of Theatre), Deborah Bestwick (Director)
52-54 Kennington Oval
London SE11 5SW
E info@ovalhouse.com
W www.ovalhouse.com

LONDON: Polish Social &
Cultural Association T 020 8741 1940
238-246 King Street, London W6 0RF

LONDON: Riverside Studios T 020 8237 1000
Crisp Road
Hammersmith
London W6 9RL
BO 020 8237 1111
E reception@riversidestudios.co.uk
W www.riversidestudios.co.uk

MAIDENHEAD: Norden Farm
Centre for the Arts T 01628 682555
Contact: Jane Corry (Chief Executive & Artistic Director)
Altwood Road
Maidenhead SL6 4PF
BO 01628 788997
E admin@nordenfarm.org
W www.nordenfarm.org

MAIDSTONE:
Hazlitt Arts Centre T 01622 753922
Contact: Mandy Hare (Theatre & Events Manager)
Earl Street, Maidstone
Kent ME14 1PL
BO 01622 758611
E theatreandevents@maidstone.gov.uk

MANCHESTER: The Lowry BO 0843 2086000
Contact: Steve Cowton (Senior Theatre Programmer)
Pier 8, Salford Quays M50 3AZ
F 0161 876 2021
E boxofficeadmin@thelowry.com
W www.thelowry.com

MILFORD HAVEN:
Torch Theatre T 01646 694192
Contact: Peter Doran (Artistic Director)
St Peter's Road, Milford Haven
Pembrokeshire SA73 2BU
BO 01646 695267
E info@torchtheatre.co.uk
W www.torchtheatre.co.uk

NORWICH:
Norwich Arts Centre T 01603 660387
St Benedicts Street, Norwich
Norfolk NR2 4PG
BO 01603 660352
E stuart@norwichartscentre.co.uk
W www.norwichartscentre.co.uk

NOTTINGHAM:
Lakeside Arts Centre T 0115 846 7777
University Park
Nottingham NG7 2RD
E lakeside-marketing@nottingham.ac.uk
W www.lakesidearts.org.uk

NUNEATON: Abbey Theatre &
Arts Centre T 024 7632 7359
Contact: Tony Deeming (Chairman)
Pool Bank Street
Nuneaton
Warks CV11 5DB
BO 024 7635 4090
E admin@abbeytheatre.co.uk
W www.abbeytheatre.co.uk

PLYMOUTH:
Plymouth Arts Centre　　T 01752 206114
Contact: Kate Sparshatt (Chief Executive Officer)
38 Looe Street, Plymouth, Devon PL4 0EB
F 01752 206118
E info@plymouthartscentre.org
W www.plymouthartscentre.org

POOLE: Lighthouse Poole
Centre for the Arts　　T 0844 4068666
Kingland Road, Poole
Dorset BH15 1UG
W www.lighthousepoole.co.uk

RADLETT: The Radlett Centre　　T 01923 857546
1 Aldenham Avenue, Radlett, Herts WD7 8HL
F 01923 857592
E admin@radlettcentre.com
W www.radlettcentre.co.uk

ROTHERHAM:
Rotherham Civic Theatre　　T 01709 823621 (T/BO)
Contact: Mark Scott (Theatre Manager)
Catherine Street, Rotherham
South Yorkshire S65 1EB
T 01709 823641 (Admin)
E theatre.tickets@rotherham.gov.uk
W www.rotherham.gov.uk/theatres

SALISBURY:
Salisbury Arts Centre　　T 01722 343020
Bedwin Street, Salisbury, Wiltshire SP1 3UT
BO 01722 321744
E info@salisburyarts.co.uk
W www.salisburyartscentre.co.uk

SHREWSBURY: The Gateway
Education & Arts Centre　　T 01743 355159
The Gateway, Chester Street
Shrewsbury, Shropshire SY1 1NB
E gateway.centre@shropshire-cc.gov.uk
W www.shropshire.gov.uk

STAMFORD:
Stamford Arts Centre　　T 01780 480846
Contact: Graham Burley (General Manager)
27 St Mary's Street, Stamford
Lincolnshire PE9 2DL
BO 01780 763203
E boxoffice@stamfordartscentre.com
W www.stamfordartscentre.com

STIRLING:
MacRobert Arts Centre　　T 01786 467155
University of Stirling, Stirling FK9 4LA
BO 01786 466666
E info@macrobert.org
W www.macrobert.org

SWANSEA:
Taliesin Arts Centre　　T 01792 295238
Contact: Sybil Crouch (Head of Cultural Services)
Swansea University, Singleton Park
Swansea SA2 8PZ
BO 01792 602060
E s.e.crouch@swansea.ac.uk
W www.taliesinartscentre.co.uk

TAUNTON: Brewhouse
Theatre & Arts Centre　　T 01823 274608
Contact: Robert Miles (Director)
Coal Orchard, Taunton, Somerset TA1 1JL
BO 01823 283244
E info@thebrewhouse.net
W www.thebrewhouse.net

TOTNES:
The Arts at Dartington　　T 01803 847074
Dartington Space
Dartington Hall
Totnes, Devon TQ9 6EN
BO 01803 847070
E arts@dartington.org
W www.dartington.org/arts

TUNBRIDGE WELLS:
Trinity Theatre　　T 01892 678670
Church Road, Tunbridge Wells
Kent TN1 1JP
BO 01892 678678
E enquiries@trinitytheatre.net

ULEY: Prema　　T 01453 860703
Contact: Gordon Scott (Director)
South Street, Uley
Nr Dursley, Glos GL11 5SS
E info@prema.demon.co.uk
W www.prema.org.uk

VALE OF GLAMORGAN:
St Donats Arts Centre　　T 01446 799099
Contact: Sharon Stone (General Manager)
St Donats Castle, The Vale of Glamorgan CF61 1WF
BO 01446 799100
E admin@stdonats.com

WAKEFIELD:
Wakefield Arts Centre　　T 01924 789815
Wakefield College
Thornes Park Centre
Thornes Park, Horbury Road, Wakefield WF2 8QZ
BO 01924 211311
W www.theatreroyalwakefield.co.uk

WASHINGTON:
The Arts Centre Washington　　T 0191 219 3455
Biddick Lane, Fatfield
Washington, Tyne & Wear NE38 8AB
F 0191 219 3458
E matthew.blyth@sunderland.gov.uk

WELLINGBOROUGH:
The Castle　　T 01933 229022
Contact: Gail Arnott (Executive Director),
Nik Ashton (Artistic Director)
Castle Way, Wellingborough
Northants NN8 1XA
BO 01933 270007
E info@thecastle.org.uk
W www.thecastle.org.uk

WIMBORNE: Layard Theatre　　T 01202 847529
Contact: Chris Thomas (Director of Drama),
Christine Haynes (Administrator)
Canford School
Canford Magna
Wimborne, Dorset BH21 3AD
BO 01202 847525
E layardtheatre@canford.com

WINDSOR: The Firestation
Centre for Arts & Culture　　T 01753 866865
The Old Court
St Leonards Road
Windsor, Berks SL4 3BL
E info@firestationartscentre.com
W www.firestationartscentre.com

WREXHAM: Oriel Wrecsam　　T 01978 292093
Rhosddu Road, Wrexham LL11 1AU
E oriel.wrecsam@wrexham.gov.uk

C

Casting Directors
Consultants
Costumes, Wigs & Make-Up
Critics

CDG
For information regarding membership of
the Casting Directors' Guild please see:

W www.thecdg.co.uk

Casting Directors

Who are casting directors?

Casting directors are employed by directors/ production companies to source the best available actors for roles across TV, film, radio, theatre and commercials. They do the groundwork and present a shortlist of artists to the director, who often makes the final selection. Many casting directors work on a freelance basis, others are employed permanently by larger organisations such as the BBC or the National Theatre. Discovering new and emerging talent also plays an important part in their job.

Why should I approach them?

If you are an actor looking for work, you can promote yourself directly to casting directors by sending them your photo and CV. They keep actors' details on file and may consider you for future productions. Bear in mind that you will not be guaranteed a response as casting directors are physically unable to reply to every one of the vast numbers of letters they receive from actors, but it is worth your while to explore this opportunity to find work.

How should I approach them?

Many of the following casting directors have indicated the method in which they prefer actors to contact them for the first time. This tends to be by post but some accept or prefer e-mails. Some are happy to receive telephone calls, but be aware that casting directors are very busy and you should not continually call them with questions or updates once you have sent your CV. If they have not specified whether they prefer postal or e-mail contact, you should send them your CV, a headshot and a covering letter by post only, as this is the traditional method of contacting casting professionals. You should **always** include a stamped-addressed envelope (SAE) big enough to contain your 10 x 8 photo and with sufficient postage. This will increase your chances of getting a reply. Write your name and telephone number on the back of your headshot in case it gets separated from your CV.

Should I send a casting director my showreel and/or voicereel?

Some casting directors have also indicated that they are happy for actors to send showreels and/ or voicereels along with their CVs and headshots, but if this is not specified, we would recommend that you leave these out of your correspondence but highlight in your covering letter that they are available. If a casting director is interested in you, they can contact you later for these items, but they usually prefer not to sift through hundreds of unsolicited showreels until they have first established an interest in an actor.

How do I target my search?

It is not advisable to send a generic CV to every casting director listed in this section. Research the names and companies and then target your letters accordingly. Find out what areas of the industry each one usually casts for (some specify this in their listing) and what productions they have previously cast. Keep an eye on TV, film and theatre credits so you become familiar with the casting directors used for different productions. Some of these casting directors have their own websites. If a casting director has 'CDG Member' after their name, it means they are a member of the Casting Directors' Guild, the professional organisation of casting directors working in the UK (see www.thecdg.co.uk for more information and their case study in this section).

How do I write an effective CV and covering letter?

Once you have made a short-list of suitable casting directors you should send them your CV, your headshot, and an individually tailored covering letter. The covering letter should demonstrate that you have researched the casting director, and ideally you will have a particular reason for contacting them at this time: perhaps you can tell them about your next showcase, or where they can see you currently appearing. Your CV should be no longer than one page, up-to-date and spell-checked. Please see the 'Promotional Services' section of Contacts for further advice on writing CVs and covering letters.

How do I prepare for a casting/audition?

Make sure you are fully prepared with accurate information about the audition time, venue, format and the people you will be meeting. Unless it's a last minute casting, you should always read the script in advance and try to have some opinions on it. If you are asked in advance to prepare a piece, always stick to the brief with something suitable and relevant.

On the day, allow plenty of time to get there so you are not flustered when you arrive. Try to be positive and enjoy yourself. Remember, the casting director doesn't want to spend several days auditioning - they want you to get the job! Never criticise previous productions you have worked on. And at the end of the casting, remember to take your script away unless you are asked to leave it, otherwise it can look as if you're not interested.

Please see 'Rehearsal Rooms and Casting Suites' for more detailed advice on preparing for and attending auditions.

Should I attend a casting in a house or flat?

Professional auditions are rarely held anywhere other than an official casting studio or venue. Be very wary if you are asked to go elsewhere. Trust your instincts. If something doesn't seem right to you, it probably isn't. Always take someone with you if you are in any doubt.

How do I become a casting director?

The best way to gain experience in this field is to work as a casting assistant. Vacancies are sometimes advertised in The Stage www.thestage.co.uk or PCR www.pcrnewsletter.com. Alternatively you could try sending your CV to casting directors asking for an internship or work experience. Just as we advise actors, remember to research any casting director you are considering approaching to make sure they actually work in the area you are interested in. Work experience is likely to be unpaid, but the experience and contacts you gain will be invaluable. You may find it helpful to refer to Equity's advice leaflet *Low Pay/No Pay* which is available to all Equity members from their website's members' area.

Casting Directors

CASE STUDY

When you read CDG after a Casting Director's name, you know he/she is a member of The Casting Directors' Guild and will therefore have a minimum of five years' experience. The current CDG Committee has the following advice for actors.

Casting directors are there to help actors and not to hinder them. We want you to do your best as that reflects back on us, and you should realise that we are only as good as the actors we submit for each role.

Much of our work consists of creating a shortlist of potential actors and reducing it to a suitably sized group to present for audition. We also spend a great deal of time watching you work. Members of the CDG endeavour to cover as many performances as possible on film, television and in the theatre. There is no substitute to seeing you act.

When asked to attend an interview or audition, an actor should feel confident in asking his/her agent any relevant questions about the role and the project. If this is not forthcoming, arrive early and seek information from the casting director or, better still, contact him/her the day before. If it is only possible to speak to the casting director on the day, preferably do so before entering the audition room, rather than in front of the director or producer. The casting director will be happy to help.

Sometimes you will only receive pages for a role, but a casting director will always endeavour to give you as much information about a character as is available. When possible, read the entire play/screenplay rather than just the scenes your 'character' appears in, and ideally be able to talk about the script as a whole during the interview. Take your time when reading; preparation is worth a lot but don't be fazed if you get lost over their script. If you feel that a scene is going terribly it's ok to start again.

For most non-theatre jobs these days you will find that your meeting will be recorded on video tape. These tapes are then shown to the various producers involved, and this is when the process can slow down. It takes time to build a company and for final casting choices to be made.

Casting is a matter of interpretation. As well as character information derived from the script, the vision of the producer, director, casting director and indeed the actor all come into play.

There are many reasons why one actor will be chosen over another, and even the best audition might not necessarily secure a part. Every aspect of the actor comes into play. Is he/she too young or too mature? Do they work as a family? Could they be mother and son? Does the chemistry work? There is also the frustrating problem of scripts, and parts, being re-written. A character may have an entirely different physical description in a later draft. Sadly we do not have control over this.

When it comes to contacting casting directors, most are happy to receive letters, updated photos and CVs. The best correspondence for casting directors to receive is performance information. Letters should be brief and to the point, with the production name, director, venue and/or TV channel clearly stated. If you are enquiring about work be as specific as possible, e.g. "I would like to be seen for the part of … in … because …" or something similar. Dear Sir or Madam letters just don't work.

CVs should be well laid out. List most recent work first and use your spell checker. 6x4 photos are fine to send but include an SAE if you want them returned. Casting directors rarely like unsolicited DVDs and showreels: you must be aware that we do get inundated. Also bear in mind that not receiving a response to your letter does not mean it hasn't been read and filed: it is virtually impossible to reply to the volume of mail received from actors.

In our greener world it's great that Spotlight and other web media now have the facility for us to view CVs, photos and showreels online. Use the technology: it's very easy to keep your CV up-to-date online and you can change your photo at any time of year without having to do a huge mail out to let people know.

Actors are a fundamental tool of this industry: CDG members are aware of this and aim to put actors at their ease. Audition nerves are a given but you should feel secure that the reason you are in the room is because someone wants you to get that role and not because they want to see you fail.

To find out more about the CDG visit www.thecdg.co.uk

Valerie Colgan

- For professional actors who need a voice production "MOT"

- Private individual classes

- Valerie Colgan and a consortium of tutors as appropriate on audition technique

Ex Head of Drama at the City Lit • 5 Drama Schools • The Actors Centre
Tel: 020 7267 2153 The Green, 17 Herbert Street, London NW5 4HA

1066 PRODUCTIONS   T 020 7193 6156
8 Blackstone House, Off Bowen Drive
West Dulwich, London SE21 8NY
E loischada@1066productions.com
W www.1066productions.com

A C A CASTING   T/F 020 7384 2635
Contact: Catherine Arton
32A Edenvale Street
London SW6 2SF
E catherine@acacasting.com

ADAMSON-PARKER, Jo   T 0113 219 2896
Northern Spirit Creative (Casting)
Studio 81, Kirkstall Road, Leeds LS3 1LH
T 07787 311270
E jo@northernspiritcreative.co.uk
W www.northernspiritcreative.co.uk

AILION, Pippa   T/F 020 8670 4816
CDG Member
3 Towton Road, London SE27 9EE
E enquiries@pippaailioncasting.co.uk

ALL DIRECTIONS OF LONDON
Contact: By Post only
7 Rupert Court, Off Wardour Street
London W1D 6EB

ANDERSON, Jane
CDG Member. Contact: By e-mail. Accepts Showreels.
Film. Television
E casting@janeandersononline.com
W www.janeandersononline.com

ANDREW, Dorothy CASTING   T 0161 344 2709
CDG Member
E dorothyandrewcasting@gmail.com

ARNOLD, Jim CASTING   T 07973 942220
Contact: By Post/e-mail only.
Accepts Showreels/Voicereels
51 St Martin's Lane, London WC2N 4EA
E jim@jacasting.co.uk
W www.jacasting.co.uk

ASHTON HINKINSON CASTING   T 020 7580 6101
Unit 15, Panther House
38 Mount Pleasant, London WC1X 0AN
E casting@ahcasting.com
W www.ashtonhinkinson.com

BAIG, Shaheen CASTING   T 020 7631 5258
PO Box 7006, London W1A 1US
E info@shaheenbaigcasting.com
W www.shaheenbaigcasting.com

BARNES, Derek   T 020 8228 7096
CDG Member
BBC DRAMA SERIES CASTING
BBC Elstree, Room N221
Neptune House, Clarendon Road
Borehamwood, Herts WD6 1JF
F 020 8228 8311

BARNETT, Briony   T 020 7836 3751
CDG Member
11 Goodwins Court, London WC2N 4LL

BEACH CASTING LTD   T 0844 5679595
Contact: Brendan McNamara
405 Strand, London WC2R 0NE
T 07903 630964
E brendan@beach-casting.com
W www.beach-casting.com

BEASTALL, Lesley CASTING   T 020 7727 6496
Contact: Lesley Beastall
41E Elgin Crescent, London W11 2JD
T 07956 516603
E lesley@lbcasting.co.uk

BEAUCHAMP, Lauren CASTING   T 07961 982198
34A Brightside, Billericay CM12 0LJ
F 01277 656147
E laurenbeauchamp@talktalk.net

BECKLEY, Rowland
BBC DRAMA SERIES CASTING
BBC Elstree, Room N222
Neptune House, Clarendon Road
Borehamwood, Herts WD6 1JF
F 020 8228 7130

BERTRAND, Leila CASTING   T/F 020 8964 0683
53 Hormead Road, London W9 3NQ
E leilabcasting@gmail.com

BEVAN, Lucy   T 020 8567 6655
CDG Member
Ealing Studios, Ealing Green
London W5 5EP

BEWICK, Maureen   T 020 8450 1604
104A Dartmouth Road
London NW2 4HB

BIRD, Sarah   T 020 7371 3248
CDG Member
PO Box 32658, London W14 0XA

BLIGH, Nicky
CDG Member
E nicky@nickyblighcasting.com

BRACKE, Siobhan   T 020 8891 5686
CDG Member. Contact: By Post
Basement Flat, 22A The Barons
St Margaret's TW1 2AP

BUCKINGHAM, Jo   T 07753 605491
CDG Member
E jo@jobuckinghamcasting.co.uk

CANDID CASTING   T 020 7490 8882
2G Woodstock Studios
36 Woodstock Grove, London W12 8LE
E mail@candidcasting.co.uk
W www.candidcasting.co.uk

CANNON, John   T 020 8228 7322
CDG Member
BBC DRAMA SERIES CASTING
BBC Elstree, Room N223, Neptune House
Clarendon Road, Borehamwood, Herts WD6 1JF
F 020 8228 8311
E john.cannon@bbc.co.uk

**CANNON DUDLEY
& ASSOCIATES**   T 020 7433 3393
*Contact: Carol Dudley (CDG Member). By Post.
Film. Stage. Television*
43A Belsize Square, London NW3 4HN
F 020 7813 2048
E cdacasting@blueyonder.co.uk

CARROLL, Anji   T 01630 647242
*CDG Member. Contact: By e-mail (Small Attachments
only). Film. Stage. Television*
T 07957 253769
E anji@anjicarroll.tv

CASTING ANGELS THE   T/F 020 8313 0443
Based in London & Paris
Suite 4, 14 College Road
Bromley, Kent BR1 3NS

CASTING COMPANY (UK) THE
Contact: Michelle Guish
E casting@michguish.com

CASTING CONNECTION THE   T 0161 432 4122
Contact: Michael Syers
Dalrossie House, 16 Victoria Grove
Stockport, Cheshire SK4 5BU

CASTING COUCH THE   T 07932 785807
Contact: Moira Townsend. No CVs/Photos by Post
213 Trowbridge Road, Bradford on Avon
Wiltshire BA15 1EU
E moira@everymansland.com

CASTING FOX THE   T 01628 771084
Contact: By e-mail only
E assistant@thecastingfox.co.uk

CATLIFF, Suzy   T 020 8442 0749
CDG Member
PO Box 39492, London N10 3YX
E soosecat@mac.com
W www.suzycatliff.co.uk

CHAND, Urvashi   T 020 8208 3861
CDG Member
Cinecraft, 69 Teignmouth Road
London NW2 4EA
E urvashi@cinecraft.biz

CHARD, Alison   T 020 7223 9125
CDG Member
23 Groveside Court, 4 Lombard Road
Battersea, London SW11 3RQ
E chardcasting@btinternet.com

CHARKHAM CASTING   T 07956 456630
Contact: Beth Charkham
Suite 361, 14 Tottenham Court Road
London W1T 1JY
E charkhamcasting@btconnect.com

CLARK, Andrea   T 020 7381 9933
Adults & Children. Commercials. Film. Stage. Television
PO Box 66300, London SW6 9FS
E andrea@aclarkcasting.com
W www.aclarkcasting.com

CLAYPOLE, Sam CASTING
PO Box 123, Darlington
Durham DL3 7WA
E contact@samclaypolecasting.com
W www.samclaypolecasting.com

CLAYTON, Rosalie   T/F 020 3605 6338
CDG Member
E rosalie@rosalieclayton.com

CLOUTER, Lou CASTING   T 07905 146271
79 Empress Avenue, Aldersbrook
London E12 5SA
E lou@loucloutercasting.com
W www.loucloutercasting.com

COGAN, Ben   T 020 8228 7516
BBC DRAMA SERIES CASTING
BBC Elstree, Room N221
Neptune House, Clarendon Road
Borehamwood, Herts WD6 1JF
F 020 8228 8311

COLLINS, Jayne CASTING   T 020 7223 0471
CDG Member
The Price Building, 110 York Road
London SW11 3RD
E info@jaynecollinscasting.com
W www.jaynecollinscasting.com

COLLYER-BRISTOW, Ellie   T 07986 607075
35 Blackheath Park, London SE3 9RW
E elliecollyerbristow@yahoo.co.uk

CORDORAY, Lin
66 Cardross Street, London W6 0DR

COTTON, Irene   T 020 8299 1595
CDG Member
25 Druce Road, Dulwich Village
London SE21 7DW
T/F 020 8299 2787
E irenecotton@btinternet.com

CRAMPSIE, Julia   T 020 8228 7170
CDG Member. Casting Executive
BBC DRAMA SERIES CASTING, BBC Elstree
Room N224, Neptune House, Clarendon Road
Borehamwood, Herts WD6 1JF
F 020 8228 8311

CRANE, Carole CASTING   T 07976 869442
E crane.shot@virgin.net

CRAWFORD, Kahleen CASTING   T 0141 425 1725
Film City Glasgow, Govan Town Hall
401 Govan Road, Glasgow G51 2QJ
T 07950 414164
E casting@kahleencrawford.com
W www.kahleencrawford.com

**CROCODILE CASTING
COMPANY THE**   T 020 8203 7009
Contact: Claire Toeman, Tracie Saban. By e-mail only
E croccast@aol.com
W www.crocodilecasting.com

CROSS, Louise   **T** 020 8341 2200
CDG Member
128A North View Road, London N8 7LP

CROWE, Sarah CASTING   **T** 020 7286 5080
75 Amberley Road
London W9 2JL
F 020 7286 5030
E sarah@sarahcrowecasting.co.uk

CROWLEY, Suzanne
CDG Member. See CROWLEY POOLE CASTING

CROWLEY POOLE CASTING   **T** 020 7379 5965
Contact: Suzanne Crowley (CDG Member),
Gilly Poole (CDG Member)
11 Goodwins Court
London WC2N 4LL

DAVIES, Jane CASTING   **T** 020 8715 1036
Contact: Jane Davies (CDG Member), John Connor
E info@janedaviescasting.co.uk

DAVIS, Leo (Miss)
See JUST CASTING

DAVY, Gary   **T** 020 7713 0888
CDG Member. Film. Television
Top Floor, 15 Crinan Street
York Way, Kings Cross
London N1 9SQ
E casting@garydavy.com

DAWES, Gabrielle   **T** 020 7435 3645
CDG Member
PO Box 52493
London NW3 9DZ
E gdawescasting@tiscali.co.uk

DAWES, Stephanie   **T** 07802 566642
CDG Member
13 Nevern Square, London SW5 9NW
E stephaniedawes5@gmail.com

DAY, Kate   **T/F** 01865 858709
Pound Cottage, 27 The Green South
Warborough, Oxon OX10 7DR

DE FREITAS, Paul
CDG Member
E info@pauldefreitas.com

DEITCH, Jane ASSOCIATES   **T** 020 7395 7525
80-81 St Martin's Lane
London WC2N 4AA
E casting@janedeitch.co.uk

DICKENS, Laura   **T** 07958 665468
CDG Member
197 Malpas Road, London SE4 1BH
E dickenscasting@aol.com
W www.lauradickens.com

DONNELLY, Laura CASTING   **T** 07917 414014
CV & Showreel on request. Film. Stage. Television
E laura@lauradonnellycasting.com
W www.lauradonnellycasting.com

DOWD, Kate   **T** 020 7828 8071
3rd Floor, 18 Buckingham Palace Road
London SW1W 0QP

DOWLING ERDELY CASTING   **T** 07958 391198
2 Eleanor Road, London N11 2QS
T 07970 071605
E info@dowlingerdely.com
W www.dowlingerdely.com

DRURY, Malcolm　　　T 020 8748 9232
CDG Member
34 Tabor Road, London W6 0BW

DUDLEY, Carol
CDG Member. See CANNON DUDLEY & ASSOCIATES

DUFF, Julia　　　T 020 7836 5557
CDG Member
PO Box 67506, London EC1P 1PH
E info@juliaduff.co.uk

DUFF, Maureen　　　T 020 7586 0532
CDG Member
PO Box 47340, London NW3 4TY
E info@maureenduffcasting.com

EAST, Irene CASTING　　　T 020 8876 5686
CDG Member. Contact: By Post. Film. Stage
40 Brookwood Avenue, Barnes
London SW13 0LR
E irneast@aol.com

EDWARDS, Daniel CASTING　　　T 020 7835 5616
CDG Member
E daniel@danieledwardscasting.com

EH7 CASTING　　　T 07711 760387
9 Claremont Bank, Edinburgh EH7 4DR
E contact@eh7casting.com
W www.eh7casting.com

EJ CASTING　　　T 020 7564 2688
PO Box 63617, London SW9 1AN
T 07891 632946
E info@ejcasting.com

EMMERSON, Chloe　　　T 020 8748 1336
Contact: By e-mail
20 Cumberland Road, London SW13 9LY
E c@chloeemmerson.com

EVANS, Camilla CASTING　　　T 07768 977050
CDG Member
E camilla@camillaevans.com
W www.thecdg.co.uk

EVANS, Richard　　　T 020 8994 6304
CDG Member
10 Shirley Road, London W4 1DD
E contact@evanscasting.co.uk
W www.evanscasting.co.uk

EYE CASTING THE　　　T 020 7377 2700
1st Floor, 92 Commercial Street
Off Puma Court, London E1 6LZ
E jody@theeyecasting.com
W www.theeyecasting.com

FEARNLEY, Ali CASTING　　　T 020 7613 7320
3rd Floor, 58-60 Rivington Street, London EC2A 3AU
T 07764 945614
E cast@alifearnley.com

FIGGIS, Susie　　　T 020 7482 2200
19 Spencer Rise, London NW5 1AR

FILDES, Bunny CASTING　　　T 020 7935 1254
CDG Member
56 Wigmore Street, London W1

FOX, Celestia　　　T 020 7720 6143
23 Leppoc Road, London SW4 9LS
E celestiafox@me.com

FRAZER, Janie
CDG Member
E janiefrazercasting@gmail.com

FRECK, Rachel　　　T/F 020 8673 2455
CDG Member
E casting@rachelfreck.com

FREE RANGE CASTING　　　T 020 7686 8676
Contact: Sandy Tedford
Highbury Barn Studio
23A Highbury Park
London N5 1TH
T 07854 794007
E sandy@freerangecasting.com
W www.freerangecasting.com

FREND, Amanda
87 Swindon Road, Horsham
West Sussex RH12 2HF
E amandafrendcasting@hotmail.co.uk

FRISBY, Jane CASTING　　　T 020 8341 4747
Contact: By e-mail. Accepts Showreels.
Commercials. Corporates. Feature Films
51 Ridge Road, London N8 9LJ
E janefrisby@hotmail.co.uk

FRUITCAKE　　　T 020 7993 6042
Studio 125, 77 Beak Street
London W1F 9DB
T 020 7993 5165
E info@fruitcakelondon.com
W www.fruitcakelondon.com

FUNNELL, Caroline　　　T 020 7326 4417
CDG Member
25 Rattray Road, London SW2 1AZ

GANE CASTING　　　T 020 8446 2551
Contact: Natasha Gane
52 Woodhouse Road, London N12 0RJ
T 07970 535911
E natasha@ganecasting.com

GILLHAM, Tracey CASTING　　　T 020 3620 8013
CDG Member
Teddington Studios
G06 Weir Cottage
Broom Road, Teddington TW11 9NT
E tracey@traceygillhamcasting.co.uk

GILLON, Tamara CASTING　　　T 020 8766 0099
26 Carson Road, London SE21 8HU
F 020 8265 6330
E tamara@tamaragillon.com
W www.tamaragillon.com

GLOBAL7　　　T/F 020 7281 7679
PO Box 56232, London N4 4XP
T 07956 956652
E global7castings@gmail.com
W www.global7casting.com

GOLD, Nina　　　T 020 8960 6099
CDG Member
117 Chevening Road, London NW6 6DU
F 020 8968 6777
E info@ninagold.co.uk

GOOCH, Miranda CASTING　　　T 020 8962 9578
Contact: By Post/e-mail. Accepts Showreels/Voicereels.
Film. Stage. Television
102 Leighton Gardens, London NW10 3PR
F 020 8962 9579
E mirandagooch@gmail.com

GREEN, Jill CASTING　　　T 020 8815 1825
CDG Member
PO Box 56927, London N10 3UR

SHEILA BURNETT

P H O T O G R A P H Y

Damian Lewis

Caroline Quentin

Kitty Lovett

Michael Absalom

020 7289 3058

www.sheilaburnett-headshots.com

Student Rates

GREENE, Francesca
CASTING   T 020 8450 5577
37 Keyes Road, London NW2 3XB
E francesca@francescagreene.co.uk
W www.francescagreenecasting.com

GROSVENOR, Angela   T 020 8244 5665
CDG Member
66 Woodland Road, London SE19 1PA
E angela.grosvenor@virgin.net

GUISH, Michelle
See CASTING COMPANY (UK) THE

HALL, Janet   T 01706 377900
3 Shore Road, Littleborough, Lances OL15 9LG
T 07956 822773
E janethall1@yahoo.co.uk

HALL, Pippa
Children. Teenagers
E pippa@pippahallcasting.com

HAMMOND, Louis   T 020 7927 8392
97 Mortimer Street, London W1W 7SU
E louis.hammond@virgin.net

HAMMOND COX
CASTING   T 07779 084425 (Thom)
Contact: Thom Hammond, Michael Cox
T 07834 362691 (Michael)
E office@hammondcoxcasting.com
W www.hammondcoxcasting.com

HAMPSON, Janet CASTING   T 07931 513223
E janet@janethampson.co.uk

HANCOCK, Gemma
CDG Member. Contact: By e-mail
E gemma@hancockstevenson.com

HARKIN, Julie CASTING   T 020 7251 6210
CDG Member
5 Albemarle Way, London EC1V 4JB
E julie@julieharkincasting.com

HAWES, Jo   T 01628 773048
CDG Member.
Children's Casting & Administration for Stage
21 Westfield Road
Maidenhead, Berkshire SL6 5AU
T 07824 337222
E jo.hawes@virgin.net
W www.johawes.com

HAWSER, Gillian CASTING   T 020 7731 5988
CDG/CSA Member. Contact: Gillian Hawser
24 Cloncurry Street, London SW6 6DS
F 020 7731 0738
E gillianhawser@btinternet.com

HB CASTING   T 020 7871 2969
Kemp House
152-160 City Road, London EC1V 2NX
T 07957 114175
E hannah@hbcasting.com
W www.hbcasting.com

HB CASTING   T 0161 241 7786
83 Ducie Street, Manchester M1 2JQ
T 07957 114175
E hannah@hbcasting.com
W www.hbcasting.com

HILL, Serena   T 00 61 2 92501727
Sydney Theatre Company, Pier 4, Hickson Road
Walsh Bay, NSW 2000, Australia
E shill@sydneytheatre.com.au

HOLM, Lissy
See JUST CASTING

HOOTKINS, Polly   T 020 7692 1184
CDG Member. Contact: By e-mail
6 Howitt Close, London NW3 4LX
T 07545 784294
E phootkins@clara.net

HORAN, Julia   T 020 7267 5261
CDG Member
26 Falkland Road, London NW5 2PX

HUBBARD CASTING   T 020 7631 4944
Contact: Dan Hubbard (CDG Member), Amy Hubbard
(CDG Member), Ros Hubbard (CDG Member),
John Hubbard (CDG Member). No Showreels
14 Rathbone Place
London W1T 1HT
F 020 7636 7117
E info@hubbardcasting.com

HUGHES, Sarah   T 020 8291 0304
CDG Member
E sarahhughescasting@gmail.com
W www.sarahhughescasting.co.uk

HUGHES, Sylvia   T 07770 520007
Casting Suite, The Deanwater
Wilmslow Road, Woodford
Cheshire SK7 1RJ
E sylviahughes007@gmail.com

IN HOUSE CASTING   T 07921 843508
12 Cliffe House
Blackwall Lane, London SE10 0RB
F 020 8588 5444
E mark@inhousecasting.com
W www.inhousecasting.com

JAFFA, Janis CASTING   T 020 8740 1629
CDG Member. Contact: By Post. Accepts Showreels
2 Landor Walk
London W12 9AP
E janis@janisjaffacasting.co.uk

JAFFREY, Jennifer   T 07973 617168
Contact: By Post
136 Hicks Avenue
Greenford, Middlesex UB6 8HB
E jennifer.jaffrey@gmail.com

JAY, Jina CASTING   T 020 8607 8888
CDG Member
Office 2, Sound Centre
Twickenham Film Studios
The Barons, St Margarets
Twickenham, Middlesex TW1 2AW
F 020 8607 8982

JENKINS, Lucy
CDG Member. See JENKINS McSHANE CASTING

JENKINS, Victor
CDG Member. See VHJ CASTING

JENKINS McSHANE CASTING   T 020 8943 5328
Contact: Lucy Jenkins (CDG Member)
74 High Street
Hampton Wick
Kingston on Thames KT1 4DQ
E lucy@jenkinsmcshanecasting.com

JENKINS McSHANE CASTING   T 020 8693 7411
Contact: Sooki McShane (CDG Member)
8A Piermont Road, East Dulwich
London SE22 0LN
E sooki@jenkinsmcshanecasting.com

JN PRODUCTION & CASTING T 020 7324 2630
Contact: Paul Hunt
27 Cowper Street, London EC2A 4AP
F 020 7253 6627
E paul@jncasting.com

JOHN, Priscilla T 020 8741 4212
CDG Member
PO Box 22477, London W6 0GT
F 020 8741 4005

JOHNSON, Alex CASTING T 020 7229 8779
15 McGregor Road, London W11 1DE
E alex@alexjohnsoncasting.com

JOHNSON, Marilyn T 020 7497 5552
CDG Member
1st Floor, 11 Goodwins Court
London WC2N 4LL
E casting@marilynjohnsoncasting.com

JONES, Doreen T 020 8746 3782
CDG Member
PO Box 22478, London W6 0WJ
F 020 8748 8533
E artists@dorcast.co.uk

JONES, Lenka T 07921 182055
Coach House, Pinewood Road
Iver Heath, Buckinghamshire SL0 0NH
E lenki13@yahoo.co.uk

JONES, Sue
CDG Member
E info@suejones.net

JUST CASTING T 020 7229 3471
20th Century Theatre, 291 Westbourne Grove
London W11 2QA
F 020 7792 2143

KATE & LOU CASTING T 07885 763429
Twitter: @kateandloucast
The Basement, Museum House
25 Museum Street, London WC1A 1JT
T 07976 252531
E cast@kateandloucasting.com
W www.kateandloucasting.com

**KENNEDY, Anna
CASTING LTD** T 020 8677 6710
8 Rydal Road, London SW16 1QN
E anna@kennedycasting.com

**KEOGH, Beverley
CASTING LTD** T 0161 273 4400
29 Ardwick Green North, Ardwick Green
Manchester M12 6DL
F 0161 273 4401
E drama@beverleykeogh.tv

KESTER, Gaby
E casting@gabykester.com

KHANDO CASTING T 020 3463 8492
1 Marlborough Court, London W1F 7EE
E casting@khandoentertainment.com
W www.khandoentertainment.com

KING, Belinda CASTING T 020 7826 8506
45 Beech Street, Barbican, London EC2Y 8AD
F 020 7826 8507
E casting@belindaking.com

KING, Cassandra CASTING T 020 8977 2345
73 Victor Road, Teddington TW11 8SP
T 07813 320673
E cassyking@yahoo.co.uk

KLIMEK, Nana CASTING T 020 3222 0035
RichMix 1st Floor West
35-47 Bethnal Green Road
London E1 6LA
E casting@nanaklimek.com
W www.nanaklimek.com

KNIGHT-SMITH, Jerry T 0161 615 6761
CDG Member
c/o Royal Exchange Theatre Company
St Ann's Square, Manchester M2 7DH

KOREL, Suzy T 020 7586 9611
CDG Member
T 07973 506793
E suzy@korel.org

KRUGER, Beatrice T 00 39 06 92956808
FBI Casting S.r.l., 17 via della Scala
00153 Roma, Italy
F 00 39 06 23328203
E beatrice.kruger@fbicasting.it
W www.fbicasting.com

KYLE, Greg T 020 8876 6763
71B North Worple Way, Mortlake
London SW14 8PR
E kylecasting@btinternet.com

LADIDA T 020 7462 0790
17 Percy Street, London W1T 1DU
F 020 7462 0791
E casting@ladidagroup.com
W www.ladidagroup.com

LARCA LTD T 07779 321954
Welsh Language/English.
Commercials. Film. Stage. Television
Ynyslas Uchaf Farm, Blackmill
Bridgend CF35 6DW
F 01656 841815
W www.leigh-annregancasting.co.uk

LEVENE, Jon T 020 7792 8501
T 07977 570899
E jonlevene@mac.com
W www.jonlevenecasting.co.uk

LINDSAY-STEWART, Karen T 020 7439 0544
CDG Member
E asst@klscasting.co.uk

LIP SERVICE CASTING LTD T 020 7734 3393
Contact: By e-mail. Accepts Voicereels. Voice Overs only
60-66 Wardour Street, London W1F 0TA
F 020 7734 3373
E bookings@lipservice.co.uk
W www.lipservice.co.uk

LITTLE NARRATIVES CASTING T 01509 828365
Contact: Clair Haynes
20 Hawcliffe Road, Mountsorrel, Leicester LE12 7AA
E info@littlenarratives.com
W www.littlenarratives.com/casting

LUNN, Maggie T 020 7420 9875
CDG Member
1st Floor, 26-28 Neal Street
Covent Garden, London WC2H 9QQ
E maggie@maggielunn.co.uk

MAD DOG CASTING LTD T 020 7269 7910
Contact: By Post/e-mail. Accepts Showreels/Voicereels.
Real People. Street Casting
2nd Floor, Holborn Hall
193-197 High Holborn, London WC1V 7BD
E info@maddogcasting.com

MAGSON, Kay T 0113 236 0251
CDG Member. Contact: By e-mail. Stage
PO Box 175, Pudsey
Leeds LS28 7WY
E kay.magson@btinternet.com

MARCH, Heather CASTING T 020 8981 4184
Contact: By e-mail. Commercials. Idents. Photographic
Unit P10 Bow Wharf
221 Grove Road
London E3 5SN
E hm@heathermarchcasting.com
W www.heathermarchcasting.com

McDAID-WREN, Ri T 07814 803808
Contact: By e-mail
Based in London
E ri@ri-mcd.com

McLEOD, Carolyn CASTING T 07946 476425
Contact: By e-mail only. Commercials. Film. Television
1st Floor, 193 Wardour Street
London W1F 8ZD
E info@cmcasting.co.uk
W www.cmcasting.co.uk

McLEOD, Thea T 07941 541314
E mcleodcasting@hotmail.com

McMURRICH, Chrissie T 020 8568 0137
Contact: By Post. Accepts Showreels
16 Spring Vale Avenue, Brentford
Middlesex TW8 9QH

McSHANE, Sooki
CDG Member. See JENKINS McSHANE CASTING

McWILLIAMS, Debbie T 020 7564 8860
T 07785 575805
E debbie@dmcwcasting.com

MEULENBERG, Thea T 00 31 20 6265846
Keizersgracht 116, 1015 CW
Amsterdam, The Netherlands
E info@theameulenberg.com
W www.theameulenberg.com

MILLER, Hannah
CDG Member. See ROYAL SHAKESPEARE COMPANY

MOISELLE, Frank T 00 353 1 2802857
7 Corrig Avenue, Dun Laoghaire
Co. Dublin, Ireland
F 00 353 1 2803277

MOISELLE, Nuala T 00 353 1 2802857
7 Corrig Avenue, Dun Laoghaire
Co. Dublin, Ireland
F 00 353 1 2803277

MOORE, Stephen T 020 8228 7109
CDG Member
BBC DRAMA SERIES CASTING
BBC Elstree, Room N222
Neptune House, Clarendon Road
Borehamwood, Herts WD6 1JF
F 020 8228 8311

MORGAN, Andy CASTING T 020 8674 5375
CDG Member
Coach House, 114 Palace Road
London SW2 3JZ

MORLEY, Adam T 07855 133836
The Lodge, Wentworth Hall
The Ridgeway
Mill Hill, London NW7 1RJ
E adam.e.morley@gmail.com

MORRISON, Melika T/F 020 7381 1571
Contact: By Post. Accepts Showreels.
Film. Radio. Television
12A Rosebank, Holyport Road
London SW6 6LG

MOUNTJOY, Lee
CASTING T 0161 850 1656 (Manchester)
T 020 7112 8353 (London)
E info@leemountjoy.com
W www.leemountjoy.com

MUGHAL, Naila
ARTISTES AGENCY T 07983 534113
All Nationalities. Actors. Dancers. Extras. Hair Stylists.
Make-up Artistes. Singers
E naila-castings@hotmail.co.uk
W www.nailamughalartistes.com

MUGSHOTS T 07880 896911
Contact: Becky Kidd

MURDER MY DARLINGS T 020 7386 0560
Contact: Sue Pocklington
Based in London
E office@murdermydarlings.com

MURPHY CHARPENTIER
CASTING T 07976 931264
Contact: Sabrina Murphy, Alix Charpentier
22 Gledhow Gardens
London SW5 0AZ
T 07956 450755
E casting@murphycharpentiercasting.com
W www.murphycharpentier.co.uk

NATIONAL THEATRE
CASTING DEPARTMENT T 020 7452 3336
Contact: Wendy Spon, Head of Casting (CDG Member),
Alastair Coomer, Deputy Head of Casting (CDG Member),
Juliet Horsley, Casting Associate (CDG Member),
Charlotte Sutton, Casting Assistant. By Post
Upper Ground, South Bank
London SE1 9PX
F 020 7452 3340
W www.nationaltheatre.org.uk

NEEDLEMAN, Sue T 020 8959 1550
CDG Member
19 Stanhope Gardens, London NW7 2JD

NORCLIFFE, Belinda T 020 8992 1333
Contact: Belinda Norcliffe, Matt Selby
23 Brougham Road
London W3 6JD
E belinda@bncasting.co.uk

NORTH, Sophie T 020 8450 6474
59A Teignmouth Road
London NW2 4EB
T 07956 516606
E sophie@sophienorthcasting.com

O'BRIEN, Debbie T 01462 742919
72 High Street, Ashwell
Nr Baldock, Herts SG7 5NS
F 01462 743110

O'CONNOR, Orla T 0131 553 0559
The Out of The Blue Drill Hall, 36 Dalmeny Street
Edinburgh EH6 8RG
E info@orlaoconnorcasting.co.uk

O'DONNELL, Rory T 07940 073165
178A Adelaide Avenue, London SE4 1JN
F 020 8690 8005
E tyrconnellpictures@hotmail.com

Affordable, naturally lit & unique headshots. Quick turnaround. London/Surrey.
t: 07899 847173 e: jess@theheadshot.co.uk w: www.theheadshot.co.uk

---

PALMER, Helena
CDG Member. See ROYAL SHAKESPEARE COMPANY

PARRISS, Susie CASTING　　T 020 8543 3326
CDG Member
PO Box 40, Morden SM4 4WJ

PETTS, Tree CASTING　　T 020 8458 8898
125 Hendon Way
London NW2 2NA
T 07966 283252
E casting@treepetts.co.uk
W www.treepettscasting.com

PLANTIN, Kate　　T 01932 782350
CDG Member
4 Riverside
Lower Hampton Road
Sunbury on Thames TW16 5PW
F 01932 783235
E kateplantin@hotmail.com

**POLENTARUTTI, Tania
CASTING**　　T 07720 299635
Contact: By e-mail
E filmtvcasting@virginmedia.com

POOLE, Gilly
CDG Member. See CROWLEY POOLE CASTING

POWELLCASTING
Contact: Annelie Powell
F annelie@powellcasting.com
W www.powellcasting.com

PROCTOR, Carl　　T 020 7681 0034
CDG Member
15B Bury Place, London WC1A 2JB
T 07956 283340
E carlproctor@btconnect.com
W www.carlproctor.com

PRYOR, Andy　　T 020 7851 8535
CDG Member
79 Wardour Street, London W1D 6QB

PURO CASTING　　T 020 7193 8799
F 07006 056678
E office@purocasting.com
W www.purocasting.com

RADCLIFFE, Gennie　　T 0161 952 1000
CDG Member
Granada Television, Quay Street
Manchester M60 9EA
F 0161 952 0573

**RANCH CASTING
COMPANY THE**　　T 020 8374 6072
*Contact: By e-mail/Telephone. Commercials. Corporate.
Idents. Photographic Campaigns. Pop Promos*
F 020 8442 9190
E info@theranchcasting.co.uk
W www.theranchcasting.co.uk

REICH, Liora　　T 020 8444 1686
25 Manor Park Road, London N2 0SN
E casting@liorareich.fsnet.co.uk

**REYNOLDS, Gillian
CASTING**　　T 028 9091 8218 (Belfast)
Based in Belfast & Dublin
Scottish Provident Building
7 Donegall Square West
Belfast, County Antrim BT1 6JH
T 0872 619718 (Dublin)
E gillianreynoldscasting@gmail.com
W www.gillianreynoldscasting.com

REYNOLDS, Simone　　T 020 8672 5443
CDG Member
60 Hebdon Road, London SW17 7NN

RHODES JAMES, Kate　　T 020 8614 2653
CDG Member
KRJ Casting, Teddington Studios
Broom Road, Teddington TW11 9NT
E office@krjcasting.com

RI McD CASTING
See McDAID-WREN, Ri

RICHTER, Ilisa　　T 020 3131 0128
Unit 106A Netil House
1 Westgate Street
London E8 3RL
E ilisarichter@live.co.uk

RIPLEY, Jane　　T 020 8340 5123
E jane@janeripleycasting.co.uk

ROBERTSON, Sasha CASTING　　T 020 8993 8118
*Contact: Sasha Robertson (CDG Member),
Maddy Hinton (Associate)*
5 Cumberland Road
London W3 6EX
E casting@sasharobertson.com
W www.sasharobertsoncasting.com

RONANE, Jessica CASTING
CDG Member
E jessica@jessicaronane.com

ROSE, Dionne **T** 01635 281673
9 Wright Way, Selsey
Chichester, West Sussex PO20 0UD
E casting@drbentertainment.co.uk
W www.drbentertainment.co.uk

ROWAN, Amy CASTING **T** 00 353 1 2140514
PO Box 10247, Blackrock
Co. Dublin, Ireland
F 00 353 1 2802005

ROWE, Annie CASTING **T** 020 8354 2699
98 St Albans Avenue, London W4 5JR
E annie@annierowe-casting.com
W www.annierowe-casting.com

**ROYAL SHAKESPEARE
COMPANY** **T** 020 7845 0530
*Contact: Hannah Miller, Head of Casting (CDG Member),
Helena Palmer (CDG Member), Matthew Dewsbury*
Casting Department, 1 Earlham Street
London WC2H 9LL
F 020 7845 0505
E suggestions@rsc.org.uk
W www.rsc.org.uk

**RUBIN, Shaila EUROPEAN
CASTING SERVICE** **T** 00 39 06 72901906
Cinecitta Studios Via Tuscolana 1055, 00173 Roma
Teatro 6/7 Stanza 8, Italy
F 00 39 06 72905183
E sernass@gmail.com

RUTHERFORD, Neil **T** 020 8371 0465
Neil Rutherford Casting
7 Falkland Avenue, London N3 1QR
T 07960 891911
E neil@neilrutherford.com
W www.neilrutherford.com

RYCROFT CASTING **T** 07958 540815
Contact: Amy Rycroft
E amy@rycroftcasting.co.uk
W www.rycroftcasting.co.uk

SALBERG, Jane **T** 01303 239277
86 Stade Street, Hythe, Kent CT21 6DY
T 07931 932103
E janesalberg@aol.com

SCHILLER, Ginny **T** 020 8806 5383
CDG Member
9 Clapton Terrace, London E5 9BW
E ginny.schiller@virgin.net

SCHOFIELD, Gilly
CDG Member
E gillyschofield1@btinternet.com

SCOTT, Laura **T** 020 7978 6336
56 Rowena Crescent, London SW11 2PT
E laurascottcasting@mac.com

SEARCHERS THE **T** 07958 922829
70 Sylvia Court, Cavendish Street
London N1 7PG
F 020 7684 5763
E waynesearcher@mac.com

SEECOOMAR, Nadira **T** 020 8892 8478
E nadira.seecoomar@gmail.com

SELECT CASTING LTD **T** 07700 059089
PO Box 748, London NW4 1TT
T 07956 131494
E info@selectcasting.co.uk
W www.selectcasting.co.uk

SHAW, David
See KEOGH, Beverley CASTING LTD

SHAW, Phil **T** 020 8715 8943
Contact: By Post. Commercials. Film. Stage. Television
Suite 476, 2 Old Brompton Road
South Kensington, London SW7 3DQ
E shawcastlond@aol.com

SHEPHERD, Debbie CASTING **T** 020 7240 0400
Suite 16, 63 St Martin's Lane
London WC2N 4JS
E casting@debbieshepherd.com

SID PRODUCTIONS **T** 01932 863194
110 Sandringham Flats
Charing Cross Road
London WC2H 0BP
E casting@sidproductions.co.uk
W www.sidproductions.co.uk

SIMPSON, Georgia **T** 028 9147 0800
CDG Member
E georgia@georgiasimpsoncasting.com
W www.georgiasimpsoncasting.com

SINGER Sandra ASSOCIATES **T** 01702 331616
Contact: By e-mail
21 Cotswold Road, Westcliff-on-Sea
Essex SS0 8AA
E sandrasingeruk@aol.com
W www.sandrasinger.com

SMITH, Michelle CASTING LTD **T** 0161 439 6825
*Contact: Michelle Smith (CDG Member). By Post.
Accepts Showreels/Voicereels.
Animation. Commercials. Corporate. Film. Television*
220 Church Lane, Stockport SK7 1PQ
F 0161 439 0622
E michelle.smith18@btinternet.com

SMITH, Suzanne **T** 020 7278 0045
CDG Member
3rd Floor, 15 Crinan Street
York Way, London N1 9SQ
E zan@dircon.co.uk

SNAPE, Janine CASTING
CDG Member
E janinesnapecasting@gmail.com

SOLOMON, Alison **T** 0121 245 2023
Birmingham Repertory Theatre
St George's Court
1 Albion Street, Birmingham B1 3AH

SPORTSCASTINGS.COM **T** 07973 863263
Contact: Penny Burrows
3 Thornlaw Road, London SE27 0SH
E info@sportsmodels.com
W www.sportsmodels.com

STAFFORD, Aaron **T** 020 8372 0611
Freelance. Commercials. Film. Television
14 Park Avenue, Enfield
Middlesex EN1 2HP
E aaron.stafford@blueyonder.co.uk

STAFFORD, Emma CASTING **T** 0161 833 4263
T 020 3137 7351
E info@emmastafford.tv
W www.emmastafford.tv

STAFFORD, Helen **T** 020 8360 6329
14 Park Avenue, Enfield
Greater London EN1 2HP
E helen.stafford@blueyonder.co.uk

SPOTLIGHT

Casting from start to finish

Spotlight Database

Browse over 40,000 actors, actresses, presenters, stunt artists, children and dancers

View performer CVs, photos, showreels, portfolios and contact details

Know that every Spotlight performer has professional training or experience

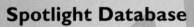

Spotlight Rooms & Studios

Hold your auditions in the heart of central London at the Spotlight Rooms & Studios

Six meeting rooms, ideal for auditions, read-throughs, production meetings and interviews

Three fully-equipped casting studios with DVD-quality video upload

Spacious waiting areas and client facilities

www.spotlight.com/spaces 020 7440 5041

Spotlight Website

E-mail casting calls to hundreds of UK agents and performers and receive responses in minutes

Find exactly the right performer for the part with our award-winning search engine

www.spotlight.com   020 7437 7631   casting@spotlight.com

STARK CASTING T 020 8800 0060
T 07956 150689
E anna@starkcasting.com
W www.starkcasting.com

STEVENS, Gail CASTING T 020 7253 6532
CDG Member
Greenhill House, 90-93 Cowcross Street
London EC1M 6BF
E office@gailstevenscasting.com

**STEVENS MILLEFIORINI,
Danny** T 00 39 389 4352200
Via Sillaro 14, Cerveteri, Rome 00052, Italy
E dannystevens62@gmail.com

STEVENSON, Sam
CDG Member
E sam@hancockstevenson.com

STOLL, Liz T 020 8228 8285
BBC DRAMA SERIES CASTING, BBC Elstree
Room N223, Neptune House, Clarendon Road
Borehamwood, Herts WD6 1JF
F 020 8228 8311

STYLE, Emma T 01628 483740
CDG Member
1 Overton Cottages, Kings Lane
Cookham, Maidenhead SL6 9BA

SUMMERS, Mark CASTING T 020 7229 8413
Formerly Casting Unlimited
1 Beaumont Avenue, West Kensington
London W14 9LP
E mark@marksummers.com
W www.marksummers.com

SYERS, Michael
See CASTING CONNECTION THE

SYSON GRAINGER CASTING T 020 7287 5327
*Contact: Lucinda Syson (CDG Member),
Elaine Grainger (CDG Member)*
Rooms 7-8, 2nd Floor
83-84 Berwick Street, London W1F 8TS
F 020 7287 3629
E office@sysongraingercasting.com

TABAK, Amanda
CDG Member. See CANDID CASTING

TOPPING, Nicci T 07802 684256
The Media Centre, 7 Northumberland Street
West Yorkshire HD1 1RL
T 01484 511988
E general@toppscasting.co.uk
W www.toppscasting.co.uk

TREVELLICK, Jill T 020 8340 2734
CDG Member
92 Priory Road, London N8 7EY
E jill@jilltrevellick.com

TREVIS, Sarah T 020 8354 2398
CDG Member
E info@sarahtrevis.com

VALENTINE HENDRY, Kelly
CDG Member. See VHJ CASTING

VAUGHAN, Sally T 020 7735 6539
CDG Member
2 Kennington Park Place, London SE11 4AS
E svaughan12@btinternet.com

VHJ CASTING T 020 7255 6146
*Contact: Kelly Valentine Hendry (CDG Member),
Victor Jenkins (CDG Member)*
Welbeck House
66-67 Wells Street
London, W1T 3PY
E assistant@vhjcasting.com
W www.vhjcasting.com

VOSSER, Anne CASTING T 01252 404716
156 Lower Farnham Road
Aldershot
Hampshire GU12 4EL
T 07968 868712
E anne@vosser-casting.co.uk
W www.vosser-casting.co.uk

WAUDBY, Melissa T 07957 284709
E melissawaudbycasting@gmail.com

WEIR, Fiona T 020 7727 5600
CDG Member
2nd Floor, 138 Portobello Road
London W11 2DZ

WEST, June
CDG Member
E junewestcasting@gmail.com

WESTERN, Matt T 020 7602 6646
150 Blythe Road, London W14 0HD
E matt@mattwestern.co.uk
W www.mattwestern.co.uk

WHALE, Toby T 020 8993 2821
CDG Member
80 Shakespeare Road, London W3 6SN
F 020 8993 8096
E toby@whalecasting.com
W www.whalecasting.com

WICKSTEED, Rose T 020 8150 7290
CSA Member
Based in London
T 07854 831636
E mail@rosewicksteed.com
W www.rosewicksteed.com

WILDMANHALL CASTING T 020 7373 2036
Contact: Vicky Wildman, Buffy Hall
1 Child's Place, London SW5 9RX
E wildmanhall@mac.com

WILLIS, Catherine T 020 7255 6130
CDG Member. Contact: By e-mail
Wellbeck House, 66-67 Wells Street
London W1T 3PY
E catherine@cwcasting.co.uk

WRIGHT, Rebecca CASTING T 020 3371 1531
CDG Member
E office@rebeccawrightcasting.com

YOUNGSTAR CASTING T 023 8047 7717
Children & Teenagers only
5 Union Castle House, Canute Road
Southampton SO14 3FJ
E info@youngstar.tv
W www.youngstar.tv

**ZIMMERMANN, Jeremy
CASTING** T 020 7478 5161
36 Marshall Street
London W1F 7EY
E info@zimmermanncasting.com

ACADEMY OF PERFORMANCE COMBAT THE T 07963 206803
Teaching Body of Stage Combat
Ivy Villa, 250 Lees New Road
Lees, Lancs OL4 5PP
E info@theapc.org.uk
W www.theapc.org.uk

ACADEMY OF PERSONAL TRAINING LTD (APT LTD) T 07776 304511
Providing Personal Training, Weight Management, Sports Specific/Conditioning, Corrective Exercise & Injury Rehabilitation Services to the Film & Media Industry
West Acre, Hurst Lane
Egham, Surrey TW20 8QJ
E alan@academypt.org

ACE FEATURE FILM - MEDIA INTERNATIONAL FOUNDATION T 07765 927029
Contact: Margaret Cooper (Executive Producer). Sourcing investors. Product Placement for Films
227 Earl's Court Road, London SW5 9BL
E acefilm1@yahoo.com
W www.i-mf.co

ACTING AUDITION SUCCESS T 020 8731 6686
Audition Coaching for Top UK Drama Schools
53 West Heath Court, London NW11 7RG
E philiproschactor@gmail.com
W www.actingauditionsuccess.co.uk

ACTING BUDDY
E info@actingbuddy.com
W www.actingbuddy.com

ACTORS ADVICE SURGERY T 07968 011163
Contact: Yvonne l'Anson (Consultant)
E yvonne@actorsadvicesurgery.co.uk
W www.actorsadvicesurgery.co.uk

ACTORS' ADVISORY SERVICE T 020 8287 2839
Provides Advice to Actors, Agents, Photographers etc
29 Talbot Road, Twickenham
Middlesex TW2 6SJ

ACTOR'S ONE-STOP SHOP THE T 020 8888 7006
Showreels for Performing Artists
1st Floor, Above The Gate Pub
Station Road, London N22 7SS
E info@actorsonestopshop.com
W www.actorsonestopshop.com

AGENTFILE T 07050 683662
Software for Agents
E admin@agentfile.com
W www.agentfile.com

AKA T 020 7836 4747
Advertising. Design. Digital. Marketing. Promotions. Sales & Ticketing
1st Floor, 115 Shaftesbury Avenue
Cambridge Circus, London WC2H 8AF
F 020 7836 8787
E aka@akauk.com
W www.akauk.com

ARIAS, Enrique T 07956 261568
Subtitles. Translations. Voice Overs
E onriqueag@gmail.com
W www.nwlondon.com/eag

ARTS VA THE T 01789 552559
Contact: Bronwyn Robertson (Experienced PA). Admin Support
T 07815 192135
E bronwyn@theartsva.com
W www.theartsva.com

ASSOCIATED STUDIOS THE T 020 8237 1080
Riverside Studios, Crisp Road, London W6 9RL
E info@associatedstudios.co.uk
W www.associatedstudios.co.uk

AUDIO DESCRIPTION
For Blind & Visually Impaired Audiences. West End & on Tour
E info@theatredescription.com

AUTOMOBILE ASSOCIATION (THE AA) T 01256 492640
Fanum House, Basing View, Basingstoke RG21 4EA
E lindsey.szegota@theaa.com

BARTERCARD T 0845 2197000
Churchill House, 1 London Road
Slough, Berkshire SL3 7FJ
E info@uk.bartercard.com
W www.bartercard.co.uk

BIG PICTURE T 020 7071 4465
Contact: Bridget Kelly. Field Marketing
13 Netherwood Road, London W14 0BL
E humanresources@ebigpicture.co.uk
W www.ebigpicture.co.uk

BLACK, Liam A. T 01383 610711
Magic & Illusion Consultant. Custom & Off-the-shelf Illusions, Magic & Special Effects Props
12 Downfield, Cowdenbeath, Fife KY4 9JE
E kandlblack@btinternet.com

BOARDMAN, Emma T 07976 294604
Creative Event Producer. Private Party Planner. Media Spokesperson for the UK Events Industry
Weybridge, Surrey KT13
E hq@thelovelypartycompany.com
W www.thelovelypartycompany.com

BRITISH ASSOCIATION OF DRAMATHERAPISTS   T/F 01242 235515
Waverley, Battledown Approach
Cheltenham, Glos GL52 6RE
E enquiries@badth.org.uk
W www.badth.org.uk

BYFORD, Simon PRODUCTION MANAGEMENT SERVICES   T 01273 623972
Production & Event Management
22 Freshfield Place, Brighton
East Sussex BN2 0BN
F 01273 606402
E simon@simonbyfordpms.com

BYRNE, John   T 07720 847831
One-to-one Advice from The Stage's Career Advisor
E johnbyrnecontact@gmail.com
W www.adviceforperformers.com

CAP PRODUCTION SOLUTIONS LTD   T 07973 432576
Technical Production Services
116 Wigmore Road, Carshalton, Surrey SM5 1RQ
F 07970 763480
E leigh@leighporter.com

CASTLE MAGICAL SERVICES   T/F 01904 709500
Contact: Michael Shepherd. Magical Effect Consultants
Broompark, 131 Tadcaster Road
Dringhouses, York YO24 1QJ
E info@castlemagicalservices.co.uk

CAULKETT, Robin Dip SM MIIRSM   T 07970 442003
Abseiling. Rope Work
3 Churchill Way, Mitchell Dean, Glos GL17 0AZ
E robincaulkett@talktalk.net

CELEBRITIES WORLDWIDE LTD   T 020 7637 4178
Celebrity Contacts & Booking
E claire@celebritiesworldwide.com
W www.celebritiesworldwide.com

CHAPERONE   T/F 020 8650 8997
For Children in Performing Arts
31 Whitecroft Way, Beckenham, Kent BR3 3AQ
T 07930 353381
E elaineboyle@msn.com

CHAPERONEAGENCY   T 07960 075928
E chaperoneagency@hotmail.co.uk
W www.chaperoneagency.com

CHAPERONES & TUTORS   T 07896 651552
141 Main Road, Nottingham
Nottinghamshire NG16 5GQ
E chaperonesandtutors@hotmail.co.uk
W www.chaperonesandtutors.co.uk

CHEKHOV, Michael CENTRE UK   T 020 8696 7372
*Information centre for the work of Michael Chekhov
in the UK including biographies, academic contacts,
international links, training links & other information*
E info@michaelchekhov.org.uk
W www.michaelchekhov.org.uk

CHILDCHAPERONE.CO.UK   T 07956 427442
*Contact: Denise Smith. Licensed Chaperone.
Stage, Television & Film Industry*
E denisesmith916@btinternet.com
W www.childchaperone.co.uk

CLASS - CARLINE LUNDON ASSOCIATES   T 07853 248957
25 Falkner Square, Liverpool L8 7NZ
E carline.lundon@ukonline.co.uk

COBO MEDIA LTD   T 020 8291 7079
Performing Arts, Entertainment & Leisure Marketing
43A Garthorne Road, London SE23 1EP
F 020 8291 4969
E admin@cobomedia.com
W www.cobomedia.com

COLCLOUGH, John   T 020 8873 1763
Practical Independent Guidance for Actors & Actresses
E info@johncolclough.com
W www.johncolclough.com

COMBAT INTERNATIONAL   T 01259 731010
27 High Street, Kincardine, Alloa FK10 4RJ
E info@clanranald.org
W www.clanranald.org

CREATIVE CULTURE   T 020 7193 3076
21E Heathmans Road, London SW6 4TJ
E m.chevalier@creativecultureint.com
W www.creativecultureint.com

CREATIVE MAGIC DIRECTOR (TONY MIDDLETON)   T 01727 838656
67 De Tany Court, St Albans
Herts AL1 1TX
T 07738 971077
E anthonyjjmiddleton@gmail.com
W www.middletonenterprisesuk.com

CROFTS, Andrew   T/F 01403 864518
Book Writing Services
Westlands Grange, West Grinstead
Horsham, West Sussex RH13 8LZ
E croftsa@aol.com
W www.andrewcrofts.com

DALLA VECCHIA, Sara   T 07877 404743
Italian Teacher
13 Fauconberg Road, London W4 3JZ
E saraitaliantuition@gmail.com
W www.italiantuition.com

EARLE, Kenneth PERSONAL MANAGEMENT   T 020 7274 1219
214 Brixton Road, London SW9 6AP
F 020 7274 9529
E kennethearle@agents-uk.com
W www.kennethearlepersonalmanagement.com

ES GLOBAL LTD   T 020 7055 7200
Bell Lane, North Woolwich Road, London E16 2AB
F 020 7055 7201
E info@esglobalsolutions.com
W www.esglobalsolutions.com

EYENNCEE.COM   T 020 7557 6650
Professional Networking Site
I.N.C Space, 9-13 Grape Street
Covent Garden, London WC2H 8ED
F 020 7557 6656
E chris@international-collective.com
W www.eyenncee.com

FACADE   T 020 8291 7079
Creation & Production of Musicals
43A Garthorne Road, London SE23 1EP
F 020 8291 4969
E facade@cobomedia.com

FERRIS ENTERTAINMENT MUSIC   T 0845 4724725
*Music for Film & Television.
London. Cardiff. Belfast. Los Angeles*
Number 8, 132 Charing Cross Road
London WC2H 0LA
E info@ferrisentertainment.com
W www.ferrisentertainment.com

FIGHT CHOREOGRAPHER & ACTION DIRECTOR T 07739 184418
Contact: Nic Main (Professional Actor, Film Fighting Choreographer)
Based in the South East
E nicmain@nicmain.com
W www.nicmain.com

FLAMES MARTIAL ARTS ACADEMY T 07950 396389
Contact: Adam Richards
Unit 2, 128 Milton Road Business Park
Gravesend, Kent DA12 2PG
E stunts@adamrichardsstunts.co.uk
W www.adamrichardsfightdirector.com

FRANCO THE MAGICIAN T/F 020 8202 4940
Flat 1, 79 Brent Street, London NW4 2EA
E franco@francomagic.co.uk
W www.francomagic.co.uk

GHOSTWRITER / AUTHOR T 01227 721071
Contact: John Parker
Dove Cottage, The Street
Ickham CT3 1QP
E ghostwriterforyourbook@ymail.com
W www.ghostwriteruk.info

GILMOUR Rev/Prof.em/Dr Glenn MscD SHsc.D Dip.Coun. BCMA.Reg T 0114 321 6500
Fully Qualified/International Medium & Clairvoyant. Healer/Counsellor. Holistic Therapist. Consultant Paranormal/Metaphysics/Occult for Radio & Television
E drglenngilmour@yahoo.com
W www.drglenngilmour.com

GLOBAL ACCESS WORLD-WIDE ENTERTAINMENT VISAS T 001 323 936 7100
4670 Wilshire Boulevard, Suite 1970
Los Angeles 90036, USA
F 001 323 936 7197

GOLDIELLE PROMOTIONS T 07977 936826
Event Management & Entertainment
68 Lynton Drive, Hillside
Southport, Merseyside PR8 4QQ
T 01704 566604
E goldielle@yahoo.co.uk
W www.goldiellepromotions.com

HANDS UP PUPPETS T 07909 824630
Contact: Marcus Clarke
7 Cavendish Vale, Nottingham NG5 4DS
E enquiries@handsuppuppets.com
W www.handsuppuppets.com

HARLEY PRODUCTIONS T 020 7580 3247
68 New Cavendish Street, London W1G 8TE
F 020 8202 8863
E harleyprods@aol.com

HAYES, Susan T 07721 927714
Choreographer
46 Warrington Crescent, London W9 1EP
E susan22@btconnect.com

HERITAGE RAILWAY ASSOCIATION T 01993 883384
10 Hurdeswell, Long Hanborough
Witney, Oxfordshire OX29 8DH
E john.crane@hra.gb.com
W www.heritagerailways.com

HITWAVE T 0844 8700496
Unit 1, 52 Churchfield Road
Acton, London W3 6DA
E info@hitwave.co.uk
W www.hitwave.co.uk

IMAGE DIGGERS T 020 8455 4564
Slide/Stills/Audio/Video Library. Theme Research
618B Finchley Road, London NW11 7RR
E lambhorn@gmail.com

IMPACT AGENCY THE T 020 7580 1770
Public Relations
1 Bedford Avenue, London WC1B 3AU
F 020 7580 7200
E mail@impactagency.co.uk
W www.theimpactagency.com

I R A - INDEPENDENT REVIEWS ARTS SERVICES T 07956 212916
Stories from the Art World
E critic@independentradioarts.com

iTREND RESEARCH LTD T 01799 531358
Audience Research. Audience Surveys. Focus Groups
The Old House, High Street
Little Chesterford
Saffron Walden
Essex CB10 1TS
E andrew@itrendresearch.com
W www.itrendresearch.com

JACKSON, Kim T 0116 253 3429
Forum Theatre Practitioner
Transforum, Studio B402
LCB Depot, 31 Rutland Street
Leicester LE1 1RW
E kim@transforum.co.uk

JOHNSON, Gareth LTD T 020 7611 0051
20-22 Stukeley Street
London WC2B 5LR
T 07770 225227
E gjltd@mac.com

JOHNSON, Gareth LTD T 01239 891368
Plas Hafren, Eglwyswrw
Crymych, Pembrokeshire SA41 3UL
T 07770 225227
E gjltd@mac.com

JORDAN, Richard PRODUCTIONS LTD T 020 7243 9001
Festivals. General Management. Production Consultancy. UK & International Productions
Mews Studios, 16 Vernon Yard
London W11 2DX
F 020 7313 9667
E richard.jordan@virgin.net

KEAN LANYON LTD T 020 7607 8453
Contact: Sharon Kean, Iain Lanyon. PR & Web/Graphic Consultants
United House, North Road
Islington, London N7 9DP
E sharon@keanlanyon.com
W www.keanlanyon.com

KELLER, Don T 020 8800 4882
Marketing Consultancy. Project Management
65 Glenwood Road
Haringey, London N15 3JS
E info@donkeller.co.uk

KIEVE, Paul T 07939 252526
Magical Effects for Film & Stage
2 St Philip's Road, London E8 3BP
E mail@stageillusion.com
W www.stageillusion.com

LAMBOLLE, Robert T 020 8455 4564
Script Evaluation & Editing
618B Finchley Road, London NW11 7RR
E lambhorn@gmail.com

LAWINSPORT.COM
Contact: Sean Cottrell (Editor). Online sports law publication providing articles of legal opinion, case law, events listings & other sports law related directories
E sean.cottrell@lawinsport.com
W www.lawinsport.com

LAWSON LEAN, David   T 01932 230273
Chaperone Service for Children in Entertainment
72 Shaw Drive
Walton-on-Thames
Surrey KT12 2LS
E dlawsonlean@aol.com
W www.davidlawsonlean.com

LEEP MARKETING & PR   T 07973 558895
Marketing. Press. Publicity
83A Albert Street, London NW1 7LX
E philip@leep.biz

**LEO MEDIA & ENTERTAINMENT
GROUP THE**   T 020 7183 3177
*Executive Production. Film, Television & Literary
Consultancy. Legal Work*
PO Box 68006
London NW4 9FW
F 07006 057893
E info@leomediagroup.com
W www.leomediagroup.com

**LOCATION TUTORS
NATIONWIDE**   T 020 7978 8898
*Fully Qualified & Experienced Teachers working with
Children on Film Sets & Covering all Key Stages of
National Curriculum*
16 Poplar Walk, Herne Hill
London SE24 0BU
F 020 7207 8794
E locationtutorsnationwide@gmail.com
W www.locationtutors.co.uk

LONDON COMPUTER DOCTOR   T 020 7652 4296
Computer Support
66 Heath Road, Clapham
London SW8 3BD
E joe@londoncomputerdoctor.com
W www.londoncomputerdoctor.com

**LONDON LITERARY PUB CRAWL
COMPANY THE**   T 020 8582 7506
*Promotes the art & literature of London through tours &
infodramas*
c/o 33A Prebend Mansions
Chiswick High Road
London W4 2LU
T 0121 444 0933
E tours@mavericktheatre.co.uk
W www.londonliterarypubcrawl.com

**LOVE, Billie HISTORICAL
PHOTOGRAPHS**   T 01983 812572
*Picture Research. Formerly 'Amanda' Theatrical
Portraiture*
3 Winton Street, Ryde
Isle of Wight PO33 2BX
E billielove@tiscali.co.uk

LUXFACTOR GROUP (UK) THE   T 0845 3700589
Twitter: @luxfactor
Fleet Place
12 Nelson Drive
Petersfield, Hampshire GU31 4SJ
F 0845 3700588
E info@luxfactor.co.uk
W www.luxfactor.co.uk

MAGICIANS.CO.UK   T 0845 0062442
Entertainers. Magic Consultants
Burnhill House, 50 Burnhill Road
Beckenham BR3 3LA
F 0845 0062443
E mail@magicians.co.uk

MAIN, Nic   T 07739 184418
*Experienced Stage, Television & Film
Action/Fight Director/Actor*
62 Kingsway, Blackwater
Camberley, Surrey GU17 0JB
E nicmain@nicmain.com
W www.nicmain.com

MATTLX GROUP   T 0845 6808692
Lighting. Design. Production Engineering. Safety. Training
Unit 3, Vinehall Business Centre, Vinehall Road
Robertsbridge, East Sussex TN32 5JW
E intray@mattlx.com
W www.mattlx.com

**MATTLX GROUP, HEALTH &
SAFETY TRAINING**   T 0845 6808692
IOSH-approved Training Provider
Unit 3 Vinehall Business Centre
Vinehall Road
Robertsbridge TN32 5DD
E training@mattlx.com
W www.mattlx.com

MAYS, Lorraine   T 01494 771029
Children's Licensed Chaperone
Park View, Stanley Avenue
Chesham, Bucks HP5 2JF
T 07778 106552
E lorrainebmays@aol.com

McKENNA, Deborah LTD   T 020 8846 0966
Celebrity Chefs & Lifestyle Presenters only
64-66 Glentham Road, London SW13 9JJ
F 020 8846 0967
E info@deborahmckenna.com
W www.dml-uk.com

MEDIA LEGAL   T 01732 460592
Jurisconsults
Town House, 5 Mill Pond Close
Sevenoaks, Kent TN14 5AW

MILDENBERG, Vanessa   T 07796 264828
Movement Director. Choreographer. Director
Flat 6, Cameford Court
New Park Road, London SW2 4LH
E vanessamildenberg@me.com
W www.vanessamildenberg.com

**MILITARY ADVISORY &
INSTRUCTION SPECIALISTS**   T 01904 491198
*Contact: Johnny Lee Harris. Advice on Weapons, Drill,
Period to Present. Ex-Army Instructor. Health & Safety.
IOSH. Military Bugler & Drummer. Actor. PSV Licence.
Own Scarlets (Scarlet Uniform), Bugle & Drum. Chieftain
Tank Driver & Gunner. Horse Rider*
38 Knapton Close, Strensall
York YO32 5ZF
T 07855 648886
E johnmusic1@hotmail.com

MINIMAL RISK   T 01432 360643
Security Consultancy
Wye Valley Court, Netherwood Road
Hereford HR2 6JG
E admin@minimalrisk.co.uk
W www.minimalrisk.co.uk

MINISTRY OF FUN THE T 020 7407 6077
Entertainment. Promotions. PR Marketing Campaigns
Unit 1, Suffolk Studios, 127-129 Great Suffolk Street
London SE1 1PP
F 020 7407 5763
E james@ministryoffun.net
W www.ministryoffun.net

**MORGAN, Jane ASSOCIATES
(JMA)** T 020 7263 9867
Marketing. Media
8 Heathville Road, London N19 3AJ
E jma@janemorganassociates.com

MUSIC SOLUTIONS LTD T 020 7866 8160
Garden Studios, 11-15 Betterton Street
London WC2H 9BP
E mail@musicsolutionsltd.com

**NEATE, Rodger PRODUCTION
MANAGEMENT** T 020 7609 9538
15 Southcote Road, London N19 5BJ
E rneate@dircon.co.uk

NEXTSTOPLAX T 001 323 798 5103
*Relocation of Entertainment Industry Professionals.
O-1 Visa Specialists*
1714 North McCadden Place, Hollywood
CA 90028, USA
T 001 323 363 9933
E info@nextstoplax.com
W www.nextstoplax.com

NORDIC NOMAD TRAINING T 07980 619165
Workshops for Performers on Business Skills
64 Tulse Hill, London SW2 2PT
E tanja@nordicnomad.com
W www.nordicnomad.com

NORTHERNALLSTARS.CO.UK T 07980 507690
Resources for Actors
2 Prince's Gardens, Sunderland SR6 8DF
E info@northernallstars.co.uk
W www.northernallstars.co.uk

**ORANGE TREE STUDIO LTD & RICHARD
PARDY MUSIC SERVICES** T 07768 146200
*Saxophone, Woodwinds, Brass Section & Bands For
Hire (Live or in Studio). Original Music/Composition &
Production*
31A New Road, Croxley Green, Herts WD3 3EJ
E richard@orangetreestudio.com
W www.redhornz.co.uk

PENROSE, Scott T 07767 336882
Magic & Illusion Effects for Film, Stage & Television
17 Berkeley Drive, Billericay
Essex CM12 0YP
E mail@stagemagician.com
W www.stagemagician.com

PINEWOOD NET T 07882 794583
Networking Group
W www.pinewoodnet.net

**POLICING EXPERIENCE
UNLEASHED** T: 020 7205 2999
Suite 36, 88-90 Hatton Garden, London EC1N 8PG
E enquiries@policingexperienceunleashed.com
W www.policingexperienceunleashed.com

PSYCHOLOGY GROUP THE T 0870 6092445
*Assessments. Counselling. Expert Opinion. Presentation.
Psychotherapy*
F 0845 2805243
E info@psychologygroup.co.uk
W www.psychologygroup.co.uk

PUKKA PRESENTING T 020 8455 1385
*Training in Television Presenting & Presentation
Techniques*
Appletree Cottage, 51 Erskine Hill
London NW11 6EY
E kathryn@pukkapresenting.co.uk
W www.pukkapresenting.co.uk

PUPPET CENTRE T 020 7228 5335
*Development & Advocacy Agency for Puppetry & Related
Animated Theatre*
BAC, Lavender Hill
London SW11 5TN
E pct@puppetcentre.org.uk
W www.puppetcentre.org.uk

**RAINBOW BIGBOTTOM &
CO LTD** T 01494 771029
Children's Warm-up Artists for Stage & Television
Park View, Stanley Avenue
Chesham, Bucks HP5 2JF
E lorrainebmays@aol.com
W www.mrpanda.co.uk

**RB HEALTH & SAFETY
SOLUTIONS LTD** T 0845 2571489
*Specialists in Stage & Production Health & Safety Audits,
Consultancy, Risk Assessments & Training*
Blacklands Business Centre, 15 Fearon Road
Hastings, East Sussex TN40 1DA
E richard@rbhealthandsafety.co.uk
W www.rbhealthandsafety.co.uk

REACH TO THE SKY LTD T 0843 2892503
Contact: Dr J. Success Life Coach
Maxet House, Liverpool Road
Luton, Bedfordshire LU1 1RS
T 07961 911027
E drtwsj@reachtothesky.com
W www.reachtothesky.com

**RED HOT ID - THE BRANDING
SERVICE FOR ACTORS** T 01279 850618
The Studio @ The Haven, Carters Lane
Hensham, Hertfordshire CM22 6AQ
F 01279 850625
E id@redhotentertainment.biz
W www.redhotentertainment.biz

RICHARDS, Adam T 07950 396389
Fight Director
Unit 2, 128 Milton Road Business Park
Gravesend, Kent DA12 2PG
E stunts@adamrichardsstunts.co.uk
W www.adamrichardsfightdirector.com

**RIPLEY-DUGGAN
PARTNERSHIP THE** T 020 7436 1392
Tour Booking
26 Goodge Street, London W1T 2QG
E info@ripleyduggan.com

ROSCH, Philip T 020 8731 0080
Audition Coaching for Top UK Drama Schools
53 West Heath Court
London NW11 7RG
E philiproschactor@gmail.com
W www.actingauditionsuccess.co.uk

SHADEÈ, Magus Lynius T 020 8378 6844
Psychic. Occult Investigator & Consultant
Suite 362, 110 Great Russell Street
London WC1B 3BC
T 07740 043156
E maguslyniusshadee@hotmail.com
W www.occultcentre.com

SHAW, Jennifer EVENTS   T 0845 1309517
Event Management & Promotions
15 Ladyhouse Lane
Milnrow OL16 4EH
E jennifer@jennifershawevents.co.uk
W www.jennifershawevents.co.uk

SHOWBIZ FRIENDS
Social Networking Website for Professional Showbiz People
W www.showbizfriends.com

SINCLAIR, Andy   T 07831 196675
Mime
E andynebular@hotmail.com
W www.andyjsinclair.co.uk

SOUTHAM FERRARI, Maggie   T 01730 814177
6 Oak Tree Court, Meadway
Midhurst, West Sussex GU29 9SE
T 07758 052325
E margaret.ferrari@virgin.net

SPORTS PROMOTIONS (UK) LTD   T 020 8771 4700
Production Advisors. Safety. Sport. Stunts
56 Church Road, Crystal Palace
London SE19 2EZ
F 020 8771 4704
E agent@sportspromotions.co.uk
W www.sportspromotions.co.uk

STAGE CRICKET CLUB   T 020 7402 7543
Cricketers & Cricket Grounds
39-41 Hanover Steps
St George's Fields
Albion Street, London W2 2YG
F 020 7262 5736
E brianjfilm@aol.com
W www.stagecc.co.uk

STUNT ACTION SPECIALISTS (S.A.S.)   T 01273 230214
Corporate & Television Stunt Work
110 Trafalgar Road, Portslade
East Sussex BN41 1GS
E mail@stuntactionspecialists.co.uk
W www.stuntactionspecialists.co.uk

STYLES, John - MAGICAL MART   T/F 020 8300 3579
Magic, Ventriloquism & Punch & Judy Consultant
42 Christchurch Road, Sidcup
Kent DA15 7HQ
W www.johnstylesentertainer.co.uk

SYNCREDIBLE MEDIA   T 020 7117 6776
Licensing & Media Marketing Communications
26-28 Hammersmith Grove, Hammersmith
London W6 7BA
E contact@syncredible.com
W www.syncredible.com

TALENT SCOUT THE   T 01924 464049
Referral Service. Agents & Managers
19 Edge Road, Thornhill
Dewsbury, West Yorkshire WF12 0QA
E connect@thetalentscout.org

THEATRE PROJECTS CONSULTANTS   T 020 7482 4224
4 Apollo Studios, Charlton Kings Road
London NW5 2SW
F 020 7284 0636
E uk@theatreprojects.com
W www.theatreprojects.com

THERAPEDIA LONDON BRIGHTON   T 07941 300871
93 Gloucester Place, London W1U 6JQ
E info@gregmadison.net
W www.gregmadison.net

TODD, Carole   T 07775 566275
Director. Choreographer
E ctdirector@gmail.com

TWINS WORLDWIDE LTD   T 0845 0523683
Special Effects for Film, Stage & Television Productions
T 07971 589186
E info@thetwinsfx.com
W www.thetwinsfx.com

UNITED KINGDOM COPYRIGHT BUREAU   T 01273 277333
Script Services
110 Trafalgar Road, Portslade
East Sussex BN41 1GS
E info@copyrightbureau.co.uk
W www.copyrightbureau.co.uk

VERNON, Doremy   T/F 020 8767 6944
Archivist. Author 'Tiller Girls'. Dance Routines Tiller Girl Style
16 Ouseley Road, London SW12 8EF

VISA WORLD   T 020 8959 6161
Passport & Visa Processing Agents. Consular Services. Travel Insurance
627 Watford Way, London NW7 3JN
F 020 8959 2888
E info@visaworld.co.uk
W www.visaworld.co.uk

VOCALEYES   T 020 7375 1043
Audio Description "Describing The Arts"
1st Floor, 54 Commercial Street
London E1 6LT
E enquiries@vocaleyes.co.uk
W www.vocaleyes.co.uk

VOICEATWORK   T 07973 871479
Voice Coach
5 Anhalt Road, London SW11 4NZ
E kateterris@voiceatwork.co.uk
W www.voiceatwork.co.uk

WELBOURNE, Jacqueline   T 07977 247287
Choreographer. Circus Trainer. Consultant
43 Kingsway Avenue
Kingswood
Bristol BS15 8AN
E jackie.welbourne@gmail.com

WHITE, Leonard   T 01273 514473
Stage & Television Credits
Highlands, 40 Hill Crest Road
Newhaven, Brighton
East Sussex BN9 9EG
E leoguy.white@virgin.net

WISE MONKEY FINANCIAL COACHING   T 01273 691223
Contact: Simonne Gnessen
14 Eastern Terrace Mews
Brighton BN2 1EP
E simonne@financial-coaching.co.uk
W www.financial-coaching.co.uk

YOUNGBLOOD   T 020 7193 3207
Fight Co-ordinators & Directors
E info@youngblood.co.uk
W www.youngblood.co.uk

ACADEMY COSTUMES T 020 7620 0771
50 Rushworth Street, London SE1 0RB
F 020 7928 6287
E info@academycostumes.com
W www.academycostumes.com

AJ COSTUMES LTD T 0871 2003343
Theatrical Costume Hire, Design & Making
Sullom Lodge, Sullom Side Lane
Barnacre, Garstang PR3 1GH
F 01253 407715
E info@squiresjohns.com
W www.squiresjohns.com

ALL-SEWN-UP T/F 01422 843407
Mechanics Institute, 7 Church Street
Heptonstall, West Yorks HX7 7NS
E nwheeler_allsewnup@hotmail.com
W www.allsewnup.org.uk

AND SEW TO DANCE T 01268 285050
Unit 11, Cornwallis House, Howard Chase
Basildon, Essex SS14 3BB
E andsewtodance@blueyonder.co.uk

ANELLO & DAVIDE T 020 7938 2255
Handmade Shoes
15 St Albans Grove, London W8 5BP
W www.handmadeshoes.co.uk

ANGELS T 020 7836 5678
Fancy Dress. Revue
119 Shaftesbury Avenue, London WC2H 8AE
F 020 7240 9527
E fun@fancydress.com
W www.fancydress.com

ANGELS THE COSTUMIERS T 020 8202 2244
1 Garrick Road, London NW9 6AA
F 020 8202 1820
E angels@angels.uk.com
W www.angels.uk.com

ANGELS WIGS T 020 8202 2244
Facial Hair Suppliers. Wig Hire/Makers
1 Garrick Road, London NW9 6AA
F 020 8202 1820
E wigs@angels.uk.com
W www.angels.uk.com

ANTOINETTE COSTUME HIRE T 020 8699 1913
Events. Film. Stage
High Street Buildings, 134 Kirkdale, London SE26 4BB
E antoinettehire@aol.com
W www.costumehirelondon.com

ARMS & ARCHERY T 01920 460335
*Armour. Banners. Chainmail. Medieval Tents. Warrior
Costumes. Weaponry*
Thrift Lane, Off London Road, Ware, Herts SG12 9QS
E armsandarchery@btconnect.com

ATTLE COSTUMIERS LTD T 020 8540 3044
Contact: Jamie Attle. Designs, Makes & Hires Costumes
4 Toynbee Road, Wimbledon
London SW20 8SS
E aalexiscolby@aol.com

BAHADLY, R. T 01625 615878
*Hair & Make-up Artist, incl. Bald Caps, Ageing
& Casualty*
47 Ploughmans Way, Macclesfield, Cheshire SK10 2UN
T 07973 553073
E rosienico@hotmail.co.uk

BERTRAND, Henry T 020 7424 7000
London Stockhouse for Silk
52 Holmes Road, London NW5 3AB
F 020 7424 7001
E sales@henrybertrand.co.uk
W www.henrybertrand.co.uk

BIRMINGHAM COSTUME HIRE T 0121 622 3158
Suites 209-210, Jubilee Centre
130 Pershore Street, Birmingham B5 6ND
F 0121 622 2758
E info@birminghamcostumehire.co.uk

BLAIR, Julia T 07917 877742
Make-up Artist. Film. Photographic. Stage. Television
6A Boston Parade, London W7 2DG
E julia0blair@gmail.com
W www.juliablair.co.uk

BRIGGS, Ron DESIGN T 020 8444 8801
*Theatrical Tailors. Costume Design & Making. Bespoke
Embroidery. Rhinestone Application*
1 Bedford Mews, London N2 9DF
E costumes@ronbriggs.com

BRODY, Shirley T 07717 855684
14 Jenner House, London WC1N 1BL
E s.brody@blueyonder.co.uk

BURLINGTONS T 0844 8008884
Hairdressers
14 John Princes Street, London W1G 0JS
E cca@newidstudios.co.uk
W www.newidstudios.co.uk

CALICO FABRICS T 020 8541 5274
*Suppliers of Unbleached Calico & other Fabrics for
Stage, Costumes, Backdrops etc*
3 Ram Passage, High Street
Kingston-upon-Thames, Surrey KT1 1HH
F 020 8546 7755
E sales@calicofabrics.co.uk
W www.calicofabrics.co.uk

CAPEZIO LONDON T 020 7379 6042
Dance Products
33 Endell Street, London WC2H 9BA
E capeziolondon@capezio.com
W www.capezio.com

CHRISANNE LTD T 020 8640 5921
Specialist Fabrics & Accessories for Dance & Stage
Chrisanne House, 110-112 Morden Road
Mitcham, Surrey CR4 4XB
F 020 8640 2106
E sales@chrisanne.com W www.chrisanne.com

CLANRANALD COSTUME T 01259 731010
27 High Street, Kincardine, Alloa FK10 4RJ
E info@clanranald.org
W www.clanranald.org

CLASSIQUE DANCE SHOP T 02392 233334
3-5 Stakes Hill Road, Waterlooville, Hampshire PO7 7JB
E audrey.hersey@ntlworld.com
W www.classiquedance.com

COLTMAN, Mike
See COSTUME CONSTRUCTION LTD

COOK, Sheila TEXTILES T 020 7603 3003
Vintage Textiles, Costumes & Accessories for Sale/Hire
26 Addison Place, London W11 4RJ
E sheilacook@sheilacook.co.uk
W www.sheilacook.co.uk

COSPROP LTD T 020 7561 7300
Accessories. Costumes
469-475 Holloway Road, London N7 6LE
F 020 7561 7310
E enquiries@cosprop.com W www.cosprop.com

COSTUME BOUTIQUE T 020 7193 6877
Costume Hire for Events & Parties
38 Great Western Studios, 65 Alfred Road
London W2 5EU
T 07973 794450
E costumeboutique@me.com
W www.costumeboutique.co.uk

**COSTUME
CONSTRUCTION LTD** T/F 01242 581847
Costumes. Masks. Props. Puppets
Unit 1 Crooks Industrial Estate, Croft Street
Cheltenham GL53 0ED
E mike@costumeconstruction.co.uk
W www.costumeconstruction.co.uk

COSTUME CREATIONS T 01902 738282
10 Olinthus Avenue, Wolverhampton WV11 3DE
E yourcostume@googlemail.com
W www.costumecreations.co.uk

COSTUME SOLUTIONS T 020 7603 9035
43 Rowan Road, London W6 7DT
E karen@costumesolutions.co.uk
W www.costumesolutions.co.uk

COSTUME STORE LTD THE T 01273 479727
Costume Accessories
16 Station Street, Lewes
East Sussex BN7 2DB
F 01273 477191
E enquiries@thecostumestore.co.uk
W www.thecostumestore.co.uk

COSTUME STUDIO LTD T 020 7275 9614
Costumes. Wigs
Montgomery House
159-161 Balls Pond Road, London N1 4BG
T/F 020 7923 9065
E costume.studio@btconnect.com
W www.costumestudio.co.uk

COSTUMEGENIE.CO.UK
113 Norwich Avenue, Southend
Essex SS2 4DH
E costume-genie@hotmail.com
W www.costumegenie.co.uk

**COUTURE BEADING
& EMBELLISHMENT** T 020 8925 2714
108 Hiltongrove Business Centre, Hatherley Mews
Walthamstow, London E17 4QP
T 07866 939401
E enquiries@couturebeading.com
W www.couturebeading.com

CRAZY CLOTHES CONNECTION T 020 7221 3989
1920's-1980's for Sale or Hire
134 Lancaster Road, Ladbroke Grove
London W11 1QU
W www.crazy-clothes.co.uk

DANCIA INTERNATIONAL T 020 7831 9483
168 Drury Lane, London WC2B 5QA
E london@dancia.co.uk
W www.dancia.co.uk/london

DARCY CLOTHING T 01273 471586
2 Mount Place, Lewes
East Sussex BN7 1YH
F 01273 475322
E sales@darcyclothing.com
W www.darcyclothing.com

**DAVIES, Bryan Philip
COSTUMES** T 01273 481004
Lavish Pantomime. Musical Shows. Opera
68 Court Road, Lewes
East Sussex BN7 2SA
T 07931 249097
E bryan@bpdcostumes.co.uk
W www.bpdcostumes.co.uk

DELAMAR ACADEMY T/F 020 8579 9511
Make-up Training
Ealing Studios, Building D, 2nd Floor
Ealing Green, London W5 5EP
E info@delamaracademy.co.uk
W www.delamaracademy.co.uk

Véronique Ebolo Hair and Make-up Artist

For Film, Television, Theatre,
Fashion, Music Video,
Advertising and more...

Website: www.veroniqueebolo.com
E-mail: ebode@hotmail.co.uk
Tel: 07500 215319

DESIGNER ALTERATIONS   T 020 7498 4360
Restyling & Remodelling of Clothes & Costumes
220A Queenstown Road, Battersea
London SW8 4LP
F 020 7622 4148
E info@designeralterations.com
W www.designeralterations.com

DR. BOO   T 020 8693 4823
22 North Cross Road, East Dulwich
London SE22 9EU
E boogirls@hotmail.co.uk
W www.drboo.co.uk

EASTON, Derek   T/F 01273 588262
Wigs For Film, Stage & Television
1 Dorothy Avenue, Peacehaven
East Sussex BN10 8LP
T 07768 166733
E wigs@derekeastonwigs.co.uk
W www.derekeastonwigs.co.uk

EBOLO, Veronique   T 07500 215319
*Hair & Make-up Artist for Film, Television, Special Effects,
Advertising & Editorial*
Flat 7, Churchfield House Hall Place, London W2 1LY
E ebode@hotmail.co.uk
W www.veroniqueebolo.com

EDA ROSE MILLINERY   T 01491 837174
Ladies' Hats. Design & Manufacture
Lalique, Mongewell
Wallingford, Oxon OX10 8BP
F 01491 835909
E edarose.lawson@btconnect.com

EIA MILLINERY DESIGN   T 001 773 975 5959
1620 West Nelson Street, Chicago
Illinois 60657-3027, USA
E info@eiahatart.com

**EVOLUTION SETS &
COSTUMES LTD**   T 01304 615333
Set & Costume Hire
Langdon Abbey, West Langdon
Dover, Kent CT15 5HJ
F 01304 615353
E dorcas@evolution-productions.co.uk

FOX, Charles H. LTD   T 020 7240 3111
The Professional Make-up Centre
22 Tavistock Street, London WC2E 7PY
F 020 7379 3410
E makeup@charlesfox.co.uk
W www.charlesfox.co.uk

FOXTROT PRODUCTIONS LTD   T 020 8964 3555
Armoury Services. Costume & Prop Hire. Firearms
3B Brassie Avenue, East Acton, London W3 7DE
E info@foxtrot-productions.co.uk
W www.foxtrot-productions.co.uk

FREED OF LONDON   T 020 7240 0432
Dance Shoes. Dancewear
94 St Martin's Lane, London WC2N 4AT
F 020 7240 3061
E shop@freed.co.uk
W www.freedoflondon.com

FUNN LTD   T 0870 8743866
*Silk, Cotton & Wool Stockings. Opaque Opera Tights.
40's Rayon Stockings*
PO Box 102, Steyning, West Sussex BN44 3EB
F 0870 8794450
E funnsales@lycos.com

GAMBA THEATRICAL
See THEATRE SHOES LTD

**GAV NICOLA
THEATRICAL SHOES**   T 07961 974278
T 00 34 673803783
E gavnicola@yahoo.com
W www.theatricalshoes.com

GENESIS UK LTD   T 01654 710137
Unit 18, Pendre Enterprise Park
Tywyn, Gwynedd LL36 9LW
E info@genesis-uk.com
W www.genesis-uk.com

GILLHAM, Felicite   T 01761 437142
Wig Makers for Film, Opera & Stage
Gallis Ash, Kilmersdon, Near Bath, Somerset BA3 5SZ
T 07802 955908
E felicite@gillywigs.co.uk

GREASEPAINT SCHOOL OF MAKE-UP & HAIR　T 020 8840 6000
143 Northfield Avenue, Ealing, London W13 9QT
E info@greasepaint.co.uk
W www.greasepaint.co.uk

GROUNDLINGS COSTUME HIRE　T 023 9273 7370
10,000 Costumes ranging from Early Man to Futuristic
Groundlings Theatre, 42 Kent Street
Portsmouth, Hampshire PO1 3BT
E wardrobe@groundlings.co.uk
W www.groundlings.co.uk

GROVE, Sue DESIGNS　T 023 8078 6849
Costume Designers & Makers. Historical Specialist
12 Ampthill Road, Shirley
Southampton, Hants SO15 8LP
E sue.grove1@tiscali.co.uk

HAIRAISERS　T 020 8965 2500
Hair Extensions. Wigs
32-34 Sunbeam Road, Park Royal
London NW10 6JL
F 020 8963 1600
E info@hairaisers.com
W www.hairaisers.com

HAND & LOCK　T 020 7580 7488
Bespoke Embroidery for Costumes, Fashion & Interiors
86 Margaret Street, London W1W 8TE
F 020 7580 7499
E enquiries@handembroidery.com
W www.handembroidery.com

HARVEYS OF HOVE　T 01273 430323
Military Specialists. Theatrical Costumes
110 Trafalgar Road, Portslade, Sussex BN41 1GS
E harveys.costume@ntlworld.com
W www.harveysofhove.co.uk

HENRY, Lewis LTD　T 020 7636 6683
Dress Makers
111-113 Great Portland Street, London W1W 6QQ
E info@lewishenrydesigns.com

HIREARCHY　T 01202 394465
Classic & Contemporary Costume
45-47 Palmerston Road, Boscombe
Bournemouth, Dorset BH1 4HW
E hirearchy1@gmail.com
W www.hirearchy.co.uk

HISTORY IN THE MAKING LTD　T 023 9225 3175
Costume Hire. Military Specialists. Bespoke Tailoring
4A Aysgarth Road, Waterlooville, Hampshire PO7 7UG
E jean@history-making.com
W www.history-making.com

HODIN, Annabel　T 020 7431 8761
Costume Designer & Stylist. Personal Shopper
12 Eton Avenue, London NW3 3EH
T 07836 754079
E annabelhodin@aol.com

HOPKINS, Trisha　T 01704 873055
6 Willow Grove, Formby L37 3NX
T 07957 368598
E trisha_hopkins@hotmail.co.uk

INTERNATIONAL DANCE SUPPLIES / GRISHKO UK LTD　T 01223 861425
Importer & Distributor of Dance Shoes & Dancewear
9 Ballard Close, Milton
Cambridge CB24 6DW
F 01223 280388
E info@grishko.co.uk
W www.grishko.co.uk

JONKMAN, Kylie　T 07960 966281
Flat 2, 50A Clive Road
Canton, Cardiff CF5 1GH
E kyliejonkman@hotmail.co.uk
W www.kyliejonkman.com

JULIETTE DESIGNS　T 020 7263 7878
Diamante Jewellery Manufacturers
90 Yerbury Road, London N19 4RS
F 020 7281 7326
E juliettedesigns@hotmail.com
W www.stagejewellery.com

KATIE'S WIGS　T 07900 250853
Wig Supplier & Maker
15 Birchwood Gardens, Idle Park
Bradford BD10 9EW
E katie.hunt@katieswigs.com

KIDD, Ella J.　T 01603 304445
Bespoke Millinery, Wigs & Head-dresses for Film, Stage & Television
W www.ellajkidd.co.uk

LARGER THAN LIFE STAGEWEAR　T 020 8466 9010
Theatrical Costumes for Hire
55C Croydon Road, Elmers End
Beckenham, Kent BR3 4AB
T 07802 717714
E info@largerthanlifestagewear.co.uk
W www.largerthanlifestagewear.co.uk

LOCK, Josie　T 07722 358425
Make-up Artist
13B Kennington Park Place, London SE11 4AS
E hello@josielock.co.uk
W www.josielockmakeup.co.uk

MADDERMARKET THEATRE COSTUME HIRE　T 01603 626292
Costume & Wig Hire. Period Clothing
St John's Alley, Norwich NR2 1DR
F 01603 661357
E mmtheatre@btconnect.com
W www.maddermarket.co.uk

MAKE-UP ARTIST & HAIR STYLIST　T 07973 216468
Freelancer
16 Tempest Avenue, Potters Bar, Hertfordshire EN6 5JX
E magui@magui.co.uk
W www.mm-mua.co.uk

MARSDEN, Chloe COSTUMES & MILLINERY　T 07786 427386
65 Grange Avenue, North Finchley
London N12 8DJ
E mail@chloemarsden.co.uk
W www.chloemarsden.co.uk

MASK, Kim   T 0845 0568482
Costume & Make-up Protection Masks
E lydia@kimmask.com
W www.keepimmaculate.com

MASTER CLEANERS THE   T 020 7431 3725
Dry Cleaning of Theatrical Costumes & Antique
Garments
189 Haverstock Hill, London NW3 4QG
E info@themastercleaners.com
W www.themastercleaners.com

McCORMACK, Mitsuki   T 07940 517757
Media Make-up Artist
Based in London SW11
E mitsukimccormack@yahoo.co.uk
W www.mitsukimccormack.webs.com

MEANANDGREEN.COM   T 0845 8991133
87 Darlington Street, Wolverhampton WV1 4EX
E custserv@meanandgreen.com
W www.meanandgreen.com

MORRIS, Heather   T 020 8771 7170
Hair Replacement. Wigs
Fortyseven, 47A Westow Street
Crystal Palace, London SE19 3RW
W www.fortysevenhair.co.uk

NATIONAL THEATRE   T 020 7820 1358 (Props)
Costume, Furniture & Props Hire
Chichester House, Kennington Park Estate
1-3 Brixton Road, London SW9 6DE
T 020 7735 4774 (Costume)
E costume_hire@nationaltheatre.org.uk

NEW ID   T 0870 8701299
Makeover & Photographic Studios
PO Box 743, Rickmansworth WD3 0JN
E bookings@newidstudios.co.uk
W www.newidstudios.co.uk

ONE MAKE UP /
ONE PHOTOGRAPHIC LTD   T 020 7467 1400
3rd Floor, 66-68 Margaret Street
London W1W 8SR
F 020 7467 1401
E info@onemakeup.com
W www.onemakeup.com

ORIGINAL KNITWEAR   T 01726 844807
Contact: Gina Pinnick. Inc. Fake Fur
Avalon, Tregoney Hill
Mevagissey, Cornwall PL26 6RG
T 07957 376855
E okgina@btinternet.com
W www.originalknitwear.co.uk

PACE, Terri MAKE-UP DESIGN   T 07939 698999
E info@terripace.com
W www.terripace.com

PAINTED LADY THE   T 07895 820041
Make-up Consultant & Trainer
581 London Road, Stoke on Trent
Staffordshire ST4 5AZ
E ashaleeblueeyes@hotmail.co.uk

PATEY (LONDON) LTD   T 020 8291 4820
The Hat Workshop
Connaught Business Park
Malham Road, London SE23 1AH
F 020 8291 6275
E trevor@pateyhats.com
W www.pateyhats.com

PEARCE, Kate   T 07749 283802
Costume Maker
Thistledown, Wellfield Road
Marshfield, Near Newport CF3 2UB
E kpearce55@hotmail.com

PINK POINTES DANCEWEAR   T/F 01708 438584
1A Suttons Lane, Hornchurch
Essex RM12 6RD
E pink.pointes@btconnect.com

POLAND DENTAL STUDIO   T 020 7935 6919
Film/Stage Dentistry
1 Devonshire Place, London W1G 6HH
F 020 7486 3952
E robpoland@btconnect.com

PORSELLI   T 0845 0170817
4 Frensham Road
Sweet Briar Industrial Estate
Norwich NR3 2BT
F 01603 406676
E porselliuk@aol.com
W www.dancewear.co.uk

PROBLOOD   T/F 01728 723865
11 Mount Pleasant, Framlingham
Suffolk IP13 9HQ

RAINBOW PRODUCTIONS LTD   T 020 8254 5300
Manufacture & Handling of Costume Characters
Unit 3, Green Lea Park, Prince George's Road
London SW19 2JD
F 020 8254 5306
E info@rainbowproductions.co.uk
W www.rainbowproductions.co.uk

REPLICA WAREHOUSE   T/F 01477 534075
Costumiers. Props
200 Main Road, Goostrey
Cheshire CW4 8PD
E lesleyedwards@replicawarehouse.co.uk
W www.replicawarehouse.co.uk

ROBBINS, Sheila   T/F 01865 735524
Wig Hire
Broombarn, 7 Ivy Cottages
Hinksey Hill, Oxford OX1 5BQ

ROYAL EXCHANGE
THEATRE COSTUME HIRE   T/F 0161 819 6660
Period Costumes & Accessories
47-53 Swan Street, Manchester M4 5JY
E costume.hire@royalexchange.co.uk
W www.royalexchange.co.uk

ROYER, Hugo
INTERNATIONAL LTD   T 01252 878811
Hair & Wig Materials
10 Lakeside Business Park, Swan Lane
Sandhurst, Berkshire GU47 9DN
F 01252 878852
E enquiries@royer.co.uk
W www.hugoroyer.com

RSC COSTUME STORE   T/F 01789 205920
28 Timothy's Bridge Road
Stratford Enterprise Park
Stratford-upon-Avon, Warwickshire CV37 9UY
E costume.store@rsc.org.uk

RUMBLE, Jane   T 020 8904 6462
Masks, Millinery & Helmets Made to Order
121 Elmstead Avenue, Wembley
Middlesex HA9 8NT

SAGUARO, Jen   T 07773 385703
35 Southey Street, Bristol BS2 9RE
E jrsaguaro@googlemail.com

SEXTON, Sallyann   T 01923 211644
Hair & Make-up Designer
c/o The Harris Agency Ltd
71 The Avenue
Watford, Herts WD17 4NU
T 07973 802842
E theharrisagency@btconnect.com

SILVESTER, Michaela   T 07595 725047
Chantry, Chapel Lane
Pirbright, Surrey GU24 0JY
E kaylasilvester@hotmail.co.uk

SINGER, Sandra ASSOCIATES   T 01702 331616
Fashion Stylists for Stage & Television.
Costume/Designer
21 Cotswold Road, Westcliff-on-Sea
Essex SS0 8AA
E sandrasingeruk@aol.com
W www.sandrasinger.com

SLEIMAN, Hilary   T 020 8555 6176
Specialist & Period Knitwear
72 Godwin Road, London E7 0LG
T 07940 555663
E hilary.sleiman@ntlworld.com

SOFT PROPS   T 020 7587 1116
Costume & Model Makers
92 Fentiman Road, London SW8 1LA
F 020 7207 0062
E jackie@softprops.co.uk

STAGEWORKS WORLDWIDE
PRODUCTIONS   T 01253 342426
Largest Costume Wardrobe in the North
525 Ocean Boulevard, Blackpool FY4 1EZ
F 01253 342702
E simone.bolajuzon@stageworkswwp.com
W www.stageworkswwp.com

STRIBLING, Joan   T 0845 4266169
BAFTA Member. Film, Television & Stage Hair, Make-up
& Prosthetics Designer (H.O.D.). BAFTA Craft Award.
BAFTA Design & Art Director's Award
Based in London / South West
T 07791 758480
E joanstribling@hotmail.com
W www.joanstribling.com

SWINFIELD, Rosemarie   T 07976 965520
Rosie's Make-up Box. Make-up Design & Training
E rosiesmake-up@uw.club.net
W www.rosemarieswinfield.com

TALK TO THE HAND PUPPETS   T 020 7627 1052
Custom Puppets for Film, Stage & Television
Studio 27B, Spaces Business Centre
15-17 Ingate Place
London SW8 3NS
T 07855 421454
E iestynmevans@hotmail.com
W www.talktothehandpuppets.com

THEATRE SHOES LTD   T 020 8529 9195
Trading as GAMBA Theatrical
Unit 1A, Lee Valley Trading Estate
Rivermead Road, London N18 3QW
F 020 8529 7995
E info@theatreshoes.com

THEATRICAL
SHOEMAKERS LTD   T 020 7474 0500
Footwear
Unit 7A
Thames Road Industrial Estate
Thames Road, Silvertown
London E16 2EZ
E ts@shoemaking.co.uk
W www.shoemaking.co.uk

TRYFONOS, Mary MASKS   T 020 7502 7883
Designer & Maker of Masks & Costume Properties
59 Shaftesbury Road
London N19 4QW
T 07764 587433
E marytryfonos@aol.com

TUTU-TOPIA   T 07999 553021
Pembrokeshire, Wales SA73
E sales@tutu-topia.co.uk
W www.tutu-topia.co.uk

WEST YORKSHIRE
FABRICS LTD   T/F 0113 225 6550
Barathea. Crepe. Linen. Stretch Fabrics. Suiting.
Venetian. Cut Lengths
Unit 5 Milestone Court
Stanningley
Leeds LS28 6HE
E neil@wyfabrics.com

WEST YORKSHIRE
PLAYHOUSE   T 0113 213 7242
Costume Hire
6 St Peter's Building, St Peter's Square
Leeds, West Yorkshire LS2 8AH
E sally.stone@wyp.org.uk
W www.wyp.org.uk/about-us/what-we-do/costume-hire

WIG EXPECTATIONS   T 07785 512011
159 Upper Brighton Road
Broadwater
Worthing BN14 9JS
E wigexpectations@aol.com
W www.wigexpectations.com

WIG ROOM THE   T 01256 415737
22 Coronation Road
Basingstoke
Hants RG21 4HA
E darren@wigroom.co.uk

WIG SPECIALITIES LTD   T 020 7724 0020
Handmade Wigs & Facial Hair, Hair Extensions
& Wig Hire
77 Ashmill Street
London NW1 6RA
F 020 7724 0069
E wigspecialities@btconnect.com
W www.wigspecialities.co.uk

WIGS, MAKE-UP &
COSTUME SPECIALIST   T 07516 323000
17 Perry Hall Road, Orpington
Kent BR6 0HT
E rachellisajones@hotmail.co.uk

WILLIAMS, Emma   T 07710 130345
Costume Designer & Stylist. Film, Stage & Television
E emmacoz@dsl.pipex.com

DAILY EXPRESS
T 020 8612 7000

Contact: Caroline Jowett (Stage, Film, Dance, Opera)
Matt Baylis (Television)
Northern Shell Building, 10 Lower Thames Street
London EC3R 6EN
E arts.editor@express.co.uk

DAILY MAIL
T 020 7938 6000

Contact: Quentin Letts (Stage)
Chris Tookey (Film)
Baz Bamigboye (Chief Showbiz Writer)
Northcliffe House
2 Derry Street
Kensington, London W8 5TT

DAILY STAR
T 020 8612 7000

Contact: Alan Frank (Film & Video)
Nigel Pauley (Showbiz Report)
Northern Shell Building
10 Lower Thames Street, London EC3R 6EN

DAILY TELEGRAPH
T 020 7931 2000

Contact: Charles Spencer, Dominic Cavendish (Stage)
Robbie Collins, Tim Robey (Film)
Gillian Reynolds (Radio)
Richard Dorment (Art)
Sarah Crompton (Arts Editor)
Mark Monahan (Dance)
Geoffrey Norris, Ivan Hewitt (Music)
111 Buckingham Palace Road
London SW1W 0DT

FINANCIAL TIMES
T 020 7873 3000

Contact: Sarah Hemming, Ian Shuttleworth (Stage)
Nigel Andrews (Film)
Martin Hoyle (Television)
1 Southwark Bridge
London SE1 9HL

GUARDIAN
T 020 3353 2000

Contact: Michael Billington (Stage)
Richard Vine (Television)
King's Place, 90 York Way
London N1 9GU

INDEPENDENT
T 020 7005 2000

Contact: Gerard Gilbert (Television)
2 Derry Street
London W8 5HF

LONDON EVENING STANDARD
T 020 3367 7000

Contact: Henry Hitchings, Fiona Mountford (Stage)
Derek Malcolm (Film)
Jane Shilling (Television)
Barry Millington (Classical Music & Opera)
Northcliffe House
2 Derry Street
Kensington, London W8 5TT
W www.thisislondon.co.uk

MAIL ON SUNDAY
T 020 7938 6000

Contact: Georgina Brown (Stage)
Jason Solomons (Cinema & DVDs)
Matthew Bond (Film)
Simon Garfield (Radio)
Review Section
Northcliffe House
2 Derry Street, London W8 5TT

MIRROR
T 020 7510 3000

Contact: Dave Edwards (Film)
James Simon, Jim Shelley (Television Previews)
Mirror Group Newspapers Ltd
1 Canada Square
Canary Wharf, London E14 5AP

MORNING STAR
T 020 8510 0815

Contact: Cliff Cocker (Arts Editor)
William Rust House
52 Beachy Road
London E3 2NS

OBSERVER
T 020 3353 2000

Contact: Susannah Clapp (Stage Contributor)
Philip French (Film Contributor)
Sarah Donaldson (Arts Editor)
Luke Jennings (Dance Contributor)
Fiona Maddocks (Opera Contributor)
King's Place
90 York Way
London N1 9GU

PEOPLE
T 020 7293 3000

Contact: Conor Nolan (Film)
John Wise (Television & Radio)
Caroline Waterson (Features)
Katie Hind (Show Business)
1 Canada Square
Canary Wharf
London E14 5AP

SUN
T 020 7782 4000

Contact: Ally Ross (Features Writer)
3 Thomas More Square
London E98 1XY

SUNDAY EXPRESS
T 020 8612 7000

Contact: Mark Shenton (Stage)
Henry Fitzherbert (Film)
David Stephenson (Television)
Clare Heal (Radio)
Clair Woodward (Arts Editor)
Clare Colvin (Opera)
Jeffery Taylor (Dance)
Northern Shell Building
10 Lower Thames Street
London EC3R 6EN

SUNDAY MIRROR
T 020 7510 3000

Contact: Kevin O'Sullivan (Stage & Television)
Mark Adams (Film)
Dean Piper (Show Business)
Mirror Group
1 Canada Square
Canary Wharf
London E14 5AP

SUNDAY TELEGRAPH
T 020 7931 2000

Contact: Tim Walker (Stage)
Jenny McCartney (Film)
Nigel Farndale (Television)
111 Buckingham Palace Road
London SW1W 0DT

SUNDAY TIMES
T 020 7782 5000

Contact: Christopher Hart (Stage)
Cosmo Landesman (Film)
A. A. Gill (Television)
Paul Donovan (Radio)
3 Thomas More Square
London E98 1XY

TIMES
T 020 7782 5000

Contact: Libby Purves (Stage)
Kate Muir (Film)
James Jackson (Television)
Ed Potton (Music)
3 Thomas More Square
London E98 1XY

D →

CDET
For information regarding membership of the
Council for Dance Education and Training
please see:

W www.cdet.org.uk

AKADEMI SOUTH ASIAN
DANCE UK   T 020 7691 3210
Hampstead Town Hall
213 Haverstock Hill
London NW3 4QP
F 020 7691 3211
E info@akademi.co.uk
W www.akademi.co.uk

ANJALI DANCE COMPANY   T 01295 251909
The Mill Arts Centre
Spiceball Park
Banbury, Oxfordshire OX16 5QE
E info@anjali.co.uk
W www.anjali.co.uk

BALLET CYMRU   T 01633 253985
30 Glasllwch Crescent
Newport, South Wales NP20 3SE
E dariusjames@welshballet.co.uk
W www.welshballet.co.uk

BALLETBOYZ   T 020 7278 5508
Sadler's Wells, Rosebery Avenue
Islington, London EC1R 4TN
E info@balletboyz.com
W www.balletboyz.com

BALLROOM, LONDON
THEATRE OF   T 020 8722 8798
Contact: Paul Harris® (Artistic Director)
24 Montana Gardens
Sutton, Surrey SM1 4FP
E office@londontheatreofballroom.com
W www.londontheatreofballroom.com

BIRMINGHAM ROYAL BALLET   T 0121 245 3500
Thorp Street
Birmingham B5 4AU
F 0121 245 3570
E brbinfo@brb.org.uk
W www.brb.org.uk

CANDOCO DANCE COMPANY   T 020 7704 6845
2T Leroy House
436 Essex Road
London N1 3QP
F 020 7704 1645
E info@candoco.co.uk
W www.candoco.co.uk

COMPANY OF CRANKS   T 07963 617981
1st Floor, 62 Northfield House
London SE15 6TN
E mimetic16@yahoo.com
W www.mimeworks.com

CREATIVE KIDZ
STAGE SCHOOL   T 07908 144802
9 Weavers Terrace
Fulham
London SW6 1QE
E info@creativekidzandco.co.uk

DAVIES, Siobhan DANCE   T 020 7091 9650
85 St George's Road
London SE1 6ER
F 020 7091 9669
E info@siobhandavies.com
W www.siobhandavies.com

DV8 PHYSICAL THEATRE   T 020 7655 0977
Artsadmin, Toynbee Studios
28 Commercial Street
London E1 6AB
F 020 7247 5103
E dv8@artsadmin.co.uk
W www.dv8.co.uk

ENGLISH NATIONAL
BALLET LTD   T 020 7581 1245
Markova House, 39 Jay Mews
London SW7 2ES
F 020 7225 0827
E comments@ballet.org.uk
W www.ballet.org.uk

ENGLISH YOUTH BALLET   T 01689 856747
Appledowne
The Hillside
Orpington, Kent BR6 7SD
T 07732 383600
E misslewis@englishyouthballet.co.uk
W www.englishyouthballet.co.uk

GREEN CANDLE DANCE
COMPANY   T 020 7739 7722
Oxford House
Derbyshire Street
Bethnal Green
London E2 6HG
E info@greencandledance.com
W www.greencandledance.com

IJAD DANCE COMPANY   T 07930 378639
22 Allison Road, London N8 0AT
E hello@ijaddancecompany.com
W www.ijaddancecompany.com

JEYASINGH, Shobana
DANCE COMPANY   T 020 7697 4444
Omnibus Office 113, 39-41 North Road
London N7 9DP
E admin@shobanajeyasingh.co.uk
W www.shobanajeyasingh.co.uk

KHAN, Akram COMPANY   T 020 7354 4333
Unit 232A, 35A Britannia Row
London N1 8QH
F 020 7354 5554
E office@akramkhancompany.net
W www.akramkhancompany.net

Dance Companies

How do I become a professional dancer?

Full-time vocational training can start from as young as ten years old. A good starting point for researching the different schools and courses available is CDET (Council for Dance Education & Training) www.cdet.org.uk. There are twenty-four dance colleges offering professional training accredited by CDET, and nearly three hundred university courses which include some form of dance training. It is estimated that over one thousand dancers graduate from vocational training schools or university courses every year, so it is a highly competitive career. Therefore anyone wanting to be a professional dancer must obtain as many years of training and experience as possible, plus go to see plenty of performances spanning different types and genres of dance. If you require further information on vocational dance schools, applying to accredited dance courses, auditions and funding, contact CDET's information line 'Answers for Dancers' on 020 7240 5703 or see their case study in this section.

What are dance companies?

There are more than two hundred dance companies in the UK, spanning a variety of dance styles including ballet, contemporary, hip hop and African. A dance company will either be resident in a venue, be a touring company, or a combination of both. Many have websites which you can visit for full information. Most dance companies employ ensemble dancers on short to medium contracts, who may then work on a number of different productions for the same company over a number of months. In addition, the company will also employ principal/leading dancers on a role-by-role basis.

What are dance organisations?

There are numerous organisations which exist to support professional dancers, covering important areas including health and safety, career development, networking and legal and financial aspects. Other organisations (e.g. regional/national dance agencies) exist to promote dance within the wider community.

I have already trained to be a dancer. Why do I need further training?

Dance training should not cease as soon as you get your first job or complete a course. Throughout your career you should continuously strive to maintain your fitness levels, enhance and develop your existing skills and keep learning new ones in order to retain a competitive edge. You must also be prepared to continuously learn new dance styles and routines for specific roles. Ongoing training and classes can help you stay fit and active, and if you go through a period of unemployment you can keep your mind and body occupied, ready to take on your next job.

How should I use these listings?

The following pages will supply you with up-to-date contact details for a wide range of dance companies and organisations, followed by listings for dance training and professional classes. Members of CDET have indicated their membership status under their name.

Always research schools and classes thoroughly, obtaining copies of prospectuses where available. Most vocational schools offer two and three year full-time training programmes, many also offer excellent degree programmes. Foundation courses offer a sound introduction to the profession, but they can never replace a full-time vocational course. Many schools, organisations and studios also offer part-time/evening classes which offer a general understanding of dance and complementary technique or the opportunity to refresh specific dance skills; they will not, however, enable a student to become a professional dancer.

How else can I find work as a dancer?

Dance also plays a role in commercial theatre, musicals, opera, film, television, live music and video, corporate events and many other industries. Dancers may also want to be represented by an agent. Agents have many more contacts within the industry than an individual dancer can have, and can offer advice and negotiate contracts on your behalf as well as submit you for jobs. A number of specialist dance agencies are listed in the 'Agents: Dance' section.

What is Spotlight Dancers?

Dancers wishing to promote themselves to these types of job opportunities should consider joining Spotlight's specialist casting directory for dancers. This is a central directory of dancers published annually which is used by dance employers throughout the UK to locate dancers and send out casting or audition information. Members receive a page in the directory containing a headshot and body shot, agency contact details and selected credits as well as an online CV. Dancers who attend CDET accredited schools receive a discount when applying in their graduating year. For more information please see www.spotlight.com/dancers

What other careers are available in dance?

Opportunities also exist to work as a teacher, choreographer, technician or manager. Dance UK www.danceuk.org is a valuable source of information for anyone considering this type of work.

What should I do to avoid injury?

An injury is more likely to occur if you are inflexible and unprepared for sudden physical exertion. The last thing you want to do is to pick up an injury, however minor, and be prevented from working, so continuous training during both employment and unemployment will help you to minimise the risk of an injury during a performance or rehearsal.

If you do sustain an injury you will want to make sure it does not get any worse by getting treatment with a specialist. The British Association for Performing Arts Medicine (BAPAM) provides specialist health support for performers, free health assessment clinics and a directory of performing arts health practitioners and specialists. Visit www.bapam.org.uk for more information. You may also find their case study in the 'Health & Wellbeing' section of Contacts useful.

I'm not a professional dancer but I enjoy dancing. Why should I use these listings?

People don't just dance to perform, teach or advise within the industry. Dance can be pursued for fun, recreation, social reasons and for health. Training and professional advice should still be pursued to ensure that you do not injure yourself while dancing and prevent yourself from working. You can also use the 'Dance Training & Professional Classes' listings to find suitable dance lessons in your area, which you could attend to make friends, keep fit and stay occupied.

Where can I find more information?

For further advice about the dance industry, you could try contacting CDET (www.cdet.org.uk) for training information, Dance UK (www.danceuk.org) regarding the importance and needs of dance and dancers, or BAPAM (www.bapam.org.uk) for health issues.

You may want to get involved with MOVE IT! – the UK's biggest dance exhibition which takes place every year in March. For more information visit www.moveitdance.co.uk

If you are looking for a dance agent to promote you to job opportunities, please see the 'Agents: Dance' section of Contacts.

Dance Companies

The Council for Dance Education and Training (CDET) is the quality assurance agency of the dance and musical theatre industries. It is the first point of contact for students and others seeking information on the quality of education and training in the United Kingdom. CDET negotiates with government agencies in this country and overseas to ensure the accredited private dance and musical theatre sectors are represented vigorously and consistently at all levels of national and international decision making.

What is a CDET Accredited School?

The Council carries out a rigorous assessment of all aspects of provision before awarding accreditation to a professional training school. Students studying at CDET accredited schools may be confident they are receiving industry endorsed training of the highest quality, training that will enable them to develop the skills to sustain them throughout their careers in the demanding worlds of professional dance and musical theatre.

What is a CDET AMS School?

An AMS School is a professional training provider working towards full accreditation, but one which has not, as yet, undergone an accreditation assessment. AMS schools must meet initial accreditation criteria as a condition of AMS membership.

What makes CDET accredited education and training so special?

Every CDET accredited institution has been inspected by a trained panel of dance and musical theatre professionals to ensure it meets the needs of both the industry and the student.

Competition for places at CDET accredited dance and musical theatre schools is fierce; consequently students will sometimes consider an offer from an unaccredited vocational trainer. Before accepting a place at an unaccredited school students should always ensure they will receive the quality of training they expect, that studio facilities and medical resources are suitable for the teaching of dance or musical theatre and that they have requested a written explanation as to why the school does not hold CDET accreditation.

What is a CDET Dance Awarding Organisation?

Dance Awarding Organisations are examining institutions offering graded and vocational graded qualifications in dance and musical theatre. Dance teachers who hold a teaching qualification from an awarding organisation may enter students for the examinations of that body. CDET has two categories of membership for Awarding Organisations:

1. Validated Dance Awarding Organisations

2. Corporate Members

Corporate Members are member organisations of CDET currently working towards validation.

What are the CDET *Recognised Awards?*

CDET's *Recognised Awards* are five industry-recognised awards available to dance and musical theatre schools and/or teachers meeting the standards of professional practice of CDET. The awards recognise dance and musical theatre schools and teachers who have committed themselves to upholding safe and professional standards. Students choosing a *Recognised* dance school or teacher may be confident in their professional standards knowing they have met CDET's *Requirements* of professional practice.

What resources are available to me?

CDET publishes the annual *The UK Guide to Professional Education and Training in Dance and Musical Theatre.* A downloadable PDF version of the guide is available on the CDET website www.cdet.org.uk. Hard copies are also available, free of charge, from French's Theatre Bookshop, London. The Council offers a comprehensive and free information service, *Answers for Dancers*, on all aspects of dance education and training. E-mail answersfordancers@cdet.org.uk or call the CDET office on 020 7240 5703.

Whatever your query regarding dance or musical theatre education and training visit the CDET website at www.cdet.org.uk or telephone the CDET office on 020 7240 5703.

Photo: Steve Cooper

Courtney George

In December 2011 Courtney George was named Young Dancer of The Year at The Dance Show after wowing the judges with her routines. As part of her prize, 18-year-old Courtney from Shelley, Huddersfield won a year's free membership to Spotlight Dancers, plus a free showreel, a contract with top dance agency Dancers Inc. and a contract to appear in Clothes Show Live's Suzuki Fashion Theatre in December 2012.

Here Courtney talks about her dance background and shares her thoughts on training for young dancers.

I started dancing at the age of 2 at my mum's theatre school, Georgie School of Theatre Arts. Ever since my passion for dance has grown. I started dancing with Northern Ballet at the age of 9, where I have built up my technique and strengthened my body. At the age of 14 I was awarded a scholarship to attend the Urdang Youth Academy which has improved my musical theatre and jazz knowledge and ability.

It felt amazing to have won the Young Dancer of the Year competition – I was so shocked it was unreal! The whole day was brilliant. I really enjoyed the process of the competition – it was so exciting getting through each round. It was just one amazing experience!

Summer schools are a great way to find out about each college and to help get you noticed.

I'll be starting my first term at Laine Theatre Arts School in September 2012. I will be studying all disciplines of dance, acting and singing. The course will be the same for everyone until my third year which is when I will get to choose either dance or musical theatre. I am so excited to start – I am ready for this move and to take this next step. I'm really looking forward to the challenge and I have been counting down the days!

I was very fortunate to have been offered full scholarships at Laine, Urdang and Bird, but it was difficult to know which would be the right place for me. As I had tried summer schools at all three, it gave me the chance to get more insight into each

college and I felt that Laine was going to suit me best.

For the scholarship I had to attend an audition at Laine where I had to do a jazz class, a ballet class, an acting workshop, a dance solo and a singing solo, which was initially just for a place at the college. To find out that I was also awarded funding straight away was amazing!

I believe that right now training is the most important thing for me. I want my training to be my focus in order to build up my strengths, so that when I do start working I will be the best I can possibly be.

After my training I would love to appear in the West End. Every show I have seen has inspired me and it is my dream to perform!

For other dancers like me preparing to start training, I think that summer schools are a great way to find out about each college and to help get you noticed. Where to study is something that only you can decide for yourself – everywhere is different and has different strengths that suit different people, so the best place is the place where you feel most at home!

The most important advice I can give is to believe in yourself. If an opportunity arises like the Young Dancer of the Year competition did for me, you have to grab it with both hands and don't let it pass by. Believe you can do it.

> **To find out more about Clothes Show Live's Suzuki Fashion Theatre visit www.clothesshowlive.com**

KOSH THE T/F 020 7263 7419
Physical Theatre
59 Stapleton Hall Road
London N4 3QF
E info@thekosh.com

LUDUS DANCE T 01524 35936
Assembly Rooms, King Street
Lancaster LA1 1RE
F 01524 847744
E info@ludusdance.org
W www.ludusdance.org

NEW ADVENTURES T 020 7713 6766
Sadler's Wells
Rosebery Avenue
London EC1R 4TN
E info@new-adventures.net
W www.new-adventures.net

NORTHERN BALLET T 0113 220 8000
2 St Cecilia Street
Quarry Hill
Leeds LS2 7PA
F 0113 220 8001
E info@northernballet.com
W www.northernballet.com

**PAVILION DANCE
SOUTH WEST** T 01202 203630
Westover Road
Bournemouth BH1 2BU
E paviliondance@dancesouthwest.org.uk
W www.paviliondance.org.uk

PHOENIX DANCE THEATRE T 0113 236 8130
2 St Cecilia Street
Quarry Hill
Leeds LS2 7PA
E info@phoenixdancetheatre.co.uk
W www.phoenixdancetheatre.co.uk

PLACE THE T 020 7121 1000
17 Duke's Road, London WC1H 9PY
F 020 7121 1142
E info@theplace.org.uk
W www.theplace.org.uk

PMB PRESENTATIONS LTD T 020 7368 3337
Vicarage House
58-60 Kensington Church Street
London W8 4DB
F 020 7368 3338
E p@triciamurraybett.com
W www.pmbpresentations.co.uk

RAMBERT DANCE COMPANY T 020 8630 0600
94 Chiswick High Road
London W4 1SH
F 020 8747 8323
E rdc@rambert.org.uk
W www.rambert.org.uk

RETINA DANCE COMPANY T 0115 947 6202
*UK-based Contemporary Dance Company Touring
Nationally & Internationally*
College Street Centre
College Street
Nottingham NG1 5AQ
E admin@retinadance.com
W www.retinadance.com

ROTIE, Marie-Gabrielle PRODUCTIONS
1 Christchurch Square
London E9 7HU
E rotieproductions@googlemail.com
W www.rotieproductions.com

ROYAL BALLET THE T 020 7240 1200 Ext 712
Royal Opera House
Covent Garden
London WC2E 9DD
F 020 7212 9121
E balletcompany@roh.org.uk
W www.roh.org.uk

SCOTTISH BALLET T 0141 331 2931
Tramway
25 Albert Drive
Glasgow G41 2PE
W www.scottishballet.co.uk

SCOTTISH DANCE THEATRE T 01382 342600
Dundee Repertory Theatre
Tay Square
Dundee DD1 1PB
F 01382 228609
E achinn@dundeereptheatre.co.uk
W www.scottishdancetheatre.com

**SLOVAK DANCE
THEATRE** T/F 00 421 2 54645811
Pribinova 25
811 09 Bratislava
Slovakia
E zahorec@sdt.sk
W www.sdt.sk

SPLITZ THEATRE ARTZ T 01223 880389
5 Cow Lane
Fulbourn
Cambridge CB21 5HB
E clare@splitz-ta.net
W www.splitz-ta.co.uk

SPRINGS DANCE COMPANY T 01634 817523
65 John Kennedy Court
Newington Green Road
London N1 4RT
T 07775 628442
E info@springsdancecompany.org.uk
W www.springsdancecompany.org.uk

**TRANSITIONS DANCE
COMPANY** T 020 8305 9471
Creekside
London SE8 3DZ
E transitions@trinitylaban.ac.uk
W www.trinitylaban.ac.uk

TWITCH EVENT CHOREOGRAPHY
E info@twitch.uk.com
W www.twitch.uk.com

UNION DANCE T 020 7836 7837
Top Floor
6 Charing Cross Road
London WC2H 0HG
F 020 7836 7847
E info@uniondance.co.uk
W www.uniondance.co.uk

ACCELERATE PRODUCTIONS LTD   **T** 07782 199181
374 Ley Street, Ilford IG1 4AE
E info@accelerate-productions.co.uk
W www.accelerate-productions.co.uk

AKADEMI SOUTH ASIAN DANCE UK   **T** 020 7691 3210
Hampstead Town Hall, 213 Haverstock Hill
London NW3 4QP
F 020 7691 3211
E info@akademi.co.uk
W www.akademi.co.uk

ALLIED DANCING ASSOCIATION **T** 0151 724 1829
137 Greenhill Road, Mossley Hill, Liverpool L18 7HQ
E carolparryada@yahoo.co.uk

ASSOCIATION OF DANCE OF THE AFRICAN DIASPORA   **T** 020 7841 7357
Urdang, The Old Finsbury Town Hall
Rosebery Avenue, London EC1R 4QT
F 020 7833 2363
E info@adad.org.uk
W www.adad.org.uk

AWARENESS THROUGH DANCE   **T** 07595 512711
Support System for Professional Dancers
77 Blackfriars Road, London SE1 8HA
E info@awarenessthroughdance.org
W www.awarenessthroughdance.org

BENESH INSTITUTE THE   **T** 020 7326 8035
36 Battersea Square, London SW11 3RA
T 020 7326 8031
E beneshinstitute@rad.org.uk
W www.benesh.org

BRITISH ARTS THE   **T** 01708 756263
12 Deveron Way, Rise Park
Romford RM1 4UL
E sally.chennelle@talk21.com
W www.britisharts.org

BRITISH ASSOCIATION OF TEACHERS OF DANCING   **T** 0141 427 3699
Pavilion, 8 Upper Level
Watermark Business Park
315 Govan Road
Glasgow G51 2SE
E enquiries@batd.co.uk
W www.batd.co.uk

BRITISH BALLET ORGANIZATION   **T** 020 8748 1241
Dance Examining Society. Teacher Training
Woolborough House
39 Lonsdale Road
Barnes, London SW13 9JP
E info@bbo.org.uk
W www.bbo.org.uk

BRITISH THEATRE DANCE ASSOCIATION   **T** 0845 1662179
Garden Street, Leicester LE1 3UA
F 0845 1662189
E info@btda.org.uk
W www.btda.org.uk

CHISENHALE DANCE SPACE   **T** 020 8981 6617
64-84 Chisenhale Road
Bow, London E3 5QZ
F 020 8980 9323
E mail@chisenhaledancespace.co.uk
W www.chisenhaledancespace.co.uk

COUNCIL FOR DANCE
EDUCATION & TRAINING (CDET)   **T** 020 7240 5703
Old Brewer's Yard, 17-19 Neal Street
Covent Garden, London WC2H 9UY
F 020 7240 2547
E info@cdet.org.uk
W www.cdet.org.uk

DANCE4   **T** 0115 941 0773
Twitter: @dance_4
College Street Centre, College Street
Nottingham NG1 5AQ
E info@dance4.co.uk
W www.dance4.co.uk

DANCE BASE NATIONAL
CENTRE FOR DANCE   **T** 0131 225 5525
14-16 Grassmarket
Edinburgh EH1 2JU
E dance@dancebase.co.uk
W www.dancebase.co.uk

DANCE EAST   **T** 01473 295230
Jerwood Dance House, Foundry Lane
Ipswich IP4 1DW
E info@danceeast.co.uk
W www.danceeast.co.uk

DANCE HOUSE   **T** 0141 552 2442
The Briggait, 141 Bridgegate
Glasgow G1 5HZ
E info@dancehouse.org
W www.dancehouse.org

DANCE IN DEVON   **T** 01392 667050
County Dance Development Agency
Exeter Phoenix, Bradnich Place
Gandy Street, Exeter EX4 3LS
E info@danceindevon.org.uk
W www.danceindevon.org.uk

DANCE INITIATIVE
GREATER MANCHESTER   **T** 0161 232 7179
Z-arts, Stretford Road
Hulme, Manchester M15 5ZA
E info@digm.org.uk
W www.digm.org

DANCE UK   **T** 020 7713 0730
Including the Healthier Dancer Programme
The Old Finsbury Town Hall
Rosebery Avenue, London EC1R 4QT
F 020 7833 2363
E info@danceuk.org
W www.danceuk.org

DANCE UMBRELLA   **T** 020 7407 1200
1 Brewery Square, London SE1 2LF
F 020 7378 8405
E mail@danceumbrella.co.uk
W www.danceumbrella.co.uk

DANCERS' CAREER
DEVELOPMENT   **T** 020 7831 1449
Plouviez House, 19-20 Hatton Place
London EC1N 8RU
F 020 7242 1462
E admin@thedcd.org.uk
W www.thedcd.org.uk

DANCEXCHANGE   **T** 0121 689 3170
National Dance Agency
Birmingham Hippodrome, Thorp Street
Birmingham B5 4TB
E info@dancexchange.org.uk
W www.dancexchange.org.uk

DAVIES, Siobhan DANCE   **T** 020 7091 9650
Professional Development for Dance Artists & Education
85 St George's Road
London SE1 6ER
F 020 7091 9669
E info@siobhandavies.com
W www.siobhandavies.com

EAST LONDON DANCE   **T** 020 8279 1050
Stratford Circus
Theatre Square
London E15 1BX
F 020 8279 1054
E office@eastlondondance.org
W www.eastlondondance.org

EVERYBODY DANCE   **T** 07870 429528
*Contact: Rachel Freeman. Aerial & Community Dance for
Disabled & Non-disabled Artists of All Ages*
Longlands Barn, Whitbourne
Worcester, Worcestershire WR6 5SG
E rfeverybodydance@gmail.com

FAME ACADEMY OF
PERFORMING ARTS   **T** 020 8882 7849
Courses. Event & Talent Management
E info@fameacademy.org.uk
W www.fameacademy.org.uk

FOUNDATION FOR
COMMUNITY DANCE   **T** 0116 253 3453
LCB Depot, 31 Rutland Street
Leicester LE1 1RE
F 0116 261 6801
E info@communitydance.org.uk
W www.communitydance.org.uk

GREENWICH DANCE   **T** 020 8293 9741
The Borough Hall, Royal Hill
London SE10 8RE
E info@greenwichdance.org.uk
W www.greenwichdance.org.uk

IDTA (INTERNATIONAL DANCE TEACHERS'
ASSOCIATION)   **T** 01273 685652
International House
76 Bennett Road
Brighton, East Sussex BN2 5JL
F 01273 674388
E info@idta.co.uk
W www.idta.co.uk

KENT YOUTH
DANCE COMPANY   **T** 01227 365013
*Giving Young Performers the Opportunity to Perform with
Professionals*
45 Western Avenue
Herne Bay, Kent CT6 8UF
E kentyouthdance@hotmail.com
W www.kentyouthdance.co.uk

LANGUAGE OF
DANCE CENTRE   **T** 020 7749 1131
Oxford House
Derbyshire Street
London E2 6HG
E info@lodc.org
W www.lodc.org

LONDON CONTEMPORARY
DANCE SCHOOL   **T** 020 7121 1111
The Place, 17 Duke's Road
London WC1H 9AT
F 020 7121 1142
E lcds@theplace.org.uk
W www.lcds.ac.uk

LUDUS DANCE　　T 01524 35936
The Assembly Rooms
King Street, Lancaster LA1 1RE
F 01524 847744
E info@ludusdance.org
W www.ludusdance.org

**MERSEYSIDE DANCE
INITIATIVE**　　T 0151 708 8810
National Dance Agency
24 Hope Street, Liverpool L1 9BX
E info@mdi.org.uk
W www.mdi.org.uk

**MIDLAND INTERNATIONAL
DANCE ARTS ASSOCIATION**　　T 0121 694 0012
29A Sycamore Road
Birmingham B23 5QP
F 0121 694 0013
E midaa.hq@hotmail.com
W www.abdance.net

**NATIONAL RESOURCE
CENTRE FOR DANCE**　　T 01483 689316
University of Surrey, Guildford GU2 7XH
F 01483 689500
E nrcd@surrey.ac.uk
W www.surrey.ac.uk/nrcd

PAVILION DANCE SOUTH WEST　　T 01202 203630
Westover Road
Bournemouth BH1 2BU
E paviliondance@dancesouthwest.org.uk
W www.paviliondance.org.uk

PLACE THE　　T 020 7121 1000
17 Duke's Road, London WC1H 9BY
F 020 7121 1142
E info@theplace.org.uk
W www.theplace.org.uk

**PROFESSIONAL TEACHERS
OF DANCING**　　T 01935 848547
Contact: Jo Pillinger
The Studios
Morcombelake
Dorset DT6 6DY
E ptdenquiries@msn.com
W www.ptdance.com

SOUTH EAST DANCE　　T 01273 696844
*National Development Organisation for Dance in South
East England*
28 Kensington Street
Brighton BN1 4AJ
F 01273 697212
E info@southeastdance.org.uk
W www.southeastdance.org.uk

SWINDON DANCE　　T 01793 601700
National Dance Agency
Town Hall Studios
Regent Circus
Swindon SN1 1QF
E info@swindondance.org.uk
W www.swindondance.org.uk

YORKSHIRE DANCE　　T 0113 243 0867
Dance Development Agency
3 St Peters Buildings
St Peters Square
Leeds LS9 8AH
F 0113 259 5700
E admin@yorkshiredance.com
W www.yorkshiredance.com

Paul Harris®

office@paulharris.uk.com
www.paulharris.uk.com

Choreography and
Coaching in Period
and Contemporary
Social Dance

Choreographer:
* The Paradise
* Da Vinci's Demons
* Great Expectations

✳ Swing ✳ Waltz ✳ Pavane ✳ Salsa ✳ Tango ✳ Quadrille ✳ Charleston ✳ Schottische

---

**ACADEMY FOR THEATRE
ARTS THE**   T 01782 631895
1 Vale View, Porthill
Newcastle under Lyme, Staffordshire ST5 0AF
F 01782 610363
E no1theacademy@aol.com
W www.jillclewes.co.uk

AIRCRAFT CIRCUS LTD   T 020 8317 8401
Unit 7A, Mellish House
Harrington Way, London SE18 5NR
E info@aircraftcircus.com
W www.aircraftcircus.com

**ARTS EDUCATIONAL
SCHOOLS LONDON**   T 020 8987 6666
CDET Member
Cone Ripman House, 14 Bath Road
Chiswick, London W4 1LY
E receptionist@artsed.co.uk
W www.artsed.co.uk

ATENEO DELLA DANZA   T 00 39 0577 222774
Professional Training Centre
Via dei Pispini 39/45, Siena 5310, Tuscany, Italy
E info@ateneodelladanza.it
W www.ateneodelladanza.it

AVIV DANCE STUDIOS   T/F 01923 250000
Watford Boys Grammar School
Rickmansworth Road, Watford WD18 7JF
E info@avivdance.com
W www.avivdance.com

**BALLROOM, LONDON
THEATRE OF**   T 020 8722 8798
Artistic Director: Paul Harris® (Mentor "Faking It")
24 Montana Gardens, Sutton, Surrey SM1 4FP
E office@londontheatreofballroom.com
W www.londontheatreofballroom.com

BELFAST TALENT SCHOOL   T 028 9024 3324
*Cheerleading, Musical Theatre Dance & Pop Style for
Children & Adults*
The Crescent Arts Centre
2-4 University Road, Belfast, Antrim BT7 1NH
E info@belfasttalent.com
W www.belfasttalentschool.com

BHAVAN CENTRE   T 020 7381 3086
*Training in Indian Classical Music, Dance, Languages
& Yoga*
4A Castletown Road, London W14 9HE
E info@bhavan.net
W www.bhavan.net

**BIRD COLLEGE DANCE MUSIC &
THEATRE PERFORMANCE**   T 020 8300 6004
*CDET Member. Dance & Theatre Performance
HE & FE Programmes*
The Centre, 27 Station Road, Sidcup, Kent DA15 7EB
F 020 8308 1370
E performance@birdcollege.co.uk
W www.birdcollege.co.uk

BODENS STUDIOS   T 020 8447 0909
Performing Arts Classes
Bodens Studios & Agency
99 East Barnet Road
New Barnet, Herts EN4 8RF
T 07545 696888
E info@bodens.co.uk
W www.bodens.co.uk

BRIGHTON DANCE DIVERSION   T 01903 770304
93 Sea Lane, Rustington
West Sussex BN16 2RS
E info@brightondancediversion.com
W www.brightondancediversion.com

**CAMBRIDGE PERFORMING
ARTS AT BODYWORK**   T 01223 314461
CDET Member
Bodywork Company Dance Studios
25-29 Glisson Road
Cambridge CB1 2HA
E admin@bodyworkds.co.uk
W www.bodywork-dance.co.uk

CANDOCO DANCE COMPANY   T 020 7704 6845
2T Leroy House, 436 Essex Road
London N1 3QP
E info@candoco.co.uk
W www.candoco.co.uk

CENTRAL SCHOOL OF BALLET   T 020 7837 6332
*Full Time Vocational Training. Open Classes Beginner/
Professional Level*
10 Herbal Hill, Clerkenwell Road
London EC1R 5EG
F 020 7833 5571
E info@csbschool.co.uk
W www.centralschoolofballet.co.uk

**CENTRE - PERFORMING
ARTS COLLEGE THE**   T 01634 848009
681 Maidstone Road
Rochester, Kent ME1 3QJ
E dance@thecentrepac.com
W www.thecentrepac.com

**CLASSIQUE SCHOOL
OF DANCE**   T 02392 233334
*Ballet. Contemporary. Jazz. Modern. Tap. Stage
(2yrs-Adult). Drama. Singing*
3-5 Stakes Hill Road
Waterlooville
Hampshire PO7 7JB
E enquiries@classiquedance.com
W www.classiquedance.com

**COLLECTIVE DANCE &
DRAMA**   T/F 020 8428 0037
The Studio
Rectory Lane
Rickmansworth
Herts WD3 1FD
E info@collectivedance.co.uk
W www.collectivedance.co.uk

**CONTI, Italia ACADEMY
OF THEATRE ARTS**   T 020 7608 0044
CDET Member. Courses: Performing Arts Diploma,
3 yr. Performing Arts with Teacher Training, 3 yr. Intensive
Performing Arts, Acting, 1 yr. Foundation Performing
Arts, 1 yr. BA (Hons) Acting, 3 yr. Foundation Acting,
2 term. Singing, 1 yr. Theatre Arts School
(academic yrs 7-11)
Italia Conti House, 23 Goswell Road
London EC1M 7AJ
F 020 7253 1430
E admin@italiaconti.co.uk
W www.italiaconti.com

**COUNCIL FOR DANCE EDUCATION &
TRAINING (CDET)**   T 020 7240 5703
Old Brewer's Yard, 17-19 Neal Street
Covent Garden, London WC2H 9UY
F 020 7240 2547
E info@cdet.org.uk
W www.cdet.org.uk

CPA STUDIOS   T 01708 766007
CDET Member
The Studios, 219B North Street
Romford, Essex RM1 4QA
E college@cpastudios.co.uk
W www.cpastudios.co.uk

**D&B SCHOOL OF PERFORMING ARTS &
D&B THEATRE SCHOOL**   T 020 8698 8880
Central Studios, 470 Bromley Road
Bromley, Kent BR1 4PQ
E info@dandbperformingarts.co.uk
W www.dandbperformingarts.co.uk

**DANCE BASE NATIONAL
CENTRE FOR DANCE**   T 0131 225 5525
14-16 Grassmarket, Edinburgh EH1 2JU
E dance@dancebase.co.uk
W www.dancebase.co.uk

DANCE COMPANY COLLEGE   T 020 8402 2424
1 yr Intensive Course
76 High Street, Beckenham BR3 1ED
E admin@dancecompanycollege.com
W www.dancecompanycollege.com

DANCE HOUSE   T 0141 552 2442
The Briggait, 141 Bridgegate
Glasgow G1 5HZ
E info@dancehouse.org
W www.dancehouse.org

**DANCE RESEARCH COMMITTEE -
IMPERIAL SOCIETY OF
TEACHERS OF DANCING**   T 01233 712469
Training in Historical Dance
c/o Ludwell House, Charing, Kent TN27 0LS
F 01233 712768
E n.gainesarmitage@tiscali.co.uk
W www.istd.org

**DANCE STUDIO
LEEDS LTD THE**   T 0113 242 1550
Mill 6, 1st Floor
Mabgate Mills, Leeds, West Yorkshire LS9 7DZ
E katie@thedancestudioleeds.com
W www.thedancestudioleeds.com

DANCEWORKS   T 020 7629 6183
Also Fitness, Yoga & Martial Arts Classes
16 Balderton Street, London W1K 6TN
E info@danceworks.net
W www.danceworks.net

DAPA   T 01254 699221
Dance. Drama. Music. Singing. All Ages & Abilities
The Wharf Studios, Eanam Wharf
Blackburn, Lancashire BB1 5BY
E info@dapacentre.co.uk
W www.dapa.info

DAVIES, Siobhan STUDIOS   T 020 7091 9650
Daily Professional Classes. Open Dance & Body
Conditioning Classes for Wider Community
85 St George's Road, London SE1 6ER
F 020 7091 9669
E info@siobhandavies.com
W www.siobhandavies.com

**DIRECTIONS THEATRE ARTS
CHESTERFIELD LTD**   T/F 01246 854455
1A-2A Sheffield Road, Chesterfield
Derbyshire S41 7LL
E julie.cox5@btconnect.com
W www.directionstheatrearts.org

D M ACADEMY   T 01274 585317
The Studios, Briggate
Shipley, Bradford, West Yorks BD17 7BT
F 01274 592502
E info@dmacademy.co.uk
W www.dmacademy.co.uk

**DUFFILL, Drusilla
THEATRE SCHOOL**   T 01444 232672
Grove Lodge, Oakwood Road
Burgess Hill, West Sussex RH15 0HZ
F 01444 232680
E drusilladschool@btclick.com
W www.drusilladuffilltheatreschool.co.uk

EAST LONDON DANCE　　　T 020 8279 1050
Stratford Circus, Theatre Square
London E15 1BX
F 020 8279 1054
E office@eastlondondance.org
W www.eastlondondance.org

**EDINBURGH'S TELFORD
COLLEGE**　　　T 0131 559 4000
350 West Granton Road
Edinburgh EH5 1QE
F 0131 559 4111
E mail@ed-coll.ac.uk
W www.ed-coll.ac.uk

**ELMHURST SCHOOL
FOR DANCE**　　　T 0121 472 6655
CDET Member
249 Bristol Road, Edgbaston
Birmingham B5 7UH
F 0121 472 6654
E enquiries@elmhurstdance.co.uk
W www.elmhurstdance.co.uk

**ENGLISH NATIONAL
BALLET SCHOOL**　　　T 020 7376 7076
CDET Member
Carlyle Building, Hortensia Road
London SW10 0QS
F 020 7376 3404
E info@enbschool.org.uk
W www.enbschool.org.uk

**EXPRESSIONS ACADEMY
OF PERFORMING ARTS**　　　T 01623 424334
CDET Member
3 Newgate Lane, Mansfield
Nottingham NG18 2LB
E expressions-uk@btconnect.com
W www.expressionsperformingarts.co.uk

**FANTASY FEET DANCE &
MUSICAL THEATRE ACADEMY**　　　T 07947 345434
The Dance Studio
Merthyr Leisure Centre
Merthyr Tydfil Leisure Village
Merthyr Tydfil, Wales CF48 1UT
T 07894 164104
E fantasyfeetdanceacademy@yahoo.co.uk
W www.fantasyfeetdance.co.uk

**GEORGIE SCHOOL OF
THEATRE ARTS**　　　T/F 01484 606994
101 Lane Head Road
Shepley, Huddersfield
West Yorkshire HD8 8DB
E donna.george@virgin.net

GREASEPAINT ANONYMOUS　　　T 020 8886 2263
4 Gallus Close
Winchmore Hill
London N21 1JR
T 07930 421216
E info@greasepaintanonymous.co.uk
W www.greasepaintanonymous.co.uk

HAMMOND SCHOOL THE　　　T 01244 305350
CDET Member
Hoole Bank, Mannings Lane
Chester CH2 4ES
F 01244 305351
E info@thehammondschool.co.uk
W www.thehammondschool.co.uk

HARRIS, Paul　　　T 07958 784462
Contact: Paul Harris®. Choreography. Movement for
Actors. Tuition in Period & Contemporary Social Dance
24 Montana Gardens, Sutton, Surrey SM1 4FP
E office@paulharris.uk.com
W www.paulharris.uk.com

ISLINGTON ARTS FACTORY　　　T 020 7607 0561
2 Parkhurst Road, London N7 0SF
E info@islingtonartsfactory.org
W www.islingtonartsfactory.org

KS DANCE LTD　　　T 01925 837693
CDET Member
9A Centre 21, Bridge Lane
Woolston, Warrington, Cheshire WA1 4AW
E simmons.k@btconnect.com
W www.ksd-online.co.uk

LAINE THEATRE ARTS　　　T 01372 724648
CDET Member
The Studios, East Street
Epsom, Surrey KT17 1HH
F 01372 723775
E webmaster@laine-theatre-arts.co.uk
W www.laine-theatre-arts.co.uk

**LIVERPOOL INSTITUTE FOR
PERFORMING ARTS THE**　　　T 0151 330 3000
CDET Member
Mount Street, Liverpool L1 9HF
E admissions@lipa.ac.uk
W www.lipa.ac.uk

**LIVERPOOL THEATRE
SCHOOL**　　　T 0151 728 7800
CDET Member. Musical Theatre & Professional Classes
19 Aigburth Road, Liverpool, Merseyside L17 4JR
T 07515 282877
E info@liverpooltheatreschool.co.uk
W www.liverpooltheatreschool.co.uk

**LONDON CONTEMPORARY
DANCE SCHOOL**　　　T 020 7121 1111
Full-time Vocational Training at Degree &
Postgraduate Level
The Place, 17 Duke's Road, London WC1H 9PY
F 020 7121 1145
E lcds@theplace.org.uk
W www.lcds.ac.uk

**LONDON SCHOOL
OF CAPOEIRA**　　　T 020 7281 2020
Unit 1-2 Leeds Place, Tollington Park, London N4 3RF
E info@londonschoolofcapoeira.com
W www.londonschoolofcapoeira.com

LONDON STUDIO CENTRE　　　T 020 7837 7741
CDET Member
artsdepot, 5 Nether Street, Tally Ho Corner
North Finchley, London N12 0GA
F 020 7837 3248
E info@london-studio-centre.co.uk
W www.london-studio-centre.co.uk

**MANN, Stella COLLEGE OF
PERFORMING ARTS LTD**　　　T 01234 213331
CDET Member. Professional Training Course for
Performers & Teachers
10 Linden Road, Bedford, Bedfordshire MK40 2DA
F 01234 217284
E stellamanncollege@hotmail.com
W www.stellamanncollege.co.uk

**MGA ACADEMY OF
PERFORMING ARTS THE**　　T 0131 466 9392
The MGA Company
207 Balgreen Road
Edinburgh EH11 2RZ
E info@themgacompany.com
W www.themgaacademy.com

**MIALKOWSKI, Andrzej - BALLROOM &
LATIN AMERICAN**　　T 01604 239755
Choreographer. Teacher. IDTA Member
Step By Step Dance School
24 Henry Street, Northampton
Northamptonshire NN1 4JE
T 07849 331430
E info@danceschool-stepbystep.com
W www.danceschool-stepbystep.com

**MIDLANDS ACADEMY OF
DANCE & DRAMA**　　T/F 0115 911 0401
CDET Member
Century House, Building B
428 Carlton Hill, Nottingham NG4 1QA
E admin@maddcollege.supanet.com
W www.maddcollege.co.uk

**MILLENNIUM PERFORMING
ARTS LTD**　　T 020 8301 8744
CDET Member
29 Thomas Street, Woolwich
London SE18 6HU
E info@md2000.co.uk
W www.md2000.co.uk

**NEW LONDON PERFORMING
ARTS CENTRE**　　T 020 8444 4544
*Performing Arts Classes (3-19 yrs). All Dance Styles.
GCSE Course. RAD & ISTD Exams*
76 St James Lane, Muswell Hill
London N10 3RD
F 020 8444 4040
E nlpac@aol.com
W www.nlpac.co.uk

NLDS THE COLLEGE　　T 020 3174 0649
Full-time Performing Arts & Teaching Qualifications
843-845 Green Lanes
Winchmore Hill
London N21 2RX
E info@nlds.org.uk
W www.nlds.org.uk

**NORTH LONDON
DANCE STUDIO**　　T 020 8360 5700
Evening & Weekend Classes (3-18 yrs)
843-845 Green Lanes
Winchmore Hill
London, N21 2RX
F 020 8360 5777
E thedancestudio@btconnect.com
W www.thedancestudio.co.uk

**NORTHERN ACADEMY OF
PERFORMING ARTS**　　T 01482 310690
Anlaby Road, Hull HU1 2PD
F 01482 212280
E napa@northernacademy.org.uk
W www.northernacademy.org.uk

NORTHERN BALLET SCHOOL　　T 0161 237 1406
CDET Member
The Dancehouse
10 Oxford Road
Manchester M1 5QA
F 0161 237 1408
E enquiries@northernballetschool.co.uk
W www.northernballetschool.co.uk

**NORTHERN SCHOOL OF CONTEMPORARY
DANCE THE**　　T 0113 219 3000
98 Chapeltown Road, Leeds LS7 4BH
E info@nscd.ac.uk
W www.nscd.ac.uk

PERFORMERS COLLEGE　　T 01375 672053
CDET Member
Southend Road, Corringham
Essex SS17 8JT
F 01375 672353
E lesley@performerscollege.co.uk
W www.performerscollege.co.uk

PINEAPPLE DANCE STUDIOS　　T 020 7836 4004
7 Langley Street
London WC2H 9JA
F 020 7836 0803
W www.pineapple.uk.com

PLACE THE　　T 020 7121 1000
17 Duke's Road, London WC1H 9BY
F 020 7121 1142
E info@theplace.org.uk
W www.theplace.org.uk

PROFESSIONAL TEACHERS
OF DANCING   T 01935 848547
Contact: Jo Pillinger
The Studios, Morcombelake
Dorset DT6 6DY
E ptdenquiries@msn.com
W www.ptdance.com

RAMBERT SCHOOL OF BALLET
& CONTEMPORARY DANCE   T 020 8892 9960
Clifton Lodge, St Margaret's Drive
Twickenham, Middlesex TW1 1QN
F 020 8892 8090
E info@rambertschool.org.uk
W www.rambertschool.org.uk

RETINA DANCE COMPANY   T 0115 947 6202
Weekly Classes. Training. Workshops. Residencies
College Street Centre, College Street
Nottingham NG1 5AQ
E leeann@retinadance.com
W www.retinadance.com

RIDGEWAY STUDIOS PERFORMING
ARTS CENTRE   T 01992 633775
Cheshunt & Cuffley Studios
Office: 106 Hawkshead Road
Potters Bar
Hertfordshire EN6 1NG
E info@ridgewaystudios.co.uk
W www.ridgewaystudios.co.uk

RIVERSIDE REFLECTIONS BATON
TWIRLING TEAM   T/F 01322 410003
34 Knowle Avenue
Bexleyheath, Kent DA7 5LX
T 07958 617976
E clare@riversidereflections.co.uk
W www.riversidereflections.co.uk

ROEBUCK, Gavin   T 020 7370 7324
Classical Ballet
51 Earls Court Square, London SW5 9DG
E info@gavinroebuck.com

ROJO Y NEGRO   T 020 8520 2726
Argentine Tango School of Dance
Latvian Club, 1st Floor
72 Queensborough Terrace, London W2 3HS
E info@rojoynegroclub.com
W www.rojoynegroclub.com

ROJO Y NEGRO   T 020 8520 2726
Argentine Tango School of Dance
Union Tavern, Above 52 Lloyd Baker Street
Farringdon, Kings Cross, London WC1X 9AA
E info@rojoynegroclub.com
W www.rojoynegroclub.com

ROYAL ACADEMY OF DANCE   T 020 7326 8000
36 Battersea Square, London SW11 3RA
F 020 7924 3129
E info@rad.org.uk
W www.rad.org.uk

SAFREY ACADEMY OF
PERFORMING ARTS   T 07956 920813
Classes at The British Home, Streatham SW16
Correspondence only:
10 St Julians Close
London SW16 2RY
F 020 8488 9121
E info@safreyarts.co.uk
W www.safreyarts.co.uk

SLP COLLEGE   T 0113 286 8136
CDET Member
Chapel Lane, Leeds LS25 1AG
E info@slpcollege.co.uk
W www.slpcollege.co.uk

STARMAKERZ
THEATRE SCHOOL   T 07771 595171
Oxted School, Bluehouse Lane
Oxted, Surrey RH8 0AB
E vicky@starmakerz.co.uk
W www.starmakerz.co.uk

TIFFANY THEATRE COLLEGE   T 01702 710069
969-973 London Road
Leigh on Sea
Essex SS9 3LB
E info@tiffanytheatrecollege.com
W www.tiffanytheatrecollege.com

TRING PARK SCHOOL FOR THE
PERFORMING ARTS   T 01442 824255
CDET Member
Tring Park, Tring
Hertfordshire HP23 5LX
E info@tringpark.com
W www.tringpark.com

TRINITY LABAN CONSERVATOIRE
OF MUSIC & DANCE   T 020 8691 8600
Creekside, London SE8 3DZ
F 020 8691 8400
E info@trinitylaban.ac.uk
W www.trinitylaban.ac.uk

URDANG ACADEMY THE   T 020 7713 7710
CDET Member
Finsbury Town Hall
Rosebery Avenue
London EC1R 4RP
F 020 7278 6727
E info@theurdangacademy.com
W www.theurdangacademy.com

VALLÉ ACADEMY OF
PERFORMING ARTS   T 01992 622862
The Vallé Academy Studios
Wilton House
Delamare Road, Cheshunt, Herts EN8 9SG
F 01992 622868
E enquiries@valleacademy.co.uk
W www.valleacademy.co.uk

WAINWRIGHT, Ben
FREELANCE   T 01709 546444
Choreography. Teaching
11 Laburnum Avenue, Sunnyside
Rotherham, South Yorkshire S66 3PR
E b-wainwright@live.co.uk

WIVELL, Betty ACADEMY OF
PERFORMING ARTS THE   T 020 8764 5500
Ballet. Jazz. Modern. Tap. Drama. Singing
52 Norbury Court Road, Norbury
London SW16 4HT
E ereeves@bettywivell.com
W www.bettywivell.com

YOUNG, Sylvia
THEATRE SCHOOL   T 020 7258 2330
1 Nutford Place, London W1H 5YZ
F 020 7724 8371
E syoung@syts.co.uk
W www.syts.co.uk

ALRA (ACADEMY OF LIVE & RECORDED ARTS) T 020 8870 6475
Studio 24-25
The Royal Victoria Patriotic Building
John Archer Way, London SW18 3SX
F 020 8875 0789
E info@alra.co.uk
W www.alra.co.uk

ARTS EDUCATIONAL SCHOOLS LONDON T 020 8987 6666
14 Bath Road, London W4 1LY
F 020 8987 6699
E receptionist@artsed.co.uk
W www.artsed.co.uk

BIRMINGHAM SCHOOL OF ACTING T 0121 331 7220
Millennium Point, Curzon Street
Birmingham B4 7XG
F 0121 331 7221
E info@bsa.bcu.ac.uk
W www.bcu.ac.uk/bsa

BRISTOL OLD VIC THEATRE SCHOOL T 0117 973 3535
1-2 Downside Road, Clifton
Bristol BS8 2XF
F 0117 980 9258
E enquiries@oldvic.ac.uk
W www.oldvic.ac.uk

CENTRAL SCHOOL OF SPEECH & DRAMA, UNIVERSITY OF LONDON T 020 7722 8183
Eton Avenue, Swiss Cottage
London NW3 3HY
E enquiries@cssd.ac.uk
W www.cssd.ac.uk

CONTI, Italia ACADEMY T 020 7733 3210
Avondale, 72 Landor Road
London SW9 9PH
E acting@italiaconti.co.uk
W www.italiaconti-acting.co.uk

CYGNET TRAINING THEATRE T/F 01392 277189
New Theatre, Friars Gate
Exeter, Devon EX2 4AZ
E cygnetarts@btconnect.com
W www.cygnetnewtheatre.com

DRAMA CENTRE LONDON T 020 7514 8760
Central Saint Martins College of Arts & Design
Granary Building
1 Granary Square, London N1C 4AA
E drama@arts.ac.uk
W www.csm.arts.ac.uk/drama

DRAMA STUDIO LONDON T 020 8579 3897
Grange Court, 1 Grange Road
London W5 5QN
F 020 8566 2035
E admin@dramastudiolondon.co.uk
W www.dramastudiolondon.co.uk

EAST 15 ACTING SCHOOL T 020 8508 5983
Hatfields, Rectory Lane
Loughton IG10 3RY
F 020 8508 7521
E east15@essex.ac.uk
W www.east15.ac.uk

GSA, GUILDFORD SCHOOL OF ACTING T 01483 684040
University of Surrey, Stag Hill Campus
Guildford, Surrey GU2 7XH
E gsaenquiries@gsa.surrey.ac.uk
W www.gsauk.org

GUILDHALL SCHOOL OF MUSIC & DRAMA T 020 7628 2571
Silk Street, Barbican
London EC2Y 8DT
E info@gsmd.ac.uk
W www.gsmd.ac.uk

LAMDA T 020 8834 0500
155 Talgarth Road
London W14 9DA
F 020 8834 0501
E enquiries@lamda.org.uk
W www.lamda.org.uk

LIVERPOOL INSTITUTE FOR PERFORMING ARTS THE T 0151 330 3000
Mount Street, Liverpool L1 9HF
F 0151 330 3131
E reception@lipa.ac.uk
W www.lipa.ac.uk

MANCHESTER SCHOOL OF THEATRE AT MANCHESTER METROPOLITAN UNIVERSITY T 0161 247 1305
The Mabel Tylecote Building
Cavendish Street
Manchester M15 6BG
E theatre@mmu.ac.uk
W www.theatre.mmu.ac.uk

MOUNTVIEW ACADEMY OF THEATRE ARTS T 020 8881 2201
Ralph Richardson Memorial Studios
1 Kingfisher Place
Clarendon Road, London N22 6XF
F 020 8829 0034
E enquiries@mountview.org.uk
W www.mountview.org.uk

OXFORD SCHOOL OF DRAMA THE T 01993 812883
Sansomes Farm Studios
Woodstock
Oxford OX20 1ER
F 01993 811220
E info@oxforddrama.ac.uk
W www.oxforddrama.ac.uk

ROSE BRUFORD COLLEGE T 020 8308 2600
Lamorbey Park
Burnt Oak Lane
Sidcup, Kent DA15 9DF
F 020 8308 0542
E enquiries@bruford.ac.uk
W www.bruford.ac.uk

ROYAL ACADEMY OF DRAMATIC ART T 020 7636 7076
62-64 Gower Street
London WC1E 6ED
F 020 7323 3865
E enquiries@rada.ac.uk
W www.rada.ac.uk

ROYAL CONSERVATOIRE OF SCOTLAND T 0141 332 4101
100 Renfrew Street
Glasgow G2 3DB
E dramaadmissions@rcs.ac.uk
W www.rcs.ac.uk

ROYAL WELSH COLLEGE OF MUSIC & DRAMA T 029 2039 1397
Drama Department, Castle Grounds
Cathays Park, Cardiff CF10 3ER
F 029 2039 1301
E admissions@rwcmd.ac.uk
W www.rwcmd.ac.uk

www.dramauk.co.uk

Drama UK is the champion of quality drama training in the UK offering advocacy, assurance and advice.

The **Drama UK** Guide to Professional Training in Drama and Technical Theatre is an ideal starting point for anyone interested in professional drama training, available to download from our website with hard copies available from French's Theatre Bookshop, email: theatre@samuelfrench-london.co.uk

Drama UK was created from the merger of the Conference of Drama Schools and the National Council for Drama Training.

To contact Drama UK please email: ro@dramauk.co.uk

ACADEMY OF PERFORMANCE COMBAT
STAGE COMBAT FOR THE 21ST CENTURY
Patrons: Sir Tom Courtenay - Kay Mellor OBE - Braham Murray - Henry Winkler OBE

Teaching includes: RSC Open Stages

Chairman: Renny Krupinski
Address: Ivy Villa,
250 Lees New Road
Lees,
Lancs,
OL4 5PP
Website: www.theapc.org.uk
E-mail: info@theapc.org.uk
Phone: 07963 206803

2 PRODUCTION   **T** 020 7993 4675
Professional Management. Voice Over Direction & CDs
E voice@2production.com
W www.2production.com

A B ACADEMY
THEATRE SCHOOL   **T/F** 0161 429 7413
Act Out Ltd, 22 Greek Street
Stockport, Cheshire SK3 8AB
E ab22actout@aol.com

ABBI ACTING MA BA Hons
Drama School Tutor/Actress. 1-2-1 Sessions in
Auditioning, Speech & Voice, Corporate Presentation,
Public Speaking, Shakespeare & Text, Relaxation
Based in London NW10
E stephanie.schonfield@googlemail.com

ABOMELI TUTORING
Contact: Charles Abomeli BA LLAM. Development
Coach. Stage & Screen Acting Technique
E charlesabm@aol.co.uk
W www.charlesabomeli.com

ACADEMY ARTS
THEATRE SCHOOL & AGENCY   **T** 01245 422595
6A The Green, Writtle
Chelmsford, Essex CM1 3DU
E info@academyarts.co.uk
W www.academyarts.co.uk

ACADEMY OF
CREATIVE TRAINING   **T** 01273 818266
Contact: Janette Eddisford
8-10 Rock Place, Brighton, East Sussex BN2 1PF
T 07740 468338
E janette@actbrighton.org
W www.actbrighton.org

ACADEMY OF PERFORMANCE
COMBAT THE   **T** 07963 206803
Teaching Body of Stage Combat
Ivy Villa, 250 Lees New Road
Lees, Lancs OL4 5PP
E info@theapc.org.uk
W www.theapc.org.uk

ACADEMY OF THE SCIENCE
OF ACTING & DIRECTING THE   **T** 020 7272 0027
9-15 Elthorne Road, London N19 4AJ
F 020 7272 0026
E info@asad.org.uk
W www.asad.org.uk

ACCENT @ THE RICHER VOICE   **T** 07967 352551
Contact: Richard Ryder. Accent Specialist
9 Kamen House
17-21 Magdalen Street
London Bridge, London SE1 2RH
E richard@therichervoice.com
W www.therichervoice.com

ACKERLEY STUDIOS OF SPEECH, DRAMA &
PUBLIC SPEAKING   **T** 0151 724 3449
Est. 1919. Contact: Margaret Parsons
16 Fawley Road, Allerton
Liverpool L18 9TF
E johnmutch@talktalk.net

ACT 2 CAM   **T** 0191 280 1345
14 Percy Road, Whitley Bay
Newcastle, Tyne and Wear NE26 2AX
E info@act2cam.com
W www.act2cam.com

ACT 2 DRAMA SCHOOL   **T** 07939 144355
Performing Arts School (5-18 yrs)
105 Richmond Avenue
Highams Park
London E4 9RR
E management@act2drama.co.uk
W www.act2drama.co.uk

ACT NOW PERFORMING
ARTS ACADEMY   **T** 07920 855410
Performing Arts Training (4-21 yrs). Part-time
Trestle Arts Base, Russett Drive
St Albans, Hertfordshire AL4 0JQ
E actnowperformingarts@mac.com
W www.actnowperformingartsschool.co.uk

ACT ONE DRAMA STUDIO   **T** 07904 339024
PO Box 4776, Sheffield S11 0EX
E info@actonedramastudio.co.uk
W www.actonedramastudio.co.uk

ACT UP   **T** 020 7924 7701
Acting Classes for Everyone. Acting Workshops. Audition
Technique. Pre-Drama School (18+ yrs). Public Speaking.
Vocal Coaching
Unit 88
Battersea Business Centre
99-109 Lavender Hill
London SW11 5QL
F 020 7924 6606
E info@act-up.co.uk
W www.act-up.co.uk

Drama Training

Why do I need drama training?

The entertainment industry is an extremely competitive one, with thousands of performers competing for a small number of jobs. In such a crowded market, professional training will increase an actor's chances of success, and professionally trained artists are also more likely to be represented by agencies. Drama training can begin at any age and should continue throughout an actor's career.

I have already trained to be an actor. Why do I need further training?

Drama training should not cease as soon as you graduate or get your first job. Throughout your career you should strive to enhance your existing skills and keep up-to-date with the techniques new actors are being taught, even straight after drama school, in order to retain a competitive edge. You must also be prepared to learn new skills for specific roles if required. Ongoing drama training and classes can help you stay fit and active, and if you go through a period of unemployment you can keep your mind and body occupied, ready to take on your next job.

What kind of training is available?

For the under 18s, stage schools provide specialist training in acting, singing and dancing. They offer a variety of full and part-time courses. After 18, students can attend drama school. The standard route is to take a three-year, full-time course, in the same way you would take a university degree. Some schools also offer one or two-year courses.

What is Drama UK?

Drama UK comprises Britain's leading drama schools. It exists in order to strengthen the voice of the member schools, to set and maintain the highest standards of training within the vocational drama sector, and to make it easier for prospective students to understand the range of courses on offer and the application process. The member schools listed in the section 'Drama Schools: Drama UK' offer courses in Acting, Musical Theatre, Directing and Technical Theatre training. For more information you can visit their website www.dramauk.co.uk

How should I use these listings?

The following listings provide up-to-date contact details for a wide range of performance courses, classes and coaches. Every company listed is done so by written request to us. Some companies have provided contact names, areas of specialisation and a selection of courses on offer.

I want to apply to join a full-time drama course. Where do I start?

Your first step should be to research as many different courses as possible. Have a look on each school's website and request a prospectus. Ask around to find out where other people have trained or are training now and who they recommend. You would be advised to begin your search by considering Drama UK courses. Please refer to the *Drama UK Guide to Professional Training in Drama & Technical Theatre* for a description of each school, its policy and the courses it offers together with information about funding, available from www.dramauk.co.uk

What types of courses are available?

Drama training courses generally involve three-year degree or diploma courses, or one-year postgraduate courses if you have already attended university or can demonstrate a certain amount of previous experience. Alternatively, short-term or part-time foundation courses are available, which can serve as an introduction to acting but are not a substitute for a full-time drama course.

When should I apply?

Deadlines for applications to drama courses vary between schools so make sure you check each school's individual deadlines. Most courses start in September. If the school you are considering requires you to apply via UCAS, you must submit your application between mid-September 2012 and 15th January 2013 to guarantee that your application will be considered for a course beginning in 2013. You can apply after that until 30th June, but the school is then under no obligation to consider your application.

See www.ucas.ac.uk/students/applying/whentoapply or contact the individual school for more details.

What funding is available to me?

Drama courses are unavoidably expensive. Most students have to fund their own course fees and other expenses, whether from savings, part-time work or a student loan. However, if you are from a low-income household you may qualify for a maintenance grant from the government to cover some of the costs. Some Drama UK accredited courses offer a limited number of students Dance and Drama Awards (DaDA) scholarships, introduced to increase access to dance, drama and stage management training for talented students. These scholarships include help with both course fees and living expenses. Find out what each school offers in terms of potential financial support before applying.

Another possibility is to raise funds from a charity, trust or foundation. As with applying to agents and casting professionals for representation and work, do your research first and target your letters to explain how your needs meet each organisation's objectives, rather than sending a generalised letter to everyone. You are much more likely to be considered if you demonstrate that you know the background of the organisation and what they can offer performers.

How can my child become an actor?

If your child is interested in becoming an actor, they should try to get as much practical experience as possible. They could also join a stage school or sign with an agent. Contact details for stage schools can be found among the listings in this section. Please also see the 'Agents: Children & Teenagers' section for more information.

What about other forms of training?

Building on your initial acting course is essential for both new and more experienced actors. There are so many new skills you can learn – you could take stage fighting classes, hire a vocal coach, attend singing and dance lessons, and many more. These will enhance your CV and will give you a competitive edge. It is also extremely useful to take occasional 'refresher' courses on audition skills, different acting techniques and so on in various forms such as one-to-one lessons, one-off workshops or evening classes, to make sure you are not rusty when your next audition comes along.

Where can I find more information?

The Actors Centre runs over 1700 classes and workshops a year to encourage performers to develop their talent throughout their career in a supportive environment. They also run introductory classes for people who are interested in becoming actors but currently have no training or experience. Visit their website www.actorscentre.co.uk for more information. You may also want to refer to the 'Dance Training & Professional Classes' section for listings which will help you to add additional skills to your CV as well as keep fit. If you are interested in a career behind rather than in front of the camera or stage, please see the *Drama UK Guide to Careers Backstage*, available from www.dramauk.co.uk

Drama Training

CASE STUDY

Anne Wittman is an actress and American dialect coach. She trained at Bristol Old Vic Theatre School, Northwestern University School of Communication, and with Stella Adler at her studio in NYC.

A few years ago, perusing the substantial array of dialect books and CDs on display at The Drama Bookshop in New York, I struck up a conversation with the man behind the counter. "You know what?" he said wryly, "If I ever want to start a really big argument among any group of people – doesn't even have to be actors – all I need to do is mention accent or dialect. Everybody has very strong opinions…and everybody disagrees! I just stand back and watch the fireworks."

Our accents and dialects are at the heart of our identities and sociology. No wonder they strike a chord.

As actors we may be lucky enough to be tasked with developing various dialects, hopefully to native standard, for a variety of roles in the course of our careers. A good coach will be able to guide you through the sound substitutions or lexical sets, placement, intonation, pitch patterns, linking and word connections, tempo and rhythm of your chosen dialect. They can answer questions and correct misunderstandings and habitual patterns that may not be serving you. As a trained, objective ear, they can assess the accuracy of your dialect and offer instruction for correction.

The Actors Centre, drama schools (some coaches there also teach privately), Representation Upson Edwards, Pronunciation Studio – and of course, the listings here in Contacts – are all good places to find dialect coaches. Choose a coach who understands your goals as an actor and tailors the work to your level of proficiency and the requirements of the role. They should balance any necessary theory, sociology and regional information with substantial practical training in the dialect's components, and give you the tools to replicate them. Hopefully, they'll have a creative approach to help keep you focused and interested. It's difficult to adopt a new dialect, but it can also be fun.

If you choose to supplement your professional tuition or work entirely on your own, be disciplined. Create a study outline and practise daily. Seek out the most authentic resources you can find: books, CDs, films, specialist dialect websites, local radio news and talk shows, oral history projects and sourcing native speakers on YouTube can all be helpful. Also be aware of aspects of their speech that are not dialect, strictly speaking, separating those out from the dialect itself. Listen, mimic and empathise. When you feel confident enough, record yourself and make corrections. Do you know a native speaker? Record them. Be adventurous! If you're lucky enough to be cast in a long-running or high-profile project, consider a reconnaissance trip to the area you're studying. Go armed with a recorder and ask people to speak with you. Discover what underpins their sound, movement and behaviour. Once your dialect is fairly solid, visit shops, cafes and pubs and strike up conversations. Test how well you pass as local. Watch as well as listen. Building a personal, multi-layered understanding of what it is to be from the area will pay dividends for your dialect and interpretation of the character.

Depending on the production or background and class of your character, you may choose to do a light version of the dialect in performance. A heavier version may be used for practice, in order to attain a good muscle memory of how the sounds are made, but then soften, integrate and own it. Some individuals and characters do have very heavy regional sounds, however. Choose the intensity consciously. Avoid the temptations of a judgmental, clichéd approach. Also, be sensitive to your audience's understanding. Does a balance need to be struck between clarity and complete authenticity? If the accent is incomprehensible to their ears, the message of the piece could be obscured.

The amount of time it takes to go from square one to sounding like a native speaker varies greatly among individuals. It's based on aptitude, any previous speech training, and how assiduously you practise the dialect on your own between class sessions. It can take the same intensity and focus to learn a dialect to native standard as it would to master anything new.

The very best approach would be to prepare the dialect before you actually need to use it. Select ones you're likely to be asked to do and make a game or hobby of it. Unless you're very experienced with dialects or have a highly musical ear, don't necessarily expect to reproduce a difficult or foreign dialect to native standard in an hour or even an afternoon or two.

A dedicated actor may find they spend the rest of their life perfecting and correcting themselves in the minutiae of a given dialect. Keep the exploration a joyous one. Hard work and perseverance, along with an attitude of playful curiosity, can get you there. Somewhere out there is a person much like the character you'll be playing. Seek accuracy of their sound, and cultivate empathy for their culture and behaviour. Tell their story the way they would have it told.

To find out more about dialect coaching with Anne Wittman visit www.spokenstates.com

Members of Drama UK (formerly the Conference of Drama Schools and NCDT) offer their students the highest quality training in the industry. Graduates from these schools are in a strong position to advise anyone thinking of following in their path. We asked two recent graduates to share their thoughts on the benefits of drama training.

Photo: David William Edwards

Faye Marsay

Faye recently graduated from Bristol Old Vic Theatre School's two-year Professional Acting course. She won the Spotlight Prize at the Spotlight Showcase 2012.

I think my decision to become an actor was based on that cliché of always wanting to perform from a young age. I went to an amateur youth group and absolutely relished being on stage and since then it's always been what I have wanted to do.

Before drama school I was part of the National Youth Theatre and did a training course with them at the age of 16. I went on to do a degree in Contemporary Acting at Newcastle College. This was a great choice as it meant I had the opportunity to work with Erica Whyman at Northern Stage.

I had auditioned for drama school when I was 18 and had been unsuccessful. So I decided to do my degree. Whilst studying I worked with an actress who had been to Bristol Old Vic Theatre School and I looked into it again from there. I had never auditioned at BOVTS and it was the only school I decided to audition for! I was very lucky to get in. I liked it because of its size and its excellent training.

The highlights of my training were the incredibly talented people I worked with on my course and being cast in Enda Walsh's *Disco Pigs*. The transition between drama school and professional work is quite scary but at the same time I am up for the challenge. I am my own business now and so I must be responsible for making the most of the opportunities that come my way.

Luckily I have a fantastic agent who I get on with very well. I am mainly auditioning at the moment and getting my face out there. I am the new kid on the block so it's important that I get myself seen for as much work as possible.

My advice to new drama students is to be focused, strong willed, hard working, polite, supportive and, most importantly for me, be real. Try to sign with an agent who you get on with and feel you can talk to openly about things. If things don't come your way straight away, hold on – you have every right to keep fighting for what you want.

Photo: Jack Ladenburg

Molly Vevers

Molly recently graduated from the Royal Conservatoire of Scotland with a BA in Acting. She won the Highly Commended Actor award at the Spotlight Showcase 2012.

I left school when I was sixteen – after taking my Higher exams – to study Acting and Performance at Edinburgh's Telford College, because even at that young age I knew I was much more passionate and driven about acting than I was about anything else. Taking the leap to pursuing it as a career was daunting but I knew it was right.

After a year at college, I did a round of auditions for drama schools up and down the country – if anything will test your commitment, it is the drama school audition slog! My poor Mum drove me up and down to lots of auditions – some which involve a brutal cut on the day, some where you won't find out anything for weeks on end. It is expensive and very stressful, and an introduction to the art of developing a thick skin.

I was lucky enough to be offered a place on the Acting course at the RCS in Glasgow. Looking back, I would say it's so important to be yourself rather than try and be what you think the teachers are looking for. Also, drama school is brilliant as it provides you with a network of people, all in the same position as you, to bounce things off and support one another – which you really begin to appreciate as your time at drama school comes to an end.

After my school showcase, I signed with an agent and since then have been auditioning for varied and exciting things. I managed to secure a job with Dundee Rep as an actor with the ensemble for a year, which I'm so pleased about and can't wait to get stuck in. Working in rep will almost be like another year of training, but in a professional context.

Having done three years of training, and coming out the other side, my advice to anyone thinking of the drama school route would be to do your research into what you want from your training, to be yourself and to remember you are there to learn, so lap up all the feedback – good or bad – you'll graduate a stronger and more flexible actor.

ACTING ANGEL THE   T 07807 103295
Acting, Audition & Career Coaching plus Industry Talks for Young Adult & Graduate Actors
E info@theactingangel.co.uk
W www.theactingangel.co.uk

ACTING AUDITION SUCCESS   T 020 8731 6686
Contact: Philip Rosch. Audition Coaching for Top UK Drama Schools. Audition Technique. Drama School Preparation. Improvisation. Private Acting Classes
53 West Heath Court
London NW11 7RG
E philiproschactor@gmail.com
W www.actingauditionsuccess.co.uk

ACTING BUDDY
E info@actingbuddy.com
W www.actingbuddy.com

ACTING COACH SCOTLAND   T/F 0800 7569535
Contact: Mark Westbrook. Acting Workshops. Audition Technique. Drama School Preparation. Private Acting Classes. Courses: Developing Acting Skills, Intro to Practical Aesthetics, Rehearsal Technique, Scene Study, all 8 week, part-time
4th Floor, 19 Queen Street
Glasgow, Lanarkshire G20 6HQ
E mark@actingcoachscotland.co.uk
W www.actingcoachscotland.co.uk

ACTION LAB   T 020 8810 0412
Contact: Miranda French, Peter Irving. Part-time Acting Courses & Private Coaching. Based in London & West Dorset
34 Northcote Avenue
London W5 3UT
T 07979 623987
E miranda@mirandafrench.com

ACTORS CENTRE THE   T 020 7632 8001
Career and Casting Advice. Voice. Accent/Dialect Coaching. Acting for Camera. Audition Technique. TV Presenting. Voice Overs. Showreels. Shakespeare. The Meisner Technique. Performance Workshops
1A Tower Street
London WC2H 9NP
E reception@actorscentre.co.uk
W www.actorscentre.co.uk

ACTORS COMPANY LA THE   T 020 8661 0226
Based in Hollywood & London
916A North Formosa Avenue
West Hollywood
Los Angeles, CA 90004, USA
E litz@theactorscompanyla.com
W www.theactorscompanyla.com

ACTORS PLATFORM LTD
Contact: Melissa Osborne.
Courses: Weekly Casting Director Workshops, Quarterly Agent Workshops, Quarterly Industry Showcases
Based in Central London
E melissa@actorsplatform.com
W www.actorsplatform.com

ACTORS STUDIO   T 01753 650951
Acting Workshops. Audition Technique. Dialect/Accent Coaching. Elocution. Improvisation. Language Tutoring. Private Acting Classes. Public Speaking. Stage School for Children. Vocal Coaching
Pinewood Film Studios
Pinewood Road
Iver Heath, Bucks SL0 0NH
F 01753 655622
E info@actorsstudio.co.uk
W www.actorsstudio.co.uk

ACTOR'S TEMPLE THE   T 020 3004 4537
13-14 Warren Street, London W1T 5LG
E info@actorstemple.com
W www.actorstemple.com

ACTORS' THEATRE SCHOOL   T 020 8450 0371
Foundation Course
32 Exeter Road, London NW2 4SB
F 020 8450 1057
E info@theactorstheatreschool.co.uk
W www.theactorstheatreschool.co.uk

ACTORWORKS   T 020 7702 0909
Contact: Daniel Brennan, Wendy Smith. Drama School (over 18 yrs). Courses: Intensive, 1 yr, Evening & Weekend. Foundation, 15 Week, Day. 1 yr, part-time, Evening
1st Floor, Raine House
16 Raine Street, Wapping, London E1W 3RL
E ask@actorworks.org
W www.actorworks.org

ACTS   T 020 8360 0352
Ayres-Clark Theatre School
c/o 12 Gatward Close
Winchmore Hill, London N21 1AS
E actsn21@talktalk.net

ALEXANDER, Helen   T 020 8543 4085
Audition Technique. Drama School Entry
14 Chestnut Road
Raynes Park
London SW20 8EB
E helen-alexander@virginmedia.com

ALL EXPRESSIONS
THEATRE SCHOOL   T 020 8898 3321
153 Waverley Avenue, Twickenham
Middlesex TW2 6DJ
E info@allexpressions.co.uk
W www.allexpressions.co.uk

ALLSORTS - DRAMA   T/F 020 8969 3249
Part-time Courses & Drama Training (3-18 yrs). Based in Kensington, Notting Hill, Hampstead, Fulham & Putney
34 Crediton Road
London NW10 3DU
E info@allsortsdrama.com
W www.allsortsdrama.com

ALRA (ACADEMY OF LIVE & RECORDED ARTS)
See DRAMA SCHOOLS: DRAMA UK

AMERICAN DIALECT COACHING   T 07956 602508
Contact: Anne Wittman.
Private Coaching in American Dialects
Based in London N8
E wittmananne@yahoo.com
W www.spokenstates.com

AMERICAN MUSICAL THEATRE ACADEMY OF LONDON   T 020 7253 3118
Europa House
13-17 Ironmomger Row, London EC1V 3QG
E info@americanacademy.co.uk
W www.americanacademy.co.uk

AMERICAN VOICES   T 07875 148755
Contact: Lynn Bains. Acting Teacher & Director.
American Accent/Dialect Coach
20 Craighall Crescent, Edinburgh EH6 4RZ
E mail@lynnbains.com

AND ALL THAT JAZZ   T 020 8993 2111
Contact: Eileen Hughes. Accompanist. Vocal Coaching
163 Gunnersbury Lane, Acton Town
London W3 8LJ

ANNA SCHER THEATRE
See SCHER, Anna THEATRE

ARABESQUE SCHOOL OF PERFORMING ARTS   T/F 01243 531144
Quarry Lane, Chichester PO19 8NY
E info@aspauk.com
W www.aspauk.com

ARDEN SCHOOL OF THEATRE THE   T 0161 909 6655
Professional Stage Practice in Acting Studies & Musical
Theatre. HNC in Drama. FD in Theatre Practice
The Manchester College, Ashton Old Road
Openshaw, Manchester M11 2WH
E enquiries@themanchestercollege.ac.uk
W www.themanchestercollege.ac.uk

ARTEMIS SCHOOL OF SPEECH & DRAMA   T/F 01342 321330
Peredur Centre of The Arts
West Hoathly Road
East Grinstead, West Sussex RH19 4NF
E office@artemisspeechanddrama.org.uk
W www.artemisspeechanddrama.org.uk

ARTEMIS STUDIOS   T 01344 429403
30 Charles Square, Bracknell
Berkshire RG12 1AY
E info@artemis-studios.co.uk
W www.artemis-studios.co.uk

ARTS EDUCATIONAL SCHOOLS LONDON
See DRAMA SCHOOLS: DRAMA UK

**ASHCROFT ACADEMY OF
DRAMATIC ART THE**   T/F 0844 8005328
Dance ISTD. Drama LAMDA. Singing (4-18 yrs)
Malcolm Primary School, Malcolm Road
Penge, London SE20 8RH
T 07799 791586
E info@ashcroftacademy.com
W www.ashcroftacademy.com

**ASHFORD, Clare BSc PGCE LLAM
ALAM (Recital) ALAM (Acting)**   T 020 8660 9609
20 The Chase, Coulsdon
Surrey CR5 2EG
E clareashford@rocketmail.com

ASSOCIATED STUDIOS   T 020 8237 1080
*Professional Development for Actors, Musical Theatre
Singers, Opera Singers & Recording Artists*
Riverside Studios, Crisp Road, London W6 9RL
E info@associatedstudios.co.uk
W www.advancedperformersstudio.com

AUDITION COACH   T 0161 969 1444
*Contact: Martin Harris. Acting Workshops. Audition
Techniques. Group Evening Classes. Private Acting
Classes*
32 Baxter Road, Sale, Manchester M33 3AL
T 07788 723570
E martin@auditioncoach.co.uk
W www.auditioncoach.co.uk

AUDITION DOCTOR   T 020 7357 8237
1 Gloucester Court, Swan Street, London SE1 1DQ
T 07764 193806
E tilly@auditiondoctor.co.uk
W www.auditiondoctor.co.uk

AUDITIONS: A PRACTICAL GUIDE
W www.auditionsapracticalguide.com

AVERY-CLARK, Kenneth   T 020 7253 3118
Musical Theatre. Voice Coach
Europa House, 13-17 Ironmonger Row
London EC1V 3QG
T 07734 509810
E ken@americanacademy.co.uk

**BAC
(BATTERSEA ARTS CENTRE)**   T 020 7326 8219
*Young People's Theatre Workshops & Performance
Projects (12-25 yrs)*
Lavender Hill, London SW11 5TN
F 020 7978 5207
E bacypt@bac.org.uk
W www.bac.org.uk

BADA   T 00 34 68 1134623
Courses for Actors
Cento De Civico, Quint Mar
Sitges, Barcelona 08010, Spain
E batemanrob@gmail.com

**BATE, Richard MA (Theatre) LGSM (TD)
PGCE (FE) Equity**   T 07940 589295
*Audition Technique. Drama School Entry. Vocal & Acting
Training*
45 Derngate, Northampton
Northamptonshire NN1 1UE
E rich.bate@yahoo.co.uk

BATES, Esme   T 0118 958 9330
*BA Hons Central School of Speech & Drama. Actress.
TEFL Teacher. Youth Theatre Director. LAMDA Teacher.
Drama Games Parties*
2 Baron Court, Western Elms Avenue
Reading, Berks RG30 2BP
T 07941 700941
E ukdramaeducation@live.co.uk
W www.ukdramaeducation.com

BELFAST TALENT SCHOOL   T 028 9024 3324
*Adults. Children. Teenagers. Classes in Acting & Dance.
Saturday Stage School*
The Crescent Arts Centre, 2-4 University Road
Belfast, Antrim BT7 1NH
E info@belfasttalent.com
W www.belfasttalentschool.com

**BENCH Paul MEd LGSM ALAM FRSA
LJBA (Hons) PGCE ACP (Lings) (Hons)
MASC (Ph) MIFA (Reg)**   T/F 01743 233164
*Audition Technique. Corporate Vocal Presentation.
LAMDA Exams, Grades to Diploma Level. Private Acting
Classes. Public Speaking. Stress Management. Vocal
Coaching*
1 Whitehall Terrace, Shrewsbury
Shropshire SY2 5AA
E pfbench@aol.com
W www.paulbench.co.uk

BERKERY, Barbara   T 020 7281 3139
Dialogue/Dialect Coach for Film & Television

BEST THEATRE ARTS   T 01727 759634
PO Box 749, St Albans AL1 4YW
E bestarts@aol.com
W www.besttheatrearts.com

BIG LITTLE THEATRE SCHOOL   T 01202 434499
*Acting Examination & Audition Prep (LAMDA). Early Years
Drama & Dance. Performance in Education Workshops.
Professional Development Programme. RAD Ballet, ISTD
Tap & Modern. Singing Technique Classes & Private
Lessons. Skills Development Classes. Summer Schools.
Youth Theatre Companies*
Garnet House
2A Harvey Road
Bournemouth, Dorset BH5 2AD
E info@biglittle.biz
W www.biglittle.biz

GORDON FAITH B.A., IPA., Dip.R.E.M. Sp., L.R.A.M.
SPEECH AND VOICE TEACHER

• Ex BBC Repertory • All Speech Work Undertaken

020-7328 0446 www.gordonfaith.co.uk 1 Wavel Mews, Priory Rd. London NW6 3AB

BIG TALENT SCHOOL &
AGENCY THE   T 029 2132 0421
Contact: Shelley Barrett-Norton
53 Mount Stuart Square, Cardiff CF10 5LR
T 07886 020923
E info@thebigtalent.co.uk
W www.thebigtalent.co.uk

BIG VOICE - LITTLE VOICE   T 01706 812420
Contact: Russell Richardson LLAM DipDram. Audition
Techniques. Drama School Preparation. LAMDA Speech
Exams. Private Acting Classes. Public Speaking. Vocal
Coaching
The Mill House, 3 Clough Mill
Walsden, West Yorkshire OL14 7QX
T 07939 215458
E russell@richardsonassoc.co.uk

BIRD COLLEGE   T 020 8300 6004
Drama/Musical Theatre College
The Centre, 27 Station Road
Sidcup, Kent DA15 7EB
F 020 8308 1370
E performance@birdcollege.co.uk
W www.birdcollege.co.uk

BIRMINGHAM SCHOOL OF ACTING
See DRAMA SCHOOLS: DRAMA UK

BIRMINGHAM THEATRE
SCHOOL THE   T 0121 440 1665
The Old Fire Station
285-287 Moseley Road
Highgate, Birmingham B12 0DX
E info@birminghamtheatreschool.co.uk
W www.birminghamtheatreschool.co.uk

BODENS STUDIOS   T 020 8447 0909
Contact: Adam Boden. Acting Workshops. Audition
Technique. Dancing. Improvisation. Part-time Performing
Arts Classes. Singing
Bodens Studios & Agency
99 East Barnet Road
New Barnet, Herts EN4 8RF
E info@bodens.co.uk
W www.bodens.co.uk

BOWES, Sara   T 07830 375389
Child Acting Coach for Film & Commercials
25 Holmes Avenue, Hove BN3 7LA
E saracrowe77@gmail.com

CYGNET TRAINING THEATRE Patron: Peter Brook

PROFESSIONAL
ACTING TRAINING
CYGNET students train
and tour as a company
playing at a wide variety
of venues. The training
gives high priority to voice
technique, musical skills
and the acting methods of
Stanislavsky and Michael
Chekhov.

www.cygnetnewtheatre.com

The Tempest

ENTRY (over 18) by audition workshop and interview
Apply to: New Theatre, Friars Gate, Exeter EX2 4AZ

Member of Drama UK   Registered Charity No. 1081824

CYGNET
PATRON: PETER BROOK

Charlie Hughes-D'Aeth 🎧

Based in London, Brighton & Stratford-Upon-Avon.

RSC resident Text and Voice Coach on 'Matilda the Musical'.
CSSD trained; 20+ years experience in theatre / actor training / singing / business; also teaches dramatic writing.

07811 010963 CHDAETH@aol.com charliehughesdaeth.co.uk

BOYD, Beth T 020 8398 6768
Private Acting Coaching
10 Prospect Road, Long Ditton
Surbiton, Surrey KT6 5PY

BRADSHAW, Irene T 020 7794 5721
Private Coach. Voice & Audition Preparation
Flat F, Welbeck Mansions, Inglewood Road
West Hampstead, London NW6 1QX
T 07949 552915
E irene@irenebradshaw.fsnet.co.uk
W www.voice-power-works.co.uk

**BRAITHWAITE'S ACROBATIC
SCHOOL** T 020 8954 5638
8 Brookshill Avenue, Harrow Weald
Middlesex HA3 6RZ

BRANSTON, Dale T 020 8696 9958
Singing Teacher. Audition Preparation. Repertoire
Ground Floor Flat, 16 Fernwood Avenue
Streatham, London SW16 1RD
T 07767 261713
E branpickle@yahoo.co.uk

**BRIDGE THEATRE
TRAINING COMPANY THE** T 020 7424 0860
*Contact: Mark Akrill. Drama School (over 18 yrs).
Acting. Dance. Film, Television & Radio Technique.
Improvisation. Movement. Professional Studies.
Singing. Stage Combat. Voice. Courses: Professional
Acting Course, 2 yr, full-time, Diploma. Postgraduate
Professional Acting Course (over 21 yrs),
1 yr, full-time, Diploma*
90 Kingsway, North Finchley
London N12 0EX
F 020 7424 9118
E admin@thebridge-ttc.org
W www.thebridge-ttc.org

BRISTOL OLD VIC THEATRE SCHOOL
See DRAMA SCHOOLS: DRAMA UK

**B.R.I.T. SCHOOL FOR PERFORMING ARTS &
TECHNOLOGY THE** T 020 8665 5242
60 The Crescent, Croydon CR0 2HN
F 020 8665 8676
E admin@brit.croydon.sch.uk
W www.brit.croydon.sch.uk

BRITISH ACTION ACADEMY LTD T 0844 4146007
Contact: Cayte Robinson. Screen Action Training
531 Maplin Park, Slough
Berkshire SL3 8YG
E cayter@britishactionacademy.com
W www.britishactionacademy.com

**BRITISH AMERICAN
DRAMA ACADEMY** T 020 7487 0730
14 Gloucester Gate
Regent's Park, London NW1 4HG
F 020 7487 0731
E info@badaonline.com
W www.badaonline.com

BROWN, Michael BA MFA T 07963 171385
*International Workshops: Physical Performance Skills,
Clown, Commedia, Mask Performance, Storytelling.
Acting Technique. Audition Technique/Preparation.
Private Acting Coach. Teacher at LAMDA & LISPA.
Workshops in UK & USA*
75 Palmerston Road, London SW14 7QA
E brown.michaelanthony@gmail.com

**CADDY, Julian
ACTING TRAINING** T 07905 120431
E training@juliancaddytraining.com
W www.sweet-uk.net

**CALDERDALE
THEATRE SCHOOL** T 07540 176724
8 Carins Walk, Halifax HX6 4JR
E jodieorange@hotmail.co.uk

CAMERON BROWN, Jo PGDVS T 07970 026621
*Dialect. Dialogue. Voice Coaching for Film, Stage,
Television & Auditions*
E jocameronbrown@me.com
W www.imdb.com/name/nm0131472

CAMPBELL, Jon T 07854 697971
36 Fentiman Road, London SW8 1LF
E jon@joncampbellacting.co.uk
W www.joncampbellacting.co.uk

**CAMPBELL, Ross
ARCM Dip RCM (Perf)** T 01252 510228
*Professor, Royal Academy of Music. Head of Singing
& Music, GSA, 2004-2012. Founder of GSA Musical
Theatre Singing Syllabus*
17 Oldwood Chase, Farnborough, Hants GU14 0QS
T 07956 465165
E rosscampbell@ntlworld.com

**CAPITAL ARTS
THEATRE SCHOOL** T/F 020 8449 2342
Contact: Kathleen Shanks
Capital Arts Studio, Wyllyotts Theatre
Darkes Lane, Potters Bar, Herts EN6 2HN
T 07885 232414
E capitalarts@btconnect.com
W www.capitalarts.org.uk

CAPITAL SCREEN ARTS T 07738 131489
*Courses in Screen-Acting. 1 Day Master Classes &
Private Coaching*
1st Floor, 75 Brownlow Road, London N11 2BN
E info@capitalscreenarts.co.uk
W www.capitalscreenarts.co.uk

CAPO FERRO FIGHT ENSEMBLE T 07791 875902
*Contact: Paul Casson-Yardley. Acting Workshops.
Drama School (over 18 yrs). Improvisation. Private Acting
Classes. Stage School for Children. Courses: Basic
Introduction to Stage Fighting, Fight Choreography,
Stage Combat Past & Present, Stage Combat with
Weapons & Props. All Abilities. All Courses Day/Half Day*
168 Richmond Road, Sheffield, Yorkshire S13 8TG
E capo.ferro.ensemble@gmail.com

the actors centre

For 34 years, thousands of actors have made their way through our doors...

The UK's leading organisation which supports actors throughout their professional careers.

A central London venue, hub, resource and theatre to network, share and create.

A year round professional development programme of high calibre, diverse and challenging workshops and masterclasses.

Direct opportunities and links with the creative industries.

Find out what becoming a member can do for you and your career.

Supported by

 Equity

www.actorscentre.co.uk

Patron: Rafe Spall @TheActorsCentre t: 020 7240 3940

Ben Eedle MA (CSSD), DIP (Webber Douglas)

-Voice Coaching
-Audition Preparation
-Monologue Structuring

Main Focus:
Classical Text &
Finding the Free Voice

07587 526 286
ben@theenglishbears.com
www.theenglishbears.com

Reasonable Rates

Find your easy vocal power

CARSHALTON COLLEGE   T 020 8544 4444
Nightingale Road, Carshalton
Surrey SM5 2EJ
F 020 8544 4440
E cs@carshalton.ac.uk
W www.carshalton.ac.uk

CARTER, Lauren   T 07879 352382
Vocal Coach for Singing
E lauren@laurencarteronline.com
W www.laurencarteronline.com

**CELEBRATION THEATRE
COMPANY FOR THE YOUNG**   T 020 8994 8886
*Contact: Neville Wortman. Drama School (over 18 yrs).
Drama School Preparation & 13-15 yrs LAMDA Bronze,
Silver & Gold Medals. Private Acting Classes. Summer
School. Vocal Coaching. Courses: Audition & Interview
Techniques, 'Shakespeare Today', Speaking in Public,
'The Confident Voice', 10 week Saturday Classes*
School of Economic Science Building
Studio 11-13 Mandeville Place, London W1U 3AJ
T 07976 805976
E neville@speakwell.co.uk
W www.speakwell.co.uk

CELEBRITY TALENT ACADEMY   T 0845 1162355
*Acting Workshops. Audition Technique. Drama School
Preparation. Improvisation. Courses: Commercial
Training, Film Studies Training, TV Training, Advanced
Acting, all part-time*
2A Tileyard Studios, Tileyard Road
Kings Cross, London N7 9AH
E celebritytalentacademy@gmail.com
W www.celebritytalentacademy.com

**CENTRAL LONDON
DRAMA COACHING**   T 07950 720868
*Audition Technique. Text Analysis. Trinity Guildhall
Examinations. Vocal Presentation Skills*
Based in WC1
E euniceroberts1@gmail.com

**CENTRAL SCHOOL OF SPEECH & DRAMA,
UNIVERSITY OF LONDON**
See DRAMA SCHOOLS: DRAMA UK

**CENTRE STAGE ACADEMY
THEATRE SCHOOL**   T 07773 416593
*Weekend Theatre School in Midhurst & Chichester
(5-20 yrs)*
9 Beech Grove, Midhurst
West Sussex GU29 9JA
E brett.east@hotmail.com
W www.csa-theatreschool.co.uk

**CENTRE STAGE SCHOOL OF
PERFORMING ARTS**   T 020 8886 4264
Students (4-18 yrs). Based in North London
The Croft, 7 Cannon Road
Southgate, London N14 7HE
F 020 8886 7555
E carole@centrestageuk.com
W www.centrestageuk.com

**CENTRE STAGE
THEATRE ACADEMY**   T 07793 058071
Performing Arts Training for Children
31 Sandpiper Way, St Mary Cray
Orpington, Kent BR5 3NS
E info@centrestagetheatreacademy.com
W www.centrestagetheatreacademy.com

**CENTRESTAGE SCHOOL OF
PERFORMING ARTS**   T 020 7328 0788
*Drama School Auditions. Private Coaching for
Professionals. Summer Courses*
Centrestage House
117 Canfield Gardens
London NW6 3DY
E vickiwoolf@centrestageschool.co.uk
W www.centrestageschool.co.uk

**CHARD, Verona
LRAM Dip RAM**   T 020 8992 1571
*Visiting Singing Tutor at Central School of Speech &
Drama. Vocal Expert X Factor Poland 2012. Coach of
Award-winning Jazz Singers. Vocal Producer for
Record Labels*
Ealing House
33 Hanger Lane, London W5 3HJ
E verona@veronachard.com

CHARKHAM, Esta   T 020 8741 2843
16 British Grove, Chiswick
London W4 2NL
E estalachark@googlemail.com

CHARRINGTON, Tim   T 020 7987 3028
Dialect/Accent Coaching
54 Topmast Point
Strafford Street, London E14 8SN
T 07967 418236
E tim.charrington@gmail.com

**CHASE, Stephan
PRODUCTIONS LTD**   T 020 8878 9112
*Private Coach for Acting, Auditions, Public Speaking &
Script Work. Originator of Managing Authentic Presence*
The Studio, 22 York Avenue
London SW14 7LG
E stephan@stephanchase.com
W www.stephanchase.com

**CHEKHOV, Michael
STUDIO LONDON**   T 020 8696 7372
*Contact: Graham Dixon. Monthly Acting Workshops.
Private Acting Classes. Summer School. Vocal Coaching*
48 Vectis Road, London SW17 9RG
E info@michaelchekhovstudio.org.uk
W www.michaelchekhovstudio.org.uk

CHERRY PIE PERFORMANCE   T 07939 422081
*Workshops for Actors, Performers, Presenters &
Professionals*
20 Coronation Court, Croston
Lancs PR26 9HF
E enquiries@cherrypieperformance.co.uk
W www.cherrypieperformance.co.uk

COURT
Theatre Training Company

train for a life in the theatre by working in the theatre...

BA (Hons) Acting
Intensive 2 Year Course

P.G. Dipl.
• Technical Theatre
• Acting
• Directing
1 Year Courses

address: Court Theatre Training Company, The Courtyard Theatre, Bowling Green Walk, 40 Pitfield St, London N1 6EU
phone/fax: 020 7739 6868   **email:** info@thecourtyard.org.uk   **web:** www.courttheatretraining.org.uk

CHRISKA STAGE SCHOOL   T 01928 739166
37-39 Whitby Road
Ellesmere Port
Cheshire L64 8AA
E chrisbooth41@hotmail.com
W www.chriska.co.uk

CHRYSTEL ARTS
THEATRE SCHOOL   T 01494 785589
Part-time Classes for Children, Teenagers & Young Adults
in Dance, Drama & Musical Theatre.
ISTD & LAMDA Examinations
Edgware Parish Hall, Rectory Lane
Edgware, Middlesex HA8 7LG
T 020 8952 6010
E chrystelarts@waitrose.com

CHUBBUCK TECHNIQUE   T 020 7732 1774
Private Coaching. Workshops
E coaching@chubbucktechnique.co.uk
W www.chubbucktechnique.co.uk

CHURCHER, Mel MA   T 07778 773019
Acting & Vocal Coach
E melchurcher@hotmail.com
W www.melchurcher.com

CHURCHER, Teresa
(Life Coach MASC)   T 07807 103295
Acting, Audition, Career & Life Coaching for Young Adult
& Graduate Actors plus Industry talks
E info@theactingangel.co.uk
W www.theactingangel.co.uk

CIRCOMEDIA   T/F 0117 947 7288
Centre for Contemporary Circus & Physical Performance
Britannia Road, Kingswood
Bristol BS15 8DB
E info@circomedia.com
W www.circomedia.com

CITY LIT THE   T 020 7492 2542
Accredited & Non-Accredited Part-time & Full-time Day &
Evening Courses. Acting Workshops. Audition Technique.
Bi-Media. Camera Training. Dancing. Dialect/Accent
Coaching. Directing. Elocution Coaching. Improvisation.
Presenting. Professional Preparation. Public Speaking.
Role-play Training. Singing. Story Telling
Keeley Street
Covent Garden
London WC2B 4BA
E drama@citylit.ac.uk
W www.citylit.ac.uk

CLANRANALD TRUST:
COMBAT INTERNATIONAL   T 01259 731010
27 High Street
Kincardine
Alloa FK10 4RJ
E info@clanranald.org
W www.clanranald.org

CLEMENTS, Anne
MA LGSM FRSA   T 020 7435 1211
Audition Technique. Back to Basics for Professional
Actors. Dialect/Accent Coaching. Preparation for Drama
School Entry. Vocal Coaching
E woodlandcreature10@hotmail.com

COLDIRON, M. J.　T 07941 920498
*Audition Preparation & Presentation Skills. Private
Coaching*
54 Millfields Road, London E5 0SB
E jiggs@blueyonder.co.uk

COLGAN, Valerie　T 020 7267 2153
Audition Technique. Voice Production
The Green, 17 Herbert Street
London NW5 4HA

**COMBER, Sharrone BA (Hons)
MAVS (CSSD) PGCE**　T 07752 029422
*Audition & Monologue Speech Technique for Drama &
Performing Arts School Entry. Vocal Coach Specialist.
Dialect & Accent Coaching. Elocution. Presentation
Skills. Private Acting Classes. Public Speaking*
E sharronecomber@hotmail.com

COMEDY COACH　T 01494 772908
Contact: Jack Milner
43 Church Street, Chesham
Buckinghamshire HP5 1HU
E jack@standanddeliver.co.uk
W www.standanddeliver.co.uk

COMPLETE WORKS THE　T 020 7377 0280
The Old Truman Brewery
91 Brick Lane, London E1 6QL
F 020 7247 7405
E info@tcw.org.uk
W www.tcw.org.uk

CONTI, Italia ACADEMY
See DRAMA SCHOOLS: DRAMA UK

**CONTI, Italia ACADEMY OF
THEATRE ARTS**　T 020 7608 0044
*Courses: Performing Arts Diploma, 3 yr. Performing Arts
with Teacher Training, 3 yr. Intensive Performing Arts,
1 yr. Foundation Performing Arts, 1 yr. BA (Hons) Acting,
3 yr. Foundation Acting, 2 term. Singing, 1 yr. Theatre
Arts School (academic yrs 7-11)*
Italia Conti House
23 Goswell Road, London EC1M 7AJ
F 020 7253 1430
E admin@italiaconti.co.uk
W www.italiaconti.com

CORNER, Clive AGSM LRAM　T 01305 860267
Qualified Teacher. Audition Training. Private Coaching
'The Belenes', 60 Wakeham
Portland DT5 1HN
E cornerassociates@btconnect.com

CORONA THEATRE SCHOOL　T 020 8941 2659
Unit B, The Kingsway Park, Oldfield Road
Hampton, London TW12 2HD
E info@coronatheatreschool.com
W www.coronatheatreschool.com

**COURT THEATRE
TRAINING COMPANY**　T/F 020 7739 6868
The Courtyard Theatre, Bowling Green Walk
40 Pitfield Street, London N1 6EU
E info@courttheatretraining.org.uk
W www.courttheatretraining.org.uk

COX, Gregory BA Joint Hons　T 07931 370135
*Bristol Old Vic Graduate with 30 Years' Experience.
Audition Coaching. Drama Coaching. Sight Reading
Skills. Voice Work*
Based in South West London
E gregoryedcox@hotmail.com

COX, Jerry MA PGCE BA (Hons)　T 07957 654027
*Acting Coach. Audition Technique. Preparation/Entry for
Drama School. Private Acting Classes*
4 Stevenson Close, London EN5 1DR
E jerrymarwood@hotmail.com

CPA COLLEGE　T 01708 766007
Full-time 3 yr Performing Arts College
The Studios, 219B North Street
Romford, Essex RM1 4QA
F 01708 766077
E college@cpastudios.co.uk
W www.cpastudios.co.uk

**CREATIVE
PERFORMANCE LTD**　T 020 8908 0502
*Mobile Workshop in Circus Skills & Drama TIE. Events
Management for Libraries, Schools, Youth Clubs &
Play Schemes*
20 Pembroke Road, North Wembley
Middlesex HA9 7PD
E creative.performance@yahoo.co.uk

CROSKIN, Phil　T 07837 712323
*RADA Trained. Auditions, Presentation Skills &
Public Profiles*
E philcroskin@fastmail.fm

CROWE, Ben　T 07952 784911
Accent, Acting & Audition Tuition
25 Holmes Avenue, Hove BN3 7LA
E bencrowe@hotmail.co.uk

CS ACADEMY　T 020 8886 4264
Foundation in Acting Course, 1 yr, part-time
The Croft, 7 Cannon Road
Southgate, London N14 7HE
F 020 8886 7555
E carole@csacademyuk.com
W www.csacademyuk.com

CYGNET TRAINING THEATRE
See DRAMA SCHOOLS: DRAMA UK

**D&B SCHOOL OF PERFORMING ARTS &
D&B THEATRE SCHOOL**　T 020 8698 8880
Central Studios
470 Bromley Road, Bromley BR1 4PQ
E info@dandbperformingarts.co.uk
W www.dandbperformingarts.co.uk

DAVIDSON, Clare　T 020 8348 0132
30 Highgate West Hill, London N6 6NP
E clare@claredavidson.co.uk
W www.claredavidson.co.uk

**DE BURGH, Luan
BA (Hons) MA, MA Dip**　T 07976 809693
*Accent Softening. Elocution. Improvisation. Presentation
Skills. Public Speaking. Vocal Coaching. Voice & Text*
E luan@luandeburgh.com
W www.deburghgroup.com

**DEBUT THEATRE SCHOOL
OF PERFORMING ARTS**　T 01274 618288
12 Tenterfields House, Meadow Road
Apperley Bridge, Bradford BD10 0LQ
E jacqui.debut@btinternet.com
W www.debuttheatreschool.co.uk

DE COURCY, Bridget　T 020 8883 8397
Singing Teacher
19 Muswell Road, London N10
E singinglessons@bridgetdecourcy.co.uk

De FLOREZ, Jane LGSM PG Dip T 020 7602 0741
Accompanist. Acting Workshops. Audition Technique.
Drama School (over 18 yrs). Drama School Preparation.
Language Tutoring. Music Theory for Singers. Public
Speaking. Singing. Vocal Coaching. Courses: Musical
Theatre, 1 yr, part-time. Classical/Opera Singing, 2 yrs,
part-time. General Singing & Music Theory, 1 yr,
part-time. Choir Preparation, 6 months, part-time
Kensington, London W14 9AS
E janedeflorez@gmail.com
W www.singingteacherlondon.com

DIGNAN, Tess MA T 07528 576915
Audition, Text & Voice Coach
004 Oregon Building, Deals Gateway
Lewisham SE13 7RR
E tess.dignan@gmail.com

DIRECTIONS THEATRE ARTS
(CHESTERFIELD) LTD T/F 01246 854455
Musical Theatre School
Studios: 1A-2A Sheffield Road
Chesterfield, Derby S41 7LL
T 07973 768144
E julie.cox5@btconnect.com
W www.directionstheatrearts.org

DOGGETT, Antonia T 07814 155090
Flat 2/2
131 Queen Margaret Drive
Glasgow G20 8PD
E antoniadoggettcontact@gmail.com
W www.antoniadoggett.co.uk

DORSET SCHOOL OF
ACTING THE T 01202 922675
c/o Lighthouse
21 Kingland Road
Poole, Dorset BH15 1UG
E admin@dorsetschoolofacting.co.uk
W www.dorsetschoolofacting.co.uk

DRAMA ASSOCIATION
OF WALES T 029 2045 2200
Summer Courses for Amateur Actors & Directors
Unit 2, The Malting
East Tyndall Street
Cardiff Bay, Cardiff CF24 5EA
E gary@dramawales.org.uk

DRAMA CENTRE LONDON
See DRAMA SCHOOLS: DRAMA UK

Jurgen Schwarz — German Speech Consultant and Coach

German Speech for Film, TV and Theatre • German Singing for Lieder, Recitals and Opera

t: 020 3411 4951   e: contact@liedercoach.com   www.liedercoach.com

---

DRAMA STUDIO
EDINBURGH THE   T 0131 453 3284
Children's Weekly Drama Workshops
19 Belmont Road
Edinburgh EH14 5DZ
E info@thedramastudio.com
W www.thedramastudio.com

DRAMA STUDIO LONDON
See DRAMA SCHOOLS: DRAMA UK

DULIEU, John   T 020 8696 9958
Acting Coach. Audition & Role Preparation
16 Fernwood Avenue, Streatham
London SW16 1RD
T 07803 289599
E john_dulieu@yahoo.com

DUNMORE, Simon
Acting & Audition Tuition
E simon.dunmore@btinternet.com
W www.simon.dunmore.btinternet.co.uk

DURRENT, Peter   T 01787 373483
Audition & Rehearsal Pianist. Vocal Coach
Blacksmiths Cottage
Bures Road, Little Cornard
Sudbury, Suffolk CO10 0NR
E tunefuldurrent@gmail.com

DYSON, Kate LRAM   T 01273 607490
Audition Technique Coaching. Drama
39 Arundel Street
Kemptown BN2 5TH
T 07812 949875
E kate.dyson@talktalk.net

EARNSHAW, Susi
THEATRE SCHOOL   T 020 8441 5010
Full-time Stage School (11-16 yrs). GCSEs &
Vocational Qualifications. Saturday Theatre School
(5-16 yrs). After School & Holiday Courses
The Bull Theatre, 68 High Street
Barnet, Herts EN5 5SJ
F 020 8364 9618
E info@sets.org.uk
W www.susiearnshaw.co.uk

EAST 15 ACTING SCHOOL
See DRAMA SCHOOLS: DRAMA UK

EASTON Helena
BPSA MA ATC (CSSD)   T 07985 931473
Acting Coach
103 Red Square, Carysfort Road
London N16 9AG
E helena.easton@gmail.com

EASTON, Lydia   T 07977 511621
Singing Teacher
72 Palmerston Road, London N22 8RF
E lydzeaston@yahoo.com

ÉCOLE INTERNATIONALE DE
THÉÂTRE JACQUES LECOQ   T 00 33 1 47704478
Acting Workshops. Drama School (over 21 yrs). Mime.
Movement & Creative Theatre. Play Writing
57 rue du Faubourg Saint-Denis
75010 Paris, France
F 00 33 1 45234014
E contact@ecole-jacqueslecoq.com
W www.ecole-jacqueslecoq.com

EDINBURGH LIGHTING &
SOUND SCHOOL (ELSS)   T 07590 015957
c/o Black Light
West Shore Trading Estate
West Shore Road, Edinburgh EH5 1QF
E contact@edinburghlightingandsoundschool.co.uk
W www.edinburghlightingandsoundschool.co.uk

EEDLE, Ben   T 07587 526286
273 Camberwell New Road, London SE5 0TF
E ben@theenglishbears.com
W www.theenglishbears.com

ELLIOTT-CLARKE THEATRE
SCHOOL & COLLEGE   T 0151 709 3323
Courses: Level 3 Musical Theatre, full-time, BTEC.
Performing Arts Performance, full-time, HND.
Saturday/Evening Classes (2-16 yrs)
35 Sefton Street, Liverpool L8 5SL
E contact@elliottclarke.co.uk

EXPRESSIONS ACADEMY OF
PERFORMING ARTS   T 01623 424334
3 Newgate Lane, Mansfield
Nottingham NG18 2LB
E expressions-uk@btconnect.com
W www.expressionsperformingarts.co.uk

FAIRBROTHER, Victoria
MA CSSD LAMDA Dip   T 07877 228990
Audition Technique. Improvisation. Private Acting
Classes. Public Speaking. Vocal Coaching
15A Devonport Road
Shepherd's Bush
London W12 8NZ
E victoriafairbrother1@hotmail.com

FAITH, Gordon
BA IPA Dip.REM.Sp LRAM   T 020 7328 0446
Speech & Voice
1 Wavel Mews, Priory Road
West Hampstead
London NW6 3AB
E gordon.faith@tiscali.co.uk
W www.gordonfaith.co.uk

FERRIS, Anna MA
(Voice Studies, CSSD)   T 01258 881098
Audition Technique. Private Acting Classes. Vocal
Coaching
Based in Dorset & South West
E atcferris@gmail.com

FERRIS ENTERTAINMENT PERFORMING ARTS   T 0845 4724725
London. Belfast. Cardiff. Los Angeles
Number 8, 132 Charing Cross Road
London WC2H 0LA
E info@ferrisentertainment.com
W www.ferrisentertainment.com

FINBURGH, Nina   T 020 7435 9484
*Sight Reading Specialist (Masterclasses & Individuals).
Audition Technique (Equity Members only)*
1 Buckingham Mansions
West End Lane
London NW6 1LR
E ninafinburgh@aol.com

FOOTSTEPS THEATRE SCHOOL & AGENCY   T/F 01274 616535
Dance, Drama & Singing Training
1st Floor, Morrisons Enterprise 5, 5 Lane Ends
Bradford, West Yorkshire BD10 8EW
E gwestman500@btinternet.com

FORD, Carole Ann ADVS   T 020 8815 1832
Acting Coach. Communication Skills
Based In N10
E emko2000@aol.com

FOURTH MONKEY   T 020 8150 0076
*Performance & Training Programme for Actors
(18-35 yrs), 1 & 2 yr, full-time & part-time*
c/o 49 South Molton Street, London W1K 5LH
E office@fourthmonkey.co.uk
W www.fourthmonkey.co.uk

FRANKLIN, Michael   T/F 020 8979 9185
Meisner Technique
Correspondence: c/o Spotlight, 7 Leicester Place
London WC2H 7RJ
E info@acteach.info

FRANKLYN, Susan   T 01306 884913
*Audition Speeches. Confidence. Interview Technique.
Presentation. Sight Reading*
T 07780 742891
E susan.franklyn1@btinternet.com

FURNESS, Simon   T 07702 619665
*Actor Training (Sanford Meisner Technique). Audition
Preparation & Technique*
c/o The Actors' Temple
13-14 Warren Street
London W1T 5LG
E simonfurness@googlemail.com

GFCA (GILES FOREMAN CENTRE FOR ACTING)   T 020 7437 3175
*Formerly Caravanserai Productions & Acting Studio.
1 yr Postgraduate Intensive Diploma & Foundation ATCL
Diploma. 7 day International Summer School. Courses:
Acting, All Levels inc Professionals, 12 week, part-time.
Movement, Voice, Improvisation, Meisner, On-Camera,
Malmgren/Laban Analysis, all 10 week, part-time. Acting
Masterclasses & Workshops. Audition Technique. Private
Acting Coaching*
Studio Soho
Royalty Mews (entrance by Quo Vadis)
22 Dean Street, London W1D 3RA
E info@gilesforeman.com
W www.gilesforeman.com

GLASGOW ACTING ACADEMY   T 0141 222 2942
Contact: Maureen Cairns, Allan Jones
2nd Floor, 34 Argyle Arcade Chambers
Buchanan Street
Glasgow G2 8BD
E info@glasgowactingacademy.com

GMA TELEVISION PRESENTER TRAINING   T 01628 673078
*Presenting for Television, Radio, Live Events. Autocue.
Improvisation. Scriptwriting. Talkback. Vocal Coaching*
86 Beverley Gardens
Maidenhead
Berks SL6 6SW
T 07769 598625
E geoff@gma-training.co.uk

GRAYSON, John T 07702 188031
Acting Workshops. Audition Technique. Improvisation. Private Acting Classes. Public Speaking. Singing. Vocal Coaching
2 Jubilee Road, St Johns
Worcester WR2 4LY
E jgbizzybee@btinternet.com

GREASEPAINT ANONYMOUS T 020 8886 2263
Youth Theatre & Training Company. Part-time Theatre Workshops run weekly through School Term Time. Holiday Courses at Easter & Summer. Acting Workshops. Dancing. Singing (4-30 yrs)
4 Gallus Close, Winchmore Hill
London N21 1JR
T 07930 421216
E info@greasepaintanonymous.co.uk

GROUT, Philip T 020 8881 1800
Theatre Director. Drama Coaching. Tuition for Students & Professionals
81 Clarence Road, London N22 8PG
E philipgrout@hotmail.com

GRYFF, Stefan T 020 7723 8181
Screen Acting Coach

GSA, GUILDFORD SCHOOL OF ACTING
See DRAMA SCHOOLS: DRAMA UK

GUILDHALL SCHOOL OF MUSIC & DRAMA
See DRAMA SCHOOLS: DRAMA UK

HANCOCK, Allison LLAM T/F 020 8891 1073
Acting. Audition Coach. Dramatic Art. Elocution. Speech Correction. Voice
38 Eve Road, Isleworth
Middlesex TW7 7HS
E allisonhancock@blueyonder.co.uk

HARLEQUIN STUDIOS PERFORMING ARTS SCHOOL T 01273 581742
Drama & Dance Training
122A Phyllis Avenue
Peacehaven
East Sussex BN10 7RQ

HARRIS, Sharon NCSD LRAM LAM STSD IPA Dip DA (London Univ) T 01923 211644
Speech & Drama Specialist Teacher. Private Acting Coach for Screen & Stage. Training for RADA, LAMDA & ESB Exams. Audition Technique. Drama School & National Youth Theatre Audition Preparation
71 The Avenue, Watford
Herts WD17 4NU
T 07956 388716
E theharrisagency@btconnect.com

HARRISON RUTHERFORD Lucie MA Voice Studies, BA (Hons) Drama T 07773 798440
Voice Tutor & Acting Coach
Based in Richmond upon Thames
E info@lucieharrison.co.uk
W www.lucieharrison.co.uk

HASS, Leontine
Vocal Coach
E leontine@associatedstudios.co.uk
W www.leontinehass.co.uk

HESTER, John LLCM (TD) T 020 8224 9580
Member of The Society of Teachers of Speech & Drama. Acting Courses for All Ages. Acting Workshops. Audition Technique. Dialect/Accent Coaching. Drama School Auditions (over 18 yrs). Elocution Coaching. Private Acting Classes. Public Speaking. Stage School for Children. Vocal Coaching
105 Stoneleigh Park Road, Epsom
Surrey KT19 0RF
E hjohnhester@aol.com

HETHERINGTON, Caro T 07723 620728
Voice & Dialect Coach
7 Dodcott Barns, Burleydam
Whitchurch, Cheshire SY13 4BQ
E carolinehetherington@gmail.com
W www.carohetherington.co.uk

HIGGS, Jessica T 020 7701 8477
Voice
34 Mary Datchelor House, 2D Camberwell Grove
London SE5 8FB
T 07940 193631
E juhiggs@aol.com

H. J. A. (HERBERT JUSTICE ACADEMY) T 020 8249 3299
Inspiration House, 38 Croydon Road
Beckenham, Kent BR3 4BJ
F 020 8650 8365
E mail@hjaworld.com
W www.hjaworld.com

HOFFMANN-GILL, Daniel T 020 8888 6045
Acting & Audition Tuition
T 07946 433903
E danielhg@gmail.com

HONEYBORNE, Jack T 020 8993 2111
Accompanist. Coach
The Studio, 165 Gunnersbury Lane
London W3 8LJ

HOOKER, Jennifer Jane T 07725 977146
Private Acting Coach
Flat 3, 16 Cosway Street
London NW1 5NR
E jj@jjhooker.com
W www.jjhooker.com

HOOPLA IMPRO T 07976 975348
Improvised Comedy, Commedia Dell'Arte, Mask & Narrative Classes. Various Venues Around London
E roezone@hotmail.com
W www.hooplaimpro.com

HOPE STREET LTD T 0151 708 8007
Professional Development Opportunities for Emerging & Established Artists
13A Hope Street, Liverpool L1 9BQ
E peter@hope-street.org
W www.hope-street.org

HOPKINS, Abigail T 07847 420882
Audition & Acting Coach
E creativeacting@hotmail.co.uk

HOPNER, Ernest LLAM T 0151 625 5641
Elocution. Public Speaking. Vocal Coaching
70 Banks Road, West Kirby CH48 0RD

HOUSEMAN, Barbara   T 07767 843737
Ex-RSC Voice Dept. Author 'Finding Your Voice' &
'Tackling Text'. Voice. Text. Acting. Confidence
E barbarahouseman@hotmail.com
W www.barbarahouseman.com

HOWARD, Ashley BA MA   T 07821 213752
Voice Coach
5 St John's Street, Aylesbury, Bucks HP20 1BS
E ashleyhowardvoicecoach@yahoo.co.uk
W www.accentsofteningandelocution.com

HUDSON, Mark   T 0161 238 8900
Film & Television Acting & Dialect Coach
14-32 Hewitt Street, Manchester M15 4GB
E actorclass@aol.com

HUGHES, Dewi   T 07836 545717
Voice. Text. Accents. Auditions
Flat 1, 4 Fielding Road
London W14 0LL
E dewi.hughes@gmail.com

HUGHES-D'AETH, Charlie   T 07811 010963
RSC Text & Voice Coach. Acting & Audition Technique.
Presentation Skills. Public Speaking. Vocal Coaching
E chdaeth@aol.com

IDENTITY DRAMA SCHOOL   T 020 7470 8711
The UK's First Black Drama School
105 Holloway Road, London N7 8LT
E space@identitydramaschool.com
W www.identitydramaschool.com

IMPULSE COMPANY THE T/F 07525 264173
Meisner-Based Core Training
E info@impulsecompany.co.uk
W www.impulsecompany.co.uk

**INDEPENDENT THEATRE
WORKSHOP THE** T 00 353 1 2600831
8 Terminus Mills, Clonskeagh
Dublin 6, Ireland
E agency@itwstudios.ie
W www.itwstudios.ie

INTERACT T 07961 982198
*Contact: Lauren Bigby (LGSM). Acting Workshops.
Audition Technique. Elocution Coaching. Private Acting
Classes. Public Speaking*
18 Knightbridge Walk, Billericay
Essex CM12 0HP
E renbigby@hotmail.com

**INTERNATIONAL PERFORMING
ARTS & THEATRE LTD** T 07760 666788
Specialises in Triple Threat (Dance, Singing & Acting)
57 Old Compton Street, Westminster
London W1D 6HP
E london@i-path.biz
W www.i-path.biz

**INTERNATIONAL SCHOOL OF
SCREEN ACTING** T 020 8555 5775
3 Mills Studios, Unit 3
24 Sugar House Lane, London E15 2QS
E office@screenacting.co.uk
W www.screenacting.co.uk

J VOX VOCAL ACADEMY T 07546 100745
*Contact: Jay Henry (Vocal Coach). Vocal Training &
Breathing. Audition Preparation. Microphone Technique*
Dunbar, Latimer Road
Barnet EN5 5NF
T 07854 596916
E info@jvox.co.uk
W www.jvoxacademy.com

JACK, Andrew T 07836 615839
Dialect Coach
Vrouwe Johanna, 24 The Moorings
Willows Riverside, Windsor, Berks SL4 5TG
W www.andrewjack.com

JACK, Paula T 07836 615839
Dialect Coach. Language Specialist
Vrouwe Johanna, 24 The Moorings
Willows Riverside, Windsor, Berks SL4 5TG
W www.paulajack.com

JAM ACADEMY THE T 01628 483808
Jam Theatre Company, 45A West Street
Marlow, Bucks SL7 3NH
E info@thejamacademy.co.uk
W www.thejamacademy.co.uk

**JAMES, Linda
RAM Dip Ed IPD LRAM** T 020 8568 2390
Dialect & Speech Coach
25 Clifden Road, Brentford
Middlesex TW8 0PB

JAQUARELLO, Roland BA T/F 020 8741 2446
*Audition Technique. Drama School Entrance.
Radio Coaching*
41 Parfrey Street, London W6 9EW
T 07808 742307
E roland@jaquarellofulham.freeserve.co.uk
W www.rolandjaquarello.com

JG DANCE LTD T 01491 572000
Melody House, 198 Grey's Road
Henley-on-Thames, Oxon RG9 1QU
E info@jgdance.co.uk
W www.jgdance.co.uk

**JIGSAW PERFORMING
ARTS SCHOOLS** T 020 8447 4530
64-66 High Street, Barnet
Herts EN5 5SJ
F 020 8447 4531
E enquiries@jigsaw-arts.co.uk
W www.jigsaw-arts.co.uk

JINGLES, Jo T 01494 778989
1 Boismore Road, Chesham, Bucks HP5 1SH
E headoffice@jojingles.co.uk
W www.jojingles.com

JOHNSON, David DRAMA T 07969 183481
PO Box 618, Oldham
Greater Manchester OL1 9GU
F 0161 620 6444
E johnsondrama@googlemail.com
W www.davidjohnsondrama.co.uk

**JONGLEURS SCHOOL
OF COMEDY** T 020 8402 2424
*1 yr Intensive Stand-up Comedy Course. Short Courses
Also Available*
76 High Street, Beckenham BR3 1ED
E admin@dancecompanystudios.co.uk
W www.jongleurs.com/schoolofcomedy

JORDAN, Daniel T 07803 684375
E daniel_jordan27@hotmail.com

**JUDE'S DRAMA ACADEMY &
MANAGEMENT** T 0161 624 5378
Manor House, Oldham Road
Springhead, Oldham OL4 4QJ
E judesdrama@yahoo.co.uk
W www.judesdrama.co.uk

KENT YOUTH THEATRE T 01227 730177
*Contact: Richard Andrews. Stage & Screen Academy.
Courses in Drama, Dance, Musical Theatre, Singing,
Film Acting/Making. Improvisation. Private Acting
Classes. Stage School for Children*
Office: Mulberry Croft, Mulberry Hill
Chilham CT4 8AJ
T/F 07967 580213
E richard@kentyouththeatre.co.uk
W www.kentyouththeatre.co.uk

KERR, Louise T 020 8509 2767
Voice Coach
20A Rectory Road, London E17 3BQ
T 07780 708102
E louise@louisekerr.com
W www.resonancevoice.com

**KINGSTON JUNIOR
DRAMA COMPANY** T 01932 230273
Workshops (10-14 yrs)
72 Shaw Drive, Walton-on-Thames
Surrey KT12 2LS
E kingstonjdc@aol.com
W www.davidlawsonlean.com

KIRKLEES COLLEGE T 01484 437047
Courses in Acting, Dance & Musical Theatre (BTEC)
Highfields Annexe, New North Road
Huddersfield HD1 5NN
E info@kirkleescollege.ac.uk

ACTING • MUSICAL THEATRE • PROFESSIONAL PRODUCTION SKILLS

Guildford School of Acting

Courses for **2013** entry

Undergraduate Courses
- Acting
- Musical Theatre
- Professional Production Skills

Postgraduate Courses
- Acting
- Musical Theatre
- Practice of Voice and Singing

We also offer
- Foundation Course
- Part-time Course
- Summer School

drama uk

TRINITY
COLLEGE LONDON
Registered Examination Centre 27006

For an application form/further details contact:

Guildford School of Acting
Stag Hill Campus, University of Surrey, Guildford GU2 7XH UK
Tel: (01483) 684040   Fax: (01483) 684070
Email: gsaenquiries@gsa.surrey.ac.uk   Web: www.gsauk.org

UNIVERSITY OF
SURREY

KNYVETTE, Sally T 07958 972425
Drama School Preparation. Drama Tuition. Specialising in
Shakespeare. All Levels
52 Burnfoot Avenue
London SW6 5EA
E salkny@gmail.com
W www.sallyknyvette.co.uk

KRIMPAS, Titania T 07957 303958
One-to-one Tuition, all levels. Tailored to suit experienced
actors & beginners
The Garden Flat, 23 Lambolle Road
London NW3 4HS
E titaniakrimpas@gmail.com

KSA PERFORMING ARTS T 020 8090 5801
Beckenham Halls, 4 Bromley Road
Beckenham BR3 5JE
E info@ksapa.co.uk
W www.ksapa.co.uk

KTPAS T 020 8799 6157
Performing Arts School. Full-time, Saturday &
Summer Courses
KT Summit House
100 Hanger Lane, London W5 1EZ
E info@kt.org
W www.kt.org/ktpas

LAINE THEATRE ARTS T 01372 724648
The Studios, East Street
Epsom, Surrey KT17 1HH
F 01372 723775
E info@laine-theatre-arts.co.uk
W www.laine-theatre-arts.co.uk

LAMDA
See DRAMA SCHOOLS: DRAMA UK

LAMONT DRAMA SCHOOL
& CASTING AGENCY T 07736 387543
Contact: Diane Lamont. Acting Skills. Audition
Technique. Coaching. Part-time Lessons
2 Harewood Avenue, Ainsdale
Merseyside PR8 2PH
E diane@lamontcasting.co.uk
W www.lamontcasting.co.uk

LAURIE, Rona T 020 7262 4909
Coach for Auditions. Public Speaking. Voice & Speech
Technique
Flat 1, 21 New Quebec Street
London W1H 7SA

LEAN, David Lawson
BA Hons PGCE T 01932 230273
Acting Tuition for Children. LAMDA Exams. Licensed
Chaperone
72 Shaw Drive, Walton-on-Thames
Surrey KT12 2LS
E dlawsonlean@aol.com
W www.davidlawsonlean.com

LEE THEATRE SCHOOL THE T 01268 793090
Office: 48 Brook Road, Benfleet
Essex SS7 5JF
E lynn.theatre@gmail.com
W www.lynnlee.co.uk

LESLIE, Maeve T 020 7834 4912
Classical & Musicals. Presentations. Singing.
Voice Production
60 Warwick Square
London SW1V 2AL

LEVENTON, Patricia BA Hons T 020 7624 5661
Audition & Dialect Coach
113 Broadhurst Gardens, West Hampstead
London NW6 3BJ
T 07703 341062
E patricia@lites2000.com

LIEDERCOACH.COM T 020 3411 4951
Contact: Jurgen Schwarz. German Singing for Lieder,
Recitals & Opera. German Speech for Film, Television
& Stage
E contact@liedercoach.com
W www.liedercoach.com

LINCOLN ACADEMY OF
DRAMATIC ARTS T 01522 837242
6-18 yrs
Sparkhouse Studios, Rope Walk
Lincoln, Lincs LN6 7DQ
F 01522 837201
E info@lada.org.uk
W www.lada.org.uk/academy

LIPTON, Rick T 07961 445247
Dialect/Accent Coaching
14 Lock Road, Richmond, Surrey TW10 7LH
E info@ricklipton.com
W www.ricklipton.com

LITTLE SHAKESPEARE
THEATRE SCHOOL T 07724 937331
Classes, Workshops & Training for Young Actors led by
Professional Actors
34 Campbell Road, Longniddry
East Lothian EH32 0NP
E michelle@littleshakespearetheatreschool.co.uk
W www.littleshakespearetheatreschool.co.uk

LIVERPOOL COMMUNITY
STAGE SCHOOL T 0151 336 4302
Community Stage School for Children. Dance. Drama.
Singing
c/o 9 Carlton Close, Parkgate
Neston, Cheshire CH64 6TD
E mail@littleactorstheatre.com
W www.littleactorstheatre.com

LIVERPOOL INSTITUTE FOR
PERFORMING ARTS THE
See DRAMA SCHOOLS: DRAMA UK

LLOYD, Gabrielle T 020 8946 4042
Audition Technique. Drama School Entrance. LAMDA
Exams. Private Acting Classes. Public Speaking.
Vocal Coaching
Based in South West London
E gubilloyd@hotmail.com

LOCATION TUTORS
NATIONWIDE T 020 7978 8898
Fully Qualified/Experienced Teachers Working with
Children on Film Sets & Covering all Key Stages of
National Curriculum
16 Poplar Walk, Herne Hill SE24 0BU
F 020 7207 8794
E locationtutorsnationwide@gmail.com
W www.locationtutors.co.uk

LONDON ACTORS WORKSHOP T 07748 846294
Workshop Studio Based in Endell Street, Covent Garden
Enquiries: 29B Battersea Rise
London SW11 1HG
E info@londonactorsworkshop.co.uk
W www.londonactorsworkshop.co.uk

LONDON DRAMA SCHOOL T 020 8830 0074
Acting. Singing. Physical Theatre. Voice. Trinity Guildhall Diplomas
30 Brondesbury Park, London NW6 7DN
F 020 8830 4992
E enquiries@startek-uk.com
W www.startek-uk.com

LONDON INTERNATIONAL SCHOOL OF PERFORMING ARTS T 020 8215 3390
The Old Lab, 3 Mills Studios
Three Mill Lane, London E3 3DU
F 020 8215 3392
E welcome@lispa.co.uk
W www.lispa.co.uk

LONDON LANGUAGE TRAINING T 07941 468639
English language coaching for overseas actors looking to improve fluency, pronunciation & intonation. All courses taught by English language teacher, trainer & author Luke Vyner
E luke@londonlanguagetraining.co.uk
W www.londonlanguagetraining.co.uk

LONDON REPERTORY COMPANY ACADEMY T/F 020 7258 1944
PO Box 59385, London NW8 1HL
E academy@londonrepertorycompany.com
W www.londonrepertorycompany.com/academy

LONDON SCHOOL OF DRAMATIC ART T 020 7581 6100
Foundation & Advanced Diplomas in Acting (full & part-time). Drama School (over 18 yrs). Short Summer Courses
4 Bute Street, South Kensington
London SW7 3EX
E enquiries@lsda-acting.com
W www.lsda-acting.com

LONDON SCHOOL OF FILM, MEDIA & PERFORMANCE T 020 7487 7505
Regent's College, Inner Circle
Regent's Park, London NW1 4NS
F 020 7487 7425
E lsfmp@regents.ac.uk
W www.regents.ac.uk/lsfmp

LONDON SCHOOL OF MUSICAL THEATRE T/F 020 7407 4455
83 Borough Road, London SE1 1DN
E info@lsmt.co.uk

LONDON STUDIO CENTRE T 020 7837 7741
Courses in Theatre Dance, 3 yrs, full-time, BA. Evening & Saturday Classes. Summer Course
artsdepot, 5 Nether Street, Tally Ho Corner
North Finchley, London N12 0GA
F 020 7837 3248
E info@london-studio-centre.co.uk
W www.london-studio-centre.co.uk

LONG OVERDUE THEATRE SCHOOL THE T 0845 8382994
16 Butterfield Drive, Amesbury, Wiltshire SP4 7SJ
E stefpearmain@hotmail.com
W www.tlots.co.uk

LONGMORE, Wyllie T 0161 881 6440
Acting Techniques. Voice & Speech. Presentation Skills.
Based in Manchester
E info@wyllielongmore.co.uk
W www.wyllielongmore.co.uk

MACKINNON, Alison T 07973 562132
Accent. Audition Preparation. Presentation. Voice
Based in London SE6
E alison.mackinnon@bruford.ac.uk

MAD RED THEATRE SCHOOL AT THE
MADDERMARKET THEATRE T 01603 628600
Contact: Jen Dewsbury. Drama School (over 18 yrs).
Drama School Preparation. Private Acting Classes. Stage
School for Children. Summer School. Courses: Arts
Awards, part-time, bronze & silver awards. Silver Stagers
(over 60 yrs), Youth/Adult Theatre Classes, all 3 terms a
year, part-time
Maddermarket Theatre
St John's Alley, Norwich NR2 1DR
F 01603 661357
E jenny.dewsbury@maddermarket.org
W www.mad-red.co.uk

MANCHESTER SCHOOL OF
ACTING T/F 0161 238 8900
14-32 Hewitt Street, Manchester M15 4GB
E info@manchesterschoolofacting.co.uk
W www.manchesterschoolofacting.co.uk

MANCHESTER SCHOOL OF THEATRE AT
MANCHESTER METROPOLITAN UNIVERSITY
See DRAMA SCHOOLS: DRAMA UK

MARLOW, Chris T 07792 309992
Voice & Speech Teacher
RDDC, 52 Bridleway, Waterfoot
Rossendale, Lancashire BB4 9DS
E rddc@btinternet.com
W www.rddc.co.uk

MARLOW, Jean LGSM T 020 8450 0371
32 Exeter Road, London NW2 4SB

MARTIN, Liza GRSM GRSM (Recital)
ARMCM (Singing & Piano) T 020 8348 0346
Piano Accompanist. Singing Tuition

MARTIN, Mandi SINGING
TECHNIQUE T 020 8950 7525
Previously at London Studio Centre & Bodywork at
Cambridge Performing Arts. Currently Coaching at
Millennium Dance 2000. Private Lessons
T 07811 758656
E mandi.martin@sky.com

MARTONE, Sergio T 07742 148418
Acting. Audition Technique. Presentation
37 Muswell Hill, Muswell Hill
London N10 3PN
E sergiomartone@mac.com

MASTERS PERFORMING
ARTS COLLEGE LTD T 01268 777351
Performing Arts Course
Arterial Road, Rayleigh
Essex SS6 7UQ
E info@mastersperformingarts.co.uk

MAVERICK YOUTH ACADEMY T 07531 138248
c/o 12 Lydney Grove, Northfield
Birmingham B31 1RB
E academy@mavericktheatre.co.uk
W www.mavericktheatre.co.uk

MAY, Maggie DRAMA T 07984 745323
The Epsom Playhouse, Ashley Avenue
Epsom, Surrey KT18 5AL
E office@maggiemayltd.com
W www.maggiemayltd.com

McDAID, Marj T 020 7923 4929
1 Chesholm Road
Stoke Newington, London N16 0DP
T 07815 993203
E marjmcdaid@hotmail.com
W www.voicings.co.uk

McDONAGH, Melanie MANAGEMENT
(ACADEMY OF PERFORMING ARTS &
CASTING AGENCY) T 07909 831409
14 Apple Tree Way
Oswaldtwistle
Accrington, Lancashire BB5 0FB
T 01254 392560
E mcdonaghmgt@aol.com
W www.mcdonaghmanagement.co.uk

McKEAND, Ian T 07768 960530
Audition Technique. Drama School Entry
Based in Lincoln
E ian.mckeand@ntlworld.com
W http://homepage.ntlworld.com/ian.mckeand1

McKELLAN, Martin T 07973 437237
Acting Workshops. Dialect/Accent Coaching. Private
Acting Classes. Vocal Coaching
Covent Garden
London WC2H 9PA
E dialectandvoice@yahoo.co.uk

MELLECK, Lydia T 020 7794 8845
Pianist & Coach for Auditions & Repertoire, RADA,
Mountview. Accompanist. Singing for Beginners. Vocal
Coaching. Workshops on Sondheim
10 Burgess Park Mansions
London NW6 1DP
E lyd.muse@yahoo.co.uk

MGA ACADEMY OF
PERFORMING ARTS THE T 0131 466 9392
The MGA Company
207 Balgreen Road
Edinburgh EH11 2RZ
E info@themgacompany.com
W www.themgaacademy.com

MICHAELJOHN'S
ACTING ACADEMY T 020 3463 8492
In association with Khando Entertainment.
Contact: Ajay Nayyar
E info@khandoentertainment.com

MICHEL, Hilary ARCM   **T** 020 8343 7243
Accompanist. Audition Songs. Diction & Languages for
Songs. Singing Teacher & Vocal Coach. Piano, Recorder
& Theory Teacher
21 Southway, Totteridge
London N20 8EB
T 07775 780182
E hilarymich@optimamail.co.uk

MILLER, Robin   **T** 07957 627677
Audition Technique. Dialect/Accent Coaching
Based in St Margarets/Twickenham
E robinjenni@hotmail.com

MONTAGE THEATRE ARTS   **T** 020 8692 7007
Contact: Judy Gordon (Artistic Director). Dance. Drama.
Singing. Children & Adults
The Albany, Douglas Way
London SE8 4AG
E office@montagetheatre.com
W www.montagetheatre.com

MORGAN, Katie BA
(Hons) PG Dip PGCE   **T** 07956 344255
Private Acting Coach. Audition Preparation. Drama
School Entry. Improvisation. Meisner Technique. Working
the Text. General Skills. Coach/Consultant for Plays/
Films. Founder of 'The Actors' Surgery'
Based in London
E theactorssurgery@gmail.com
W www.theactorssurgery.com

MORLEY COLLEGE   **T** 020 7450 1889
Acting, Writing & Public Speaking Courses for all levels.
Accredited Courses for Vocational Study. Courses:
Acting, Audition Workshops, Directing, Drama Theory,
Improvisation, Mime, Physical Theatre, Presentation
Skills, Public Speaking, Scriptwriting, Shakespeare,
Stand-up
61 Westminster Bridge Road, London SE1 7HT
E drama@morleycollege.ac.uk
W www.morleycollege.ac.uk

MORRISON, Elspeth   **T** 07790 919870
Accent & Dialect Coach
E elsp.morrison@talk21.com

MORRISON, Stuart MA Voice Studies
FVCM(TD)(Hons) FIfL FRSA   **T** 07411 864580
Voice, Speech & Acting Coach
24 Deans Walk, Coulsdon
Surrey CR5 1HR
E stuartvoicecoach@yahoo.co.uk
W www.voiceandspeech.org.uk

MOTHERWELL COLLEGE   **T** 01698 232323
Courses: Acting, Musical Theatre, HNC/D, BA Hons
1 Enterprise Way, Motherwell ML1 2TX
E information@motherwell.co.uk
W www.motherwell.co.uk

MOUNTVIEW ACADEMY OF THEATRE ARTS
See DRAMA SCHOOLS: DRAMA UK

MTA THE   **T** 020 8882 8181
T 07904 987493
E info@themta.co.uk
W www.themta.co.uk

MURRAY, Barbara
LGSM LALAM   **T** 01923 823182
129 Northwood Way, Northwood
Middlesex HA6 1RF
E barbarahalliwell@gmail.com

RICK LIPTON DIALECT, DIALOGUE AND VOICE COACH

- American Accent Coaching from an American in London
- Digital Recordings of your sessions provided
- Film, Television, Theatre, Auditions, Private Lessons
- 10+ years experience, 1000+ actors trained and coached

07961445247   rl@ricklipton.com   www.ricklipton.com

MUSICAL KIDZ COMPANY THE   T 07989 353673
Spires Meade, 4 Bridleways
Wendover, Bucks HP22 6DN
F 01296 623696
E themusicalkidz@aol.com
W www.themusicalkidz.co.uk

NATHENSON, Zoe   T 07956 833850
Audition Technique. Film Acting. Sight Reading.
Group Classes
55 St James's Lane, London N10 3DA
E zoe.act@btinternet.com
W www.zoenathenson.com

NEIL, Andrew   T/F 020 7262 9521
Audition Technique. Private Acting Classes. Public
Speaking
2 Howley Place, London W2 1XA
T 07979 843984
E andrewneil@talktalk.net

NEO - NUNCHAKU EXERCISE
ORGANISATION   T 020 8337 6181
Fight Scene Staging, Planning & Training. Training in the
use of Nunchaku vs Nunchaku & Other Weapons. Venue
based in Kingston, London
202 Bridgewood Road, Worcester Park
Sutton, Surrey KT4 8XU
E neo@neo-nunchaku.co.uk
W www.neo-nunchaku.co.uk

NESTON THEATRE SCHOOL   T 0151 336 4302
Dance, Drama & Singing Training (2-11 yrs)
9 Carlton Close, Parkgate
Neston, Cheshire CH64 6TD
E mail@littleactorstheatre.com
W www.littleactorstheatre.com

NEW LONDON PERFORMING
ARTS CENTRE   T 020 8444 4544
Courses in Performing Arts (3-19 yrs). Dance. Drama.
GCSE Courses, LAMDA, ISTD & RAD
76 St James Lane, Muswell Hill
London N10 3DF
F 020 8444 4040
E nlpac@aol.com
W www.nlpac.co.uk

NEWNHAM, Caryll   T 01255 670973
Singing Teacher
69 Old Road, Frinton, Essex CO13 9BX
T 07976 635745
E caryllcollins@gmail.com

NOBLE, Penny
PSYCHOTHERAPY   T 07506 579895
Character-centred Counselling & Training. Character
Development. Performance Support. Safe Emotion
Memory Work. Script Work. Self-esteem & Confidence
8 Shaftesbury Gardens, Victoria Road
North Acton, London NW10 6LJ
E pennynobletherapy@googlemail.com
W www.pennynoblepsychotherapy.com

NORTHERN ACADEMY OF
PERFORMING ARTS   T 01482 310690
Anlaby Road, Hull HU1 2PD
F 01482 212280
E napa@northernacademy.org.uk
W www.northernacademy.org.uk

NORTHERN FILM & DRAMA   T/F 01977 681949
Acting Workshops. Television Audition Technique.
Drama School. Residential Courses (over 18 yrs). Film &
Television Training. Improvisation. Private Acting Classes.
Stage School for Children
The Studio
21 Low Street
South Milford, Leeds LS25 5AR
E info@northernfilmanddrama.com
W www.northernfilmanddrama.com

NPAS @ THE STUDIOS   T/F 00 353 1 8944660
NPAS The Factory, 35A Darrow Street
Dublin 4, Ireland
E info@npas.ie
W www.npas.ie

O.J. SONUS   T 020 8963 0702
Voice Over Workshops. Voicereel Production with
Professional Coaching Available
14-15 Main Drive
East Lane Business Park
Wembley HA9 7NA
T 07929 859401
E info@ojsonus.com
W www.ojsonus.com

OLLERENSHAW, Maggie
BA (Hons) Dip Ed   T 020 7286 1126
Acting Workshops. Audition Technique. Career
Guidance. Private Acting. Television & Theatre Coaching
151D Shirland Road
London W9 2EP
T 07860 492699
E maggieoll@aol.com

OLSON, Lise   T 0121 331 7220
Acting Through Song. American Accents. Vocal
Coaching. Working with Text
c/o Birmingham School of Acting
Millennium Point
Curzon Street, Birmingham B4 7XG
E lise.olson@bcu.ac.uk

OMOBONI, Lino   T/F 020 8741 2038
Private Acting Classes
2nd Floor, 12 Weltje Road, London W6 9TG
T 07525 187468
E bluewand@btinternet.com

OPEN VOICE   T 07704 704930
Contact: Catherine Owen. Auditions. Consultancy.
Personal Presentations
9 Bellsmains
Gorebridge, Near Edinburgh EH23 4QD
E catherineowenopenvoice@gmail.com

MOUNTVIEW
ACADEMY OF THEATRE ARTS

Ralph Richardson Memorial Studios,
Kingfisher Place, Clarendon Road,
Wood Green, London N22 6XF

Tel: 020 8881 2201
Fax: 020 8829 0034

enquiries@mountview.org.uk
www.mountview.org.uk

Undergraduate & Postgraduate Courses

Plus an exciting programme of Part-time and Summer Courses

Mountview is committed to equal opportunities

Musical Theatre

Acting

Production Arts

OPPOSITE LEG LTD　　T 07950 824123
Contact: David Windle. Acting Workshops. Classroom
Presence for Teachers. Corporate Voice & Body Training.
Improvisation. Presentation Skills Training. Private Acting
Classes. Public Speaking. Teenage Drama Workshops.
Vocal Coaching
132 Bethwin Road, London SE5 0YY
E david@oppositeleg.co.uk
W www.oppositeleg.co.uk

ORAM, Daron　　T 07905 332497
Voice, Text & Accent Coach. Senior Voice Teacher, Arts
Educational Schools London. RSC, West End &
National Tours
Based in W4/SE10
E darono@yahoo.com

OSBORNE HUGHES, John　　T 020 8653 7735
Spiritual Psychology of Acting
Miracle Tree Productions Training Department
51 Church Road
London SE19 2TE
T 07801 950916
E info@miracletreeproductions.com
W www.spiritualpsychologyofacting.com

OSCARS THEATRE ACADEMY　　T 01484 545519
Contact: Paula Danholm
Oscars Management, Spring Bank House
1 Spring Bank, New North Road
Huddersfield, West Yorkshire HD1 5NR
E management@oscarsacademy.co.uk

OXFORD SCHOOL OF DRAMA THE
See DRAMA SCHOOLS: DRAMA UK

PALMER, Jackie
STAGE SCHOOL　　T 01494 510597
30 Daws Hill Lane, High Wycombe
Bucks HP11 1PW
F 01494 510479
E jackie.palmer@btinternet.com
W www.jackiepalmer.co.uk

PARKES, Frances MA AGSM　　T/F 020 8542 2777
Contact: Frances Parkes, Sarah Upson. Dialect/Accent
Coaching & Script Coach. Interview Skills for Castings.
Presenting. Private Acting Classes. Public Speaking.
Speak English Clearly Programme for Actors with English
as a Second Language
Suite 5, 3rd Floor, 1 Harley Street
London W1G 9QD
T 01782 827222 (Upson Edwards)
E frances@maxyourvoice.com
W www.maxyourvoice.com

PERFORMANCE BUSINESS THE　　T 01932 888885
78 Oatlands Drive, Weybridge
Surrey KT13 9HT
E michael@theperformance.biz
W www.theperformance.biz

PERFORMANCE FACTORY
STAGE SCHOOL THE　　T 01792 701570
c/o 26 Pine Crescent, Swansea SA6 6AR
E info@tpfwales.com
W www.tpfwales.com

PERFORMANCE FREQUENCY　　T 07876 298613
9 Tennyson Road, Stoke
Coventry, West Midlands CV2 5HX
E info@performancefrequency.com
W www.performancefrequency.com

PERFORMERS COLLEGE　　T 01375 672053
Contact: Brian Rogers, Susan Stephens
Southend Road, Corringham
Essex SS17 8JT
F 01375 672353
E lesley@perfomerscollege.co.uk
W www.performerscollege.co.uk

PERFORMERS
THEATRE SCHOOL　　T 0151 708 4000
Classes in Drama, Dance & Singing. Stage School for
Children. Holiday & Summer Schools
8 Vernon Street, Liverpool L2 2AY
E info@performerstheatre.co.uk
W www.performerstheatre.co.uk

PERFORMERZONE
(BRIGHTON & LONDON)　　T 07973 518643
Contact: William Pool (ARCM). Singing. Tuition.
Workshops
33A Osmond Road, Hove
East Sussex BN3 1TD
E pool.william@gmail.com
W www.performerzone.co.uk

PG COACHING　　T 07786 512841
One-to-one tuition & Meisner training in small groups
with qualified acting coach based in Altrincham, South
Manchester & Leek, North Staffordshire. Courses
arranged elsewhere on request
E coaching@pruegillett.com
W www.pruegillett.com/coaching

PINPOINT　　T 020 8963 0702
Voice Over Workshops. Voicereel Production with
Professional Coaching Available
14-15 Main Drive, East Lane Business Park
Wembley HA9 7NA
T 07929 859401
E info@voice-overstudio.co.uk
W www.voice-overstudio.co.uk

POLLYANNA TRAINING
THEATRE　　T 020 7481 1911
1 Knighten Street, Wapping, London E1W 1PH
E pollyanna_mgmt@btinternet.com
W www.pollyannatheatre.org

POLYDOROU, Anna MA　　T 07833 545292
Vocal Coaching. MA Voice Studies, Central School of
Speech & Drama
147C Fernhead Road, Maida Hill
Queens Park W9 3ED
E annahebe@yahoo.co.uk

POOR SCHOOL　　T 020 7837 6030
242 Pentonville Road, London N1 9JY
E acting@thepoorschool.com
W www.thepoorschool.com

POPPIES YOUTH
THEATRE & AGENCY　　T 07795 370678
Stockbrook House, 8 King Street
Duffield, Derbyshire DE56 4EU
E poppies09@live.co.uk
W www.poppies-yta.co.uk

PRECINCT THEATRE THE　　T 020 7359 3594
Units 2-3 The Precinct, Packington Square
London N1 7UP
F 020 7359 3660
E theatre@breakalegman.com
W www.breakalegman.com

PRICE, Janis R.　　　T 07977 630829
Voice Coach
E janis@janisprice.sfnet.co.uk

PRIMOATTO PRODUCTIONS　　T 07830 120536
2/21 Culmington Road, Ealing, London W13 9NJ
E mg@primoattoproductions.com
W www.primoattoproductions.com

PROJECTURVOICE.COM　　T 01273 204779
*Contact: Dee Forrest (Deputy Head of Voice,
Mountview). Audition Technique. Confidence Building/
NLP. Public Speaking. Vocal Coaching.*
London & Brighton Studios
20 Landseer Road, Hove BN3 7AF
T 07957 211065
E dee_forrest@yahoo.com
W www.projecturvoice.com

**QUEEN MARGARET UNIVERSITY,
EDINBURGH**　　T 0131 474 0000
Queen Margaret University Drive, Musselburgh
East Lothian EH21 6UU
F 0131 474 0001
E admissions@qmu.ac.uk
W www.qmu.ac.uk

**QUESTORS THEATRE
EALING THE**　　T 020 8567 0011
12 Mattock Lane, London W5 5BQ
F 020 8567 2275
E jane@questors.org.uk
W www.questors.org.uk

**RAPIERSHARP
(STAGE & SCREEN COMBAT)**　　T 07710 763735
*Performance combat & fight directing services for stage,
film & television. Specialised weapons & unarmed
combat training leading to British Academy of Dramatic
Combat (BADC) qualifications. Training & workshops for
all levels. Consultancy & weapon hire*
E info@rapiersharp.com
W www.rapiersharp.com

RAVENSCOURT THEATRE SCHOOL
See CORONA THEATRE SCHOOL

**RAZZAMATAZ
THEATRE SCHOOLS**　　T 01228 550129
2nd Floor, Atlas Works, Nelson Street
Denton Holme, Carlisle CA2 5NB
E franchise@razzamataz.co.uk
W www.razzamataz.co.uk

RC-ANNIE LTD T 020 8123 5936
Stage & Screen Combat Training.
Theatrical Blood Supplies
34 Pullman Place, London SE9 6EG
E info@rc-annie.com
W www.rc-annie.com

REALLY YOUTHFUL
THEATRE COMPANY THE T/F 01926 494533
Audition Technique. LAMDA/Trinity Guildhall.
Private Acting Classes. Stage School for Children.
Summer School
17 West End Court, Crompton Street
Warwick, Warwickshire CV34 6NA
T 07970 627916
E info@rytc.co.uk
W www.rytc.co.uk

REBEL SCHOOL OF THEATRE ARTS &
CASTING AGENCY LTD T 07808 803637
Based in Leeds & Huddersfield
PO Box 169, Huddersfield HD8 1BE
E sue@rebelschool.co.uk
W www.rebelschool.co.uk

REDROOFS THEATRE SCHOOL T 01628 674092
26 Bath Road, Maidenhead
Berkshire SL6 4JT
T 07531 355835
E sam@redroofs.co.uk
W www.redroofs.co.uk

REP COLLEGE THE T 0118 942 1144
17 St Mary's Avenue, Purley on Thames
Berks RG8 8BJ
E tudor@repcollege.co.uk
W www.repcollege.co.uk

RICHMOND
DRAMA SCHOOL T 020 8891 5907 ext 4018
Contact: Dr Fern-Chantele Carter (Director of Courses).
Acting Workshops. Audition Technique. Drama School
(over 18 yrs). Drama School Preparation. Public
Speaking. Courses: Access to HE Drama, BTEC Ext
Cert L2 Performing Arts (Acting), RACC Certificate,
Richmond Drama School Advanced Certificate,
all 1 yr, part-time
Richmond Adult & Community College, Parkshot
Richmond, Surrey TW9 2RE
E fern-chantelecarter@racc.ac.uk

RIDGEWAY STUDIOS
PERFORMING ARTS COLLEGE T 01992 633775
Office: 106 Hawkshead Road
Potters Bar, Hertfordshire EN6 1NG
E info@ridgewaystudios.co.uk
W www.ridgewaystudios.co.uk

RISING STARS DRAMA SCHOOL T 0845 2570127
Contact: Jessica Andrews. Acting Workshops.
Audition Technique. Filming Techniques. Films Made.
Improvisation. LAMDA Examinations
10 Orchard Way, Measham, Derbyshire DE12 7JZ
E info@risingstarsdramaschool.co.uk
W www.risingstarsdramaschool.co.uk

ROSCH, Philip T 020 8731 6686
Contact: Philip Rosch. Audition Coaching for Top UK
Drama Schools. Audition Technique. Drama School
Preparation. Improvisation. Private Acting Classes
53 West Heath Court, London NW11 7RG
E philiproschactor@gmail.com
W www.actingauditionsuccess.co.uk

ROSE BRUFORD COLLEGE
See DRAMA SCHOOLS: DRAMA UK

ROSS, David ACTING
ACADEMY THE T 07957 862317
Contact: David Ross. Acting Workshops. Audition
Technique. Dialect/Accent Coaching. Drama School
Preparation. Improvisation. Stage School for Children.
Vocal Coaching
8 Farrier Close, Sale
Cheshire M33 2ZL
E info@davidrossacting.com
W www.davidrossacting.com

ROSSENDALE DANCE &
DRAMA CENTRE T 01706 211161
Contact: Chris Marlow. LAMDA LCM TCL Grade &
Diploma Courses & Exams. Acting Workshops. Audition
Technique. Dancing. Dialect/Accent Coaching. Drama
School (over 18 yrs). Elocution. Improvisation. Private
Acting Classes. Public Speaking. Stage School for
Children. Vocal Coaching
52 Bridleway, Waterfoot
Rossendale, Lancs BB4 9DS
E rddc@btinternet.com

ROYAL ACADEMY OF DRAMATIC ART
See DRAMA SCHOOLS: DRAMA UK

ROYAL ACADEMY OF MUSIC T 020 7873 7483
Musical Theatre Department
Marylebone Road, London NW1 5HT
E mth@ram.ac.uk
W www.ram.ac.uk/mth

ROYAL CONSERVATOIRE OF SCOTLAND
See DRAMA SCHOOLS: DRAMA UK

ROYAL WELSH COLLEGE OF MUSIC & DRAMA
See DRAMA SCHOOLS: DRAMA UK

RUMBELOW, Sam T 020 7622 9742
Acting & Method Acting Coach. Classes held at
Brick Lane E1
84 Union Road, London SW4 6JU
E samson@methodacting.co.uk
W www.methodacting.co.uk

SALES, Stephanie T 020 8995 9127
61 Brookfield Road, Chiswick
London W4 1DF
E steph@stephaniesales.co.uk
W www.stephaniesales.co.uk/dramacoaching

SAMPSON PILATES T 01328 712116
Pilates Teacher Training (NVQ3 - Cert).
Physical Coaching
7A Park Road, Holkham Village
Wells next the Sea, Norfolk NR23 1RG
E info@sampsonpilates.com
W www.sampsonpilates.com

SAMUELS, Marianne T 07974 203001
Accents. Text & Business Voice. Voice Coach
Based in Ealing, West London
E marianne@voice-ms.com

SATURDAY ACTING
ACADEMY THE T 07500 878300
Taught Entirely by Industry Professionals
10A Gloucester Drive, Finsbury Park
London N4 2LW
E info@thesaturdayacademy.co.uk
W www.thesaturdayacademy.co.uk

SCALA SCHOOL OF PERFORMING ARTS   T 0113 250 6823
Audition Technique. Dancing. Dialect/Accent Coaching. Improvisation. Singing. Stage School for Children. Vocal Training
Office: 42 Rufford Avenue
Yeadon, Leeds LS19 7QR
F 0113 250 8806
E office@scalakids.com
W www.scalakids.com

SCHER, Anna THEATRE   T 020 3093 5422
St Silas Church, Pentonville
Penton Street, London N1 9UL
E enquiries@nicknightmanagement.com
W www.nicknightmanagement.com

SEMARK, Rebecca LLAM   T 07956 850330
Elocution. Voice & Vocal Coaching. Audition Technique. Drama School Preparation. LAMDA Exams. Private Acting Classes & Public Speaking for Children & Adults. Stage School entry for Children including Singing
Based in Epping, Essex
E rebecca@semark.biz
W www.semark.biz

SHAPES IN MOTION   T 07802 709933
Contact: Sarah Perry. Movement & Acting Coaching. Laban. Yoga
Based in London
E sarah@shapesinmotion.com
W www.shapesinmotion.com

SHAW, Phil   T 020 8715 8943
Actors' Consultancy Service. Acting Workshops. Audition Technique. Drama School Preparation. Private Acting Classes. Vocal Coaching
Suite 476
2 Old Brompton Road
South Kensington, London SW7 3DQ
E shawcastlond@aol.com

SHENEL, Helena   T 020 7724 8793
Singing Teacher
80 Falkirk House,165 Maida Vale, London W9 1QX
T 020 7328 2921

SHINE TIME MUSICAL THEATRE & ACTING   T 07880 721689
Contact: Laura Green. Audition Technique. Dancing. Drama School Preparation. Improvisation. LAMDA Acting Solo Examinations. Musical Theatre & Acting Holiday Workshops. Private Acting Classes. Singing. Stage School for Children. Vocal Coaching
Flat 10, Valentine House, Church Road
Guildford, Surrey GU1 4NG
E shinetime@hotmail.co.uk
W www.shinetimeworkshops.com

SHOWSONG ACCOMPANIST   T 020 8993 2111
163 Gunnersbury Lane, London W3 8LJ

SIMMONS, Ros MA   T 020 8347 8089
Accents/Dialects. Voice. Auditions. Presentations
The Real Speaking Company, 120 Hillfield Avenue
Crouch End, London N8 7DN
T 07957 320572
E info@realspeaking.co.uk
W www.realspeaking.co.uk

SIMPKIN, Heather   T 01491 574349
Morriston, Fairmile
Henley-on-Thames, Oxon RG9 2JX
E heathersimpkin@btinternet.com

SINGER, Sandra ASSOCIATES   T 01702 331616
LAMDA & ISTD Exams. Acting Workshops. Audition Technique. Dancing. Dialect/Accent Coaching. Part time Drama School (over 18 yrs). Improvisation. Private Acting Classes. Singing. Stage School for Children. Vocal Coaching
21 Cotswold Road, Westcliff-on-Sea, Essex SS0 8AA
E sandrasingeruk@aol.com
W www.sandrasinger.com

SINGER STAGE SCHOOL　　T 01702 331616
Part-time Vocational Stage School & Summer School.
Adult Classes (16+ yrs) for Singing, Acting & Tap.
Acting Workshops. Audition Technique. Dancing.
Dialect/Accent Coaching. Drama School (over 18 yrs).
Improvisation. ISTD. Private Acting Classes. Singing.
Stage School for Children. Vocal Coaching
Office: 21 Cotswold Road
Westcliff-on-Sea, Essex SS0 8AA
E sandrasingeruk@aol.com
W www.sandrasinger.com

SLP COLLEGE　　T 0113 286 8136
5 Chapel Lane, Garforth
Leeds, West Yorkshire LS25 1AG
F 0113 287 4487
E info@slpcollege.co.uk
W www.slpcollege.co.uk

SOCIETY OF TEACHERS OF
SPEECH & DRAMA THE　　T 01623 627636
Registered Office:
73 Berry Hill Road, Mansfield
Notts NG18 4RU
E ann.k.jones@btinternet.com
W www.stsd.org.uk

SONNETS THEATRE
ARTS SCHOOL　　T 0845 0038910
Thorneycombe, Vernham Dean
Andover, Hampshire SP11 0JY
E sonnetsagency@hotmail.co.uk
W www.sonnets-tas.co.uk

SPEAK EASILY　　T 020 3174 1316
Voice, Speech & Accent Specialists
92-93 Great Russell Street
London WC1B 3PS
E info@speak-easily.com
W www.speak-easily.com

SPEAKE, Barbara
STAGE SCHOOL　　T 020 8743 1306
East Acton Lane, London W3 7EG
F 020 8743 2746
E speakekids3@aol.com
W www.barbaraspeake.com

SPEED, Anne-Marie
Hon ARAM MA (Voice Studies)
CSSD ADVS BA　　T 07957 272554
Vanguard Estill Practitioner. Accents. Auditions.
Coaching. Vocal Technique for Speaking & Singing
E info@thevoiceexplained.com
W www.thevoiceexplained.com

SPIRITUAL PSYCHOLOGY OF
ACTING THE　　T 020 8653 7735
51 Church Road, London SE19 2TE
E info@spiritualpsychologyofacting.com
W www.spiritualpsychologyofacting.com

SPLITZ THEATRE ARTZ　　T 01223 880389
5 Cow Lane, Fulbourn
Cambridge CB21 5HB
E clare@splitz-ta.net
W www.splitz-ta.net

SPONTANEITY SHOP THE　　T 020 7788 4080
85-87 Bayham Street
London NW1 0AG
E info@the-spontaneity-shop.com
W www.the-spontaneity-shop.com

STAGE2 YOUTH THEATRE　　T 07961 018841
Based at: Millennium Point, Curzon Street
Birmingham B4 7XG
E info@stage2.org
W www.stage2.org

STAGE2 YOUTH THEATRE　　T 07961 018841
Administration: 12 Valentine Road, Kings Heath
Birmingham, West Midlands B14 7AN
E info@stage2.org
W www.stage2.org

STAGE 84 YORKSHIRE SCHOOL
OF PERFORMING ARTS　　T 01274 569197
Evening & Weekend Classes & Summer Schools
Old Bell Chapel, Town Lane
Idle, West Yorks BD10 8PR
T 07785 244984
E valeriejackson@stage84.com

STAGECOACH THEATRE ARTS　　T 01932 254333
The Courthouse, Elm Grove
Walton-on-Thames, Surrey KT12 1LZ
F 01932 222894
E mail@stagecoach.co.uk
W www.stagecoach.co.uk

STAGEFIGHT　　T 07813 308672
138 Wilden Lane, Stourport-on-Severn
Worcestershire DY13 9LP
E raph@stagefight.co.uk
W www.stagefight.co.uk

STEP ON STAGE ACADEMY OF
PERFORMING ARTS　　T 020 8408 0633
Contact: Emma-Louise Tinniswood. Stage School
for Children. Acting Workshops & Audition Coaching.
Musical Theatre Courses & Workshops. Acting for Stage
& Screen. Dancing. Singing. Summer School. School
Workshops & Teacher INSET. Courses: GCSE Drama,
1 yr, part-time. LAMDA, 1 term-1 yr, part-time. Acting,
Musical Theatre, Audition Technique, Film Acting, Stage
Make-up, Stage Combat
5 Poulett Gardens, Twickenham
Middlesex TW1 4QS
T 07973 900196
E info@steponstageacademy.co.uk
W www.steponstageacademy.co.uk

STEPHENSON, Sarah
GMusRNCM PGDip RNCM　　T 020 8425 1225
Vocal Coach. Piano Accompanist. Audition Technique
8A Edgington Road, Streatham, London SW16 5BS
T 07581 716233
E s.stephenson@ntlworld.com

STEWART, Carola
LRAM NCSD LUD　　T 020 8444 5994
Audition Technique. CV Advice. Dialect/Accent
Coaching. Elocution. Interview Technique. LAMDA
Exams. Private Acting Classes. Public Speaking
13 Church Lane, East Finchley
London N2 8DX
E carolastewart@msn.com

STIRLING ACADEMY　　T 01204 848333
Contact: Glen Mortimer. Acting Workshops. Audition
Techniques. Audition Training for Camera. Drama
School. Improvisation. Private Acting Classes. Showreels
490 Halliwell Road, Bolton, Lancashire BL1 8AN
F 0844 4128689
E admin@stirlingacademy.co.uk
W www.stirlingacademy.co.uk

STOCKTON RIVERSIDE COLLEGE　　T 01642 865400
Further Education & Training
Harvard Avenue, Thornaby
Stockton TS17 6FB
W www.stockton.ac.uk

STOMP! THE SCHOOL OF PERFORMING ARTS　　T 020 8446 9898
Stage School for Children. Street Dance. Acting & Singing Classes (6-19 yrs). Evenings & Weekends.
Mill Hill Area
c/o Suite 6, Fiboard House
5 Oakleigh Gardens, London N20 9AB
E stompschoolnw7@aol.com
W www.stompschool.com

STREETON, Jane　　T 020 8556 9297
Singing Teacher, RADA
24 Richmond Road, Leytonstone
London E11 4BA
E janestreetonsop@aol.com

STUDIOS THE　　T 01628 777853
Office: 47 Furze Platt Road
Maidenhead SL6 7NF
E julie.fox@virgin.net

SUPERSTARS IN THE MAKING　　T 07531 814820
PO Box 187, Barry
Vale of Glamorgan CF63 9EL
E superstars@radio.fm
W www.superstarsinthemaking.com

SUPPORT ACT SERVICES　　T 07980 300927
Contact: Ian McCracken. Services for Actors including Stage Combat Instruction
197 Church Road
Northolt UB5 5BE
E info@supportact.co.uk
W www.supportact.co.uk

TALENT TIME THEATRE SCHOOL　　T 07904 771980
Show Company
Parkwood Health & Fitness Centre
Darkes Lane
Potters Bar, Herts EN6 1AA
T 07930 400647
E talenttimeyouth@aol.com
W www.talenttimetheatre.com

TALENTED KIDS PERFORMING ARTS SCHOOL & AGENCY　　T/F 00 353 45 485464
Contact: Maureen V. Ward. Acting Workshops. Audition Technique. Dance. Drama School (over 18 yrs). Elocution. Improvisation. Modelling. Musical Theatre. Singing. Stage School for Children. Vocal Coaching
23 Burrow Manor, Calverstown
Kilcullen, Co. Kildare, Ireland
T 00 353 87 2480348
E talentedkids@hotmail.com
W www.talentedkidsireland.com

THAT'S A WRAP PERFORMING ARTS SCHOOL　　T 01753 650951
Accompanist. Acting Workshops. Audition Technique. Dialect & Accent Coaching. Elocution. Improvisation. Private Acting Classes. Singing. Stage School for Children
The Actors Studio, Pinewood Studios
Pinewood Road, Iver Heath, Bucks SL0 0NH
E info@actorsstudio.co.uk
W www.actorsstudio.co.uk

THEATRETRAIN　　T 01327 300498
Annual West End Productions Involving All Pupils (6-18 yrs)
Orchard Studio, PO Box 42
Hitchin, Herts SG4 8FS
E admin@theatretrain.co.uk
W www.theatretrain.co.uk

THREE4ALL THEATRE COMPANY　　T 020 8402 7858
77 Victoria Road, Bromley BR2 9PL
E alison@three4all.org
W www.three4all.org/dramatraining.php

TIP TOE STAGE SCHOOL　　T 07940 521864
Dance, Drama, Singing & Performing Arts Part-time Training
For correspondence only:
65 North Road, South Ockendon, Essex RM15 6QH
E julie@tiptoestageschool.co.uk
W www.tiptoestageschool.co.uk

TO BE OR NOT TO BE　　T 07958 990227
Contact: Anthony Barnett. LAMDA Exams. Showreels. Theatre/Audition Pieces. Television/Film Acting Technique
40 Gayton Road, King's Lynn, Norfolk PE30 4EL
E anthony.barnett10@virginmedia.com
W www.showreels.org.uk

TODD, Paul　　　　**T** 020 7229 9776
Singing. Audition Technique. Acting. Percussion.
Improvisation. Vocal Coaching. Any age, any level
3 Rosehart Mews, London W11 3JN
T 07813 985092
E paultodd@talk21.com

TOMORROW'S TALENT　　　**T** 01245 200555
Theatre School & Agency for Young Performers. Acting.
Singing. Dance. Musical Theatre. Audition Preparation.
Drama School Coaching
Based in Chelmsford, Essex
E enquiries@tomorrowstalent.co.uk
W www.tomorrowstalent.co.uk

TOP HAT STAGE &
SCREEN SCHOOL　　　　**T/F** 01727 812666
Contact: Warren Bacci. Acting Workshops. Dancing.
Singing. Stage School for Children. Courses: School
Term Weekends, part-time. Easter & Summer Holidays,
part-time. Youth Theatre, Weeknights, part-time. Schools
in Potters Bar, Welwyn, Stevenage, St Albans & Hertford
PO Box 860, St Albans
Herts AL1 9BR
E admin@tophatstageschool.co.uk
W www.tophatstageschool.co.uk

TRING PARK SCHOOL FOR THE
PERFORMING ARTS　　　**T** 01442 824255
Dance, Drama & Musical Theatre Training School
(8-19 yrs)
Tring Park, Tring
Hertfordshire HP23 5LX
E info@tringpark.com
W www.tringpark.com

TROLLOPE, Ann　　　　**T** 07943 816276
Voice/Acting Coach
Harpsford, St. Peters Lane
Solihull B92 0DR
E ann-t@uwclub.net

TROTTER, William
BA MA PGDVS　　　　**T/F** 020 8459 7594
25 Thanet Lodge, Mapesbury Road
London NW2 4JA
T 07946 586719
E william.trotter@ukspeech.co.uk
W www.ukspeech.co.uk

TUCKER, John　　　　**T** 07903 269409
Speech & Voice Coaching. Singing Lessons. Accents.
Audition & Role Preparation
503 Mountjoy House, Barbican
London EC2Y 8BP
E mail@john-tucker.com
W www.john-tucker.com

TURNBULL, Mark　　　　**T** 07742 070122
Private Acting & Vocal Tuition. West End Musical Theatre
Specialist
E pootles@sky.com

TV ACTING CLASSES　　　**T** 07885 621061
Contact: Elisabeth Charbonneau
E ejcharbonneau@aol.com

TWICKENHAM THEATRE
WORKSHOP FOR CHILDREN　**T** 020 8898 5882
29 Campbell Road
Twickenham
Middlesex TW2 5BY
E frabbt@aol.com

URQUHART, Moray　　　**T** 020 7731 3604
Private Coaching for Auditions, Schools, Showbiz etc
61 Parkview Court
London SW6 3LL
E nmuphelps@yahoo.co.uk

VALLÉ ACADEMY OF
PERFORMING ARTS　　　**T** 01992 622862
The Vallé Academy Studios, Wilton House
Delamare Road, Cheshunt, Herts EN8 9SG
F 01992 622868
E enquiries@valleacademy.co.uk
W www.valleacademy.co.uk

VERRALL, Charles　　　**T** 020 7833 1971
19 Matilda Street, London N1 0LA
E info@charlesverrall.com
W www.learntoact.co.uk

VIVIAN, Michael　　　　**T** 020 8876 2073
Acting Workshops. Audition Technique. Improvisation.
Private Acting Classes. Public Speaking
15 Meredyth Road, Barnes
London SW13 0DS
T 07958 903911
E vivcalling@aol.com

VOCAL CONFIDENCE　　　**T** 07958 450382
Contact: Alix Longman. Accent & Dialect Coaching. Fast,
Effective Vocal & Acting Technique. Audition Preparation.
Presentation. Singing. Vocal Problems
E alix@vocalconfidence.com
W www.vocalconfidence.com

VOICE & DIALECT COACH　　**T** 07723 620728
Contact: Caroline Hetherington
7 Dodcott Barns, Burleydam
Whitchurch SY13 4BQ
E voice@carohetherington.co.uk
W www.carohetherington.co.uk

VOICE MASTER
INTERNATIONAL　　　　**T** 020 8455 1666
Creators of the Hudson Voice Technique: the only
Technique in the World for Voiceovers, Actors & Autocue
88 Erskine Hill, London NW11 6HR
T 07921 210400
E info@voicemaster-international.com
W www.voicemaster.co.uk

VOICES & PERFORMANCE　　**T** 07712 624083
Contact: Julia Gaunt ALCM TD-Musical Theatre. Audition
Technique. Corporate Training. Singing. Stage School
for Children. Summer School. Courses: Singing for
Beginners, part-time. Singing for Musical Theatre, 1-2
days. Voice Care, 1 day
1 Brandreth Drive, Giltbrook
Nottinghamshire
E joolsmusicbiz@aol.com
W www.joolsmusicbiz.com

VOICES LONDON　　　　**T** 07774 445637
Specialist Vocal Coaching
36 Wigmore Street, London W1U 2BP
T 07775 810572
E info@voicesvocal.co.uk
W www.voicesvocal.co.uk

VOXTRAINING LTD　　　**T** 020 7434 4404
Demo CDs. Voice Over Training
20 Old Compton Street, London W1D 4TW
E info@voxtraining.com
W www.voxtraining.com

WALLACE, Elaine BA T 07856 098334
Voice
249 Goldhurst Terrace, London NW6 3EP
E im@voicebiz.biz

WALSH, Anne T 07932 440043
Accents. Dialect. Speech
The Pronunciation Rooms, The Garden Studios
71-75 Shelton Street, London WC2H 9JQ
E anne@confidentlyspeaking.co.uk
W www.confidentlyspeaking.co.uk

WALSH, Genevieve T 020 7627 0024
Acting Tuition. Audition Coaching
37 Kelvedon House, Guildford Road
Stockwell, London SW8 2DN

WALTZER, Jack T 07855 114394 (London)
Professional Acting Workshops
5 Minetta Street Apt 2B, New York NY 10012, USA
T 001 212 840 1234
E jackwaltzer@hotmail.com
W www.jackwaltzer.com

WEAKLIAM, Brendan PGDipMusPerf
BMusPerf Dip ABRSM T 07724 558955
Singing Teacher. Voice Coach
23 Alders Close, Wanstead
London E11 3RZ
E brendanweakliam@gmail.com

WEBB, Bruce T 01508 518703
Audition Technique. Singing
Abbots Manor, Kirby Cane
Bungay, Suffolk NR35 2HP

WELBOURNE, Jacqueline T 07977 247287
Choreographer. Circus Trainer. Consultant
43 Kingsway Avenue, Kingswood, Bristol BS15 8AN
E jackie.welbourne@gmail.com

WESTMINSTER
KINGSWAY COLLEGE T 0870 0609800
Performing Arts
Regent's Park Centre, Longford Street
London NW1 3HB
F 020 7391 6400
E courseinfo@westking.ac.uk
W www.westking.ac.uk

WHITE, Chris T 07971 234829
Head of Acting Rose Bruford, BSA, Italia Conti
E chrisjohnwhite40@aol.com

WHITE, Susan BA TEFL LGSM
MA Voice Studies Distinction T 020 7244 0402
*Coach of Professional Spoken Voice & Personal
Presence via 1-2-1 Days for Individuals &
Summer 'Pause Presence' Master Class*
Based in Central London
E susan@per-sona.com
W www.per-sona.com

WILDCATS THEATRE SCHOOL &
POST-16 ACADEMY T 07725 915333
*Contact: Caz Dolby. Dancing. Public Speaking. Singing.
Stage School for Children. Summer School. Courses:
Acting, Musical Theatre, Public Speaking, Verse & Prose,
all LAMDA. Part-time & full-time Extended Diploma in
Performing Arts (no course fees)*
PO Box 1198, Stamford
Lincolnshire PE2 2JE
E admin@wildcats-uk.com
W www.wildcatstheatreschool.co.uk

John Colclough Advisory

Practical independent guidance for actors and actresses

t: 020 8873 1763   e: info@johncolclough.com   www.johncolclough.com

---

WILDER, Andrea T 07919 202401
23 Cambrian Drive
Colwyn Bay, Conwy LL28 4SL
F 07092 249314
E andreawilder@fastmail.fm
W www.awagency.co.uk

WILSON, Holly T 020 8878 0015
3 Worple Street, Mortlake
London SW14 8HE
E hbwilson@fastmail.co.uk

WIMBUSH, Martin Dip GSMD T 020 8877 0086
Audition Technique. Drama School Entry. Elocution.
Public Speaking. Vocal Coaching
Flat 4, 289 Trinity Road
Wandsworth Common
London SW18 3SN
T 07930 677623
E martinwimbush@btinternet.com
W www.martinwimbush.com

WINDLEY, Joe T 07867 780856
Accent, Speech, Voice, Text & Presentation Skills for
Film, Stage & Television
91 Lyric Road, Barnes
London SW13 9QA
E joe.windley@gmail.com

WINDSOR, Judith Ph. D T 01782 827222
American Accents/Dialects
Woodbine, Victoria Road
Deal, Kent CT14 7AS
F 01782 728004
E sarah.upson@voicecoach.tv

**WOOD, Tessa Teach Cert AGSM
CSSD PGDVS** T 020 8896 2659
Voice Coach
43 Woodhurst Road, London W3 6SS
E tessaroswood@aol.com

**WOODHOUSE, Alan
AGSM ADVS** T 07748 904227
Acting Coach. Acting Workshops. Audition Technique.
Drama School Preparation. Elocution. Private Acting
Classes. Public Speaking. Vocal Coaching
33 Burton Road, Kingston upon Thames
Surrey KT2 5TG
E alanwoodhouse50@hotmail.com
W www.woodhouse-voice.co.uk

WORTMAN, Neville T 020 8994 8886
Speech Coach. Voice Training
11 Mandeville Place
London W1U 3AJ
T 07976 805976
E neville@speakwell.co.uk
W www.speakwell.co.uk

WYNN, Madeleine T 01394 450265
Acting Workshops. Audition Technique. Directing &
Acting Coach. Drama School (over 18 yrs). LAMDA
Exams. Private Acting Classes. Public Speaking
40 Barrie House
Hawksley Court
Albion Road, London N16 0TX
E madeleinewynn@toucansurf.com
W www.plainspeaking.co.uk

**YOUNG, Sylvia
THEATRE SCHOOL** T 020 7258 2330
Full-time Academic/Vocational School. Part-time Acting
Workshops. Audition Technique. Dancing. Improvisation.
Singing. Vocal Coaching
1 Nutford Place
London W1H 5YZ
F 020 7724 8371
E syoung@syts.co.uk
W www.syts.co.uk

YOUNG ACTORS THEATRE T 020 7278 2101
70-72 Barnsbury Road
London N1 0ES
E info@yati.org.uk
W www.yati.org.uk

**YOUNGSTAR TELEVISION &
FILM ACTING SCHOOL** T 023 8047 7717
Part-time Schools across the UK (8-20 yrs)
Twitter: @ystvproductions
Head Office
20 Hilldene Way
Westend, Southampton SO30 3DW
F 023 8045 5816
E info@youngstar.tv
W www.youngstar.tv

**YOUNGSTARS THEATRE
SCHOOL & AGENCY** T 020 8950 5782
Contact: Coralyn Canfor-Dumas. Part-time Children's
Theatre School (4-18 yrs). Commercials. Dance. Drama.
Film. Singing. Stage. Television. Voice Overs
4 Haydon Dell, Bushey
Herts WD23 1DD
T 07966 176756
E youngstarsagency@gmail.com
W www.youngstarsagency.co.uk

ZANDER, Peter T 020 7437 4767
Acting for Stage, Opera, Screen & Radio. Audition
Preparation. Breathing. Improvisation. Mime. Movement.
Private Acting Classes. Relaxation. Speech/Voice
Coaching in English & German
22 Romilly Street
London W1D 5AG
T 07920 125509
E peterzan.berlin@virgin.net

F

Festivals

What do I need to know about the listed festivals?

The festivals listed in this section are all dedicated to creative and performing arts. Festivals are an opportunity for like-minded people to gather together to appreciate and learn from both well-established and new and up-and-coming acts and performers.

Why should I get involved?

Being a spectator at a festival is a chance to see others in action and to see a variety of shows that are not necessarily mainstream. This is an opportunity to see talent in its rawest form, which is exactly why casting directors often attend drama festivals: they may spot someone who is just what they are looking for, who would otherwise have gone unnoticed in a pile of CVs.

Taking part in festivals will be something else to add to your CV and will help develop your skills. This not only means performance skills but social skills as well: you will meet hundreds of new faces with the same passion for their work as you, so this is a great opportunity to make friends and useful contacts in the industry.

What do I need to bear in mind?

Before committing to performing at a festival, there are a number of issues to take into consideration. You will usually be unpaid and you will have to set aside enough money to fund the time spent rehearsing for and performing at the festival, not to mention travel, accommodation and food expenses. Not only that, you must also consider that you will be putting yourself out of the running for any paid work offered to you during this time. Make sure you let your agent know the dates you will be unavailable for work. You may find it helpful to refer to Equity's advice leaflet *Low Pay/No Pay* which is available to all Equity members from their website's members' area.

You may be required to not just perform but help out with any odd jobs involved with your show, such as setting up the stage and handing out flyers. If you are considering taking your own show to a festival, you will have to think well in advance about entrance fees, choosing and hiring a suitable venue, publicising your show, casting if necessary, finding technicians, buying or hiring props, costumes, sets, and so on. You must weigh up the financial outlays and potential headaches

with the learning and networking opportunities that come with being involved in festivals.

How can I get involved?

If you are a performer at a festival, casting professionals could be there looking for you! Let them know that you will be performing and where and when. Send them a covering letter giving details and enclose your CV and headshot if you have not already done so in previous correspondence. You could do the same with agents if you are currently searching for new representation.

Spotlight members performing at the Edinburgh Festival Fringe can access a number of free services including a Spotlight VIP area, a series of career advice seminars, one-to-one advice sessions with a Spotlight expert and free Wi-Fi. For full information or to book tickets for seminars please visit www.edfringe.com from June onwards and enter 'Spotlight' in the show/performer field.

Most festivals have websites which you can browse for further information on what to expect and how to get involved. Even if you simply go as a spectator to a festival, you will learn a lot and will have the opportunity to network. If you are performing in or organising a show, make sure you know exactly what you are letting yourself in for and make the most of your time there!

CASE STUDY

PERFORM 2013 is a live event designed to offer anyone interested in a future in the performing arts a chance to find out about training opportunities, get tips on building a career and meet organisations and individuals who can help. The event takes place from 8-10 March 2013 at London's Olympia, Kensington. Creative Director Georgina Harper discusses how performers can utilise live events to get an edge on the competition...

Every performer is looking for ways to enhance their CV and help make themselves stand out from the crowd, as well as make those vital connections that help you break into the industry. There are loads of ways to achieve this, from networking online to attending seminars at events, 'working' your personal contact book and scouring the web for cost-effective training opportunities.

PERFORM is a newly emerging event created by the producers of the hugely successful MOVE IT dance show which aims to gather a huge number of these opportunities under one roof, and shine a light on the multiple ways performers can get the edge on the competition, improve their craft and network with the companies, organisation and industry experts that count. It's for anyone looking for a future in the performing arts, either as a performer, a creative or in one of the many other roles from management to technical theatre.

As Creative Director of the event, I wanted to design a programme of activity which offered a variety of ways for performers to engage with the key issues, debates and developments in the industry. We work with leading companies and organisations including Spotlight, Equity and The Stage to identify the hottest topics and we have created a new feature stage which will host interviews and live demonstrations, bringing to life some of the most important aspects of a career in performance. There are also seminars where people can try out different techniques and hear talks on various subjects straight from those people making the industry tick. The value of bringing so many of the people working in the performing arts together in one space, face-to-face, cannot be underestimated. From the unexpected meetings and incidental conversations the most incredible ideas, projects and connections can spring.

I have seen time and again the difference between performers who thrive on networking and those who fear it. The beauty of a live event is that the environment is designed to facilitate conversations and new links can be made so much more easily. My advice to anyone attending events to help enhance their career prospects falls into three main categories:

Be ready to work the room

Research online which organisations are going to be there and what they offer, so you can speak directly to their staff and ask the right questions. By doing this, you might find out about a new scheme they are developing or an upcoming training programme that is not yet being advertised. Let people know what you are looking for – are you after advice on how to improve your

CV? Keen to find the best photographer to help you get some killer new headshots? Is it to find out which technical theatre courses have the best record for getting their students employment at top theatres? Come armed with your questions and with a list of the organisations you think can help.

Keep an open mind

PERFORM gathers loads of related companies and organisations under one roof and hosts hundreds of seminars, interviews and talks. Whilst setting off on a mission to meet the key organisations on your list, you also need to keep your eyes open for organisations you haven't heard of or anything unexpected that catches your interest. You might encounter a stage fighting workshop (perfect preparation for your audition next week), hear a top casting director discussing the ten most common mistakes actors make in auditions (perhaps a few you are guilty of?) or you might even bump into someone you used to go to school with who is now a producer... and casting their new show. You need to be there with an open mind to the possibilities.

Follow up your leads

At live events, everyone is there to make new connections, so the atmosphere is usually friendly and the people approachable. Make the most of this environment to take people's cards or leaflets and follow up the following week – no later! This gives them time to recover from the event but it is still fresh in their mind. People are usually more than happy to help, particularly if they have met you face-to-face the week before. You just need to send a simple email saying: "Great to meet you at the event last week. I was wondering if you could put me in touch with that agent you mentioned? I'd be really interested in chatting to them about my career development..." It might be the connection you've been looking for!

To find out more about PERFORM 2013 visit www.performshow.co.uk

Festivals

Photo: Laura Brown Fitzgibbons

CASE STUDY

The National Student Drama Festival (NSDF) is a week-long celebration of theatre and live performance, presenting outstanding productions from young theatre makers aged 16 to 25.

To celebrate the year of the London Olympics, NSDF teamed up with Sheffield Theatres, the University of Sheffield and Sheffield Hallam University to create a one-off International Student Drama Festival (ISDF) in June 2012, attended by student performers and industry professionals from all over the world.

A professional team of actors, directors and producers watched every production submitted for consideration and chose just 20 shows to perform at ISDF. Produced and performed by both UK and international college students, they represented a talented new generation of actors and actresses.

After nine unforgettable days of theatre, the ISDF judges presented a handful of young actors and actresses with the Judges' Awards for Acting in recognition of their outstanding performances. We asked a few of the winners to share their ISDF experiences in the build-up to and aftermath of the event: read on for their advice to other drama festival-goers.

The next NSDF will take place in Scarborough on 23-29 March 2013. Production submission is open to any student aged 16 to 25 up to a year after graduating.

If you're an aspiring actor, director, producer, stage manager, designer, technician, production manager or carpenter, NSDF can also offer professional workshops, masterclasses and a technical training programme to give you the experience and knowledge you need, as well as the opportunity to watch the shows.

To find out more, submit your production for consideration or buy tickets visit www.nsdf.org.uk

Mariel Pettee

Mariel is a member of the Harvard University class of 2014 pursuing a joint concentration in Physics and Math with a secondary in Astrophysics. At ISDF 2012 she won the Judges' Award for Acting for the part of Lucy in *CryHurtFood*.

An unspoken, rather dangerous agreement amongst all of us participants permeated the International Student Drama Festival: art is not a choice.

I say "dangerous" quite honestly because ISDF made realise I needed to discard a future that I had been clinging onto for years but would never really have made me happy: a life of pure scientific research in which art came as an afterthought in infrequent, mild, forgettable bursts.

ISDF showed me that pursuing art throughout my life was not the "risky" choice but perhaps the most important one. The professional artists whom I was lucky enough to engage with on a regular, honest, and friendly basis were living proof that inspiring others is an essential action that defines us as humans. At ISDF, the apparent disparity between my loves for science and art evolved from a tug-of-war in my mind to a revitalising challenge. How could I best craft all of my interests into a career of inspiration?

Leading up to the festival, I found myself pacing along a thin wire stretched between passion and addiction, envious of those who were able to confidently pursue the careers they felt they were destined to follow without looking back. Within the ISDF crowd, however, I began to understand how art was as necessary and easy as breath. The Crucible Bar blossomed with a dizzying energy after each night of conversation and newly forged friendships.

I witnessed innovation made manifest in performances like Curious Directive's *Your Last Breath*, which explored science and geometry through gorgeous choreography and projection, in workshops where I learned to uniquely blend text and physicality, and especially in my peers' breathtaking performances. ISDF empowered me with the skills and drive necessary to forge my own career path of blended interests. I can only hope that someday I might inspire others as I have been by the passionate artists I've met through ISDF and beyond.

Festivals

Phoebe Sparrow

Photo: Jennifer Eggleton

Phoebe studied English Literature and Theatre Studies at the University of Leeds, receiving a BA (Int). She spent one year studying abroad at Arizona State University's Theatre and Film School. At ISDF 2012 she won the Judges' Award for Acting for the part of Meg in *The Birthday Party.*

The most exciting aspect of this year's festival was undoubtedly the addition of international shows. From watching the passion and tenacity of the Japanese performers to dancing alongside the cast of the Zimbabwe production *Umfazi,* each of the nine days was at once fascinating and educational.

Being given the chance to meet with professionals working within the theatre industry who are so willing to share their knowledge and offer advice was absolutely invaluable. For me, leaving student drama behind to begin trying to carve a path as a professional actor is incredibly daunting, but ISDF makes this transition seem so much more tangible, with so many opportunities available to everyone attending.

Being given the chance to meet with professionals working within the industry was absolutely invaluable.

Alongside attending workshops and watching the other shows, we were re-staging our production of Pinter's *The Birthday Party.* After our original run seven months ago, I didn't expect to play the character of Meg again but getting the opportunity to re-engage with the text was a great challenge and I felt lucky to be able to perform in front of so many talented students at the festival.

Since ISDF I have accepted a place at Mountview Academy of Theatre Arts and begun rehearsals for the Edinburgh Festival Fringe where I will be performing with DugOut Theatre.

Tom Coxon

Photo: Megan Taylor

Tom is currently studying for a BA in his final year of Architecture: Spaces and Objects at Central Saint Martins College of Arts and Design. At ISDF 2012 he won the Judges' Award for Acting for the part of Ariel in *If Room Enough.*

I was previously involved in NSDF in 2009 with Wings Theatre Company's *Sad Since Tuesday,* a play which was devised in our final year of school. We had been cooking up a few ideas for quite a while and decided at the start of the following year to try to create a show for the Edinburgh Festival Fringe. However, we knew we would benefit from the expertise and input of the NSDF team and found ourselves entering ISDF instead. It was a good way to make us push hard for a finished product by the end of the first devising week, which we rehearsed in the Christmas holidays. This was the only time we could with the company of nine all having different term dates and being at opposite ends of the country.

My last acting experience was in 2009 when I was part of the NSDF ensemble *Touched* by Chris Thorpe, which was performed at North Wall and Latitude. I haven't really had the chance to get involved with anything at university, which was what motivated me to get the company back together for ISDF.

The festival was just such a shock; we never expected to have such a great reception and response. Taking a piece of adapted Shakespeare from a small theatre in Giggleswick to an international festival in the Crucible in Sheffield was quite a daunting prospect, but after our first performance we were just blown away.

I'm still very much undecided about what to do once I've graduated but I'm definitely giving acting and the theatre company more thought after having this experience. Along with the people I have met and the contacts I've made it is something I now feel more confident doing.

We are taking the show to the Edinburgh Festival Fringe for 2013 and we have already started working on our next devised project. My advice to other festival performers would be to throw yourself into every situation and always be the last at the bar and the first to the dance floor…

Festivals

Photo: Eitan Tal

Zlil-hen Saks

Zlil-hen is a graduate of the 2010 acting class in the Kibbutzim College School of the Arts. At ISDF 2012 she won the Judges' Award for Acting for her three roles in *Good.*

Imagine yourselves in an artistic bubble, if you will, far away from the place you usually call home. A bubble that the minute you're in it feels like you've been there all the time without even knowing. You know the roads by heart; every person is a friend. You can be whoever you want to be. Which, in a funny way, leads you towards being yourself, in the most honest way you have ever been.

I have no clever words for those who want to try and participate next year, except *do it.*

"You don't always get what you want", but you do choose what to give. And it's not a cliché: you get as much as you give. I know it's maybe a little bit weird or hard to understand. But I came to Sheffield for an experience, to meet new people, to see innovative theatre. And I went home with new friends, a new desire for learning, and a whole lot of love. I felt at home.

I have no clever words for those who want to try and participate next year, except *do it.* Come open minded, as actors and artists should. And believe me you'll benefit from it.

The next step for me will hopefully be a year of postgraduate studies in London. So cross your fingers for me, and hopefully, I promise, we'll meet again.

Photo: Peter J. Stone

Milly Falkner-Lee

Milly has just graduated from Newcastle University with a First Class BA Hons degree in Geography. At ISDF 2012 she won the Judges' Award for Acting for the part of Mrs Lovett in *Sweeney Todd.*

Performing at ISDF was a once-in-a-lifetime opportunity, and an experience I will never forget.

We, Newcastle University Theatre Society, were selected with our production of *Sweeney Todd* in November 2011. We decided to get involved with ISDF following our experience with a show last year. Unfortunately the production wasn't selected, however we learnt a lot from the feedback session and this inspired us to apply again.

After the initial excitement of realising our success, we soon discovered that organising a company of 40 was not going to be a walk in the park. However, book as much as possible as early as possible and life will become considerably easier!

In terms of performance preparation, we spent two solid weeks rehearsing 8-10 hours a day prior to the festival. This intense rehearsal period was the only option given every member of the cast had end-of-year exams, and most had finals right up until the day we started rehearsing. Factor in getting 26 heads, some of them new, around Sondheim's masterful score and you can imagine it wasn't a terribly relaxing couple of weeks. It was, however, a prime example of hard work paying off.

Performing at The Crucible was a towering highlight of my acting career to date. This wasn't just because of the incredible facilities and technicians available to help your production reach its full potential, but also because at ISDF you have the opportunity to meet people from all over the industry, learn staggering amounts from a huge range of workshops and be inspired to make that next step in your career.

Performing at ISDF has given me the confidence to step back and realise that acting is the career I want to pursue. I am hoping to apply to drama school to study postgraduate acting this year in order to follow my passion and develop my skills. The piece of advice I would like to offer future performers is that opportunities like ISDF don't come along every day, so make the most of every minute.

24:7 THEATRE FESTIVAL   T 0845 4084101
19-26 July 2013
PO Box 247, Manchester M60 2ZT
E info@247theatrefestival.co.uk
W www.247theatrefestival.co.uk

**ALDEBURGH FESTIVAL OF
MUSIC & THE ARTS**   T 01728 687100
7-23 June 2013
Aldeburgh Music, Snape Maltings Concert Hall
Snape, Suffolk IP17 1SP
BO 01728 687110
E enquiries@aldeburgh.co.uk   W www.aldeburgh.co.uk

**BATH INTERNATIONAL
MUSIC FESTIVAL**   T 01225 462231
22 May-2 June 2013
Bath Festivals, Abbey Chambers
Kingston Buildings, Bath BA1 1NT
BO 01225 463362
E info@bathfestivals.org.uk
W www.bathmusicfest.org.uk

BATH LITERATURE FESTIVAL   T 01225 462231
1-10 March 2013
Bath Festivals, Abbey Chambers
Kingston Buildings, Bath BA1 1NT
BO 01225 463362
E info@bathfestivals.org.uk   W www.bathlitfest.org.uk

**BRIGHTON DOME &
FESTIVAL LTD**   T 01273 700747
1-31 May 2013.
Contact: Andrew Comben (Chief Executive)
12A Pavilion Buildings, Castle Square, Brighton BN1 1EE
BO 01273 709709
E info@brightonfestival.org   W www.brightonfestival.org

BRIGHTON FRINGE   T 01273 764900
4 May-2 June 2013.
England's Largest Arts Festival
5 Palace Place, Brighton BN1 1EF
E info@brightonfringe.org   W www.brightonfringe.org

BUXTON FESTIVAL   T 01298 70395
5-23 July 2013 (Provisional)
3 The Square, Buxton, Derbyshire SK17 6AZ
BO 0845 1272190
E info@buxtonfestival.co.uk
W www.buxtonfestival.co.uk

**CHESTER SUMMER
MUSIC FESTIVAL**   T 01244 405631
8-14 July (Provisional).
Contact: Kate Sawallisch (Festival Manager)
Chester Festivals Ltd, Chester Railway Station
1st Floor, West Wing Offices
Station Road, Chester CH1 3NT
BO 0845 2417868
E k.sawallisch@chesterfestivals.co.uk
W www.chesterfestivals.co.uk/site/music

**CHICHESTER FESTIVITIES (Not Chichester
Festival Theatre)**   T 01243 785718
End June-Mid July 2013
Canon Gate House, South Street
Chichester, West Sussex PO19 1PU
F 01243 528356
E info@chifest.org.uk   W www.chifest.org.uk

DANCE UMBRELLA   T 020 7407 1200
*October 2013. Dance Umbrella brings brave new
dance to London as part of its leading international
dance festival*
1 Brewery Square, London SE1 2LF
F 020 7378 8405
E mail@danceumbrella.co.uk
W www.danceumbrella.co.uk

DUBLIN THEATRE
FESTIVAL   T 00 353 1 6778439
26 September-13 October 2013 (Provisional)
44 East Essex Street
Temple Bar, Dublin 2, Ireland
F 00 353 1 6797709
E marketing@dublintheatrefestival.com
W www.dublintheatrefestival.com

EDINBURGH FESTIVAL
FRINGE   T 0131 226 0026
2-26 August 2013
Festival Fringe Society Ltd, 180 High Street
Edinburgh EH1 1QS
BO 0131 226 0000
E admin@edfringe.com
W www.edfringe.com

EDINBURGH
INTERNATIONAL FESTIVAL   BO 0131 473 2000
9 August-1 September 2013
The Hub, Castlehill, Edinburgh EH1 2NE
E boxoffice@eif.co.uk
W www.eif.co.uk

HARROGATE
INTERNATIONAL FESTIVAL   T 01423 562303
July 2013
Raglan House, Raglan Street
Harrogate, North Yorkshire HG1 1LE
F 01423 521264
E info@harrogate-festival.org.uk
W www.harrogateinternationalfestival.com

HENLEY FRINGE
(TRUST) THE   T 07742 059762
15-20 July 2013
Aston Farm House, Remenham Lane
Henley on Thames, Oxon RG9 3DE
E info@henleyfringe.org
W www.henleyfringe.org

KING'S LYNN FESTIVAL   T 01553 767557
14-27 July 2013
5 Thoresby College, Queen Street
King's Lynn, Norfolk PE30 1HX
F 01553 767688
W www.kingslynnfestival.org.uk

LIFT   T 020 7968 6800
Biennial Festival. Next Festival 2014
3rd Floor, Institute of Contemporary Arts
12 Carlton House Terrace, London SW1Y 5AH
E kate@liftfestival.com
W www.liftfestival.com

LUDLOW FESTIVAL
SOCIETY LTD   T 01584 875070
22 June-7 July 2013
Festival Office, Castle Square
Ludlow, Shropshire SY8 1AY
BO 01584 872150
E admin@ludlowfestival.co.uk
W www.ludlowfestival.co.uk

MOVE IT 2013   T 020 7288 6734
8-10 March 2013
Olympia Exhibition Centre, Warwick Road
London SW5 9TA
E info@moveitdance.co.uk
W www.moveitdance.co.uk

PERFORM 2013   T 020 7288 6625
8-10 March 2013
Olympia Exhibition Centre
Warwick Road
London SW5 9TA
E info@performshow.co.uk
W www.performshow.co.uk

SUNDAY TIMES NATIONAL STUDENT DRAMA
FESTIVAL THE   T 020 7036 9027
23-29 March 2013. Scarborough. Contact:
Michael Brazier (Director), Chris Wootton (Administrator)
23-29 March 2013
Woolyard
54 Bermondsey Street
London SE1 3UD
E admin@nsdf.org.uk
W www.nsdf.org.uk

ULSTER BANK BELFAST FESTIVAL AT
QUEEN'S   T 028 9097 1034
19 October-4 November 2013
8 Fitzwilliam Street, Belfast BT9 6AW
BO 028 9097 1197
E festivalservice@qub.ac.uk
W www.belfastfestival.com

WEST END LIVE   T 020 7641 3297
22-23 June 2013 (Provisional)
E westendlive@westminster.gov.uk
W www.westendlive.co.uk

WINCHESTER HAT FAIR, FESTIVAL OF
STREET THEATRE   T 01962 849841
6-7 July 2013
5A Jewry Street, Winchester
Hampshire SO23 8RZ
E info@hatfair.co.uk
W www.hatfair.co.uk

**ACTOR'S ONE-STOP
SHOP THE**　　T 020 8888 7006
Showreels for Performing Artists
1st Floor, Above The Gate Pub
Station Road, London N22 7SS
E info@actorsonestopshop.com
W www.actorsonestopshop.com

ALBANY THE　　T 020 8692 4446
Douglas Way, London SE8 4AG
F 020 8469 2253
E hires@thealbany.org.uk
W www.thealbany.org.uk

ANVIL POST PRODUCTION　　T 020 8799 0555
Contact: Mike Anscombe (Studio Manager)
Perivale Park, Horsenden Lane South
Perivale UB6 7RL
E mike.anscombe@technicolor.com
W www.technicolor.com

ARRI MEDIA　　T 01895 457100
3 Highbridge, Oxford Road
Uxbridge, Middlesex UB8 1LX
F 01895 457101
E info@arrimedia.com
W www.arrimedia.com

**CAUTIOUS TRAIN
PRODUCTIONS**　　T 00 353 86 6627337
Promo Videos. Showreels
The Forge, Newcastle
Co. Wicklow, Ireland
E info@cautioustrain.com
W www.cautioustrain.com

CENTRAL FILM FACILITIES　　T 01694 771544
Film Unit Drivers & Location Finders
Myddle Cottage, Plaish
Church Stretton, Shropshire SY6 7HX
T 07966 421878
E mansell323@btinternet.com
W www.centralfilmfacilities.com

CENTRELINE VIDEO LTD　　T 0118 941 0033
138 Westwood Road, Tilehurst
Reading RG31 6LL
W www.centrelinevideo.co.uk

CHANNEL 2020 LTD　　T 0844 8402020
2020 House, 26-28 Talbot Lane
Leicester LE1 4LR
F 0116 222 1113
E info@channel2020.co.uk
W www.channel2020.co.uk

CHANNEL 2020 LTD　　T 0844 8402020
The Clerkenwell Workshops
27/31 Clerkenwell Close
London EC1R 0AT
E info@channel2020.co.uk
W www.channel2020.co.uk

CLICKS MEDIA STUDIOS　　T 01634 723838
Contact: Peter Snell
Amp House, Grove Road
Rochester, Kent ME2 4BX
E info@clicksmediastudios.com
W www.clicksmediastudios.com

CRYSTAL MEDIA　　T 0131 240 0988
28 Castle Street, Edinburgh EH2 3HT
F 0131 240 0989
E hello@crystal-media.co.uk
W www.crystal-media.co.uk

DE LANE LEA　　T 020 7432 3800
Film & TV Sound Dubbing & Editing Suite
75 Dean Street, London W1D 3PU
F 020 7494 3755
E solutions@delanelea.com
W www.delanelea.com

DELUXE 142　　T 020 7878 0000
Post-production Facilities
Film House, 142 Wardour Street
London W1F 8DD
F 020 7878 7800
W www.deluxe142.co.uk

DENMAN PRODUCTIONS　　T 020 8891 3461
3D Computer Animation. Video Production
60 Mallard Place, Strawberry Vale
Twickenham TW1 4SR
E info@denman.co.uk
W www.denman.co.uk

DIVERSE PRODUCTION LTD　　T 020 7603 4567
Pre & Post-production
Network House, 1 Ariel Way
London W12 7SL
F 020 3189 3200
E reception@diverse.tv
W www.diverse.tv

EXECUTIVE AUDIO VISUAL　　T 020 7723 4488
DVD Editing & Duplication Service. Photography Services
E chris.jarvis60@gmail.com

FROME SILK MILL STUDIOS　　T 01373 473246
Westbrook House, 33 Vicarage Street
Frome BA11 1PU
T 07811 440584
E silkmillstudios@macace.net

**GREENPARK
PRODUCTIONS LTD**　　T 01566 782107
Film & Video Archives
Illand, Launceston
Cornwall PL15 7LS
E info@greenparkimages.co.uk
W www.greenparkimages.co.uk

HARLEQUIN PRODUCTIONS　　T 020 8653 2333
15-17 Church Road, London SE19 2TF
E neill@harlequinproductions.co.uk
W www.harlequinproductions.co.uk

HARVEY HOUSE FILMS LTD　　T 07968 830536
*Animation. Full Pre/Post-production. Graphics.
Showreels*
71 Southfield Road, London W4 1BB
E chris@harveyhousefilms.co.uk
W www.harveyhousefilms.co.uk

HIREACAMERA.COM　　T 01435 873028
*Equipment Hire. Video & Photography. Accessories.
Lenses*
Unit 5, Wellbrook Farm
Berkeley Road, Mayfield, East Sussex TN20 6EH
F 01435 874841
E info@hireacamera.com
W www.hireacamera.com

**HUNKY DORY
PRODUCTIONS LTD**　　T 020 8440 0820
Crew. Facilities. Also Editing: Non-linear
57 Alan Drive, Barnet, Herts EN5 2PW
T 07973 655510
E adrian@hunkydory.tv
W www.hunkydory.tv

MPC (THE MOVING PICTURE COMPANY) T 020 7434 3100
Post-production
127 Wardour Street, London W1F 0NL
F 020 7287 5187
E mailbox@moving-picture.com
W www.moving-picture.com

OCEAN OPTICS T 01268 523786
Underwater Camera Sales & Operator Rental
Archer Fields, Burnt Mills Industrial Estate
Basildon, Essex SS13 1DL
E optics@oceanoptics.co.uk
W www.oceanoptics.co.uk

ONSIGHT LTD T 020 7637 0888
Film Equipment Rental
Shepperton Studios, Studios Road
Middlesex TW17 0QD
F 01932 592246
E hello@onsight.co.uk
W www.onsight.co.uk

PANAVISION UK T 020 8839 7333
The Metropolitan Centre, Bristol Road
Greenford, Middlesex UB6 8GD
F 020 8839 7300
W www.panavision.co.uk

PLACE THE T 020 7121 1000
17 Duke's Road
London WC1H 9BY
F 020 7121 1142
E info@theplace.org.uk
W www.theplace.org.uk

PRO-LINK RADIO SYSTEMS LTD T 01527 577788
Radio Microphones & Communications
8 Wynall Lane, Stourbridge, West Midlands DA9 9AQ
F 01527 577757
E admin@prolink-radio.com
W www.prolink-radio.com

RICH TV LTD T 0161 635 6207
Houldsworth Mill, Houldsworth Street
Reddish, Stockport, Cheshire SK5 6DA
E sales@richtv.co.uk
W www.richtv.co.uk

SALON LTD T 020 8963 0530
Editing Equipment Hire. Post-production
D12 Genesis Business Park
Whitby Avenue
London NW10 7SE
E hire@salonrentals.com
W www.salonrentals.com

SOUNDHOUSE THE T 0161 832 7299
2nd Floor, Astley House
Quay Street
Manchester M3 4AE
F 0161 832 7266
E mike@thesoundhouse.com
W www.thesoundhouse.tv

TEN80MEDIA T 07814 406251
Studio: 517 Foleshill Road
Coventry
West Midlands CV6 5AU
E info@ten80media.com
W www.ten80media.com

VIDEO INN PRODUCTION T 01604 864868
AV Equipment Hire. Conferences & Events
Glebe Farm
Wooton Road
Quinton, Northampton NN7 2EE
E enquiries@videoinn.co.uk
W www.videoinn.co.uk

VSI - VOICE & SCRIPT INTERNATIONAL T 020 7692 7700
Dubbing. DVD Encoding & Authoring Facilities. Editing. Subtitling. Voice Overs
132 Cleveland Street, London W1T 6AB
F 020 7692 7711
E info@vsi.tv
W www.vsi.tv

W6 STUDIO T 020 7385 2272
Editing Facilities. Music Videos. Photography. Showreels. Video Production
359 Lillie Road, Fulham
London SW6 7PA
T 07836 357629
E kazkam@w6studio.fsnet.co.uk
W www.w6studio.co.uk

1066 PRODUCTIONS T 020 7193 6156
8 Blackstone House, Off Bowen Drive
West Dulwich, London SE21 8NY
E admin@1066productions.com
W www.1066productions.com

30 BIRD PRODUCTIONS T 07970 960995
17 Emery Street, Cambridge CB1 2AX
E info@30birdproductions.org
W www.30birdproductions.org

303 PRODUCTIONS T 020 7494 0955
2nd Floor, 23 Heddon Street
London W1B 4BQ
F 020 7734 7597
E henry@303productions.co.uk

ACADEMY T 020 7395 4155
16 West Central Street, London WC1A 1JJ
F 020 7240 0355
E post@academyfilms.com
W www.academyfilms.com

AGILE FILMS T 020 7000 2882
Unit 1, 68-72 Redchurch Street
London E2 7DP
E info@agilefilms.com
W www.agilefilms.com

**AN ACQUIRED TASTE
TV CORP** T 020 8686 1188
51 Croham Road, South Croydon CR2 7HD
F 020 8686 5928
E cbennetttv@aol.com

ARIEL PRODUCTIONS LTD
Contact: By Post
46 Melcombe Regis Court
59 Weymouth Street
London W1G 8NT

ASF PRODUCTIONS LTD T 07770 277637
*Contact: Alan Spencer, Malcolm Bubb. Commercials.
Corporate Videos. Documentaries. Feature Films. Films*
38 Clunbury Court, Manor Street
Berkhamsted, Herts HP4 2FF
E info@asfproductions.co.uk

**ASHFORD ENTERTAINMENT
CORPORATION LTD THE** T 020 8660 9609
*Contact: Frazer Ashford. By e-mail. Documentaries.
Drama. Feature Films. Films. Television*
20 The Chase, Coulsdon
Surrey CR5 2EG
E info@ashford-entertainment.co.uk
W www.ashford-entertainment.co.uk

ASSOCIATED PRESS T 020 7482 7400
The Interchange, Oval Road
Camden Lock, London NW1 7DZ
F 020 7413 8312

AVALON TELEVISION LTD T 020 7598 8000
4A Exmoor Street, London W10 6BD
F 020 7598 7313

BAILEY, Catherine LTD T 020 7483 3330
110 Gloucester Avenue, Primrose Hill
London NW1 8JA
W www.cbltd.net

BANANA PARK LTD T 020 7228 7136
Animation
Banana Park, 6 Cranleigh Mews
London SW11 2QL
F 020 7738 1887
E studio@bananapark.co.uk
W www.bananapark.co.uk

BARFORD PRODUCTIONS T 020 7324 1466
Magdalen House, 148 Tooley Street
London SE1 2TU
E info@barford.co.uk
W www.barford.co.uk

BBC WORLDWIDE LTD T 020 8433 2000
Media Centre, Media Village
201 Wood Lane W12 7TQ
W www.bbcworldwide.com

BLACKBIRD PRODUCTIONS T 020 7924 6440
6 Molasses Row
Plantation Wharf
Battersea, London SW11 3UX
E enquiries@blackbirdproductions.co.uk

BRUNSWICK FILMS LTD T 020 8960 0066
Formula One Motor Racing Archive
26 Macroom Road, Maida Vale
London W9 3HY
F 020 8960 4997
E info@brunswickfilms.com
W www.brunswickfilms.com

BRYANT WHITTLE LTD T 020 8311 8752
49 Federation Road, Abbey Wood
London SE2 0JT
E amanda@bryantwhittle.com
W www.bryantwhittle.com

BURDER FILMS T 07950 287039
37 Braidley Road, Meyrick Park
Bournemouth BH2 6JY
E burderfilms@aol.com
W www.johnburder.co.uk

CARDINAL BROADCAST T 01753 639210
Room 114
N&P Building, Pinewood Studios
Iver Heath, Bucks SL0 0NH
W www.mentalhealthtv.co.uk

**CENTRE SCREEN
PRODUCTIONS** T 0161 832 7151
Eastgate, Castle Street
Castlefield, Manchester M3 4LZ
F 0161 832 8934
E info@centrescreen.co.uk
W www.centrescreen.co.uk

CHANNEL 2020 LTD T 0844 8402020
2020 House, 26-28 Talbot Lane
Leicester LE1 4LR
F 0116 222 1113
E info@channel2020.co.uk
W www.channel2020.co.uk

**CHANNEL TELEVISION
PRODUCTION** T 01534 816816
The Television Centre
La Pouquelaye
St Helier, Jersey JE1 3ZD
F 01534 816817
E production@channeltv.co.uk
W www.channelonline.tv

CHANNEL X LTD T 0845 9002940
4 Gandover Street, London W1W 7DJ
F 020 7580 8016
E gary.matsell@channelx.co.uk
W www.channelx.co.uk

CINEMANX LTD T 020 7637 2612
3rd Floor, 12 Great Portland Street
London W1W 8QN
F 020 7636 5481

CLASSIC MEDIA   **T** 01784 438700
The Studio, Drew Cottage
Vicarage Road, Egham
Surrey TW20 8NN
E robert.garofalo@classic-media-group.com

CLASSIC MEDIA   **T** 020 8762 6200
3rd Floor, Royalty House
72-74 Dean Street
London W1D 3SG
F 020 8762 6299
E enquiries@classicmedia.tv
W www.classicmedia.tv

CLAW FILMS LTD
71-75 Shelton Street, London WC2H 9JQ
E info@clawfilms.com
W www.clawfilms.com

CLEVER BOY MEDIA LTD   **T** 01753 650951
Pinewood Film Studios
Pinewood Road
Iver Heath, Bucks SL0 0NH
E tim@cleverboymedia.com
W www.cleverboymedia.com

**COLLINGWOOD O'HARE
PRODUCTIONS LTD**   **T** 020 8993 3666
10-14 Crown Street
Acton, London W3 8SB
F 020 8993 9595
E info@crownstreet.co.uk
W www.collingwoodohare.com

COMMERCIAL BREAKS   **T** 0844 8816789
Anglia House, Norwich NR1 3JG
F 0844 8816790
E commercialbreaks@itv.com
W www.commercialbreaks.co.uk

COMMUNICATOR LTD   **T** 020 7700 0777
Omnibus Business Centre
39-41 North Road, London N7 9DP
E info@communicator.ltd.uk

COMPLETE WORKS THE   **T** 020 7377 0280
The Old Truman Brewery
91 Brick Lane, London E1 6QL
F 020 7247 7405
E info@tcw.org.uk
W www.tcw.org.uk

COMTEC LTD   **T** 0844 8805238
Tandridge Court Farm
Tandridge Lane
Oxted, Surrey RH8 9NJ
F 0844 8805239
E info@comtecav.co.uk
W www.comtecav.co.uk

COURTYARD PRODUCTIONS   **T** 01732 700324
Television
Little Postlings Farmhouse
Four Elms, Kent TN8 6NA
E courtyard@mac.com

CPL PRODUCTIONS LTD   **T** 020 7240 8101
38 Long Acre, London WC2E 9JT
F 020 7836 9633
E info@cplproductions.co.uk
W www.cplproductions.co.uk

CREATIVE PARTNERSHIP THE   **T** 020 7439 7762
13 Bateman Street
London W1D 3AF
F 020 7437 1467
W www.creativepartnership.co.uk

CROFT TELEVISION   **T** 01628 668735
*Contact: Nick Devonshire. By e-mail. Commercials.
Corporate Videos. Live Events*
Croft House, Progress Business Centre, Whittle Parkway
Slough, Berkshire SL1 6DQ
F 01628 668791
E nick@croft-tv.com
W www.croft-tv.com

CROSSROADS FILMS   **T** 020 7395 4848
2nd Floor, 83 Long Acre
London WC2E 9NG
F 020 7395 4849
E info@crossroadsfilms.co.uk
W www.crossroadsfilms.co.uk

CUPSOGUE PICTURES   **T** 020 3411 2058
40 Hayway, Irthlingborough
Wellingborough NN9 5QP
E enquiries@cupsoguepictures.com
W www.cupsoguepictures.com

DALTON FILMS LTD   **T** 020 7328 6169
127 Hamilton Terrace, London NW8 9QR
E robindalton1@gmail.com

DANCETIME LTD   **T/F** 020 8742 0507
1 The Orchard, Chiswick
London W4 1JZ
E berry@tabletopproductions.com
W www.tabletopproductions.com

**DARLOW SMITHSON
PRODUCTIONS LTD**   **T** 020 7482 7027
1st Floor, Shepherds Building Central
Charecroft Way
Shepherd's Bush, London W14 0EE
F 020 7482 7039
E mail@darlowsmithson.com
W www.darlowsmithson.com

DELUXE 142   **T** 020 7878 0000
Film House, 142 Wardour Street
London W1F 8DD
F 020 7878 7800
W www.deluxe142.co.uk

**DIALOGICS
CONSULTANCY LTD**   **T** 020 8960 6069
Hub Kings Cross, 34B York Way
London N1 9AB
E dialogue@dialogics.com
W www.dialogics.com

DISNEY, Walt COMPANY THE   **T** 020 8222 1000
3 Queen Caroline Street, Hammersmith
London W6 9PE
F 020 8222 2795
W www.disney.co.uk

**DISTANT OBJECT
PRODUCTIONS LTD**   **T** 01635 281760
*Video Production. Corporate. Documentary. Internet
Broadcasting*
11 Lime Tree Mews, 2 Lime Walk
Headington, Oxford OX3 7DZ
E production@distantobject.com
W www.distantobject.com

DLT ENTERTAINMENT UK LTD   **T** 020 7631 1184
10 Bedford Square, London WC1B 3RA
F 020 7636 4571

DRAMATIS PERSONAE LTD   **T** 020 7834 9300
Contact: Nathan Silver, Nicolas Kent
19 Regency Street, London SW1P 4BY
E ns@nathansilver.com

DRB ENTERTAINMENT
TV & FILM PRODUCTIONS   T 01635 281673
9 Wright Way, Selsey
Chichester, West Sussex PO20 0UD
E mail@drbentertainment.co.uk
W www.drbentertainment.co.uk

DREAMING WILL
INITIATIVE THE   T/F 020 7793 9755
PO Box 38155, London SE17 3XP
E londonswo@hotmail.com
W www.lswproductions.co.uk

ECOSSE FILMS LTD   T 020 7371 0290
Brigade House, 8 Parsons Green
London SW6 4TN
F 020 7736 3436
E info@ecossefilms.com
W www.ecossefilms.com

EDGE PICTURE
COMPANY LTD THE   T 020 7836 6262
20-22 Shelton Street, London WC2H 9JJ
F 020 7836 6949
E ask.us@edgepicture.com
W www.edgepicture.com

EFFINGEE PRODUCTIONS LTD   T 07946 586939
Contact: Lesley Kiernan. By e-mail. Television
E info@effingee.com
W www.effingee.com

ENDEMOL UK PLC   T 0870 3331700
Including Endemol UK Productions, Initial, Brighter
Pictures, Victoria Real, Remarkable & Zeppotron
Shepherds Building Central, Charecroft Way
Shepherd's Bush, London W14 0EE
F 0870 3331800
E info@endemoluk.com
W www.endemoluk.com

ENGINE CREATIVE   T 01604 453177
The Church Rooms, Agnes Road
Northampton, Northants NN2 6EU
E wecancreate@enginecreative.co.uk
W www.enginecreative.co.uk

ENLIGHTENMENT
INTERACTIVE   T 01695 727555
East End House, 24 Ennerdale
Skelmersdale WN8 6AJ
W www.trainingmultimedia.co.uk

EON PRODUCTIONS LTD   T 020 7493 7953
Eon House, 138 Piccadilly, London W1J 7NR
F 020 7408 1236

EXTRA DIGIT LTD
10 Wyndham Place, London W1H 2PU
W www.extradigit.com

EYE FILM & TELEVISION   T 0845 6211133
Epic Studios, 112-114 Magdalen Street
Norwich NR3 1JD
E production@eyefilmandtv.co.uk
W www.eyefilmandtv.co.uk

FARNHAM FILM COMPANY THE   T 01252 710313
34 Burnt Hill Road, Lower Bourne, Farnham GU10 3LZ
F 01252 725855
E Info@farnfilm.com
W www.farnfilm.com

FEELGOOD FICTION LTD   T 020 8746 2535
49 Goldhawk Road, London W12 8QP
F 020 8740 6177
E feelgood@feelgoodfiction.co.uk
W www.feelgoodfiction.co.uk

FENIXX PRODUCTIONS   T 07837 338990
Music Video Specialists. Commercial Production
Company & Creative Team
32 Dale Court, York Road
Kingston KT2 6JQ
E us.fenixx@gmail.com
W www.fenixx.tv

FERRIS ENTERTAINMENT
FILMS   T 0845 4724725
London. Belfast. Cardiff. Los Angeles
Number 8, 132 Charing Cross Road
London WC2H 0LA
E info@ferrisentertainment.com
W www.ferrisentertainment.com

FESTIVAL FILM &
TELEVISION LTD   T 020 8297 9999
Festival House, Tranquil Passage, London SE3 0BJ
F 020 8297 1155
E info@festivalfilm.com
W www.festivalfilm.com

FILMS OF RECORD LTD   T 020 7428 3100
6 Anglers Lane, Kentish Town, London NW5 3DG
F 020 7284 0626
W www.filmsofrecord.com

FIREFLY PRODUCTIONS   T 01725 514462
Twin Oaks, Hale Purlieu
Fordingbridge, Hampshire SP6 2NN
T 07956 675276
E theonlyfirefly@aol.com
W www.fireflyproductions.info

FLYING DUCKS GROUP LTD   T 01902 842888
Duck HQ, The Old Mill
The Upper Hattons
Pendeford Hall Lane, Coven WV9 5BD
E enquiries@flyingducks.biz
W www.flyingducks.biz

FOCUS PRODUCTIONS
PUBLICATIONS   T 01789 298948
58 Shelley Road, Stratford-upon-Avon
Warwickshire CV37 7JS
F 01789 294845
E maddern@focuspublishers.co.uk
W www.focusproductions.co.uk

FORSTATER, Mark
PRODUCTIONS   T 07771 665382
11 Keslake Road, London NW6 6DJ
E mforstater@msn.com

FREMANTLEMEDIA
TALKBACKTHAMES   T 020 7691 6000
1 Stephen Street, London W1T 1AL
F 020 7691 6100
W www.freemantlemedia.com

FRICKER, Ian (FILMS) LTD   T 020 7836 3090
3rd Floor, 146 Strand
London WC2R 1JD
F 020 7836 3078
E mail@ianfricker.com

FUNNY FACE FILMS LTD
8A Warwick Road, Hampton Wick
Surrey KT1 4DW
E stevendrew40@hotmail.com

GALA PRODUCTIONS LTD   T 020 8741 4200
25 Stamford Brook Road, London W6 0XJ
F 020 8741 2323
E info@galaproductions.co.uk
W www.galaproductions.co.uk

GALLEON FILMS LTD	T 020 8310 7276
Head Office:
50 Openshaw Road, London SE2 0TE
E alice@galleontheatre.co.uk
W www.galleontheatre.co.uk

GAY, Noel TELEVISION LTD	T 01344 887507
Orchard Lea, Drift Road
Windsor SL4 4RU
E charles.armitage@virgin.net

GHA GROUP	T 020 7439 8705
33 Newman Street, London W1T 1PY
F 020 7636 4448
E info@ghagroup.co.uk
W www.ghagroup.co.uk

GLASS PAGE LTD THE	T 0116 249 2199
15 De Montfort Street, Leicester LE1 7GE
F 0116 249 2188
E info@glass-page.com
W www.glass-page.com

GOLDHAWK ESSENTIAL	T 020 7439 7113
Radio Productions
20 Great Chapel Street, London W1F 8FW
F 020 7287 3597
E lucinda@essentialmusic.co.uk

**GRANT NAYLOR
PRODUCTIONS LTD**	T 01932 592175
David Lean Building, Shepperton Studios
Studios Road, Shepperton, Middlesex TW17 0QD
F 01932 592484

GREAT GUNS LTD	T 020 7692 4444
43-45 Camden Road, London NW1 9LR
F 020 7692 4422
E reception@greatguns.com
W www.gglondon.tv

GUERILLA FILMS LTD	T 020 8758 1716
35 Thornbury Road, Isleworth
Middlesex TW7 4LQ
E david@guerilla-films.com
W www.guerilla-films.com

**HAMMERWOOD FILM
PRODUCERS**	T 01273 277333
110 Trafalgar Road, Portslade
Sussex BN41 1GS
E filmangels@freenetname.co.uk
W www.filmangel.co.uk

HANDS UP PRODUCTIONS LTD	T 07909 824630
7 Cavendish Vale, Sherwood
Nottingham NG5 4DS
E marcus@handsuppuppets.com
W www.handsuppuppets.com

HARTSWOOD FILMS	T 020 8607 8736
Twickenham Film Studios, The Barons, St Margaret's
Twickenham, Middlesex TW1 2AW
F 020 8607 8744
W www.hartswoodfilms.co.uk

HEAD, Sally PRODUCTIONS	T 020 8607 8730
Twickenham Film Studios, The Barons, St Margaret's
Twickenham, Middlesex TW1 2AW
F 020 8607 8964
E admin@shpl.demon.co.uk

HEAVY ENTERTAINMENT LTD	T 020 7494 1000
111 Wardour Street, London W1F 0UH
F 020 7494 1100
E info@heavy-entertainment.com
W www.heavy-entertainment.com

**HERMES ENTERTAINMENT
INC LTD (HE)**	T 07875 628299
*Production & Distribution. Television. Video. Based in
Paris & London*
72/6 Grove Lane, Camberwell Green
London SE5 8TW
F 020 7703 7927
E moneymodeste@yahoo.com

HIT ENTERTAINMENT LTD	T 020 7554 2500
5th Floor, Maple House
149 Tottenham Court Road, London W1T 7NF
F 020 7388 9321
E creative@hitentertainment.com
W www.hitentertainment.com

**HOLMES ASSOCIATES &
OPEN ROAD FILMS**	T 020 7813 4333
The Studio, 37 Redington Road
London NW3 7QY
E holmesassociates@blueyonder.co.uk

HOWARD, Danny	T 01625 875170
*Director. 30 years of Television, Video & Online Web
Production Experience*
AmbitActivate Ltd, 52 Shrigley Road
Poynton, Cheshire SK12 1TF
E danny@ambitactivate.co.uk
W www.ambitactivate.co.uk

HUNGRY MAN LTD	T 020 7239 4550
1-2 Herbal Hill, London EC1R 5EF
F 020 7239 4589
E ukreception@hungryman.com
W www.hungryman.com

**HUNKY DORY
PRODUCTIONS LTD**	T 020 8440 0820
57 Alan Drive, Barnet, Herts EN5 2PW
T 07973 655510
E adrian@hunkydory.tv
W www.hunkydory.tv

HURICA PRODUCTIONS
89 Birchanger Lane, Bishop Stortford CM23 5QF
E huricaproductions@gmail.com
W www.wix.com/hurica/huricaproductions

HURRICANE FILMS LTD	T 0151 707 9700
17 Hope Street, Liverpool L1 9BQ
E info@hurricanefilms.co.uk
W www.hurricanefilms.net

IAMBIC RIGHTS LTD	T 0117 923 7222
89 Whiteladies Road, Clifton, Bristol BS8 2NT
F 0117 923 8343
E admin@iambic.tv
W www.iambic.tv

ICE PRODUCTIONS LTD	T 01926 864800
Warwick Corner, 42 Warwick Road
Kenilworth, Warwickshire CV8 1HE
E admin@ice-productions.com
W www.ice-productions.com

ICON FILMS LTD	T 0117 910 2030
3rd Floor College House, 32-36 College Green
Bristol BS1 5SP
F 0117 910 2031
W www.iconfilms.co.uk

IMAGE PRODUCTIONS	T 07729 304795
Makes Films with Children for Children
PO Box 133, Bourne
Lincolnshire PE10 1DE
E info@imageproductions.co.uk
W www.imageproductions.co.uk

INFORMATION TRANSFER LLP   T 01223 312227
Training Video Packages
Burleigh House, 15 Newmarket Road
Cambridge CB5 8EG
F 01223 310200
W www.informationtransfer.com

**INGLENOOK
PRODUCTIONS LTD**   T 07814 077708
83 Wistaston Road, Willaston
Nantwich, Cheshire CW5 6QP
E hello@inglenookproductions.com
W www.inglenookproductions.com

JACKSON, Brian FILMS LTD   T 020 7402 7543
39-41 Hanover Steps
St George's Fields
Albion Street, London W2 2YG
F 020 7262 5736
W www.brianjacksonfilms.com

J. I. PRODUCTIONS   T 07732 476409
90 Hainault Avenue, Giffard Park
Milton Keynes, Bucks MK14 5PE
E jasonimpey@live.com
W www.jasonimpey.co.uk

JMP-MEDIA   T 07947 241821
Corporate Videos. Television
18 Westmead, Princes Risborough
Buckinghamshire HP27 9HR
E carolyn@jmp-media.tv
W www.jmp-media.tv

JMS GROUP LTD THE   T 01603 811855
Park Farm Studios, Hethersett
Norwich, Norfolk NR9 3DL
F 01603 812255
E info@jms-group.com
W www.jms-group.com

JUNCTION 15 PRODUCTIONS   T 01782 836600
EMMY Award Winners. Corporate. Television
The Burslem School of Art, Queen Street
Stoke-on-Trent, Staffordshire ST6 3EJ
E info@junction15.com
W www.junction15.com

KHANDO ENTERTAINMENT   T 020 3463 8492
Contact: By Post (for Script Submissions)
1 Marlborough Court
London W1F 7EE
E production@khandoentertainment.com

KNOWLES, Dave FILMS LTD   T 023 8084 2190
*Contact: Jenny Knowles. Corporate, Training & Project
Documentary Video Productions*
34 Ashleigh Close, Hythe SO45 3QP
E mail@dkfilms.co.uk
W www.dkfilms.co.uk

LANDSEER PRODUCTIONS LTD   T 020 7794 2523
27 Arkwright Road, London NW3 6BJ
E ken@landseerproductions.com
W www.landseerfilms.com

**LIGHT AGENCY &
PRODUCTIONS LTD**   T 020 7228 6558
*Contact: Lucy Misch. By Post/e-mail/Telephone.
Commercials. Corporate Videos. Documentaries.
Music Videos. Television. Showreel Editing.
Software Developement*
12 Molasses Row, Plantation Wharf
London SW11 3UX
E agency@lightproductions.tv
W www.lightproductions.tv

LIME PICTURES   T 0151 722 9122
Campus Manor, Childwall
Abbey Road, Liverpool L16 0JP
F 0151 722 6839

**MALLINSON TELEVISION
PRODUCTIONS**   T 0141 332 0589
Commercials
29 Lynedoch Street
Glasgow G3 6EF
F 0141 332 6190
E reception@mtp.co.uk

MANS, Johnny PRODUCTIONS   T 01992 470907
Incorporating Encore Magazine
PO Box 196, Hoddesdon
Herts EN10 7WG
T 07974 755997
E johnnymansagent@aol.com
W www.johnnymansproductions.co.uk

**MANSFIELD, Mike
PRODUCTIONS**   T 020 8947 6884
4 Ellerton Road, London SW20 0EP
E mikemantv@aol.com

**MARTIN, William
PRODUCTIONS**   T 01865 390258
The Studio
Tubney Warren Barns
Tubney, Oxfordshire OX13 5QJ
F 01865 390148
E info@wmproductions.co.uk
W www.wmproductions.co.uk

MAVERICK TELEVISION   T 0121 771 1812
Progress Works, Heath Mill Lane
Birmingham B9 4AL
F 0121 771 1550
E mail@mavericktv.co.uk
W www.mavericktv.co.uk

MBP TV   T 01403 741620
Saucelands Barn, Coolham
Horsham, West Sussex RH13 8QG
F 01403 741647
E info@mbptv.com
W www.mbptv.com

**McINTYRE, Phil
ENTERTAINMENTS LTD**   T 020 7291 9000
3rd Floor, 85 Newman Street
London W1T 3EU
F 020 7291 9001
E info@mcintyre-ents.com
W www.mcintyre-ents.com

MENTORN   T 020 7258 6800
77 Fulham Palace Road, London W6 8JA
F 020 7258 6888
E reception@mentorn.tv

MET FILM PRODUCTION   T 020 0200 9127
Ealing Studios, Ealing Green
London W5 5EP
F 020 8280 9111
E assistant@metfilm.co.uk
W www.metfilm.co.uk

MINAMONFILM   T 020 8674 3957
*Contact: Min Clifford. By e-mail/Telephone. Corporate
Videos. Documentaries. Drama. Films*
117 Downton Avenue
London SW2 3TX
E studio@minamonfilm.co.uk
W www.minamonfilm.co.uk

MINISTRY OF VIDEO   T 020 8369 5956
*Contact: Chris, Andy. By e-mail/Telephone. Casting
Videos. Children's Entertainment. Commercials.
Corporate Videos. Live Events. Live Stage Productions.
Music Videos. Showreels*
1533 High Road, Whetstone
London N20 9PP
E info@ministryofvideo.co.uk
W www.ministryofvideo.co.uk

MIRA MOTION PICTURES LTD   T 07790 917476
*Commercials. Documentaries. Educational/Training.
Film. Live Events. Music Videos. Promotional. Based in
London & South Wales*
20 Vineyard Vale, Valley Road
Saundersfoot SA69 9DA
E miramotionpictures@googlemail.com
W www.miramotionpictures.com

MISTRAL FILMS LTD   T 020 7284 2300
31 Oval Road, London NW1 7EA
F 020 7284 0547
E info@mistralfilm.co.uk

MONITON PICTURES   T 07753 865511
Mercantile Chambers, 2nd Floor
53 Bothwell Street, Glasgow G2 6TS
E andy@monitonpictures.com
W www.monitonpictures.com

**MOVE A MOUNTAIN
PRODUCTIONS**   T 020 8743 3017
5 Ashchurch Park Villas, London W12 9SP
E mail@moveamountain.com
W www.moveamountain.com

MUMMU LTD   T 020 7012 1673
*Independent Studio Creating Animated, Filmed &
Illustrated Content*
Unit 1.1, 128 Hoxton Street, London N1 6SH
E info@mummu.co.uk
W www.mummu.co.uk

MURPHY, Patricia FILMS LTD   T 020 7267 0007
Lock Keepers Cottage, Lyme Street, London NW1 0SF
F 020 7485 0555
E office@patriciamurphy.co.uk

MY SPIRIT PRODUCTIONS LTD   T 01634 323376
Paranormal & Psychic Radio & Television Production
Maidstone TV Studios, Vinters Park
Maidstone ME14 5NZ
E info@myspiritradio.com
W www.myspiritradio.com

NANAK FILM PVT LTD   T 00 91 22 23511363
*Producers & Distributors of Films, Tele-films, Television,
Serials, Documentaries & Music Videos*
132, 1st Floor
Arun Chambers, Next to Tardeo A.C. Market
Tardeo Road, Bombay 400 034, India
F 00 91 22 23510328
E info@devnani23.com
W www.devnani23.com

**NEAL STREET
PRODUCTIONS LTD**   T 020 7240 8890
1st Floor, 26-28 Neal Street, London WC2H 9QQ
F 020 7240 7099
E post@nealstreetproductions.com
W www.nealstreetproductions.com

NEW MOON TELEVISION   T 020 7479 7010
63 Poland Street, London W1F 7NY
F 020 7479 7011
E production@new-moon.co.uk
W www.new-moon.co.uk

NEW PLANET FILMS LTD   T 020 8426 1090
PO Box 640, Pinner HA5 9JB
E info@newplanetfilms.com
W www.newplanetfilms.com

NEXUS PRODUCTIONS LTD   T 020 7749 7500
*Animation, Mixed Media, Live Action & Interactive
Production for Commercials, Broadcast, Pop Promos &
Title Sequences*
113-114 Shoreditch High Street, London E1 6JN
F 020 7749 7501
E info@nexusproductions.com
W www.nexusproductions.com

NFD PRODUCTIONS LTD   T/F 01977 681949
*Contact: By Post/e-mail/Telephone. Children's
Entertainment. Commercials. Corporate Videos. Drama.
Films. Television. Short Films. Showreels
Twitter: @platform2c*
The Studio, 21 Low Street
South Milford, Leeds, Yorkshire LS25 5AR
T 07966 473455
E contact@nfdproductions.com
W www.nfdproductions.com

OMNI PRODUCTIONS LTD   T 0117 954 7170
14-16 Wilson Place, Bristol BS2 9HJ
E info@omniproductions.co.uk
W www.omniproductions.co.uk

ON COMMUNICATION   T 020 7558 8314
*Science & Technology. Work across all Media in
Business Communications*
5 East St Helen Street, Abingdon
Oxford OX14 5EG
F 01235 530581
E info@oncommunication.com
W www.oncommunication.com

**ON SCREEN
PRODUCTIONS LTD**   T 01291 636300
Ashbourne House, 33 Bridge Street
Chepstow, Monmouthshire NP16 5GA
F 01291 636301
E action@onscreenproductions.com
W www.onscreenproductions.com

**OPEN SHUTTER
PRODUCTIONS LTD**   T 01753 841309
*Contact: John Bruce. Documentaries. Drama. Films.
Television*
100 Kings Road, Windsor, Berkshire SL4 2AP
T 07753 618875
E openshutterproductions@googlemail.com

OVC MEDIA LTD   T 020 7402 9111
*Contact: Eliot M. Cohen. By e-mail. Animation.
Documentaries. Drama. Feature Films. Films. Television*
88 Berkeley Court, Baker Street, London NW1 5ND
F 020 7723 3064
E eliot@ovcmedia.com
W www.ovcmedia.com

P4FILMS   T 01242 542760
Film & Video for Television, Commercials & Corporate
Cheltenham Film Studios, Hatherley Lane
Cheltenham, Gloucestershire GL51 6PN
E info@p4films.com
W www.p4films.com

PAPER MOON PRODUCTIONS   T/F 01628 829819
Wychwood House
Burchetts Green Lane
Littlewick Green, Maidenhead
Berkshire SL6 3QW
E insight@paper-moon.co.uk

PARK VILLAGE LTD T 020 7387 8077
1 Park Village East, London NW1 7PX
F 020 7388 3051
E info@parkvillage.co.uk

PASSION PICTURES LTD T 020 7323 9933
Animation. Documentary. Television
2nd Floor, 33-34 Rathbone Place
London W1T 1JN
F 020 7323 9030
E info@passion-pictures.com

PATHE PICTURES LTD T 020 7323 5151
4th Floor, 6 Ramillies Place
London W1F 7TY
F 020 7631 3568
W www.pathe.co.uk

**PENSIVE PENGUIN
PRODUCTIONS** T 01204 848333
37 Oldstead Grove, Ferncrest
Bolton, Lancs BL3 4XW
E glenmortimer@btinternet.com
W www.shadowhawkinternational.com/seeingsmokephotos.htm

**PICTURE LOCK
PRODUCTIONS** T 07508 810449
3rd Floor, Unit 17
8 Lower Ormond Street
Manchester M20 2SB
E info@picturelock.co.uk
W www.picturelock.co.uk

PICTURE PALACE FILMS LTD T 020 7586 8763
13 Egbert Street, London NW1 8LJ
F 020 7586 9048
E info@picturepalace.com
W www.picturepalace.com

PIER PRODUCTIONS LTD T 01273 691401
8 St Georges Place, Brighton BN1 4GB
E info@pierproductionsltd.co.uk

PINBALL LONDON T 0845 2733893
20 Attneave Street
London WC1X 0DX
E info@pinballonline.co.uk
W www.pinballonline.co.uk

PODCAST COMPANY THE T 07956 468344
101 Wardour Street, London W1F 0UG
E info@thepodcastcompany.co.uk
W www.thepodcastcompany.co.uk

PODCAST COMPANY THE T 0844 5041226
3 The Avenue, London N3 2LB
E info@thepodcastcompany.co.uk
W www.thepodcastcompany.co.uk

POSITIVE IMAGE LTD T 01753 842248
25 Victoria Street, Windsor
Berkshire SL4 1HE
E theoffice@positiveimage.co.uk

**POTBOILER
PRODUCTIONS LTD** T 020 7734 7372
9 Greek Street, London W1D 4DQ
F 020 7287 5228
E info@potboiler.co.uk
W www.potboiler.co.uk

POZZITIVE TELEVISION LTD T 020 7255 1112
1st Floor, 25 Newman Street
London W1T 1PN
F 020 7255 1116
E pozzitive@pozzitive.co.uk
W www.pozzitive.co.uk

PRETTY CLEVER PICTURES T 01730 817899
Hurst Cottage, Old Buddington Lane
Hollist Lane, Eastbourne
Midhurst, West Sussex GU29 0QN
T 07836 616981
E pcpics@globalnet.co.uk

PRISM ENTERTAINMENT T 020 3463 8630
Television Production & Website Design Company
Euston Tower, 33rd Floor
286 Euston Road, London NW1 3DP
E info@prismdigitalsolutions.com
W www.prismdigitalsolutions.com

PRODUCERS THE T 020 7636 4226
11 Priory Road, London NW6 3NN
E info@theproducersfilms.co.uk
W www.theproducersfilms.co.uk

PSA FILMS T 0161 924 0011
52 The Downs, Altrincham WA14 2QJ
F 0161 924 0022
E andy@psafilms.co.uk

QUADRILLION T 01628 487522
17 Balvernie Grove, London SW18 5RR
E enqs@quadrillion.tv
W www.quadrillion.tv

RAW TALENT COMPANY THE T 0131 510 0133
*Contact: Helen Raw. Film & Stage. Actor Training
Workshops*
E info@therawtalentcompany.co.uk
W www.therawtalentcompany.co.uk

READ, Rodney T 020 8891 2875
45 Richmond Road, Twickenham
Middlesex TW1 3AW
T 07956 321550
E rodney_read@blueyonder.co.uk
W www.rodney-read.com

REAL MAX MEDIA THE T 01487 823608
Contact: Martin Franks. Drama. Comedy. Corporate
The Lilacs, West End
Woodhurst, Huntingdon, Cambridge PE28 3BH
E martin@therealmaxmedia.com
W www.therealmaxmedia.com

**RECORDED PICTURE
COMPANY LTD** T 020 7636 2251
24 Hanway Street, London W1T 1UH
F 020 7636 2261
E rpc@recordedpicture.com

RED KITE ANIMATION T 0131 554 0060
89 Giles Street, Edinburgh EH6 6BZ
F 0131 553 6007
E info@redkite-animation.com
W www.redkite-animation.com

RED ROSE CHAIN T 01473 603388
Gippeswyk Hall, Gippeswyk Avenue
Ipswich, Suffolk IP2 0AF
E info@redrosechain.co.uk
W www.redrosechain.co.uk

REDWEATHER PRODUCTIONS T 0117 941 5854
Easton Business Centre
Felix Road, Bristol BS5 0HE
F 0117 941 5851
E production@redweather.co.uk
W www.redweather.co.uk

REEL THING LTD THE T 020 8660 9609
20 The Chase, Coulsdon, Surrey CR5 2EG
E info@reelthing.tv
W www.reelthing.tv

RENIERMEDIA T 01462 892669
Television Production & Consulting
11 The Twitchell
Baldock SG7 6DN
E renierv@aol.com
W www.reniermedia.com

REPLAY LTD T 020 7637 0473
Contact: Danny Scollard. Animation. Corporate Videos.
Documentaries. Drama. E-Learning. Live Events. Script
Writing. Web Design
Museum House, 25 Museum Street
London WC1A 1JT
E sales@replayfilms.co.uk
W www.replayfilms.co.uk

REUTERS LTD T 020 7250 1122
The Thompson Reuters Building, South Collonade
Canary Wharf, London E14 5EP

RIVERSIDE TV STUDIOS T 020 8237 1123
Riverside Studios, Crisp Road
London W6 9RL
F 020 8237 1121
E info@riversidetv.co.uk
W www.riversidetv.co.uk

ROEBUCK PRODUCTIONS T 01937 835900
Commer House, Station Road
Tadcaster, North Yorkshire LS24 9JF
F 01937 835901
E john@roebuckproductions.com
W www.roebuckproductions.com

ROOKE, Laurence
PRODUCTIONS T 020 8674 3128
14 Aspinall House, 155 New Park Road
London SW2 4EY
T 07765 652058

RSA FILMS T 020 7437 7426
42-44 Beak Street, London W1F 9RH
F 020 7734 4978
W www.rsafilms.com

SANDS FILMS T 020 7231 2209
82 St Marychurch Street, London SE16 4HZ
F 020 7231 2119
E info@sandsfilms.co.uk
W www.sandsfilms.co.uk

SCALA PRODUCTIONS LTD T 020 7916 4771
249 Gray's Inn Road, London WC1X 8QZ
E scalaprods@aol.com

SCIMITAR FILMS LTD T 020 7734 8385
219 Kensington High Street, London W8 6BD
F 020 7602 9217
E winner@ftech.co.uk

SCREEN FIRST LTD T 01248 716973
Cil-y-Coed, Llansadwrn
Menai Bridge, Anglesey LL59 5SE
E paul.madden@virgin.net

SEPTEMBER FILMS LTD T 020 8563 9393
Glen House, 22 Glenthorne Road
Hammersmith, London W6 0NG
F 020 8741 7214
E september@septemberfilms.com

SEVENTH ART PRODUCTIONS T 01273 777678
63 Ship Street, Brighton BN1 1AE
F 01273 323777
E info@seventh-art.com
W www.seventh-art.com

SHED PRODUCTIONS T 020 7239 1010
85 Gray's Inn Road, London WC1X 8TX
F 020 7239 1011
E mail@walltowall.co.uk
W www.shedproductions.com

SHELL FILM & VIDEO UNIT T 020 7934 3318
Shell Centre, York Road, London SE1 7NA
E jane.poynor@shell.com

SIGHTLINE T 01483 813311
Videos for the Web. DVDs. E-Learning.
Interactive CD-ROM. Promotion. Touch Screens.
Training. Websites.
Based in Guildford
F 01483 813317
E keith@sightline.co.uk
W www.sightline.co.uk

SILK SOUND T 020 7434 3461
Commercials. Corporate Videos. Documentaries
13 Berwick Street, London W1F 0PW
F 020 7494 1748
E bookings@silk.co.uk
W www.silk.co.uk

SINDIBAD FILMS LTD T 020 7259 2707
Tower House, 226 Cromwell Road, London SW5 0SW
E info@sindibad.co.uk
W www.sindibad.co.uk

SITCOM SOLDIERS LTD T 07712 669097
Windy Yetts, Windy Harbour Lane
Bromley Cross, Bolton BL7 9AP
E info@sitcomsoldiers.com
W www.sitcomsoldiers.com

SNEEZING TREE FILMS T 020 7436 8036
1st Floor, 37 Great Portland Street, London W1W 8QH
E firstname@sneezingtree.com
W www.sneezingtree.com

SOLOMON THEATRE
COMPANY LTD T/F 01725 518760
Penny Black, High Street, Damerham
Nr Fordingbridge, Hampshire SP6 3EU
E office@solomon-theatre.co.uk
W www.solomon-theatre.co.uk

SONY PICTURES T 020 7533 1000
25 Golden Square, London W1F 9LU
F 020 7533 1015

SPACE CITY PRODUCTIONS T 020 7371 4000
77-79 Blythe Road, London W14 0HP
F 020 7371 4001
E info@spacecity.co.uk
W www.spacecity.co.uk

SPEAKEASY PRODUCTIONS LTD T 01738 828524
Wildwood House, Stanley, Perth PH1 4NH
F 01738 828419
E info@speak.co.uk
W www.speak.co.uk

SPECIFIC FILMS LTD T 020 7580 7476
33 Percy Street, London W1T 2DF
F 020 7636 6886
E info@specificfilms.com

SPIRAL PRODUCTIONS LTD T 020 7428 9948
Unit 17-18, The Dove Centre
109 Bartholomew Road, London NW5 2BJ
F 020 7485 1845
E info@spiral.co.uk
W www.spiral.co.uk

STAFFORD, Jonathan PRODUCTIONS　T 01932 562611
Shepperton Studios, Studios Road
Shepperton, Middlesex TW17 0QD
E jon@staffordproductions.com

STAMP PRODUCTIONS　T 020 8743 5555
Ugli Campus, 56 Wood Lane
London W12 7SB
E info@stamp-productions.com
W www.stamp-productions.com

STANDFAST FILMS　T 020 8466 5580
The Studio, 14 College Road
Bromley, Kent BR1 3NS

STANTON MEDIA　T 01296 489539
6 Kendal Close, Aylesbury
Bucks HP21 7HR
E info@stantonmedia.com
W www.stantonmedia.com

STONE PRODUCTIONS CREATIVE LTD　T 01255 822172
Lakeside Studio, 62 Mill Street
St Osyth, Essex CO16 8EW
F 01255 822160
E kevin@stone-productions.co.uk
W www.stone-productions.co.uk

STUDIO AKA　T 020 7434 3581
Animation
30 Berwick Street, London W1F 8RH
F 020 7437 2309
E nikki@studioaka.co.uk
W www.studioaka.co.uk

TABARD PRODUCTIONS LTD　T 020 7497 0830
Contact: John Herbert. By e-mail. Corporate Videos.
Documentaries
Adam House, 7-10 Adam Street
London WC2N 6AA
F 020 7497 0850
E johnherbert@tabard.co.uk
W www.tabardproductions.com

TABLE TOP PRODUCTIONS　T 020 8994 1269
Contact: Ben Berry. By e-mail. Drama. Feature Films
1 The Orchard, Bedford Park
Chiswick, London W4 1JZ
T/F 020 8742 0507
E berry@tabletopproductions.com

TAKE 3 PRODUCTIONS LTD　T 020 7288 1818
Business Design Centre, 52 Upper Street
London N1 0QH
E mail@take3.co.uk
W www.take3.co.uk

TAKE FIVE PRODUCTIONS　T 020 7287 2120
37 Beak Street, London W1F 9RZ
F 020 7287 3035
E info@takefivestudio.com
W www.takefivestudio.com

TALKBACKTHAMES　T 020 7861 8000
20-21 Newman Street, London W1T 1PG
F 020 7861 8001
W www.talkbackthames.tv

TALKING PICTURES　T 01753 650000
Pinewood Studios
Pinewood Road
Iver Heath, Bucks SL0 0NH
F 01865 890504
E info@talkingpictures.co.uk
W www.talkingpictures.co.uk

TANDEM CREATIVE　T 01442 261576
Contact: By e-mail. Corporate Videos. Documentaries
Charleston House, 13 High Street
Hemel Hempstead, Herts HP1 3AA
E info@tandem.tv
W www.tandem.tv

THEATRE WORKSHOP　T 0131 555 3854
Film. Theatre
Out of the Blue Drill Hall, 36 Dalmeny Street
Edinburgh EH6 8RG
W www.theatre-workshop.com

THEOTHER COMPANY LTD　T 020 8858 6999
Contact: Sarah Boote. By e-mail. Showreels. Corporate
Videos. Documentaries. Drama. Music Videos
30 Glenluce Road, Blackheath
London SE3 7SB
E contact@theothercompany.co.uk
W www.theothercompany.co.uk

THIN MAN FILMS　T 020 7734 7372
9 Greek Street, London W1D 4DQ
F 020 7287 5228
E info@thinman.co.uk

TIGER ASPECT PRODUCTIONS　T 020 7434 6700
Shepherds Buidling Central, Charecroft Way
London W14 0EE
F 020 8222 4700
E general@tigeraspect.co.uk
W www.tigeraspect.co.uk

TOP BANANA　T 01562 700404
The Studio, Stourbridge
West Midlands DY9 0HA
F 01562 700930
E enquiries@top-b.com
W www.top-b.com

TOPICAL TELEVISION LTD　T 023 8071 2233
61 Devonshire Road, Southampton SO15 2GR
F 023 8033 9835
E post@topical.co.uk

TRAFALGAR 1 LTD　T 020 7722 7789
Contact: Hasan Shah. By Post/e-mail. Documentaries.
Feature Films. Films. Music Videos. Television
153 Burnham Towers, Fellows Road
London NW3 3JN
F 020 7483 0662
E t1ltd@blueyonder.co.uk

TV PRODUCTION PARTNERSHIP LTD　T 01264 861440
4 Fullerton Manor, Fullerton
Hants SP11 7LA
E dbj@tvpp.tv
W www.tvpp.tv

TVF　T 020 7837 3000
375 City Road, London EC1V 1NB
F 020 7833 2185

TWOFOUR　T 01752 727400
Corporate Videos. Documentaries. Live Events.
Television
Twofour Studios, Estover
Plymouth PL6 7RG
F 01752 727450
E enquiries@twofour.co.uk
W www.twofour.co.uk

TYBURN ENTERTAINMENT LTD　T 01753 516767
Cippenham Court, Cippenham Lane
Cippenham, Nr Slough, Berkshire SL1 5AU
F 01753 691785

Film, Radio, Television & Video Production Companies

VECTOR PRODUCTIONS   T 0845 0535400
Corporate Videos. Television
Moulton Park Industrial Estate
Northampton NN3 6AQ
E production@vectortv.co.uk
W www.vectortv.co.uk

VERA PRODUCTIONS LTD   T 020 7292 1480
165 Wardour Street, London W1F 8WW
F 020 7292 1481
E info@vera.co.uk

VIDEO ARTS   T 020 7400 4800
Elsinore House, 4th Floor
77 Fulham Palace Road, London W6 8JA
F 020 7400 4900
E info@videoarts.co.uk

VIDEO ENTERPRISES   T 01494 534144
Contact: Maurice Fleisher. Corporate Videos.
Documentaries. Live Events. Television
12 Barbers Wood Road
High Wycombe, Bucks HP12 4EP
T 07831 875216
E videoenterprises@ntlworld.com
W www.videoenterprises.co.uk

VIDEOTEL PRODUCTIONS   T 020 7299 1800
Corporate Videos
84 Newman Street, London W1T 3EU
F 020 7299 1818

VILLAGE PRODUCTIONS   T 020 8984 0322
4 Midas Business Centre, Wantz Road
Dagenham, Essex RM10 8PS
F 020 8593 0198
E village000@btclick.com

**VSI - VOICE & SCRIPT
INTERNATIONAL**   T 020 7692 7700
132 Cleveland Street, London W1T 6AB
E info@vsi.tv
W www.vsi.tv

W3KTS LTD   T 01904 647822
10 Portland Street, York YO31 7EH
T 0845 8727949
E info@w3kts.com

W6 STUDIO   T 020 7385 2272
Editing Facilities. Music Video. Photography. Video
Production
359 Lillie Road, Fulham, London SW6 7PA
E kazkam@w6studio.fsnet.co.uk
W www.w6studio.co.uk

WALKING FORWARD   T 01438 310157
Unit 5E, Business & Technology Centre
Bessemer Drive, Stevenage SG1 2DX
E info@walkingforward.co.uk
W www.walkingforward.co.uk

WALKOVERS VIDEO LTD   T 01249 750428
Facilities. Production
Kington Langley, Chippenham
North Wiltshire SN15 5NU
T 07831 828022
E walkoversvideo@btinternet.com

WALSH BROS LTD   T/F 020 8858 6870
Contact: By e-mail. Animation. Documentaries. Drama.
Feature Films. Films. Television
29 Trafalgar Grove, Greenwich, London SE10 9TB
E info@walshbros.co.uk
W www.walshbros.co.uk

**WARNER BROS
PRODUCTIONS LTD**   T 01923 882500
Warner Suite
Warner Bros Studios Leavesden
Aerodrome Way
Leavesden, Herts WD25 7LS

**WARNER SISTERS
PRODUCTIONS LTD**   T 020 8567 6655
Ealing Studios, Ealing Green
London W5 5EP
E ws@warnercini.com

WEST DIGITAL   T 020 8743 5100
Broadcast Post-production
65 Goldhawk Road
London W12 8EG
F 020 8743 2345
E luci@westdigital.co.uk

WHITEHALL FILMS   T 020 8785 3737
6 Embankment, Putney
London SW15 1LB
F 020 8788 2340
E whitehallfilms@gmail.com

WINNER, Michael LTD   T 020 7734 8385
219 Kensington High Street
London W8 6BD
F 020 7602 9217
E winner@ftech.co.uk

WORKING TITLE FILMS LTD   T 020 7307 3000
26 Aybrook Street, London W1U 4AN
F 020 7307 3001
W www.workingtitlefilms.com

**WORLD PRODUCTIONS &
WORLD FILM SERVICES LTD**   T 020 3002 3113
101 Finsbury Pavement, London EC2A 1RS
T 020 3002 3120
W www.world-productions.com

WORLD WIDE PICTURES   T 020 7613 6580
103 The Timber Yard
Drysdale Street
London N1 6ND
F 020 7613 6581
E info@worldwidepictures.tv
W www.worldwidepictures.tv

WORLD'S END TELEVISION   T 020 7386 4900
16-18 Empress Place
London SW6 1TT
F 020 7386 4901
E info@worldsendproductions.com
W www.worldsendproductions.com

WORTHWHILE MOVIE LTD   T 00 1 416 4690459
Providing the services of Bruce Pittman as Film Director
191 Logan Avenue
Toronto, Ontario
Canada M4M 2NT
E bruce.pittman@sympatico.ca

XINGU FILMS   T 020 7451 0600
12 Cleveland Row
London SW1A 1DH
F 020 7451 0601
W www.xingufilms.com

ZEPHYR FILMS LTD   T 020 7255 3555
33 Percy Street, London W1T 2DF
F 020 7255 3777
E info@zephyrfilms.co.uk

BRIGHTON FILM SCHOOL   T 01273 602070
Head of School: Gary Barber. Short Courses
in Filmmaking & Screenwriting. Pre-Masters in
Cinematography & Directing. HNC Filmmaking
The Brighton Forum, 95 Ditchling Road
Brighton BN1 4ST
E info@brightonfilmschool.co.uk
W www.brightonfilmschool.co.uk

LEEDS METROPOLITAN
UNIVERSITY   T 0113 812 8000
MA Filmmaking. BA (Hons) Film & Moving Image
Production. Cert HE/FdA Film & Television Production.
BA (Hons) Animation
Northern Film School, Leeds Metropolitan University
Electric Press, 1 Millennium Square, Leeds LS2 3AD
F 0113 812 8080
E filmenquiries@leedsmet.ac.uk
W www.leedsmet.ac.uk

LONDON COLLEGE OF
COMMUNICATION   T 020 7514 6569
Film & Video Course
Elephant & Castle, London SE1 6SB
F 020 7514 6843
E info@lcc.arts.ac.uk
W www.lcc.arts.ac.uk

LONDON FILM ACADEMY   T 020 7386 7711
The Old Church, 52A Walham Grove
London SW6 1QR
F 020 7381 6116
E info@londonfilmacademy.com
W www.londonfilmacademy.com

LONDON FILM SCHOOL THE   T 020 7836 9642
2 yr MA Course Filmmaking. 1 yr MA Screenwriting.
1 yr MA Film Curating. Specialised Professional Short
Courses & Workshops
24 Shelton Street, London WC2H 9UB
F 020 7497 3718
E info@lfs.org.uk
W www.lfs.org.uk

LONDON SCHOOL OF FILM,
MEDIA & PERFORMANCE   T 020 7487 7505
Regent's College, Inner Circle
Regent's Park, London NW1 4NS
F 020 7487 7425
E lsfmp@regents.ac.uk
W www.regents.ac.uk/lsfmp

MIDDLESEX UNIVERSITY   T 020 8411 5555
School of Arts & Education
Television Production, Hendon Campus
The Burroughs, Hendon
London NW4 4BT
W www.mdx.ac.uk

NATIONAL FILM &
TELEVISION SCHOOL   T 01494 671234
MA & Diploma Courses in the Key Filmmaking Disciplines.
Short Courses for Freelancers
Beaconsfield Studios
Station Road
Beaconsfield, Bucks HP9 1LG
F 01494 674042
E info@nfts.co.uk
W www.nfts.co.uk

NORTHERN FILM SCHOOL   T 0113 812 8000
Leeds Metropolitan University
Electric Press
1 Millennium Square, Leeds LS2 3AD
E filmenquiries@leedsmet.ac.uk
W www.leedsmet.co.uk

RAINDANCE FILM
PARTNERSHIP LLP   T 020 7287 3833
Short Courses. 1 yr Postgraduate Degrees
10 Craven Street, London WC2N 5PE
E info@raindance.co.uk
W www.raindance.org

UNIVERSITY FOR THE
CREATIVE ARTS   T 01252 892883
Pre-degree, Undergraduate & Postgraduate Degrees in
Creative Arts Courses
Falkner Road, Farnham
Surrey GU9 7DS
E enquiries@ucreative.ac.uk
W www.ucreative.ac.uk

UNIVERSITY OF WESTMINSTER SCHOOL OF
MEDIA ARTS & DESIGN   T 020 7911 5000
Undergraduate Courses: Film & Television Production.
Contemporary Media Practice. Postgraduate Courses:
Screenwriting & Producing, Film & Television. Theory,
Culture & Industry
Admissions & Enquiries:
Watford Road, Northwick Park
Harrow, Middlesex HA1 3TP
W www.westminster.ac.uk/film

Film & Television Schools

What are film and television schools?

The schools listed in this section offer various courses to those who wish to become part of the behind-camera world of the entertainment industry. These courses include filmmaking, producing, screenwriting and animation, to name a few. Students taking these courses usually have to produce a number of short films in order to graduate. The following advice has been divided into two sections: for potential students and for actors.

Advice for filmmakers/writers:

Why should I take a course?

The schools listed here offer courses which enable a budding filmmaker or script writer to develop their skills with practical training. These courses are designed to prepare you for a career in a competitive industry. They also provide you with an opportunity to begin networking and making contacts with industry professionals.

How should I use these listings?

Research a number of schools carefully before applying to any courses. Have a look at the websites of the schools listed first to get an idea of the types of courses on offer, what is expected from students, and the individual values of each school. Request a prospectus from the school if they do not have full details online. Word of mouth recommendations are invaluable if you know anyone who has attended or taught at a school. You need to decide what type of course suits you – don't just sign up for the first one you read about. See what is available and give yourself time to think about the various options.

Advice for actors:

Why should I get involved?

Student films can offer new performers the chance to develop skills and experience in front of a camera, learning scripts, working with other actors and working with crew members. Making new contacts and learning how to get on with those you are working with, whether in front of or behind camera, is a vital part of getting along in the acting community.

In addition, you are likely to receive a certain amount of exposure from the film. The student filmmaker may show it to teachers, other students, other actors, and most importantly directors when applying for jobs, and you would normally be given your own copy of the film which you can show to agents or casting directors if requested, or use a clip of it in your showreel.

For more experienced actors, working on a student film can offer the opportunity to hone existing skills and keep involved within the industry. It can also be useful to observe new actors and keep up-to-date with new training ideas and techniques.

How do I get involved?

It may be helpful to see if the schools' websites have any advice for actors interested in being considered for parts in student films and suggesting how they should make contact. If there is no advice of this kind, it would be worth either phoning or e-mailing to ask if the school or its students would consider actors previously unknown to them. If this is the case, ask who CVs and headshots should be sent to, and whether they would like to see a showreel or voicereel (for animation courses).

If you are asked to play a role in a student film, make sure you are not going to a student's home and that someone knows where you are going and when. Equity also recommends that actors request a contract when working on any film; you could receive payment retrospectively if the film becomes a success. You may find it helpful to refer to Equity's advice leaflet *Low Pay/No Pay* which is available to all Equity members from their website's members' area.

Should I use a clip of a student film on my showreel?

Casting directors would generally prefer to see some form of showreel than none at all. If you do not have anything else you can show that has been professionally broadcast, or do not have the money to get a showreel made from scratch, then a student film is an acceptable alternative. See the 'Promotional Services' section for more information on showreels.

Where can I find more information?

Students and actors may want to visit Shooting People's website www.shootingpeople.org for further advice and daily e-mail bulletins of student/short film and TV castings. Filmmakers can upload their films to the site for others to view.

3 MILLS STUDIOS T 020 7363 3336
Three Mill Lane, London E3 3DU
F 0871 5944028
E info@3mills.com
W www.3mills.com

ANIMAL PROMOTIONS T 07778 156513
White Rocks Farm, Underriver
Sevenoaks, Kent TN15 0SL
F 01732 763767
E happyhoundschool@yahoo.co.uk
W www.whiterocksfarm.co.uk

ARDMORE STUDIOS LTD T 00 353 1 2862971
Herbert Road, Bray
Co. Wicklow, Ireland
F 00 353 1 2861894
E film@ardmore.ie
W www.ardmore.ie

BBC TELEVISION T 020 8743 8000
Television Centre, Wood Lane
Shepherds Bush, London W12 7RJ

BRAY FILM STUDIOS T 01628 622111
Down Place, Water Oakley
Windsor, Berkshire SL4 5UG
F 01628 770381

CLAPHAM ROAD STUDIOS T 020 7582 9664
Animation. Live Action
161 Clapham Road, London SW9 0PU
W www.claphamroadstudios.co.uk

EALING STUDIOS T 020 8567 6655
Ealing Green, London W5 5EP
F 020 8758 8658
E info@ealingstudios.com
W www.ealingstudios.com

ELSTREE STUDIOS T 020 8953 1600
Shenley Road, Borehamwood
Herts WD6 1JG
F 020 8905 1135
E info@elstreestudios.co.uk
W www.elstreestudios.co.uk

LONDON STUDIOS THE T 020 7157 5555
London Television Centre
Upper Ground
London SE1 9LT
F 020 7157 5757
E sales@londonstudios.co.uk
W www.londonstudios.co.uk

PINEWOOD STUDIOS T 01753 651700
Pinewood Road, Iver Heath
Buckinghamshire SL0 0NH
W www.pinewoodgroup.com

REUTERS TELEVISION T 020 7250 1122
The Reuters Thompson Building
South Colonnade
Canary Wharf, London E14 5EP

RIVERSIDE STUDIOS T 020 8237 1000
Crisp Road, London W6 9RL
F 020 8237 1001
E reception@riversidestudios.co.uk
W www.riversidestudios.co.uk

**SANDS FILMS COSTUMES LTD /
ROTHERHITHE STUDIOS** T 020 7231 2209
82 St Marychurch Street
London SE16 4HZ
F 020 7231 2119
E info@sandsfilms.co.uk
W www.sandsfilms.co.uk

SHEPPERTON STUDIOS T 01932 562611
Studios Road, Shepperton
Middlesex TW17 0QD
F 01932 568989
W www.pinewoodgroup.com

SILVER ROAD STUDIOS T 020 8746 2000
*Green Screen Studios. Filming/Photographic Studios.
Conference/Function Room. Cinema/Screening Room.
Casting Room. Make-up. Voice Overs. Maintenance.
Equipment Hire*
2 Silver Road, White City
London W12 7SG
E info@silverroadstudios.co.uk
W www.silverroadstudios.co.uk

TEDDINGTON STUDIOS T 020 8977 3252
Broom Road, Teddington
Middlesex TW11 9NT
F 020 8943 4050
W www.pinewoodgroup.com

**TWICKENHAM FILM
STUDIOS LTD** T 020 8607 8888
The Barons, St Margaret's
Twickenham
Middlesex TW1 2AW
F 020 8607 8889
E enquiries@twickenhamstudios.com
W www.twickenhamstudios.com

Film London

Supports over 1,000 film, TV and advertising projects every year. Make us your first point of contact for filming in the capital.

www.filmlondon.org.uk

MAYOR OF LONDON

Awarding funds from
The National Lottery®

G

Good Digs Guide
Compiled by Janice Cramer
and David Banks

This is a list of digs recommended by those
who have used them.

To keep the list accurate please send
recommendations for inclusion to:

Good Digs Guide
Spotlight, 7 Leicester Place
London WC2H 7RJ

E contacts@spotlight.com

If you are a digs owner wishing
to be listed, your application must
contain a recommendation from
a performer who has stayed
in your accommodation.

ABERDEEN: Milne, Mrs A.   T 01224 638951
5 Sunnyside Walk, Aberdeen AB24 3NZ

ABERDEEN: Woods, Pat   T 01224 586324
62 Union Grove, Aberdeen AB10 6RX

ABERYSTWYTH:
Vegetarian Penrhiw   T 07837 712323
Farmhouse near Aberystwyth providing Accommodation
& Vegetarian Breakfasts
Penrhiw, Llanafan
Aberystwyth, Dyfed SY23 4BA
E penrhiw@fastmail.fm
W www.vegetarianpenrhiw.com

AYR: Dunn, Sheila   T 01292 284531
The Dunn-Thing Guest House
13 Park Circus
Ayr KA7 2DJ

BATH: Hutton, Mrs Celia   T 01225 442238
Bath Holiday Homes
4 Edgar Buildings
Bath BA1 2EE
E bookings@bathandcountryholidays.co.uk
W www.bathholidayhomes.co.uk

BATH: Tapley, Jane   T 01225 446561
Camden Lodgings
3 Upper Camden Place
Bath BA1 5HX
E peter@tapley.ws

BIRMINGHAM: Hurst, Mr P.   T 0121 449 8220
41 King Edward Road, Moseley
Birmingham B13 8HR
E phurst1com@aol.com

BIRMINGHAM:
Mountain, Marlene P.   T 0121 454 5900
268 Monument Road, Edgbaston
Birmingham B16 8XF

BIRMINGHAM: Wilson, Mrs   T 0121 440 5182
17 Yew Tree Road, Edgbaston
Birmingham B15 2LX
E yolandewilson17@gmail.com

BLACKPOOL: Lees, Jean   T 01253 621059
Ascot Flats, 6 Hull Road
Central Blackpool FY1 4QB

BLACKPOOL:
Somerset Apartments   T/F 01253 346743
22 Barton Avenue, Blackpool FY1 6AP
W www.blackpool-somerset-apartments.co.uk

BLACKPOOL:
Waller, Veronica & Bob   T 01253 627003
The Brooklyn Hotel, 7 Wilton Parade
Blackpool FY1 2HE
E enquiries@brooklynhotel.co.uk
W www.brooklynhotel.co.uk

BOLTON: Duckworth, Paul   T 07762 545129
19 Burnham Avenue, Bolton BL1 6BD
E pauljohnathan@msn.com

BOURNEMOUTH: Sitton, Martin   T 01202 293318
Flat 2, 9 St Winifreds Road
Meyrick Park, Bournemouth BH2 6NX
E martinbmouth@hotmail.co.uk

BRADFORD: Smith, Theresa   T 01274 778568
8 Moorhead Terrace, Shipley
Bradford BD18 4LA
E theresaannesmith@hotmail.com

BRIGHTON: Benedict, Peter   T 020 7703 4104
19 Madeira Place, Brighton BN2 1TN
T 07752 810122
E peter@peterbenedict.co.uk
W www.madeiraplace.co.uk

BRIGHTON: Chance, Michael &
Drinkel, Keith   T 01273 779585
6 Railway Street, Brighton BN1 3PF
T 07876 223359
E mchance@lineone.net

BRIGHTON: Dyson, Kate   T 01273 607490
39 Arundel Street, Kemptown BN2 5TH
T 07812 949875
E kate.dyson@talktalk.net

BRISTOL: Ham, Phil & Jacqui   T 0117 902 5213
78 Stackpool Road, Bristol BS3 1NN
T 07956 962422
E jacquic@tiptopmusic.com

BURY ST EDMUNDS:
Bird, Mrs S.   T 01284 754492
30 Crown Street, Bury St Edmunds, Suffolk IP33 1QU
E josandsue@homebird2.plus.com

BURY ST EDMUNDS:
Harrington-Spier, Sue   T 01284 768986
39 Well Street, Bury St Edmunds, Suffolk IP33 1EQ
E sue.harringtonspier@googlemail.com

BUXTON: Kitchen, Mrs G.   T 01298 26555
Silverlands Holiday Apartments
c/o 156 Brown Edge Road
Buxton, Derbyshire SK17 7AA
T 01298 79381
E swiftcaterequip2@aol.com

CAMBRIDGE: Dunn, Anne   T 01954 210291
The Dovecot, 1 St Catherine's Hall
Coton, Cambridge CB23 7GU
T 07774 131797
E dunn@annecollet.fsnet.co.uk

CANTERBURY: Ellen, Nikki   T 01227 720464
Crockshard Farmhouse, Wingham
Canterbury CT3 1NY
E crockshard_bnb@yahoo.com
W www.crockshard.com

CARDIFF: Blade, Mrs Anne   T 029 2022 5860
25 Romilly Road, Canton
Cardiff CF5 1FH

CARDIFF: Kelly, Sheila   T 029 2039 5078
166 Llandaff Road, Canton, Cardiff CF11 9PX
T 07875 134381
E mgsmkelly1@gmail.com

CARDIFF: Kennedy, Rosie   T 07746 946118
Duffryn Mawr Farm House, Pendoylan
Vale of Glamorgan
E rosie@duffrynmawrcottages.com
W www.duffrynmawrcottages.co.uk

CARDIFF: Lewis, Nigel   T 029 2049 4008
66 Donald Street, Roath, Cardiff CF24 4TR
T 07813 069822
E nigel.lewis66@btinternet.com

CHESTERFIELD:
Cook, Linda & Chris   T 01246 202631
27 Tennyson Avenue, Chesterfield
Derbyshire
T 07929 850561
E chris_cook@talk21.com

CHESTERFIELD:
Foston, Mr & Mrs   **T** 01246 235412
Anis Louise Guest House, 34 Clarence Road
Chesterfield S40 1LN
E anislouise@gmail.com
W www.anislouiseguesthouse.co.uk

CHESTERFIELD:
Popplewell, Mr & Mrs   **T** 01246 201738
Alfred House, 23 Tennyson Avenue
Chesterfield S40 4SN

COVENTRY:
Snelson, Paddy & Bob   **T** 01926 852850
Banner Hill Farmhouse, Rouncil Lane
Kenilworth CV8 1NN

DARLINGTON: Bird, Mrs   **T** 01748 822771
Gilling Old Mill, Gilling West
Richmond, N Yorks DL10 5JD
E admin@yorkshiredales-cottages.com

DARLINGTON: George Hotel   **T** 01325 374576
Contact: Reception
Piercebridge
Darlington DL2 3SW
W www.georgeontees.co.uk

DARLINGTON: Graham, Anne   **T** 01325 374280
Holme House, Piercebridge
Darlington DL2 3SY
E graham.holmehouse@gmail.com
W www.holmehouse.com

DERBY: Boddy, Susan   **T** 01332 701384
St Wilfrids, Church Lane
Barrow-upon-Trent, Derbyshire DE73 7HB

DERBY: Coxon, Mary   **T** 01332 347460
Short Term Accommodation. Theatricals only
1 Overdale Road, Derby DE23 6AU
T 07850 082943
E marycoxon@hotmail.co.uk

DUNDEE: Hill, Mrs J.   **T** 01382 450831
Ash Villa, 216 Arbroath Road
Dundee DD4 7RZ
E ashvilla_guesthouse@talk21.com

EASTBOURNE: Allen, Peter   **T** 07712 439289
16 Enys Road, Eastbourne BN21 2DN

EASTBOURNE: Guess, Maggie   **T** 01323 736689
3 Hardy Drive, Langney Point
Eastbourne, East Sussex BN23 6ED
T 07710 273288
E guesswhom@btinternet.com

EDINBURGH: ACS Properties   **T** 01620 826880
Contact: Ashley Smith, Carole Smith.
Short Term Letting in Edinburgh
Office: 7 St Lawrence, Haddington
East Lothian EH41 3RL
T 07875 667752
E ashley@acs-properties.com
W www.acs-properties.com

EDINBURGH: Glen Miller, Edna   **T** 0131 556 4131
25 Bellevue Road
Edinburgh EH7 4DL

EDINBURGH: Tyrrell, Helen   **T** 0131 229 7219
Two single rooms in flat overlooking park. 10 mins walk
from several Edinburgh theatres
9 Lonsdale Terrace, Edinburgh EH3 9HN
T 07929 960510
E hkmtyrrell@gmail.com

GLASGOW: Baird, David W.   **T** 0141 423 1340
6 Beaton Road, Maxwell Park
Glasgow G41 4LA
T 07842 195597
E b050557@yahoo.com

GLASGOW:
Leslie-Carter, Simon   **T** 01436 810264
52 Charlotte Street, Glasgow G1 5DW
T 07814 891351
E slc@52charlottestreet.co.uk
W www.52charlottestreet.co.uk

INVERNESS: Blair, Mrs   **T** 01463 232878
McDonald House Hotel, 1 Ardross Terrace
Inverness IV3 5NQ
E f.blair@homecall.co.uk

INVERNESS:
Kerr-Smith, Jennifer   **T** 01463 233131
Ardkeen Tower, 5 Culduthel Road
Inverness IV2 4AD

IPSWICH: Ball, Bunty   **T** 01473 256653
56 Henley Road, Ipswich IP1 3SA
E bunty.ball.t21@btinternet.com

IPSWICH: Bennett, Liz   **T** 01473 623343
Gayfers, Playford, Ipswich IP6 9DR
E lizzieb@clara.co.uk

KESWICK: Bell, Miss A.   **T** 07740 949250
Flat 4, Skiddaw View
Penrith Road, Keswick CA12 5HF

LEEDS: Byrne, Ralph   **T** 0113 249 5303
16 Oakwell Crescent, Leeds LS8 4AF
T 07763 572183
E ralphjbyrne@googlemail.com

LEEDS: Cannon, Rosie   **T** 0113 262 3550
14 Toronto Place, Chapel Allerton
Leeds LS7 4LJ
T 07969 832955

LINCOLN: Carnell, Andrew   **T** 01522 569892
Tennyson Court Cottages, 3 Tennyson Street
Lincoln LN1 1LZ
E andrew@tennyson-court.co.uk
W www.tennyson-court.co.uk

LINCOLN: Sharpe, Mavis S.   **T** 01522 534477
Bight House, 17 East Bight
Lincoln LN2 1QH

LIVERPOOL: Maloney, Anne   **T** 0151 734 4839
16 Sandown Lane, Wavertree, Liverpool L15 8HY
T 07977 595040

LLANDUDNO:
Blanchard, Mr D. & Mrs A.   **T** 01492 877822
Oasis Hotel, 4 Neville Crescent
Central Promenade, Llandudno LL30 1AT
E oasishotel@unicombox.com

LONDON: Allen, Mrs I.   **T** 020 7723 3979
Flat 2, 9 Dorset Square
London NW1 6QB
E neddyallen@mypostoffice.co.uk

LONDON: Cardinal, Maggie   **T** 020 7681 7376
17A Gaisford Street, London NW5 2EB

LONDON:
Cavanah, Anne Marie   **T** 07939 220299
Upper Flat, 66 Elsinore Road
Forest Hill, London SE23 2SL
E anmariecavanah@aol.com

LONDON: Home Rentals B&B T 020 8840 1071
7 Park Place, Ealing
London W5 5NQ
E home_rentals@btinternet.com

LONDON: Horn, Cryn T 07958 107620
27 Donald Road
Upton Park, London E13 0QF
E crynhorn@easynet.co.uk

LONDON: Kempton, Victoria T 020 8888 5595
66 Morley Avenue
London N22 6NG
T 07946 344697
E vjkempton@onetel.com

LONDON: Long, Hilary T 020 8856 5023
56 Sutlej Road, Charlton
London SE7 7DB
F 07092 315384
E rainbowtheatrelondoneast@yahoo.co.uk

LONDON: Mesure, Nicholas T 020 8853 4337
16 St Alfege Passage
Greenwich, London SE10 9JS
T 07941 043841
E info@st-alseges.co.uk

LONDON: Montagu, Beverley T 020 7263 3883
13 Hanley Road
London N4 3DU

LONDON: Rothner, Stephanie T 020 8446 1604
44 Grove Road, North Finchley
London N12 9DY
T 07956 406446

LONDON: Shaw, Lindy T 020 8567 0877
11 Baronsmede, London W5 4LS
E lindy.shaw@talktalk.net

LONDON: Walsh, Genevieve T 020 7627 0024
37 Kelvedon House
Guildford Road
Stockwell, London SW8 2DN

LONDON: Warren, Mrs Sally T 020 8994 0560
28 Prebend Gardens, Chiswick
London W4 1TW

LONDON: Wilson, Sylvia T 07758 265351
1 Marlborough Mansions
39 Bromells Road
Clapham SW4 0BA

MALVERN: McLeod, Mr & Mrs T 01684 574994
Sidney House
40 Worcester Road
Malvern WR14 4AA
E info@sidneyhouse.co.uk
W www.sidneyhouse.co.uk

MANCHESTER: Cox, Lucia T 0161 860 6005
22 Woodlawn Court, Manchester M16 9RH
T 07805 337742
E lougrand76@hotmail.com

**MANCHESTER:
Dyson, Mrs Edwina** T 0161 434 5410
33 Danesmoor Road, West Didsbury
Manchester M20 3JT
T 07947 197755
E edwinadyson@hotmail.com

**MANCHESTER:
Heaton, Miriam** T 0161 773 4490
58 Tamworth Avenue, Whitefield
Manchester M45 6UA

MANCHESTER: Higgins, Mark T 07904 520898
New build less than 1 mile from town
72 Camp Street, Manchester M7 1LG
E icenlemon30@hotmail.com
W www.theatredigsmanchester.co.uk

**MANCHESTER:
Jones, Miss P. M.** T 0161 766 9243
'Forget-me-not Cottages'
12 Livsey Street
Whitefield, Manchester M45 6AE
E patricia@whitefieldcottages.co.uk

**MANCHESTER:
Prichard, Fiona & John** T 0161 434 4877
45 Bamford Road, Didsbury
Manchester M20 2QP
T 07771 965651
E fionaprichard@hotmail.com

MANCHESTER: Twist, Susan T 0161 225 1591
45 Osborne Road, Levenshulme
Manchester M19 2DU
E sue.twist@o2.co.uk

MANSFIELD: Ward, Judith T 01623 431359
16 Watson Avenue, Mansfield
Nottinghamshire NG18 2BS
T 07800 727659
E judithaward@hotmail.com

**MILFORD HAVEN:
Henricksen, Bruce & Diana** T 01646 695983
Belhaven House Hotel
29 Hamilton Terrace
Milford Haven SA73 3JJ
T 07825 237386
E brucehenricksen@mac.com
W www.westwaleshotel.com

**NEWCASTLE UPON TYNE:
Rosebery Hotel** T 0191 281 3363
Contact: The Manager
2 Rosebery Crescent, Jesmond
Newcastle upon Tyne NE2 1ET
W www.roseberyhotel.co.uk

**NEWCASTLE UPON TYNE:
Theatre Digs Newcastle** T 0191 226 1345
73 Moorside North
Newcastle upon Tyne NE4 9DU
E pclarerowntree@yahoo.co.uk
W www.theatredigsnewcastle.co.uk

NEWPORT: Price, Mrs Dinah T 01633 420216
Great House, Isca Road
Old Village, Caerleon, Gwent NP18 1QG
E dinahprice123@btinternet.com
W www.greathousebb.co.uk

NORWICH: Busch, Julia T 01603 612833
8 Chester Street, Norwich NR2 2AY
T 07920 133250
E juliacbusch@aol.com

NOTTINGHAM: Davis, Barbara T 0115 947 4179
3 Tattershall Drive, The Park
Nottingham NG7 1BX

NOTTINGHAM: Offord, Mrs T 0115 947 6924
5 Tattershall Drive, The Park
Nottingham NG7 1BX

NOTTINGHAM: Santos, Mrs S. T 0115 966 3018
Eastwood Farm, Hagg Lane
Epperstone, Nottingham NG14 6AX
E info@eastwoodfarm.co.uk

NOTTINGHAM: Seymour Road Studios
Bed & Breakfast   T 07946 208211
42 Seymour Road, West Bridgford
Nottingham NG2 5EF
E fran@seymourroadstudios.co.uk

NOTTINGHAM:
Walker, Christine   T 0115 947 2485
18A Cavendish Crescent North
The Park, Nottingham NG7 1BA
E walker.ce@virgin.net

OXFORD: Petty, Susan   T 01993 703035
Self-catering Cottages
74 Corn Street, Witney
Oxford OX28 6BS
E ianpetty@btinternet.com

PETERBOROUGH: Smith, J.   T 01733 211847
Fen-Acre, 20 Barber Drove North
Crowland, Peterborough PE6 0BE
T 07759 661896
E julie@fen-acreholidaylet.com
W www.fen-acreholidaylet.com

PLYMOUTH: Ball, Fleur   T 01752 670967
3 Hoe Gardens, Plymouth PL1 2JD
E fleurball@blueyonder.co.uk

PLYMOUTH: Carson, Mr & Mrs   T 01752 872124
6 Beech Cottages
Parsonage Road
Newton Ferrers, Nr Plymouth PL8 1AX
E beechcottages@aol.com

PLYMOUTH:
Humphreys, John & Sandra   T 01752 220176
Lyttleton House, 4 Crescent Avenue
Plymouth PL1 3AN

PLYMOUTH: Mead, Teresa   T 01752 664046
Ashgrove House, 218 Citadel Road
The Hoe, Plymouth PL1 3BB
E ashgroveho@aol.com

PLYMOUTH:
Spencer, Hugh & Eloise   T 01752 664066
10 Grand Parade
Plymouth PL1 3DF
T 07966 412839
E hugh.spencer@hotmail.com

POOLE: Saunders, Mrs   T 01202 741637
1 Harbour Shallows
15 Whitecliff Road
Poole BH14 8DU
E saunders.221@btinternet.com

RAMSGATE: Waugh, Gilda   T 01843 448149
2 Bed, 1 Bath Victorian House. Rooms for Theatricals
to Rent
14 Hatfield Road, Ramsgate
Kent CT11 9SS
E gildawaugh@hotmail.co.uk

SALISBURY: Brumfitt, Ms S.   T 01722 334877
26 Victoria Road, Salisbury
Wilts SP1 3NG
E slbrumfitt@gmail.com

SHEFFIELD: Slack, Penny   T 0114 234 0382
Rivelin Glen Quarry
Rivelin Valley Road
Sheffield S6 5SE
E pennyslack@aol.com
W www.quarryhouse.org.uk

SHOREHAM: Cleveland, Carol   T 01273 567954
Near Brighton
1 Oxen Court, Oxen Avenue
Shoreham-by-Sea BN43 5AS
T 07973 363939
E info@carolcleveland.com

SOUTHSEA & PORTSMOUTH:
Tyrell, Wendy   T 023 9282 1453
Douglas Cottage, 27 Somerset Road
Southsea PO5 2NL

STOKE-ON-TRENT:
Hindmoor, Mrs   T 01782 264244
Self-catering & B&B
Verdon Guest House, 44 Charles Street
Hanley, Stoke-on-Trent ST1 3JY
E debbietams@ymail.com
W www.verdonguesthouse.co.uk

STOKE-ON-TRENT:
Meredith, Mr K.   T 01782 502160
2 Bank End Farm Cottage, Hammond Avenue
Brown Edge, Stoke-on-Trent, Staffs ST6 8QU
E kenmeredith@btinternet.com

STRATFORD-UPON-AVON:
Caterham House   T 01789 267309
58-59 Rother Street
Stratford-upon-Avon CV37 6LT
E caterhamhousehotel@btconnect.com

TAUNTON: Parker, Sue   T 01278 458580
Admirals Rest, 5 Taunton Road
Bridgwater TA6 3LW
E info@admiralsrest.co.uk

TAUNTON: Read, Mary   T 01823 334148
Pyreland Farm, Cheddon Road
Taunton, Somerset TA2 7QX

WINCHESTER:
South Winchester Lodges   T 01962 820490
The Green, South Winchester Golf Club
Winchester, Hampshire SO22 5SW

WOLVERHAMPTON:
Riggs, Peter A.   T 01902 846081
'Bethesda', 56 Chapel Lane
Codsall, Nr Wolverhampton WV8 2EJ
T 07930 967809

WORTHING: Stewart, Mollie   T 01903 206823
School House, 11 Ambrose Place
Worthing BN11 1PZ

WORTHING: Symonds, Mrs Val   T 01903 201557
23 Shakespeare Road, Worthing BN11 4AR
T 07951 183252

YORK: Blacklock, Tom   T 01904 620487
155 Lowther Street, York YO31 7LZ
E thomas.blacklock@btinternet.com

YORK: Blower, Iris & Dennis   T 01904 626801
Dalescroft Guest House
10 Southlands Road
York YO23 1NP
E info@dalescroft-york.co.uk
W www.dalescroft-york.co.uk

YORK: Harrand, Greg   T 01904 637404
Hedley House Hotel & Apts
3 Bootham Terrace
York YO30 7DH
E greg@hedleyhouse.com

H →

Health & Wellbeing

Health & Wellbeing

How should I use these listings?

You will find a variety of companies in this section which could help you enhance your health and wellbeing physically and mentally. They include personal fitness and lifestyle coaches, counsellors, exercise classes and beauty consultants amongst others. It is worth researching any company or service you are considering using. Many of these listings have websites which you can browse. Even if you feel you have your career and lifestyle under control, you may still find the following advice helpful:

Your body is part of your business

Your mental and physical health is vital to your career as a performer. Just from a business perspective, your body is part of your promotional package and it needs to be maintained. Try to keep fit and eat healthily to enhance both your outward appearance and your inner confidence. This is particularly important if you are unemployed. You need to ensure that if you are suddenly called for an audition you look suitable for and feel positive about the part you are auditioning for.

Injury

Keeping fit also helps you to minimise the risk of an injury during a performance. The last thing you want to do is to be prevented from working. An injury is more likely to occur if you are inflexible and unprepared for sudden physical exertion. If you do pick up an injury or an illness you will want to make sure it does not get any worse by getting treatment with a specialist.

Mental health

Mental health is just as important as bodily health. Just as you would for any physical injury or illness, if you suffer from a psychological problem such as stage fright, an addiction or depression, you should make sure that you address your concerns and deal with the issues involved. You may need to see a counsellor or a life coach for guidance and support.

Unemployment

If you are unemployed, it can be difficult to retain a positive mindset. The best thing you can do is to keep yourself occupied. You could join a dance or drama class, which would help to maintain your fitness levels as well as developing contacts and keeping involved within the industry. Improve your CV by learning to speak a new language or play a musical instrument. Think about taking on temporary or part-time work outside of acting to earn money until the next job comes along (see the 'Non-Acting Jobs' section), or you could put yourself forward for acting work in a student film (see 'Film & Television Schools' for more information).

Where can I find more information?

For more information on health and wellbeing you may wish to contact the British Association for Performing Arts Medicine (BAPAM) www.bapam.org.uk. You may also find their case study in this section helpful. Please refer to the 'Drama Training, Schools & Coaches' and 'Dance Training & Professional Classes' sections if you are interested in taking drama or dance courses or lessons to improve your fitness, keep your auditioning skills sharp between jobs and/or stay occupied and motivated.

Health & Wellbeing

CASE STUDY

Actors who are never out of work are rare creatures. But you can use your resting periods to invest in your physical and mental health. Here are a few suggestions from BAPAM, the charity that provides free health-assessment clinics and reduced-price treatments to artists with performance-related health problems.

Look after your health on a budget

If you can't justify the cost of keeping up your gym membership, go for cheaper forms of exercise.

Walk or cycle instead of driving or using public transport. If you haven't ridden a bike for years, build your confidence by taking a course.

Run in the open air instead of on a treadmill at a gym. It's much better to be in the fresh air – and it's more sociable.

Swimming is a cheap and effective form of exercise. Think about taking lessons to make your stroke more efficient and avoid putting unnecessary pressure on your joints – especially your neck.

Team sports combine fresh air and being sociable; now could be the time to take up football or netball again. Be careful, though – you wouldn't want a sports injury to come between you and your next job!

Learn a technique to help with **posture**, such as Alexander Technique, Feldenkrais or Pilates. Techniques that are taught one-to-one can be expensive, but you can often find taster sessions at adult education colleges. BAPAM could also help you find an affordable teacher in their Directory of Practioners.

Take a refresher in all those stagecraft skills (breathing; warm-up exercises; stage fighting) you learned at drama school. Enrol on a short course or read some books. When the next job comes up you need to be in peak condition and able to perform safely.

Think about your diet while you're resting

Everyone knows that eating well has a positive effect on your mental and physical wellbeing – especially important when you need to keep your spirits up.

Learn about **healthy eating**, and expand your repertoire of recipes. Farmers' markets save money and you'll learn what's in season. Then you can maintain good habits when you're running around or on tour.

If you ration your **treats**, you make them more special. If a treat becomes a daily habit you won't enjoy real treats so much.

Now is the time to **phase out junk food**. Why spend money on processed food when you could eat so much better for less? See the BAPAM factsheet *Sensible eating for performers*.

Don't rely on **alcohol** to keep you going. You develop expectations around alcohol, and that will take its toll on your liver (and your wallet!). Try to make a drink last longer, or alternate alcohol and water over the course of an evening. See the BAPAM factsheet *The drinks are on me!* for more information about drinking responsibly.

Invest in your mental health too

Think strategically about your career. Do a **skills** audit, remembering all the skills you've accumulated (numeracy, fundraising, any IT skills). Be creative about how you can put them to use, and fill any skill gaps. Focusing on something developmental can take your mind off your current circumstances.

Use quiet periods to **organise** your paperwork and electronic filing systems. You will feel empowered when you know everything is in order; it saves time and stress when you do get busy if you already have a workable system in place. Learn to use **spreadsheets** to keep track of your finances. You'll save yourself endless headaches when it's time to file your tax return, *and* you'll save yourself money on an accountant.

Volunteering is great for stopping you feeling isolated. Try and find an activity that involves **physical exercise** – such as working in a community garden. It might even lead to a job!

Remember, there's no need to suffer alone if being out of work is beginning to get you down. A few sessions with a **counsellor** can make a big difference. Check out the BAPAM Directory online at www.bapam.org.uk to locate a performer-friendly counsellor in your area.

To find out more about performance-related health issues and BAPAM services visit www.bapam.org.uk

CASE STUDY

Dance UK's Healthier Dancer Programme (HDP) has been providing information and resources to support dancers' health for over 20 years. The HDP provides dancers with educational resources, information, and talks; a free directory of specialist dance healthcare practitioners; expert health advice; and the only free specialist dancers' health clinic in the UK, as well as keeping the dance sector connected to the most up-to-date research in dance medicine and science.

National Institute for Dance Medicine and Science (NIDMS)

This year, in partnership with Birmingham Royal Ballet, Trinity Laban, the Royal National Orthopaedic Hospital, and the Universities of Wolverhampton and Birmingham, Dance UK has launched NIDMS. It aims, through shared expertise and a network of multidisciplinary hub-sites and partners, to provide access for all dancers to high quality, evidence-based, dance-specific healthcare and dance science services. It will:

- offer fast, affordable, specialist healthcare and injury treatment for dancers, including the first NHS-based dance injury clinic accessible free via GP referral;

- provide education for dancers, teachers, scientists, healthcare and medical practitioners;

- be a focus for cutting edge research into dancers' health, injury and performance, co-ordinating research nationally which will lead to more effective injury prevention.

Supporting this work, Dance UK's HDP is a key part of the NIDMS education strand, and is now offering workshops in dancers' health and performance. For more information on accessing the free dancers' health clinic, or to learn more about NIDMS and educational talks, check out Dance UK's website: www.danceuk.org/healthier-dancer-programme

Healthcare Practitioners Directory

Supporting the work of NIDMS' dance injury clinic in London, the Dance UK Healthcare Practitioners Directory provides information on medical and complimentary practitioners across the UK with specific experience caring for dancers. The directory is searchable by postcode, practitioner type, or practitioner name and can be found at: www.danceuk.org/medical-practitioners-directory

Psychological Approaches and Support

Improving performance can sometimes just be a matter of changing your attitude or finding motivation and support to improve technical skills or solve ongoing problems. Dance UK's HDP can help dancers find advice, information, and practitioners to help with clinical topics, such as eating disorders and burnout, as well as methods for enhancing performance through mental skills. Skills such as goal setting, imagery and motivation can help dancers overcome performance anxiety, optimise training, and gain confidence. The Foundations for Excellence website has a range of resources on mental training for performers including developing self-esteem and motivation, and practising goal setting: www.foundations-for-excellence.org/resources/preparation-for-performance

Resources: Information Sheets, Books and Links

Dance UK's Information Sheets, publications, and website cover a wide variety of topics essential for keeping dancers fit including nutrition and hydration, warm up and cool down, proper dancer floors and spaces, and safe and effective practices for dance teachers, choreographers, and dancers. Information about health-related events and conferences, industry standards, and healthy recipes for dancers are also available on the HDP pages: www.danceuk.org/healthier-dancer-programme

International Association of Dance Medicine and Science (IADMS)

IADMS offers resources for teachers and dancers on dance fitness, bone health, nutrition, pointe work, proprioception, and motor learning as well as a Bulletin for Teachers, plus a Studio Teachers' Network. More information is available on their website: www.iadms.org

IADMS have also partnered with Trinity College London on the Certificate in Safe and Effective Dance Practice: a Level 5 qualification suitable for all dance professionals working within any dance style, to gain knowledge of anatomy and physiology, injury management, and nutrition. More information on the certificate and entering can be found at: www.trinitycollege.co.uk/site/?id=1598

Rudolf Nureyev Foundation Medical Website

This website contains up-to-date and relevant information contributed by experienced doctors and scientists about dancers' health, dance medicine, and safe practice across dance styles. Resources include advice on safe practice and caring for common dance injuries, and over 300 articles and research reports on topics in dancers' health, as well as a new international listing of health practitioners who specialise in treating dancers. The website also has listings of events and helpful links, frequently asked questions about dance medicine and science, and a forum for dancers to ask questions: www.nureyev-medical.org

For dance-related queries and advice visit www.danceuk.org or www.facebook.com/healthier dancerprogramme

1ST SUCCESS
T 01628 780470
Empowerment, Confidence & Stress Therapies.
Challenge Blocks, Anxieties, Stresses & Fears
10 Gillott Court, St Lukes Road
Maidenhead, Berks SL6 7AD
E joanna@1stsuccess.com
W www.1stsuccess.com

ALEXANDER ALLIANCE
T 01727 843633
Alexander Technique. Audition & Voice Coaching
3 Hazelwood Drive
St Albans, Herts
E bev.keech@ntlworld.com
W www.alextech.co.uk

ALEXANDER TECHNIQUE
T 020 7731 1061
Contact: Jackie Coote MSTAT
27 Britannia Road
London SW6 2HJ
E jackiecoote@alexandertec.co.uk
W www.alexandertec.co.uk

ALEXANDER TECHNIQUE
T 07956 852303
Contact: Robert Macdonald
4 Droot Street, London W10 4DQ
W www.voice.org.uk

ALKALI
T 020 8788 8588
Cosmetic Dentistry. Straightening. Whitening
226A Upper Richmond Road
Putney, London SW15 6TG
E hello@alkaliaesthetics.co.uk
W www.alkaliaesthetics.co.uk

ARTS CLINIC THE
T 020 7935 1242
Personal & Professional Development. Psychological
Counselling
14 Devonshire Place
London W1G 6HX
F 020 7224 6256
E mail@artsclinic.co.uk

ASPEY ASSOCIATES / COACHING
FOR LEADERS LTD
T 0845 1701300
Executive Coaching. Management & Team Development
& Training
90 Long Acre, Covent Garden
London WC2E 9RZ
E hr@aspey.com
W www.aspey.com

AURA DENTAL SPA
T 020 7722 0040
5 Queens Terrace, London NW8 6DX
E info@auradentalspa.com
W www.auradentalspa.com

BLOOMSBURY ALEXANDER
CENTRE THE
T 020 7404 5348
Alexander Technique
Bristol House
80A Southampton Row
London WC1B 4BB
T 07884 015954
E enquiries@alexcentre.com
W www.alexcentre.com

BODY CLINIC THE
T 0800 5424809
Skincare Specialists
Harley Street W1G
E info@thebodyclinic.co.uk
W www.thebodyclinic.co.uk

BODY CLINIC THE
T 0800 5424809
Skincare Specialists
South Woodford E18
E info@thebodyclinic.co.uk
W www.thebodyclinic.co.uk

BODY CLINIC THE
T 0800 5424809
Skincare Specialists
Gidea Park RM2
E info@thebodyclinic.co.uk
W www.thebodyclinic.co.uk

BODYWISE YOGA &
NATURAL HEALTH
T 020 3116 2098
30 Hanbury Street, London E1 6QR
E info@bodywisehealth.org
W www.bodywisehealth.org

BOXMOOR HOUSE
DENTAL PRACTICE
T 01442 253253
451 London Road
Hemel Hempstead HP3 9BE
F 01442 244454
E d-gardner@btconnect.com

BREATHE FITNESS
PERSONAL TRAINING
T 07840 180094
20 Enford Street, Marylebone
London W1H 1DG
E anthony@breathefitness.uk.com
W www.breathefitness.uk.com

BURGESS, Chris
T 07985 011694
Counsellor. Psychotherapist
New Road Consultancy Practice
28 New Road
Brighton BN1 1NG
E chrisburgess@netcom.co.uk

BURT, Andrew
T 020 8992 5992
Counselling
74 Mill Hill Road, London W3 8JJ
E burt.counsel@tiscali.co.uk
W www.andrewburtcounselling.co.uk

COGNITIVE BEHAVIOURAL THERAPY (CBT)
Based in West & North London
E info@therapycbt.co.uk
W www.therapycbt.co.uk

COLLEGE PRACTICE THE
T 020 7267 6445
Massage. Osteopathy. Pilates. Podiatry. Sports Therapy
60 Highgate Road, London NW5 1PA
E info@thecollegepractice.com
W www.thecollegepractice.com

CONFIDENT PERFORMER THE
T 07859 914501
NLP Coaching & Therapy
E info@theconfidentperformer.com
W www.theconfidentperformer.com

CONSTRUCTIVE
TEACHING CENTRE LTD
T 020 7727 7222
Alexander Technique Teacher Training
E constructiveteachingcentre@gmail.com
W www.constructiveteachingcentre.com

CORTEEN, Paola MSTAT
T 020 8882 7898
Alexander Technique
10A Eversley Park Road
London N21 1JU
E pmcorteen@yahoo.co.uk

COURTENAY, Julian　　T 07973 139376
NLP Hypnotherapy
42 Langdon Park Road
London N6 5QG
E julian@mentalfitness.uk.com

CRAIGENTINNY DENTAL CARE　T 0131 669 2114
57 Duddingston Crescent, Milton Road
Edinburgh EH15 3AY
E office@craigentinny.co.uk
W www.craigentinny.co.uk

CROWE, Sara　　T 07830 375389
Holistic Massage. Pregnancy Treatment. Reflexology
25 Holmes Avenue, Hove BN3 7LB
E saracrowe77@gmail.com

**DAVIES, Siobhan
DANCE STUDIOS**　　T 020 7091 9650
Treatment Room
85 St George's Road, London SE1 6ER
F 020 7091 9669
E info@siobhandavies.com
W www.siobhandavies.com

DREAM　　T 07973 731026
*Massage, Reflexology & Yoga for the Workplace &
Events. Yoga Holidays & Retreats in Goa*
117B Gaisford Street
London NW5 2EG
E heidi@dreamtherapies.co.uk
W www.dreamtherapies.co.uk

**EDGE OF THE WORLD
HYPNOTHERAPY & NLP**　　T 01206 391050
*Contact: Graham Howes. ASHPH GHR Registered.
GHSC Regulated. Gastric Band/Weight Loss
Hypnotherapy. Specialist Help for Performers: Anxiety,
Audition/Stage Fright, Problems with Line Learning,
Stress. Quit Smoking*
Based in Central London, Essex/Suffolk
T 07875 720623
E info@edgehypno.com
W www.edgehypno.com

**EDWARDS, Simon MCAHyp DABCH MHS MHA
MAPHP SQHP**　　T 020 7467 8498
*Hypnotherapy for Professionals in Film,
Stage & Television*
10 Harley Street, London W1G 9PF
T 07889 333680
E simonedwardsharleystreet@gmail.com
W www.simonedwards.com

ELITE SPORTS SKILLS
*Personal Training. Sports Coaching. Level 4 in Fitness
& Coaching*
E esskills@hotmail.com
W www.elitesportsskills.com

ENLIGHTENED SELF INTEREST　T 07910 157064
56 Bloomsbury Street
London WC1B 3QT
E maggie@enlightenedselfinterest.com

**EXPERIENTIAL FOCUSING
THERAPY SESSIONS**　　T 07941 300871
Contact: Dr Greg Madison
93-95 Gloucester Place, London W1
E info@gregmadison.net
W www.gregmadison.net

**EXPERIENTIAL FOCUSING
THERAPY SESSIONS**　　T 07941 300871
Contact: Dr Greg Madison
40 Wilbury Road
Brighton BN1
E info@gregmadison.net
W www.gregmadison.net

**EXPLORING U
COUNSELLING LTD**　　T 01787 829141
Practices in Colchester, Long Melford & Saffron Walden
The Workshop
9 Hall Street, Long Melford
Nr Sudbury
Suffolk CO10 9JF
T 07841 979450
E euc@exploringUcounselling.co.uk
W www.exploringUcounselling.co.uk

FABULOUS-LIFESTYLES　　T 07958 984195
*Corporate Impact/Confidence Coach. Hypnotherapy.
Lifestyle & Presentation Coaching. NLP*
E nicci@fabulous-lifestyles.com
W www.fabulous-lifestyles.com

**FAITH, Gordon
BA MCHC (UK) Dip.REM.Sp**　T 020 7328 0446
*Focusing. Hypnotherapy. Obstacles to Performing.
Positive Affirmation*
1 Wavel Mews, Priory Road
West Hampstead, London NW6 3AB
E gordon.faith@tiscali.co.uk
W www.hypnotherapy.gordonfaith.co.uk

FIT 4 THE PART　　T 07702 590464
*Contact: Jon Trevor. Celebrity Trainer. Lifestyle Guru.
Media Presenter*
Based in North London
E info@fit4thepart.com
W www.fit4thepart.com

FITNESS COACH THE　　T 020 7300 1414
Contact: Jamie Baird
Agua at The Sanderson
50 Berners Street
London W1T 3NG
T 07970 782476
E jamie@thefitnesscoach.com

**FOOTPRINT COACHING &
PERSONAL TRAINING**　　T 07984 251903
Based in London & Kent
E georgina@georginaburnett.com
W www.footprintcoaching.org.uk

**HAMMOND, John B.
Ed (Hons) ICHFST**　　T/F 01277 632830
Fitness Consultancy. Sports & Relaxation Massage
4 Glencree, Billericay
Essex CM11 1EB
T 07703 185198
E johnhammond69@googlemail.com

HARLEY HEARING CENTRE　T 020 7935 5486
*Hearing Protection. Invisible Hearing Aids. Tinnitus
Maskers*
109 Harley Street
London W1G 6AN
E info@hearing-aid-devices.co.uk

HARLEY STREET
VOICE CENTRE THE   T 020 7224 2350
The Harley Street ENT Clinic, 109 Harley Street
London W1G 6AN
F 020 7935 7701
E info@harleystreetent.com
W www.harleystreetent.com

HAYWARD, Sarah   T 07834 608833
Reflexology, Reiki, Meditation & Other Therapies
27C Lyford Road, London SW18 3LU
E eyelovelight2012@gmail.com
W www.eyelovelight.co.uk

HILTON HOLISTICS   T 07548 896333
Hilton Hall, Hilton Lane
Essington, Staffordshire WV11 2BQ
E susan@cmc-technologies.co.uk

HYL ENERGISER   T 07768 321092
10 Little Newport Street, London WC2H 7JJ
E info@hylenergiser.com
W www.hylenergiser.com

HYPNOSIS WORKS   T 020 7237 5815
19 Glengall Road, London SE15 6NJ
E melissa@hypnosisdoeswork.net
W www.hypnosisdoeswork.net

INSPIRATIONAL WELLBEING
Energy Healer
E inspirationalwellbeing@gmail.com
W www.inspirationalwellbeing.com

JLP FITNESS   T 07930 304809
Personal Trainer. Strength & Conditioning Coach
E info@jlpfitness.com
W www.jlpfitness.com

JOSHI CLINIC THE   T 020 7487 5456
Holistic Healthcare
57 Wimpole Street, London W1G 8YW
E reception@joshiclinic.co.uk
W www.joshiclinic.co.uk

LIFE PRACTICE UK LTD   T/F 01462 451473
Specialists in Coaching, Mentoring, NLP & Hypnotherapy
Woodlands, Preston Road
Gosmore, Hitchin, Herts SG4 7QS
E info@lifepractice.co.uk
W www.lifepractice.co.uk

LUCAS, Hazel   T 07870 862939
Qualified Holistic Masseur
119 Brightwell Avenue, Westcliff-on-Sea
Essex SS0 9EQ
E onedaylucas@blueyonder.co.uk

MAGIC KEY PARTNERSHIP THE   T 0844 3320234
Contact: Lyn Burgess. Media Life Coach
151A Moffat Road, Thornton Heath
Surrey CR7 8PZ
E lyn@magickey.co.uk
W www.magickey.co.uk

MATRIX ENERGY
FIELD THERAPY   T 01304 379466
Accredited Healer
Deal Castle House, 31 Victoria Road
Deal, Kent CT14 7AS
T 07762 821828
E donnie@lovingorganization.org

McCALLION, Anna   T 020 7602 5599
Alexander Technique. Voice
Flat 2, 11 Sinclair Gardens, London W14 0AU
E hildegarde007@yahoo.com

MIESSENCE   T 01494 611249
Organic Natural Skincare. Wholefood Superfood Nutritionals
Mulkern House, 6 Springfield Road
Chesham, Bucks HP5 1PW
E rob@minaturals.co.uk
W www.freefromskincare.com

MINDSCI CLINIC   T/F 020 8948 2439
Clinical Hypnotism
34 Willow Bank, Ham
Richmond, Surrey TW10 7QX
E bt@mindsci-clinic.com
W www.mindsci-clinic.com

NOBLE, Penny
PSYCHOTHERAPY   T 07506 579895
8 Shaftesbury Gardens, Victoria Road
North Acton, London NW10 6LJ
E pennynobletherapy@googlemail.com
W www.pennynoblepsychotherapy.com

NORTON, Michael R.   T 020 7486 9229
Implant/Reconstructive Dentistry
104 Harley Street, London W1G 7JD
F 020 7486 9119
E linda@nortonimplants.com
W www.nortonimplants.com

NUTRITIONAL THERAPY
FOR PERFORMERS   T 07962 978763
Contact: Vanessa May BSc CNHC NTC & BANT Reg
18 Oaklands Road, Ealing, London W7 2DR
E vanessa@wellbeingandnutrition.co.uk
W www.wellbeingandnutrition.co.uk

ODYSSEY FITNESS   T 07527 571443
Berwick-upon-Tweed TD15 1PX
E lyons.a.michelle@gmail.com

OGUNLARU, Rasheed   T 020 7207 1082
Life & Business Coach
The Coaching Studio, 223A Mayall Road
London SE24 0PS
E rasheed@rasaru.com
W www.rasaru.com

OWOADE, Simon   T 07877 520266
Author. Motivational Speaker
Based in West London
E beinspiredtosucceed@hotmail.com
W www.simonowoade.co.uk

PEAK PERFORMANCE
TRAINING   T 01628 633509
Contact: Tina Reibl. Hypnotherapy. NLP. Success Strategies
42 The Broadway, Maidenhead, Berkshire SL6 1LU
E tina.reibl@tesco.net
W www.maidenhead-hypnotherapy.co.uk

POLAND, Ken
DENTAL STUDIOS   T 020 7935 6919
Film & Stage Dentistry
1 Devonshire Place, London W1G 6HH
F 020 7486 3952
E robpoland@btconnect.com

**PSYCHOTHERAPY &
MEDICAL HYPNOSIS** T 020 7794 5843
*Contact: Karen Mann DCH DHP. Including Performance
Improvement & Let Go of the Past*
10 Harley Street, London W1G 9PF
E emailkarenmann@googlemail.com
W www.karenmann.co.uk

REACH TO THE SKY LTD T 0843 2892503
Contact: Dr J. Success Life Coach
Maxet House, Liverpool Road
Luton, Bedfordshire LU1 1RS
T 07961 911027
E drtwsj@reachtothesky.com
W www.reachtothesky.com

ROBERTS, Dan TRAINING LTD
Boutique Personal Training
Twitter: @DanRobertsPT
9-13 Grape Street, London WC2H 8ED
E info@danrobertstraining.com
W www.danrobertstraining.com

**SEYRI, Kayvan MSc NSCA-CPT*D CSCS*D
NASM-PES CES** T 07881 554636
Athletic Performance Specialist. Master Personal Trainer
E info@ultimatefitpro.com
W www.ultimatefitpro.com

SHAPES IN MOTION T 07802 709933
*Contact: Sarah Perry. Movement Coaching. Yin, Viniyoga
& Children's Yoga*
Based in London
E yoga@shapeinmotion.com
W www.shapeinmotion.com

SHENAS, Dr DENTAL CLINIC T 020 7589 2319
51 Cadogan Gardens, Sloane Square
Chelsea, London SW3 2TH
E info@shenasdental.co.uk
W www.shenasdental.co.uk

SHER SYSTEM THE T 01784 227805
Helping Skin with Acne & Rosacea
PO Box 573, Staines
Middlesex TW18 9FJ
F 01784 463410
E skincare@sher.co.uk
W www.sher.co.uk

SHIATSU HEALTH CENTRE T 01908 679834
E japaneseyoga@btinternet.com
W www.shiatsuhealth.com

SMILE NW T 020 8458 2333
*Contact: Dr Veronica Morris (Cosmetic & General
Dentist)*
17 Hallswelle Parade, Finchley Road
Temple Fortune, London NW11 0DL
F 020 8458 5681
E enquiries@smile-nw.co.uk
W www.smile-nw.co.uk

SMILE SOLUTIONS T 020 7440 1760
Dental Practice
24 Englands Lane
London NW3 4TG
F 020 7449 1769
E enquiries@smile-solutions.info
W www.smile-solutions.info

SPORTS MEDICINE ON SCREEN T 07796 936442
1 Louis Drive East
London SS6 9DU
E administrator@starinjuries.com
W www.starinjuries.com

**STAT (THE SOCIETY OF TEACHERS OF THE
ALEXANDER TECHNIQUE)** T 020 7482 5135
1st Floor Linton House, 39-51 Highgate Road
London NW5 1RT
F 020 7482 5435
E enquiries@stat.org.uk
W www.stat.org.uk

THEATRICAL DENTISTRY T/F 020 7580 9696
*Contact: Richard D. Casson (Cosmetic Dentist).
Cosmetic. Orthodontic*
6 Milford House, 7 Queen Anne Street
London W1G 9HN
E smile@richardcasson.com
W www.richardcasson.com

TOP NOTCH NANNIES T 020 7824 8209
142 Buckingham Palace Road
London SW1W 9TR
T 020 7881 0893
E jean@topnotchnannies.com
W www.topnotchnannies.com

VITAL TOUCH (UK) LTD THE T 07976 263691
50 Greenham Road, Muswell Hill
London N10 1LP
E suzi@thevitaltouch.com
W www.thevitaltouch.com

WALK-IN BACKRUB T/F 020 7436 9875
On-site Massage Company
14 Neals Yard, London WC2H 9DP
E info@walkinbackrub.co.uk
W www.walkinbackrub.co.uk

**WALSH, Gavin
PERSONAL TRAINING** T 07782 248687
22 Stirling Court, Tavistock Street
London WC2E 7NU
E gavin@gavinwalsh.co.uk
W www.gavinwalsh.co.uk

WELLBEING T 07957 333921
Contact: Leigh Jones. Personal Training. Tai Chi. Yoga
22 Galloway Close
Broxbourne
Herts EN10 6BU
E williamleighjones@hotmail.com

**WOODFORD HOUSE
DENTAL PRACTICE** T 020 8504 2704
162 High Road, Woodford Green
Essex IG8 9EF
E info@improveyoursmile.co.uk
W www.improveyoursmile.co.uk

WORSLEY, Victoria T 07711 088765
*Feldenkrais Practitioner. Addresses habits of moving,
breathing, speaking & singing which limit range or
cause pain*
32 Clovelly Road, London N8 7RH
E v.worsley@virgin.net
W www.feldenkraisworks.co.uk

N →

Non-Acting Jobs

42ND STREET RECRUITMENT   T 020 7734 4422
Linen Hall, 162-168 Regent Street, London W1B 5TD
E info@42ndstreetrecruitment.com
W www.42ndstreetrecruitment.com

ACHIEVE RECRUITMENT   T 020 7138 3170
Temporary & Permanent Recruitment
Hanover House, 2nd Floor
7 Hanover Square, London W1S 1HQ
F 0845 3632007
E ben.davidson@achieverecruit.co.uk
W www.achieverecruit.co.uk

**AT YOUR SERVICE EVENT
STAFFING LTD**   T 020 7610 8610
Temporary Event Staff
Unit 12, The Talina Centre
Bagley's Lane, Fulham, London SW6 2BW
F 020 7610 8616
E sara@ays.co.uk   W www.apply.ays.co.uk

ATTITUDE EVENTS   T 020 7953 7935
Event Consultation & Staffing
412 Coppergate House,
16 Brune Street, London E1 7NJ
E nikki@attitude-events.com
W www.attitude-events.com

BREEZE PEOPLE   T 07903 012859
Promotional Staffing Agency
12 Warren Road, London SW19 2HX
T 07903 012861
E peepz@breezepeople.co.uk
W www.breezepeople.co.uk

**BRISTOW, Lucy
APPOINTMENTS**   T 0117 925 5988
Recruitment for Office Staff
12 Orchard Street, Bristol BS1 5EH
E enquire@lucybristow.com   W www.lucybristow.com

CATERINGTEMPS.COM LTD   T 020 7713 8772
*Suppliers of Temporary Staff to the Catering &
Hospitality Industry*
108-110 Judd Street, London WC1H 9PX
F 020 7713 6297
E office@cateringtemps.com
W www.cateringtemps.com

**CENTRAL EMPLOYMENT
AGENCY**   T 0191 232 4816
34-36 St Mary's Place
Newcastle upon Tyne NE1 7PQ
F 0191 261 2203
E info@centralemployment.co.uk
W www.centralemployment.co.uk

COVENT GARDEN BUREAU   T 020 7734 3374
Recruitment Consultants
5-6 Argyll Street, London W1F 7TE
E cv@coventgardenbureau.co.uk
W www.coventgardenbureau.co.uk

DIAMOND RESOURCING PLC   T 020 7929 2977
Generalist Recruitment Consultancy
29-30 Leadenhall Market, London EC3V 1LR
E info@diamondresourcing.com
W www.diamondresourcing.com

FAIRYTALE PROMOTIONS   T 01636 605291
Event Management, Promotional & Modelling Agency
6 Milton Street, New Balderton
Newark, Nottinghamshire NG24 3AW
E info@fairytalepromotions.com
W www.fairytalepromotions.com

FISHER, Judy ASSOCIATES   T 020 7437 2277
Media & Arts Recruitment Specialists
7 Swallow Street, London W1B 4DE
E cv@judyfisher.co.uk
W www.judyfisher.co.uk

Judy fisher
A S S O C I A T E S

Media Recruitment Specialists

020 7437 2277
www.judyfisher.co.uk
7 Swallow Street London W1B 4DE

**FOUR SEASONS
RECRUITMENT**　　　T 020 8237 8900
Recruitment Company. Beauty. Fashion. Retail
The Triangle
5-17 Hammersmith Grove, London W6 0LG
F 020 8237 8999
E jo@fsrl.co.uk
W www.fsrl.co.uk

GOGEN　　　T 020 7923 8130
Telephone Fundraising
T 020 7242 6991
E ciara.lloyd@brookstreet.co.uk
W www.gogen.org

HANDLE RECRUITMENT　　　T 020 7569 9999
*Recruitment for Arts, Media, Entertainment &
Inspirational Brands*
7 Portman Mews South, London W1H 6AY
E david.bishop@handle.co.uk
W www.handle.co.uk

ID STAFFING　　　T 020 7428 1444
Highgate Studios, 53-79 Highgate Road
London NW5 1TL
E recruitment@idstaffing.com
W www.idexperiential.co.uk/idstaffing

JAM STAFFING LTD　　　T 020 7237 2228
Events Company. Part-time Flexible Bar & Waiting Work
Unit 104, The Light Box
111 Power Road, London W4 5PY
E katie@jamstaffing.com
W www.jamstaffing.com

JFL SEARCH & SELECTION　　　T 020 7009 3500
Recruitment Consultants
27 Beak Street, London W1F 9RU
F 020 7734 6501
W www.jflrecruit.com

LEISUREJOBS　　　T 020 7622 8500
*Temporary, Promotional & Permanent Positions
within Leisure*
Cloisters House
8 Battersea Park Road, London SW8 4BG
E info@leisurejobs.com
W www.leisurejobs.com

**LUMLEYS HOSPITALITY
& CATERING**　　　T 020 7630 0545
Private & Corporate Hospitality, Catering & Events
Grosvenor Gardens House
35-37 Grosvenor Gardens
London SW1W 0BS
E admin@lumleyscooks.co.uk
W www.lumleyscooks.co.uk

MORTIMER, Angela　　　T 020 7287 7788
*Recruitment Specialists for Perm & Temp PAs & Support
Staff in the UK & Europe*
37-38 Golden Square, London W1F 9LA
E info@angelamortimer.com
W www.angelamortimer.com

NETWORK THE　　　T 020 8742 4336
Field Marketing & Promotions
Merlin House, 20 Belmont Terrace
Chiswick, London W4 5UG
F 020 8742 4051
E recruitment@thenetwork-uk.com
W www.thenetwork-uk.com

OFF TO WORK　　　T 020 7381 8222
*Non-acting Employment. Promotional Work at Events
across the UK*
3rd Floor, 79 Knightsbridge
London SW1X 7RB
E platinum@offtowork.co.uk
W www.offtowork.co.uk

OFFICETEAM　　　T 020 7389 6900
Grand Buildings, 1-3 Strand
London WC2N 5HR
E london@officeteamuk.com
W www.officeteamuk.com

**PERTEMPS RECRUITMENT
PARTNERSHIP**　　　T 020 7621 1304
Recruitment Consultancy
1st Floor, 106 Leadenhall Street
London EC3A 4AA
F 020 7626 6671
E jamie.so@pertemps.co.uk
W www.pertemps.co.uk

RSVP (MEDIA RESPONSE) LTD　　　T 020 7536 3500
Call Centre Work for Performers only
Northern & Shell Tower, 4 Selsdon Way
London E14 9GL
E jobs@rsvp.co.uk
W www.rsvp.co.uk

SENSE STAFFING　　　T 020 7034 2000
Promotional Staffing for Experiential Marketing
2nd Floor, 100 Oxford Street, London W1D 1LN
E staff@senselondon.com
W www.senselondon.com

SEYNER BENSON　　　T 020 7813 2121
*Temporary Non-acting Positions available in Museums &
Galleries in London*
Tudor House, 35 Gresse Street, London W1T 1QY
F 020 7813 1414
E admin@seynerbenson.com

**SMITH, Amanda
RECRUITMENT LTD**　　　T 020 7681 6180
*Recruitment of Temporary, Permanent & Contract Office
Support Staff*
88 Kingsway, Holborn, London WC2B 6AA
E info@as-recruitment.co.uk

STUCKFORSTAFF.CO.UK　　　T 0844 5869595
Promotions, Field Marketing & Brand Experience
116 Zellig, Custard Factory
Gibb Street, Birmingham B9 4AA
E info@stuckforstaff.com
W www.stuckforstaff.co.uk

TRIBE MARKETING LTD　　　T 020 7702 3600
Experiential Marketing & Promotional Staffing Agency
The Wool House, 74 Back Church Lane
Whitechapel, London E1 1LX
E dan.campbell@tribemarketing.co.uk
W www.tribemarketing.co.uk

O →

Opera Companies
Organisations

CARL ROSA PRODUCTIONS LTD
T 020 7613 0777
359 Hackney Road
London E2 8PR
F 020 7613 0859
E info@carlrosaopera.co.uk
W www.carlrosaopera.co.uk

CO-OPERA CO
T 020 8699 8650
Touring Productions. Education. Training. Workshops
5 Metro Business Centre
Kangley Bridge Road
London SE26 5BW
E admin@co-opera-co.org
W www.co-opera-co.org

ENGLISH NATIONAL OPERA
T 020 7836 0111
London Coliseum
St Martin's Lane
London WC2N 4ES
F 020 7845 9277
W www.eno.org

ENGLISH TOURING OPERA
T 020 7833 2555
Contact: James Conway
1st Floor, 52-54 Rosebery Avenue
London EC1R 4RP
F 020 7713 8686
E admin@englishtouringopera.org.uk
W www.englishtouringopera.org.uk

GARSINGTON OPERA
T 01865 368201
The Old Garage, The Green
Great Milton, Oxford OX44 7NP
F 01865 961545
W www.garsingtonopera.org

GLYNDEBOURNE
T 01273 812321
Lewes, East Sussex BN8 5UU
E info@glyndebourne.com
W www.glyndebourne.com

GRANGE PARK OPERA
T 01962 737360
24-26 Broad Street, Alresford
Hampshire SO24 9AQ
E info@grangeparkopera.co.uk
W www.grangeparkopera.co.uk

GUBBAY, Raymond LTD
T 020 7025 3750
Dickens House, 15 Tooks Court
London EC4A 1QH
F 020 7025 3751
E info@raymondgubbay.co.uk
W www.raymondgubbay.co.uk

KENTISH OPERA
T 01732 700993
Contact: Sally Langford
Lakefields Farmhouse
Ide Hill Road, Bough Beech
Kent TN8 7PW
E sl.sweald@fsmail.net
W www.kentishopera.com

LONDON CHILDREN'S OPERA COMPANY
T/F 020 8449 2342
*Capital Arts Opera Minor Foundation. For Students aged
6-18. Rehearsals at Covent Garden Dragon Hall*
E capitalarts@btconnect.com
W www.capitalarts.org.uk

MUSIC THEATRE LONDON
T 07831 243942
c/o Capriol Films
The Old Reading Room
The Street, Brinton
Melton Constable
Norfolk NR24 2QF
E info@capriolfilms.co.uk
W www.capriolfilms.co.uk

OPERA DELLA LUNA
T 01869 325131
7 Cotmore House, Fringford
Bicester, Oxfordshire OX27 8RQ
E enquiries@operadellaluna.org
W www.operadellaluna.org

OPERA NORTH
T 0113 243 9999
Grand Theatre
46 New Briggate
Leeds LS1 6NU
F 0113 244 0418
E info@operanorth.co.uk
W www.operanorth.co.uk

OPERAUK LTD
T 020 7628 0025
Charity
177 Andrewes House
Barbican, London EC2Y 8BA
E rboss4@aol.com
W www.operauk.co.uk

PEGASUS OPERA COMPANY LTD
T/F 020 7501 9501
The Brix, St Matthew's
Brixton Hill, London SW2 1JF
E admin@pegopera.org
W www.pegopera.org

PIMLICO OPERA
T 01962 737360
24 Broad Street, Alresford
Hampshire SO24 9AQ
E pimlico@grangeparkopera.co.uk
W www.grangeparkopera.co.uk

PMB PRESENTATIONS LTD
T 020 7368 3337
Vicarage House
58-60 Kensington Church Street
London W8 4DB
F 020 7368 3338
E p@triciamurraybett.com
W www.pmbpresentations.co.uk

ROYAL OPERA THE
T 020 7240 1200
Royal Opera House, Bow Street
Covent Garden, London WC2E 9DD
W www.roh.org.uk

SCOTTISH OPERA
T 0141 248 4567
39 Elmbank Crescent
Glasgow G2 4PT
E information@scottishopera.org.uk
W www.scottishopera.org.uk

WELSH NATIONAL OPERA
T 029 2063 5000
Wales Millennium Centre
Bute Place
Cardiff CF10 5AL
F 029 2063 5099
E marketing@wno.org.uk
W www.wno.org.uk

A STAGE KINDLY　　　**T** 07947 074887
Develops & Produces New Musicals
7 Northiam, Cromer Street, London WC1H 8LB
E mail@astagekindly.com
W www.astagekindly.com

ABTT (ASSOCIATION OF BRITISH THEATRE TECHNICIANS)　　**T** 020 7242 9200
4th Floor, 55 Farringdon Road, London EC1M 3JB
F 020 7242 9303
E office@abtt.org.uk
W www.abtt.org.uk

ACADEMY OF PERFORMANCE COMBAT THE　　**T** 07963 206803
Teaching Body of Stage Combat
Ivy Villa, 250 Lees New Road, Lees, Lancs OL4 5PP
E info@theapc.org.uk
W www.theapc.org.uk

ACTORS' BENEVOLENT FUND　　**T** 020 7836 6378
6 Adam Street, London WC2N 6AD
F 020 7836 8978
E office@abf.org.uk
W www.actorsbenevolentfund.co.uk

ACTORS CENTRE (LONDON) THE　　**T** 020 7632 8001
Charity. 1700 workshops & courses per year for professional actors. Advice & Information.
Introductory Courses
1A Tower Street, London WC2H 9NP
E reception@actorscentre.co.uk
W www.actorscentre.co.uk

ACTORS' CHARITABLE TRUST　　**T** 020 7636 7868
Provides Advice & Support. Grants for Actors' Children
58 Bloomsbury Street, London WC1B 3QT
F 020 7637 3368
E robert@tactactors.org

ACTORS' CHURCH UNION　　**T** 020 7240 0344
St Paul's Church, Bedford Street, London WC2E 9ED
E actorschurchunion@gmail.com

ADVERTISING ASSOCIATION　　**T** 020 7340 1100
7th Floor North, Artillery House
11-19 Artillery Row, London SW1P 1RT
F 020 7222 1504
E aa@adassoc.org.uk
W www.adassoc.org.uk

AGENTS' ASSOCIATION (GREAT BRITAIN)　　**T** 020 7834 0515
54 Keyes House, Dolphin Square, London SW1V 3NA
E association@agents-uk.com
W www.agents-uk.com

ARTS & BUSINESS　　**T** 020 7566 8650
137 Shepherdess Walk, London N1 7RQ
E info@bitc.org.uk
W www.bitc.org.uk

ARTS CENTRE GROUP　　**T** 0845 4581881
c/o Paintings in Hospitals, 51 Southwark Street
London SE1 1RU
T 020 7407 1881
E info@artscentregroup.org.uk
W www.artscentregroup.org.uk

ARTS COUNCIL ENGLAND
T 0845 3006200
T 020 7973 6564 (Textphone)
W www.artscouncil.org.uk

ARTS COUNCIL OF NORTHERN IRELAND
T 028 9038 5200
MacNeice House, 77 Malone Road
Belfast BT9 6AQ
F 028 9066 1715
E info@artscouncil-ni.org
W www.artscouncil-ni.org

ARTS COUNCIL OF WALES
T 01492 533440
36 Prince's Drive, Colwyn Bay
Conwy LL29 8LA
F 01492 533677
E funding@artswales.org.uk
W www.artswales.org.uk

ARTS COUNCIL OF WALES
T 0845 8734900
4-6 Gardd Llydaw, Jackson Lane
Carmarthen SA31 1QD
F 01267 233084
E funding@artswales.org.uk
W www.artswales.org.uk

ARTS COUNCIL OF WALES
T 029 2044 1360
Bute Place, Cardiff CF10 5AL
F 029 2044 1400
E funding@artswales.org.uk
W www.artswales.org.uk

ARTSLINE
T 020 7388 2227
Disability Access Information Service
c/o 21 Pine Court, Wood Lodge Gardens
Bromley BR1 2WA
E admin@artsline.org.uk
W www.artsline.org.uk

ASSOCIATION OF LIGHTING DESIGNERS
T 07817 060189
PO Box 955, Southsea PO1 9NF
E office@ald.org.uk
W www.ald.org.uk

ASSOCIATION OF MODEL AGENTS
T 020 7422 0699
11-29 Fashion Street, London E1 6PX
E amainfo@btinternet.com
W www.associationofmodelagents.org

BASCA - BRITISH ACADEMY OF SONGWRITERS, COMPOSERS & AUTHORS
T 020 7636 2929
2nd Floor, British Music House
26 Berners Street, London W1T 3LR
F 020 7636 2212
E info@basca.org.uk
W www.basca.org.uk

BFI SOUTH BANK
T 020 7928 3232
Belvedere Road, South Bank, London SE1 8XT
W www.bfi.org.uk

BRITISH ACADEMY OF FILM & TELEVISION ARTS
T 020 7734 0022
195 Piccadilly, London W1J 9LN
E info@bafta.org
W www.bafta.org

BRITISH ACADEMY OF FILM & TELEVISION ARTS LOS ANGELES
T 001 323 658 6590
8469 Melrose Avenue, West Hollywood
CA 90069, USA
E office@baftala.org
W www.bafta.org/losangeles

BRITISH ACADEMY OF STAGE & SCREEN COMBAT
T 07981 806265
Suite 280, 10 Great Russell Street
London WC1B 3BQ
E info@bassc.org
W www.bassc.org

BRITISH ASSOCIATION FOR PERFORMING ARTS MEDICINE (BAPAM)
T 020 7404 8444
Charity
4th Floor, Totara Park House
34-36 Gray's Inn Road
London WC1X 8HR
E clinic@bapam.org.uk
W www.bapam.org.uk

BRITISH ASSOCIATION OF DRAMATHERAPISTS THE
T 01242 235515
Waverley, Battledown Approach
Cheltenham, Glos GL52 6RE
E enquiries@badth.org.uk
W www.badth.org.uk

BRITISH BOARD OF FILM CLASSIFICATION
T 020 7440 1570
3 Soho Square, London W1D 3HD
F 020 7287 0141
W www.bbfc.co.uk

BRITISH COUNCIL
T 020 7389 3194
Arts Group
10 Spring Gardens, London SW1A 2BN
E arts@britishcouncil.org
W www.britishcouncil.org/arts

BRITISH EQUITY COLLECTING SOCIETY
T 020 7670 0360
1st Floor, Guild House
Upper St Martin's Lane
London WC2H 9EG
E becs@equity.org.uk
W www.equitycollecting.org.uk

BRITISH FILM INSTITUTE
T 020 7255 1444
21 Stephen Street, London W1T 1LN
F 020 7436 0165
W www.bfi.org.uk

BRITISH LIBRARY SOUND ARCHIVE
T 020 7412 7831
96 Euston Road, London NW1 2DB
F 020 7412 7691
E sound-archive@bl.uk
W www.bl.uk/soundarchive

BRITISH MUSIC HALL SOCIETY
T 01727 768878
Contact: Daphne Masterton (Secretary). Charity
45 Mayflower Road, Park Street
St Albans, Herts AL2 2QN
W www.music-hall-society.com

CATHOLIC ASSOCIATION OF PERFORMING ARTS
T 020 7240 1221
Contact: Ms Molly Steele (Hon Secretary). By Post (SAE)
1 Maiden Lane
London WC2E 7NB
E secretary@caapa.org.uk
W www.caapa.org.uk

CELEBRITY BULLETIN THE
T 020 8672 3191
98 Battersea Studios
80 Silverthorne Road
London SW8 3HE
F 020 8672 2282
E enquiries@celebrity-bulletin.co.uk

WE CAN HELP ACTORS' CHILDREN

Are you:

- a professional actor?
- the parent of a child under 21?
- having trouble with finances?

Please get in touch for a confidential chat.

The Actors' Charitable Trust
020 7636 7868
robert@tactactors.org

TACT can help in many ways: with regular monthly payments, one-off grants, and long-term support and advice.
We help with clothing, child-care, music lessons, school trips, special equipment and adaptations, and in many other ways.

Our website has a link to a list of all the theatrical and entertainment charities which might be able to help you if you do not have children: www.tactactors.org

TACT, 58 Bloomsbury Street, London C1B 3QT.
Registered charity number 206809.

CIDA CO　　　　　　**T** 0113 373 1754
The Creative & Innovation Company
Munro House, Duke Street
Leeds LS9 8AG
E info@cida.org
W www.cida.org

CINEMA & TELEVISION
BENEVOLENT FUND (CTBF)　**T** 020 7437 6567
22 Golden Square, London W1F 9AD
F 020 7437 7186
E charity@ctbf.co.uk
W www.ctbf.co.uk

CINEMA EXHIBITORS'
ASSOCIATION　　　　**T** 020 7734 9551
22 Golden Square, London W1F 9JW
F 020 7734 6147
E info@cinemauk.org.uk
W www.cinemauk.org.uk

CLUB FOR ACTS &
ACTORS　　　　**T** 020 7836 2884 (Members)
Incorporating Concert Artistes Association
20 Bedford Street, London WC2E 9HP
T 020 7836 3172 (Office)
E office@thecaa.org
W www.thecaa.org

COMPANY OF CRANKS　**T** 07963 617981
1st Floor, 62 Northfield House
Frensham Street, London SE15 6TN
E mimetic16@yahoo.com
W www.mimeworks.com

CONCERT ARTISTES ASSOCIATION
See CLUB FOR ACTS & ACTORS

COUNCIL FOR DANCE EDUCATION &
TRAINING (CDET)　　　**T** 020 7240 5703
Old Brewer's Yard, 17-19 Neal Street
London WC2H 9UY
F 020 7240 2547
E info@cdet.org.uk
W www.cdet.org.uk

CREATIVE SCOTLAND　**T** 0141 302 1700
249 West George Street, Glasgow G2 4QE
F 0141 302 1711
E enquiries@creativescotland.com
W www.creativescotland.com

CRITICS' CIRCLE THE　**T** 020 7483 1181
c/o Catherine Cooper Events
PO Box 59382
London NW8 1HG
W www.criticscircle.org.uk

DANCE HOUSE　　　**T** 0141 552 2442
The Briggait, 141 Bridgegate
Glasgow G1 5HZ
E info@dancehouse.org
W www.dancehouse.org

DANCE UK　　　　**T** 020 7713 0730
*Including the Healthier Dancer Programme & 'The UK
Choreographers' Directory'. Professional Body & Charity,
providing Advice, Information & Support*
The Urdang, The Old Finsbury Town Hall
Rosebery Avenue
London EC1R 4QT
F 020 7833 2363
E info@danceuk.org
W www.danceuk.org

DENVILLE HALL　　　**T** 01923 825843
*Provides residential & nursing care to actors & other
theatrical professions*
62 Ducks Hill Road, Northwood
Middlesex HA6 2SB
E office@denvillehall.org.uk
W www.denvillehall.org.uk

DIRECTORS UK　　　**T** 020 7240 0009
Inigo Place, 31 & 32 Bedford Street
London WC2E 9ED
F 020 7845 9700
E info@directors.uk.com
W www.directors.uk.com

DON'T PLAY ME PAY ME CAMPAIGN
*Campaigning for a Greater Representation of Disabled
Talent in the Entertainment Industry*
E peoplenotpunchlines@gmail.com
W www.dontplaymepayme.com

D'OYLY CARTE
OPERA COMPANY　　**T** 0844 6060007
295 Kennington Road, London SE11 4QE
F 020 7820 0240
E ian@doylycarte.org.uk
W www.doylycarte.org.uk

DRAMA ASSOCIATION
OF WALES　　　　**T** 029 2045 2200
Specialist Drama Lending Library
Unit 2, The Maltings
East Tyndall Street
Cardiff Bay, Cardiff CF24 5EA
E teresa@dramawales.org.uk
W www.dramawales.org.uk

DRAMA UK　　　　**T** 020 7407 3686
*Formerly Conference of Drama Schools & National
Council for Drama Training*
23 Tavistock Street, London WC2E 7NX
E info@dramauk.co.uk
W www.dramauk.co.uk

DRAMATURGS' NETWORK　**T** 07939 270566
*UK-wide Voluntary Network of Professional
Dramaturgs. Explores Dramaturgy & Supports
Practitioners' Development*
Twitter: @dramaturgs_net
16 Warner Road, London E17 7DZ
E info@dramaturgy.co.uk
W www.dramaturgy.co.uk

ENGLISH FOLK DANCE &
SONG SOCIETY　　　**T** 020 7485 2206
Cecil Sharp House
2 Regent's Park Road, London NW1 7AY
F 020 7284 0534
E info@efdss.org
W www.efdss.org

EQUITY CHARITABLE TRUST　**T** 020 7831 1926
Plouviez House, 19-20 Hatton Place
London EC1N 8RU
E info@equitycharitabletrust.org.uk

FILM LONDON　　　**T** 020 7613 7676
Suite 6.10, The Tea Building
56 Shoreditch High Street, London E1 6JJ
F 020 7613 7677
E info@filmlondon.org.uk
W www.filmlondon.org.uk

❖

THE RALPH AND MERIEL RICHARDSON FOUNDATION

Please support us as we provide grants to relieve the need, hardship, or distress of British actors and actresses, their spouses and children.

Please consider including the Foundation in your Will, or sending a donation to the address below, as any amount will be warmly welcomed.

Please help to spread awareness of this very special charity and encourage anyone who needs assistance to be in contact with us.

Address: C/o Suite 23, 19 Cavendish Square, London W1A 2AW
W: sirralphrichardson.org.uk   E: manager@sirralphrichardson.org.uk   T: 020 7636 1616

GLASGOW FILM OFFICE   T 0141 287 0424
Free Advice & Liaison Support for all Productions
231 George Street
Glasgow G1 1RX
F 0141 287 0311
E info@glasgowfilm.com

**GRAND ORDER OF
WATER RATS**   T 020 7278 3248
328 Gray's Inn Road
London WC1X 8BZ
E info@gowr.net
W www.gowr.net

GROUP LINE   T 020 7580 6793
Group Bookings for London Theatre
22-24 Torrington Place
London WC1E 7HJ
F 020 7436 6287
E tix@groupline.com
W www.groupline.com

**HAMMER FILMS
PRESERVATION SOCIETY**   T 020 8854 7383
Fan Club
14 Kingsdale Road, Plumstead
London SE18 2DG
E maylott@btinternet.com

**INDEPENDENT THEATRE
COUNCIL (ITC)**   T 020 7403 1727
*Professional Body offering Advice, Information,
Support & Political Representation*
The Albany, Douglas Way
London SE8 4AG
F 020 7403 1746
E admin@itc-arts.org
W www.itc-arts.org

INTERNATIONAL CENTRE FOR VOICE
Central School of Speech & Drama
Eton Avenue
London NW3 3HY
E icv@cssd.ac.uk
W www.icvoice.co.uk

IRVING SOCIETY THE   T 020 8566 8301
Contact: Michael Kilgarriff (Hon. Secretary)
10 Kings Avenue
London W5 2SH
E secretary@theirvingsociety.org.uk
W www.theirvingsociety.org.uk

ITC
See INDEPENDENT THEATRE COUNCIL (ITC)

**LONDON SCHOOL
OF CAPOEIRA THE**   T 020 7281 2020
Units 1 & 2 Leeds Place, Tollington Park
London N4 3RF
E info@londonschoolofcapoeira.com
W www.londonschoolofcapoeira.com

**LONDON SHAKESPEARE
WORKOUT**   T/F 020 7793 9755
PO Box 31855, London SE17 3XP
E londonswo@hotmail.com
W www.lswproductions.co.uk

**NATIONAL ASSOCIATION OF
YOUTH THEATRES (NAYT)**   T 07515 651481
*Contact: Henry Raby. Founded in 1982, NAYT works
with over 1,000 groups & individuals to support the
development of youth theatre activity through information
& support services, advocacy, training, participation &
partnerships*
c/o York Theatre Royal, St Leonards Place
York YO1 7HD
E info@nayt.org.uk
W www.nayt.org.uk

**NATIONAL CAMPAIGN
FOR THE ARTS**   T 020 7240 4698
17 Tavistock Street, London WC2E 7PA
E nca@artscampaign.org.uk
W www.artscampaign.org.uk

**NATIONAL RESOURCE CENTRE
FOR DANCE**   T 01483 689316
University of Surrey, Guildford, Surrey GU2 7XH
F 01483 689500
E nrcd@surrey.ac.uk
W www.surrey.ac.uk/nrcd

**NODA (National Operatic &
Dramatic Association)**   T 01733 865790
*Charity, providing Advice, Information & Support. Largest
umbrella body for amateur theatre in the UK offering
advice & assistance on all aspects of amateur theatre
plus workshops, summer school and social events*
Noda House, 58-60 Lincoln Road
Peterborough PE1 2RZ
F 01733 319506
E info@noda.org.uk
W www.noda.org.uk

NORTH WEST PLAYWRIGHTS T/F 0161 237 1978
*Charity. Independent Agency Developing & Supporting
Scriptwriters in All Media. Provides Training, Advice,
Workshops & Information*
18 Express Networks, 1 George Leigh Street
Manchester M4 5DL
E newplaysnw@hotmail.com
W www.northwestplaywrights.co.uk

OFCOM T 0300 1234000
Ofcom Media Office, Riverside House
2A Southwark Bridge Road, London SE1 9HA
E ofcomnews@ofcom.org.uk
W www.ofcom.org.uk

PACT T 020 7380 8230
*Trade Association for Independent Television, Feature
Film & New Media Production Companies*
3rd Floor, Fitzrovia House
153-157 Cleveland Street, London W1T 6QW
E info@pact.co.uk
W www.pact.co.uk

PRS FOR MUSIC T 020 7580 5544
29-33 Berners Street, London W1T 3AB
F 020 7306 4455
W www.prsformusic.com

**RICHARDSON, Ralph & Meriel
FOUNDATION** T 020 7636 1616
c/o Suite 23, 19 Cavendish Square, London W1A 2AW
F 020 7664 4489
E manager@sirralphrichardson.org.uk
W www.sirralphrichardson.org.uk

ROYAL TELEVISION SOCIETY T 020 7822 2810
Kildare House, 3 Dorset Rise, London EC4Y 8EN
F 020 7822 2811
E info@rts.org.uk
W www.rts.org.uk

ROYAL THEATRICAL FUND T 020 7836 3322
11 Garrick Street, London WC2E 9AR
F 020 7379 8273
E admin@trtf.com

SAMPAD SOUTH ASIAN ARTS T 0121 446 3260
*Promotes the Appreciation & Practice of South
Asian Arts*
c/o Mac, Cannon Hill Park, Birmingham B12 9QH
E info@sampad.org.uk
W www.sampad.org.uk

SOCIETY OF AUTHORS T 020 7373 6642
*Trade Union for Professional Writers. Providing Advice,
Funding, Information & Support*
84 Drayton Gardens, London SW10 9SB
E info@societyofauthors.org
W www.societyofauthors.org

**SOCIETY OF BRITISH
THEATRE DESIGNERS** T 020 8308 2664
*Professional Body. Charity. Providing Advice &
Information*
Rose Bruford College of Theatre & Performance
Burnt Oak Lane
Sidcup, Kent DA15 9DF
E admin@theatredesign.org.uk
W www.theatredesign.org.uk

**SOCIETY OF LONDON
THEATRE THE (SOLT)** T 020 7557 6700
32 Rose Street, London WC2E 9ET
F 020 7557 6799
E enquiries@solttma.co.uk

**SOCIETY OF TEACHERS OF SPEECH &
DRAMA THE** T 01623 627636
Registered Office: 73 Berry Hill Road, Mansfield
Nottinghamshire NG18 4RU
E ann.k.jones@btinternet.com
W www.stsd.org.uk

**SOCIETY OF THEATRE
CONSULTANTS** T 020 7419 8767
27 Old Gloucester Street, London WC1N 3AX
W www.theatreconsultants.org.uk

STAGE CRICKET CLUB T 020 7402 7543
39-41 Hanover Steps, St George's Fields
Albion Street, London W2 2YG
F 020 7262 5736
E brianjfilm@aol.com
W www.stagecc.co.uk

STAGE GOLFING SOCIETY T 020 8940 8861
Sudbrook Park, Sudbrook Lane
Richmond, Surrey TW10 7AS
E sgs@richmondgolfclub.co.uk

**STAGE MANAGEMENT
ASSOCIATION** T 020 7403 7999
*Providing Advice, Information & Support. Promotes,
represents & champions stage management & all its
practitioners. Provides help finding work, training &
networking opportunities & advice*
89 Borough High Street, London SE1 1NL
E admin@stagemanagementassociation.co.uk
W www.stagemanagementassociation.co.uk

STAGE ONE T 020 7557 6737
Operating Name of The Theatre Investment Fund Ltd
32 Rose Street, London WC2E 9ET
F 020 7557 6799
E enquiries@stageone.uk.com
W www.stageone.uk.com

**THEATREMAD (THEATRE: MAKING
A DIFFERENCE)** T 020 7240 8206
*The Make A Difference Trust raises funds to support
people living with HIV, AIDS & other long-term medical
conditions. UK Charity Registration No. 1124014*
c/o The Make A Difference Trust, 1st Floor
28 Denmark Street
London WC2H 8NJ
F 020 7240 3573
E office@madtrust.org.uk
W www.madtrust.org.uk

THEATRES TRUST THE T 020 7836 8591
*Contact: Kate Carmichael (Resources Officer). National
Advisory Public Body for Theatres, Protecting Theatres
for Everyone. Charity. Social Membership. Provides
Advice, Support & Information*
22 Charing Cross Road, London WC2H 0QL
F 020 7836 3302
E info@theatrestrust.org.uk
W www.theatrestrust.org.uk

THEATRICAL GUILD THE T 020 7240 6062
Charity for Theatre Staff
11 Garrick Street, London WC2E 9AR
E admin@ttg.org.uk
W www.ttg.org.uk

**TMA (THEATRICAL MANAGEMENT
ASSOCIATION)** T 020 7557 6700
32 Rose Street, London WC2E 9ET
F 020 7557 6799
E enquiries@solttma.co.uk
W www.tmauk.org

TYA - UK CENTRE OF ASSITEJ T 0121 245 2092
*International Association of Theatre for Children & Young
People. Network for makers & promoters of professional
theatre for young audiences*
c/o Birmingham Repertory Theatre, St George's Court
Albion Street, Birmingham B1 2EP
E secretary@tya.uk.org
W www.tya-uk.org

UK CHOREOGRAPHERS' DIRECTORY THE
See DANCE UK

UK THEATRE CLUBS T 020 8459 3972
54 Swallow Drive, London NW10 8TG
E uktheatreclubs@aol.com

**UNITED KINGDOM
COPYRIGHT BUREAU** T 01273 277333
110 Trafalgar Road, Portslade
East Sussex BN41 1GS
E info@copyrightbureau.co.uk
W www.copyrightbureau.co.uk

**UNIVERSITY OF BRISTOL
THEATRE COLLECTION** T 0117 331 5086
Formerly Mander & Mitcheson Theatre Collection
Department of Drama, Cantocks Close
Bristol BS8 1UP
F 0117 331 5082
E theatre-collection@bristol.ac.uk

**VARIETY & LIGHT ENTERTAINMENT
COUNCIL (VLEC)** T 020 7798 5622
54 Keyes House, Dolphin Square, London SW1V 3NA
E association@agents-uk.com
W www.vlec.org.uk

**VARIETY, THE CHILDREN'S
CHARITY** T 020 7428 8100
Variety Club House
93 Bayham Street
London NW1 0AG
F 020 7428 8111
E info@variety.org.uk
W www.variety.org.uk

WILLIAMS, Tim AWARDS T 020 7793 9755
*In memory of LSW's late musical director. Seeking to
support excellence in the composition of theatrical song*
PO Box 31855, London SE17 3XP
E londonswo@hotmail.com
W www.lswproductions.co.uk

**WOMEN IN FILM &
TELEVISION (UK)** T 020 7287 1400
*Contact: Nelle Strange. WFTV is the premier
membership organisation for women working in creative
media in the UK and part of an international network
of over 10,000 women worldwide. Provides Advice,
Information, Social Membership & Support*
Unit 2, Wedgwood Mews
12-13 Greek Street
London W1D 4BB
E info@wftv.org.uk
W www.wftv.org.uk

**YOUTH MUSIC THEATRE UK
(YMT)** T 0844 4154858
40 Parkgate Road, Battersea
London SW11 4JH
E mail@ymtuk.org
W www.youthmusictheatreuk.org

P

Photographers: Advertisers Only
Promotional Services:
CVs, Showreels, Websites etc
Properties & Trades
Publications: Print & Online
Publicity & Press Representatives

Each photographer listed in this section
has taken an advertisement in this edition.
See Index to Advertisers pages to view
each advertisement.

Photographers

How do I find a photographer?

Having a good quality, up-to-date promotional headshot is crucial for every performer. Make sure you choose your photographer very carefully: do some research and try to look at different examples. Photographers' adverts run throughout this edition, featuring many sample shots, although to get a real feel for their work you should also try to see their portfolio or website since this will give a more accurate impression of the quality of their photography.

If you live in or around London, please feel free to visit the Spotlight offices and look through current editions of our directories to find a style you like. We also have nearly sixty photographers' portfolios available for you to browse, many of them from photographers listed in this edition. Our offices are open Monday - Friday, 10.00am - 5.30pm at 7 Leicester Place, London WC2H 7RJ (nearest tube is Leicester Square).

What should I expect from the photo shoot?

When it comes to your photo shoot, bear in mind that a casting director, agent or production company will want to see a photo of the 'real' you. Keep your appearance as neutral as possible so that they can imagine you in many different roles, rather than type-casting yourself from the outset and limiting your opportunities.

Your eyes are your most important feature, so make sure they are visible: face the camera straight-on and try not to smile too much because it makes them harder to see. Wear something simple and avoid jewellery, hats, scarves, glasses or props, since these will all add character. Do not wear clothes that detract from your face such as polo necks, big collars, busy patterns or logos. Always keep your hands out of the shot.

Also consider the background: some photographers like to do outdoor shots. A contrast between background and hair colour works well, whereas dark backgrounds work less well with dark hair, and the same goes for light hair on light backgrounds.

Which photograph should I choose?

When you get your contact sheet or digital proofs back from the photographer, make sure you choose a photo that looks like you - not how you would like to look. If you are unsure, ask friends or your agent for an honest opinion. Remember, you will be asked to attend meetings and auditions on the basis of your photograph, so if you turn up looking completely different you will be wasting everyone's time.

Due to copyright legislation, you must always credit the photographer when using the photo.

How should I submit my photo to Spotlight and to casting professionals?

All photographs submitted to Spotlight must be of the highest possible quality, otherwise casting professionals will not see you in the best possible light. If you are sending your photo by hard copy, we would expect a 10 x 8 sized print, which is the industry standard. It is not necessary to provide an original print: a high quality, clear focused repro is fine. If you are sending a digital image by e-mail or disk, we have certain technical specifications which can be found on our website. We would recommend that you follow similar guidelines when sending your headshot directly to casting professionals.

What are Spotlight portfolio photographs?

Every Spotlight performer can also add extra photographs onto their web page, in addition to their principal photograph. These are called portfolio photos, and they give you the opportunity to show yourself in a range of different shots and/or roles. Members can upload up to 15 digital photos to their online CV free of charge by logging on with their update PIN to www.spotlight.com

Please visit www.spotlightcom/ artists/multimediaphotoguidelines for further information.

ALLEN, Stuart
T 07776 258829
W www.stuartallenphotos.com

AM LONDON
T 020 7193 1868
T 07974 188105
W www.am-london.com

ANKER, Matt
T 07835 241835
W www.mattanker.com

ANNAND, Simon
T 07884 446776
W www.simonannand.com

BACON, Ric
T 07970 970799
E ricbacon@gmail.com
W www.ricbacon.co.uk

BADRAN, Zina
T 07813 845849
E headshots@zinabadran.com
W www.zinabadran.com

BARTLETT, Pete
T 07971 653994
E info@petebartlett.com
W www.petebartlettheadshots.co.uk

BISHOP, Brandon
T 020 7275 7468
T 07931 383830
W www.brandonbishopphotography.com

BOSTOCK, Richard
T 07702 131557
W www.richardbostockphotography.co.uk

BURNETT, Sheila
T 020 7289 3058
W www.sheilaburnett-headshots.com

CABLE, Paul
T 07958 932764
E info@paulcable.com
W www.paulcable.com

CLARK, John
T 07702 627237
W www.johnclarkphotography.com

EVANS, Maxine
T 07966 130426
E maxinevans@aol.com
W www.maxineevansphotography.co.uk

GREGAN, Nick
T 020 8533 3003
T 07774 421878
E info@nickgregan.com
W www.nickgregan.com

GROGAN, Claire
T 020 7272 1845
T 07932 635381
E claire@clairegrogan.co.uk
W www.clairegrogan.co.uk

THEHEADSHOT.CO.UK
T 07899 847173
E jess@theheadshot.co.uk
W www.theheadshot.co.uk

HOSKIN, Ian
T 07773 902071
E info@ianhoskin.co.uk
W www.ianhoskin.co.uk

HULL, Anna
T 07778 399419
E info@annahullphotography.com
W www.annahullphotography.com

JAMIE, Matt
T 07976 890643
E photos@mattjamie.co.uk
W www.mattjamie.co.uk/portraits

LADENBURG, Jack
T 07932 053743
E info@jackladenburg.co.uk
W www.jackladenburg.co.uk

LATIMER, Carole
T 020 7727 9371
E carole@carolelatimer.com
W www.carolelatimer.com

LAWTON, Steve
T 07973 307487
W www.stevelawton.com

M.A.D. PHOTOGRAPHY
T 07949 581909
E mad.photo@talktalk.net
W www.mad-photography.co.uk

MERCHANT, Natasha
T 07932 618111
E natashamerchant@mac.com
W www.natashamerchant.com

PROCTOR, Carl
T 07956 283340
E carlphotos@btconnect.com
W www.carlproctorphotography.com

RED BOX STUDIOS
T 01253 406392
T 07785 587920
W www.redboxstudios.co.uk

RUOCCO, Alex
T 07732 293231
W www.alexruoccophotography.co.uk

SAVAGE, Robin
T 07901 927597
E contact@robinsavage.co.uk
W www.robinsavage.co.uk

SAYER, Howard
T 020 8123 0251
E info@howardsayer.co.uk
W www.howardsayer.co.uk

SCOTT, Karen
T 07958 975950
E info@karenscottphotography.com
W www.karenscottphotography.com

SELL, David
T 07957 302934
E david@davidsell.co.uk
W www.davidsell.co.uk

SHAKESPEARE LANE, Catherine
T 020 7226 7694
W www.csl-art.co.uk

SIMPKIN, Peter
T 020 8364 2634
T 07973 224084
E petersimpkin@aol.com
W www.petersimpkin.co.uk

THORN, Gavin
T 01483 299993
E contacts@gavinthorn.com
W www.gavinthorn.com/contacts

TOMKINSON, Simon
T 07812 181415
W www.simontomkinson.com

ULLATHORNE, Steve
T 07961 380969
W www.steveullathorne.com

VALENTINE, Vanessa
T 07904 059541
W www.vanessavalentinephotography.com

VANDYCK, Katie
W www.excellentheadshots.co.uk

WADE, Philip
T 020 7226 3088
T 07956 599691
E pix@philipwade.com
W www.philipwade.com

WEBSTER, Caroline
T 07867 653019
E caroline@carolinewebster.co.uk
W www.carolinewebster.co.uk

WHARLEY, Michael
W www.michaelwharley.com

WORKMAN, Robert
T 020 7385 5442
W www.robertworkman.demon.co.uk

Promotional Services

What are promotional services?

This section contains listings for companies who provide practical services to help performers promote themselves. You might need to improve or create your CV; record a showreel or voicereel; design your own website; duplicate CDs; or print photographic repros, CVs or Z-cards: all essential ways to create a good impression with those that count in the industry.

Why do I need to promote myself?

Performers need to invest in marketing and promotion as much as any other self-employed businessperson. Even if you have trained at a leading drama school, have a well-known agent, or have just finished work on a popular TV series, you should never sit back and wait for your phone to ring or for the next job opportunity just to knock on your door. In such a competitive industry, successful performers are usually the ones who market themselves pro-actively and treat their careers as a 'business'.

Having up-to-date and well-produced promotional material makes a performer look professional and serious about their career: and hence a desirable person for a director or agent to work with.

Why is my CV important?

Poor presentation, punctuation and grammar create a bad first impression and you risk your CV being dismissed before it is even read. Make sure that you continually update your CV – you don't want it to look as if you haven't been working recently when you have, and you don't want to miss out on an audition because you haven't included skills you have put time and effort into achieving. Your CV should be kept to a maximum of one page and printed on good-quality paper.

Why do I need a covering letter?

Always include a covering letter to introduce your CV and persuade casting professionals that it is worth reading. Remember that they receive hundreds each week. Keep your communication concise and be professional at all times. We also recommend that your letter has some kind of focus: perhaps you can tell them about your next showcase, or where they can see you currently appearing on stage. Ideally this should be addressed to an individual, not "Dear Sir or Madam".

Why is my headshot important?

Your CV should feature, or be accompanied by, a recent headshot which is an accurate current likeness. See the 'Photographers' section for more information about promotional photography. You may need to print copies of your headshot through a repro company, some of whom are listed over the following pages.

Why do I need a voicereel?

If you are interested in voice-over and/or radio work, you will need a professional-sounding voicereel to show agents, casting directors and potential employers what your voice is capable of. For commercial and corporate voice-over work this should be no more than two minutes long with a number of short clips demonstrating your range, but showcase the strengths of your natural voice as much as possible. It should contain a mixture of commercials and narrations.

A radio voicereel should be around eight minutes long, with four clips no longer than two minutes each, and read in your natural voice. To achieve a good balance of material, one clip should be 'classical', one 'contemporary', one 'comic' and one a poem. This is designed to give an overview of your suitability to various areas of radio work.

Record your voicereel in a professional studio to ensure a high-quality result, otherwise you are unlikely to be considered in this competitive industry. For further information please see the 'Agents: Voice-Over' and 'Radio' sections.

Why do I need a showreel?

Some casting directors nowadays will only consider a performer for an audition if they have first seen them demonstrating their skills in a showreel. A CV and headshot give some indication of their potential, but can only provide a basic summary.

What should I do if I don't currently have anything on film?

Showreels are expensive to produce if you don't currently have any broadcasted material to use, but it is advisable to get one professionally recorded and edited if at all possible. Showreels help you to promote yourself, but a casting director may be put off by a poor quality one. You might want to consider a Spotlight Intro as a temporary alternative to a full showreel (see the next page). It may also be worth considering working on a student film. Students are usually willing to let you keep a copy of their film and casting professionals would consider this an acceptable alternative. See 'Film & Television Schools' for further advice and listings.

How long should my showreel be?

We would recommend no more than three or four minutes. Casting professionals receive thousands of CVs and showreels and do not have time to watch every actor for ten minutes each. This is why we suggest you do not send your showreel out with your CV, but instead mention in your covering letter that one is available.

What should I use in my showreel?

Rather than one long excerpt, it is more beneficial to demonstrate your versatility with a number of different clips. Focus on your strongest characters to enable the casting director to picture you in the roles you play best.

The first 30 seconds are the most important in your showreel, and can be the only part a busy casting director or agent has time to look at. You may wish to start with a brief montage summarising the clips that are to follow, or with a headshot of yourself so that they know who to watch out for. Avoid noisy musical/uptempo soundtracks where possible and cut straight to the action.

The focus should be on you, not on the other actors, so close-up shots ought to be included. You should be speaking most if not all of the time. A visual contrast is good, whether this means filming in a different location or setting, or changing your outfit. You should avoid well-known scripts in order to prevent drawing comparisons between yourself and previous successful interpretations.

What is a *Spotlight Intro?*

If you are a Spotlight member, a *Spotlight Intro* is your opportunity to give casting professionals a quick introduction to you, your character and your voice with a one or two minute video as part of your Spotlight CV. Think of it as a video version of a covering letter you might enclose with a paper CV. It could also be used as a temporary alternative to a showreel, although ideally you should include both. For further please visit www.spotlight.com/spotlightintro

How should I use these listings?

If you are looking for a company to help you with any of these promotional items, browse through this section carefully and get quotes from a number of places to compare. If you are a Spotlight member, some companies offer a discount on their services. Always ask to see samples of a company's work, and ask friends in the industry for their own recommendations.

Promotional Services

CASE STUDY

Marina Caldarone is Drama Producer for Crying Out Loud, a company specialising in making voicereels, now in its 14th year. She is also an acting coach, a radio drama producer and theatre director. She is co-author of the best-selling *Actions: The Actor's Thesaurus.*

What are voicereels?

It's all about expanding your casting possibilities, be it radio drama, advertising, corporate, animation, gaming, narrative etc. Without a voicereel, producers of content can't translate your CV into what you sound like… in spite of your credits. They are an essential part of this multi-media landscape.

How do you choose a voicereel company?

It's partly about taste – some studios will have a chat with you over the phone, get the measure of your voice and e-mail you material that might be a perfect fit for you to come in and record later; others don't have this 'consultation' at all but prefer you to turn up at the studio and be given material there and then to try, live on the microphone; whilst others have the consultation face-to-face in order to ensure that the choice is spot on, and then record a few days/weeks later – it goes without saying that meeting the company face-to-face to select content is by far the best route.

Look at each company's testimonials, check out their previous clients, and listen to examples of their work on their website. If these examples don't exist, be wary. You could spend anything from £150 to £500. You should also expect to be directed by at least one professional producer, not by a studio manager or technician – you need to know you are in safe hands and be guided through the recording session.

What material to include?

Play to your strengths, but also be realistic about the market for your voice: bring your ideas to the table, but let the voicereel company guide you. The case is subjective. You should include at least three commercials, each showing a different 'sell' in your natural range, plus a documentary, drama (this is where you can include your non-native but exceptionally good accent if you really feel you need to show another accent), and an extract from a novel, perhaps, if that's an obvious place for your voice; if not, then a contrasting documentary or drama or even corporate styles would do.

It goes without saying that not all voices suit all areas of voice-over work – a good voicereel company will guide you in the right direction so as to maximise on your chances of breaking into voice-overs that fall naturally within your range.

What to expect

You should expect to receive a full recording of all the tracks you recorded, and 2 one-minute megamixes, divided firstly into a commercials megamix and secondly into a drama/narrative megamix: these are 'best of' compilations that you can use on your Spotlight profile.

You may prefer to have an all-in-one megamix of no longer than two minutes, but increasingly commercial studios are expressing a preference for a commercial reel and a narrative/drama reel.

Once you have your voicereel

Think of yourself as a brand – all brands need marketing. After recording your reel, *do your homework:* have a good listen to the talent on voice-over agents' websites and contact ones where you think your voice would fit alongside their current clients. Be objective. Send them your two megamix clips and be sure to include your Spotlight View PIN. Chase any agent that expresses an interest but do not be a pest. Tip: forward-thinking agents will accept e-mail submissions these days so don't rush into burning 100 copies of your voicereel CD! You can also tackle the list of contacts that your voicereel company should have given you with your reel, and methodically target each and every relevant potential employer with your voice clips – it costs nothing and it's all electronic – just be sure to be professional, courteous and upbeat.

The animation CD

This is totally different from your regular voicereel. If you're interested in animation then ask your production company to include an animation track that illustrates some of your skills in that area.

Top tip!

Some studios charge you a hire fee for the studio and engineer and invite you to bring your own material – this can be extremely risky and we'd only recommend this if you are an experienced voice-over and know exactly where your voice sits. The right material is a critical part of the process – if it isn't right for you, however well you lift it off the page, however cleverly it is edited, it won't be 'right'. This judgment should be made by you *with* the company making the reel: they can best assess your voice objectively.

> **To find out more about Crying Out Loud Productions visit www.cryingoutloud.co.uk**

SHOWREELS
ACTORS
PRESENTERS
SINGERS
MAGICIANS
STUNTS

WWW.STAGESCAPTURETHEMOMENT.COM

TEL: 020 7193 8519
MOB: 07786 813812

10X8PRINTS.COM　　T 07783 590509
E info@10x8prints.com
W www.10x8prints.com

2PRODUCTION　　T 020 7993 4675
Professional Management Voice Over Direction & CDs
E voice@2production.com
W www.2production.com

A1 VOX LTD　　T 020 7434 4404
Audio Clips. Demo CDs. ISDN Links. Spoken
Word Audio
20 Old Compton Street
London W1D 4TW
E info@a1vox.com
W www.a1vox.com

ABBEY ROAD STUDIOS　　T 020 7266 7000
3 Abbey Road, St John's Wood
London NW8 9AY
F 020 7266 7250
E bookings@abbeyroad.com
W www.abbeyroad.com

ABBEY SHOWREELS　　T 020 8544 1944
10B, The 1929 Shop
Merton Abbey Mills
London SW19 2RD
E info@abbeyshowreels.co.uk
W www.abbeyshowreels.co.uk

ABSOLUTE WORKS LTD　　T 01525 385400
Danson House, Manor Farm Lane
Ledburn, Bucks LU7 0UG
T 07778 934307
E absoluteworks@btinternet.com
W www.absoluteworks.com

ACTOR SHOWREELS　　T 07853 637965
Showreel Service
97B Central Hill, London SE19 1BY
E post@actorshowreels.co.uk
W www.actorshowreels.co.uk

ACTORS CENTRE　　T 020 7240 3940
1A Tower Street
London WC2H 9NP
E film@actorscentre.co.uk
W www.actorscentre.co.uk

ACTOR'S ONE-STOP
SHOP THE　　T 020 8888 7006
Showreels, Photography, CVs & Websites for
Performing Artists
1st Floor, Above The Gate Pub
Station Road, London N22 7SS
E info@actorsone-stopshop.com
W www.actorsone-stopshop.com

ACTORSHOP.CO.UK　　T 07970 381944
Showreels. Voicereels. Websites
E info@actorshop.co.uk
W www.actorshop.co.uk

ACTUALLYACTORS.COM　　T 020 8325 1946
Websites
3 Milestone Road
London SE19 2LL
E mail@actuallyactors.co.uk
W www.actuallyactors.com

AIR-EDEL RECORDING
STUDIOS LTD　　T 020 7486 6466
18 Rodmarton Street
London W1U 8BJ
F 020 7224 0344
E tom.bullen@air-edel.co.uk
W www.air-edelstudios.co.uk

ANGEL RECORDING
STUDIOS LTD　　T 020 7354 2525
311 Upper Street
London N1 2TU
F 020 7226 9624
E bookings@angelstudio.co.uk

ANT FARM STUDIOS
VOICE-OVERS　　T 01992 714664
Southend Farm
Southend Lane
Waltham Abbey EN9 3SE
E antfarmstudio@yahoo.co.uk
W www.antfarmstudios.co.uk

APPLE VIDEO FACILITIES　　T 01204 847974
The Studio
821 Chorley Old Road
Bolton, Lancs BL1 5SL
F 01204 495020
E info@applevideo.co.uk
W www.applevideo.co.uk

ARTS HOSTING　　T 0845 2508688
46 Glenmore Drive, Birmingham
West Midlands B38 8YR
E hosting@artshosting.co.uk
W www.artshosting.co.uk

BESPOKE REELS
T 020 7580 3773
Contact: Charlie Lort-Phillips
3rd Floor, 83 Charlotte Street
London W1T 4PR
T 07538 257748
E charlie@bespokereels.com
W www.bespokereels.com

BEWILDERING PICTURES
T 07974 916258
Contact: Graeme Kennedy. Showreel Service
& Duplication
Based in West London
E gk@bewildering.co.uk
W www.bewildering.co.uk

BLUE CHECKBOX
T 0843 2894414
Website Design
13 Portman House
136 High Road
London N22 6DF
E contact@bluecheckbox.com
W www.bluecheckbox.com

CAKE & CUSTARD
T 020 7503 6216
E info@cakeandcustard.co.uk
W www.cakeandcustard.co.uk

CHANNEL 2020 LTD
T 0844 8402020
2020 House, 26-28 Talbot Lane
Leicester LE1 4LR
F 0116 222 1113
E info@channel2020.co.uk
W www.channel2020.co.uk

CHANNEL 2020 LTD
T 0844 8402020
The Clerkenwell Workshops
27-31 Clerkenwell Close
London EC1R 0AT
E info@channel2020.co.uk
W www.channel2020.co.uk

CHASE, Stephan
PRODUCTIONS LTD
T 020 8878 9112
Producer of Voice Overs & Showreels
The Studio
22 York Avenue
London SW14 7LG
E stephan@stephanchase.com
W www.stephanchase.com

CLAW FILMS LTD
71-75 Shelton Street
London WC2H 9JQ
E info@clawfilms.com
W www.clawfilms.com

CLICKS MEDIA STUDIOS
T 01634 723838
Contact: Peter Snell
Grove Road, Rochester
Kent ME2 4BX
E info@clicksmediastudios.com
W www.clicksmediastudios.com

CONSIDER CREATIVE
T 020 3397 3816
22 Butlers & Colonial Wharf
Shad Thames
London SE1 2PX
E phil@considercreative.co.uk

CONSIDER THIS
T 01895 619900
Design. Marketing. Print. Web
Brook House, 54A Cowley Mill Road
Uxbridge, Middlesex UB8 2QE
F 01895 251048
E develop@considerthisuk.com
W www.considerthisuk.com

COURTWOOD
PHOTOGRAPHIC LTD
T 01736 741222
Photographic Reproduction
Profile Prints
Freepost TO55
Penzance, Cornwall TR20 8DU
F 01736 741255
E images@courtwood.co.uk
W www.courtwood.co.uk

CRICKCRACK PRODUCTIONS
T 01268 416195
Contact: Charlie Wilson. Professionally Equipped
Recording Facility for Voice Overs
23 Kings Road, Laindon
Basildon, Essex SS15 4AB
E charlie@crickcrack.com
W www.crickcrackproductions.com

CROWE, Ben
T 07952 784911
Voice Clip Recording
25 Holmes Avenue
Hove BN3 7LB
E bencrowe@hotmail.co.uk

CRYING OUT LOUD
PRODUCTIONS
T 07809 549887
Contact: Simon Cryer, Marina Caldarone. Voice Over
Specialists. Demo CDs. Voice Training
Chester House, Unit 1:04
1-3 Brixton Road
London SW9 6DE
T 07946 533108
E simon@cryingoutloud.co.uk
W www.cryingoutloud.co.uk

CRYSTAL MEDIA
T 0131 240 0988
28 Castle Street
Edinburgh EH2 3HT
F 0131 240 0989
E hello@crystal-media.co.uk
W www.crystal-media.co.uk

DARKSIDE REPROS
T 07990 543370
Photographic Repro Service
E info@darksidephoto.co.uk
W www.darksidephoto.co.uk

DE LANE LEA SOUND
T 020 7432 3800
Post-production. Re-recording Studios
75 Dean Street
London W1D 3PU
F 020 7494 3755
E solutions@delanelea.com
W www.delanelea.com

DELUXE 142
T 020 7878 0000
Film House
142 Wardour Street, London W1F 8DD
F 020 7878 7800
W www.deluxe142.co.uk

DENBRY REPROS LTD   T 01442 242411
Photographic Reproduction
57 High Street
Hemel Hempstead
Herts HP1 3AF
E info@denbryrepros.com
W www.denbryrepros.com

DV2BROADCAST   T 0161 736 5300
3 Carolina Way
Salford M50 2ZY
E info@dv2broadcast.co.uk
W www.dv2broadcast.co.uk

DYNAMIC ISLE STUDIO   T 07956 951090
58 Selhurst New Road
South Norwood
London SE25 5PU
E olympicrecords@tiscali.co.uk
W www.olympicrecordsuk.com

ELMS STUDIOS   T 020 8518 8629
*Contact: Phil Lawrence. Composing/Scoring for
Film & Television*
10 Empress Avenue
London E12 5ES
T 07956 275554
E info@elmsstudios.com
W www.elmsstudios.com

ESSENTIAL MUSIC   T 020 7439 7113
20 Great Chapel Street
London W1F 8FW
E david@essentialmusic.co.uk

EXECUTIVE AUDIO VISUAL   T/F 020 7723 4488
*DVD Duplication Service. Showreels for Actors &
Presenters*
E chris.jarvis60@gmail.com

FLIXELS LTD   T 020 8960 2577
Unit 7 Rutland Studios
Cumberland Park
Scrubs Lane, London NW10 6RE
E info@flixels.co.uk
W www.flixels.co.uk

**GENESIS TEE SHIRTS
& HOODIES**   T 01654 710137
18 Pendre Enterprise Park
Tywyn, Gwynedd LL36 9LW
F 01654 712461
E info@genesis-uk.com
W www.genesis-uk.com

GLITTERGAL WEBS   T 07931 318021
E info@glittergalwebs.com
W www.glittergalwebs.com

GYROSCOPE STUDIOS   T 00 46 86 459223
Contact: Frank Sanderson
Hökmossevägen 34
SE12638 Hägersten, Sweden
E frank@gyroscope-studios.com
W www.gyroscope-studios.com

HARVEY HOUSE FILMS LTD   T 07968 830536
Animation. Showreels. Video Production
80-82 Chiswick High Road, London W4 1SY
E chris@harveyhousefilms.co.uk
W www.harveyhousefilms.co.uk

HEAVY ENTERTAINMENT LTD   T 020 7494 1000
111 Wardour Street
London W1F 0UH
F 020 7494 1100
E info@heavy-entertainment.com
W www.heavy-entertainment.com

HOTQS CREATIVE   T 07903 017819
Animation. Graphics. Showreels. Websites
RichMix
1st Floor West
35-47 Bethnal Green Road
London E1 6LA
E pat@hotqs-creative.com
W www.hotqs-creative.com

HOTREELS   T 020 7952 4362
Voice & Showreels
E info@hotreels.co.uk
W www.hotreels.co.uk

IMAGE PHOTOGRAPHIC   T 020 7602 1190
PO Box 125, Swanley
Kent BR8 9BF
E digital@imagephotographic.com
W www.imagephotographic.com

JMS GROUP LTD THE
T 01603 811855
Park Farm Studios
Norwich Road
Hethersett, Norfolk NR9 3DL
F 01603 812255
E info@jms-group.com
W www.jms-group.com

KEAN LANYON LTD
T 020 7697 8453
Design of Websites, Print & Front of House, from Touring to West End
United House, North Road
Islington, London N7 9DP
E iain@keanlanyon.com
W www.keanlanyon.com

KORUPT MEDIA
T 07791 580600
Specialises in Shooting & Editing Showreels, Corporate & Music Videos
54 Balls Pond Road, London N1 4AP
E koruptmedia@gmail.com
W www.koruptmedia.com

LONDON SHOWREELS
T 07986 863550
Based in London N22
E sales@londonshowreels.co.uk

MINAMONFILM
T 020 8674 3957
Specialist in Showreels
117 Downton Avenue, London SW2 3TX
E studio@minamonfilm.co.uk
W www.minamonfilm.co.uk

MOF STUDIOS
T 020 7407 6077
Unit 1 Suffolk Studios
127-129 Great Suffolk Street, London SE1 1PP
E studio@ministryoffun.net
W www.mofstudios.net

MOO.COM
T 020 7392 2780
Online Printers. Business Cards
32-38 Scrutton Street, London EC2A 4RQ
W www.moo.com

MOTIVATION
SOUND STUDIOS
T 020 7328 8305
35A Broadhurst Gardens, London NW6 3QT
F 020 7624 4879
E info@motivationsound.co.uk
W www.motivationsound.co.uk

MUSIC IN MOTION LTD
T 07813 070961
4 Ravenshaw Street
London NW6 1NN
E neil@neilmyers.com
W www.neilmyers.com

NICOLINA MARKETING &
COMMUNICATIONS
T 07729 757006
Branding. Creative. Marketing. Social Media. Strategies. Websites
16 The Grange, London SW19 4PS
E consulting@nicolina-online.com
W www.lifestylemarketingcommunications.yolasite.com

O.J. SONUS
T 020 8963 0702
Recording Studio, Voice Over Recording. Voicereel Production. Voice Over Workshops. Professional Coaching Available
14-15 Main Drive
East Lane Business Park, Wembley HA9 7NA
T 07929 859401
E info@ojsonus.com
W www.ojsonus.com

PINPOINT
T 020 8963 0702
Specialised Voice Over Studio. Voice Over Recording. Voicereel Production. Voice Over Workshops. Professional Coaching Available
14-15 Main Drive, East Lane Business Park
Wembley HA9 7NA
T 07929 859401
E info@voice-overstudio.co.uk
W www.voice-overstudio.co.uk

PROFILE PRINTS
T 01736 741222
Photographic Reproduction
Unit 2, Plot 1A
Rospeath Industrial Estate
Crowlas, Cornwall TR20 8DU
F 01736 741255
E sales@courtwood.co.uk
W www.courtwood.co.uk

RE:AL
T 01622 200123
Printing. Creative. Marketing. Digital
Unit 2, Tovil Green Business Park
Maidstone, Kent ME15 6TA
E info@realprintandmedia.com
W www.realprintandmedia.com

RED FACILITIES
T 0131 555 2288
61 Timber Bush, Leith
Edinburgh EH6 6QH
F 0131 555 0088
E doit@redfacilities.com
W www.redfacilities.com

REEL DEAL
SHOWREEL CO THE
T 020 8647 1235
6 Charlotte Road
Wallington, Surrey SM6 9AX
E info@thereel-deal.co.uk
W www.thereel-deal.co.uk

REEL GEEKS.COM THE
T 07951 757024
Based in West Kensington, London
E thereelgeeks@hotmail.com
W www.thereelgeeks.com

REEL McCOY THE
T 07708 626477
Showreel Editing Service
21 Urquhart Court, 109 Park Road
Beckenham BR3 1QL
E reelmccoyservice@aol.com
W www.jameshyland.co.uk/reelmccoy

REPLAY LTD
T 020 7637 0473
Showreels & Performance Recording
Museum House
25 Museum Street
London WC1A 1JT
E sales@replayfilms.co.uk
W www.replayfilms.co.uk

RETRO REELS
T 07896 299932
Showreels. Voicereels. Websites. Shoots From Scratch
Flat 1, 29 Park Avenue
London NW2 5AN
E mail@retroreels.co.uk
W www.retroreels.co.uk

RJ THEATRE ARTS
T 020 8858 6999
Web Design
49 Priory Road, Croydon CR0 3QZ
T 07929 939534
E info@rjtheatrearts.com
W www.webdesign.rjtheatrearts.com

ROUND ISLAND SHOWREELS
& VOICEREELS   T 07939 540458
Contact: Ben Warren, Guy Michaels
T 07973 445328
E mail@roundisland.net
W www.roundisland.net

SCARLET INTERNET   T 0870 7771820
15 Red House Yard, Gislingham Road
Thornham Magna, Suffolk IP23 8HH
F 0870 2241418
E info@scarletinternet.com
W www.scarletinternet.com

SETTLE THE SCORE   T 07853 643346
E toby@settlethescore.co.uk
W www.settlethescore.co.uk

SHOE STRING FILMING   T 07955 736926
E showreels@shoestringfilming.com
W www.shoestringfilming.com

SHOOT FROM SCRATCH
SHOWREELS   T 020 8449 7133
Actors Showreels
74 Normandy Avenue, Barnet, Herts EN5 2JA
E info@shootfromscratch.com
W www.shootfromscratch.com

SHOWREEL THE   T 020 7043 8660 (Bookings)
Voice Over Demo Services. Training & Workshops
140 Buckingham Palace Road
London SW1W 9SA
E info@theshowreel.com
W www.theshowreel.com

SHOWREELS 4 U   T 01923 352385
Actors Showreels Filmed & Edited in HD. Voicereels.
Based near Elstree
15 Pippin Close
Shenley, Radlett, Herts WD7 9EU
E showreels4u@hotmail.com
W www.showreels4u.blogspot.com

SHOWREELZ   T 020 8994 7927
28 Eastbury Grove
Chiswick
London W4 2JZ
T 07885 253477
E brad@showreelz.com
W www.showreelz.com

SILVER-TONGUED
PRODUCTIONS   T 020 8309 0659
Specialising in the Recording & Production of Voicereels
E contactus@silver-tongued.co.uk
W www.silver-tongued.co.uk

SILVERTIP FILMS LTD   T 01483 407533
Actor Showreel Production. Edits Existing Material.
Shoots New Material
8 Quadrum Park
Old Portsmouth Road
Guildford, Surrey GU3 1LU
E info@silvertipfilms.co.uk
W www.silvertipfilms.co.uk

SLICK SHOWREELS   T 07543 016194
Watergate House
York Buildings, London WC2N 6JU
E info@slickshowreels.co.uk
W www.slickshowreels.co.uk

SMALL SCREEN SHOWREELS   T 020 8816 8896
Showreel Editing for Actors, Presenters, Dancers
& Models
The Edit Suite, 17 Knole Road
Crayford, London
E info@smallscreenshowreels.co.uk
W www.smallscreenshowreels.co.uk

SOHO SHOWREELS   T 0844 5040731
101 Wardour Street
London W1F 0UG
E info@sohoshowreels.co.uk
W www.sohoshowreels.co.uk

SONICPOND STUDIO　　T 020 7690 8561
Specialising in Voicereels. MT Demos. Showreels
70 Mildmay Grove South
Islington, London N1 4PJ
E info@sonicpond.co.uk
W www.sonicpond.co.uk

SOUND　　T 0117 924 5853
Pembroke House
7 Brunswick Square
Bristol BS2 8PE
E kenwheeler@mac.com
W www.soundat4.com

SOUND COMPANY LTD　　T 020 7580 5880
23 Gosfield Street
London W1W 6HG
F 020 7580 6454
E bookings@sound.co.uk
W www.sound.co.uk

SOUND HOUSE LTD THE　　T 0161 832 7299
2nd Floor, Astley House
Quay Street, Manchester M3 4AE
F 0161 832 7266
E mail@thesoundhouse.tv
W www.thesoundhouse.tv

SOUND MARKETING　　T 01225 701600
Strattons House, Strattons Walk
Melksham, Wiltshire SN12 6JL
F 01225 701601
E nicki@soundm.com
W www.soundm.com

**STAGES CAPTURE
THE MOMENT**　　T 020 7193 8519
Showreels
31 Evensyde, Croxley Green
Watford, Herts WD18 8WN
T 07786 813812
E info@stagescapturethemoment.com
W www.stagescapturethemoment.com

STAMP PRODUCTIONS　　T 020 8743 5555
Ugli Campus, 56 Wood Lane
London W12 7SB
E info@stamp-productions.com

**SUGAR LENS
PRODUCTIONS LTD**　　T 07943 805423
Showreels
10 Foreland Close, Christchurch, Dorset BH23 2TQ
E info@sugarlensproductions.com
W www.sugarlensproductions.com

SUGAR POD PRODUCTIONS　　T 020 8829 8969
Voice Showreels & Production Studio
Studio 8C, Chocolate Factory 2
Coburg Road, Wood Green
London N22 6UJ
T 07967 673552
E info@sugarpodproductions.com
W www.sugarpodproductions.com

SYNCREDIBLE AGENCY　　T 020 7117 6776
26-28 Hammersmith Grove, London W6 7BA
E contact@syncredible.com
W www.syncredible.com

crickcrack voices
A personal and professional studio for voice reels and VOs
• Relaxed & helpful • Free guidance notes • Discounts available
• www.crickcrackproductions.com • charlie@crickcrack.com
01268 416195

TAKE FIVE CASTING STUDIO T 020 7287 2120
Showreels
37 Beak Street, London W1F 9RZ
F 020 7287 3035
E info@takefivestudio.com
W www.takefivestudio.com

**TM PHOTOGRAPHY &
DESIGN LTD** T 020 8530 4382
Suites 14-15
Marlborough Business Centre
96 George Lane
South Woodford, London E18 1AD
E info@tmphotography.co.uk
W www.tmphotography.co.uk

**TOUCHWOOD AUDIO
PRODUCTIONS** T 0113 278 7180
6 Hyde Park Terrace, Leeds
West Yorkshire LS6 1BJ
T 07745 377772
E bruce@touchwoodaudio.com
W www.touchwoodaudio.com

**TV PRESENTER TRAINING -
ASPIRE** T 0800 0305471
3 Mills Studios
Three Mill Lane, London E3 3DU
E info@aspirepresenting.com
W www.aspirepresenting.com

TWITCH FILMS T 020 7266 0946
Showreels
22 Grove End Gardens
18 Abbey Road, London NW8 9LL
E post@twitchfilms.co.uk
W www.twitchfilms.co.uk

**UNIVERSAL SOUND
(JUST PLAY LTD)** T 01494 723400
Old Farm Lane
London Road East
Amersham, Buckinghamshire HP7 9DH
E foley@universalsound.co.uk
W www.universalsound.co.uk

VC STUDIOS T 05602 625262
6 Millan Court
Lumphanan
Aberdeenshire AB31 4QF
E richard.edgar@vcstudios.co.uk
W www.vcstudios.co.uk

VISUALEYES T 020 7323 7430
Photographic Reproduction
95 Mortimer Street, London W1W 7ST
F 020 7323 7438
E imaging@visualeyes.co.uk
W www.visualeyes.co.uk

**VOICE MASTER
INTERNATIONAL** T 020 8455 1666
*Creators of the Hudson Voice Technique, the only
Technique in the World for Voice Overs*
88 Erskine Hill, London NW11 6HR
T 07921 210400
E info@voicemaster-international.com
W www.voicemaster.co.uk

VOICEREELS.CO.UK T 07989 602880
Based in London SW16
E rob@voicereels.co.uk
W www.voicereels.co.uk

**VSI - VOICE & SCRIPT
INTERNATIONAL** T 020 7692 7700
*Foreign Language Specialists. Casting. Dubbing. Editing.
Recording Studios. Subtitling. Translation*
132 Cleveland Street, London W1T 6AB
F 020 7692 7711
E info@vsi.tv
W www.vsi.tv

WE THEATRE T 020 3327 3877
*Flyer, Poster, Programme & Website Design for
Fringe Theatre*
239 Lewisham Way, London SE4 1XF
E info@wetheatre.co.uk
W www.wetheatre.co.uk

WEBVID.CO.UK T 020 8133 1728
*Contact: Neil Bentley (Heart, Capital, Galaxy), James,
Vince. Web & Video Production Company. Bespoke
Website Design & Video Filming/Editing*
Based in South London
E hello@webvid.co.uk
W www.webvid.co.uk

WORLDWIDE PICTURES LTD T 020 7613 0500
103 The Timber Yard
Drivedale Street, London N1 6ND
F 020 7613 6581
E info@worldwidepictures.tv
W www.worldwidepictures.tv

**10 OUT OF 10
PRODUCTIONS LTD**   T 020 8659 2558
Lighting & Sound. Design. Hire. Installation. Sales
5 Metro Business Centre, Kangley Bridge Road
London SE26 5BW
E sales@10outof10.co.uk
W www.10outof10.co.uk

147RESEARCH   T 01635 200147
*Will source anything needed for period or modern
productions*
Chaucers, Oare, Hermitage, Thatcham RG18 9SD
T 07778 002147
E jenniferdalton@147research.com
W www.147research.com

3D CREATIONS LTD   T 01493 652055
*Production Design. Prop Makers. Scenery Contractors.
Scenic Artists*
Berth 33, Malthouse Lane
Gorleston, Norfolk NR31 0GW
F 01493 443124
E info@3dcreations.co.uk
W www.3dcreations.co.uk

AC FLUTES   T 020 8123 5925
*Handmade Native American-style Flutes. Handmade
Wood & Leather Crafts*
E info@acflutes.co.uk
W www.acflutes.co.uk

ACROBAT PRODUCTIONS   T 01923 518989
Advisors. Artistes
2 The Grove, Whippendell
Chipperfield, Kings Langley, Herts WD4 9JF
E roger@acrobatproductions.com
W www.acrobatproductions.com

ACTION 99 CARS LTD   T 01923 266373
Westwick Road Farm, Westwick Row
Hemel Hempstead HP2 4UB
E david@nineninecars.com
W www.nineninecars.com

ACTION CARS LTD   T 01753 785690
Contact: Steven Royffe
Room 49A, D Block, Pinewood Studios
Pinewood Road, Iver Heath, Bucks SL0 0NH
E steve@actioncars.co.uk
W www.actioncars.co.uk

ADAMS ENGRAVING   T 01483 725792
Unit G1A, The Mayford Centre, Mayford Green
Woking GU22 0PP
E adamsengraving@pncl.co.uk
W www.adamsengraving.co.uk

**AIRBOURNE SYSTEMS
INTERNATIONAL**   T 01245 268772
*All Skydiving Requirements Arranged. Parachute Hire
(Period & Modern)*
8 Burns Crescent, Chelmsford, Essex CM2 0TS

**ALCHEMICAL
LABORATORIES ETC**   T 01636 707836
*Medieval Science & Technology Recreated for
Museums & Films*
2 Stapleford Lane, Coddington
Newark, Nottinghamshire NG24 2QZ
E alchemyjack@gmail.com
W www.jackgreene.co.uk

ALL SCENE ALL PROPS   T 01892 752223
Props, Masks, Painting & Scenery Makers
Buckhurst Works, Bells Yew Green
Tunbridge Wells, East Sussex TN3 9BN
F 01892 752221
E pr@allscene.net
W www.allscene.net

ALL STARS AMERICAN LIMOS   T 07747 130685
Field Gate, Station Road, Northiam, Rye TN31 6QT
E limohire@live.co.uk
W www.limo-hire-sussex-kent.co.uk

AMERICAN DREAMS   T 0800 8488032
Vehicle Supply
PO Box 11038, St Osyth
Clacton on Sea, Essex CO16 8SY
E tphj47@aol.com
W www.americandreams.co.uk

ANELLO & DAVIDE   T 020 7938 2255
Handmade Shoes
15 St Albans Grove, London W8 5BP
W www.handmadeshoes.co.uk

**ANNUAL CLOWNS
DIRECTORY THE**   T 01268 745791
Contact: Salvo The Clown
13 Second Avenue, Kingsleigh Park
Thundersley, Essex SS7 3QD
E salvo@annualclownsdirectory.com
W www.annualclownsdirectory.com

AQUATECH SURVEY LTD   T 01452 740559
Camera Boats
2 Cobbies Rock, Epney, Gloucestershire GL2 7LN
F 01452 741958
E office@aquatech-uk.com
W www.aquatech-uk.com

ARCHERY CENTRE THE   T 01424 777183
Archery Tuition & Equipment
PO Box 39, Battle, East Sussex TN33 0ZT
E sales@archerycentre.co.uk
W www.archerycentre.co.uk

ARMS & ARCHERY   T 01920 460335
Armour. Chainmail. Longbows. Tents. Weaponry. X-bows
Thrift Lane, Off London Road, Ware, Herts SG12 9QS
E armsandarchery@btconnect.com

ART *
Art Consultant. Supplier of Paintings & Sculpture
E h@art8star.co.uk
W www.art8star.co.uk

**ART DIRECTORS &
TRIP PHOTO LIBRARY**   T 020 8642 3593
Digital Scans & Colour Slides (All Subjects)
57 Burdon Lane, Cheam, Surrey SM2 7BY
F 020 8395 7230
E images@artdirectors.co.uk
W www.artdirectors.co.uk

A. S. DESIGNS   T 01279 722416
*Theatrical Designer. Costumes, Heads, Masks, Puppets,
Sets etc*

ASH, Riky   T 01476 407383
Equity Registered Stunt Performer/Co-ordinator
T 07850 471227
E stuntmanriky@fallingforyou.tv
W www.fallingforyou.tv

AWESOME UPHOLSTERY   T 01480 461195
Custom Upholstery Specialists
Unit 7, Monsal Works
Somersham Road, St Ives, Cambridgeshire PE27 3LY
E info@awesome.eu.com
W www.awesome.eu.com

BAPTY (2000) LTD   T 020 8574 7700
Dressing, Props, Weapons etc
1A Witley Gardens, Norwood Green
Southall, Middlesex UB2 4ES
F 020 8571 5700
E hire@bapty.demon.co.uk
W www.bapty.co.uk

BEAT ABOUT THE BUSH LTD   T 020 8960 2087
Musical Instrument Hire
Unit 23, Enterprise Way, Triangle Business Centre
Salter Street (Off Hythe Road), London NW10 6UG
F 020 8969 2281
E info@beataboutthebush.com
W www.beataboutthebush.com

**BIANCHI AVIATION
FILM SERVICES**   T 01494 449810
Historic & Other Aircraft
Wycombe Air Park, Booker Marlow
Buckinghamshire SL7 3DP
F 01494 461236
E info@bianchiaviation.com
W www.bianchiaviation.com

BIG BREAK CARDS   T 01386 438952
*Theatrical greetings cards featuring hamlet the pig,
drawn by Harry Venning, as seen in The Stage. Made by
actors for actors*
E info@bigbreakcards.co.uk
W www.bigbreakcards.co.uk

BLUE MILL LTD   T 0116 248 8130
Dyers. Finishers
84 Halstead Street, Leicester LE5 3RD
F 0116 253 7633
E info@bluemill.co.uk
W www.bluemill.co.uk

BLUEBELL RAILWAY PLC   T 01825 720800
*Period Stations. Pullman Coaches. Steam Locomotives.
Much Film Experience*
Sheffield Park Station, East Sussex TN22 3QL
F 01825 720804
E info@bluebell-railway.co.uk
W www.bluebell-railway.com

**BOLDGATE COMMERCIAL
SERVICES LTD**   T 01753 610525
The Crossbow Centre, 40 Liverpool Road
Slough, Berkshire SL1 4QZ
F 01753 610587
E info@boldgate.co.uk   W www.boldgate.co.uk

BOSCO LIGHTING   T 020 8769 3470
Design/Technical Consultancy
47 Woodbourne Avenue
London SW16 1UX
E boscolx@lineone.net

**BOUNCY CASTLES BY
P. A. LEISURE**   T 01282 453939
Specialists in Amusements & Fairground Equipment
Delph House, Park Bridge Road
Towneley Park
Burnley, Lancs BB10 4SD
T 07968 399053
E info@paleisure.co.uk
W www.paleisure.co.uk

BRISTOL (UK) LTD   T 01923 779333
Scenic Paint & StageFloor Duo Suppliers. VFX Solutions
Unit 3, Sutherland Court
Tolpits Lane, Watford WD18 9SP
F 01923 779666
E tech.sales@bristolpaint.com
W www.bristolpaint.com

BRODIE & MIDDLETON LTD   T 020 7836 3289
Theatrical Suppliers. Glitter, Paints, Powders etc
68 Drury Lane, London WC2B 5SP
F 020 7497 0554
E info@brodies.net
W www.brodies.net

**BRUNEL'S THEATRICAL
SERVICES**   T 0117 907 7855
Removal Services
20A Walnut Lane, Kingswood
Bristol BS15 4JG
E enquiries@brunelsremoval.co.uk
W www.brunelsremoval.co.uk

BURTON EXECUTIVE CARS   T 0845 6013944
Parkway House, Second Avenue, Burton on Trent
Burton, Staffordshire DE14 2WF
T 07792 013117
E dganley@burtonexecutivecars.co.uk
W www.burtonexecutivecars.co.uk

CANDLE MAKERS SUPPLIES   T 020 7602 1812
Rear of 102-104 Shepherds Bush Road
(Entrance in Batoum Gardens)
London W6 7PD
E candles@candlemakers.co.uk
W www.candlemakers.co.uk

CARLINE PRIVATE HIRE   T 01293 430430
12A Bridge Industrial Estate
Balcombe Road
Horley, West Sussex RH6 9HU
F 01293 430432
E carlinehire@yahoo.co.uk
W www.albioncarsgatwick.co.uk

CAULFIELD PRODUCTIONS LTD   T 07902 974108
Technical & Production Services
71 Turner Road, Walthamstow
London E17 3JG
E office@caulfieldproductions.co.uk
W www.caulfieldproductions.co.uk

**CHASE 55 SUPERHIRE
PROPS LTD**   T 0871 2310900
Prop Hire Specialist. Victorian to Present Day
55 Chase Road, London NW10 6LU
F 020 8965 8107
E trez@superhire.com
W www.superhire.com

CHRISANNE LTD   T 020 8640 5921
Specialist Fabrics & Accessories for Theatre & Dance
Chrisanne House, 110-112 Morden Road
Mitcham, Surrey CR4 4XB
F 020 8640 2106
E sales@chrisanne.com
W www.chrisanne.com

CIRCUS PROMOTIONS   T 01892 537964
Entertainers
36 St Lukes Road
Tunbridge Wells, Kent TN4 9JH
E mike@heypresto.orangehome.co.uk
W www.heyprestoentertainment.co.uk

CLASSIC CAR AGENCY THE   T 07788 977655
Advertising. Film. Promotional. Publicity
PO Box 427, Dorking
Surrey RH5 6WP
E theclassiccaragency@btopenworld.com
W www.theclassiccaragency.com

CLASSIC CAR HIRE   T 020 8398 8304
Over 30 Classic & Vintage Vehicles
Unit 2 Hampton Court Estate
Summer Road
Thames Ditton KT7 0RG
E info@classic-hire.co.uk
W www.classic-hire.com

CLASSIC OMNIBUS   T 01303 248999
Vintage Open-Top Buses & Coaches
44 Welson Road, Folkestone
Kent CT20 2NP
W www.opentopbus.co.uk

COBO MEDIA LTD   T 020 8291 7079
Performing Arts, Entertainment & Leisure Marketing
43A Garthorne Road, London SE23 1EP
F 020 8291 4969
E admin@cobomedia.com
W www.cobomedia.com

COMPTON, Mike & Rosi   T 020 8680 4364
Costumes. Models. Props
11 Woodstock Road, Croydon
Surrey CR0 1JS
T 07900 258646
E mikeandrosicompton@btopenworld.com

CONCEPT ENGINEERING LTD   T 01628 825555
Smoke, Fog, Snow etc
7 Woodlands Business Park
Woodlands Park Avenue
Maidenhead, Berkshire SL6 3UA
F 01628 826261
E info@conceptsmoke.com
W www.concept-smoke.co.uk

COOK, Sheila TEXTILES   T 020 7603 3003
Textiles, Costumes & Accessories for Hire/Sale
26 Addison Place, London W11 4RJ
E sheilacook@sheilacook.co.uk
W www.sheilacook.co.uk

**COSTUMES &
SHOWS UNLIMITED**   T 01253 827092
*Costume Rental & Design. Ice Rink Rental. Show
Production*
Crammond, Hillylaid Road
Thornton-Cleveleys, Lancs FY5 4EG
T 07881 970398
E iceshowpro@aol.com
W www.ice-shows-and-costumes-unlimited.co.uk

CRESTA BLINDS LTD   T 01902 714143
Supplier of Vertical Blinds
Unit 23, Hollies Industrial Estate
Graiseley Row
Wolverhampton WV2 4HE
F 01902 715518
E info@crestablindsltd.co.uk
W www.crestablindsltd.co.uk

CROFTS, Andrew   T/F 01403 864518
Book Writing Services
Westlands Grange, West Grinstead
Horsham, West Sussex RH13 8LZ
E croftsa@aol.com
W www.andrewcrofts.com

**CUE ACTION POOL
PROMOTIONS**   T 07881 828077
Advice for UK & US Pool, Snooker, Trick Shots
4 Hillview Close, Rowhedge
Colchester, Essex CO5 7HT
E sales@cueaction.com
W www.stevedaking.com

DAVEY, Brian
See NOSTALGIA AMUSEMENTS

DESIGN PROJECTS   T 01883 730262
Perrysfield Farm, Broadham Green
Old Oxted, Surrey RH8 9PG
F 01883 723707
W www.designprojects.co.uk

**DEVEREUX
DEVELOPMENTS LTD**   T 01642 560854
Haulage. Removals. Trucking
Daimler Drive, Cowpen Industrial Estate
Billingham, Cleveland TS23 4JD
F 01642 566664
E mikebell@britdev.com

**DORANS PROPMAKERS /
SET BUILDERS**   T/F 01335 300064
53 Derby Road, Ashbourne
Derbyshire DE6 1BH
E info@doransprops.com
W www.doransprops.com

DRAMA T'S   T 07587 094808
*Branded Merchandise for Stage Professionals
(T-shirts/Hoodies)*
Based in London
E info@dramats.com
W www.dramats.com

DURRENT, Peter　　T 01787 373483
Audition & Rehearsal Pianist. Cocktail Pianist.
Composer. Vocalist
Blacksmiths Cottage
Bures Road, Little Cornard
Sudbury, Suffolk CO10 0NR
E tunefuldurrent@gmail.com

EAT TO THE BEAT　　T 01494 790700
Production & Location Caterers
Global Infusion Court
Nashleigh Hill, Chesham
Bucks HP5 3HE
F 01494 790701
E enquiries@eattothebeat.com
W www.globalinfusiongroup.com

ELECTRO SIGNS LTD　　T 020 8521 8066
97 Vallentin Road, London E17 3JJ
F 020 8520 8127
E info@electrosigns.co.uk

ELMS LESTERS
PAINTING ROOMS　　T 020 7836 6747
Locations. Rehearsal Rooms
1-3-5 Flitcroft Street
London WC2H 8DH
F 020 7379 0789
E info@elmslesters.co.uk

ESCORT GUNLEATHER　　T 01268 792769
Custom Leathercraft
602 High Road
Benfleet, Essex SS7 5RW
F 01268 566775
E info@escortgunleather.com
W www.escortgunleather.com

FACADE　　T 020 8291 7079
Musical Production Services
43A Garthorne Road, London SE23 1EP
F 020 8291 4969
E facade@cobomedia.com

FELLOWES, Mark
TRANSPORT SERVICES　　T 020 7386 7005
Transport. Storage
59 Sherbrooke Road, London SW6 7QL
T 07850 332818
W www.fellowesproductions.com

FILM MEDICAL SERVICES　　T 020 8961 3222
Units 5 & 7, Commercial Way
Park Royal, London NW10 7XF
F 020 8961 7427
E info@filmmedical.co.uk
W www.filmmedical.co.uk

FINAL CREATION　　T 01530 249100
Unit 19, The Loft Studio
Hill Lane Industrial Estate
Markfield, Leicestershire LE67 9PN
F 01530 249400
E gemma@finalcreation.co.uk
W www.finalcreation.co.uk

FIREBRAND　　T/F 01546 870310
Flambeaux Hire & Sales
Leac Na Ban, Tayvallich
By Lochgilphead, Argyll PA31 8PF
E firebrand.props@btinternet.com

FIRST NIGHT DESIGN　　T 07773 770781
Greeting Cards & Gifts
E info@firstnightdesign.co.uk
W www.firstnightdesign.co.uk

FLAME RETARDING LTD   T 01621 818477
Grove Farm, Grove Farm Road
Tolleshunt Major, Maldon, Essex CM9 8LR
F 07092 036931
E email@flameretarding.co.uk
W www.flameretarding.co.uk

FLAMENCO PRODUCTIONS   T 01905 424083
Entertainers
Sevilla 4 Cormorant Rise, Lower Wick
Worcester WR2 4BA
E delphineflamenco@tiscali.co.uk

FLINT HIRE & SUPPLY LTD   T 020 7703 9786
Queen's Row, London SE17 2PX
F 020 7708 4189
E sales@flints.co.uk
W www.flints.co.uk

FLYING BY FOY   T 020 8236 0234
Flying Effects for Stage, Television, Corporate Events etc
Unit 4, Borehamwood Enterprise Centre
Theobald Street, Borehamwood, Herts WD6 4RQ
F 020 8236 0235
E mail@flyingbyfoy.co.uk
W www.flyingbyfoy.co.uk

FRANCO THE MAGICIAN   T/F 020 8202 4940
Flat 1, 79 Brent Street, London NW4 2EA
E franco@francomagic.co.uk
W www.francomagic.co.uk

FROST, John NEWSPAPERS
Historical Newspaper Archives
E andrew@johnfrostnewspapers.com
W www.johnfrostnewspapers.com

GARRATT, Jonathan FRSA   T 01725 517700
Suppliers of Traditional & Unusual Garden Pots &
Installations. Glazed Tableware
Hare Lane Farmhouse, Cranborne, Dorset BH21 5QT
E jonathan.garratt@talk21.com
W www.jonathangarratt.com

**GAV NICOLA
THEATRICAL SHOES**   T 07961 974278
T 00 34 673803783
E gavnicola@yahoo.com
W www.theatricalshoes.com

GENESIS UK LTD   T 01654 710137
Unit 18, Pendre Enterprise Park
Tywyn, Gwynedd LL36 9LW
E info@genesis-uk.com
W www.genesis-uk.com

GET STUFFED   T 020 7226 1364
Taxidermy
105 Essex Road, London N1 2SL
T 07831 260062
E taxidermy@thegetstuffed.co.uk
W www.thegetstuffed.co.uk

GHOSTWRITER / AUTHOR   T 01227 721071
Contact: John Parker
Dove Cottage, The Street, Ickham CT3 1QP
E ghostwriterforyourbook@ymail.com
W www.ghostwriteruk.info

GORGEOUS GOURMETS LTD   T 020 8944 7771
Equipment Hire
Gresham Way, Wimbledon SW19 8ED
E hire@gorgeousgourmets.co.uk
W www.gorgeousgourmets.co.uk

GOULD, Gillian ANTIQUES   T 020 8458 7673
Scientific & Marine Antiques & Collectables
38 Denman Drive South, London NW11 6RH
T 07831 150060
E gillgould@dealwith.com
W www.gilliangouldantiques.co.uk

GRADAV HIRE & SALES LTD   T 020 8803 7400
Lighting & Sound Hire/Sales
Units C6 & C9 Hastingwood Trading Estate
Harbet Road, Edmonton, London N18 3HU
F 020 8803 5060
E office@gradav.co.uk

GRAND HIRE   T 020 7281 9555
Short & Long Term Piano Hire
465 Hornsey Road
London N19 4DR
F 020 7263 0154
E piano@grandhire.co.uk
W www.grandhire.co.uk

GRAY, Robin COMMENTARIES   T 01420 23347
Voice Overs. Hunting Attire. Racing Colours. Saddles
Comptons, Isington
Alton, Hampshire GU34 4PL
T 07831 828424
E comptons1@hotmail.co.uk

GREENPROPS   T 01398 361531
Prop Suppliers. Artificial Flowers, Fruit, Grass, Plants,
Trees etc
E trevor@greenprops.org
W www.greenprops.org

**GREENSOURCE
SOLUTIONS LTD**   T 0845 3100200
Providers of Mobile Phone Props. Supplies & Recycles
Printer Consumables
14 Kingsland Trading Estate
St Phillips Road, Bristol BS2 0JZ
F 0117 304 2391
E props@greensource.co.uk
W www.greensource.co.uk

GROWING CONCERNS
Things Rustic, Rural & Recycled. Artefacts, Artworks,
Furniture & Tools for Stage, Film, Television, Photo Sets
etc. Buy, Hire or Finders-Service
E info@growingconcern.co.uk

HAMPTON COURT HOUSE   T 020 8943 0889
Hampton Court Road
East Molesey KT8 9BS
F 020 8977 5357
W www.hamptoncourthouse.co.uk

HANDS UP PUPPETS   T 07909 824630
7 Cavendish Vale, Nottingham
Nottinghamshire NG5 4DS
E marcus@handsuppuppets.com
W www.handsuppuppets.com

**HARLEQUIN FLOORS
(BRITISH HARLEQUIN PLC)**   T 01892 514888
Floors for Dance, Display, Entertainment &
the Performing Arts
Festival House, Chapman Way
Tunbridge Wells
Kent TN2 3EF
T 0800 289932
E enquiries@harlequinfloors.com
W www.harlequinfloors.com

HERON & DRIVER   T 020 7394 8688
Scenic Furniture & Prop Makers
Unit 7, Dockley Road Industrial Estate
Rotherhithe, London SE16 3SF
E mail@herondriver.co.uk
W www.herondriver.co.uk

HI-FLI   T 0161 278 9352
Flying Effects
18 Greencourt Drive
Manchester M38 0BZ
E mikefrost@hi-fli.co.uk

GREENPROPS

Foliage * Flowers * Fruit & Veg
Importers, Stockists & Makers

The Artificial STAGE SUPPLIERS, serving The West End, The UK and Europe
T: 01398 361531   trevor@greenprops.org   www.greenprops.org

IIIIIIIIIIIIIIIIIIIIIIIIIIIIIIIIIIIIIIIIIIIIIIIIIIIIIIIIIIIIIIIIIIIIIIIIIIIIIIIIIIIIIIIIIIIIIIIIIIIIIIIIIIIIIIIIIIIIIIIIIIIIIIIIII

HISTORICAL INTERPRETER & ROLE PLAYING   T 020 8866 2997
Contact: Donald Clarke
80 Warden Avenue, Rayners Lane
Harrow, Middlesex HA2 9LW
T 07811 606285
E info@historicalinterpretations.co.uk
W www.historicalinterpretations.co.uk

HISTORY IN THE MAKING LTD   T 023 9225 3175
Weapon & Costume Hire
4A Aysgarth Road, Waterlooville, Hampshire PO7 7UG
E enquiries@history-making.com
W www.history-making.com

HOME JAMES CHAUFFEUR SERVICE   T 0121 323 4717
Moor Lane, Witton, Birmingham B6 7HH
E enquiries@homejamescars.com
W www.homejamescars.com

HOMESITE ESTATE AGENTS   T 020 7243 3535
16 Lambton Place, London W11 2SH
F 020 7243 5794
E info@homesite.co.uk
W www.homesite.co.uk

HOWARD, Rex DRAPES   T 020 8955 6940
Trading division of Hawthorns
Unit F, Western Trading Estate
London NW10 7LU
E hire@hawthorns.uk.com

IMPACT   T 020 8579 9922
Private & Contract Hire of Coaches
1 Leighton Road, Ealing, London W13 9EL
F 020 8840 4880
E sales@impactgroup.co.uk
W www.impactgroup.co.uk

IMPACT MARKETING   T 020 7729 5978
Print Distribution & Display
Tuscany Wharf, 4B Orsman Road, London N1 5QJ
F 020 7729 5994
E contactus@impactideas.co.uk
W www.impactideas.co.uk

IMPACT PERCUSSION   T 020 8299 6700
Percussion Instruments for Sale
Unit 7 Goose Green Trading Estate
47 East Dulwich Road, London SE22 9BN
F 020 8299 6704
E sales@impactpercussion.com

IMPACT SCHOOL OF MOTORING   T 01202 666001
Expert Driving Instructors on All Vehicles
85 Dorchester Road, Oakdale
Poole BH15 3QZ
T 07775 713780
E andyd@mail2world.com

JAPAN PROMOTIONS   T/F 020 7278 4099
Japanese Costumes & Props
200 Russell Court, 3 Woburn Place, London WC1H 0ND
E info@japan-promotions.co.uk
W www.japan-promotions.co.uk

JULIETTE DESIGNS   T 020 7263 7878
Diamante Jewellery Manufacturer: Necklaces, Crowns etc
90 Yerbury Road, London N19 4RS
F 020 7281 7326
E juliettedesigns@hotmail.com
W www.stagejewellery.com

KEIGHLEY & WORTH VALLEY LIGHT RAILWAY LTD   T 01535 645214
Crew. Props. Carriages, Engines & Stations
The Railway Station, Haworth
Keighley, West Yorkshire BD22 8NJ
F 01535 647317
E admin@kwvr.co.uk
W www.kwvr.co.uk

KENSINGTON EYE CENTRE   T/F 020 7937 8282
Opticians. Special Eye Effects
37 Kensington Church Street, London W8 4LL
E kensingtoneyecentre@gmail.com

KEW BRIDGE STEAM MUSEUM   T 020 8568 4757
Green Dragon Lane
Brentford, Middlesex TW8 0EN
F 020 8569 9978
E info@kbsm.org
W www.kbsm.org

KIRBY'S AFX LTD   T/F 020 8723 8552
8 Greenford Avenue, Hanwell, London W7 3QP
T 07958 285608
E mail@afxuk.com
W www.kirbysflying.co.uk

KNEBWORTH HOUSE, GARDENS & PARK   T 01438 812661
Knebworth, Herts SG3 6PY
E info@knebworthhouse.com
W www.knebworthhouse.com

LAREDO, Alex   T 01306 889423
Expert with Ropes, Bullwhips, Shooting & Riding
29 Lincoln Road, Dorking, Surrey RH4 1TE
T 07745 798118

LAREDO WILD WEST TOWN   T 01580 891790
Wild West Entertainment
1 Bower Walk, Staplehurst, Tonbridge, Kent TN12 0LU
T 07947 652771
E colin.winter123@btinternet.com
W www.laredo.org.uk

LEES-NEWSOME LTD   T 0845 0708005
Manufacturers of Flame Retardant Fabrics
Ashley Works, Unit 2, Rule Business Park
Grimshaw Lane, Middleton, Manchester M24 2AE
F 0845 0708006
E info@leesnewsome.co.uk
W www.leesnewsome.co.uk

LEIGHTON HALL   T 01524 734474
Historic House
Carnforth, Lancashire LA5 9ST
F 01524 720357
E info@leightonhall.co.uk
W www.leightonhall.co.uk

LEVRANT, Stephen - HERITAGE ARCHITECTURE LTD T 020 8748 5501
Architects. Historic Building Consultants
62 British Grove, Chiswick, London W4 2NL
F 020 8748 4992
E info@heritagearchitecture.co.uk

LIMELIGHT ENTERTAINMENT T 020 8853 9570
Theatre Merchandise
Unit 13, The io Centre
The Royal Arsenal, Seymour Street, London SE18 6SX
F 020 8853 0979
E enquiries@thelimelightgroup.co.uk

LONDON QUALITY DRY CLEANERS LTD T 020 7935 7316
Dry Cleaners. Dyers. Launderers. Costumes & Stage Curtains
222 Baker Street, London NW1 5RT

LONO DRINKS CO T 0800 8250035
23-24 Failsworth Industrial Estate
Greenhalgh Street
Failsworth, Manchester M35 0BN
E info@lono.co.uk
W www.lono.co.uk

LOS KAOS T 01291 680074
Animatronics. Puppetry. Street Theatre
Quay House, Quayside
Brockweir, Gloucestershire NP16 7NQ
E kaos@loskaos.co.uk
W www.loskaos.co.uk

LUCKINGS T 020 8332 2000
Stage Hands. Storage. Transporters
Boston House, 69-75 Boston Manor Road
Brentford, Middlesex TW8 9JJ
F 020 8332 3000
E info@luckings.co.uk
W www.luckings.co.uk

LUCKINGS SCREEN SERVICES T 020 8332 2000
Artists' Trailers/Splits/2-3 Ways
Boston House, 69-75 Boston Manor Road
Brentford, Middlesex TW8 9JJ
F 020 8332 3000
E info@luckings.co.uk
W www.luckings.co.uk

LYON EQUIPMENT T 01539 626250
Petzl & Beal Rope Access Equipment (PPE) for Industrial & Theatrical Work
Junction 38, M6, Tebay, Cumbria CA10 3SS
F 01539 624857
E work.rescue@lyon.co.uk
W www.lyon.co.uk

M A C T 0161 969 8311
Sound Hire
1-2 Attenburys Park, Park Road
Altrincham, Cheshire WA14 5QE
F 0161 962 9423
E hire@macsound.co.uk
W www.macsound.co.uk

MACKIE, Sally LOCATIONS T 01451 830294
Location Finding & Management
Cownham Farm, Broadwell
Moreton-in-Marsh, Gloucestershire GL56 0TT
E sally@mackie.biz
W www.sallymackie-locations.com

MAGICAL MART T/F 020 8300 3579
Magic. Punch & Judy. Ventriloquists' Dolls. Hire & Advising. Callers by Appointment
42 Christchurch Road, Sidcup
Kent DA15 7HQ
W www.johnstylesentertainer.co.uk

MAINSTREAM LEISURE GROUP T 020 3044 29234
Riverboat/Canal Boat Hire
Trident Court, 1 Oakcroft Road
Chessington, Surrey KT9 1BD
F 020 3044 2926
E info@mainstreamleisure.co.uk
W www.mainstreamleisure.co.uk

MARCUS HALL PROPS T 020 7252 6291
Contact: Chris Marcus, Jonathan Hall
Unit 2B/C Vanguard Court
Rear of 36-38 Peckham Road, London SE5 8QT
E chris@marcushallprops.com
W www.marcushallprops.com

MARKSON PIANOS T 020 7935 8682
8 Chester Court, Albany Street, London NW1 4BU
F 020 7224 0957
E info@marksonpianos.com
W www.marksonpianos.com

MATTLX GROUP T 0845 6808692
Audio Visual. Health & Safety. Lighting. Production Design
Unit 3, Vinehall Business Centre
Vinehall Road, Robertsbridge, East Sussex TN32 5JW
E intray@mattlx.com
W www.mattlx.com

McNEILL, Brian T 01706 812291
Vintage Truck & Coaches
Hawk Mount, Kebs Road
Todmorden, Lancashire OL14 8SB
E autotrans@uk2.net
W www.rollingpast.com

MIDNIGHT ELECTRONICS T 0191 224 0088
Sound Hire
Off Quay Building, Foundry Lane
Newcastle upon Tyne NE6 1LH
E info@midnightelectronics.co.uk
W www.midnightelectronics.co.uk

MILITARY, MODELS & MINATURES T 020 7700 7036
Model Figures
38A Horsell Road, London N5 1XP
F 020 7700 4624
E minaturesmodels@aol.com

MODDED MOTORS AGENCY T 07989 128131
Suppliers of Modified Cars
38 Williamson Way, Rickmansworth
Hertfordshire WD3 8GL
E daniellechristie@hotmail.com
W www.moddedmotorsagency.com

MODELBOX T 01837 810923
Computer Aided Design. Design Services
41C Market Street, Hatherleigh, Devon EX20 3JP
E info@modelbox.co.uk
W www.modelboxplans.com

MOORFIELDS PHOTOGRAPHIC LTD T 0151 236 1611
2 Old Hall Street, Liverpool L3 9RQ
E info@moorfieldsphoto.com
W www.moorfieldsphoto.com

MORGAN, Dennis T 07915 662767
Cameraman
241 Crystal Palace Road, London SE22 9JQ
E info@dennismorgan.co.uk

MORTON, G. & L. T 01430 860185
Farming. Horses
Hashome Carr, Holme-on-Spalding Moor
Yorkshire YO43 4BD
E janet_morton@hotmail.com

MOTORHOUSE HIRE LTD T 020 7495 1618
Contact: Michael Geary. Action Vehicles
Oatleys Hall, Turweston, Northants NN13 5JX
F 01280 704944
E michael@motorhouseltd.co.uk

MPG BOOKS GROUP LTD T 01208 265300
Quality Book Manufacturers
Victoria Square, Bodmin
Cornwall PL31 1EB
F 01208 73603
E print@mpg-books.co.uk
W www.mpg-booksgroup.com

NATIONAL MOTOR MUSEUM T 01590 612345
John Montagu Building, Beaulieu
Brockenhurst, Hampshire SO42 7ZN
F 01590 612624
E info@beaulieu.co.uk
W www.beaulieu.co.uk

NEWMAN HIRE COMPANY T 020 8743 0741
Lighting Hire
16 The Vale, Acton
London W3 7SB
E info@newmanhire.co.uk

NORTHERN LIGHT T 0131 622 9100
Assembly Street, Leith
Edinburgh EH6 7RG
F 0131 622 9101
E enquiries@northernlight.co.uk
W www.northernlight.co.uk

NOSTALGIA AMUSEMENTS T 020 8398 2141
Contact: Brian Davey
22 Greenwood Close, Thames Ditton
Surrey KT7 0BG
T 07973 506869

NOTTINGHAM JOUSTING ASSOCIATION SCHOOL OF NATIONAL EQUITATION LTD T 01509 852366
Jousting & Medieval Tournaments. Horses & Riders for Films & Television
Bunny Hill Top, Costock
Loughborough, Leicestershire LE12 6XN
E info@bunnyhill.co.uk
W www.bunnyhill.co.uk

OCEAN LEISURE T 020 7930 6060
Scuba Diving. Watersports Retail
11-14 Northumberland Avenue, London WC2N 5AQ
F 020 7930 3032
E info@oceanleisure.co.uk
W www.oceanleisure.co.uk

OFFSTAGE BOOKS T 020 8444 4717
BlackGull Bookshop, 121 High Road
London N2 8AG
E offstagebooks@gmail.com

PAPERFLOW PLC T 020 8331 2000
Office Equipment. Stationery
Units 5 & 6, Meridian Trading Estate
20 Bugsbys Way, Charlton, London SE7 7SJ
F 020 8331 2001
E sales@paperflowgroup.com

PAPERPROPMAKER T 07545 281486
Paper Props Created for Stage, Film & Television. Letters, Notebooks, Paper Ephemera etc. Handwritten or Printed. Any Style or Period Reproduced
Based in London
E sianwillis@live.co.uk

PATCHETTS EQUESTRIAN CENTRE T 01923 852255
Location
Hillfield Lane, Aldenham
Watford, Herts WD25 8PE
F 01923 859289
E info@patchetts.co.uk
W www.patchetts.co.uk

PATERSON, Helen T 020 7730 6428
Typing Services
40 Whitelands House, London SW3 4QY
E pater@waitrose.com

PERIOD PETROL PUMP COLLECTION T 01379 643978
c/o Diss Ironworks
7 St Nicholas Street
Diss, Norfolk IP22 4LB
E info@dissironworks.co.uk
W www.periodpetrolpump.co.uk

PHOSPHENE T 01449 770011
Lighting & Sound. Design. Hire. Sales
Milton Road South, Stowmarket
Suffolk IP14 1EZ
E phosphene@btconnect.com
W www.phosphene.co.uk

PIANO PEOPLE THE T 0845 6076713
Piano Hire & Transport
74 Playford Road, London N4 3PH
E info@pianopeople.co.uk
W www.pianopeople.co.uk

PICTURES PROPS CO LTD T 020 8749 2434
Film & Television Prop Hire
12-16 Brunel Road, London W3 7XR
F 020 8740 5846
E picturesprops@tiscali.co.uk

PINK POINTES DANCEWEAR T/F 01708 438584
1A Suttons Lane, Hornchurch
Essex RM12 6RD
E pink.pointes@btconnect.com

PLUNGE PRODUCTIONS T 01273 421819
Creative Services. Graphic Design. Props
Unit 3, Bestwood Works
Drove Road, Brighton BN41 2PA
E info@plungeproductions.com
W www.plungeproductions.com

PLUS FILM LTD T 01489 895559
All Periods Vehicle Hire
1 Mill House Cottages
Winchester Road
Bishop's Waltham SO32 1AH
T 07885 619783
E stephen.lamonby@gmail.com
W www.plusfilm.com

POLAND, Anna: SCULPTOR & MODELMAKER   T 023 8040 5166
Sculpture, Models, Puppets, Masks etc
Salterns, Old Bursledon
Southampton, Hampshire SO31 8DH
E polandanna@hotmail.com

POLLEX PROPS / FIREBRAND   T/F 01546 870310
Prop Makers
Leac Na Ban, Tayvallich
Lochgilphead, Argyll PA31 8PF
E firebrand.props@btinternet.com

PRAETORIAN ASSOCIATES / PROCUREMENT SERVICES - SA   T 020 7096 1827
Personal Safety & Anti-Stalking Consultancy. Services for Film & Television Industry within South Africa
Tintagel, 1 St Clairs Road
St Osyth, Essex CO16 8QG
T 07973 505981
E martin.beale@praetorianasc.com
W www.praetorianasc.com

PREMIER CHAUFFEUR SERVICES   T 01925 299112
164 Haydock Street, Newton-le-Willows
Merseyside WA12 9DH
T 07890 661050
E mike.vizard@hotmail.co.uk

PRINTMEDIA GROUP
E info@printmediagroup.eu
W www.printmediagroup.eu

PROBLOOD   T/F 01728 723865
11 Mount Pleasant, Framlingham
Suffolk IP13 9HQ

PROFESSOR PATTEN'S PUNCH & JUDY   T 01707 873262
Hire & Performances. Advice on Traditional Show
14 The Crest, Goffs Oak, Hertfordshire EN7 5NP
W www.dennispatten.co.uk

PROP FARM LTD   T 01909 723100
Contact: Pat Ward
Grange Farm, Elmton
Nr Creswell, North Derbyshire S80 4LX
F 01909 721465
E pat@propfarm.co.uk

PROP STUDIOS LTD   T 01444 250088
Unit 3 Old Kiln Works
Ditchling Common Industrial Estate
Hassocks BN6 8SG
F 01444 250089
E info@propstudios.co.uk
W www.propstudios.co.uk

PUNCH & JUDY PUPPETS & BOOTHS   T/F 020 8300 3579
Hire & Advisory Service. Callers by Appointment
42 Christchurch Road, Sidcup, Kent DA15 7HQ
W www.johnstylesentertainer.co.uk

RAINBOW PRODUCTIONS LTD   T 020 8254 5300
Creation & Appearances of Costume Characters. Stage Shows
Unit 3, Greenlea Park
Prince George's Road, London SW19 2JD
F 020 8254 5306
E info@rainbowproductions.co.uk
W www.rainbowproductions.co.uk

RE:AL   T 01622 200123
Print. Creative. Marketing. Digital
Unit 2, Tovil Green Business Park
Maidstone, Kent ME15 6TA
E info@realprintandmedia.com
W www.realprintandmedia.com

RENT-A-CLOWN   T/F 020 7608 0312
Contact: Mattie Faint
37 Sekeforde Street, Clerkenwell
London EC1R 0HA
E mattiefaint@gmail.com

REPLAY LTD   T 020 7637 0473
Showreels. Television Facilities Hire
Museum House, 25 Museum Street
London WC1A 1JT
E sales@replayfilms.co.uk
W www.replayfilms.co.uk

ROBERTS, Chris INTERIORS   T 07956 512074
Specialist Painters & Decorators to the Film Industry
117 Colebrook Lane, Loughton IG10 2HP

ROOTSTEIN, Adel LTD   T 020 7381 1447
Mannequin Manufacturer
9 Beaumont Avenue, London W14 9LP
F 020 7386 9594
W www.rootstein.com

ROYAL HORTICULTURAL HALLS THE   T 0845 3704606
Film Location: Art Deco & Edwardian Buildings. Conferences. Events. Exhibitions. Fashion Shows
80 Vincent Square, London SW1P 2PE
F 020 7834 2072
E horthalls@rhs.org.uk
W www.rhhonline.co.uk

RUDKIN DESIGN   T 01327 301770
Design Consultants. Advertising, Brochures, Corporate etc
10 Cottesbrooke Park, Heartlands Business Park
Daventry, Northamptonshire NN11 8YL
E arudkin@rudkindesign.co.uk
W www.rudkindesign.co.uk

RUMBLE, Jane   T 020 8904 6462
Props to Order. No Hire
121 Elmstead Avenue, Wembley
Middlesex HA9 8NT

SABAH MICHELLE   T/F 001 954 566 6219
UK Stylist/Designer Based in Florida. Fashion. Props. Wardrobe
2841 N. Ocean Boulevard Apt 501
Fort Lauderdale, Florida 33308, USA
T 001 954 383 2179
E sabah561@aol.com

SALVO THE CLOWN   T 01268 745791
13 Second Avenue, Kingsleigh Park
Thundersley, Essex SS7 3QD
E salvo@annualclownsdirectory.com
W www.annualclownsdirectory.com

SAPEX SCRIPTS   T 020 8236 1600
The Maxwell Building, Elstree Film Studios
Shenley Road, Borehamwood, Herts WD6 1JG
F 020 8324 2771
E scripts@sapex.co.uk
W www.sapex.co.uk

SCHULTZ & WIREMU FABRIC EFFECTS LTD   T/F 020 8469 0151
Distressing. Dyeing. Printing
Unit B202 Faircharm Studios, 8-12 Creekside
London SE8 3DX
E swfabricfx@london.com
W www.schultz-wiremufabricfx.co.uk

SCRIPTRIGHT   T 020 8749 9179
Contact: S.C. Hill. Script & Manuscript Typing Services. Script Reading & Assessment Services
St Saviour's Vicarage Cottage, Cobbold Road
London W12 9LN
E samc.hill@virgin.net

SCRIPTS BY ARGYLE   T 07905 293319
Play, Film & Book Typing/Editing in Professional Layout.
London Collection of Manuscript on Request
43 Clappers Lane, Fulking
West Sussex BN5 9ND
E argyle.associates@me.com

SHAOLIN WAY   T 020 7734 6391
Martial Arts Supplies. Lion Dance & Kung Fu Instruction
10 Little Newport Street
London WC2H 7JJ
T 07768 321092
E shaolinway@btconnect.com
W www.shaolinway.com

SHIRLEY LEAF &
PETAL COMPANY   T/F 01424 427793
Flower Makers Museum & Manufacturers
58A High Street, Old Town
Hastings, East Sussex TN34 3EN

SIDE EFFECTS   T 020 7587 1116
FX. Models. Props
92 Fentiman Road, London SW8 1LA
F 020 7207 0062
E sfx@lineone.net

SNOW BUSINESS   T/F 01453 840077
Snow & Winter Effects on Any Scale
The Snow Mill, Bridge Road
Ebley, Stroud
Gloucestershire GL5 4TR
E snow@snowbusiness.com
W www.snowbusiness.com

SOFT PROPS   T 020 7587 1116
Modelmakers
92 Fentiman Road, London SW8 1LA
F 020 7207 0062
E jackie@softprops.co.uk

STANSTED AIRPORT TAXIS
& CHAUFFEURS   T 0845 6436705
55 Croasdaile Road
Stansted Airport
Essex CM24 8DW
E enquiries@stanstedtaxiservice.co.uk
W www.stanstedtaxiservice.co.uk

STEELDECK RENTALS /
SALES LTD   T 020 7833 2031
Modular Staging. Stage Equipment Hire
Unit 58, T Marchant Trading Estate
42-72 Verney Road, London SE16 3DH
F 020 7232 1780
E rentals@steeldeck.co.uk
W www.steeldeck.co.uk

STEVENSON, Scott   T 07739 378579
Prop Maker
60 Ripley Road. Sawmills
Belper, Derbyshire DE56 2JQ
E scott@bodymechprops.co.uk
W www.bodymechprops.co.uk

STOKE BRUERNE BOAT
COMPANY LTD   T 07966 503609
Passenger Boat Operator
Wharf Cottage, Stoke Bruerne
Northants NN12 7SE
W www.stokebruerneboats.co.uk

SUFFOLK SCENERY   T 01449 736305
Curtain Tracks & Drapes only
Pie Hatch Farm, Brettenham Road
Buxall, Stowmarket, Suffolk IP14 3DZ
T 07787 548744
E piehatch@aol.com
W www.suffolkscenery.info

SUPERSCRIPTS   T 01256 769376
1 Bluehaven Walk, Hook
Hampshire RG27 9SX
T 07793 160138
E super_scripts@sky.com

SUPERSCRIPTS   T 020 8898 7933
Audio Typing. Post-Prod Scripts. Rushes
56 New Road, Hanworth
Middlesex TW13 6TQ
T 07971 671011
E jackie@superscripts.fsnet.co.uk

TALK TO THE HAND PUPPETS   T 020 7627 1052
Custom Puppets for Film, Stage & Television
Studio 27B
Spaces Business Centre
15-17 Ingate Place
London SW8 3NS
T 07855 421454
E iestynmevans@hotmail.com
W www.talktothehandpuppets.com

TAYLOR, Charlotte   T 020 8876 9085
Props Buyer. Stylist
18 Eleanor Grove, Barnes
London SW13 0JN
T 07836 708904
E charlottetaylor1@blueyonder.co.uk

THAMES LUXURY
CHARTERS LTD   T 020 7357 7751
Eagle Wharf
53 Lafone Street
London SE1 2LX
F 020 7378 1359
E sales@thamesluxurycharters.co.uk
W www.thamesluxurycharters.co.uk

THEATRESEARCH   T 01423 780497
Theatre Consultants
Dacre Hall, Dacre
North Yorkshire HG3 4ET
F 01423 781957
E info@theatresearch.co.uk
W www.theatresearch.co.uk

THEATRICAL
SHOEMAKERS LTD   T 020 7474 0500
Footwear
Unit 7A
Thames Road Industrial Estate
Thames Road, Silvertown
London E16 2EZ
E ts@shoemaking.co.uk
W www.shoemaking.co.uk

THEME TRADERS LTD   T 020 8452 8518
Props. Prop Hire. Party Planners. Productions
The Stadium, Oaklands Road, London NW2 6DL
F 020 8450 7322
E mailroom@themetraders.com
W www.themetraders.com

TOP SHOW   T/F 01904 750022
Props. Scenery. Conference Specialists
North Lane, Huntington
Yorks YO32 9SU

TRACK THAT   T 07941 234254
Tracking Vehicle/Camera Car Supplier
Based in Wandsworth, London SW18
E info@trackthat.co.uk
W www.trackthat.co.uk

TRANSCRIPTS   T 07973 200197
*Conferences. Interviews. Post-production Scripts.
Proofreading. Videos. Working Formats: Digital,
CD/DVD, Tapes*
E lucy@transcripts.demon.co.uk

**TRISTAR WORLDWIDE
CHAUFFEUR SERVICES**   T 01895 432000
Unit 1-2, Horton Road
West Drayton UB7 8BQ
E reservations@tristarworldwide.com
W www.tristarworldwide.com

TRYFONOS, Mary MASKS   T 020 7502 7883
Mask, Headdress & Puppet Specialist
59 Shaftesbury Road, London N19 4QW
T 07764 587433
E marytryfonos@aol.com

TURN ON LIGHTING   T/F 020 7359 7616
Antique Lighting c1850-1950
11 Camden Passage, London N1 8EA

**UK SAME DAY
DELIVERY SERVICE**   T 07785 717179
Contact: Philip Collings
18 Billingshurst Road, Broadbridge Heath
Horsham, West Sussex RH12 3LW
F 01403 266059
E philcollings60@hotmail.com

UPBEAT EVENT DESIGN   T 01494 790700
Corporate Hospitality Caterers
Global Infusion Court, Nashleigh Hill
Chesham, Bucks HP5 3HE
F 01494 790701
E enquiries@upbeateventdesign.com
W www.upbeateventdesign.com

UPSTAGE   T 020 7403 6510
Live Communications Agency
Studio A, 7 Maidstone Buildings Mews
72-76 Borough High Street, London SE1 1GD
F 020 7403 6511
E post@upstagelivecom.co.uk
W www.upstagelivecom.co.uk

**VENTRILOQUIST
DOLLS HOME**   T/F 020 8300 3579
Hire & Helpful Hints. Callers by Appointment
42 Christchurch Road, Sidcup
Kent DA15 7HQ
W www.johnstylesentertainer.co.uk

VENTRILOQUIST DUMMY HIRE   T 01707 873262
Contact: Dennis Patten. Hire & Advice
14 The Crest, Goffs Oak
Herts EN7 5NP
W www.dennispatten.co.uk

VINMAG ARCHIVE LTD   T 020 8533 7588
84-90 Digby Road
London E9 6HX
F 020 8525 9209
E piclib@vinmagarchive.com
W www.vinmagarchive.com

VINTAGE CARRIAGES TRUST   T 01535 680425
*Owners of the Museum of Rail Travel at Ingrow
Railway Centre*
Keighley
West Yorkshire BD21 5AX
F 01535 610796
E admin@vintagecarriagestrust.org
W www.vintagecarriagestrust.org

VOCALEYES   T 020 7375 1043
*Providers of Audio Description for Theatrical
Performance*
1st Floor, 54 Commercial Street
London E1 6LT
F 020 7247 5622
E enquiries@vocaleyes.co.uk
W www.vocaleyes.co.uk

WALKING YOUR DOG   T 020 8316 1175
Dog Walking & Pet Services for South East London
T 07867 502333
E info@walkingyourdog.net
W www.walkingyourdog.net

**WEBBER, Peter HIRE /
RITZ STUDIOS**   T 020 8870 1335
Music Equipment Hire. Rehearsal Studios
110-112 Disraeli Road
London SW15 2DX
E ben@peterwebberhire.com

**WESTED LEATHERS
COMPANY**   T 01322 660654
Suede & Leather Suppliers/Manufacturers
Little Wested House
Wested Lane
Swanley, Kent BR8 8EF
F 01322 667039
E wested@wested.com

WESTWARD, Lynn BLINDS   T 020 8742 8333
Window Blind Specialist
458 Chiswick High Road
London W4 5TT
F 020 8742 8444
E info@lynnwestward.com
W www.lynnwestward.com

WHITE ROOM STUDIO   T 020 8674 8151
Unit 03, 45 Morrish Road
London SW2 4EE
E info@whiteroomstudio.co.uk
W www.whiteroomstudio.co.uk

WILTSHIRE A. F. LLP   T 01483 200516
Agricultural Vehicle Engineers, Repairs etc
The Agricultural Centre
Alfold Road
Dunsfold, Surrey GU8 4NP
F 01483 200491
E team@afwiltshire.co.uk

WORBEY, Darryl STUDIOS   T 020 7639 8090
Specialist Puppet Design & Construction
Ground Floor, 33 York Grove
London SE15 2NY
T 07815 671564
E info@darrylworbeystudios.com

ACADEMY PLAYERS DIRECTORY
See PLAYERS DIRECTORY

A C I D PUBLICATIONS　　T/F 07050 205206
The Basement, Minus One House
Lyttelton Road, London E10 5NQ
E acidnews@aol.com

**ACTIONS: THE ACTORS'
THESAURUS**　　T 020 8749 4953
By Marina Caldarone & Maggie Lloyd-Williams
Nick Hern Books, The Glasshouse
49A Goldhawk Road, London W12 8QP
F 020 8735 0250
E info@nickhernbooks.co.uk
W www.nickhernbooks.co.uk

ACTORS' YEARBOOK　　T 020 7494 2111
Methuen Drama, Bloomsbury Publishing Plc
50 Bedford Square, London WC1B 3DP
F 020 7434 0151
E methuen.drama@bloomsbury.com
W www.methuendrama.com

**ANNUAIRE DU CINEMA
BELLEFAYE**　　T 00 33 1 42335252
*French Actors' Directory, Production, Technicians & All
Technical Industries & Suppliers*
30 rue Saint Marc, 75002 Paris, France
F 00 33 1 42333303
E contact@bellefaye.com
W www.bellefaye.com

ARTISTES & AGENTS　　T 020 7224 9666
Richmond House Publishing Co Ltd
70-76 Bell Street
Marylebone, London NW1 6SP
F 020 7224 9688
E sales@rhpco.co.uk
W www.rhpco.co.uk

AUDITIONS: A PRACTICAL GUIDE
W www.auditionsapracticalguide.com

AUDITIONS UNDRESSED　　T 020 7839 4888
By Dan Bowling
c/o Global Artists, 23 Haymarket
London SW1Y 4DG
E michaelgarrett@globalartists.co.uk

**AURORA METRO PRESS
(1989)**　　T 020 3261 0000
*Biography, Drama, Fiction, Humour, Reference &
International Literature in English Translation*
67 Grove Avenue
Twickenham TW1 4HX
E info@aurorametro.com
W www.aurorametro.com

BEAT MAGAZINE　　T 01753 866865
Arts & Culture Magazine
c/o Firestation Centre for Arts & Culture
The Old Court, St Leonards Road
Windsor, Berks SL4 3BL
E editor@beatmagazine.co.uk
W www.beatmagazine.co.uk

**BRITISH PERFORMING
ARTS YEARBOOK**　　T 020 7333 1729
Rhinegold Publishing
Rhinegold House
20 Rugby Street, London WC1N 3QZ
E bpay@rhinegold.co.uk
W www.rhinegold.co.uk

**BRITISH THEATRE
DIRECTORY**　　T 020 7224 9666
Richmond House Publishing Co Ltd
70-76 Bell Street, Marylebone, London NW1 6SP
F 020 7224 9688
E sales@rhpco.co.uk
W www.rhpco.co.uk

BROADCAST　　T 020 7728 5507
Greater London House
Hampstead Road, London NW1 7EJ
T 0844 8488859 (Subscriptions)
E bro@subscription.co.uk
W www.broadcastnow.co.uk

BROADWAY BABY　　T 020 3327 3872
*Reviewer at Edinburgh & Brighton Fringe & also in
London. Print & Online Reviews*
239 Lewisham Way, London SE4 1XF
E pressreleases@broadwaybaby.com
W www.broadwaybaby.com

CASTCALL　　T 01582 456213
Casting Information Services. Incorporating Castfax
106 Wilsden Avenue, Luton LU1 5HR
E admin@castcall.co.uk
W www.castcall.co.uk

CASTWEB　　T 020 7720 9002
7 St Luke's Avenue, London SW4 7LG
E info@castweb.co.uk
W www.castweb.co.uk

CELEBRITY BULLETIN THE　　T 020 8672 3191
G8 Battersea Studio 1
80 Silverthorne Road
London SW8 3HE
E enquiries@celebrity-bulletin.co.uk

CHAPPELL OF BOND STREET　　T 020 7432 4400
*Sheet Music. Musical Instruments. Guitars.
Keyboards. Pianos*
152-160 Wardour Street
London W1F 8YA
F 020 7432 4410
E enquiries@chappellofbondstreet.co.uk
W www.chappellofbondstreet.co.uk

**CONFERENCE & INCENTIVE
TRAVEL MAGAZINE**　　T 020 8267 4307
22 Bute Gardens, London W6 7HN
F 020 8267 4442
E cit@haymarket.com
W www.citmagazine.com

**CREATIVE REVIEW
HANDBOOK**　　T 020 7970 6455
Centaur Media Plc, 79 Wells Street
London W1T 3QN
W www.chb.com

DANCERS SPOTLIGHT　　T 020 7437 7631
Twitter: @SpotlightUK
7 Leicester Place, London WC2H 7RJ
F 020 7437 5881
E questions@spotlight.com
W www.spotlight.com

EQUITY MAGAZINE　　T 020 7670 0211
Guild House, Upper St Martin's Lane
London WC2H 9EG
F 020 7379 7001
E ppemberton@equity.org.uk
W www.equity.org.uk

FORESIGHT-NEWS T 020 7190 7777
Centaur Media Plc, Wells Point
London W1T 3QN
F 020 7900 3684
E info@foresightnews.co.uk
W www.foresightnews.co.uk

FOURTHWALL MAGAZINE T 020 7701 4536
Incorporating The Drama Student Magazine
Top Floor 3, 66 Wansey Street, London SE17 1JP
F 07092 846523
E editor@fourthwallmagazine.co.uk
W www.fourthwallmagazine.co.uk

HERN, Nick BOOKS T 020 8749 4953
Theatre Publishers. Performing Rights Agents
The Glasshouse, 49A Goldhawk Road
London W12 8QP
F 020 8735 0250
E info@nickhernbooks.co.uk
W www.nickhernbooks.co.uk

**KAY'S UK & EUROPEAN
PRODUCTION MANUALS** T 020 8960 6900
Pinewood Studios, Pinewood Road
Iver Heath, Bucks SL0 0NH
E info@kays.co.uk
W www.kays.co.uk

KFTV T 020 7549 2532
Formerly KEMPS
Wilmington Publishing & Information Ltd
6-14 Underwood Street, London N1 7JQ
E skeegan@wilmington.co.uk
W www.kftv.com

KNOWLEDGE THE
6-14 Underwood Street, London N1 7JQ
E knowledge@wilmington.co.uk
W www.theknowledgeonline.com

LIMELIGHT THE T 00 27 11 7937231
Limelight Publications, Contacts & Casting Directory
PO Box 760, Randpark Ridge
2156, Gauteng, South Africa
F 00 27 86 5457231
E info@limelight.co.za
W www.limelight.co.za

METHUEN DRAMA T 020 7631 5840
50 Bedford Square, London WC1B 3DP
F 020 7631 5800
E methuendrama@bloomsbury.com
W www.methuendrama.com

MOVIE MEMORIES MAGAZINE
Devoted to Films & Stars of the 40s, 50s & 60s
10 Russet Close, Scunthorpe, N. Lincs DN15 8YJ
E crob.mvm@ntlworld.com

**OFFICIAL LONDON
SEATING PLAN GUIDE THE** T 020 7224 9666
Richmond House Publishing Co Ltd, 70-76 Bell Street
Marylebone, London NW1 6SP
F 020 7224 9668
E sales@rhpco.co.uk
W www.rhpco.co.uk

PA ENTERTAINMENT T 0870 1203200
292 Vauxhall Bridge Road, Victoria
London SW1V 1AE
F 0870 1203201
E events@pressassociation.com
W www.pressassociation.com

PCR
See PRODUCTION & CASTING REPORT

PINTER & MARTIN LTD T 020 7737 6868
6 Effra Parade, Brixton
London SW2 1PS
E info@pinterandmartin.com
W www.pinterandmartin.com

PLAYERS DIRECTORY T 001 310 247 3058
*Casting Directory Published in January & July. Hard
Copy & eBook. Contains Actor Photos, Representation,
Resume & Demo Reels. Published since 1937*
2210 W. Olive Avenue, Suite 320
Burbank, California 91506, USA
E info@playersdirectory.com
W www.playersdirectory.com

PLAYS INTERNATIONAL T 020 7720 1950
33A Lurline Gardens, London SW11 4DD
E info@playsinternational.org
W www.playsinternational.org.uk

PRESENTERS CLUB THE T 07782 224207
Presenter Promotions
123 Corporation Road
Gillingham, Kent ME7 1RG
E info@presenterpromotions.com
W www.presenterpromotions.com

PRESENTERS SPOTLIGHT T 020 7437 7631
Twitter: @SpotlightUK
7 Leicester Place, London WC2H 7RJ
F 020 7437 5881
E questions@spotlight.com
W www.spotlight.com

**PRODUCTION &
CASTING REPORT** T 020 7566 8282
Editorial
6-14 Underwood Street, London N1 7JQ
E info@pcrnewsletter.com
W www.pcrnewsletter.com

**PRODUCTION &
CASTING REPORT** T 020 7549 2578
Subscriptions
Marketing Department
6-14 Underwood Street, London N1 7JQ
E info@pcrsubscriptions.com
W www.pcrnewsletter.com

**PRODUCTION
INTELLIGENCE** T 020 7549 2596
Hosted on The Knowledge. Contact: Sarah Keegan
6-14 Underwood Street
London N1 7JQ
E skeegan@wilmington.co.uk
W www.theknowledgeonline.com/production-intelligence

RADIO TIMES T 020 8433 1200
Formerly published by BBC Magazines
Immediate Media, Media Centre
201 Wood Lane, London W12 7TQ
E enquiries@immediate.co.uk
W www.radiotimes.com

**RICHMOND HOUSE
PUBLISHING COMPANY LTD** T 020 7224 9666
70-76 Bell Street, Marylebone
London NW1 6SP
F 020 7224 9688
E sales@rhpco.co.uk
W www.rhpco.co.uk

ROUTLEDGE PUBLISHING   T 020 7017 6000
2 Park Square, Milton Park, Abington, Oxon OX14 4RN
F 020 7017 6336
E book.orders@tandf.co.uk
W www.routledge.com

SBS LTD   T 020 7372 6337
1 Goodwin's Court, London WC4N 4LL
E office@sbscasting.co.uk

SCREEN INTERNATIONAL   T 020 7728 5000
Greater London House, Hampstead Road
London NW1 7EJ
E mai.le@emap.com
W www.screendaily.com

SHOWBIZ FRIENDS
*Social Networking Website for Professional
Showbiz People*
W www.showbizfriends.com

SHOWCASE   T 01892 557825
*Annual Handbook for the Worldwide Music
Production Industry*
25 Southmead Close, Mayfield, East Sussex TN20 6UJ
E james@showcase-music.com
W www.showcase-music.com

SHOWCAST   T 00 61 2 46209464
PO Box 2001, Leumeah, NSW 2560 Australia
E danelle@showcast.com.au
W www.showcast.com.au

SHOWDIGS.CO.UK
E info@showdigs.co.uk
W www.showdigs.co.uk

SIGHT & SOUND   T 020 7255 1444
British Film Institute, 21 Stephen Street, London W1T 1LN
E s&s@bfi.org.uk
W www.bfi.org.uk/sightandsound

**SOCIETY OF LONDON
THEATRE THE (SOLT)**   T 020 7557 6700
Latest News & London Theatre Listings
32 Rose Street
London WC2E 9ET
E enquiries3@solttma.co.uk
W www.officiallondontheatre.co.uk

**SO YOU WANT TO
BE AN ACTOR?**   T 020 8749 4953
By Timothy West & Prunella Scales
Nick Hern Books, The Glasshouse
49A Goldhawk Road, London W12 8QP
F 020 8735 0250
E info@nickhernbooks.co.uk
W www.nickhernbooks.co.uk

**SO YOU WANT TO BE A
THEATRE DIRECTOR?**   T 020 8749 4953
By Stephen Unwin
Nick Hern Books, The Glasshouse
49A Goldhawk Road, London W12 8QP
F 020 8735 0250
E info@nickhernbooks.co.uk
W www.nickhernbooks.co.uk

**SO YOU WANT TO BE A
THEATRE PRODUCER?**   T 020 8749 4953
By James Seabright
Nick Hern Books, The Glasshouse
49A Goldhawk Road, London W12 8QP
F 020 8735 0250
E info@nickhernbooks.co.uk
W www.nickhernbooks.co.uk

SPOTLIGHT
85th Anniversary

Spotlight has been providing casting information to the entertainment industry for 85 years

www.spotlight.com

1927: First edition of Spotlight printed

CHILDREN A-Z

First editions of other titles

SO YOU WANT TO BE A TV PRESENTER?   **T** 020 8749 4953
By Kathryn Wolfe
Nick Hern Books, The Glasshouse
49A Goldhawk Road, London W12 8QP
F 020 8735 0250
E info@nickhernbooks.co.uk
W www.nickhernbooks.co.uk

SO YOU WANT TO DO A SOLO SHOW?   **T** 020 8749 4953
By Gareth Armstrong
Nick Hern Books, The Glasshouse
49A Goldhawk Road, London W12 8QP
F 020 8735 0250
E info@nickhernbooks.co.uk
W www.nickhernbooks.co.uk

SPOTLIGHT   **T** 020 7437 7631
Twitter: @SpotlightUK
7 Leicester Place, London WC2H 7RJ
F 020 7437 5881
E questions@spotlight.com
W www.spotlight.com

STAGE NEWSPAPER LTD THE   **T** 020 7939 8483
47 Bermondsey Street, London SE1 3XT
F 020 7939 8478
E editor@thestage.co.uk
W www.thestage.co.uk

SUPERNOVA BOOKS   **T** 020 3261 0000
Contact: Rebecca Gillieron (Publisher/Editor). Publishing Books on Film, Music, Art & Music
67 Grove Avenue, Twickenham TW1 4HX
E rebecca@aurorametro.com
W www.supernovabooks.co.uk

TELEVISUAL MEDIA UK LTD   **T** 020 3008 5750
48 Charlotte Street, London W1T 2NS
F 020 3008 5784
E advertising@televisual.com
W www.televisual.com

THEATRE RECORD   **T/F** 01243 539437
131 Sherringham Avenue
London N17 9RU
E editor@theatrerecord.com
W www.theatrerecord.com

TIME OUT GROUP LTD   **T** 020 7813 3000
Universal House
251 Tottenham Court Road
London W1T 7AB
F 020 7813 6001
W www.timeout.com

TV TIMES   **T** 020 3148 5615
IPC Media, Blue Fin Building
110 Southwark Street, London SE1 0SU
F 020 3148 8115

VARIETY NEWSPAPER   **T** 020 7911 1924
3rd Floor, 31 Southampton Row
London WC1B 5HJ
T 020 7911 1906
W www.variety.com

WHITE BOOK THE   **T** 020 8971 8282
Mash Media Group Ltd, 4th Floor, Sterling House
6-10 St Georges Road, London SW19 4DP
E spascal@mashmedia.net
W www.whitebook.co.uk

ARTHUR LEONE PR   T 020 7836 7660
Suite 5, 17 Shorts Gardens
London WC2H 9AT
E info@arthurleone.com
W www.arthurleone.com

AVALON PUBLIC RELATIONS   T 020 7598 8000
Arts. Marketing
4A Exmoor Street, London W10 6BD
F 020 7598 7223
E sophias@avalonuk.com
W www.avalonuk.com

BEIGE LONDON   T 020 7404 3000
65 Clerkenwell Road, London EC1R 5BL
F 020 7404 5000
E beige@beigelondon.com
W www.beigelondon.com

**BOLTON, Erica &
QUINN Jane LTD**   T 020 7221 5000
6 Addison Avenue, London W11 4QR
F 020 7221 8100
E name@boltonquinn.com
W www.boltonquinn.com

CHESTON, Judith PUBLICITY   T 01608 661198
30 Telegraph Street, Shipston-on-Stour
Warwickshire CV36 4DA
F 01608 663772
E jacheston@tiscali.co.uk

CLARKE, Duncan PR   T 01904 345247
24 Severus Street, York
North Yorkshire YO24 4NL
E duncanclarkepr@live.co.uk
W www.duncanclarkepr.wordpress.com

**CLOUT
COMMUNICATIONS LTD**   T 020 8362 0803
15 Carlton Road, London N11 3EX
E enquiries@cloutcom.co.uk
W www.cloutcom.co.uk

DDA PUBLIC RELATIONS LTD   T 020 7932 9800
192-198 Vauxhall Bridge Road
London SW1V 1DX
F 020 7932 4950
E info@ddapr.com
W www.ddapr.com

DS MANAGEMENT   T 020 8743 7777
St Martin's Theatre, West Street, London WC2N 9NH
T 07711 245848
E ds@denisesilvey.com

ELSON, Howard PROMOTIONS   T 07768 196310
Management. Marketing. PR
16 Penn Avenue, Chesham
Buckinghamshire HP5 2HS
F 01494 784760
E howardelson@btinternet.com

EMPICA LTD   T 01275 394400
1 Lyons Court, Long Ashton Business Park
Yanley Lane, Bristol BS41 9LB
F 01275 393933
E info@empica.com
W www.empica.com

**FIVEASH, Nick
PR & MANAGEMENT**   T 07971 240987
4 Baxendale Street, London E2 7BY
E nickfiveash@me.com

GADABOUTS LTD   T 020 8445 5450
Theatre Marketing & Promotions
54 Friary Road, London N12 9PB
F 0870 7059140
E info@gadabouts.co.uk
W www.gadabouts.co.uk

GAYNOR, Avril ASSOCIATES   T 07958 623013
126 Brudenell Road, London SW17 8DE
E gaynorama@aol.com

GENERATE PR   T 07545 499254
Contact: Fran Walker
9 Winchester Way, Peterborough PE3 6HL
E fran@generatepr.co.uk

**GOODMAN, Deborah
PUBLICITY (DGPR)**   T 020 8959 9980
25 Glenmere Avenue, London NW7 2LT
F 020 8959 7875
E publicity@dgpr.co.uk
W www.dgpr.co.uk

GRIFFIN, Alison ASSOCIATES
3rd Floor, 146 Strand, London WC2R 1JD
E alison@alisongriffin.co.uk

**HYMAN, Sue
ASSOCIATES LTD**   T 020 7379 8420
St Martin's House, 59 St Martin's Lane
London WC2N 4JS
T 07976 514449
E sue.hyman@btinternet.com
W www.suehyman.com

IMPACT AGENCY THE   T 020 7580 1770
1 Bedford Avenue, London WC1B 3AU
F 020 7580 7200
E mail@impactagency.co.uk
W www.theimpactagency.com

KEAN LANYON LTD   T 020 7697 8453
Contact: Sharon Kean
United House, North Road, Islington, London N7 9DP
T 07973 843133
E sharon@keanlanyon.com
W www.keanlanyon.com

KELLER, Don   T 020 8800 4882
Arts Marketing
65 Glenwood Road, Harringay, London N15 3JS
E info@donkeller.co.uk

LEEP MARKETING & PR   T 07973 558895
Marketing. Press. Publicity
83A Albert Street, London NW1 7LX
E philip@leep.biz

LONDON FLAIR PR   T 020 3371 7945
*Entertainment Specialists for Actors & Celebrities.
Film. Television*
6th Floor, International House
223 Regents Street, London W1B 2QD
E cls@londonflairpr.com
W www.londonflairpm.com

MATTHEWS, Liz PR   T 020 7253 1639
8 Smokehouse Yard, 44-46 St John Street
London EC1M 4DF
E liz@lizmatthewspr.com
W www.lizmatthewspr.com

MAYER, Anne PR   T 020 7254 7391
82 Mortimer Road, London N1 4LH
T 07764 192842
E annemayer@btopenworld.com

**McAULEY ARTS MARKETING LTD /
MAKESTHREE**   T 020 7021 0927
25 Short Street, London SE1 8LJ
E sam@makesthree.org
W www.makesthree.org

MITCHELL, Jackie   T 01372 465041
JM Communications
4 Sims Cottages, The Green, Claygate, Surrey KT10 0JH
F 01372 471073
E pr@jackiem.com   W www.jackiem.com

MOBIUS T 020 7269 9929
The Crypt, St Georges Church
6-7 Little Russell Street
London WC1A 2HR
E info@mobiusindustries.com
W www.mobiusindustries.com

**MORGAN, Jane
ASSOCIATES (JMA)** T 020 7263 9867
Marketing. Media
8 Heathville Road, London N19 3AJ
E jma@janemorganassociates.com

**NELSON BOSTOCK
GROUP LTD** T 020 7229 4400
Compass House, 22 Redan Place
London W2 4SA
F 020 7727 2025
E info@nelsonbostock.com
W www.nelsonbostock.com

**NICOLINA MARKETING &
COMMUNICATIONS** T 07729 757006
16 The Grange, London SW19 4PS
E consulting@nicolina-online.com
W www.lifestylemarketingcommunications.yolasite.com

OATWAY, Christopher T 07873 485265
495 Altrincham Road, Baguley Hall
Manchester M23 1AR
E christopherjoatway@gmail.com

PR PEOPLE THE T 0161 976 2729
1 St James Drive, Sale
Cheshire M33 7QX
E graham@pr-people.uk.com
W www.pr-people.uk.com

PREMIER PR T 020 7292 8330
91 Berwick Street
London W1F 0NE
F 020 7734 2024
W www.premierpr.com

**PRESS COMPLAINTS
COMMISSION** T 020 7831 0022
Halton House, 20/23 Holborn
London EC1N 2JD
E complaints@pcc.org.uk
W www.pcc.org.uk

**PUBLIC EYE
COMMUNICATIONS LTD** T 020 7351 1555
Suite 313, Plaza
535 Kings Road, London SW10 0SZ
F 020 7351 1010
E assistant@publiceye.co.uk

**PURPLE REIGN
PUBLIC RELATIONS** T 07809 110982
28 Undercliff Road
Lewisham
London SE13 7TT
E info@purplereignpr.co.uk
W www.purplereignpr.co.uk

**RICHMOND TOWERS
COMMUNICATIONS LTD** T 020 7388 7421
26 Fitzroy Square, London W1T 6BT
F 020 7388 7761
W www.rt-com.com

RKM COMMUNICATIONS LTD T 020 3130 7090
Based in London & Los Angeles
2nd Floor, 4 New Burlington Street
London W1S 2JG
F 020 7287 1704
E info@rkmcom.com
W www.rkmcom.com

S & X MEDIA T 0121 604 6366
Contact: Paul Phedon
The Gatehouse, 2B Victoria Works
Vittoria Street, Birmingham B1 3PE
F 0121 694 6494
E paul@sx-media.com
W www.sx-media.com

SAVIDENT, Paul T 020 3287 0960
Marketing. Press Management
The Office, 27 St Dunstan's Road
London W7 2EY
E paul@savident.com
W www.savident.com

**SHIPPEN, Martin
MARKETING & MEDIA** T 020 8968 1943
88 Purves Road, London NW10 5TB
T 07956 879165
E m.shippen@virgin.net

SKPR THEATRE PUBLICITY T 07966 578607
Theatre PR Consultancy
1 Heath Hall Lodge, French Hill
Thursley, Godalming, Surrey GU8 6NQ
E sheridan@sheridanskitchen.com

SNELL, Helen LTD T 020 7240 5537
4th Floor, 80-81 St Martin's Lane
London WC2N 4AA
F 020 7240 2947
E info@helensnell.com

**SOCIETY OF LONDON
THEATRE THE (SOLT)** T 020 7557 6727
Contact: Alison Duguid (Senior Press Officer)
32 Rose Street, London WC2E 9ET
E alison@solttma.co.uk

STOTT, Barbara T 020 7350 1159
20 Sunbury Lane, London SW11 3NP
E b-stott@talktalk.net

TARGET LIVE LTD T 020 3372 0950
Design. Marketing. Media. Press
45-51 Whitfield Street, London W1T 4HD
F 020 3372 0951
E info@target-live.co.uk
W www.target-live.co.uk

**TAYLOR HERRING
PUBLIC RELATIONS** T 020 8206 5151
11 Westway Centre, 69 St Marks Road
London W10 6JG
F 020 8206 5155
E james.herring@taylorherring.com
W www.taylorherring.com

TRE-VETT, Eddie T 01425 475544
Brink House, Avon Castle
Ringwood, Hampshire BH24 2BL

**WILLIAMS, Tei PRESS &
ARTS MARKETING** T 01869 337940
Post Office Cottage, Clifton
Oxon OX15 0PD
T 07957 664116
E artsmarketing@btconnect.com

**WILSON, Stella PUBLICITY &
PERSONAL MANAGEMENT** T 07860 174301
293 Faversham Road, Seasalter
Whitstable, Kent CT5 4BN
E stella@stellawilson.com

**WINGHAM, Maureen
PRESS & PUBLIC RELATIONS** T 01449 771200
69 Bury Street, Stowmarket
Suffolk IP14 1HD
E maureen.wingham@mwmedia.uk.com

R →

Radio
- BBC Radio
- BBC Local
- Independent

Rehearsal Rooms & Casting Suites

Role Play Companies / Theatre Skills in Business

BBC RADIO

BBC Broadcasting House
Portland Place, London W1A 1AA
T 020 7580 4468 (Main Switchboard)

The BBC has relocated a number of its departments to a new site at MediaCityUK, Salford Quays, Salford. Departments include BBC Children's, BBC Radio 5 live, parts of Future Media & Technology, BBC Learning, BBC Sport and BBC Breakfast. For further information about BBC North please contact the BBC's main London switchboard.

If you are interested in working for the BBC in a production role, you can submit your CV to the BBC Production Talent website at www.bbcproductiontalent.co.uk

• DRAMA

Head of Audio Drama	Alison Hindell (BBC Wales)

Production

Editor, Drama	Toby Swift
Editor, Readings	Di Speirs
Production Executive & RDC	Rebecca Wilmshurst
Executive Producer	Jeremy Mortimer

Drama Producers – London

Sally Avens	Marion Nancarrow
Marc Beeby	Tracey Neale
Jessica Dromgoole	Jonquil Panting
David Hunter	Mary Peate
Peter Kavanagh	Saha Yevtushenko
Development	Abigail le Fleming

Readings Producers - London

Elizabeth Allard	Duncan Minshull
Emma Harding	Justine Willett
Gemma Jenkins	

Drama Producers - Manchester

Gary Brown	Nadia Molinari
Pauline Harris	
Editor	Sue Roberts
Development	Charlotte Riches

Drama Producers, The Archers - Birmingham

Julie Beckett	Rosemary Watts
Kim Greengrass	
Editor	Vanessa Whitburn
Development	Sarah Bradshaw

Drama Producer - BBC Wales Kate McAll

Drama Producers - BBC Scotland

Gaynor Macfarlane	Kirsty Williams
David Ian Neville	
Editor	Bruce Young

Drama Producers - BBC Northern Ireland

All enquiries to Gemma McMullan

Writersroom

Director	Kate Rowland

• RADIO COMEDY/RADIO PRODUCTION

Head, Radio Comedy	Jane Berthoud

Executive Producers

Steven Canny	Alison Vernon-Smith

Producers

Colin Anderson	Claire Jones
Sam Bryant	Victoria Lloyd
Leanne Coop	Julia McKenzie
Carl Cooper	Sam Michell

Lyndsey Fenner	Ed Morrish
Tilusha Ghelani	Katie Tyrrell
Production Executive	Mel Almond
Production Manager	Hayley Nathan

• NEWS AND CURRENT AFFAIRS

Director, News	Helen Boaden
Deputy Director, BBC News & Head of Multimedia Programmes	Stephen Mitchell
Head of BBC Newsroom	Mary Hockaday
Head of Newsgathering	Fran Unsworth
Controller of BBC News Channel (incl. News at One) & Deputy Head of BBC Newsroom	Kevin Bakhurst
Head of Editorial Development	Sam Taylor
Technology Controller, Journalism	Peter Coles
Head of Political Programmes, Analysis & Research	Sue Inglish
Executive Editor & Commissioning Editor for Current Affairs	Clive Edwards
Executive Editor, Radio Current Affairs	Nicola Meyrick
Editor, Six & Ten o'clock News	James Stephenson
Editor, Newsnight	Peter Rippon
Editor, Breakfast	Alison Ford
Editor, Panorama	Tom Giles
Editor, BBC News Website	Steve Herrmann

Radio Programmes

Editor, Today	Ceri Thomas
Editor, PM/Broadcasting House	Joanna Carr
The World This Weekend/ The World at One	Nick Sutton
Editor, Newsbeat, Radio 1	Rod McKenzie

• RADIO SPORT

Head of BBC Sports News & BBC Radio Sport	Richard Burgess
Deputy Controller/Commissioning Editor, Radio 5 live	Jonathan Wall

• CONTROLLERS

Director of Audio & Music	Tim Davie

RADIO 1

Controller	Ben Cooper

RADIO 2

Controller	Bob Shennan

RADIO 3

Controller	Roger Wright

RADIO 4 & RADIO 4 EXTRA

Controller	Gwyneth Williams

RADIO 5 LIVE

Controller	Adrian Van Klaveren

• BBC NEW WRITING

BBC Writersroom
BBC Broadcasting House
Portland Place, London W1A 1AA
T 020 8743 8000 (Main Switchboard)
E writersroom@bbc.co.uk
W www.bbc.co.uk/writersroom

Creative Director	Kate Rowland
Development Producer	Paul Ashton

Radio

Why should I work in radio?

To make a smooth transition from stage or camera to radio acting, everything that would otherwise be conveyed through body language and facial expressions must all be focused into the tone and pitch of the actor's voice.

If you have only ever considered visual acting work before, pursuing radio work would certainly enable you to expand your horizons and add additional skills to your CV. It is an opportunity to work in a different way and meet new requirements. Rehearsal and recording time is reduced in radio, which may allow you to pursue visual and radio acting alongside each other. Time constraints can be a pressure, and you have to get used to working without props (just sound effects), but this 'back to basics' existence is appealing to a lot of actors.

How can I become a radio presenter?

Presenting work in any medium comes under a different category as this is not classed as acting. It is a skill in its own right. Please refer to the 'Agents: Presenters' section for more information.

Do I need a voicereel?

This has to be your first and most important step into getting work as a radio actor. Your CV is not enough to get you a job without a professional-sounding voicereel. Voice-over work in commercial and corporate sectors requires a different type of reel. Please see the 'Promotional Services' section for more detailed voicereel advice in either area.

Do I need an agent?

It is not strictly necessary to have an agent for radio work. The BBC is by far the main producer of radio drama and welcomes applications directly from actors, but some independent radio stations prefer using agents to put actors forward. It might be worth doing some research on your local radio stations and finding out their preferred method of contact and making a decision from there. If you are looking for a new agent and are interested in radio work as well as straight acting work, find out whether they deal with this area of the industry before signing up. If you only want to pursue radio and/or voice-over work, or are looking for a specialist agent in addition to your main agent, please see the 'Agents: Voice-over' section for further advice and listings.

How do I find work in radio?

You can send your CV and voicereel directly out to producers of radio drama, but make sure you target your search. Listen to radio plays and make a note of any producers whose work you particularly liked. This may also help you to identify what types of dramas you feel your voice would be most suited to.

Once you have done your research and made a shortlist, send your voicereel with a personalised letter. Mention the plays you liked and explain that you feel he or she will be able to use your voice in productions like these. This method is likely to be much more effective than sending out a generic covering letter en masse, and will make you stand out.

You don't need to send a headshot with your CV, but you could incorporate your photo in the body of your CV. It would be a good idea to have your name and contact details professionally printed onto your voicereel CD in case it becomes separated from your CV – see 'Promotional Services' for listings of companies that can do this for you.

Radio

Di Speirs is the Editor of Readings, BBC Radio, London. After five years in professional theatre, Di worked for ABC Australia before joining Woman's Hour on BBC Radio 4. She edited the Woman's Hour serial reading for five years and edited two collections of Woman's Hour short stories. Since 1997 she has produced readings and drama across Radio 4 and 3, particularly Book at Bedtime. She runs and judges the BBC National Short Story Award and was Chair of the Orange Award for New Writers in 2010.

The world of audio can be an overlooked one for actors, especially those starting out or who have perhaps come up through a screen route. And yet, on BBC Radio alone, there are hours of readings and radio drama every week and the commercial audiobook market is now taking advantage of the rapid growth of new media, from downloads to apps. For those whose voice is a strong part of their acting armoury there are opportunities, be they the most established of names and or at the beginning of their careers. And audio, particularly radio, is exciting and empowering for actors. It's a medium where they can take on roles they could never realistically hope to play in more visual mediums, stage or screen. The shortest actress can play that 'painted maypole', Helena, and in readings in particular, there's an unrivalled opportunity to not only give voice to both genders and all age ranges, but to people a whole cast.

As with anything in life, knowing the market is key to starting to work in it. In my area of radio readings, the bulk of the output is on BBC Radio 4, though Radio 3 also has proms and twenty minute interval slots, which are often stories, as well as The Essay. On Radio 4 there are three main strands: Book of the Week, 9.45am Monday to Friday, which is non-fiction; standalone short readings on Fridays and Sundays, a mix of contemporary and classic commissioned and published stories and non-fiction; and Book at Bedtime, the original reading slot, which goes out at 10.45pm Monday to Friday and is usually a ten part abridgement of a new or classic novel.

Beyond this lie the riches of radio drama - with the Woman's Hour drama serial, the Afternoon Play at 2.45pm, the Saturday Play, and the Classic Serial on Sunday afternoons (repeated on Saturday evenings), not to mention The Archers. And then there are the plays on Radio 3 and occasional originations, often of science fiction, on Radio 7.

Radio is exciting and empowering for actors. It's a medium where they can take on roles they could never realistically hope to play in more visual mediums.

For many actors, radio has a special appeal, despite the smaller fees on offer. It is swift and frequently very convenient – a reading or a role in a radio drama can often be fitted in around the demands of a filming or a rehearsal schedule, or can be an ideal job once a play is running. BBC Radio has a devoted, loyal and large audience – often of over a million listeners – so you, and your talent, reaches many ears and may prompt other work. The variety of the work is enormous. Casting can be counter-intuitive and certainly allows a performer to explore areas they might not reach otherwise. If you still sound younger than your advancing years, you may yet get a coveted romantic lead; similarly the most able and versatile voice artists are able to adopt nationalities at will. Over two decades I have directed the same actress creating characters who were Welsh-Maltese, Ukrainian, Italian and Danish in different Book at Bedtimes.

The quality of the writing is, by and large, also extremely high. Radio is an unforgiving medium in that sense and poor writing shows. Given the wealth of literature on offer and the comparatively few slots available, the books that are chosen for broadcast are amongst the best of contemporary and classic writing and hopefully a pleasure to work on. Similarly the cost of dramatising a great classic, whilst still high in radio budget terms, remains feasible. And radio's ability to paint the best pictures through sound, part of which is of course through the performances, make it a challenging and satisfying environment to work in.

Beyond that, there is a magic about the intimacy of radio which is something actors, producers and directors relish. Listen out and you will hear the greatest British acting talent on our airwaves. It is always a small team – with readings a very small one – but that also means that there is a real sense of collaboration when working, and a real sense of connection, on a one-to-one basis, with that great unseen audience.

Getting your voice heard in the first place is the next question. I cast largely from theatre (which has some affinity) rather than film – and from other radio productions. BBC Radio maintains a unique theatrical institution – The Radio Drama Company – which began in the midst of the Blitz to keep a small company of actors safe and at hand for productions during the war. These days, while no longer 50 strong, the RDC consists of a group of actors on contract for a matter of months who appear in numerous dramas across the networks. Through its Soundstart programme, BBC Audio Drama also runs two major awards – The Carleton Hobbs and the Norman Beaton awards. For details on these and advice on how to get started in radio do look at the Soundstart webpages at www.bbc.co.uk/soundstart. There are many independent companies making productions for the audio market and for the BBC. It is worth sending demo tapes to them too.

There is a magic about the intimacy of radio which is something actors, producers and directors relish.

If you are particularly interested in readings I would suggest including fairly long passages in any demo, which demonstrate not only the ability to create a host of characters (please don't over-characterise though – shading is usually more successful) but also that more elusive element – the narrator. Also take advantage of the useful facility on Spotlight to upload voice clips and include narration on the audio content. It's impossible to judge the ability of a potential reader or actor from an advertising voice-over. And if you are good at dialects, include a couple on your Spotlight page, as well as listing them. Listen to the output and get a sense of the tone of the network or outlet as well as the book. If sent the original book as well as the abridgement, try to read at least some of it. They tend to be sent because the background information will inform your performance. And prepare your scripts before either an audition or a job. There is nothing more disheartening than actors who clearly hope to sight read!

Great actors are not necessarily good readers – as we've all discovered. An empathy for storytelling and for literature, and an intelligence and interest in language does matter. It is quite an exposed place if you are used to working with a larger cast and there is nowhere to hide. It is tiring spending a day alone in a studio, often going over the same material for small nuances. But please don't let that put you off. I hope it's also one of the great unsung pleasures of a broad acting career.

To find out more about BBC Radio Drama's Soundstart programme visit www.bbc.co.uk/soundstart

BBC RADIO BRISTOL   **T** 0117 974 1111
Contact: Tim Pemberton (Managing Editor)
Bristol Broadcasting House
Whiteladies Road
Bristol BS8 2LR
E radio.bristol@bbc.co.uk
W www.bbc.co.uk/bristol

**BBC RADIO
CAMBRIDGESHIRE**   **T** 01223 259696
Contact: Dave Harvey (Managing Editor)
Cambridge Business Park
Cowley Road
Cambridge CB4 0WZ
E cambs@bbc.co.uk
W www.bbc.co.uk/cambridgeshire

BBC RADIO CORNWALL   **T** 01872 275421
Contact: Pauline Causey (Managing Editor)
Phoenix Wharf, Truro
Cornwall TR1 1UA
F 01872 240679
W www.bbc.co.uk/cornwall

**BBC COVENTRY &
WARWICKSHIRE**   **T** 024 7655 1000
Contact: Sue Curtis (News Desk Editor)
Priory Place, Coventry CV1 5SQ
F 024 7655 2000
E coventry.warwickshire@bbc.co.uk
W www.bbc.co.uk/coventry

BBC RADIO CUMBRIA   **T** 01228 592444
Contact: Mark Elliot (Managing Editor)
Annetwell Street, Carlisle
Cumbria CA3 8BB
F 01228 511195
E radio.cumbria@bbc.co.uk
W www.bbc.co.uk/radiocumbria

BBC RADIO DERBY   **T** 01332 361111
Contact: Simon Cornes (Managing Editor)
56 St Helen's Street
Derby DE1 3HY
E radio.derby@bbc.co.uk
W www.bbc.co.uk/derby

BBC RADIO DEVON   **T** 01752 260323
Contact: Mark Grinnell (Managing Editor)
PO Box 1034
Plymouth PL3 5BD
F 01752 234595
E radio.devon@bbc.co.uk
W www.bbc.co.uk/devon

BBC ESSEX   **T** 01245 616000
Contact: Gerald Main (Managing Editor)
PO Box 765, Chelmsford
Essex CM2 9AB
F 01245 616025
E essex@bbc.co.uk
W www.bbc.co.uk/essex

**BBC RADIO
GLOUCESTERSHIRE**   **T** 01452 308585
Contact: Mark Hurrell (Managing Editor)
London Road, Gloucester GL1 1SW
E radio.gloucestershire@bbc.co.uk
W www.bbc.co.uk/gloucestershire

BBC GUERNSEY   **T** 01481 200600
Contact: Robert Wallace (Managing Editor),
Kay Langlois (Assistant Editor),
David Earl (Senior Broadcast Journalist)
Broadcasting House, Bulwer Avenue
St Sampsons, Guernsey GY2 4LA
F 01481 200361
E bbcguernsey@bbc.co.uk
W www.bbc.co.uk/guernsey

**BBC HEREFORD &
WORCESTER**   **T** 01905 748485
Contact: Jeremy Pollock (Managing Editor)
Hylton Road, Worcester WR2 5WW
W www.bbc.co.uk/herefordandworcester

BBC RADIO HUMBERSIDE   **T** 01482 323232
Contact: Simon Pattern (Managing Editor)
Queens Court, Queens Gardens
Hull HU1 3RH
F 01482 226409
E radio.humberside@bbc.co.uk
W www.bbc.co.uk/humberside

BBC RADIO JERSEY   **T** 01534 870000
Contact: Jon Gripton (Editor),
Matthew Price (Assistant Editor)
18 & 21 Parade Road, St Helier
Jersey JE2 3PL
F 01534 732569
E radiojersey@bbc.co.uk
W www.bbc.co.uk/jersey

BBC RADIO KENT   **T** 01892 670000
Contact: Paul Leaper (Managing Editor)
The Great Hall
Mount Pleasant Road
Tunbridge Wells, Kent TN1 1QQ
E radio.kent@bbc.co.uk
W www.bbc.co.uk/kent

BBC RADIO LANCASHIRE   **T** 01254 262411
Contact: John Clayton (Editor)
20-26 Darwen Street, Blackburn
Lancashire BB2 2EA
E radio.lancashire@bbc.co.uk
W www.bbc.co.uk/lancashire

BBC RADIO LEEDS   **T** 0113 244 2131
Contact: Rozina Breen (Managing Editor)
BBC Yorkshire, 2 St Peter's Square
Leeds LS9 8AH
F 0113 224 7316
E radioleeds@bbc.co.uk
W www.bbc.co.uk/leeds

BBC RADIO LEICESTER   **T** 0116 251 6688
Contact: Jane Hill (Managing Editor)
9 St Nicholas Place
Leicester LE1 5LB
F 0116 251 1463
E radio.leicesternews@bbc.co.uk
W www.bbc.co.uk/leicester

BBC RADIO LINCOLNSHIRE   **T** 01522 511411
Contact: Charlie Partridge (Managing Editor)
Newport, Lincoln LN1 3XY
F 01522 511058
W www.bbc.co.uk/lincolnshire

BBC LONDON
94.9 FM   **T** 020 7224 2000 (Live Studio)
Contact: David Robey (Managing Editor)
Egton House, Portland Place, London W1A 1AA
T 020 8743 8000 (Switchboard)
E yourlondon@bbc.co.uk
W www.bbc.co.uk/london

BBC RADIO MANCHESTER   **T** 0161 335 6000
Contact: John Ryan (Managing Editor)
MediaCityUK, Salford M50 2EQ
W www.bbc.co.uk/manchester

BBC RADIO MERSEYSIDE   **T** 0151 708 5500
Contact: Sue Owen (Managing Editor)
PO Box 95.8, Liverpool L69 1ZJ
E radio.merseyside@bbc.co.uk
W www.bbc.co.uk/liverpool

BBC NEWCASTLE   **T** 0191 232 4141
Contact: Matthew Barraclough (Editor)
Broadcasting Centre, Barrack Road
Newcastle upon Tyne NE99 1RN
F 0191 221 0796
E bbcnewcastle.news@bbc.co.uk
W www.bbc.co.uk/tyne

BBC RADIO NORFOLK   **T** 01603 617411
Contact: David Clayton (Managing Editor)
The Forum, Millennium Plain, Norwich NR2 1BH
E norfolk@bbc.co.uk
W www.bbc.co.uk/norfolk

BBC NORTHAMPTON   **T** 01604 239100
Contact: Jess Rudkin (Manager)
Broadcasting House, Abington Street
Northampton NN1 2BH
F 01604 230709
E northampton@bbc.co.uk
W www.bbc.co.uk/northampton

BBC RADIO NOTTINGHAM   **T** 0115 955 0500
Contact: Mike Bettison (Editor)
London Road, Nottingham NG2 4UU
F 0115 902 1984
E radio.nottingham@bbc.co.uk
W www.bbc.co.uk/nottingham

BBC RADIO SHEFFIELD   **T** 0114 273 1177
Contact: Martyn Weston (Managing Editor)
54 Shoreham Street, Sheffield S1 4RS
F 0114 267 5454
E radio.sheffield@bbc.co.uk
W www.bbc.co.uk/sheffield

BBC RADIO SHROPSHIRE   **T** 01743 248484
Contact: Tim Beech (Editor),
Tracey Higgins (Senior Broadcast Journalist News)
2-4 Boscobel Drive, Shrewsbury, Shropshire SY1 3TT
F 01743 271702
E radio.shropshire@bbc.co.uk
W www.bbc.co.uk/shropshire

BBC RADIO SOLENT   **T** 023 8063 1311
Contact: Chris Carnegy (Managing Editor)
Broadcasting House, 10 Havelock Road
Southampton SO14 7PW
F 023 8033 9648
E radio.solent@bbc.co.uk
W www.bbc.co.uk/solent

BBC RADIO STOKE   **T** 01782 208080
Contact: Gary Andrews (Managing Editor)
Cheapside, Hanley
Stoke-on-Trent, Staffordshire ST1 1JJ
F 01782 289115
E radio.stoke@bbc.co.uk
W www.bbc.co.uk/stoke

BBC RADIO SUFFOLK   **T** 01473 250000
Contact: Peter Cook (Editor)
Broadcasting House
St Matthews Street
Ipswich IP1 3EP
F 01473 210887
E radiosuffolk@bbc.co.uk
W www.bbc.co.uk/suffolk

BBC SURREY   **T** 01273 320400
Contact: Sara David (Managing Editor)
Broadcasting Centre
Guildford, Surrey GU2 7AP
F 01483 304952
E sussex@bbc.co.uk
W www.bbc.co.uk/sussex

BBC SUSSEX   **T** 01273 320400
Contact: Sara David (Managing Editor)
40-42 Queen's Road
Brighton BN1 3YB
F 01483 304952
E sussex@bbc.co.uk
W www.bbc.co.uk/sussex

BBC TEES   **T** 01642 225211
Contact: Dan Thorpe (Acting Managing Editor)
Broadcasting House
Newport Road
Middlesbrough TS1 5DG
F 01642 211356
E tees.studios@bbc.co.uk
W www.bbc.co.uk/tees

BBC THREE
COUNTIES RADIO   **T** 01582 637400
Contact: Laura Moss (Managing Editor)
1 Hastings Street, Luton LU1 5XL
F 01582 401467
E 3cr@bbc.co.uk
W www.bbc.co.uk/threecounties

BBC WEST MIDLANDS   **T** 0121 567 6767
The Mailbox, Birmingham B1 1RF
E midlandstoday@bbc.co.uk
W www.bbc.co.uk/westmidlands

BBC WILTSHIRE   **T** 01793 513626
Contact: Tony Worgan (Managing Editor)
Broadcasting House
56-58 Prospect Place
Swindon SN1 3RW
E radio.wiltshire@bbc.co.uk
W www.bbc.co.uk/wiltshire

BBC RADIO YORK   **T** 01904 641351
Contact: Sarah Drummond (Managing Editor)
20 Bootham Row
York YO30 7BR
E radio.york@bbc.co.uk
W www.bbc.co.uk/york

ABERDEEN:
Northsound Radio T 01224 337000
Abbotswell Road, West Tullos
Aberdeen AB12 3AJ
F 01224 400003
W www.northsound.com

AYR: West Sound Radio T 01292 283662
Incorporating West Sound 1035 AM & West 96.7 FM
Radio House, 54A Holmston Road, Ayr KA7 3BE
E carolyn.mcallister@westsound.co.uk
W www.westsound.co.uk

BELFAST:
City Beat 96.7 FM & 102.5 FM T 028 9023 4967
2nd Floor, Arena Building
85 Ormeau Road, Belfast BT7 1SH
F 028 9089 0100
E newsdesk@citybeat.co.uk
W www.citybeat.co.uk

BELFAST: Cool FM T 028 9181 7181
Kiltonga Industrial Estate, Newtownards
Co Down BT23 4ES
E info@coolfm.co.uk
W www.coolfm.co.uk

BELFAST: Downtown Radio T 028 9181 5555
Kiltonga Industrial Estate, Newtownards
Co Down BT23 4ES
E info@downtown.co.uk
W www.downtown.co.uk

BERKSHIRE & NORTH
HAMPSHIRE: Heart T 0118 945 4400
PO Box 2020, Reading, Berkshire RG31 7FG
E thamesvalley.news@heart.co.uk
W www.heart.co.uk

BIRMINGHAM:
Free Radio 96.4 & Gold T 0121 566 5200
9 Brindleyplace, 4 Oozells Square, Birmingham B1 2DJ
F 0121 566 5209
W www.freeradio.co.uk

BORDERS THE: Radio Borders T 01896 759444
Tweedside Park, Galashiels TD1 3TD
F 0845 3457080
E info@radioborders.com
W www.radioborders.com

BRADFORD:
Sunrise Radio Yorkshire T 01274 735043
55 Leeds Road, Bradford BD1 5AF
F 01274 728534
W www.sunriseradio.fm

BRADFORD, HUDDERSFIELD, HALIFAX,
KEIGHLEY & DEWSBURY:
Pulse 2 T 01274 203040
Forster Square, Bradford BD1 5NE
E general@pulse.co.uk
W www.pulse2.net

CAMBRIDGESHIRE &
PETERBOROUGH: Heart T 01733 281370
Enterprise House, Division Park
Histon, Cambridgeshire CB24 9ZR
T 01733 460460
E cambridgeshire.news@heart.co.uk
W www.heart.co.uk

CARDIFF & NEWPORT:
Capital FM & Gold FM T 029 2066 2066
Global Radio
The Red Dragon Centre, Cardiff Bay
Cardiff CF10 4DJ
W www.capitalfm.com

CHESTER, NORTH WALES
& WIRRAL: Heart T 01978 752202
Contact: Paul Holmes (Programme Controller)
The Studios, Mold Road
Wrexham LL11 4AF
E northwestwales.news@heart.co.uk
W www.heart.co.uk

DUMFRIES: West Sound FM T 01387 250999
Unit 40, The Loreburn Centre
High Street, Dumfries DG1 2BD
F 01387 265629
W www.westsoundradio.com

DUNDEE & PERTH:
Radio Tay AM T 01382 200800
6 North Isla Street, Dundee DD3 7JQ
E tayam@radiotay.co.uk
W www.radiotay.co.uk

DUNDEE & PERTH:
Radio Tay FM T 01382 200800
6 North Isla Street, Dundee DD3 7JQ
E tayfm@radiotay.co.uk
W www.radiotay.co.uk

EAST MIDLANDS:
Capital East Midlands T 0115 873 1500
Incorporating Ram FM, Leicester Sound & Trent FM
Chapel Quarter
Maid Marian Way
Nottingham NG1 6HQ
W www.capitalfm.com

EDINBURGH: Radio Forth Ltd T 0131 556 9255
Forth House, Forth Street
Edinburgh EH1 3LE
E info@radioforth.com
W www.radioforth.com

EXETER & TORBAY: Heart T 01392 354200
Hawthorn House
Exeter Business Park
Exeter EX1 3QS
F 01392 354209
W www.heart.co.uk

FALKIRK: Central FM T 01324 611164
201-203 High Street
Falkirk FK1 1DU
F 01324 611168
W www.centralfm.co.uk

GLASGOW: Radio Clyde Ltd T 0141 565 2200
3 South Avenue
Clydebank Business Park
Glasgow G81 2RX
W www.clyde1.com

GLASGOW: Radio Clyde 2 T 0141 565 2200
3 South Avenue
Clydebank Business Park
Glasgow G81 2RX
W www.clyde2.com

GLOUCESTER &
CHELTENHAM: Heart 102.4   T 01452 572400
The Mall, Gloucester GL1 1SS
F 01452 572409
W www.heart.co.uk

GREAT YARMOUTH &
NORWICH: Heart   T 01603 630621
St Georges Plain, 47-49 Colegate
Norwich NR3 1DB
W www.heart.co.uk

GUILDFORD: 96.4 Eagle Radio   T 01483 300964
Eagle Radio Ltd, Dolphin House, 3 North Street
Guildford, Surrey GU1 4AA
F 01483 454443
E onair@964eagle.co.uk
W www.964eagle.co.uk

HEREFORD & WORCESTER:
Free Radio   T 01905 545500
1st Floor, Kirkham House
John Comyn Drive, Worcester WR3 7NS
W www.freeradio.co.uk

HOME COUNTIES: Heart   T 01604 795600
Bedford, Beds, Bucks, Herts, Milton Keynes &
Northamptonshire
4th Floor, CBX11
382-428 Midsummer Boulevard
Milton Keynes MK9 2EA
T 01582 676200
E fourcounties.news@heart.co.uk
W www.heart.co.uk

INVERNESS:
Moray Firth Radio   T 01463 224433
PO Box 271, Scorguie Place
Inverness IV3 8UJ
F 01463 227714
E mfr@mfr.co.uk
W www.mfr.co.uk

ISLE OF WIGHT:
Isle of Wight Radio   T 01983 822557
Dodnor Park, Newport
Isle of Wight PO30 5XE
F 01983 822109
E studio@iwradio.co.uk
W www.iwradio.co.uk

KENT: Heart   T 01227 772004
Radio House, John Wilson Business Park
Whitstable, Kent CT5 3QX
E news.kent@heart.co.uk
W www.heart.co.uk

LEEDS:
Radio Aire 96.3 & Magic 828   T 0113 283 5500
51 Burley Road, Leeds LS3 1LR
F 0113 283 5501
W www.radioaire.com

LIVERPOOL: Radio City   T 0151 472 6800
St John's Beacon, 1 Houghton Street
Liverpool L1 1RL
W www.radiocity.co.uk

LONDON: Absolute Radio   T 020 7434 1215
1 Golden Square, London W1F 9DJ
W www.absoluteradio.co.uk

LONDON: Choice FM   T 020 7766 6810
Global Radio
30 Leicester Square
London WC2H 7LA
F 020 7766 6100
W www.choice-fm.co.uk

LONDON: Classic FM   T 020 7343 9000
Global Radio
30 Leicester Square, London WC2H 7LA
F 020 7344 2789
W www.classicfm.com

LONDON: Gold   T 020 7054 8000
Global Radio
30 Leicester Square, London WC2H 7LA
W www.mygoldmusic.co.uk

LONDON:
Independent Radio News   T 020 7182 8591
Mappin House, 4 Winsley Street
London W1W 8HF
E irn@bskyb.com
W www.irn.co.uk

LONDON:
London Greek Radio   T 020 8349 6950
437 High Road, Finchley
London N12 0AP
W www.lgr.co.uk

LONDON: Magic 105.4 FM   T 020 7182 8233
Mappin House, 4 Winsley Street
London W1W 8HF
W www.magic.co.uk

LONDON: Smooth Radio   T 0161 886 8800
26-27 Castlereagh Street, London W1H 5DL
E info@smoothradio.co.uk
W www.smoothradio.co.uk

MANCHESTER:
Key 103 FM & Magic 1152   T 0161 288 5000
Piccadilly Radio Ltd, Castle Quay
Castle Field, Manchester M15 4PR
F 0161 288 5151
W www.key103.co.uk

NORTHAMPTONSHIRE: Connect FM 97.2,
106.8 FM & 107.4 FM   T 01536 513664
55 Headlands, Kettering
Northampton NN15 7EU
W www.connectfm.com

OXFORD & BANBURY: Heart   T 01865 871000
The Chase, Calcot
Reading RG31 7RB
W www.heart.co.uk

PLYMOUTH & DEVON: Heart   T 01752 275600
Hawthorn House
Exeter Business Park EX1 3QS
W www.heart.co.uk

PORTSMOUTH & SOUTHAMPTON:
Capital South Coast   T 01489 589911
Global Radio
Radio House, Whittle Avenue
Segensworth West
Fareham, Hampshire PO15 5SX
W www.capitalfm.com

**PORTSMOUTH &
SOUTHAMPTON: Heart**   T 01489 589911
Global Radio
Radio House, Whittle Avenue
Segensworth West
Fareham, Hampshire PO15 5SX
W www.heart.co.uk

**SOUTH MANCHESTER &
CHESHIRE: Imagine 104.9 FM**   T 0161 476 7340
Waterloo Place, Watson Square
Stockport, Cheshire SK1 3AZ
E sales@imaginefm.net
W www.imaginefm.net

**STOKE-ON-TRENT &
STAFFORD: Signal Radio**   T 01782 441300
Stoke Road, Stoke-on-Trent
Staffordshire ST4 2SR
E info@signalradio.com
W www.signalone.co.uk

SUSSEX: Heart   T 01273 430111
Radio House, Franklin Road
Portslade, East Sussex BN41 1AS
F 01273 316909
W www.heart.co.uk

SWANSEA: The Wave 96.4 FM   T 01792 511964
Victoria Road, Gowerton
Swansea SA4 3AB
W www.thewave.co.uk

TEESSIDE: Magic 1170   T 01642 888222
Yale Crescent, Teesdale
Thornaby, Stockton on Tees TS17 6AA
W www.magic1170.co.uk

TEESSIDE: TFM Radio   T 01642 888222
Yale Crescent, Teesdale
Thornaby, Stockton on Tees TS17 6AA
W www.tfmradio.com

**TYNE & WEAR, NORTHUMBERLAND
& DURHAM: Magic 1152**   T 0191 230 6100
55 Degrees North, Pilgrim Street
Newcastle upon Tyne NE1 6BF
W www.magic1152.co.uk

**TYNE & WEAR, NORTHUMBERLAND &
DURHAM: Metro Radio**   T 0191 230 6100
55 Degrees North, Pilgrim Street
Newcastle upon Tyne NE1 6BF
W www.metroradio.co.uk

WEST COUNTRY: Heart   T 0117 984 3200
1 Passage Street, Bristol BS2 0JF
F 0117 984 3229
W www.heart.co.uk

**WOLVERHAMPTON & BLACK COUNTRY /
SHREWSBURY & TELFORD:
Free Radio**   T 01902 461200
267 Tettenhall Road
Wolverhampton WV6 0DE
W www.freeradio.co.uk

**YORKSHIRE:
Hallam FM & Magic AM**   T 0114 209 1000
Radio House, 900 Herries Road
Hillsborough, Sheffield S6 1RH
W www.hallamfm.co.uk

YORKSHIRE: Seaside Radio   T 07903 729993
Community Radio for Southern Holderness
Shores Centre
29-31 Seaside Road
Withernsea, East Yorkshire HU19 2DL
E justin@seasideradio.co.uk
W www.seasideradio.co.uk

**YORKSHIRE & LINCOLNSHIRE: Viking 96.9 FM
& Magic 1161 AM**   T 01482 325141
Commercial Road, Hull HU1 2SG
W www.vikingfm.co.uk

Rehearsal Rooms & Casting Suites

How should I prepare for an audition?

When you are called to a casting you should make sure you are fully prepared with accurate information about the audition time, venue and format. Research the casting director too: look on his or her website and pay attention to media news. What productions have they worked on previously? What do they seem to look for and expect from the actors they cast?

For most auditions you will be given a script to learn, but you could be provided with a brief in advance and asked to find something suitable yourself. It would be advisable to have about five or six pieces ready to choose from that demonstrate your range before you are even called to a casting. You should select two relevant but contrasting pieces of about two to three minutes each for your audition, with the others as backups. If you can, read the whole play in addition to your speech.

It is generally best not to use 'popular' or very well-known pieces and instead to use original modern speeches, as this prevents the likelihood of the casting director comparing you, perhaps unfavourably, with anyone else. Having said this, however, you should still rehearse at least one Shakespeare piece. To find suitable speeches you should read widely for inspiration, or you could search online. If you are still struggling, think about who your favourite playwrights are and find out if they have written anything that is not too well-known.

What should I expect when I arrive at the audition?

Arrive early for your audition, but be prepared to wait! Time slots are allocated but auditions can overrun for various reasons. Be presentable and think about how your character might choose to dress, but overall you will feel more comfortable and confident if you don't differ too much from what you would normally wear. Don't come in costume unless specifically asked.

When you enter the audition room, you may have just the casting director in the room, or you could be confronted with a panel including the director and/or producer, and an editor and cameraman

if you are being filmed. Don't let this disconcert you. Nerves are to be expected, but try to be positive and enjoy yourself. Remember, the casting director doesn't want to spend several days auditioning – they want you to get the job!

Take a few moments to work out where you should stand and where everything is. Don't ask too many questions as this can be irritating but you could ask whether to address your monologue to the casting director/camera, or whether to speak into the 'middle distance'. Make sure that your face, and in particular your eyes, can be seen as much as possible.

Once you have performed your monologue, pause and wait for the casting director to speak to you. Don't ask if they want to see a second speech. If they want another one, and if there's time, they will ask you. You may be asked your opinion on the speech so be prepared with possible answers. Never criticise previous productions you have worked on. At the end of the casting, remember to take your script away unless you are asked to leave it, otherwise it can look as if you're not interested.

Auditions are never a waste of time, even if you don't get the part. You may have performed well but you might not have been quite right for that particular role. Every audition is great practice and experience, and the casting director may very well keep you in mind for future productions.

Should I attend a casting in a house or flat?

Professional auditions are rarely held anywhere other than an official casting studio or venue. Be very wary if you are asked to go elsewhere. Trust your instincts. If something doesn't seem right to you, it probably isn't. Always take someone with you if you are in any doubt.

101 IDENTITY REHEARSAL & PERFORMANCE STUDIOS   T 020 7470 8711
73-75 Shacklewell Lane, London E8 2EB
E info@theidentitystudios.com
W www.theidentitystudios.com

3 MILLS STUDIOS   T 020 7363 3336
Three Mill Lane, London E3 3DU
F 0871 5944028
E info@3mills.com
W www.3mills.com

ABACUS ARTS   T 020 7277 2880
2A Browning Street, Southwark, London SE17 1LN
E info@abacus-arts.org.uk
W www.abacus-arts.org.uk

ACTING SUITE LTD   T 020 7462 0792
Fully Equipped Film, Television, Commercial & Theatrical Casting Studios
17 Percy Street, London W1T 1DU
E jimmy@actingsuite.com
W www.actingsuite.com

ACTORS CENTRE (LONDON) THE   T 020 7632 8012
Auditioning. Casting. Rehearsals. Room Hire
1A Tower Street
London WC2H 9NP
T 020 7240 3940
E operations@actorscentre.co.uk
W www.actorscentre.co.uk

ACTORS STUDIO REHEARSAL & CASTING SPACE   T 01753 650951
Pinewood Studios
Pinewood Road
Iver Heath, Bucks SL0 0NH
E info@actorsstudio.co.uk
W www.actorsstudio.co.uk

ACTOR'S TEMPLE THE   T 020 3004 4537
13-14 Warren Street, London W1T 5LG
E info@actorstemple.com
W www.actorstemple.com

AIRCRAFT CIRCUS   T 020 3004 6173
Hangar Arts Trust
Unit 7A, Mellish House
Harrington Way
London SE18 5NR
E aduncan@hangarartstrust.org
W www.aircraftcircus.com

ALBANY THE   T 020 8692 0231
Douglas Way, Deptford
London SE8 4AG
F 020 8469 2253
E hires@thealbany.org.uk
W www.thealbany.org.uk

ALFORD HOUSE   T 020 7735 1519
Aveline Street, London SE11 5DQ
E tim@alfordhouse.org.uk
W www.alfordhouse.org.uk

ALL TALENT, THE SONIA SCOTT AGENCY   T 0141 418 1074
Unit 325, 95 Morrison Street
Glasgow G5 8BE
T 07971 337074
E enquiries@alltalentuk.co.uk
W www.alltalentuk.co.uk

ALRA (ACADEMY OF LIVE & RECORDED ARTS)   T 020 8870 6475
The Royal Victoria Patriotic Building
John Archer Way, London SW18 3SX
F 020 8875 0789
E info@alra.co.uk
W www.alra.co.uk

AMERICAN CHURCH IN LONDON THE   T 020 7580 2791
Whitefield Memorial Church
79A Tottenham Court Road, London W1T 4TD
F 020 7580 5013
E latchcourt@amchurch.co.uk
W www.latchcourt.com

ARCH 468 THEATRE STUDIO   T 07973 302908
Arch 468, 209A Coldharbour Lane
London SW9 8RU
E rebecca@arch468.com
W www.arch468.com

ARTEMIS STUDIOS LTD   T 01344 429403
30 Charles Square, Bracknell, Berkshire RG12 1AY
E info@artemis-studios.co.uk
W www.agency.artemis-studios.co.uk

ARTSADMIN   T 020 7247 5102
Toynbee Studios
28 Commercial Street
London E1 6AB
F 020 7247 5103
E admin@artsadmin.co.uk
W www.artsadmin.co.uk

AVIV DANCE STUDIOS   T/F 01923 250000
Watford Boys Grammar School
Rickmansworth Road, Watford WD18 7JF
E info@avivdance.com
W www.avivdance.com

BAC (BATTERSEA ARTS CENTRE)   T 020 7326 8211
Lavender Hill, London SW11 5TN
F 020 7978 5207
E venues@bac.org.uk
W www.bac.org.uk/hires

BIG CITY STUDIOS   T 020 7241 6655
Montgomery House, 159-161 Balls Pond Road
Islington, London N1 4BG
F 020 7241 3006
W www.pineappleagency.com

BLOOMSBURY THEATRE THE   T 020 7679 2777
15 Gordon Street
London WC1H 0AH
E admin@thebloomsbury.com
W www.thebloomsbury.com

**BRIDGE THEATRE
TRAINING COMPANY THE**   T 020 7424 0860
Various Large Studios & Meeting Rooms
90 Kingsway, Tally Ho Corner
North Finchley, London N12 0EX
E admin@thebridge-ttc.org
W www.thebridge-ttc.org

BRIXTON COMMUNITY BASE   T 020 7326 4417
Formerly Brixton St Vincent's Community Centre
Talma Road, London SW2 1AS
T 07958 448690
E info@brixtoncommunitybase.org
W www.bsvcc.org

**CALDER THEATRE
BOOKSHOP LTD THE**   T 020 7620 2900
*Central London Rehearsal Space, Fringe Venue &
Theatre Bookshop*
51 The Cut, London SE1 8LF
E info@calderbookshop.com
W www.calderbookshop.com

CARDINBROOK LTD   T 020 7373 1665
32 Barkston Gardens
London SW5 0EN
E info@ycbc.co.uk
W www.ycbc.co.uk/roomhire.htm

CASTING CABIN LTD THE   T 020 7278 0114
Panther House, 38 Mount Pleasant
Holborn, London WC1X 0AN
T 07767 445640
E thecastingcabin@gmail.com
W www.castingcabin.com

CECIL SHARP HOUSE   T 020 7485 2206
2 Regent's Park Road
London NW1 7AY
F 020 7284 0534
E hire@efdss.org
W www.efdss.org

**CENTRAL LONDON
GOLF CENTRE**   T 020 8871 2468
Burntwood Lane, London SW17 0AT
F 020 8874 7447
E info@clgc.co.uk
W www.clgc.co.uk

CENTRAL STUDIOS   T 020 8698 8880
470 Bromley Road, Bromley
Kent BR1 4PQ
E info@dandbperformingarts.co.uk
W www.dandbperformingarts.co.uk

CHARING CROSS THEATRE   T 020 7930 5868
Formerly New Players Theatre
The Arches
Off Villiers Street
London WC2N 6NL
E info@charingcrosstheatre.co.uk
W www.charingcrosstheatre.co.uk

CHATS PALACE   T 020 8533 0227
42-44 Brooksby's Walk
Hackney, London E9 6DF
E info@chatspalace.com
W www.chatspalace.co.uk

CHELSEA THEATRE   T 020 7349 7811
Contact: Francis Alexander
World's End Place, King's Road
London SW10 0DR
T 020 7352 1967
E admin@chelseatheatre.org.uk
W www.chelseatheatre.org.uk

**CLAPHAM COMMUNITY
PROJECT**   T/F 020 7720 8731
St Anne's Hall, 31-33 Bromells Road
London SW4 0BN
E admin@claphamcommunityproject.org.uk
W www.rehearseatccp.co.uk

CLEAN BREAK   T 020 7482 8600
2 Patshull Road, London NW5 2LB
F 020 7482 8611
E general@cleanbreak.org.uk
W www.cleanbreak.org.uk

CLUB FOR ACTS & ACTORS   T 020 7836 3172
Incorporating Concert Artistes Association
20 Bedford Street, London WC2E 9HP
E office@thecaa.org
W www.thecaa.org

COLOMBO CENTRE THE   T 020 7261 1658
Audition & Rehearsal Space
34-68 Colombo Street, London SE1 8DP
E colombodm@jubileehalltrust.org
W www.colombo-centre.org

**COPTIC STREET
STUDIO LTD**   T 020 7636 2030
9 Coptic Street, London WC1A 1NH
E studio@copticstreet.com

**COVENT GARDEN
DRAGON HALL TRUST**   T 020 7404 7274
17 Stukeley Street, London WC2B 5LT
E director@dragonhall.org.uk
W www.dragonhall.org.uk

CUSTARD FACTORY   T 0121 224 7777
Gibb Street, Digbeth
Birmingham B9 4AA
F 0121 604 8888
E info@custardfactory.co.uk
W www.custardfactory.co.uk

Rehearsal Spaces for hire

Two new, purpose built studios for hire just 15 minutes by tube from the West End. Suitable for dance, musicals, large scale rehearsals, meetings or intimate one on one work.

For full details visit our website:
www.losttheatre.co.uk
or call us on 020 7622 9208

Tube: Stockwell (Victoria & Northern Lines)
Vauxhall (Northern & Overground lines)

DANCE ATTIC STUDIOS T 020 7610 2055
368 North End Road, Fulham
London SW6 1LY
F 020 7610 0995
E danceattic@hotmail.com

DANCE COMPANY STUDIOS T 020 8402 2424
76 High Street
Beckenham BR3 1ED
E hire@dancecompanystudios.co.uk
W www.dancecompanystudios.co.uk

DANCEWORKS T 020 7318 4100
16 Balderton Street
London W1K 6TN
E info@danceworks.net
W www.danceworks.net

DAVIES Siobhan STUDIOS T 020 7091 9650
85 St George's Road
London SE1 6ER
F 020 7091 9669
E info@siobhandavies.com
W www.siobhandavies.com

DIE-CAST STUDIOS T 020 7494 4630
39A Berwick Street, Soho
London W1F 8RU
E studio@diecaststudios.co.uk
W www.diecaststudios.co.uk

EALING STUDIOS T 020 8567 6655
Ealing Green, London W5 5EP
F 020 8758 8658
E bookings@ealingstudios.com
W www.ealingstudios.com

BLOOMSBURY THEATRE

REHEARSAL STUDIO

Attractive and modern, 11m x 8m (36ft x 26ft 4in)
Sprung dance floor, mirrored wall, piano,
kitchenette, adjustable lighting.
Shop and café on site.

Easily accessible central location

Available Mon through Sat, daytime and evening

Contact the Administration Officer
on **020 7679 2777**

15 Gordon Street, London WC1H 0AH
www.thebloomsbury.com

**ELMS LESTERS
PAINTING ROOMS** T 020 7836 6747
1-3-5 Flitcroft Street, London WC2H 8DH
F 020 7379 0789
E info@elmslesters.co.uk
W www.elmslesters.co.uk

**ENGLISH FOLK DANCE &
SONG SOCIETY** T 020 7485 2206
Cecil Sharp House, 2 Regent's Park Road
London NW1 7AY
F 020 7284 0534
E hire@efdss.org
W www.efdss.org

ENGLISH NATIONAL OPERA T 020 7624 7711
Lilian Baylis House
165 Broadhurst Gardens
London NW6 3AX
F 020 7625 3398
E receptionlbh@eno.org
W www.eno.org

ENGLISH TOURING THEATRE T 020 7450 1990
25 Short Street, Waterloo
London SE1 8LJ
F 020 7633 0188
E admin@ett.org.uk
W www.ett.org.uk

ETCETERA THEATRE T 020 7482 4857
(Above the Oxford Arms)
265 Camden High Street
London NW1 7BU
F 020 7482 0378
E etc@etceteratheatre.com
W www.etceteratheatre.com

**EUROKIDS &
EKA CASTING STUDIOS** T 01925 761088
Contact: Amy Musker (Senior Casting Agent)
The Warehouse Studios, Glaziers Lane
Culcheth, Warrington, Cheshire WA3 4AQ
T 01925 761210
E castings@eka-agency.com
W www.eka-agency.com

EXCHANGE THE T 01258 475137
Old Market Hill, Sturminster Newton DT10 1FH
E info@stur-exchange.co.uk
W www.stur-exchange.co.uk

EXPRESSIONS STUDIOS T 020 7813 1580
Linton House, 39-51 Highgate Road
London NW5 1RT
E info@expressionsstudios.org.uk
W www.expressionsstudios.org.uk

**FACTORY FITNESS &
DANCE CENTRE THE**   T 020 7272 1122
407 Hornsey Road, London N19 4DX
E info@factorylondon.com
W www.factorylondon.com

FSU LONDON STUDY CENTRE   T 020 7813 3223
99 Great Russell Street
London WC1B 3LH
F 020 7813 3270

GRAEAE THEATRE COMPANY   T 020 7613 6900
Bradbury Studios, 138 Kinsland Road
London E2 8DY
E info@graeae.org
W www.graeae.org

**GREAT EASTERN
DINING ROOM**   T 020 7613 4545
54-56 Great Eastern Street
Shoreditch, London EC2A 3QR
E greateastern@rickerrestaurants.com
W www.rickerrestaurants.com

**GREEN ROOM
CASTING STUDIO THE**   T 020 7734 3057
7 D'Arblay Street, London W1F 8DW
E casting@thegreenroom.eu
W www.thegreenroom.eu

GROUNDLINGS THEATRE   T 023 9273 7370
42 Kent Street, Portsmouth
Hampshire PO1 3BT
E richard@groundlings.co.uk
W www.groundlings.co.uk

HAMPSTEAD THEATRE   T 020 7449 4200
Eton Avenue, Swiss Cottage
London NW3 3EU
F 020 7449 4201
E info@hampsteadtheatre.com
W www.hampsteadtheatre.com

HANGAR ARTS TRUST   T 020 8317 8401
Unit 7A, Mellish House
Harrington Way, London SE18 5NR
E info@hangarartstrust.org
W www.hangarartstrust.org

HEYTHROP COLLEGE   T 020 7795 6600
University of London
23 Kensington Square
London W8 5HN
E conferences@heythrop.ac.uk
W www.heythrop.ac.uk

**HOLLY LODGE
COMMUNITY CENTRE**   T 020 8342 9524
*2 Halls for Hire for Afternoons, Evenings & Weekends.
Community & Family Centres*
Holly Lodge Estate, Family Centre
Oakshott Avenue, London N6 6NT
E hollylodgelondon@hotmail.com
W www.hollylodge.org.uk

**HOLLY LODGE
COMMUNITY CENTRE**   T 020 8342 9524
*2 Halls for Hire for Afternoons, Evenings & Weekends.
Community & Family Centres*
30 Makepeace Avenue
Highgate, London N6 6HL
E hollylodgelondon@hotmail.com
W www.hollylodge.org.uk

HOLY INNOCENTS CHURCH   T 020 8748 2286
Paddenswick Road, London W6 0UB
E bookings@hisj.co.uk
W www.hisj.co.uk

TAKE FIVE STUDIO

Commercial & Film Casting Studio
Online Casting
Skype Casting
Showreels

**37 Beak Street, London W1F 9RZ
Tel +44 (0) 20 7287 2120
Fax +44 (0) 20 7287 3035
info@takefivestudio.com
www.takefivestudio.com**

Questors, Ealing's Playhouse

Rehearsal Rooms
For Hire **Daytimes** Monday – Friday
- Shaw Room 12m x 8.5m
- Emmet Room 11m × 9m *(sprung floor)*
- Redgrave Room 11m x 8.5m
- Piano available by arrangement
- See photos at ealingtheatre.com

Additional Facilities: On-Site Car Park, Café, Break-Out Spaces

Quiet and attractive location, opposite park with shopping centre nearby.
8 mins' walk from Ealing Broadway Tube and mainline station (District and Central lines).

The Questors Theatre
12 Mattock Lane, London W5 5BQ
020 8567 0011
enquiries@questors.org.uk

ealingtheatre.com

Registered Charity 207516

HOLY TRINITY W6 T 020 7603 3832
Holy Trinity Parish Centre, 41 Brook Green
London W6 7BL
E brookgreen@rcdow.org.uk
W www.holytrinityw6.org

HOMES FOR ISLINGTON T 020 7527 8632
Highbury House
5 Highbury Crescent
London N5 1RN
E service.development@homesforislington.org.uk
W www.homesforislington.org.uk

HOPE STREET LTD T 0151 708 8007
13A Hope Street, Liverpool L1 9BQ
F 0151 709 3242
E peter@hope-street.org
W www.hope-street.org

HOXTON HALL THEATRE &
YOUTH ARTS CENTRE T 020 7684 0060
130 Hoxton Street, London N1 6SH
E info@hoxtonhall.co.uk
W www.hoxtonhall.co.uk

IMT GALLERY T 020 8980 5475
Unit 2
210 Cambridge Heath Road
London E2 9NQ
E mail@imagemusictext.com
W www.imagemusictext.com

INC SPACE T 020 7557 6658
9-13 Grape Street, Covent Garden
London WC2H 8ED
F 020 7557 6656
E debbie@international-collective.com
W www.inc-space.com

INVISIBLE DOT THE T 020 7424 8918
2 Northdown Street, London N1 9BG
E hire@theinvisibledot.com
W www.theinvisibledot.com

ISLINGTON ARTS FACTORY T 020 7607 0561
2 Parkhurst Road, London N7 0SF
E info@islingtonartsfactory.org
W www.islingtonartsfactory.org

JACKSONS LANE T 020 8340 5226
Various Spaces including Rehearsal Rooms &
Theatre Hire
269A Archway Road, London N6 5AA
E reception@jacksonslane.org.uk
W www.jacksonslane.org.uk

JAM THEATRE STUDIOS T 01628 483808
Air-conditioned Studios
Archway Court, 45A West Street
Marlow, Buckinghamshire SL7 2LS
E office@jamtheatre.co.uk
W www.jamtheatre.co.uk

JERWOOD SPACE T 020 7654 0171
171 Union Street, London SE1 0LN
F 020 7654 0172
E space@jerwoodspace.co.uk
W www.jerwoodspace.co.uk

LIVE THEATRE T 0191 261 2694
Broad Chare, Quayside
Newcastle upon Tyne NE1 3DQ
E info@live.org.uk
W www.live.org.uk

LONDON BUBBLE
THEATRE COMPANY LTD T 020 7237 4434
5 Elephant Lane, London SE16 4JD
E admin@londonbubble.org.uk
W www.londonbubble.org.uk

LONDON SCHOOL
OF CAPOEIRA T 020 7281 2020
Units 1 & 2 Leeds Place, Tollington Park
London N4 3RF
E studiohire@londonschoolofcapoeira.com
W www.londonschoolofcapoeira.com

LONDON STUDIO CENTRE T 020 7837 7741
artsdepot, 5 Nether Street, Tally Ho Corner
North Finchley, London N12 0GA
F 020 7837 3248
E info@london-studio-centre.co.uk
W www.london-studio-centre.co.uk

LONDON THEATRE THE T 020 8694 1888
Lower Space, 443 New Cross Road
New Cross, London SE14 6TA
E thelondontheatre@live.co.uk
W www.thelondontheatre.com

LONDON WELSH CENTRE T 020 7837 3722
157-163 Gray's Inn Road, London WC1X 8UE
E administrator@lwcentre.demon.co.uk
W www.londonwelsh.org

LYRIC HAMMERSMITH T 020 8741 6850
King Street, London W6 0QL
F 020 8741 5965
E enquiries@lyric.co.uk
W www.lyric.co.uk

MACKINTOSH, Cameron
REHEARSAL STUDIO T 020 7372 6611
The Tricycle, 269 Kilburn High Road, London NW6 7JR
F 020 7328 0795
E admin@tricycle.co.uk
W www.tricycle.co.uk

MAKEBELIEVE ARTS T 020 8691 3803
2 Spaces Available for Hire
The Deptford Mission
1 Creek Road, London SE8 3BT
E info@makebelievearts.co.uk
W www.rehearsalspacelondon.co.uk/studio-hire-south-of-the-river

MENIER CHOCOLATE
FACTORY T 020 7378 1712
53 Southwark Street, London SE1 1RU
F 020 7234 0447
E office@menierchocolatefactory.com
W www.menierchocolatefactory.com

REHEARSAL SPACE FOR HIRE KING'S CROSS & CAMDEN TOWN

Studio 8.6m x 5.0m
Blue Room 4.9m x 4.9m
Northdown Street, N1 9BG
100m from King's Cross St Pancras Station

Studio 8.3m x 5.5m
Camden Stables Market, Chalk Farm Road, NW1 8AH
400m from Camden Town Station

COMPETITIVE RATES FOR REHEARSALS, CASTINGS & MEETINGS

020 7424 8918
hire@theinvisibledot.com
www.theinvisibledot.com

MOBERLY SPORTS & EDUCATION CENTRE T 020 7641 4807
101 Kilburn Lane, Kensal Rise, London W10 4AH
F 020 7641 5878
E moberly@westminster.gov.uk

MOVING EAST STUDIO T 020 7503 3101
Harlequin Sprung Floor. Quadrophonic Sound System
St Matthias Church Hall, Wordsworth Road
London N16 8DD
E admin@movingeast.co.uk
W www.movingeast.co.uk

NATIONAL YOUTH THEATRE OF GREAT BRITAIN T 020 7281 3863
443-445 Holloway Road, London N7 6LW
E info@nyt.org.uk
W www.nyt.org.uk

NEALS YARD MEETING ROOMS T/F 020 7436 9875
14 Neals Yard, Covent Garden, London WC2H 9DP
E info@walkinbackrub.co.uk
W www.meetingrooms.org.uk

NEW DIORAMA THEATRE THE T 020 7916 5467
81 Seat Blackbox Theatre.
16 New Rooms from May 2013
15-16 Triton Street, Regents Place
London NW1 3BF
W www.newdiorama.com

NLPAC PERFORMING ARTS T 020 8444 4544
Casting & Production Office Facilities
76 St James Lane, Muswell Hill, London N10 3RD
F 020 8444 4040
E nlpac@aol.com
W www.nlpac.co.uk

OBSERVATORY STUDIOS THE T 020 7437 2823
45-46 Poland Street, London W1F 7NA
F 020 7437 2830
E info@theobservatorystudios.com
W www.theobservatorystudios.com

OCTOBER GALLERY T 020 7831 1618
24 Old Gloucester Street, London WC1N 3AL
F 020 7405 1851
E rentals@octobergallery.co.uk
W www.octobergallery.co.uk

OLD VIC THEATRE THE T 020 7928 2651
The Cut, London SE1 8NB
E hires@oldvictheatre.com
W www.oldvictheatre.com

ONLY CONNECT UK T 0845 3707990
32 Cubitt Street, London WC1X 0LR
T 020 7278 8939
E info@oclondon.org
W www.oclondon.org

OPEN DOOR COMMUNITY CENTRE T/F 020 8871 8172
Beaumont Road, Wimbledon, London SW19 6TF
E dconstantinou@wandsworth.gov.uk
W www.wandsworth.gov.uk

OUT OF JOINT T 020 7609 0207
7 Thane Works, Thane Villas, London N7 7NU
F 020 7609 0203
E ojo@outofjoint.co.uk
W www.outofjoint.co.uk

COVENT GARDEN DRAGON HALL TRUST

Photo: David Andrew

17 Stukeley Street, Covent Garden
London, WC2B 5LT

020 7404 7274
bookings@dragonhall.org.uk
www.dragonhall.org.uk

OVAL HOUSE　　T 020 7582 0080
52-54 Kennington Oval
London SE11 5SW
E hire@ovalhouse.com
W www.ovalhouse.com

PAINES PLOUGH REHEARSAL &
AUDITION SPACE　　T 020 7240 4533
4th Floor, 43 Aldwych
London WC2B 4DN
F 020 7240 4534
E office@painesplough.com
W www.painesplough.com

PEOPLE SHOW　　T 020 7729 1841
3 Rehearsal Rooms. Casting Suites. Set Building
Workshop. Sound & Lighting Equipment for Hire
People Show Studios, Pollard Row
London E2 6NB
F 020 7739 0203
E people@peopleshow.co.uk
W www.peopleshow.co.uk

PEREGRINES PIANOS　　T 020 7242 9865
Auditioning. Casting. Filming. Piano Hire
137A Gray's Inn Road, London WC1X 8TU
E info@peregrines-pianos.com
W www.peregrines-pianos.com

PHA CASTING SUITE　　T 0161 273 4444
Tanzaro House
Ardwick Green North
Manchester M12 6FZ
F 0161 273 4567
E info@pha-agency.co.uk
W www.pha-agency.co.uk

PINEAPPLE DANCE STUDIOS　　T 020 7836 4004
7 Langley Street, Covent Garden
London WC2H 9JA
F 020 7836 0803
W www.pineapple.uk.com

PLACE THE　　T 020 7121 1000
17 Duke's Road
London WC1H 9PY
F 020 7121 1142
E info@theplace.org.uk
W www.theplace.org.uk

PLAYGROUND STUDIO THE　　T/F 020 8960 0110
Unit 8, Latimer Road
London W10 6RQ
E info@the-playground.co.uk
W www.the-playground.co.uk

POOR SCHOOL THE　　T 020 7837 6030
242 Pentonville Road, London N1 9JY
E acting@thepoorschool.com
W www.thepoorschool.com

PRECINCT THEATRE THE　　T 020 7359 3594
Units 2-3 The Precinct
Packington Square
London N1 7UP
F 020 7359 3660
E agency@breakalegman.com
W www.breakalegman.com

PRETZEL FILMS　　T 020 7580 9595
142-144 New Cavendish Street
London W1W 6YF
E grace@pretzelfilms.com
W www.pretzelfilms.com

QUESTORS THEATRE
EALING THE　　T 020 8567 0011
12 Mattock Lane, London W5 5BQ
F 020 8567 2275
E alice@questors.org.uk
W www.questors.org.uk

RAG FACTORY THE　　T 020 7183 3048
16-18 Heneage Street
London E1 5LJ
E hello@ragfactory.org.uk
W www.ragfactory.org.uk

RAMBERT DANCE COMPANY　　T 020 8630 0600
94 Chiswick High Road
London W4 1SH
F 020 8747 8323
E rdc@rambert.org.uk
W www.rambert.org.uk

REALLY USEFUL GROUP
THEATRES　　T 020 7557 7300
Contact: Michael Townsend
65 Drury Lane, London WC2B 5SP
F 020 7240 2511
E mike.townsend@reallyuseful.co.uk
W www.reallyuseful.com

RIDGEWAY STUDIOS　　T 01992 633775
Office:
106 Hawkshead Road
Potters Bar, Herts EN6 1NG
E info@ridgewaystudios.co.uk

RITZ STUDIOS　　T 020 8870 1335
Provides Backline Hire for Musicians
110-112 Disraeli Road
London SW15 2DX
E lee@ritzstudios.com
W www.ritzstudios.com

RIVERSIDE STUDIOS　　T 020 8237 1000
Crisp Road, Hammersmith
London W6 9RL
T 020 8237 1004
E staceysmith@riversidestudios.co.uk
W www.riversidestudios.co.uk

ROAR CASTING SUITE　　T 020 7427 5680
ROAR House, 46 Charlotte Street
London W1T 2GS
E info@colekitchenn.com

ROCHELLE SCHOOL　　T 020 7033 3539
Arnold Circus, London E2 7ES
E info@rochelleschool.org
W www.rochelleschool.org

ROOFTOP STUDIO THEATRE   **T** 01785 761233
Rooftop Studio
High Street Arcade
Stone, Staffordshire ST15 8AU
F 01785 818176
E elaine@pssa.co.uk
W www.rooftopstudio.co.uk

ROOMS ABOVE THE   **T** 0845 6860802
Westheath Yard
(Opposite The Emmanuel School)
174 Mill Lane
West Hampstead, London NW6 1TB
F 020 8201 9464
E info@theroomsabove.org.uk
W www.theroomsabove.org.uk

ROSE STUDIO & GALLERY   **T** 020 8546 6983
Rose Theatre, Kingston
24-26 High Street
Kingston upon Thames
Surrey KT1 1HL
F 020 8546 8783
E hiresandevents@rosetheatrekingston.org
W www.rosetheatrekingston.org

ROTHERHITHE STUDIOS   **T** 020 7231 2209
82 St Marychurch Street
London SE16 4HZ
F 020 7231 2119
E ostockman@sandsfilms.co.uk
W www.sandsfilms.co.uk

ROYAL ACADEMY OF DANCE   **T** 020 7326 8000
36 Battersea Square
London SW11 3RA
F 020 7924 3129
E info@rad.org.uk
W www.rad.org.uk

ROYAL ACADEMY OF
DRAMATIC ART   **T** 020 7908 4826
Including The RADA Studios
62-64 Gower Street, London WC1E 6ED
F 020 7908 4811
E bookings@radaenterprises.org
W www.rada.ac.uk/venues

ROYAL SHAKESPEARE
COMPANY   **T** 020 7845 0500
35 Clapham High Street
London SW4 7TW
F 020 7819 8708
W www.rsc.org.uk

RTM STUDIOS   **T** 07892 816283
Central Chambers
93 Hope Street
Glasgow G2 6LD
F 0141 221 8622
E kay@revolutiontalentmanagement.com
W www.revolutiontalentmanagement.com

RUDEYE STUDIOS   **T** 020 7014 3023
73 St John Street, Farringdon
London EC1M 4NJ
E info@rudeye.com
W www.rudeye.com

SADLER'S WELLS THEATRE   **T** 020 7863 8065
Rosebery Avenue, London EC1R 4TN
F 020 7863 8061
E events@sadlerswells.com
W www.sadlerswells.com/page/corporate-hire

SHEPHERDS BUSH CLUB   **T** 020 8743 1624
205 Goldhawk Road, Shepherds Bush
London W12 8EP
E mark@chiswickalbion.com

SOHO GYMS
T 0845 6778890
Borough Gym, Empire Square
Long Lane, London SE1 4NA
F 020 7234 9397
E borough@sohogyms.com
W www.sohogyms.com

SOHO GYMS
T 020 7482 4524
Camden Town Gym, 193-199 Camden High Street
London NW1 7BT
F 020 7267 0500
W www.sohogyms.com

SOHO GYMS
T 020 7720 0321
Clapham Common Gym, 95-97 Clapham High Street
London SW4 7TB
F 020 7720 6510
E clapham@sohogyms.com
W www.sohogyms.com

SOHO GYMS
T 020 7242 1290
Covent Garden Gym, 12 Macklin Street
London WC2B 5NF
F 020 7242 0899
W www.sohogyms.com

SOHO GYMS
T 020 7370 1402
Earl's Court Gym, 254 Earl's Court Road
London SW5 9AD
F 020 7244 6893
W www.sohogyms.com

SOHO GYMS
T 020 7261 9798
Waterloo Gym, 11-15 Brad Street
London SE1 8TG
F 020 7928 8623
W www.sohogyms.com

SOHO THEATRE
T 020 7287 5060
21 Dean Street, London W1D 3NE
F 020 7287 5061
E hires@sohotheatre.com
W www.sohotheatre.com

SOUTH LONDON
DANCE STUDIOS
T 020 7978 8624
130 Herne Hill, London SE24 9QL
E info@southlondondancestudios.co.uk
W www.southlondondancestudios.co.uk

SPACE @ CLARENCE MEWS
T 020 8986 5260
40 Clarence Mews, London E5 8HL
E frith.salem@virgin.net
W www.movingarchitecture.com

SPACE ARTS CENTRE THE
T 020 7515 7799
269 Westferry Road, London E14 3RS
E info@space.org.uk
W www.space.org.uk

SPACE CITY STUDIOS
T 020 7371 4000
79 Blythe Road, London W14 0HP
F 020 7371 4001
E info@spacecity.co.uk
W www.spacecitystudios.co.uk

SPOTLIGHT
T 020 7440 5041
Casting Studios. Room Hire
Twitter: @SpotlightUK
7 Leicester Place, London WC2H 7RJ
F 020 7287 1201
E rooms@spotlight.com
W www.spotlight.com/rooms

ST AGNES CHURCH
T 020 7582 0032
St Agnes Place, Kennington Park, London SE11 4BB
E keith.potter@talk21.com

ST ANDREW'S CHURCH
T 020 7633 9819
Casting Suites. Meetings. Rehearsal Room.
Workshops & Classes
Short Street, Southbank, London SE1 8LJ
E bookings@stjohnswaterloo.org
W www.stjohnswaterloo.co.uk

ST GEORGE'S CHURCH
BLOOMSBURY
T 020 7242 1979
Vestry Hall, 6 Little Russell Street
London WC1A 2HR
E hiring@stgb.org.uk
W www.stgeorgesbloomsbury.org.uk

ST JAMES'S CHURCH,
PICCADILLY
T 020 7292 4861
197 Piccadilly, London W1J 9LL
E roomhire@st-james-piccadilly.org
W www.st-james-piccadilly.org

ST MARTIN-IN-THE-FIELDS
T 020 7766 1130
5 St Martin's Place, London WC2N 4JJ
E jennifer.lang@smitf.org
W www.smitf.org

ST MARY ABBOTS CENTRE
T 020 7937 8885
Vicarage Gate, Kensington, London W8 4HN
E manager@smacentre.com
W www.smacentre.com

ST SWITHUN'S CHURCH
T 020 8852 5088
Meetings. Workshops
Hither Green Lane, Lewisham SE13 6QE
W www.saintswithuns.org.uk

STUDIO THE
T 01746 787153
Burwarton, Nr Bridgnorth
Shropshire WV16 6QJ
E meghawkins@btinternet.com
W www.meghawkins.com

STUDIO SOHO
T 020 7437 3175
Also known as The Giles Foreman Centre For Acting.
2 Large Air-conditioned Newly Customised Spaces.
Wi-Fi. Reception. Kitchen. Changing Room. Showers
Royalty Mews (entrance by Quo Vadis)
22 Dean Street, London W1D 3RA
E info@gilesforeman.com
W www.gilesforeman.com

SUMMERS Mark
CASTING STUDIOS
T 020 7229 8413
1 Beaumont Avenue, West Kensington
London W14 9LP
E louise@marksummers.com
W www.marksummers.com

SUMMIT STUDIOS
T 020 8840 2200
2-4 Spring Bridge Mews, Spring Bridge Road
Ealing, London W5 2AB
F 020 8840 2446
E info@summitstudios.co.uk
W www.summitstudios.co.uk

TAKE FIVE CASTING STUDIO
T 020 7287 2120
Casting Suite
37 Beak Street, London W1F 9RZ
F 020 7287 3035
E info@takefivestudio.com
W www.takefivestudio.com

THEATRE ALIBI
T/F 01392 217315
Emmanuel Hall, Emmanuel Road
Exeter EX4 1EJ
E info@theatrealibi.co.uk
W www.theatrealibi.co.uk/hire.php

THEATRO TECHNIS   T 020 7387 6617
26 Crowndale Road, London NW1 1TT
E info@theatrotechnis.com
W www.theatrotechnis.com

**TOOTING & MITCHAM
COMMUNITY SPORTS CLUB**   T 020 8685 6193
Imperial Fields, Bishopsford Road
Morden, Surrey SM4 6BF
F 020 8685 6190
E info@tmcsc.co.uk
W www.tmcsc.co.uk

TREADWELL'S   T 020 7419 8507
33 Store Street, Bloomsbury
London WC1E 7BS
E info@treadwells-london.com
W www.treadwells-london.com/rehearsal_space.html

TRESTLE ARTS BASE   T 01727 850950
Home of Trestle Theatre Company
Russet Drive, St Albans
Herts AL4 0JQ
F 01727 855558
E admin@trestle.org.uk
W www.trestle.org.uk

TRICYCLE THE   T 020 7372 6611
269 Kilburn High Road, London NW6 7JR
F 020 7328 0795
E trish@tricycle.co.uk
W www.tricycle.co.uk

TT DANCE STUDIO   T 07904 771980
Parkwood Health & Fitness Centre
Darkes Lane, Potters Bar
Herts EN6 1AA
T 07930 400647
E info@talenttimetheatre.com
W www.talenttimetheatre.com

UNICORN THEATRE   T 020 7645 0500
147 Tooley Street, London SE1 2HZ
E sd.supervisor@unicorntheatre.com
W www.unicorntheatre.com

URDANG ACADEMY THE   T 020 7713 7710
The Old Finsbury Town Hall
Rosebery Avenue
London EC1R 4RP
F 020 7278 6727
E studiohire@theurdangacademy.com
W www.theurdangacademy.com

WALKING FORWARD LTD   T 01438 310157
Unit 5E, Business & Technology Centre
Bessemer Drive, Stevenage SG1 2DX
E info@walkingforward.co.uk
W www.walkingforward.co.uk

WATERMANS   T 020 8232 1019
40 High Street, Brentford TW8 0DS
F 020 8232 1030
E info@watermans.org.uk
W www.watermans.org.uk

WHIRLED CINEMA   T 07528 048491
Contact: Rob Lindsay
259-260 Hardess Street
London SE24 0HN
W www.whirledart.co.uk

**Y TOURING THEATRE
COMPANY**   T 020 7520 3090
One KX, 120 Cromer Street
London WC1H 8BS
E d.jackson@ytouring.org.uk
W www.theatreofdebate.com

**YOUNG, Sylvia
THEATRE SCHOOL**   T 020 7258 2336
1 Nutford Place
London W1H 5YZ
T 020 7258 2339
E syoung@syts.co.uk
W www.syts.co.uk

YOUNG ACTORS THEATRE   T 020 7278 2101
70-72 Barnsbury Road, London N1 0ES
E info@yati.org.uk
W www.yati.org.uk

Is your CV up-to-date?
Top tips for promoting yourself!

> **Keep your credits up-to-date**
An absolute must – always take responsibility for updating your own CV, as and when you gain credits and new skills.

> **Review your skills**
Add new skills as they are learnt; remove old skills that you can no longer complete. The more skilled you are the more you maximise your marketability.

> **Make sure your professional training appears**
Also, remember to update this section as you undertake further training across your career.

> **Update your photograph**
Ensure that you are representing yourself as you would now appear at an audition.

> **For online CVs add a few additional photographs and multimedia**
Make sure casting professionals can view a range of photos and see and hear just how good you are with video and voice-clips.

ACT UP T 020 7924 7701
Unit 88, 99-109 Lavender Hill
London SW11 5QL
F 020 7924 6606
E info@act-up.co.uk
W www.act-up.co.uk

ACTIVATION T 020 8783 9494
Riverside House
Feltham Avenue
Hampton Court, Surrey KT8 9BJ
F 020 8783 9345
E info@activation.co.uk
W www.activation.co.uk

APROPOS INTERNATIONAL T 020 7739 2857
PO Box 63581
London N6 9BH
E info@aproposltd.com
W www.aproposltd.com

**BROWNE, Michael
ASSOCIATES LTD** T/F 01462 812483
The Cloisters
168C Station Road
Lower Stondon
Bedfordshire SG16 6JQ
E enquiries@mba-roleplay.co.uk
W www.mba-roleplay.co.uk

CRAGRATS T 0844 8111184
Lawster House
140 South Street
Dorking, Surrey RH4 2EU
E enquiries@cragrats.com
W www.cragrats.com

DRAMANON UNLIMITED T 01753 647795
Langtons House
Templewood Lane
Farnham Common
Buckinghamshire SL2 3HD
F 01753 647783
E info@dramanon.co.uk
W www.dramanon.co.uk

FRANK PARTNERS T 0117 908 5384
14 Brynland Avenue
Bishopton
Bristol BS7 9DT
E neil@frankpartners.co.uk
W www.frankpartners.co.uk

GLOBAL7 T/F 020 7281 7679
PO Box 56232
London N4 4XP
T 07956 956652
E global7castings@gmail.com
W www.global7casting.com

INTERACT T 020 7793 7744
138 Southwark Bridge Road, London SE1 0DG
F 020 7793 7755
E cv@interact.eu.com
W www.interact.eu.com

LADA PRODUCTIONS T 01522 837242
Sparkhouse Studios
Ropewalk, Lincoln, Lincs LN6 7DQ
F 01522 837201
E productions@lada.org.uk
W www.lada.org.uk

**LOVELY PARTY
COMPANY THE** T 01732 669812
2 Whitefriars Wharf
Tonbridge, Kent TN9 1QP
E hq@thelovelypartycompany.com
W www.thelovelypartycompany.com

NV MANAGEMENT LTD
Central Office
Minerva Mill Innovation Centre
Station Road, Alcester
Warwickshire B49 5ET
E hello@nvmanagement.co.uk
W www.nvmanagement.co.uk

**PERFORMANCE
BUSINESS THE** T 01932 888885
The Coach House, 78 Oatlands Drive
Weybridge, Surrey KT13 9HT
E lucy@theperformance.biz
W www.theperformance.biz

RADA IN BUSINESS T 020 7908 4810
The Royal Academy of Dramatic Art
18-22 Chenies Street
London WC1E 7PA
F 020 7908 4811
E admin@radaenterprises.org
W www.radaenterprises.org

ROLEPLAY UK T 0333 121 3003
The Grey House
3 Broad Street
Stamford PE9 1PG
E info@roleplayuk.com
W www.roleplayuk.com

**STEPS DRAMA LEARNING
DEVELOPMENT** T 020 7403 9000
Suite 10
Baden Place
Crosby Row
London SE1 1YW
F 020 7403 0909
E mail@stepsdrama.com
W www.stepsdrama.com

THEATRE& LTD T 01484 532967
Church Hall
St James Road
Marsh
Huddersfield HD1 4QA
F 01484 532962
E cmitchell@theatreand.com
W www.theatreand.com

S →

**Set Construction, Lighting,
Sound & Scenery**

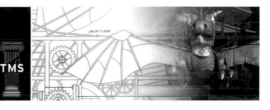

3D SET COMPANY LTD   T 0161 273 8831
Construction. Exhibition Stands. Scenery Design. Sets
Unit 8 Temperance Street
Manchester M12 6HR
F 0161 273 6786
E twalsh@3dsetco.com
W www.3dsetco.com

**ALBEMARLE SCENIC
STUDIOS**   T 0845 6447021
Suppliers of Scenery & Costumes Construction/Hire
Admin: PO Box 240
Rotherfield TN6 9BN
E albemarle.productions@virgin.net
W www.albemarleproductions.com

ALL SCENE ALL PROPS   T 01892 752223
CNC Routing Specialists. Prop Makers. Scenery Builders
Buckhurst Works
Bells Yew Green
Tunbridge Wells
East Sussex TN3 9BN
F 01892 752221
E pr@allscene.net
W www.allscene.net

BONDINI LTD   T 01763 852691
*Cabaret, Magic & Illusion. Scenery Construction.
Venue Decor. AV Equipment*
Low Farm, Brook Road
Bassingbourn, Royston
Herts SG8 5NT
F 01763 853946
E hello@bondini.co.uk
W www.bondini.co.uk

BRISTOL (UK) LTD   T 01923 779333
Scenic Paint
Unit 3, Southerland Court
Tolpits Lane
Watford WD18 9SP
F 01923 779666
E tech.sales@bristolpaint.com
W www.bristolpaint.com

BRITISH HARLEQUIN PLC   T 01892 514888
Festival House
Chapman Way
Tunbridge Wells
Kent TN2 3EF
F 01892 514222
E enquiries@harlequinfloors.com
W www.harlequinfloors.com

**CAP PRODUCTION
SOLUTIONS**   T 07973 432576
116 Wigmore Road
Carshalton
Surrey SM5 1RQ
E leigh@leighporter.com

CCT LIGHTING UK LTD   T 0115 985 8919
Lighting. Dimmers. Sound & Stage Machinery
Unit 3, Ellesmere Business Park
Haydn Road, Sherwood
Nottingham NG5 1DX
F 0115 985 7091
E office@cctlighting.co.uk
W www.cctlighting.com

COD STEAKS   T 0117 980 3910
*Costume. Design. Exhibitions. Model Making.
Set Construction*
2 Cole Road, Bristol BS2 0UG
E mail@codsteaks.com
W www.codsteaks.com

CREWCO   T 0845 4589400
Stage & Technical Crew for London & Midlands
Admin Office: Unit 4, Old Road
Long Compton, Warwickshire CV36 5LE
F 0845 4589411
E contactus@crewco.net
W www.crewco.net

DAP STUDIO   T 07973 406830
55 Longdown Lane North
Epsom, Surrey KT17 3JB
E info@dapstudio.co.uk
W www.dapstudio.co.uk

DMN DESIGN BUILD   T 0844 8711801
Unit 1, Calder Trading Estate, Lower Quarry Road
Bradley, Huddersfield HD5 0RR
E enquiries@dmndesignbuild.co.uk
W www.dmndesignbuild.com

EVANS, Peter STUDIOS LTD   T 01582 725730
Scenic Embellishment. Vacuum Forming
12-14 Tavistock Street, Dunstable, Bedfordshire LU6 1NE
F 01582 481329
E sales@peterevansstudios.co.uk
W www.peterevansstudios.co.uk

FULL EFFECT THE
T 020 7836 0562
Event Designers & Producers
30 Maiden Lane
London WC2E 7JS
F 020 7836 1044
E mark.harrison@tfe.co.uk
W www.thefulleffect.co.uk

FUTURIST SOUND & LIGHT LTD
T 0113 279 0033
Unit 1, White Swan Yard
Boroughgate, Otley LS21 1AE
F 0113 242 0022
E info@futurist.co.uk
W www.futurist.co.uk

GAUGE AUDIO VISUAL
T 01243 641404
Gauge Theatre Sound. Consultancy. Design.
Hire. Installation. Sales
Tithe Barn Cottage, Rookery Lane
Sidlesham, West Sussex PO20 7ND
E jonathan@gauge-av.com
W www.gauge-av.com

GILL, Perry
T 07815 048164
Installation. Production Management. Set Construction
E perry_gill100@hotmail.com

GROWING CONCERNS
Rustic Vintage Furniture & Tools
286 Church Road
Kessingland
Suffolk NR33 7SB
E ak@growingconcerns.co.uk

HALL STAGE LTD
T 0845 3454255
Unit 4, Cosgrove Way
Luton, Beds LU1 1XL
F 0845 3454256
E sales@hallstage.com
W www.hallstage.com

HALO LIGHTING
T 0844 8440484
98-124 Brewery Road
London N7 9PG
E info@halo.co.uk
W www.halo.co.uk

HAND & LOCK
T 020 7580 7488
Embroidery for Costumes & Interiors
86 Margaret Street
London W1W 8TE
F 020 7580 7499
E enquiries@handembroidery.com
W www.handembroidery.com

HENSHALL, John
T 01367 710191
Director of Lighting & Photography
68 High Street
Stanford in the Vale
Oxfordshire SN7 8NL
E john@epi-centre.com

HERON & DRIVER
T 020 7394 8688
Scenic Furniture & Structural Prop Makers
Unit 7, Dockley Road Industrial Estate
Rotherhithe, London SE16 3SF
E mail@herondriver.co.uk
W www.herondriver.co.uk

IOGIG LTD
T 020 7112 8907
Production Services including Set, Lighting, Sound & Stage/Production Management
39 Equinox House
Wakering Road
Barking, Essex IG11 8RN
E info@iogig.com
W www.iogig.com

LIGHT WORKS LTD
T 020 7249 3627
2A Greenwood Road
London E8 1AB
F 020 7254 0306

MALTBURY STAGING
T 0333 800 8881
Portable Staging Sales & Consultancy
87 Church Road
Hove BN3 2BB
F 0333 800 8882
E info@maltbury.com
W www.maltbury.com

MATTLX GROUP
T 0845 6808693
Lighting. Design. Production Engineering. Safety. Training
Unit 3, Vinehall Business Centre
Vinehall Road, Robertsbridge
East Sussex TN32 5JW
E intray@mattlx.com
W www.mattlx.com

MODELBOX
T 01837 810923
Computer Aided Design. Design Services
41C Market Street
Hatherleigh
Devon EX20 3JP
E info@modelbox.co.uk
W www.modelboxplans.com

MODERNEON LONDON LTD
T 020 8650 9690
Lighting. Signs
Cromwell House
27 Brabourne Rise
Park Langley, Beckenham
Kent BR3 6SQ
F 020 8658 2770
E info@moderneon.co.uk
W www.moderneon.co.uk

MOUNSEY, Matthew
T 07941 355450
Scenic Artist
E matthewmounsey@hotmail.com

NEED, Paul J.
T 020 8659 2558
Lighting Designer
5 Metro Business Centre
Kangley Bridge Road
London SE26 5BW
F 020 8778 9217
E paul@10outof10.co.uk
W www.pauljneed.co.uk

NORTHERN LIGHT
T 0131 622 9100
Communications, Lighting, Sound & Stage Equipment
Assembly Street, Leith
Edinburgh EH6 7RG
F 0131 622 9101
E info@northernlight.co.uk
W www.northernlight.co.uk

ORBITAL   T 020 7501 6868
Sound Hire & Design
57 Acre Lane, Brixton
London SW2 5TN
F 020 7501 6869
E hire@orbitalsound.co.uk
W www.orbitalsound.co.uk

PANALUX   T 020 8233 7000
12 Waxlow Road, London NW10 7NU
F 020 8233 7001
E info@panalux.biz
W www.panalux.biz

**PMB THEATRE
EXHIBITION SERVICES LTD**   T 01763 852691
Low Farm, Brook Road, Bassingbourn
Royston, Herts SG8 5NT
F 01763 853946
E pmb@creatingtheimpossible.co.uk
W www.creatingtheimpossible.co.uk

PRODUCTION STORE   T 0845 6808692
Consumables. Parts. Tapes. Tools
Unit 3, Vinehall Business Centre
Vinehall Road, Robertsbridge
East Sussex TN32 5JW
E sales@mattlx.com
W www.productionstore.net

**REVOLVING STAGE
COMPANY LTD THE**   T 024 7668 7055
Unit F5, Little Heath Industrial Estate
Old Church Road, Coventry
Warwickshire CV6 7ND
F 024 7668 9355
E enquiries@therevolvingstagecompany.co.uk
W www.therevolvingstagecompany.co.uk

RK RESOURCE   T 01233 750180
2 Wyvern Way, Henwood
Ashford, Kent TN24 8DW
F 01233 750133
E rkresource2007@aol.co.uk
W www.rk-resourcekent.com

**S + H TECHNICAL
SUPPORT LTD**   T 01271 866832
Starcloths. Drapes
Starcloth Way, Mullacott Industrial Estate
Ilfracombe, Devon EX34 8PL
F 01271 865423
E shtsg@aol.com
W www.starcloth.co.uk

S2 EVENTS   T 020 7928 5474
*Design, Equipment Hire, Production, Scenery/Set
Construction & Technical Services for Creative Live Events*
3-5 Valentine Place
London SE1 8QH
F 020 7928 6082
E info@s2events.co.uk
W www.s2events.co.uk

SCENA PRODUCTIONS LLP   T 020 7703 4444
Set Construction
240 Camberwell Road, London SE5 0DP
F 020 7703 7012
E info@scenapro.com
W www.scenapro.com

SCENIC WORKSHOPS LTD   T 0151 933 6677
Baltic Road, Bootle
Liverpool L20 1AW
F 0151 933 6699
E info@scenicworkshops.co.uk
W www.scenicworkshops.co.uk

**SCOTT FLEARY
PRODUCTIONS LTD**   T 0870 4441787
Unit 1-4, Vale Industrial Park
170 Rowan Road
London SW16 5BN
F 0870 4448322
E info@scottfleary.com

SET CREATIONS   T 020 7274 2044
Unit 41, MG Industrial Estate
Milkwood Road
London SE24 0JF
F 020 7738 3099
E info@setcreations.com
W www.setcreations.com

SHOWSTORM LTD   T 020 8123 3453
24 The Poplars
Littlehampton BN17 6GZ
E mark@showstorm.tv
W www.showstorm.tv

SMITH, Paul Don   T 07949 710306
Graffiti Mural Artist. Graphics. Scenery
11A Cadogan Road
Surbiton, Surrey KT6 4DQ
E firedon_1@hotmail.com
W www.pauldonsmith.com

SPICKNELL, Jackie   T 07752 831095
Freelance Scenic Painter
34 Shirley Gardens
Hornchurch
Essex RM12 4NH
E jackie_jackiecool@hotmail.com
W www.jacquelinespicknell.webeden.co.uk

SPLINTER   T 0161 633 6787
Supplier of Touring Theatre Scenery
The Gasworks, Higginshaw Lane
Oldham, Greater Manchester OL1 3LB
F 0161 633 6851
E splintermail@aol.com
W www.splinterscenery.co.uk

**STAGE MANAGEMENT
COMPANY**   T 01274 669259
Audio. Lighting. Production
Unit 12 Commerce Court
Challenge Way
Bradford BD4 8NW
E info@stagemanagementcompany.com
W www.stagemanagementcompany.com

STAGE SYSTEMS   T 01509 611021
*Designers & Suppliers of Modular Staging, Tiering &
Auditorium Seating*
Stage House
Prince William Road
Loughborough LE11 5GU
F 01509 233146
E info@stagesystems.co.uk
W www.stagesystems.co.uk

STAGE TEAM   T 0844 8700497
2A Moorend Crescent
Cheltenham
Gloucestershire GL53 0EL
E info@stageteam.co.uk
W www.stageteam.co.uk

**STAGECRAFT TECHNICAL
SERVICES LTD**   T 0845 8382015
*Hire & Sales of Audio Visual, Lighting, Sound & Staging
for Conference & Live Events*
Porton Business Centre, Porton
Wiltshire SP4 0ND
F 0845 8382016
E hire@cpsgroup.co.uk
W www.stagecraft.co.uk

**STAGEWORKS WORLDWIDE
PRODUCTIONS**   T 01253 342426
Lighting. Props. Scenery. Sound
525 Ocean Boulevard
Blackpool FY4 1EZ
F 01253 342702
E info@stageworkswwp.com
W www.stageworkswwp.com

STEWART, Helen   T 07887 682186
Theatre Designer
29C Hornsey Rise Gardens
London N19 3PP
E helen@helenstewart.co.uk
W www.helenstewart.co.uk

STORM LIGHTING LTD   T 01483 757211
Warwick House
Monument Way West
Woking, Surrey GU21 5EN
F 01483 757710
E hire@stormlighting.co.uk
W www.stormlighting.co.uk

TITAN TOUR PRODUCTIONS   T 07894 868750
55 Hereford Road, Eccles
Greater Manchester M30 9BX
E charlotte@titantourproductions.com
W www.titantourproductions.com

TMS THEATRICAL LTD   T 020 7394 9519
Set Construction & Painting
306 St James's Road
London SE1 5JX
F 020 7232 2347
E administration@tmstheatrical.com
W www.tmstheatrical.com

TOP SHOW   T 01904 750022
Props. Scenery. Conference Specialists
North Lane, Huntington
York YO32 9SU

WEST, John   T 07753 637451
Art Director. Draughtsman
103 Abbotswood Close
Winyates Green, Redditch
Worcestershire B98 0QF
E johnwest@blueyonder.co.uk
W www.johnwestportfolio.com

T

BBC TELEVISION
Wood Lane
London W12 7RJ
T 020 8743 8000

The BBC has relocated a number of its departments to a new site at MediaCityUK, Salford Quays, Salford. Departments include BBC Children's, BBC Radio 5 live, parts of Future Media & Technology, BBC Learning, BBC Sport and BBC Breakfast. For further information about BBC North please contact the BBC's main London switchboard.

If you are interested in working for the BBC in a production role, you can submit your CV to the BBC Production Talent website at www.bbcproductiontalent.co.uk

•TALENT & RIGHTS NEGOTIATION GROUP
Room 3400
201 Wood Lane
White City
London W12 7TS

Head of Talent Rights & Negotiation	Roger Leatham
Head of Copyright Contracting	Rob Kirkham
Head of Performance Contracting	Annie Thomas

LITERARY COPYRIGHT
Room 3206
BBC White City
London W12 7TS

Manager	Neil Hunt

Senior Executives

Sue Dickson	Julieann May
Julie Gallagher	Sally Millwood
David Knight	Hilary Sagar

MUSIC COPYRIGHT & MUSIC ENTERTAINMENT PERFORMANCE
Room 3370
BBC White City
London W12 7TS

Manager	Catherine Grimes
Executives	
Laura Amphlett	Celine Palavioux
Sally Dunsford	Natasha Pullin
Madeline Hennessy	Debbie Rogerson
Sam Nicholas	Vicki Willis

BBC JOURNALISM, COMEDY & ENTERTAINMENT
Room 3029
BBC Television Centre
London W12 7RJ

Manager	Tessa Beckett
Rights Executives	
John Arnold	Gary Casey
Mike Bickerdike	Jemma McGee

LONDON FACTUAL & ARTS
Room 401, MC4 DI Media Centre
201 Wood Lane, London W12 7TQ

Rights Manager	Jane Armstrong
Executives	
Alice Brandon	Stuart Krelle
Selena Harvey	Shelagh Morrison
Matthew Hickling	
Classical Music Rights Manager	Simon Brown

TV DRAMA & RADIO DRAMA/COMEDY
Room 3370
BBC White City
London W12 7TS

Rights Manager	Tessa Beckett
Executives – TV Drama	
Lorraine Clark	Candice Nichols
Fiona Dourado	
Executives – Radio Drama/Comedy	
Stephanie Beynon	Ian Heydon

PERFORMANCE CONTRACTING BBC NORTH
3rd Floor, Dock House
MediaCityUK
Salford M50 2HL

Rights Manager	Simon Ashwood
Executives	
Colleen Burrows	Sarah McHugh
Teresa Cordall	Collette Tanner

PERFORMANCE CONTRACTING BBC BIRMINGHAM
Level 10
The Mailbox
102-107 Wharfside Street
Birmingham B1 1AY

Rights Manager	Simon Ashwood
Executives	
Rachel Amos	Jill Ridley
Andrea Coles	

•DRAMA
BBC Drama Production
Lighthouse Building
Media Village
201 Wood Lane
London W12 7TQ
T 020 8743 8000 (Main Switchboard)

Director, Drama Production	Nicolas Brown
Controller, Series & Serials	Kate Harwood
Controller, Drama Production & New Talent	John Yorke
Head of Production	Susy Liddell
Creative Director, Drama Production	Katie McAleese
Executive Producers - Drama Production	
Phillippa Giles	Hilary Salmon

Sue Hogg — Will Trotter
Anne Pivcevic — Jonathan Young
Jess Pope
Executive Producer, EastEnders Lorraine Goodman

•COMMISSIONING

Director, BBC Vision — George Entwistle
Head of Independent Drama — Polly Hill
Commissioning Editor,
  Independent Drama — Lucy Richer
Controller, Drama Production Studios — John Yorke
Controller, BBC Four — Richard Klein
Head of Knowledge Commissioning — Emma Swain
Controller, Series & Serials — Kate Harwood
Controller, Drama Commissioning — Ben Stephenson

•NEWS GROUP

BBC News (Television & Radio)
BBC Broadcasting House
Portland Place
London W1A 1AA
T 020 7580 4468 (Main Switchboard)

Director, News — Helen Boaden
Director, Global News — Peter Horrocks
Head of Programmes, News — Stephen Mitchell
Head of Newsgathering — Fran Unsworth
Head of Newsroom — Mary Hockaday
Head of Political Programmes,
  Research & Analysis — Sue Inglish
Controller of Production, News — Jenny Baxter
Controller, English Regions — David Holdsworth
Controller, BBC Parliament — Peter Knowles
Editor, News Online — Steve Herrmann
Editor, Andrew Marr Show — Barney Jones
Editor, This Week & Daily Politics — Robbie Gibb
Editor, The Politics Show — Gavin Allen

London Factual Executive Producers

All based in the Media Centre
at White City Media Village
T 020 8743 8000 (Main Switchboard)

Arts
Jonty Claypole — Basil Comely
Documentaries & Features
Colin Barr — Gary Hunter
Tina Fletcher — Clare Sillery
Eamon Hardy
Consumer — Lisa Ausden
Science
Andrew Cohen — Jonathan Renouf
Tina Fletcher — Helen Thomas
Horizon Editor — Aidan Laverty
Business & History — Dominic Crossley-Holland

History
Chris Granlund — Eamon Hardy
Editor, The Culture Show — Janet Lee
Editor, The One Show — Sandy Smith

•CHILDREN

Director — Joe Godwin
Controller, CBBC — Cheryl Taylor
Controller, CBeebies — Kay Benbow
Head of In-house Production — Helen Bullough
Head of Children's Programmes,
  Scotland — Sara Harkins

•MUSIC

Head of Television,
  Classical Music & Performance — Peter Maniura
Managing Editor, Classical Music,
  Television — Caroline Speed
Editor Music Programmes, Television,
  Classical Music & Performance — Oliver Macfarlane
Talent Producer/Programme
  Development Manager — Victoria Jones
Executive Producer — Celina Parker
Producers/Directors
Dominic Best — Andy King-Dabbs
Jonathan Haswell — Helen Mansfield
Francesca Kemp
Production Executive — Ian Taitt

•SPORT

Director of Sport — Barbara Slater
Head of Major Events — Dave Gordon
Head of TV Sport — Philip Bernie
Head of Interactive & Formula 1 — Ben Gallop
Head of Sports News &
  BBC Radio Sport — Richard Burgess
Head of Production — Jackie Myburgh
HR Partner — Andrea Wilkinson
Head of Sports Rights — David Murray
Head of Marketing & Communications,
  Sports & Events — Louise Fyans
Finance Partner — Daniel Chaffer

•NEW WRITING

BBC Writersroom
BBC Broadcasting House
Portland Place
London W1A 1AA
T 020 8743 8000 (Main Switchboard)
E writersroom@bbc.co.uk
W www.bbc.co.uk/writersroom

Creative Director — Kate Rowland
Development Producer — Paul Ashton

BBC BIRMINGHAM & BLACK COUNTRY

The Mailbox
Birmingham B1 1AY
F 0121 567 6875   T 0121 567 6767

English Regions

Controller, English Regions	David Holdsworth
Head of New Media Services, English Regions	Laura Ellis
Chief Operating Officer, English Regions	Ian Hughes
Senior Officer, Press & PR	Caroline Boots
Secretary, BBC Trust	Louise Hall
Head of Regional & Local Programmes, West Midlands	Cath Hearne

Vision Productions

Head of Birmingham & Manchester Factual	Nick Patten
Head of Production Talent, Birmingham & Manchester	Manjit Ahluwalia

Audio & Music Factual

Head of Rural Affairs & Audio & Music Production	Andrew Thorman
Deputy Editor	Fran Barnes

Drama

BBC Birmingham TV Drama Village
Archibald House
1059 Bristol Road, Selly Oak
Birmingham B29 6LT   T 0121 567 7417

Executive Producer   Will Trotter

BBC BRISTOL

Broadcasting House
Whiteladies Road
Bristol BS8 2LR   T 0117 973 2211

Network Television Features & Documentaries

Head of Bristol Factual	Nick Patten
Editor, Daytime	Kate Beetham
Head of Talent	Christopher Hutchins

Executive Producers

Robi Dutta	Michael Poole
Pete Lawrence	Simon Shaw
Julian Mercer	

Series Producers

Kate Broome	Alastair Laurence
Hannah Corneck	Ben Southwell
John Das	

BBC Audio & Musical Production, Bristol (BBC Radio 4)

Head of Production for Audio & Music	Clare McGinn
Production Manager	Kate Chaney

Producers

John Byrne	Chris Ledgard
Sara Davies	Beth O'Dea
Tim Dee	Mark Smalley
Christine Hall	Mary Ward-Lowery
Jolyon Jenkins	Miles Warde
Kirsten Lass	

BBC Natural History Unit, Bristol

Contact: Emily Ash
(Assistant to Head of Natural History Unit)
Head of Natural History Unit   Wendy Darke

Executive Producers

Chris Cole	Brian Leith
Alastair Fothergill	Tim Martin
Mike Gunton	Tim Scoones
Julian Hector	

BBC LONDON

2nd Floor
Egton Wing Broadcasting House
10-22 Portland Place
London W1A 1AA   T 020 8743 8000

BBC London News

TV: The Politics Show
Radio: BBC London Radio 94.9FM
Online: BBC London online

Head of BBC London	Michael MacFarlane
TV Editor	Antony Dore
Editor, Inside Out	Dippy Chaudhary
Managing Editor, BBC Radio London 94.9FM	David Robey
Political Editor	Tim Donovan
Editor, BBC London Online	Claire Timms

BBC NORTH WEST

New Broadcasting House
Oxford Road
Manchester M60 1SJ

W www.bbc.co.uk/manchester
W www.bbc.co.uk/liverpool
W www.bbc.co.uk/lancashire   T 0161 200 2020

Entertainment & Features

Editor, Entertainment & Features	Helen Bullough

Religion & Ethics

Head of Religion & Ethics & Commissioning Editor for Religion TV	Aaqil Ahmed
Executive Editor & Head of Radio, Religion & Ethics	Christine Morgan
Head of Television Religion	Tommy Nagra

Regional & Local Programmes

Head of Regional & Local Programmes, North West	Aziz Rashid
Head of Regional & Local Programmes, North East & Cumbria	Phil Roberts

BBC SOUTH

Havelock Road
Southampton SO14 7PU   **T 023 8022 6201**

Head of Regional & Local Programmes	Jason Horton
TV News Editor	Lee Desty
Editor, BBC Oxford	Marianne Bell
Managing Editor, BBC Solent	Chris Carnegy
Managing Editor, BBC Radio Berkshire	Duncan McLarty

BBC SOUTH EAST

The Great Hall Arcade
Mount Pleasant Road
Tunbridge Wells
Kent TN1 1QQ   **T 01892 670000**

Head of Regional & Local Programmes, BBC South East	Michael Rawsthorne
Managing Editor, BBC Radio Kent	Paul Leaper
Managing Editor, BBC Radio Surrey & BBC Radio Sussex	Nicci Holliday
Editor, BBC South East Today	Quentin Smith
Editor, Inside Out	Linda Bell
Assistant Editor, Politics Show	Dan Fineman

BBC SOUTH WEST

Seymour Road
Mannamead
Plymouth PL3 5BD   **T 01752 229201**

Head of BBC South West	Leo Devine
Editor, TV Current Affairs	Simon Willis
Output Editor	Simon Read

BBC WEST

Broadcasting House
Whiteladies Road
Bristol BS8 2LR   **T 0117 973 2211**

For the latest local news and information about your area, visit our websites:

Bristol:	www.bbc.co.uk/bristol
Gloucestershire:	www.bbc.co.uk/gloucestershire
Somerset:	www.bbc.co.uk/somerset
Wiltshire/ Swindon:	www.bbc.co.uk/wiltshire
Points West:	www.bbc.co.uk/pointswest

Head of Regional & Local Programmes, including BBC West, BBC Radio Bristol, BBC Somerset, BBC Gloucestershire, BBC Wiltshire	Lucio Mesquita
Editor, TV News	Neil Bennett

BBC SCOTLAND

40 Pacific Quay
Glasgow G51 1DA
W www.bbc.co.uk/scotland   **T 0141 422 6000**

Scottish Executive Board

Director, Scotland	Ken MacQuarrie
Head of Programmes & Services	Donalda MacKinnon
Head of Public Policy	Ian Small
Chief Operating Officer	Bruce Malcolm
Head of Talent & Operations	Donald-Iain Brown
Head of HR & Development	Wendy Aslett
Head of Marketing & Communications	Mairead Ferguson
Head of Strategy	Catherine Smith
Head of News & Current Affairs	John Boothman
Commissioning Editor, Television & Head of Sport	Ewan Angus
Head of Radio, Scotland	Jeff Zycinski

Genre Heads

Head of Service, BBC Alba	Margaret Mary Murray
Service Editor, BBC Alba	Marion MacKinnon
Head of Factual	Andrea Miller
Head of Drama, Television	Christopher Aird
Head of Drama, Radio	Bruce Young
Creative Director, Children's Scotland	Sara Harkins
Head of Entertainment & Events	Eileen Herlihy
Head of New Media, Learning & Outreach	Matthew Lee
Director, BBC Scottish Symphony Orchestra	Gavin Reid

Commissioning

Executive Editor, Entertainment Commissioning	Alan Tyler
Commissioning Executive, BBC Daytime, Scotland & Northern Ireland	Jo Street
Executive Producer, Scotland, Knowledge Commissioning	Sam Anthony

BBC Scotland provides television and radio programmes for Scotland and the UK networks as well as online and interactive content. Based in Glasgow's digital headquarters, there are also centres throughout Scotland which includes City Halls, the home of the BBC Scottish Symphony Orchestra.

Aberdeen

Broadcasting House
Beechgrove Terrace
Aberdeen AB15 5ZT   **T 01224 625233**

Dumbarton

Dumbarton Studios
Studio Way
Dumbarton G82 2AP   **T 01389 736666**

Dumfries

Elmbank, Lover's Walk
Dumfries DG1 1NZ   **T 01387 268008**

Dundee
Nethergate Centre
4th Floor, 66 Nethergate
Dundee DD1 4ER   T 01382 202481

Edinburgh
The Tun, 4 Jackson's Entry
111 Holyrood Road
Edinburgh EH8 8PJ   T 0131 557 5888

Glasgow
Glasgow City Halls
(BBC Scottish Symphony Orchestra)
87 Albion Street
Glasgow G1 1NQ   T 0141 552 0909

Inverness
7 Culduthel Road
Inverness IV2 4AD   T 01463 720720

Orkney
Castle Street, Kirkwall
Orkney KW15 1DF   T 01856 873939

Portree
Clydesdale Bank Buildings
Somerled Square

Portree
Isle of Skye IV51 9BT   T 01478 612005

Selkirk
Unit 1, Ettrick Riverside
Dunsdale Road
Selkirk TD7 5EB   T 01750 724567

Shetland
Pitt Lane, Lerwick
Shetland ZE1 0DW   T 01595 694747

Stornoway
Radio nan Gaidheal
Rosebank
52 Church Street

Stornoway
Isle of Lewis HS1 2LS   T 01851 705000

BBC CYMRU/WALES
Broadcasting House
Llandaff
Cardiff CF5 2YQ   T 029 2032 2000

Director	Rhodri Talfan-Davies
Head of Programmes & Services (Welsh)	Sian Gwynedd
Head of Programmes & Services (English)	Adrian Davies
Head of Marketing, Communications & Audiences	Richard Thomas
Head of News & Current Affairs	Mark O'Callaghan
Head of HR & Development	Jude Gray
Chief Operating Officer	Gareth Powell
Head of Drama	Faith Penhale
Head of Sport	Geoff Williams
Acting Head of Factual & Music	Judith Winnan
Editor, Radio Wales	Steve Austins
Editor, Radio Cymru	Sian Gwynedd
Editor, New Media	Iain Tweedale

BBC NORTHERN IRELAND
Belfast
BBC Broadcasting House
Ormeau Avenue
Belfast BT2 8HQ   T 028 9033 8000
W www.bbc.co.uk/ni

Director, BBC Northern Ireland	Peter Johnston
Head of Programmes	Ailsa Orr
Head of Drama	Stephen Wright
Head of News	Kathleen Carragher
Chief Operating Officer	Mark Taylor
Head of Corporate & Community Affairs	Mark Adair
Head of Marketing, Communications & Audiences	Kathy Martin
Head of TV Current Affairs	Jeremy Adams
Editor, Sport	Shane Glynn
Head of Local TV Commissioning	Susan Lovell
Head of Radio Ulster	Fergus Keeling
Editor, Radio Foyle	Michael Tumelty

BBC Radio Ulster
BBC Broadcasting House
Ormeau Avenue
Belfast BT2 8HQ   T 028 9033 8000
W www.bbc.co.uk/radioulster

BBC Radio Foyle
8 Northland Road
Londonderry BT48 7JD   T 028 7126 2244

CHANNEL 4 TELEVISION CORPORATION

London Office
124 Horseferry Road
London SW1P 2TX
Textphone 020 7396 8691   **T 020 7396 4444**

Members of the Board

Chairman	Lord Terry Burns
Deputy Chairman	Lord David Puttnam
Chief Executive	David Abraham
Chief Creative Officer	Jay Hunt
Chief Operating Officer	Anne Bulford

Non-Executive Directors

Monica Burch	Mark Price
Martha Lane-Fox	Mt Rainy
Lord Tony Hall	Richard Rivers
Alicja Lesniak	Josie Rourke
Paul Potts	

Executives

Director, Human Resources	Diane Herbert
Director, Audience Technology & Insight	Gill Whitehead
Director, Marketing & Communications	Dan Brooke

Heads of Departments

Board Secretary	Paula Carter
Head of Commercial Affairs	Martin Baker
Channel Manager	Richard Brent
Controller, Channel Management	George Dixon
Director, Commercial & Business Development	Sarah Rose
Head of Business Assurance	Jeff O'Sullivan
Head of Corporate Relations	Sophie Jones
Director, Creative Diversity	Stuart Cosgrove
Head of Distribution & Broadcast Technology	David Dorans
Head of Comedy	Shane Allen
Head of Entertainment	Justin Gorman
Head of Corporate Services	Julie Kortens
Head of Factual Entertainment	Liam Humphreys
Controller, Film & Drama	Tessa Scantlebury
Director, Finance	Glyn Isherwood
Head of HR Operations	Rosie Ranganathan
Controller, Legal & Compliance	Prash Naik
Head of News & Current Affairs	Dorothy Byrne
Head of Online	Richard Davidson-Houston
Head of Portfolio & Airtime Management	Merlin Inkley
Head of Acquisitions	Gill Hay
Head of Specialist Factual	Ralph Lee
Director, Strategy	Keith Underwood
Chief Information Officer	Kevin Gallagher
Chief Technology Officer	Bob Harris
Head of Agency Sales	Damon Lafford
Controller, Press & Publicity	Jane Fletcher
Head of Production, 4Creative	Claire Finn
Head of Music	Mary Seiler
Head of Film4	Mark Adams
Head of Business Affairs, Film4 & Scripted	Julia Mortimer
Head of Production, Film4	Geraldine Atlee
Head of Rights	Tracey Josephs
Head of T4 & Music	Jeremy Kimberlin
	Neil McCallum

CHANNEL 5 BROADCASTING LTD

10 Lower Thames Street
London EC3R 6EN
W www.channel5.com   **T 020 8612 7000**

Chairman	Richard Desmond
Director of Programmes	Jeff Ford
Executive Assistant to Director of Programmes	Kelly Hornsby
Head of Scheduling	Craig Morris
Head of News & Factual	Andrew O'Connell
Head of Factual Entertainment & Head of Sport	Steve Gowans
Commissioning Editor, Entertainment, Daytime & Soaps	Greg Barnett
Commissioning Editor, Children's	Jessica Symons
Head of Digital Channels	Kate Barnes
Head of Acquisitions	Kate Keenan
Marketing Director	Zoe Harris
Creative Director	Rich Thrift
Head of Marketing	Iain Sawbridge
Commercial Sales Director	Nick Bampton
Director of Legal & Commercial Affairs	Marcus Lee
Group Finance Director	Rob Sanderson

CHANNEL TELEVISION LTD

Registered Office
The Television Centre
La Pouquelaye, St Helier
Jersey JE1 3ZD, Channel Islands
F 01534 816817
W www.channelonline.tv   **T 01534 816816**

Channel Islands: Weekday and Weekend

Senior Executive	Karen Rankin
Programme Producer	Laura Holgate
Managing Director, Commercial	Mike Elsey
Director of Resources & Transmission	Kevin Banner
Programme Editor	Eric Blakeley

INDEPENDENT TELEVISION NEWS

200 Gray's Inn Road
London WC1X 8XZ   T 020 7833 3000

Chief Executive	John Hardie
Editor, ITV News	Deborah Turness
Editor, Channel 4 News	Jim Gray

ITV PLC

Registered Office

The London Television Centre
Upper Ground
London SE1 9LT
F 020 7849 9344
W www.itv.com   T 020 7157 3000

Management Board

Chairman	Archie Norman
Chief Executive	Adam Crozier
Director of Television, Channels & Online	Peter Fincham
Director of Strategy & Development	Carolyn Fairbairn
Group Director of Communications	Ruth Settle
Group Finance Director	Ian Griffiths
Managing Director, ITV Studios	Lee Bartlett
HR Director	Andy Doyle
Group Legal Director & Company Secretary	Andrew Garard
Managing Director, ITV Brand & Commercial	Rupert Howell

Casting Directors at ITV Studios

Manchester

Casting Director	Gennie Radcliffe
Assistant Casting Director	Katy Belshaw

Leeds

Casting Director	Faye Styring
Casting Assistant	Amy Hill

If you would like one of the casting teams to cover your performance in a stage production, please e-mail casting@itv.com including your name, the theatre and the dates.

ITV ANGLIA

Head Office

Anglia House
Norwich NR1 3JG
Twitter: @ITVAnglia
E anglianews@itv.com
W www.itv.com/anglia   T 0844 8816900

East of England: Weekday & Weekend

Regional News Centres

Cambridge

Link House
Station Road
Great Shelford
Cambridge CB22 5LT   T 0844 8816985 (News)

Northampton

Portfolio Innovation Centre
University of Northampton
St George's Avenue
Northampton NN2 6JD   T 0844 8816974

ITV BREAKFAST

London Television Centre
Upper Ground, London SE1 9TT
F 020 7827 7001
W www.itv.com/daybreak   T 020 7827 7000

Editor	David Kermode
Deputy Editor	Abi Donald
Head of News	Pete Meikle
Head of Features	Vivek Sharma
Head of Planning	Caroline Sigley
Head of Entertainment	Corinne Bishop
Head of Graphics	Fiona Skinner
Production Executive	Helen Killeen

Lorraine

Creative Director	Emma Gormley
Series Editor	Pauline Haase
Head of Features	Annemarie Leahy

ITV MERIDIAN

ITV Meridian is part of ITV Plc

Fusion 3
1200 Parkway
Whiteley, Hants PO15 7AD
F 0844 8812074   T 0844 8812000

Meridian Board

Regional Sales Manager	Matt Corse

Executives

Finance Manager	Malcolm Beasley
Head of News	Robin Britton

ITV TYNE TEES & ITV BORDER

Television House, The Watermark
Gateshead NE11 9SZ   T 0844 8815000

Teesside News Gathering
20 Manor Way, Belasis Hall Technology Park
Billingham, Cleveland TS23 4HN
E tttvnews@itv.com   T 0844 8815000

North East and North Yorkshire: Weekday and Weekend

Executive Chair ITV	Adam Crozier
Head of News	Lucy West
Managing Director, SignPost	Malcolm Wright

ITV WALES

Television Centre
Culverhouse Cross
Cardiff CF5 6XJ
E news@itvwales.com
W www.itv.com/wales   T 0844 8810100

Wales: All week

Head of News & Programmes	Phil Henfrey

ITV WEST & ITV WESTCOUNTRY

470 Bath Road
Bristol BS4 3HG   T 0844 8812345

Head of News   Terence Brennan

ITV YORKSHIRE

The Television Centre
Leeds LS3 1JS
F 0113 244 5107
W www.itv.com   T 0113 222 7000

London Office

London Television Centre
Upperground
London SE1 9LT   T 020 7620 1620

Executives

Head of News   Margaret Emsley
Creative Director ITV Studios   John Whiston

S4C

Parc Tŷ Glas, Llanishen
Cardiff CF14 5DU
F 029 2075 4444
E s4c@s4c.co.uk
W www.s4c.co.uk   T 029 2074 7444

The Welsh Fourth Channel Authority

Chair   Huw Jones

Authority Members

John Davies   Dr Glenda Jones
Dyfrig Jones   Rheon Tomos

Senior Staff

Chief Executive   Ian Jones
Director of Commissioning   Dafydd Rhys
Director of Communications,
  Marketing & Partnerships   Garffild Lloyd Lewis
Director of Finance   Kathryn Morris
Director of Corporate & Commercial   Elin Morris

SKY SATELLITE TELEVISION BRITISH SKY BROADCASTING LTD (BSkyB)

Grant Way, Isleworth
Middlesex TW7 5QD
W www.sky.com/corporate   T 020 7705 3000

Chief Executive   Jeremy Darroch
Chief Financial Officer   Andrew Griffith
Managing Director,
  Entertainment & News   Sophie Turner Laing
Director for People   Deborah Baker
Chief Operating Officer   Mike Darcey
Group Director of
  Corporate Affairs   Graham McWilliam

General Counsel   James Conyers
Managing Director, Sky Sports   Barney Francis
Managing Director, Product Design &
  Development   Alun Webber
Chief Technology Officer   Didier Lebrat
Group Director,
  Business Performance   William Mellis
Managing Director, Customer Group   Andrea Zappia
Group Director of Strategy   Mia Fyfield

STV

Glasgow Office

Pacific Quay
Glasgow G51 1PQ
F 0141 300 3030
W www.stv.tv   T 0141 300 3000

Aberdeen Office

Television Centre
Craigshaw Business Park
West Tullos
Aberdeen AB12 3QH
W www.stv.tv   T 01224 848848

London Office

21-25 St Anne's Court
London W1F 0BJ
W www.stv.tv   T 020 7494 5747

Director of Channels   Bobby Hain
Head of News & Current Affairs   Gordon MacMillan
Chief Executive   Rob Woodward
Director of Content   Alan Clements
Deputy Director of Content   Liam Hamilton
Head of Entertainment   Gary Chippington
Head of Drama   Margaret Enefer

UTV MEDIA PLC

Ormeau Road
Belfast BT7 1EB
F 028 9024 6695
E info@u.tv
W www.utvmedia.com   T 028 9032 8122

Northern Ireland: Weekday and Weekend

Contact:

Sarah McCaffrey
Broadcast Marketing Executive   T 028 9026 2186

Chairman   J B McGuckian BSc (Econ)
Group Chief Executive   J McCann BSc, FCA
Group Financial Director   Jim Downey
Managing Director, Television   Michael Wilson
Head of Communications   Orla McKibbin
Head of News & Current Affairs   Rob Morrison
Sales Director   Paul Hutchinson

Theatre Producers

What is a theatre producer?

A theatre producer is someone who oversees and organises a theatre show. He or she will find, or arrange for other professionals to find, a suitable script, design, director and cast for each production, while also managing all finances and marketing.

How should I use these listings?

Theatre producers tend to use casting directors to put forward suitable actors for the parts in forthcoming productions, but you could also try approaching them yourself.

Rather than sending your CV and headshot to every producer listed, it would be best to do some research first in order to target your search. You need to decide what type of work you want to do first, as there is no need to waste your time and the producer's time sending your CV to unsuitable companies. Then find out what each company has produced in the past, what they are currently working on, and if possible what they are considering producing in the future, and only send your CV to those most relevant to the roles you want to play.

Don't forget to include a covering letter which states why you are contacting this producer in particular: this could be because you feel you are perfect for a particular role in their next production, for example. Personalising and targeting your correspondence in this way gives you the best chance of your CV being considered in a favourable light.

How should I approach theatre producers?

You should contact theatre producers by post or e-mail only. We would advise against calling them, especially when approaching them for the first time. Address your correspondence to an individual within the company, as this demonstrates that you have done your research. If you are unsure as to the best method of applying to theatre producers, as with other casting professionals it is safest to post your CV and headshot in the traditional way rather than e-mailing it.

Remember to put your name and telephone number on the back of the photo in case it gets separated from your CV. It would be a good idea to include a SAE big enough to contain your 10 x 8 photo and with sufficient postage to increase your chances of getting a reply. Do not enclose your showreel but you can mention that you have one available in your covering letter, and if the producer is interested in viewing it they will contact you.

When should I approach theatre producers?

Listen to industry news and have a look at theatre producers' websites for forthcoming production details. The casting process usually takes place around three months prior to rehearsals, so bear this in mind when you are writing your covering letter.

How do I become a theatre producer?

The best way to learn about producing is to work in producing. Internships are a good way to get to grips with the industry; research the theatre producers listed over the following pages by checking their websites' jobs sections for vacancies. Remember to make sure they actually work in the area you are interested in before making contact. You should also try to build up a good general knowledge of the industry by going to see as many theatrical productions as you can and keeping track of which producers work on which types of shows.

CASE STUDY

Chickenshed is an inclusive theatre company based in London that brings people of all ages, backgrounds and abilities together to create groundbreaking and exciting new theatre. Their mission is to produce original and creative theatre of the highest quality which entertains and challenges audiences, and which demonstrates that the performing arts belong to everyone.

The role of producer at Chickenshed is slightly different to a similar role at other theatres I would think. Working for a large arts provider, I can find myself communicating with theatres, schools, consortiums – whoever wishes to find out more about our performances. Maybe it's easiest to talk in terms of just one project.

Crime of the Century is Chickenshed's theatre production that addresses issues of knife crime and gang violence. It was originally developed in 2008, has been on a UK tour and continues to be performed in colleges and communities as part of our outreach work.

In 2008, as the piece began to develop, I was looking into an initial Edinburgh run. Contacts were made with ZOO Venues in Edinburgh. We have worked with the ZOO team before and I'm familiar with their venues (this is always a good starting point!). In the past we have always started with an Edinburgh run; it's a great way of putting the work in front of bookers and promoters, good for a burst of press reviews and good for audience reaction. However the cost of the exercise and the proliferation of other industry events is leading me to consider alternative models including a much reduced, but targeted, run in Edinburgh.

Chickenshed is well known for its 'wrap-around', 'added value', (call it what you will) workshop programmes, so we will often be targeting schools and other organisations. Partner organisations are an essential tool for us. For instance during a recent tour of another production (*as the mother of a brown boy…*) we partnered with INQUEST. Together we produced post-show forums which also gave us access to their mailing list and website and ultimately supported audience numbers. I always presume that any tour venue is working with you and not for you. The more help we can provide in audience development the better for all. In my experience theatres are very keen on these wrap-around events. Workshops in, and with, local schools are an essential part of what we do and are never considered to be an annoying extra – that's important to remember!

So, having booked the venue for Edinburgh it's important that we let bookers and press know – where, what, who etc. Never forget there are two thousand plus shows in Edinburgh – that's a lot of competition – so get prepared. Make it easy for people. Where possible I hang around before and after the show. Sometimes people will want to make immediate contact – have too many business cards. There's nothing worse (and I've done it!) than scribbling details on a serviette in the bar. Edinburgh feels like a mad bun fight for producers, performers, directors and reviewers alike so the easier, smoother and more relaxed you can make things for people, the better.

For *Crime of the Century* the follow-up tour was planned for the spring/summer terms the following year which means I'm on the phone immediately – booking dates, negotiating prices, discussing packages. We will often look at an alternative kind of residency – based on providing a series of workshops with one or two performances over a week. This is where I will have to juggle between theatres and schools in the area. Some theatres have their own school contacts that they will pursue on your behalf. Sometimes the request comes from the school. On more than one occasion a school has approached me to provide workshop and performance. I've then approached the local theatre and said, "Look, there's a guaranteed schools audience – I think this will be worth doing," and theatres usually react very positively to that as local community engagement ticks a lot of boxes for them.

Crime of the Century was a good tour for combining education and theatre work – the show itself sits happily in a school hall with no lights or in a venue like the Oxford Playhouse with lighting rig, sound system and cyc. Flexibility can be useful but it makes for added complications elsewhere so it's always a balancing act. As long as your work is honest and true then you shouldn't go wrong. In my experience things tend to go pear-shaped when you pretend to be something you're not in order to get bookings or interest.

When's a good time to contact producers? When they're looking for you is the best answer, but as that's beyond your control avoid the usual bad times in anyone's diary such as just before Christmas, just before the summer holidays and that sort of thing.

Final advice? Know what you want and go for it!

To find out more visit www.chickenshed.org.uk or find Chickenshed on Twitter @CHICKENSHED_UK or at www.facebook.com/chickenshed

**10TH PLANET
PRODUCTIONS** T/F 020 8442 2659
75 Woodland Gardens, London N10 3UD
E admin@10thplanetproductions.com
W www.10thplanetproductions.com

30 BIRD PRODUCTIONS T 07501 922816
Twitter: @30Bird
Future Business, Milton Road
Cambridge, Cambridgeshire CB4 1UY
E info@30birdproductions.org
W www.30birdproductions.org

A STAGE KINDLY LTD T 07947 074887
7 Northiam, Cromer Street
London WC1H 8LB
E mail@astagekindly.com
W www.astagekindly.com

**ACORN
ENTERTAINMENTS LTD** T 01285 644622
PO Box 64, Cirencester, Glos GL7 5YD
F 01285 642291
E info@acornents.co.uk
W www.acornents.co.uk

ACT PRODUCTIONS LTD T 020 3077 8900
20-22 Stukeley Street, 3rd Floor
London WC2B 5LR
F 020 7242 3548
E info@actproductions.co.uk
W www.actproductions.co.uk

ACTORS PLATFORM LTD
Showcases for Professional Actors
Based in Central London
E melissa@actorsplatform.com
W www.actorsplatform.com

ACTOR'S TEMPLE THE T 020 3004 4537
13-14 Warren Street, London W1T 5LG
E info@actorstemple.com
W www.actorstemple.com

ACTORS TOURING COMPANY T 020 7930 6014
Contact: Nick Williams (Executive Director)
Institute of Contemporary Arts (ICA)
12 Carlton House Terrace, London SW1Y 5AH
E atc@atctheatre.com
W www.atctheatre.com

AJTC THEATRE COMPANY T/F 01483 232795
28 Rydes Hill Crescent, Guildford
Surrey GU2 9UH
W www.ajtctheatre.co.uk

**AMBASSADOR
THEATRE GROUP** T 020 7534 6100
39-41 Charing Cross Road, London WC2H 0AR
F 020 7534 6109
E ccreception@theambassadors.com
W www.atgtickets.com

ANTIC DISPOSITION T 020 7284 0760
4A Oval Road, London NW1 7EB
E info@anticdisposition.co.uk
W www.anticdisposition.co.uk

AOD (ACTORS OF DIONYSUS) T/F 01273 692604
14 Cuthbert Road, Brighton BN2 0EN
E info@actorsofdionysus.com
W www.actorsofdionysus.com

ARCADE PRODUCTIONS LTD
*Contact: Henry Filloux-Bennett, Stephen Makin,
Nick Rogers, Kellie Spooner (Producers)*
418 St John Street, Angel
London EC1V 4NJ
E info@arcadeproductions.co.uk
W www.arcadeproductions.co.uk

ARDEN ENTERTAINMENT T 07970 033785
7 Maiden Place, London NW5 1HZ
E douglas@arden-entertainment.co.uk
W www.arden-entertainment.co.uk

ARIA ENTERTAINMENT T 07947 074887
7 Northiam, Cromer Street
London WC1H 8LB
E info@aria-entertainment.com
W www.aria-entertainment.com

**ASHTON GROUP
THEATRE THE** T 01229 430636
The Old Fire Station, Abbey Road
Barrow-in-Furness, Cumbria LA14 1XH
E theashtongroup@btconnect.com
W www.ashtongroup.co.uk

**ATTIC THEATRE
COMPANY (LONDON) LTD** T 020 8640 6800
Mitcham Library, 157 London Road
Mitcham CR4 2YR
E info@attictheatrecompany.com
W www.attictheatrecompany.com

**BEE & BUSTLE
ENTERPRISES** T 020 8450 0371
32 Exeter Road, London NW2 4SB
F 020 8450 1057
E info@beeandbustle.co.uk
W www.beeandbustle.co.uk

**BIRMINGHAM STAGE
COMPANY THE** T 020 7437 3391
Suite 228, The Linen Hall
162 Regent Street, London W1B 5TB
F 020 7437 3395
E info@birminghamstage.com
W www.birminghamstage.com

**BLUE BOX
ENTERTAINMENT LTD** T 020 7395 7520
Top Floor, 80-81 St Martin's Lane, London WC2N 4AA
F 020 3292 1699
E info@newbluebox.com
W www.newbluebox.com

BLUE STAR PRODUCTIONS T 020 7836 6220
Contact: Barrie Stacey, Keith Hopkins
7-8 Shaldon Mansions, 132 Charing Cross Road
London WC2H 0LA
T 020 7836 4128
E bluestar.london.2000@gmail.com

BLUE THEATRE COMPANY
31 Beach Street, Deal CT14 6HY
E fen.wilson@gmail.com

BORDER CROSSINGS T 020 8829 8928
13 Bankside, Enfield EN2 8BN
F 020 8366 5239
E info@bordercrossings.org.uk
W www.bordercrossings.org.uk

BOTELLO, Catalina T 020 7935 1360
48 New Cavendish Street, London W1G 8TG
T 07939 060434
E contact@catalinabotello.com
W www.outoftheboxproductions.org

BRIT-POL THEATRE LTD T 020 7266 0323
10 Bristol Gardens, London W9 2JG
E admin@britpoltheatre.com
W www.britpoltheatre.com

**BRITISH THEATRE
SEASON IN MONACO** T 020 8455 3278
1 Hogarth Hill, London NW11 6AY
E mail@montecarlotheatre.co.uk
W www.montecarlotheatre.com

BROADHOUSE
PRODUCTIONS LTD   T 01984 640773
Lodge Rocks House, Bilbrook
Minehead, Somerset TA24 6RD
F 01984 641027
E admin@broadhouse.co.uk

BROOKE, Nick LTD   T 020 7240 3901
2nd Floor, 80-81 St Martin's Lane, London WC2N 4AA
F 020 7240 2947
E nick@nickbrooke.com
W www.nickbrooke.com

BUDDY WORLDWIDE LTD   T 020 7240 9941
PO Box 293, Letchworth Garden City, Herts SG6 9EU
F 01462 684851
E info@buddyshow.com
W www.buddythemusical.com

BUSH THEATRE   T 020 8743 3584
7 Uxbridge Road, Shepherd's Bush, London W12 8LJ
E info@bushtheatre.co.uk
W www.bushtheatre.co.uk

CAHOOTS THEATRE
COMPANY   T 020 8743 7777
Contact: Denise Silvey
St Martin's Theatre, West Street
London WC2N 9NH
E ds@denisesilvey.com

CAP PRODUCTION
SOLUTIONS LTD   T 07973 432576
116 Wigmore Road, Carshalton, Surrey SM5 1RQ
F 07970 763480
E leigh@leighporter.com

CENTRELINE PRODUCTIONS &
THE TOURING CONSORTIUM
THEATRE COMPANY   T 07710 522438
41 Beresford Road, London N8 0AL
E jenny@centrelinenet.com
W www.touringconsortium.com

CHAIN REACTION
THEATRE COMPANY   T/F 020 8534 0007
Three Mills Studios, Sugar House Yard
Sugar House Lane, London E15 2QS
E mail@chainreactiontheatre.co.uk
W www.chainreactiontheatre.co.uk

CHANNEL THEATRE
PRODUCTIONS LTD   T 01843 587950
Penistone House, 5 High Street
St Lawrence, Ramsgate, Kent CT11 0QH
E info@channel-theatre.co.uk
W www.channel-theatre.co.uk

CHAPMAN, Duggie
ASSOCIATES   T/F 01253 403177
Concerts. Musicals. Pantomime
Clifton House, 106 Clifton Drive
Blackpool FY4 1RR
E info@duggiechapmanassociates.co.uk
W www.duggiechapman.co.uk

CHEEK BY JOWL   T 020 7382 7304
Contact: Beth Byrne
Stage Door, Barbican Centre
Silk Street, London EC2Y 8DS
E info@cheekbyjowl.com
W www.cheekbyjowl.com

CHICHESTER
FESTIVAL THEATRE   T 01243 784437
Oaklands Park, Chichester, West Sussex PO19 6AP
F 01243 787288
E admin@cft.org.uk
W www.cft.org.uk

Richard Jordan Productions Ltd
- Producing
- General Management
  UK and International Productions,
  and International Festivals
- Consultancy
- Richard Jordan Productions Ltd
  Mews Studios, 16 Vernon Yard
  London W11 2DX
  Tel: 020 7243 9001
  Fax: 020 7313 9667
  e-mail: richard.jordan@virgin.net

CHICKENSHED   T 020 8351 6161
Chase Side, Southgate, London N14 4PE
E info@chickenshed.org.uk
W www.chickenshed.org.uk

CHOL THEATRE   T 01484 536008
Contact: Susan Burns (Director)
Twitter: @choltheatre
48A Byram Arcade, Westgate, Huddersfield HD1 1ND
E info@choltheatre.co.uk
W www.choltheatre.co.uk

CHURCHILL THEATRE
BROMLEY LTD   T 020 8464 7131
Producing Theatre
The Churchill, High Street, Bromley, Kent BR1 1HA
F 020 8290 6968
W www.atgtickets.com/churchill

CLEAN BREAK   T 020 7482 8600
Theatre Education. New Writing
2 Patshull Road, London NW5 2LB
F 020 7482 8611
E general@cleanbreak.org.uk
W www.cleanbreak.org.uk

CODRON, Michael
PLAYS LTD   T 020 7240 8291
Aldwych Theatre Offices, London WC2B 4DF
F 020 7240 8467

COLE KITCHENN   T 020 7427 5682
ROAR House, 46 Charlotte Street, London W1T 2GS
E guy@colekitchenn.com

COMPLICITE   T 020 7485 7700
14 Anglers Lane, London NW5 3DG
F 020 7485 7701
E email@complicite.org
W www.complicite.org

CONCORDANCE   T 020 7244 7439
Contact: Neil McPherson
Finborough Theatre, 118 Finborough Road
London SW10 9ED
E admin@concordance.org.uk
W www.concordance.org.uk

CONTEMPORARY STAGE COMPANY
9 Finchley Way, London N3 1AG
E contemp.stage@hotmail.co.uk

CONWAY, Clive CELEBRITY
PRODUCTIONS LTD   T 01865 514830
32 Grove Street, Oxford OX2 7JT
F 01865 514409
E admin@celebrityproductions.org
W www.celebrityproductions.info

CREATIVE BLAST PRODUCTIONS　T 07545 009830
The Training Centre, Radford Way
Billericay, Essex CM12 0DX
E info@creativeblastcompany.com
W www.creativeblastcompany.com

CREATIVE MANAGEMENT & PRODUCTIONS (CMP) LTD　T 020 7240 3033
1st Floor, 26-28 Neal Street, London WC2H 9QQ
F 020 7240 3037
E mail@cmplimited.com
W www.cmplimited.com

CROI8 PRODUCTIONS　T 00 353 85 1420683
Galway, Co. Galway, Ireland
E croiproductions@yahoo.co.uk

DEAD EARNEST THEATRE　T 0114 321 0450
Sheffield Design Studio, 40 Ball Street
Sheffield S3 8DB
E info@deadearnest.co.uk
W www.deadearnest.co.uk

DEAN, Lee　T 020 7497 5111
PO Box 10703, London WC2H 9ED
E admin@leedean.co.uk

DEBUT PRODUCTIONS　T 07505 677994
Actor Showcases in London's West End & Manchester
65 Norton Way North, Letchworth, Herts SG6 1BH
E submissions@debutproductions.co.uk
W www.debutproductions.co.uk

DISNEY THEATRICAL PRODUCTIONS (UK)　T 020 7845 0900
Lyceum Theatre, 21 Wellington Street
London WC2E 7RQ
F 020 7845 0999

DONEGAN, David LTD　T 07957 358909
PO Box LB689, London W1A 9LB
E daviddonegan@hotmail.co.uk

DRAMATIS PERSONAE LTD　T 020 7834 9300
Contact: Nathan Silver, Nicolas Kent
19 Regency Street, London SW1P 4BY
E ns@nathansilver.com

EASTERN ANGLES THEATRE COMPANY　T 01473 218202
Hiring The Sir John Mills Theatre
Gatacre Road, Ipswich, Suffolk IP1 2LQ
F 01473 384999
E admin@easternangles.co.uk
W www.easternangles.co.uk

EASY TIGER PRODUCTIONS LTD　T/F 020 3539 8769
Hurlingham Studios, London SW6 3PA
E mail@easytigerproductions.com
W www.easytigerproductions.com

ELLIOTT, Paul LTD　T 020 7379 4870
16 Westbourne Park Road, London W2 5PH
E pre@paulelliott.ltd.uk

ENGLISH NATIONAL OPERA　T 020 7836 0111
London Coliseum, St Martin's Lane
London WC2N 4ES
F 020 7845 9277
W www.eno.org

ENGLISH STAGE COMPANY LTD　T 020 7565 5050
Royal Court Theatre, Sloane Square
London SW1W 8AS
F 020 7565 5001
E info@royalcourttheatre.com
W www.royalcourttheatre.com

ENGLISH TOURING THEATRE (ETT)　T 020 7450 1990
25 Short Street, London SE1 8LJ
F 020 7633 0188
E admin@ett.org.uk
W www.ett.org.uk

ENTERTAINMENT BUSINESS LTD THE　T 020 7766 5274
Cameo House
11 Bear Street, London WC2H 7AS
F 020 7766 5275
E info@entbiz.co.uk
W www.entbiz.co.uk

EUROPEAN THEATRE COMPANY THE
15 Beverley Avenue, London SW20 0RL
E admin@europeantheatre.co.uk
W www.europeantheatre.co.uk

EXCESS ALL AREAS LTD　T/F 020 7737 5300
1st & 2nd Floors, 20 Stansfield Road
Stockwell, London SW9 9RZ
E paul@excessallareas.co.uk
W www.excessallareas.co.uk

FACADE　T 020 8291 7079
Musicals
43A Garthorne Road, London SE23 1EP
F 020 8291 4969
E facade@cobomedia.com

FAIRBANK PRODUCTIONS
27 Harcourt Road, London E15 3DX
E info@fairbankproductions.co.uk
W www.fairbankproductions.co.uk

FEATHER PRODUCTIONS LTD　T 020 8940 2335
Unit 3, Blade House
77 Petersham Road, Richmond
E anna@featherproductions.com
W www.featherproductions.com

FIELD, Anthony ASSOCIATES LTD　T 020 7240 5453
Top Floor, 80-81 St Martin's Lane
London WC2N 4AA
F 020 7240 2947
E info@anthonyfieldassociates.com
W www.anthonyfieldassociates.com

FIERY ANGEL LTD　T 020 7907 7040
22-24 Torrington Place, London WC1E 7HJ
E mail@fiery-angel.com
W www.fiery-angel.com

FORBIDDEN THEATRE COMPANY　T 07852 942588
56 Handsworth Road, London N17 6DE
E info@forbidden.org.uk
W www.forbidden.org.uk

FORD, Vanessa PRODUCTIONS　T 01483 278203
Upper House Farm, Upper House Lane
Shamley Green, Surrey GU5 0SX
E vanessa@vanessafordproductions.co.uk

FOSTER, Sharon PRODUCTIONS　T 0121 443 4865
15A Hollybank Road, Birmingham B13 0RF
E mail@sharonfoster.co.uk
W www.sharonfosterproductions.co.uk

FOX, Robert LTD　T 020 7584 6855
6 Beauchamp Place, London SW3 1NG
F 020 7225 1638
E info@robertfoxltd.com
W www.robertfoxltd.com

FRANK, Lina B. / AUSFORM
Circus. Dance. Live Arts. Theatre
Cube Cinema, Bristol BS2 8NQ
E lina@ausform.co.uk
W www.ausform.co.uk

**FRANKLIN
PRODUCTIONS LTD**   T 020 7720 3718
187 Drury Lane, London WC2B 5QD
E office@franklinproductions.co.uk

FREEDMAN, Bill LTD   T 020 7226 5554
Colebrooke House, 10-12 Gaskin Street
London N1 2RY

**FRESH GLORY
PRODUCTIONS**   T 020 7240 1941
59 St Martin's Lane, London WC2N 4JS
E fg@freshglory.com
W www.freshglory.com

**FRICKER, Ian
(THEATRE) LTD**   T 020 7836 3090
3rd Floor, 146 Strand, London WC2R 1JD
F 020 7836 3078
E mail@ianfricker.com
W www.ianfricker.com

**FRIEDMAN, Sonia
PRODUCTIONS**   T 020 7845 8750
Duke of York's Theatre, 104 St Martin's Lane
London WC2N 4BG
F 020 7845 8759
E office@soniafriedman.com
W www.soniafriedman.com

**GALLEON THEATRE
COMPANY LTD**   T 020 8310 7276
Contact: Alice De Sousa
Head Office, Greenwich Playhouse
50 Openshaw Road, London SE2 0TE
E boxoffice@galleontheatre.co.uk
W www.galleontheatre.co.uk

GBM PRODUCTIONS LTD   T 01837 871522
Bidlake Toft, Roadford Lake
Germansweek, Devon EX21 5BD
E gbm@bidlaketoft.com
W www.musicaltheatrecreations.com

GIANT STEPS LTD   T/F 020 8741 2446
41 Parfrey Street, London W6 9EW
T 07808 742307
E giantstepstheatre@googlemail.com
W www.giantsteps.info

**GOODNIGHTS
ENTERTAINMENT LTD**   T 01908 672077
74 Pannier Place, Milton Keynes MK14 7QP
E goodnights@talk21.com
W www.goodnights.org

GOUCHER, Mark LTD   T 020 7438 9570
3rd Floor, 20-22 Stukeley Street, London WC2B 5LR
F 020 7438 0677
E jess@markgoucher.com

GRAEAE THEATRE COMPANY   T 020 7613 6900
Bradbury Studios, 138 Kingsland Road
London E2 8DY
E info@graeae.org
W www.graeae.org

**GRAHAM, David
ENTERTAINMENT LTD**   T 0870 3211600
72 New Bond Street, London W1S 1RR
F 0870 3211700
E info@davidgraham.co.uk
W www.davidgrahamentertainment.com

**HAMPSTEAD THEATRE
PRODUCTIONS LTD**   T 020 7449 4200
Eton Avenue, Swiss Cottage, London NW3 3EU
F 020 7449 4201
E info@hampsteadtheatre.com
W www.hampsteadtheatre.com

HAPPYSTORM THEATRE   T 07547 711839
Contact: By e-mail
Based in Salford
E info@happystormtheatre.co.uk
W www.happystormtheatre.co.uk

HARLEY PRODUCTIONS   T 020 7580 3247
68 New Cavendish Street, London W1G 8TE
F 020 8202 8863
E harleyprods@aol.com

HARRISON, Garth   T 01508 530849
Stage Further Productions, Michaelmas Barn
Long Stratton, Norfolk NR15 2PY
E garthsfp@hotmail.co.uk

**HAYDEN SCOTT
PRODUCTIONS**   T 07879 897900
Contact: Daniel Sparrow, Mike Walsh
44B Floral Street, London WC2E 9DA
E info@danielsparrowproductions.com
W www.danielsparrowproductions.com

HAYMARKET THE   T 01256 819797
c/o The Anvil Trust, Wote Street
Basingstoke, Hampshire RG21 7NW
F 01256 331733
E christine.bradwell@anvilarts.org.uk
W www.anvilarts.org.uk

HEADLONG THEATRE LTD   T 020 7478 0270
3rd Floor, 34-35 Berwick Street, London W1F 8RP
F 020 7438 1749
E info@headlongtheatre.co.uk
W www.headlongtheatre.co.uk

**HENDERSON, Glynis
PRODUCTIONS LTD**   T 020 7580 9644
69 Charlotte Street, London W1T 4PJ
F 020 7436 1489
E info@ghmp.co.uk
W www.ghmp.co.uk

**HENDRY, Jamie
PRODUCTIONS LTD**   T/F 020 7183 5630
23 Garrick Street, 1st Floor
Covent Garden, London WC2E 9BN
E office@jamiehendryproductions.com
W www.jamiehendryproductions.com

HENNEGAN, Nicholas   T 020 8582 7506
33A Prebend Mansions, Chiswick High Road
London W4 2LU
E info@nicholashennegan.com
W www.nicholashennegan.com

**HESTER, John
PRODUCTIONS**   T/F 020 8224 0580
Intimate Mysteries Theatre Company
105 Stoneleigh Park Road, Epsom
Surrey KT19 0RF
E hjohnhester@aol.com

**HISS & BOO
COMPANY LTD THE**   T 01444 881707
Contact: Ian Liston. By Post (SAE). No unsolicited scripts
Nyes Hill, Wineham Lane
Bolney, West Sussex RH17 5SD
F 01444 882057
E email@hissboo.co.uk
W www.hissboo.co.uk

HISTORIA THEATRE COMPANY   T 020 7837 8008
8 Cloudesley Square, London N1 0HT
T 07811 892079
E kateprice@lineone.net
W www.historiatheatre.com

HOIPOLLOI   T 01223 322748
Office F, Dale's Brewery
Gwydir Street, Cambridge CB1 2LJ
E info@hoipolloi.org.uk
W www.hoipolloi.org.uk

HOLLOW CROWN PRODUCTIONS   T 07930 530948
2 Old Hall Farm, Halesworth Road
Reydon, Suffolk IP18 6SG
E enquiries@hollowcrown.co.uk
W www.hollowcrown.co.uk

HOLMAN, Paul ASSOCIATES LTD   T 020 8845 9408
Morritt House, 58 Station Approach
South Ruislip, Middlesex HA4 6SA
F 020 8839 3124
E enquiries@paulholmanassociates.co.uk
W www.paulholmanassociates.co.uk

HOLT, Thelma LTD   T 020 7812 7455
Noel Coward Theatre
85 St Martin's Lane
London WC2N 4AU
F 020 7812 7550
E thelma@dircon.co.uk
W www.thelmaholt.co.uk

HUGHES, Steve   T 07816 844024
17 Albert Road, Henley-on-Thames
Oxfordshire RG9 1SD
E steve@hughes-productions.com
W www.hughes-productions.com

HULL TRUCK THEATRE   T 01482 224800
50 Ferensway, Hull HU2 8LB
F 01482 581182
E admin@hulltruck.co.uk
W www.hulltruck.co.uk

IAN, David PRODUCTIONS   T 020 7257 6380
Third Floor, 33 Henrietta Street
London WC2E 8NA
F 020 7257 6381
E enquiries@davidianproductions.com
W www.davidianproductions.com

IBSEN STAGE COMPANY   T 07958 566274
Flat 1, 1 Thurleigh Road, London SW12 8UB
E ask@ibsenstage.com
W www.ibsenstage.com

ICARUS THEATRE COLLECTIVE   T 020 7998 1562
32 Portland Place, London W1B 1NA
E info@icarustheatre.co.uk
W www.icarustheatre.co.uk

IMAGE MUSICAL THEATRE   T 020 8743 9380
23 Sedgeford Road, Shepherd's Bush
London W12 0NA
F 020 8749 9294
E brian@imagemusicaltheatre.co.uk
W www.imagemusicaltheatre.co.uk

INCISOR   T 07979 498450
41 Edith Avenue, Peacehaven
East Sussex BN10 8JB
E sarahmann7@hotmail.co.uk
W www.theatre-company-incisor.com

INDIGO ENTERTAINMENTS   T 01978 790211
Tynymynydd, Bryneglwys
Corwen, Denbighshire LL21 9NP
E info@indigoentertainments.com
W www.indigoentertainments.com

INGRAM, Colin LTD   T 020 7038 3906
Suite 526, Linen Hall
162-168 Regent Street, London W1B 5TE
F 020 7038 3907
E info@coliningramltd.com
W www.coliningramltd.com

INSIDE INTELLIGENCE   T/F 020 8986 8013
Theatre. Contemporary Opera. Music Theatre
13 Athlone Close, London E5 8HD
E admin@inside-intelligence.org.uk
W www.inside-intelligence.org.uk

INSTANT WIT   T 0117 974 5734
Comedy Improvisation Theatre Show. Corporate/ Conference Entertainment Show. Drama Based Training
6 Worrall Place, Worrall Road
Clifton, Bristol BS8 2WP
T 07711 644094
E info@instantwit.co.uk
W www.instantwit.co.uk

JAM THEATRE COMPANY   T 01628 483808
Jam Theatre Studios, Archway Court
45A West Street, Marlow
Buckinghamshire SL7 2LS
E office@jamtheatre.co.uk
W www.jamtheatre.co.uk

JOHNSON, David   T 020 7284 3733
85B Torriano Avenue, London NW5 2RX
E david@johnsontemple.co.uk

JOHNSON, Gareth LTD   T 01239 891368
20-22 Stukeley Street, London WC2B 5LR
T 07770 225227
E gjltd@mac.com

JOHNSON, Gareth LTD   T 01239 891368
Plas Hafren, Eglwyswrw
Crymych, Pembrokeshire SA41 3UL
T 07770 225227
E gjltd@mac.com

JORDAN, Andy PRODUCTIONS LTD   T 07775 615205
130 Newland Street West, Lincoln LN1 1PH
E andyjandyjordan@aol.com

JORDAN, Richard PRODUCTIONS LTD   T 020 7243 9001
Mews Studios
16 Vernon Yard, London W11 2DX
F 020 7313 9667
E richard.jordan@virgin.net

JORDAN PRODUCTIONS LTD   T 01323 417745
Phoenix Auction Rooms
142 Langney Road
Eastbourne, East Sussex BN22 8AQ
F 01323 417766
E info@jordanproductionsltd.co.uk

JQ PRODUCTIONS
Contact: James Quaife
E jamesquaife@gmail.com
W www.jamesquaife.com

KEAN PRODUCTIONS   T 020 3151 2710
Communications House, 26 York Street
London W1U 6PZ
E info@keanprods.com
W www.keanprods.com

KELLY, Robert C.　**T** 0141 533 5856
PO Box 5597, Glasgow G77 9DH
E office@robertckelly.co.uk
W www.robertckelly.co.uk

KENWRIGHT, Bill LTD　**T** 020 7446 6200
BKL House, 1 Venice Walk, London W2 1RR
F 020 7446 6222
E info@kenwright.com
W www.kenwright.com

**KING, Belinda
CREATIVE PRODUCTIONS**　**T** 01604 720041
157 Clarence Avenue, Northampton NN2 6NY
F 01604 721448
E office@belindaking.com
W www.belindaking.com

KING'S HEAD THEATRE　**T** 020 7226 8561
Contact: Adam Spreadbury-Maher (Artistic Director)
115 Upper Street
Islington, London N1 1QN
BO 020 7478 0160
E info@kingsheadtheatre.com
W www.kingsheadtheatre.com

**LANGUAGE LAID BARE
PRODUCTIONS**　**T** 07545 704016
Top Floor, 298 Brockley Road, London SE4 2RA
E languagelaidbare@yahoo.co.uk

LATCHMERE THEATRE　**T** 020 7978 2620
Contact: Chris Fisher
Unit 5A, Spaces Business Centre
Ingate Place, London SW8 3NS
F 020 7978 2631
E latchmere@fishers.org.uk

LEIGH-PEMBERTON, David　**T** 020 7112 8445
43-44 Berners Street, London W1T 3ND
E david@leigh-pemberton.co.uk
W www.davidleigh-pemberton.co.uk

LHP LTD　**T** 07973 938634
9 Coombe Court, Hayne Road
Beckenham, Kent BR3 4XD
E lhpltd@msn.com

LIMELIGHT PRODUCTIONS　**T** 020 8853 9570
Unit 13, The io Centre, The Royal Arsenal
Seymour Street, London SE18 6SX
F 020 8853 9579
E enquiries@thelimelightgroup.co.uk

LINNIT PRODUCTIONS LTD　**T** 020 7352 7722
123A King's Road, London SW3 4PL
F 020 7352 3450

LIVE THEATRE　**T** 0191 261 2694
Broad Chare, Quayside
Newcastle upon Tyne NE1 3DQ
E info@live.org.uk
W www.live.org.uk

**LONDON BUBBLE
THEATRE COMPANY LTD**　**T** 020 7237 4434
5 Elephant Lane, London SE16 4JD
E admin@londonbubble.org.uk
W www.londonbubble.org.uk

LONDON CLASSIC THEATRE　**T** 020 8395 2095
The Production Office, 63 Shirley Avenue
Sutton, Surrey SM1 3QT
E admin@londonclassictheatre.co.uk
W www.londonclassictheatre.co.uk

LONDON PRODUCTIONS LTD　**T** 020 7497 5111
PO Box 10703, London WC2H 9ED
E admin@leedean.co.uk

**LONDON REPERTORY
COMPANY**　**T/F** 020 7258 1944
PO Box 59385, London NW8 1HL
E info@londonrepertorycompany.com
W www.londonrepertorycompany.com

MACKINTOSH, Cameron LTD　**T** 020 7637 8866
Contact: Paul Wooller (Casting Assistant)
1 Bedford Square, London WC1B 3RB
F 020 7436 2683
E paul@camack.co.uk

MACNAGHTEN PRODUCTIONS　**T** 01223 577974
19 Grange Court, Grange Road
Cambridge CB3 9BD

**MALCOLM, Christopher
PRODUCTIONS LTD**　**T** 07850 555042
26 Rokeby Road, London SE4 1DE
E cm@christophermalcolm.co.uk
W www.christophermalcolm.co.uk

MANS, Johnny PRODUCTIONS　**T** 01992 470907
Incorporating Encore Magazine
PO Box 196, Hoddesdon, Herts EN10 7WG
T 07974 755997
E johnnymansagent@aol.com
W www.johnnymansproductions.co.uk

**MASTERSON, Guy
PRODUCTIONS**　**T/F** 01707 330360
The Hawthorne Theatre, Campus West
Welwyn Garden City, Herts AL8 6BX
E admin@theatretoursinternational.com
W www.theatretoursinternational.com

McKITTERICK, Tom LTD　**T/F** 001 212 431 7697
113 Greene Street
New York 10012, USA
E tommckitterick@aol.com

**MEADOW, Jeremy
& ROSENTHAL, Suzanna**　**T** 020 7436 2244
26 Goodge Street, London W1T 2QG
F 0870 7627882
E info@jeremymeadow.com

MENZIES, Lee LTD　**T** 020 7611 0050
3rd Floor, 20-22 Stukeley Street
London WC2B 5LR
F 020 7681 3670
E leemenzies@leemenzies.co.uk
W www.leemenzies.co.uk

**MIDDLE GROUND
THEATRE CO LTD**　**T** 01684 577231
3 Gordon Terrace, Malvern Wells
Malvern, Worcestershire WR14 4ER
F 01684 574472
E middleground@middlegroundtheatre.co.uk
W www.middlegroundtheatre.co.uk

MITCHELL, Matthew LTD　**T/F** 01273 842572
New Barn Farm, London Road
Hassocks, West Sussex BN6 0ND
E info@matthewmitchell.org

MJE PRODUCTIONS LTD　**T** 020 7395 0260
Contact: Carole Winter, Michael Edwards
1st Floor, 18 Exeter Street, London WC2E 7DU
F 020 7395 0261
E info@mjeproductions.com
W www.mjeproductions.com

MMP　**T** 020 7494 4007
4 D'Arblay Street, Soho
London W1F 8DJ
E mailbox@michaelmccabe.net
W www.michaelmccabe.net

MOKITAGRIT   T 07980 564849
6 Addington Road, London N4 4RP
E mail@mokitagrit.com
W www.mokitagrit.com

MOVING THEATRE   T 01323 815726
16 Laughton Lodge, Nr Lewes
East Sussex BN8 6BY
F 01323 815736
E info@movingtheatre.com
W www.movingtheatre.com

MUSIC THEATRE LONDON   T 07831 243942
c/o Capriol Films, The Old Reading Room
The Street, Brinton
Melton Constable, Norfolk NR24 2QF
E info@capriolfilms.co.uk
W www.capriolfilms.co.uk

NADINE'S WINDOW
Theatre Company
E nadineswindow@yahoo.co.uk
W www.nadineswindow.com

NATIONAL ANGELS   T 020 7376 4878
123A Kings Road, London SW3 4PL
F 020 7352 3450
E admin@nationalangels.com

NATIONAL THEATRE   T 020 7452 3333
Upper Ground, South Bank
London SE1 9PX
F 020 7452 3344
W www.nationaltheatre.org.uk

**NEAL STREET
PRODUCTIONS LTD**   T 020 7240 8890
1st Floor, 26-28 Neal Street, London WC2H 9QQ
F 020 7240 7099
E post@nealstreetproductions.com

**NEW PERSPECTIVES
THEATRE COMPANY**   T 0115 927 2334
Regional & National New Writing Touring Theatre
Park Lane Business Centre, Park Lane
Basford, Nottinghamshire NG6 0DW
E info@newperspectives.co.uk
W www.newperspectives.co.uk

NEWPALM PRODUCTIONS   T 020 8349 0802
26 Cavendish Avenue, London N3 3QN
F 020 8346 8257
E newpalm@btopenworld.com
W www.newpalm.co.uk

**NICHOLAS, Paul &
IAN, David ASSOCIATES LTD**   T 020 7257 6380
c/o 3rd Floor, 33 Henrietta Street, London WC2E 8NA
F 020 7257 6381
E enquiries@davidianproductions.com

NITRO   T 020 7609 1331
E info@nitro.co.uk
W www.nitro.co.uk

**NORDIC NOMAD
PRODUCTIONS**   T 07980 619165
*Contact: Tanja Raaste (Creative Producer).
Specialising in New Writing, Site Specific & Interactive
Work and Tango & Dance Events. Training & Workshops:
Business Skills for Performers*
64 Tulse Hill, London SW2 2PT
E info@nordicnomad.com
W www.nordicnomad.com

**NORTHERN BROADSIDES
THEATRE COMPANY**   T 01422 369704
Dean Clough, Halifax HX3 5AX
E sue@northern-broadsides.co.uk
W www.northern-broadsides.co.uk

**NORTHERN STAGE (THEATRICAL
PRODUCTIONS) LTD**   T 0191 242 7200
Barras Bridge, Newcastle upon Tyne NE1 7RH
F 0191 242 7257
E info@northernstage.co.uk
W www.northernstage.co.uk

**NORTHUMBERLAND
THEATRE COMPANY (NTC)**   T 01665 602586
The Playhouse, Bondgate Without
Alnwick, Northumberland NE66 1PQ
F 01665 605837
E admin@northumberlandtheatre.co.uk
W www.northumberlandtheatre.co.uk

OLD VIC PRODUCTIONS PLC   T 020 7928 2651
The Old Vic Theatre, The Cut, Waterloo, London SE1 8NB
F 020 7981 0991
E becky.barber@oldvictheatre.com

**ONE NIGHT BOOKING
COMPANY THE**   T 020 8455 3278
1 Hogarth Hill, London NW11 6AY
E mail@onenightbooking.com
W www.onenightbooking.com

OUT OF JOINT   T 020 7609 0207
7 Thane Works, Thane Villas, London N7 7PH
F 020 7609 0203
E ojo@outofjoint.co.uk
W www.outofjoint.co.uk

OVATION   T 020 8340 4256
Upstairs at The Gatehouse, The Gatehouse
Highgate Village, London N6 4BD
F 020 8340 3466
E events@ovationproductions.com
W www.ovationtheatres.com

PAINES PLOUGH   T 020 7240 4533
4th Floor, 43 Aldwych, London WC2B 4DN
F 020 7240 4534
E office@painesplough.com
W www.painesplough.com

**PAPATANGO
THEATRE COMPANY**   T 07834 958804
37A Harold Road, London SE19 3PL
E papatango.theatre@gmail.com
W www.papatango.co.uk

**PAPER MOON
THEATRE COMPANY**   T 020 7060 0550
*Contact: Jan Hunt (Producer/Director). Specialising in
Traditional Victorian Music Hall*
6 Thames Meadow, West Molesey, Surrey KT8 1TQ
E jan@papermoontheatre.co.uk

**PASSWORD
PRODUCTIONS LTD**   T 020 7284 3733
Contact: John Mackay
85B Torriano Avenue, London NW5 2RX
E johnmackay2001@aol.com

PENDLE PRODUCTIONS LTD   T 01253 839375
Bridge Farm, 249 Hawes Side Lane, Blackpool FY4 4AA
F 01253 792930
E admin@pendleproductions.co.uk
W www.pendleproductions.co.uk

PENTABUS THEATRE   T 01584 856564
Bromfield, Ludlow, Shropshire SY8 2JU
E elizabeth@pentabus.co.uk
W www.pentabus.co.uk

PEOPLE SHOW   T 020 7729 1841
People Show Studios, Pollard Row, London E2 6NB
F 020 7739 0203
E people@peopleshow.co.uk
W www.peopleshow.co.uk

PERFECT PITCH MUSICALS LTD   T 020 7930 1087
5A Irving Street, London WC2H 7AT
E info@perfectpitchmusicals.com
W www.perfectpitchmusicals.com

PERFORMANCE BUSINESS THE   T 01932 888885
78 Oatlands Drive, Weybridge
Surrey KT13 9HT
E info@theperformance.biz
W www.theperformance.biz

PILOT THEATRE   T 01904 635755
Performance Work Across Platforms & National Touring
York Theatre Royal, St Leonard's Place, York YO1 7HD
E info@pilot-theatre.com
W www.pilot-theatre.com

PLANTAGENET PRODUCTIONS   T 01635 253322
Drawing Room Recitals
Westridge Open Centre, Star Lane
Highclere, Nr Newbury RG20 9PJ

PLAYFUL PRODUCTIONS   T 020 7811 4600
5th Floor, Haymarket House, 1 Oxendon Street
London SW1Y 4EE
F 020 7811 4622
E aboutus@playfuluk.com
W www.playfuluk.com

POLKA THEATRE   T 020 8545 8323
240 The Broadway, Wimbledon SW19 1SB
F 020 8545 8365
E stephen@polkatheatre.com
W www.polkatheatre.com

POPULAR PRODUCTIONS LTD   T 020 8347 0221
448 Muswell Hill Broadway, Muswell Hill
London N10 1BS
E info@popularproductions.com
W www.popularproductions.com

PORTER, Richard LTD   T 07884 183404
214 Grange Road, London SE1 3AA
E office@richardporterltd.com
W www.richardporterltd.com

POSTER, Kim   T 020 7240 3098
4th Floor, 80-81 St Martin's Lane
London WC2N 4AA
F 020 7504 8656
E admin@stanhopeprod.com

PROMENADE PRODUCTIONS   T 020 7240 3407
20 Thayer Street, London W1U 2DD
E hharrison@promenadeproductions.com
W www.promenadeproductions.com

PUGH, David & ROGERS, Dafydd   T 020 7292 0390
David Pugh Ltd, Wyndhams Theatre
Charing Cross Road, London WC2H 0DA
F 020 7292 0399
E dpl@davidpughltd.com

PURSUED BY A BEAR PRODUCTIONS   T 01252 745445
Farnham Maltings, Bridge Square
Farnham GU9 7QR
E pursuedbyabear@yahoo.co.uk
W www.pursuedbyabear.co.uk

PW PRODUCTIONS LTD   T 020 7395 7580
2nd Floor, 80-81 St Martin's Lane
London WC2N 4AA
F 020 7240 2947
E info@pwprods.co.uk
W www.pwprods.co.uk

QDOS ENTERTAINMENT   T 01723 500038
Qdos House, Queen Margaret's Road
Scarborough, North Yorkshire YO11 2YH
F 01723 361958
E info@qdosentertainment.co.uk
W www.qdosentertainment.com

QUANTUM THEATRE   T 020 8317 9000
The Old Button Factory, 1-11 Bannockburn Road
Plumstead, London SE18 1ET
E office@quantumtheatre.co.uk
W www.quantumtheatre.co.uk

RAGS & FEATHERS THEATRE COMPANY   T 020 8224 2203
80 Summer Road, Thames Ditton, Surrey KT7 0QP
T 07958 724374
E jilldowning.tls@gmail.com

RAIN OR SHINE THEATRE COMPANY   T/F 01452 521575
25 Paddock Gardens, Longlevens, Gloucester GL2 0ED
E theatre@rainorshine.co.uk
W www.rainorshine.co.uk

RATTLING TONGUE THEATRE COMPANY
44 Fairfield South, Kingston Upon Thames
Surrey KT1 2UW
E info@rattlingtongue.com
W www.rattlingtongue.com

REAL CIRCUMSTANCE THEATRE COMPANY
22 Erle Harvard Road, West Bergholt
Colchester CO6 3BW
E info@realcircumstance.com
W www.realcircumstance.com

REALLY USEFUL THEATRE COMPANY THE   T 020 7240 0880
22 Tower Street, London WC2H 9TW
F 020 7240 1204

RED ROOM THE   T 020 7470 8790
The Garden Studio, 71-75 Shelton Street
London WC2H 9JQ
E admin@theredroom.org.uk
W www.theredroom.org.uk

RED ROSE CHAIN   T 01473 603388
Gippeswyk Hall, Gippeswyk Avenue
Ipswich, Suffolk IP2 9AF
E info@redroscchain.co.uk
W www.redrosechain.co.uk

RED SHIFT THEATRE COMPANY   T/F 020 8540 1271
PO Box 60151, London SW19 2TB
E redshift100@gmail.com
W www.redshifttheatreco.co.uk

REDROOFS THEATRE COMPANY
Contact: By Post
Novello Theatre, High Street, Sunninghill, Ascot SL5 9NE
W www.novellotheatre.co.uk

REGENT'S PARK THEATRE LTD   T 0844 3753460
Open Air Theatre
Stage Door Gate, Inner Circle
Regent's Park, London NW1 4NU
W www.openairtheatre.com

REVEAL THEATRE COMPANY LTD   T 01782 294871
The Creative Village
Staffordshire University Business Village
72 Leek Road, Stoke on Trent ST4 2AR
E enquiries@revealtheatre.co.uk
W www.revealtheatre.co.uk

RGC PRODUCTIONS T 07740 286727
260 Kings Road, Kingston, Surrey KT2 5HX
E info@rgcproductions.com
W www.rgcproductions.com

RHO DELTA LTD T 020 7436 1392
Contact: Greg Ripley-Duggan
26 Goodge Street, London W1T 2QG
E info@ripleyduggan.com

ROCKET THEATRE T 0161 969 1444
32 Baxter Road, Sale
Manchester M33 3AL
T 07788 723570
E martin@rockettheatre.co.uk
W www.rockettheatre.co.uk

ROGERS, Nick LTD T 020 7100 1123
212 Strand, London WC2R 1AP
E info@nickrogerslimited.com
W www.nickrogerslimited.com

ROSE, Michael LTD T 01202 522711
The Old Dairy, Throop Road
Holdenhurst, Bournemouth, Dorset BH8 0DL
F 01202 522311
E nicky@michaelroseltd.com

ROSE, Michael LTD T 0845 3101050
4th Floor, Eon House, 138 Piccadilly, London W1J 7NR
F 0845 3101060
E dbell@michaelroseltd.com

ROSE THEATRE, KINGSTON T 020 8546 6983
Contact: Stephen Unwin (Artistic Director),
Lisa Lepki (PA to Artistic Director)
24-26 High Street, Kingston Upon Thames
Surrey KT1 1HL
F 020 8546 8783
E admin@rosetheatrekingston.org
W www.rosetheatrekingston.org

ROSENTHAL, Suzanna LTD
See MEADOW, Jeremy & ROSENTHAL, Suzanna

ROYAL COURT THEATRE
PRODUCTIONS LTD T 020 7565 5050
Sloane Square, London SW1W 8AS
F 020 7565 5001
E info@royalcourttheatre.com
W www.royalcourttheatre.com

ROYAL EXCHANGE THEATRE T 0161 833 9333
St Ann's Square, Manchester M2 7DH
W www.royalexchange.co.uk

ROYAL SHAKESPEARE
COMPANY T 020 7845 0500
1 Earlham Street, London WC2H 9LL
F 020 7845 0505
W www.rsc.org.uk

ROYAL SHAKESPEARE
COMPANY T 01789 296655
Royal Shakespeare Theatre, Waterside
Stratford-upon-Avon CV37 6BB
F 01789 403710
W www.rsc.org.uk

RUBINSTEIN, Mark LTD T 020 7021 0787
25 Short Street, London SE1 8LJ
F 0870 7059731
E info@mrluk.com

SCAMP THEATRE LTD T 01462 734843
Sutherland Callow Arts Management & Production
44 Church Lane, Arlesey, Beds SG15 6UX
T 07710 491111
E admin@scamptheatre.com
W www.scamptheatre.com

SCENE THREE CREATIVE T 07899 825152
Creative Services. Project Management.
Theatre Production. Writing
5 High Street, St Lawrence
Ramsgate, Kent CT11 0QH
E info@scenethreecreative.co.uk
W www.scenethreecreative.co.uk

SEABRIGHT
PRODUCTIONS LTD T 020 7439 1173
Palace Theatre, Shaftesbury Avenue
London W1D 5AY
F 020 7183 6023
E office@seabrights.com
W www.seabrights.com

SELL A DOOR THEATRE
COMPANY LTD T 07709 498055
Athelney House, 161-165 Greenwich High Road
London SE10 8JA
E info@selladoor.com
W www.selladoor.com

SHAKESPEARE'S MEN T 01708 222938
10 Dee Close, Upminster
Essex RM14 1QD
E terence@terencemustoo.com
W www.terencemustoo.com

SHARED EXPERIENCE T 01865 305321
c/o Oxford Playhouse, Beaumont Street
Oxford OX1 2LW
E admin@sharedexperience.org.uk
W www.sharedexperience.org.uk

SHOW OF STRENGTH T 0117 902 0235
74 Chessel Street, Bedminster
Bristol BS3 3DN
E info@showofstrength.org.uk
W www.showofstrength.org.uk

SHOWCASE ENTERTAINMENTS
INTERNATIONAL LTD T 01325 316224
Contact: Geoffrey J.L. Hindmarch (Executive Producer),
Paul Morgan (Creative Director). Theatre. Cruises.
Hotels. Corporate
2 Lumley Close, Newton Aycliffe
Co Durham DL5 5PA
E gjl@showcaseproductions.co.uk
W www.showcaseproductions.co.uk

SIMPLY THEATRE T 00 41 22 8600518
Chemin des Couleuvres 8B
1295 Tannay, Switzerland
E info@simplytheatre.com
W www.simplytheatre.com

SINDEN, Marc PRODUCTIONS T 020 8455 3278
1 Hogarth Hill, London NW11 6AY
E mail@sindenproductions.com
W www.sindenproductions.com

SIXTEENFEET PRODUCTIONS T 020 7326 4417
25 Rattray Road, London SW2 1AZ
T 07958 448690
E info@sixteenfeet.co.uk
W www.sixteenfeet.co.uk

SOHO THEATRE COMPANY T 020 7287 5060
21 Dean Street, London W1D 3NE
F 020 7287 5061
W www.sohotheatre.com

SPARROW, Daniel &
WALSH, Mike PRODUCTIONS T 020 7240 2720
1A Neal's Yard, London WC2H 9AW
T 07879 897900
E info@danielsparrowproductions.com
W www.danielsparrowproductions.com

SPHINX THEATRE COMPANY　T 07768 332564
76 Lyford Road, London SW18 3JW
E info@sphinxtheatre.co.uk
W www.sphinxtheatre.co.uk

SPLATS ENTERTAINMENT　T 07944 283659
5 Denmark Street, London WC2H 8LP
E admin@splatsentertainment.com
W www.splatsentertainment.com

SPLITMOON THEATRE　T 020 7252 8126
PO Box 58891, London SE15 9DE
E info@splitmoontheatre.org
W www.splitmoontheatre.org

**SQUAREDEAL
PRODUCTIONS LTD**　T 020 7249 5966
Contact: Jenny Topper
24 De Beauvoir Square, London N1 4LE
F 020 7275 7553
E jenny@jennytopper.com

**SQUIRES & JOHNS
PRODUCTIONS LTD**　T 0871 2003343
Sullon Lodge, Sullon Side Lane
Garstang PR3 1GH
F 01253 407715
E info@squiresjohns.com
W www.squiresjohns.com

**STAGE ENTERTAINMENT
UK LTD**　T 020 7025 6970
6th Floor, Swan House, 52 Poland Street
London W1F 7NQ
F 020 7025 6971
W www.stage-entertainment.co.uk

**STANHOPE
PRODUCTIONS LTD**　T 020 7240 3098
4th Floor, 80-81 St Martin's Lane
London WC2N 4AA
F 020 7504 8656
E admin@stanhopeprod.com

**STEPHENSON, Ian
PRODUCTIONS LTD**　T 07960 999374
E soholondon@aol.com

**STRAIGHT LINE
PRODUCTIONS**　T 020 8393 4220
58 Castle Avenue, Epsom, Surrey KT17 2PH
F 020 8393 8079
E hilary@straightlinemanagement.co.uk

TALAWA THEATRE COMPANY　T 020 7251 6644
Ground Floor, 53-55 East Road, London N1 6AH
F 020 7251 5969
E hq@talawa.com
W www.talawa.com

**TAMASHA THEATRE
COMPANY**　T 020 7749 0090
RichMix, 35-47 Bethnal Green Road, London E1 6LA
F 020 7729 8906
E info@tamasha.org.uk
W www.tamasha.org.uk

TBA MUSIC　T 0845 1203722
1 St Gabriels Road, London NW2 4DS
F 0700 607 0808
E peter@tbagroup.co.uk

TEG PRODUCTIONS LTD
See MEADOW, Jeremy & ROSENTHAL, Suzanna

**THAT'S ENTERTAINMENT
PRODUCTIONS**　T 01903 263454
PO Box 4766, Worthing BN11 9NY
E info@thatsentertainmentproductions.co.uk
W www.thatsentertainmentproductions.co.uk

THEATRE ABSOLUTE　T 07799 292957
Shop Front Theatre, 38 City Arcade
Coventry CV1 3HW
E info@theatreabsolute.co.uk
W www.theatreabsolute.co.uk

THEATRE ALIVE!
13 St Barnabas Road, London E17 8JZ
E theatrealive@tiscali.co.uk
W www.theatrealive.org.uk

**THEATRE OF COMEDY
COMPANY LTD**　T 020 7379 3345
Shaftesbury Theatre, 210 Shaftesbury Avenue
London WC2H 8DP
F 020 7836 8181
E info@shaftesburytheatre.com

**THEATRE ROYAL
HAYMARKET PRODUCTIONS**　T 020 7930 8890
Theatre Royal Haymarket, 18 Suffolk Street
London SW1Y 4HT
E nigel@trh.co.uk

**THEATRE ROYAL
STRATFORD EAST**　T 020 8534 0310
Gerry Raffles Square, Stratford
London E15 1BN
F 020 8534 8381
E theatreroyal@stratfordeast.com
W www.stratfordeast.com

THEATRE SANS FRONTIERES　T 01434 652484
Queen's Hall Arts Centre, Beaumont Street
Hexham NE46 3LS
F 01434 607206
E info@tsf.org.uk
W www.tsf.org.uk

**THEATRE TOURS
INTERNATIONAL**　T/F 01707 330360
Contact: Guy Masterson
The Hawthorne Theatre, The Campus West
Welwyn Garden City, Herts AL8 6BX
E admin@theatretoursinternational.com
W www.theatretoursinternational.com

THEATRE WORKOUT LTD　T 020 8144 2290
13A Stratheden Road, Blackheath
London SE3 7TH
E enquiries@theatreworkout.co.uk
W www.theatreworkout.com

TIATA FAHODZI　T/F 020 3538 6257
The Africa Centre, 38 King Street
London WC2E 8JT
E info@tiatafahodzi.com
W www.tiatafahodzi.com

TOLD BY AN IDIOT　T 020 7407 4123
Twitter: @toldbyanidiot93
Unit LF 1.7 Lafone House, The Leathermarket
11-13 Weston Street, London SE1 3ER
F 020 7407 9002
E info@toldbyanidiot.org
W www.toldbyanidiot.org

TOPPER, Jenny　T 020 7249 5966
SquaredDeal Productions Ltd
24 De Beauvoir Square, London N1 4LE
F 020 7275 7553
E jenny@jennytopper.com

TOWER THEATRE COMPANY　T/F 020 7353 5700
Full-time Non-professional
St Bride Foundation, Bride Lane
London EC4Y 8EQ
E info@towertheatre.freeserve.co.uk
W www.towertheatre.org.uk

TREAGUS, Andrew ASSOCIATES LTD
32-33 St James's Place, London SW1A 1NR
E admin@at-assoc.co.uk

TRESTLE THEATRE COMPANY   T 01727 850950
Visual/Physical Theatre. Music. Choreography.
New Writing
Trestle Arts Base, Russet Drive
Herts, St Albans AL4 0JQ
F 01727 855558
E admin@trestle.org.uk
W www.trestle.org.uk

TRICYCLE THEATRE
COMPANY   T 020 7372 6611
269 Kilburn High Road, London NW6 7JR
F 020 7328 0795
E admin@tricycle.co.uk
W www.tricycle.co.uk

TRIUMPH PROSCENIUM
PRODUCTIONS LTD   T 01243 527186
The Cottage, West Lavant
Chichester, West Sussex PO18 9AH

TURTLE KEY ARTS   T 020 8964 5060
Ladbroke Hall, 79 Barlby Road
London W10 6AZ
F 020 8964 4080
E admin@turtlekeyarts.org.uk
W www.turtlekeyarts.org.uk

TWO'S COMPANY   T 020 8299 4593
244 Upland Road
London SE22 0DN
E graham@2scompanytheatre.co.uk

UK ARTS INTERNATIONAL   T 01905 26424
1st Floor, 6 Shaw Street
Worcester WR1 3QQ
F 01905 22868
E janryan@ukarts.com
W www.ukarts.com

UK PRODUCTIONS LTD   T 01483 423600
Churchmill House, Ockford Road
Godalming, Surrey GU7 1QY
F 01483 418486
E mail@ukproductions.co.uk
W www.ukproductions.co.uk

UNRESTRICTED VIEW   T 020 7704 2001
Above Hen & Chickens Theatre Bar
109 St Paul's Road
London N1 2NA
E henandchickens@aol.com
W www.henandchickens.com

VANDER ELST, Anthony
PRODUCTIONS   T 020 8466 5580
The Studio, 14 College Road
Bromley, Kent BR1 3NS

VAYU NAIDU COMPANY   T 020 7720 0707
Storytellers & Actors
Unit C16, The Old Imperial Laundry
71 Warriner Gardens
Battersea, London SW11 4XW
E vayunaidu@vayunaiducompany.org.uk
W www.vayunaiducompany.org.uk

VOLCANO THEATRE
COMPANY LTD   T 01792 464790
229 High Street
Swansea SA1 1NY
E mail@volcanotheatre.co.uk
W www.volcanotheatre.co.uk

WALKING FORWARD LTD   T 01438 310157
Business & Technology Centre
Bessemer Drive
Stevenage, Hertfordshire SG1 2DX
E info@walkingforward.co.uk
W www.walkingforward.co.uk

WALLACE, Kevin LTD   T 020 7812 7238
Amadeus House
27B Floral Street
London WC2E 9DP
E info@kevinwallace.co.uk

WAREHOUSE THEATRE
COMPANY   T 020 8681 1257
Dingwall Road
Croydon CR0 2NF
F 020 8688 6699
E ted@warehousetheatre.co.uk
W www.warehousetheatre.co.uk

WAX, Kenny LTD   T 020 7437 1736
3rd Floor, 25 Lexington Street
London W1F 9AG
W www.kennywax.com

WELDON, Duncan C.
PRODUCTIONS LTD   T 01243 527186
The Cottage, West Lavant
Chichester
West Sussex PO18 9AH

WHITALL, Keith   T 01323 844882
25 Solway, Hailsham
East Sussex BN27 3HB

WHITEHALL, Michael   T/F 020 8785 3737
6 Embankment, Putney
London SW15 1LB
E whitehallfilms@gmail.com

WILLS, Newton
MANAGEMENT   T 07989 398381
12 St Johns Road, Isleworth
Middlesex TW7 6NN
F 00 33 4 68218685
E newtoncttg@aol.com
W www.newtonwills.com

WORD & MUSIC
COMPANY THE   T 020 8237 1080
Riverside Studios
Crisp Road
London W6 9RL
E info@associatedstudios.co.uk
W www.wordandmusiccompany.co.uk

WORTMAN UK /
POLESTAR PICTURES   T 020 8994 8886
Theatre & Film Productions
48 Chiswick Staithe
London W4 3TP
T 07976 805976
E neville@speakwell.co.uk
W www.speakwell.co.uk

YELLOW EARTH THEATRE   T 020 7734 5988
3rd Floor, 20 Rupert Street
London W1D 6DF
E admin@yellowearth.org
W www.yellowearth.org

YOUNG VIC THEATRE   T 020 7922 2800
66 The Cut, London SE1 8LZ
F 020 7922 2801
E info@youngvic.org
W www.youngvic.org

Theatre

There are hundreds of theatres and theatre companies in the UK, varying dramatically in size and type. The theatre sections are organised under headings which best indicate a theatre's principal area of work. A summary of each of these is below.

Alternative & Community

Many of these companies tour to arts centres, small and middle-scale theatres, and non-theatrical venues which do not have a resident company, or they may be commissioned to develop site-specific projects. The term 'alternative' is sometimes used to describe work that is more experimental in style and execution.

Children, Young People & TIE

The primary focus of these theatre companies is to reach younger audiences. They often tour to smaller theatres, schools and non-theatrical venues. Interactive teaching – through audience participation and workshops – is often a feature of their work.

English Speaking Theatre Companies in Europe

These work principally outside of the UK. Some are based in one venue whilst others are touring companies. Their work varies enormously and includes theatre for young people, large-scale musicals, revivals of classics and dinner theatre. Actors are employed either for an individual production or a 'season' of several plays.

London Theatres

Larger theatres situated in the West End and Central London. A few are producing houses, but most are leased to theatre producers who take responsibility for putting together a company for a run of a single show. In such cases it is they and not the venue who cast productions (often with the help of casting directors). Alternatively, a production will open outside London and tour to provincial theatres, then subsequently, if successful, transfer to a London venue.

Outer London, Fringe & Venues

Small and middle-scale theatres in Outer London and around the country. Some are producing houses, others are only available for hire. Many of the London venues have provided useful directions on how they may be reached by public transport.

Provincial / Touring

Theatre producers and other companies sell their ready-made productions to the provincial/touring theatres, a list of larger venues outside London. A run in each theatre varies between a night and several weeks, but a week per venue for tours of plays is usual. Even if a venue is not usually a producing house, most provincial theatres and arts centres put on a family show at Christmas.

Puppet Theatre Companies

Some puppet theatres are one-performer companies who literally create their own work from scratch. The content and style of productions varies enormously. For example, not all are aimed at children, and some are more interactive than others. Although we list a few theatres with puppet companies in permanent residence, this kind of work often involves touring. As with all small and middle scale touring, performers who are willing, and have the skills, to involve themselves with all aspects of company life are always more valuable.

Repertory (Regional) Theatres

Theatres situated outside London which employ a resident company of actors (i.e. the 'repertory company') on a play-by-play basis or for a season of several plays. In addition to the main auditorium (usually the largest acting space) these theatres may have a smaller studio theatre attached, which will be home to an additional company whose focus is education or the production of new plays (see 'Theatre: Children, Young People & TIE'). In recent years the length of repertory seasons has become shorter; this means that a number of productions are no longer in-house. It is common for gaps in the performance calendar to be filled by tours mounted by theatre producers, other repertory theatres and non-venue based production companies.

Theatre

CASE STUDY

Park Theatre is a brand new arts venue, situated less than a minute's walk from Finsbury Park tube station. The £2.5 million privately funded building will comprise a 200-seat and a 90-seat theatre with a late licence cafe and bar. Freelance publicist and Press & PR Manager for Park Theatre, Nouska Hanly, tells us about the theatre's journey so far.

Over the course of my now two-year involvement with Park Theatre, many people have wondered who on earth is behind this project and who would be brave enough to build a new theatre in the middle of an economic recession? The answer to that is husband and wife team Jez and Melli Bond and from the moment I met these two, there has never been a doubt in my mind that their venture would be anything other than successful. I decided to make it my business to help them.

By the time I joined the project in September 2010 the building had been acquired after a six-year search across London for the perfect location. The remit was for a site very near a tube station, situated in an area that would benefit greatly from the emergence of a new theatre.

The next search was for the right architectural firm to design the space. The design process has been a completely collaborative journey between Jez Bond, our artistic director, and our architect, Dave Hughes. For Jez, the fact that Dave had not designed a theatre before was an advantage as it represented a blank canvas from which to create something new. The plans which have emerged embed the technical requirements of a theatre, whilst allowing a space which enhances the ceremony and collective experience of a theatre visit.

The specifications of the building have been expertly thought through, with exhaustive research into every area. Jez and Dave visited nearly forty different theatres in order to research the very best design features for Park Theatre. From the latest lighting rig technology to the optimum facilities for actors' dressing rooms and the most efficient ticketing systems front of house, every aspect of the build has been carefully considered with no detail overlooked or rushed.

Park Theatre will focus on building a reputation through world-class productions and a broad artistic programme. We will seek to give equal programming opportunities to male and female talent and address the balance of male and female roles on our stages. Ultimately we're not following a formula. We have an opportunity to do things a little differently – not for the sake of it but because we believe in creativity and pushing the boundaries of what a theatre can be.

Along the way Park Theatre has received a huge amount of attention, featuring in over forty articles across the national and international press since the beginning of this year and even making New York theatre networks as a representative model of arts organisations bucking the economic recession. We have been delighted to receive overwhelming support from many of the most distinguished members of the industry including Sir Ian McKellen, Celia Imrie, Tamzin Outhwaite, Alan Rickman, Roger Lloyd Pack and Sean Mathias, all of whom have offered their help after visiting the site.

Eighteen months into the build, the dream is becoming a reality. Our challenge now is to raise the last £150,000 for our education floor. Having this facility on-site will enable us to offer unprecedented access to the theatre for our local community. In partnership with the award-winning Islington Community Theatre, we will deliver theatre workshops for young people in the area and help inspire their interest in the arts.

Park Theatre has always maintained its original intention to serve its community and help rejuvenate an area. The venue has already been cited as an aspirational symbol of regeneration after the leaders of Islington, Hackney and Haringey councils met on-site to sign The Finsbury Park Accord, a new political agreement which promises improvements for the area.

At the heart of the project is a shared belief in the power of theatre to transform lives. We want to be a catalyst for change and a force for good. Many of us have spent our careers working in this industry and we want to be part of building something great from the ground up. The team is a passionate, ambitious, positive group of individuals with a touch of the maverick about them all. An infectious collective energy drives the whole thing forward through triumphs and struggles. Jez likens the process of building the theatre to putting on a show; only this one will be the biggest show of his life.

To find out more visit www.parktheatre.co.uk, follow @ParkTheatreLive on Twitter or e-mail nouska.hanly@parktheatre.co.uk

1623 THEATRE COMPANY   T 01332 285434
QUAD, Market Place
Cathedral Quarter, Derby DE1 3AS
E messages@1623theatre.co.uk
W www.1623theatre.co.uk

ABERYSTWYTH ARTS CENTRE   T 01970 621512
Penglais, Aberystwyth
Ceredigion SY23 3DE
F 01970 622883
E ggo@aber.ac.uk
W www.aber.ac.uk/artscentre

ADMIRATION THEATRE   T 07010 041579
E email@admirationtheatre.com
W www.admirationtheatre.com

**AGE EXCHANGE
THEATRE TRUST**   T 020 8318 9105
*Contact: Suzanne Lockett (Director of Training & Support
Services)*
The Reminiscence Centre
11 Blackheath Village
London SE3 9LA
E administrator@age-exchange.org.uk
W www.age-exchange.org.uk

ALTERNATIVE ARTS   T 020 7375 0441
Top Studio, Montefiore Centre
Hanbury Street, London E1 5HZ
F 020 7375 0484
E info@alternativearts.co.uk
W www.alternativearts.co.uk

ANGLES THEATRE THE   BO 01945 474447
Alexandra Road, Wisbech
Cambridgeshire PE13 1HQ
E office@anglestheatre.co.uk

ARUNDEL JAILHOUSE   T/F 01903 889821
Arundel Town Hall, Arundel
West Sussex BN18 9AP
E info@arundeljailhouse.co.uk
W www.arundeljailhouse.co.uk

**ASHTON GROUP
THEATRE THE**   T 01229 430636
The Old Fire Station, Abbey Road
Barrow-in-Furness, Cumbria LA14 1XH
E theashtongroup@btconnect.com
W www.ashtongroup.co.uk

ATTIC THEATRE COMPANY   T 020 8640 6800
Mitcham Library, 157 London Road
Mitcham CR4 2YR
E info@attictheatrecompany.com
W www.attictheatrecompany.com

BANNER THEATRE   T 0845 4581909
Greenspring Training
Raleigh Industrial Estate
176 Camp Lane, Handsworth
Birmingham B21 8JF
E info@bannertheatre.co.uk

BECK THEATRE   T 020 8561 7506
Grange Road, Hayes
Middlesex UB3 2UE
T 020 8561 8371
E enquiries@becktheatre.org.uk
W www.becktheatre.org.uk

**BENT BACK TULIPS
THEATRE COMPANY**   T 07971 159940
59B Crystal Palace Park Road
Crystal Palace
London SE26 6UT
E info@bentbacktulips.com
W www.bentbacktulips.com

BISHOPS GREAVES THEATRE   T 01522 583700
Bishop Grosseteste University College, Newport
Lincoln, Lincolnshire, LN1 3DY
E theatre@bishopg.ac.uk
W www.bishopg.ac.uk/theatre

BLANK PAGES
*Double-bills of New Writing put
on in Feb, May, Aug & Nov*
89 Birchanger Lane, Bishop Stortford
Herts CM23 5QF
E contactblankpages@gmail.com
W www.wix.com/blankpages1/blankpages

**BLUE MOON
THEATRE COMPANY**   T 01278 458253
20 Sandpiper Road, Blakespool Park
Bridgwater, Somerset TA6 5QU
E info@bluemoontheatre.co.uk
W www.bluemoontheatre.co.uk

**BLUEYED THEATRE
PRODUCTIONS**   T 07799 137487
59B Crystal Palace Park Road
London SE26 6UT
T 07971 159940
E info@blueyedtheatreproductions.co.uk
W www.blueyedtheatreproductions.co.uk

**BLUNDERBUS
THEATRE COMPANY LTD**   T 01636 678900
The Studio, The Palace Theatre
Appletongate, Newark, Notts NG24 1JY
E admin@blunderbus.co.uk
W www.blunderbus.co.uk

**CAPITAL ARTS
YOUTH THEATRE**   T/F 020 8449 2342
Capital Arts Studio
Wyllyotts Centre, Darkes Lane
Potters Bar, Herts EN6 2HN
T 07885 232414
E capitalarts@btconnect.com
W www.capitalarts.org.uk

CARIB THEATRE COMPANY   T/F 020 8903 4592
73 Lancelot Road, Wembley
Middlesex I IA0 2AN
E antoncarib@yahoo.co.uk

**CENTRE FOR
PERFORMANCE RESEARCH**   T 01970 622133
The Foundry, Parry Williams
Penglais Campus SY23 3AJ
F 01970 622132
E info@thecpr.org.uk
W www.thecpr.org.uk

**CHAIN REACTION
THEATRE COMPANY**   T/F 020 8534 0007
Three Mills Studios
Sugar House Yard
Sugar House Lane, London E15 2QS
E mail@chainreactiontheatre.co.uk
W www.chainreactiontheatre.co.uk

CHALKFOOT THEATRE ARTS
c/o Channel Theatre Productions Ltd
Penistone House, 5 High Street
St Lawrence, Ramsgate
Kent CT11 0QH
E info@chalkfoot.org.uk
W www.chalkfoot.org.uk

CHATS PALACE   T 020 8533 0227
42-44 Brooksby's Walk, Hackney
London E9 6DF
E info@chatspalace.com
W www.chatspalace.co.uk

CHICKENSHED   T 020 8351 6161
Chase Side, Southgate
London N14 4PE
BO 020 8292 9222
E susanj@chickenshed.org.uk
W www.chickenshed.org.uk

CHOL THEATRE   T 01484 536008
Contact: Susan Burns (Director)
Lawrence Batley Theatre, 8 Queen Street
Huddersfield, West Yorkshire HD1 2SP
F 01484 425336
E info@choltheatre.co.uk
W www.choltheatre.co.uk

**CLOSE FOR COMFORT
THEATRE COMPANY**   T 07710 258290
34 Boleyn Walk, Leatherhead
Surrey KT22 7HU
T 01372 378613
E close4comf@aol.com
W www.closeforcomforttheatre.co.uk

COMPLETE WORKS THE   T 020 7377 0280
The Old Truman Brewery, 91 Brick Lane
London E1 6QL
F 020 7247 7405
E info@tcw.org.uk
W www.tcw.org.uk

**CORNELIUS & JONES
ORIGINAL PRODUCTIONS**   T/F 01908 612593
49 Carters Close, Sherington
Newport Pagnell, Buckinghamshire MK16 9NW
E admin@corneliusjones.com
W www.corneliusjones.com

CUT-CLOTH THEATRE   T 07950 542346
41 Beresford Road, Highbury
London N5 2HR

EALDFAEDER   T 01787 238257
Anglo Saxon Living History & Re-enactment
12 Carleton Close, Great Yeldham
Essex CO9 4QJ
E pete@gippeswic.demon.co.uk
W www.ealdfaeder.org

ELAN WALES   T 07837 101038
5 Grange Gardens, Cardiff CF11 7LJ
E info@elanwales.org
W www.elanwales.org

ELECTRIC CABARET   T 01280 700956
107 High Street, Brackley
Northants NN13 7BN
T 07714 089763
E richard@electriccabaret.co.uk
W www.electricccabaret.co.uk

EUROPEAN THEATRE COMPANY THE
15 Beverley Avenue, London SW20 0RL
E admin@europeantheatre.co.uk
W www.europeantheatre.co.uk

**FEMME FATALE
THEATRE COMPANY**   T 07779 611414
30 Creighton Avenue, Muswell Hill
London N10 1NU
E dianelefley@yahoo.com
W www.femmefataletheatrecompany.com

**FOREST FORGE
THEATRE COMPANY**   T 01425 470188
The Theatre Centre, Endeavour Park, Crow Arch Lane
Ringwood, Hampshire BH24 1SF
F 01425 471158
E info@forestforge.co.uk
W www.forestforge.co.uk

FOUND THEATRE   T 01629 813083
The Byways, Church Street
Monyash, Derbyshire DE45 1JH
E found_theatre@yahoo.co.uk
W www.foundtheatre.org.uk

**FRANTIC THEATRE
COMPANY**   T/F 0870 1657350
32 Woodlane, Falmouth TR11 4RF
E bookings@frantictheatre.com
W www.frantictheatre.com

**GALLEON THEATRE
COMPANY LTD**   T 020 8310 7276
Head Office, Greenwich Playhouse
50 Openshaw Road, London SE2 0TE
E boxoffice@galleontheatre.co.uk
W www.galleontheatre.co.uk

GRANGE ARTS CENTRE   T 0161 785 4239
Rochdale Road, Oldham
Greater Manchester OL9 6EA
F 0161 785 4263
E grangearts@oldham.ac.uk
W www.grangeartsoldham.co.uk

GREASEPAINT ANONYMOUS   T 020 8886 2263
Youth Theatre Company
4 Gallus Close, Winchmore Hill, London N21 1JR
T 07930 421216
E info@greasepaintanonymous.co.uk

HALL FOR CORNWALL   T 01872 321971
Contact: Isobel King (Education Manager)
Back Quay, Truro, Cornwall TR1 2LL
E admin@hallforcornwall.org.uk
W www.hallforcornwall.co.uk

**HEBE THEATRE
COMPANY THE**   T 01473 785672
Paradise Now, Mow Hill
Witnesham, Ipswich IP6 9EH
E c.mugleston672@btinternet.com
W www.thehebetheatrecompany.onesuffolk.net

HIJINX THEATRE   T 029 2030 0331
*Touring Theatre Company. Producers of Inclusive
Theatre*
Wales Millennium Centre
Bute Place, Cardiff CF10 5AL
F 029 2030 0332
E info@hijinx.org.uk
W www.hijinx.org.uk

**HISTORIA THEATRE
COMPANY**   T 020 7837 8008
8 Cloudesley Square, London N1 0HT
T 07811 892079
E kateprice@lineone.net
W www.historiatheatre.com

ICON THEATRE   T 01634 813179
The Brook Theatre, Old Town Hall
Chatham, Kent ME4 4SE
E nancy@icontheatre.org.uk
W www.icontheatre.org.uk

IMAGE MUSICAL THEATRE   T 020 8743 9380
23 Sedgeford Road, Shepherd's Bush
London W12 0NA
F 020 8749 9294
E brian@imagemusicaltheatre.co.uk
W www.imagemusicaltheatre.co.uk

IMMEDIATE THEATRE   T 020 7923 8180
Unit 18, Springfield House
5 Tyson Street, London E8 2LY
E info@immediate-theatre.com
W www.immediate-theatre.com

INOCENTE ART & FILM LTD T 07973 518132
Film. Multimedia. Music Videos. Two Rock 'n' Roll
Musicals
Flat 2, 76 Highdown Road
Hove BN3 6EB
E tarascas@btopenworld.com

ISOSCELES T 020 8946 3905
7 Amity Grove, Raynes Park
London SW20 0LQ
E patanddave@isosceles.biz
W www.isosceles.biz

KING'S HEAD THEATRE BO 020 7478 0160
Contact: Adam Spreadbury-Maher (Artistic Director)
115 Upper Street, Islington
London N1 1QN
T 020 7226 8561
E info@kingsheadtheatre.com
W www.kingsheadtheatre.com

KNEEHIGH T 01872 267910
15 Walsingham Place, Truro
Cornwall TR1 2RP
E office@kneehigh.co.uk
W www.kneehigh.co.uk

KNUTSFORD CIVIC CENTRE T 01565 633005
Cheshire East Council
Toft Road, Knutsford
Cheshire WA16 0PE
E knutsfordcinema@cheshireeast.gov.uk
W www.cheshireeast.gov.uk/cinemas

KOMEDIA T 01273 647101
44-47 Gardner Street
Brighton BN1 1UN
F 01273 647102
E info@komedia.co.uk
W www.komedia.co.uk

KORU THEATRE T 020 8579 1029
11 Clovelly Road, London W5 5HF
E info@korutheatre.com
W www.korutheatre.com

LADDER TO THE MOON T 020 7794 2593
Branch Hill House, Branch Hill
Hampstead, London NW3 7LS
E info@laddertothemoon.co.uk

LIVE THEATRE T 0191 261 2694
New Writing
Broad Chare, Quayside
Newcastle upon Tyne NE1 3DQ
F 0191 232 2224
E info@live.org.uk
W www.live.org.uk

LONDON ACTORS
THEATRE COMPANY T 020 7978 2620
Unit 5A, Imex Business Centre
Ingate Place, London SW8 3NS
F 020 7978 2631
E latchmoro@fichorc.org.uk

LONDON BUBBLE
THEATRE COMPANY LTD T 020 7237 4434
5 Elephant Lane, London SE16 4JD
E admin@londonbubble.org.uk
W www.londonbubble.org.uk

LONG OVERDUE THEATRE
COMPANY THE T 0845 8382994
16 Butterfield Drive
Amesbury
Wiltshire SP4 7SJ
E stefpearmain@hotmail.com
W www.tlots.co.uk

LSW JUNIOR INTER-ACT T/F 020 7793 9755
PO Box 31855, London SE17 3XP
E londonswo@hotmail.com
W www.londonshakespeare.org.uk

LSW PRISON PROJECT T/F 020 7793 9755
PO Box 31855, London SE17 3XP
E londonswo@hotmail.com
W www.lswproductions.co.uk

LSW SENIOR RE-ACTION T/F 020 7793 9755
PO Box 31855, London SE17 3XP
E londonswo@hotmail.com
W www.lswproductions.co.uk

M6 THEATRE COMPANY T 01706 355898
Studio Theatre
Hamer CP School
Albert Royds Street, Rochdale OL16 2SU
F 01706 712601
E info@m6theatre.co.uk
W www.m6theatre.co.uk

MADDERMARKET THEATRE T 01603 626560
Resident Community Theatre Company. Small-scale
Producing & Receiving House
St John's Alley, Norwich NR2 1DR
E mmtheatre@btconnect.com
W www.maddermarket.co.uk

MAGIC HAT PRODUCTIONS T 07769 560991
Based in London
E general@magichat-productions.com
W www.magichat-productions.com

MANCHESTER
ACTORS COMPANY T 0161 227 8702
c/o 31 Leslie Street, Manchester M14 7NE
E dramaticnights@aol.com
W www.manactco.org.uk

MAVERICK THEATRE
COMPANY LTD T 0121 444 0933
33A Prebend Mansions
Chiswick High Road
London W4 2LU
T 07531 138248
E info@mavericktheatre.co.uk
W www.mavericktheatre.co.uk

MIKRON THEATRE
COMPANY LTD T 01484 843701
Marsden Mechanics, Peel Street
Marsden, Huddersfield HD7 6BW
E admin@mikron.org.uk
W www.mikron.org.uk

MONTAGE THEATRE ARTS T 020 8692 7007
Contact: Judy Gordon (Artistic Director)
The Albany, Douglas Way
London SE8 4AG
E office@montagetheatre.com
W www.montagetheatre.com

NATURAL THEATRE COMPANY T 01225 469131
Street Theatre. Touring. Corporate
Widcombe Institute
Widcombe Hill
Bath BA2 6AA
E info@naturaltheatre.co.uk
W www.naturaltheatre.co.uk

NEW PERSPECTIVES
THEATRE COMPANY T 0115 927 2334
Regional/National New Writing Touring Theatre
Park Lane Business Centre, Park Lane
Basford, Nottinghamshire NG6 0DW
E info@newperspectives.co.uk
W www.newperspectives.co.uk

NEWFOUND THEATRE COMPANY
Contact: By e-mail
E newfoundtheatre@gmail.com
W www.newfoundtheatre.com

NORTH COUNTRY THEATRE   T 01748 825288
3 Rosemary Lane
Richmond
North Yorkshire DL10 4DP
E office@northcountrytheatre.com
W www.northcountrytheatre.com

NORTHERN STAGE (THEATRICAL PRODUCTIONS) LTD   T 0191 242 7200
Barras Bridge
Newcastle upon Tyne NE1 7RH
F 0191 242 7257
E info@northernstage.co.uk
W www.northernstage.co.uk

NORTHUMBERLAND THEATRE COMPANY (NTC)   T 01665 602586
Touring Regionally & Nationally
The Playhouse, Bondgate Without
Alnwick, Northumberland NE66 1PQ
F 01665 605837
E admin@northumberlandtheatre.co.uk
W www.northumberlandtheatre.co.uk

NUFFIELD THEATRE   T 023 8031 5500
Projects. Touring
University Road
Southampton SO17 1TR
F 023 8031 5511
E annie.reilly@nuffieldtheatre.co.uk
W www.nuffieldtheatre.co.uk

OLD TYME PLAYERS THEATRE COMPANY   T 01425 612830
Music Hall. Comedy. Revues. Locally Based
35 Barton Court Avenue
Barton on Sea
Hants BH25 7EP
E oldetymeplayers@tiscali.co.uk
W www.oldetymeplayers.com

OPEN STAGE PRODUCTIONS   T/F 0121 777 9086
49 Springfield Road, Moseley
Birmingham B13 9NN
E info@openstage.co.uk
W www.openstage.co.uk

OXFORDSHIRE THEATRE COMPANY   T 07802 287703
c/o Mercer Lewin
41 Cornmarket Street
Oxford OX1 3HA
E info@oxfordshiretheatrecompany.co.uk
W www.oxfordshiretheatrecompany.co.uk

PASCAL THEATRE COMPANY   T 020 7383 0920
35 Flaxman Court
Flaxman Terrace
Bloomsbury, London WC1H 9AR
E pascaltheatrecompany@gmail.com
W www.pascal-theatre.com

PEOPLE'S THEATRE COMPANY THE
69 Manor Way, Guildford
Surrey GU2 7RR
E ptc@ptc.org.uk
W www.ptc.org.uk

PHANTOM CAPTAIN THE   T 020 8455 4564
618B Finchley Road, London NW11 7RR
E lambhorn@gmail.com

PLAYTIME THEATRE COMPANY   T 01227 266272
18 Bennells Avenue, Whitstable, Kent CT5 2HP
F 01227 266648
E playtime@dircon.co.uk
W www.playtimetheatre.co.uk

POWERHOUSE THEATRE COMPANY   T 01483 444787
Contact: Geoff Lawson (Artistic Director)
The Electric Theatre, Onslow Street
Guildford GU1 4SZ
T 07949 821567
E powerhousetheatre@hotmail.co.uk
W www.powerhousetheatre.co.uk

POWYS ART   T 01597 824444
The Drama Centre, Tremont Road
Llandrindod Wells, Powys LD1 5EB
F 01597 824381
E lucy.bevan@powys.gov.uk
W www.theatrpowys.co.uk

PRIME PRODUCTIONS   T/F 0131 449 4055
54 Hermiston Village
Currie EH14 4AQ
E primeproductions@talktalk.net
W www.primeproductions.co.uk

PROTEUS THEATRE COMPANY   T 01256 354541
Multimedia & Cross-artform Work
Queen Mary's College
Cliddesden Road
Basingstoke, Hampshire RG21 3HF
E info@proteustheatre.com
W www.proteustheatre.com

PURSUED BY A BEAR PRODUCTIONS   T 01252 745445
Farnham Maltings
Bridge Square
Farnham GU9 7QR
E pursuedbyabear@yahoo.co.uk
W www.pursuedbyabear.co.uk

Q20 THEATRE LTD   T 01274 221360
Dockfield Road, Shipley
West Yorkshire BD17 7AD
E info@q20theatre.co.uk

RIDING LIGHTS THEATRE COMPANY   T 01904 655317
Friargate Theatre, Lower Friargate
York YO1 9SL
F 01904 651532
E info@rltc.org
W www.ridinglights.org

SALTMINE THEATRE COMPANY   T 01384 454807
61 The Broadway, Dudley DY1 3EB
E creative@saltmine.org
W www.saltminetrust.org.uk

SPANNER IN THE WORKS   T 020 7193 7995
PO Box 239, Sidcup DA15 0DP
T 07850 313986
E info@spannerintheworks.org.uk
W www.spannerintheworks.org.uk

SPARE TYRE T/F 020 7061 6454
Contact: Arti Prashar (Artistic Director). Theatre Without Prejudice. For performers who are female, older or have learning disabilities
Unit 3.22, Canterbury Court, Kennington Park
1-3 Brixton Road, London SW9 6DE
E info@sparetyre.org
W www.sparetyre.org

SPECTACLE THEATRE T 01443 430700
Coleg Morgannwg Rhondda
Llwynypia
Tonypandy CF40 2TQ
F 01443 439640
E info@spectacletheatre.co.uk
W www.spectacletheatre.co.uk

SPONTANEITY SHOP THE T 020 7788 4080
85-87 Bayham Street
London NW1 0AG
E info@the-spontaneity-shop.com
W www.the-spontaneity-shop.com

TAG CITIZENS T 0141 429 5561
Citizens' Theatre, 119 Gorbals Street
Glasgow G5 9DS
F 0141 429 7374
E info@citz.co.uk
W www.citz.co.uk

TAKING FLIGHT THEATRE COMPANY T 029 2022 6072
31 Brunswick Street, Canton
Cardiff CF5 1LH
E takingflighttheatre@yahoo.co.uk
W www.takingflighttheatre.co.uk

TARA ARTS GROUP LTD T 020 8333 4457
Tara Theatre, 356 Garratt Lane, London SW18 4ES
F 020 8870 9540
E tara@tara-arts.com
W www.tara-arts.com

THEATRE& LTD T 01484 532967
Church Hall, St James Road
Marsh, Huddersfield HD1 4QA
F 01484 532962
E cmitchell@theatreand.com
W www.theatreand.com

THEATRE & FILM WORKSHOP T 0131 555 3854
Out of the Blue Drill Hall
36 Dalmeny Street
Edinburgh EH6 8RG
W www.theatre-workshop.com

THEATRE IS... T 01582 481221
The Hat Factory, 65-67 Bute Street
Luton, Bedfordshire LU1 2EY
E info@theatreis.org
W www.theatreis.org

THEATRE PECKHAM T 020 7708 5401
Havil Street
London SE5 7SD
E admin@theatrepeckham.co.uk
W www.theatrepeckham.co.uk

TOBACCO FACTORY THEATRE T 0117 902 0345
Raleigh Road, Southville
Bristol BS3 1TF
E theatre@tobaccofactorytheatre.com
W www.tobaccofactorytheatre.com

TRAFFORD MARGARETIANS AOS T 0161 718 5398
2 Shows per year. Monday Rehearsals
5 Newgate Road, Sale
Cheshire M33 4NQ
T 07980 931345
E tmaos@hotmail.co.uk
W www.tmaos.co.uk

WAREHOUSE THEATRE COMPANY T 020 8681 1257
Dingwall Road, Croydon CR0 2NF
F 020 8688 6699
E ted@warehousetheatre.co.uk
W www.warehousetheatre.co.uk

WINCHESTER HAT FAIR, FESTIVAL OF STREET THEATRE T 01962 849841
5A Jewry Street, Winchester
Hampshire SO23 8RZ
E info@hatfair.co.uk
W www.hatfair.co.uk

WOMEN & THEATRE BIRMINGHAM LTD T 0121 449 7117
The Old Lodge, Uffculme
50 Queensbridge Road
Moseley, Birmingham B13 8QY
F 0121 449 0785
E info@womenandtheatre.co.uk

Y TOURING THEATRE COMPANY T 020 7520 3090
One KX, 120 Cromer Street
London WC1H 8BS
E d.jackson@ytouring.org.uk
W www.theatreofdebate.com

YELLOW EARTH THEATRE T 020 7734 5988
3rd Floor, 20 Rupert Street
London W1D 6DF
E admin@yellowearth.org
W www.yellowearth.org

YELLOWCHAIR PERFORMANCE EXPERIENCE THE
First Breaks on the London Fringe for New Talent
89 Birchanger Lane
Bishop Stortford CM23 5QF
E contacttype@gmail.com
W www.wix.com/yellowchair/type

YORICK INTERNATIONALIST THEATRE ENSEMBLE T/F 020 7836 7637
Yorick Theatre & Film
4 Duval Court, 36 Bedfordbury
Covent Garden, London WC2N 4DQ
E yorickx@hotmail.com

YOUNG VIC THEATRE T 020 7922 2000
66 The Cut, London SE1 8LZ
BO 020 7922 2922
E info@youngvic.org
W www.youngvic.org

ZIP THEATRE T 01902 572250
Newhampton Arts Centre
Dunkley Street
Wolverhampton WV1 4AN
F 01902 572251
E admin@ziptheatre.co.uk
W www.ziptheatre.co.uk

A THOUSAND CRANES T 07801 269772
48 Brunswick Crescent, London N11 1EB
E kumiko@athousandcranes.org.uk
W www.athousandcranes.org.uk

ACTION STATION UK LTD THE T 0870 7702705
4-6 Canfield Place, London NW6 3BT
E info@theactionstation.co.uk
W www.theactionstation.co.uk

ACTION TRANSPORT THEATRE T 0151 357 2120
*New Writing. Professional Production for, by & with
Young People*
Whitby Hall, Stanney Lane
Ellesmere Port, Cheshire CH65 9AE
E info@actiontransporttheatre.org
W www.actiontransporttheatre.org

**ACTIONWORK
WORLDWIDE LTD** T 01934 815163
Theatre & Film Productions with Young People
PO Box 433, Weston-super-Mare
Somerset BS24 0WY
E admin@actionwork.com   W www.actionwork.com

**AESOP'S TOURING
THEATRE COMPANY** T/F 01483 724633
Touring Arts Centres, Schools & Theatres Nationally
The Arches, 38 The Riding, Woking, Surrey GU21 5TA
T 07836 731872
E info@aesopstheatre.co.uk
W www.aesopstheatre.co.uk

**AKADEMI SOUTH
ASIAN DANCE UK** T 020 7691 3210
Hampstead Town Hall
213 Haverstock Hill, London NW3 4QP
F 020 7691 3211
E info@akademi.co.uk   W www.akademi.co.uk

**ARTY-FACT THEATRE
COMPANY LTD** T 07020 962096
18 Weston Lane, Crewe, Cheshire CW2 5AN
F 07020 982098
E artyfact@talktalk.net   W www.arty-fact.co.uk

ASHCROFT YOUTH THEATRE T 0844 8005328
Ashcroft Academy of Dramatic Art
Malcolm Primary School
Malcolm Road, Penge, London SE20 8RH
T 07799 791586
E info@ashcroftacademy.com
W www.ashcroftacademy.com

**BARKING DOG
THEATRE COMPANY** T 020 7117 6321
14 Leaside Mansions, Fortis Green, London N10 3EB
T 07803 773160
E mike@barkingdog.co.uk   W www.barkingdog.co.uk

BECK THEATRE T 020 8561 7506
Grange Road, Hayes, Middlesex UB3 2UE
T 020 8561 8371
E enquiries@becktheatre.org.uk
W www.becktheatre.org.uk

BIG WOODEN HORSE T 020 8567 8431
30 Northfield Road, West Ealing, London W13 9SY
E info@bigwoodenhorse.com
W www.bigwoodenhorse.com

**BIRMINGHAM STAGE
COMPANY THE** T 020 7437 3391
*Contact: Neal Foster (Actor/Manager),
Philip Compton (Executive Producer)*
Suite 228, The Linen Hall, 162 Regent Street
London W1B 5TB
F 020 7437 3395
E info@birminghamstage.com
W www.birminghamstage.com

BITESIZE THEATRE COMPANY T 01978 358320
8 Green Meadows, New Broughton, Wrexham LL11 6SG
F 01978 756308
E admin@bitesizetheatre.co.uk
W www.bitesizetheatre.co.uk

**BLUE MOON THEATRE
COMPANY** T 01278 458253
20 Sandpiper Road, Blakespool Park
Bridgwater, Somerset TA6 5QU
E info@bluemoontheatre.co.uk
W www.bluemoontheatre.co.uk

**BLUNDERBUS THEATRE
COMPANY LTD** T 01636 678900
The Studio, The Palace Theatre
Appletongate, Newark, Notts NG24 1JY
E admin@blunderbus.co.uk
W www.blunderbus.co.uk

**BOOSTER CUSHION
THEATRE LTD** T 01727 873874
75 How Wood, Park Street, St Albans, Herts AL2 2RW
F 01727 872597
E admin@booster-cushion.co.uk
W www.booster-cushion.co.uk

BRIDGE HOUSE THEATRE T 01926 776437
Professional & School Productions. Visiting Companies
Warwick School Site, Myton Road
Warwick CV34 6PP
E info@bridgehousetheatre.co.uk
W www.bridgehousetheatre.co.uk

BRIEF CANDLE THEATRE T 01629 735576
Oaker View, Wensleys
Darley Bridge, Matlock, Derbyshire DE4 2JZ
E office@briefcandle.co.uk
W www.briefcandle.co.uk

**CAMBRIDGE
TOURING THEATRE** T/F 01223 246533
29 Worts Causeway, Cambridge CB1 8RJ
E info@cambridgetouringtheatre.co.uk
W www.cambridgetouringtheatre.co.uk

CAUGHT IN THE ACT T 01608 659555
Conygree House, Church Street
Kingham, Oxfordshire OX7 6YA
E cita@caughtintheact.co.uk
W www.caughtintheact.co.uk

**CHAIN REACTION THEATRE
COMPANY** T/F 020 8534 0007
Three Mills Studios, Sugar House Yard
Sugar House Lane, London E15 2QS
E mail@chainreactiontheatre.co.uk
W www.chainreactiontheatre.co.uk

CHALKFOOT THEATRE ARTS
Contact: Philip Dart (Artistic Director)
c/o Channel Theatre Productions Ltd
Penistone House, 5 High Street
St Lawrence, Ramsgate, Kent CT11 0QH
E info@chalkfoot.org.uk
W www.chalkfoot.org.uk

CHICKENSHED T 020 8351 6161
Chase Side, Southgate, London N14 4PE
BO 020 8292 9222
E susanj@chickenshed.org.uk
W www.chickenshed.org.uk

**CLWYD THEATR CYMRU
THEATRE FOR YOUNG PEOPLE** T 01352 701575
Contact: Nerys Edwards (Education Administrator)
Raikes Lane, Mold, Flintshire CH7 1YA
F 01352 701558
E education@clwyd-theatr-cymru.co.uk
W www.ctctyp.co.uk

COMPLETE WORKS THE　T 020 7377 0280
Contact: Phil Evans (Artistic Director)
The Old Truman Brewery, 91 Brick Lane, London E1 6QL
F 020 7247 7405
E info@tcw.org.uk
W www.tcw.org.uk

CRAGRATS　T 0844 8111184
Lawster House, 140 South Street
Dorking, Surrey RH4 2EU
E enquiries@cragrats.com
W www.cragrats.com

DAYLIGHT THEATRE　T 01453 763808
66 Middle Street, Stroud
Gloucestershire GL5 1EA

DONNA MARIA COMPANY　T 020 8670 7814
16 Bell Meadow, Dulwich, London SE19 1HP
E info@donnamariasworld.co.uk
W www.donna-marias-world.co.uk

DRAGON DRAMA　T 07590 452436
Theatre Company. Parties. Tuition. Workshops.
347 Hanworth Road, Hampton TW12 3EJ
E askus@dragondrama.co.uk
W www.dragondrama.co.uk

**EUROPA CLOWN
THEATRE SHOW**　T 01892 537964
36 St Lukes Road, Tunbridge Wells, Kent TN4 9JH
E mike@heypresto.orangehome.co.uk
W www.clowneuropa.co.uk

EUROPEAN THEATRE COMPANY THE
Contact: By Post/e-mail
15 Beverley Avenue, London SW20 0RL
E admin@europeantheatre.co.uk
W www.europeantheatre.co.uk

**FUSE: NEW THEATRE
FOR YOUNG PEOPLE CO LTD**　T 0151 708 0877
*Contact: Michael Quirke (General Manager),
Andrew Raffle (Artistic Producer)*
13 Hope Street, Liverpool L1 9BH
F 0151 707 9950
E info@fusetheatre.com
W www.fusetheatre.com

FUTURES THEATRE COMPANY　T 020 7928 2832
St John's Crypt, 73 Waterloo Road, London SE1 8UD
F 020 7928 6724
E info@futurestheatrecompany.co.uk
W www.futurestheatrecompany.co.uk

GAZEBO THEATRE COMPANY　T 01902 497222
The Town Hall, Church Street
Bilston, West Midlands WV14 0AP
F 01902 497244
E admin@gazebotie.org
W www.gazebotie.org

**GRANT, Derek
ORGANISATION LTD**　T 01202 855777
13 Beechwood Road, West Moors, Dorset BH22 0BN
E admin@derekgrant.co.uk
W www.derekgrant.co.uk

**GREENWICH & LEWISHAM YOUNG PEOPLE'S
THEATRE (GLYPT)**　T 020 8854 1316
The Tramshed, 51-53 Woolwich New Road
London SE18 6ES
F 020 8317 8595
E info@glypt.co.uk
W www.glypt.co.uk

GROUP 64 YOUTH THEATRE　T 020 8788 6935
Putney Arts Theatre, Ravenna Road
London SW15 6AW
E info@putneyartstheatre.org.uk
W www.putneyartstheatre.org.uk

GWENT THEATRE　T 01873 853167
The Drama Centre Pen-y-pound, Abergavenny
Monmouthshire NP7 5UD
F 01873 853910
E gwenttie@uwclub.net

**HALF MOON YOUNG
PEOPLE'S THEATRE**　T 020 7265 8138
43 White Horse Road, London E1 0ND
F 020 7709 8914
E admin@halfmoon.org.uk
W www.halfmoon.org.uk

HOXTON HALL　T 020 7684 0060
130 Hoxton Street, London N1 6SH
E getcreative@hoxtonhall.co.uk
W www.hoxtonhall.co.uk

IMAGE MUSICAL THEATRE　T 020 8743 9380
23 Sedgeford Road, Shepherd's Bush
London W12 0NA
F 020 8749 9294
E brian@imagemusicaltheatre.co.uk
W www.imagemusicaltheatre.co.uk

INDIGO MOON THEATRE　T 07855 328552
35 Waltham Court, Beverley, East Yorkshire HU17 9JF
E info@indigomoontheatre.com
W www.indigomoontheatre.com

INTERACT YOUTH THEATRE　T 07778 579005
New Writing for Young People
9 Carlton Close, Parkgate
Neston, Cheshire CH64 6TD
E interact@littleactorstheatre.com
W www.littleactorstheatre.com

INTERPLAY THEATRE　T 0113 263 8556
Armley Ridge Road, Leeds LS12 3LE
E info@interplayleeds.co.uk
W www.interplayleeds.co.uk

**KINETIC THEATRE
COMPANY LTD**　T 020 8286 2613
Suite H, The Jubilee Centre
Lombard Road, Wimbledon, London SW19 3TZ
F 020 8286 2645
E sarah@kinetictheatre.co.uk
W www.kinetictheatre.co.uk

KOMEDIA　T 01273 647101
44-47 Gardner Street, Brighton BN1 1UN
E info@komedia.co.uk
W www.komedia.co.uk

**LEAVENERS THE
(QUAKER COMMUNITY ARTS)**　T 0121 414 0099
1 The Lodge, 1046 Bristol Road
Birmingham B29 6LJ
E enquiries@leaveners.org
W www.leaveners.org

**LEIGHTON BUZZARD
YOUTH THEATRE**　T 01525 377222
6 Hillside Road, Leighton Buzzard LU7 3BU
T 07803 966369
E sarah.cavender@tesco.net
W www.lbyt.org

**LITTLE ACTORS
THEATRE COMPANY**　T 0151 336 4302
9 Carlton Close, Parkgate
Cheshire CH64 6TD
E mail@littleactorstheatre.com

M6 THEATRE COMPANY　T 01706 355898
Studio Theatre, Hamer CP School
Albert Royds Street, Rochdale OL16 2SU
F 01706 712601
E info@m6theatre.co.uk
W www.m6theatre.co.uk

MAGIC CARPET THEATRE　　T 01482 709939
18 Church Street, Sutton-on-Hull HU7 4TS
F 01482 787362
E admin@magiccarpettheatre.com
W www.magiccarpettheatre.com

**NATIONAL ASSOCIATION
OF YOUTH THEATRES (NAYT)**　　T 07515 651481
*Works with youth theatres & other organisations in
regional venues to host festivals & events*
c/o York Theatre Royal, St Leonard's Place
York YO1 7HD
E info@nayt.org.uk
W www.nayt.org.uk

**NATIONAL STUDENT
DRAMA FESTIVAL**　　T 020 7036 9027
Woolyard, 54 Bermondsey Street, London SE1 3UD
E info@nsdf.org.uk
W www.nsdf.org.uk

**NATIONAL YOUTH
MUSIC THEATRE**　　T 020 7802 0386
Adrian House, 27 Vincent Square, London SW1P 2NN
F 020 7821 0458
E enquiries@nymt.org.uk　　W www.nymt.org.uk

**NATIONAL YOUTH
THEATRE OF GREAT BRITAIN**　　T 020 7281 3863
Woolyard, 52 Bermondsey Street, London SE1 3UD
F 020 7036 9031
E info@nyt.org.uk
W www.nyt.org.uk

**NOTTINGHAM
PLAYHOUSE ROUNDABOUT**　　T 0115 873 6203
Nottingham Playhouse, Wellington Circus
Nottingham NG1 5AF
F 0115 947 5759
E kittyp@nottinghamplayhouse.co.uk

OILY CART　　T 020 8672 6329
*Creates work for the under 6s & for young people 3-19
with profound & multiple learning disabilities
(PMLD) or ASD*
Smallwood School Annexe, Smallwood Road
London SW17 0TW
F 020 8672 0792
E oilies@oilycart.org.uk　　W www.oilycart.org.uk

ONATTI PRODUCTIONS LTD　　T 01594 562033
Contact: Andrew Bardwell (Artistic Director)
The Old Chapel, Yorkley, Gloucestershire GL15 4SB
F 0870 1643629
E info@onatti.co.uk　　W www.onatti.co.uk

OUTLOUD PRODUCTIONS LTD　　T 07946 357521
TIE Company. Drama Workshops
21-23 Glendale Gardens, Leigh on Sea, Essex SS9 2PA
E info@outloudproductions.co.uk
W www.outloudproductions.co.uk

**PANDEMONIUM
TOURING PARTNERSHIP**　　T 029 2047 2060
228 Railway Street, Cardiff CF24 2NJ
T 07885 280635
E paul@pandemoniumtheatre.com

**PIED PIPER
THEATRE COMPANY**　　T/F 01428 684022
1 Lilian Place, Coxcombe Lane
Chiddingfold, Surrey GU8 4QA
E twpiedpiper@aol.com
W www.piedpipertheatre.co.uk

PILOT THEATRE　　T 01904 635755
Performance Work Across Platforms. National Touring
York Theatre Royal, St Leonard's Place, York YO1 7HD
E info@pilot-theatre.com
W www.pilot-theatre.com

PLAY HOUSE THE　　T 0121 464 5712
Language Alive!
Longmore Street, Birmingham B12 9ED
F 0121 464 5713
E info@theplayhouse.org.uk
W www.theplayhouse.org.uk

**PLAYTIME THEATRE
COMPANY**　　T 01227 266272
18 Bennells Avenue
Whitstable, Kent CT5 2HP
F 01227 266648
E playtime@dircon.co.uk
W www.playtimetheatre.co.uk

POLKA THEATRE　　T 020 8545 8323
240 The Broadway, Wimbledon SW19 1SB
F 020 8545 8365
E stephen@polkatheatre.com
W www.polkatheatre.com

Q20 THEATRE LTD　　T 01274 221360
Creative Arts Hub, Dockfield Road
Shipley, West Yorkshire BD17 7AD
F 0871 9942226
E info@q20theatre.co.uk

QUANTUM THEATRE　　T 020 8317 9000
*Contact: Michael Whitmore, Jessica Selous
(Artistic Directors)*
The Old Button Factory, 1-11 Bannockburn Road
Plumstead, London SE18 1ET
E office@quantumtheatre.co.uk
W www.quantumtheatre.co.uk

**RAINBOW BIGBOTTOM &
CO LTD**　　T 01494 771029
Parkview 1A, Stanley Avenue
Chesham, Bucks HP5 2JF
T 07778 106552
E lorrainebmays@aol.com
W www.mrpanda.co.uk

**RAINBOW THEATRE
LONDON EAST**　　T 020 8856 5023
56 Sutlej Road, Charlton, London SE7 7DB
F 07092 315384
E rainbowtheatrelondoneast@yahoo.co.uk
W www.rainbow-theatre.com

REDROOFS THEATRE COMPANY
Contact: By Post
The Novello Theatre, Sunninghill
Nr Ascot, Berkshire SL5 9NE
W www.novellotheatre.co.uk

ROYAL & DERNGATE　　T 01604 626222
19-21 Guildhall Road
Northampton NN1 1DP
E arts@royalandderngate.co.uk
W www.royalandderngate.co.uk

SCOTTISH YOUTH THEATRE　　T 0141 552 3988
The Old Sheriff Court, 105 Brunswick Street
Glasgow G1 1TF
E info@scottishyouththeatre.org
W www.scottishyouththeatre.org

**SHAKESPEARE 4 KIDZ
THEATRE COMPANY THE**　　T 01342 894548
Drewshearne Barn, Crowhurst Lane End
Oxted, Surrey RH8 9NT
F 01342 893754
E theatre@shakespeare4kidz.com
W www.shakespeare4kidz.com

SHAKESPEAREWORKS　　T/F 01865 241281
22 Chilswell Road, Oxford OX1 4PJ
E info@shakespeareworks.co.uk
W www.shakespeareworks.co.uk

**SHARED EXPERIENCE
YOUTH THEATRE** T 01865 305321
13 Riverside House
27-29 Vauxhall Grove, London SW8 1SY
F 020 7735 0374
E admin@sharedexperience.org.uk
W www.sharedexperience.org.uk

SHEFFIELD THEATRES TRUST T 0114 249 5999
Contact: Sue Burley (Education Administrator),
Dan Bates (Chief Executive)
55 Norfolk Street, Sheffield S1 1DA
F 0114 249 6003
E info@sheffieldtheatres.co.uk
W www.sheffieldtheatres.co.uk/creativedevelopmentprogramme

**SOLOMON THEATRE
COMPANY** T/F 01725 518760
Penny Black, High Street
Damerham, Fordingbridge, Hants SP6 3EU
E office@solomon-theatre.co.uk
W www.solomon-theatre.co.uk

SOUTH WEST YOUTH THEATRE T 07778 579005
New Writing for Young People. Based in London SW18
c/o 9 Carlton Close, Parkgate
Neston, Cheshire CH64 6TD
E swyt@littleactorstheatre.com
W www.littleactorstheatre.com

SPECTACLE THEATRE T 01443 430700
Coleg Morgannwg, Rhondda, Llwynypia
Tonypandy CF40 2TQ
F 01443 439640
E info@spectacletheatre.co.uk
W www.spectacletheatre.co.uk

**STOPWATCH THEATRE
COMPANY** T 023 8078 3800
Unit 318 Solent Business Centre, Millbrook Road West
Southampton SO15 0HW
E info@stopwatchtheatre.com
W www.stopwatchtheatre.com

**STORYTELLERS THEATRE
COMPANY THE** T 01253 839375
Bridge Farm, 249 Hawes Side Lane, Blackpool FY4 4AA
F 01253 792930
E admin@pendleproductions.co.uk
W www.pendleproductions.co.uk

SUPPORT ACT PRODUCTIONS T 07980 300927
Contact: Ian McCracken
197 Church Road, Northolt UB5 5BE
E info@supportact.co.uk
W www.supportact.co.uk

**TALEGATE THEATRE
PRODUCTIONS** T 01777 708333
5 Station Road, Retford, Nottinghamshire DN22 7DE
E info@talegatetheatre.co.uk
W www.talegatetheatre.co.uk

THEATR IOLO LTD T 029 2061 3782
The Old School Building, Cefn Road
Mynachdy, Cardiff CF14 3HG
F 029 2052 2225
E info@theatriolo.com   W www.theatriolo.com

THEATRE& LTD T 01484 532967
Church Hall, St James Road
Marsh, Huddersfield HD1 4QA
F 01484 532962
E cmitchell@theatreand.com
W www.theatreand.com

THEATRE ALIBI T/F 01392 217315
Adults & Young People
Emmanuel Hall, Emmanuel Road, Exeter EX4 1EJ
E info@theatrealibi.co.uk   W www.theatrealibi.co.uk

THEATRE CENTRE T 020 7729 3066
National Touring. New Writing for Young Audiences
Shoreditch Town Hall, 380 Old Street, London EC1V 9LT
F 020 7739 9741
E admin@theatre-centre.co.uk
W www.theatre-centre.co.uk

**THEATRE COMPANY
BLAH BLAH BLAH** T 0113 274 0030
The West Park Centre
Spen Lane, Leeds LS16 5BE
E cas@blahs.co.uk
W www.blahs.co.uk

THEATRE HULLABALOO T 01325 352004
The Meeting Rooms, 5 Skinner Gate
Darlington, County Durham DL3 7NB
F 01325 369404
E info@theatrehullabaloo.org.uk
W www.theatrehullabaloo.org.uk

THEATRE IS... T 01582 481221
The Hat Factory, 65-67 Bute Street
Luton, Bedfordshire LU1 2EY
E info@theatreis.org
W www.theatreis.org

THEATRE NA N'OG T 01639 641771
Unit 3, Millands
Road Industrial Estate, Neath SA11 1NJ
F 01639 647941
E drama@theatr-nanog.co.uk
W www.theatr-nanog.co.uk

THEATRE WORKOUT LTD T 020 8144 2290
13A Stratheden Road
Blackheath, London SE3 7TH
E enquiries@theatreworkout.co.uk
W www.theatreworkout.com

TICKLISH ALLSORTS SHOW T/F 01722 744949
57 Victoria Road, Wilton
Salisbury, Wiltshire SP2 0DZ
E garynunn@ntlworld.com
W www.ticklishallsorts.co.uk

TRICYCLE THEATRE T/F 020 7372 6611
Contact: Gillian Christie (Education Director)
269 Kilburn High Road, London NW6 7JR
E education@tricycle.co.uk
W www.tricycle.co.uk

UNICORN THEATRE T 020 7645 0500
147 Tooley Street, London SE1 2HZ
F 020 7645 0550
E jenny.skene@unicorntheatre.com
W www.unicorntheatre.com

**WEST YORKSHIRE
PLAYHOUSE** T 0113 213 7225
Touring Company
Playhouse Square, Quarry Hill, Leeds LS2 7UP
E gail.mcintyre@wyp.org.uk
W www.wyp.org.uk

WIZARD THEATRE T 0800 5832373
Contact: Leon Hamilton (Director), Emmy Bradbury
(Company Manager), Oliver Gray (Associate Producer)
175 Royal Crescent
Ruislip, Middlesex HA4 0PN
E admin@wizardtheatre.co.uk
W www.wizardtheatre.co.uk

**YOUNG SHAKESPEARE
COMPANY** T 020 8368 4828
Contact: Christopher Geelan, Sarah Gordon
(Artistic Directors)
213 Fox Lane, Southgate, London N13 4BB
E youngshakespeare@mac.com
W www.youngshakespeare.org.uk

AUSTRIA, VIENNA:
Vienna's English Theatre　　T/F 01304 813330
Main House Representative:
VM Theatre Productions Ltd, 16 The Street, Ash
Canterbury, Kent CT3 2HJ
E vanessa@vmtheatre.demon.co.uk
W www.englishtheatre.at

AUSTRIA, VIENNA:
Vienna's English Theatre　　T 020 8946 3400
School Tours Representative:
The European Production Co
15 Beverley Avenue, London SW20 0RL
E europeanproductions@virginmedia.com
W www.englishtheatre.at

DENMARK, COPENHAGEN:
The London Toast Theatre　　T 00 45 33228686
Contact: Vivienne McKee (Artistic Director),
Soren Hall (Administrator)
Kochsvej 18
DK-1812 Frb. C, Denmark
E mail@londontoast.dk
W www.londontoast.dk

FRANCE, LYON: Theatre From Oxford
(Touring Europe & Beyond)
Contact: Robert Southam. By Post
B.P. 10, F-42750 St-Denis-de-Cabanne
France
E theatre.oxford@virgin.net

FRANCE, PARIS:
ACT Company　　T 00 33 1 46562050
Contact: Andrew Wilson (Artistic Director),
Anne Wilson (Administrator)
25 Avenue Mal Leclerc, 92240 Malakoff, France
E andrew@actheatre.com
W www.actheatre.com

GERMANY, FRANKFURT AM MAIN: The English
Theatre Frankfurt　　T 00 49 69 24231615
Contact: Daniel Nicolai (Artistic & Managing Director)
Gallusanlage 7, 60329
Frankfurt am Main
Germany
F 00 49 69 24231614
E mail@english-theatre.de
W www.english-theatre.de

GERMANY, HAMBURG: The English Theatre of
Hamburg　　T 00 49 40 2277925
Contact: Robert Rumpf, Clifford Dean
Lerchenfeld 14, 22081 Hamburg
Germany
BO 00 49 40 2277089
W www.englishtheatre.de

GERMANY, TOURING GERMANY:
White Horse Theatre　　T 00 49 29 21339339
Contact: Peter Griffith, Michael Dray
Boerdenstrasse 17, 59494 Soest, Germany
F 00 49 29 21339336
E theatre@white-horse-theatre.eu
W www.whitehorse.de

HUNGARY, BUDAPEST:
Átrium Film-Theatre　　T 00 36 1 3179338
Contact: László Magács (Director)
Margit Körút 55, 1024 Budapest, Hungary
E info@atriumarts.hu
W www.atriumarts.hu

ICELAND, REYKJAVIK: Light Nights -
The Summer Theatre　　T 00 354 5519181
Contact: Kristine G. Magnus (Artistic Director)
The Travelling Theatre, Baldursgata 37
IS-101 Reykjavik, Iceland
E info@lightnights.com
W www.lightnights.com

ITALY, SANREMO: Theatrino & Melting Pot
Theatre - ACLE　　T 00 39 0184 506070
Via Roma 54, 18038 Sanremo (IM), Italy
F 00 39 0184 509996
E info@acle.org
W www.acle.org

SWITZERLAND, TANNAY:
Simply Theatre　　T 00 41 22 8600518
Chemin des Couleuvres 8B
1295 Tannay, Switzerland
F 00 41 22 8600519
E info@simplytheatre.com
W www.simplytheatre.com

UNITED KINGDOM, YORKLEY:
Onatti Productions Ltd　　T 01594 562033
Contact: Andrew Bardwell
The Old Chapel, Yorkley
Gloucestershire GL15 4SB
F 0870 1643629
E info@onatti.co.uk
W www.onatti.co.uk

ADELPHI T 020 7836 1166
411-412 Strand, London WC2R 0NS
BO 0844 4124651

ALDWYCH T 020 7836 5537
Aldwych, London WC2B 4DF
W www.aldwychtheatre.com

ALMEIDA T 020 7288 4900
Almeida Street, London N1 1TA
BO 020 7359 4404
E info@almeida.co.uk

AMBASSADORS T 020 7828 0600
West Street, London WC2H 9ND
BO 0844 8112334
E enquiries@theambassadorstheatre.co.uk
W www.theambassadorstheatre.co.uk

APOLLO T 020 7494 5834
Shaftesbury Avenue, London W1D 7EZ
BO 0844 4124658
E enquiries@nimaxtheatres.com
W www.nimaxtheatres.com

APOLLO VICTORIA T 020 7834 6318
17 Wilton Road, London SW1V 1LG
W www.apollovictorialondon.org.uk

ARTS T 020 7836 8463 (T/BO)
6-7 Great Newport Street, London WC2H 7JB
E info@artstheatrewestend.co.uk
W www.artstheatrewestend.co.uk

BARBICAN T 020 7628 3351
Barbican Centre, Stage Door
Silk Street, London EC2Y 8DS
BO 0845 1207511
E theatre@barbican.org.uk
W www.barbican.org.uk

BLOOMSBURY T 020 7679 2777
15 Gordon Street, London WC1H 0AH
BO 020 7388 8822
E admin@thebloomsbury.com
W www.thebloomsbury.com

BUSH T 020 8743 3584
7 Uxbridge Road, London W12 8LJ
BO 020 8743 5050
E info@bushtheatre.co.uk
W www.bushtheatre.co.uk

CAMBRIDGE T 020 7850 8710
Earlham Street, Seven Dials
Covent Garden, London WC2H 9HU
BO 020 7850 8715
W www.reallyuseful.com

CHARING CROSS T 020 7930 5868
Formerly New Players Theatre
The Arches, Off Villiers Street, London WC2N 6NL
E info@charingcrosstheatre.co.uk
W www.charingcrosstheatre.co.uk

**COLISEUM
(ENGLISH NATIONAL OPERA)** T 020 7836 0111
St Martin's Lane, London WC2N 4ES
BO 020 7845 9300
W www.eno.org

CRITERION T 020 7839 8811
2 Jermyn Street, Piccadilly, London SW1Y 4XA
BO 0844 8471778
E admin@criterion-theatre.co.uk
W www.criterion-theatre.co.uk

DOMINION T 020 7927 0900
268-269 Tottenham Court Road, London W1T 7AQ
BO 0844 8471775
W www.dominiontheatre.com

DONMAR WAREHOUSE T 020 7240 4882
41 Earlham Street, London WC2H 9LX
BO 0844 8717624
E office@donmarwarehouse.com
W www.donmarwarehouse.com

DRURY LANE T 020 7850 8790
Theatre Royal, Catherine Street, London WC2B 5JF
BO 020 7494 5060
W www.rutheatres.com

DUCHESS T 020 7632 9601
Catherine Street, London WC2B 5LA
BO 0844 4124659
E enquiries@nimaxtheatres.com

DUKE OF YORK'S T 020 7565 6500
St Martin's Lane, London WC2N 4BG
BO 0844 8717623

FORTUNE T 020 7010 7900
Russell Street, Covent Garden, London WC2B 5HH
BO 0844 8717627

GARRICK T 020 7520 5692
2 Charing Cross Road, London WC2H 0HH
BO 020 7520 5693
E enquiries@nimaxtheatres.com

GIELGUD T 020 7292 1320
Shaftesbury Avenue, London W1D 6AR
BO 0844 4825130

HACKNEY EMPIRE T 020 8510 4500
291 Mare Street, London E8 1EJ
BO 020 8985 2424
E info@hackneyempire.co.uk
W www.hackneyempire.co.uk

HAMMERSMITH APOLLO T 020 8563 3800
Queen Caroline Street, London W6 9QH
BO 0844 8444748
W www.hammersmithapollo.net

HAMPSTEAD T 020 7449 4200
Eton Avenue, Swiss Cottage, London NW3 3EU
BO 020 7722 9301
E info@hampsteadtheatre.com
W www.hampsteadtheatre.com

HAROLD PINTER T 020 7321 5300
Formerly Comedy Theatre. Ambassador Theatre Group
Panton Street, London SW1Y 4DN
BO 0870 0606637
E jaybourley@theambassadors.com

HER MAJESTY'S T 020 7850 8750
Haymarket, London SW1Y 4QL
BO 0844 4122707

LONDON PALLADIUM T 020 7850 8770
Argyll Street, London W1F 7TF
BO 0844 4122957

LYCEUM T 020 7420 8100
21 Wellington Street, London WC2E 7RQ
BO 0844 8713000

LYRIC T 020 7494 5840
29 Shaftesbury Avenue, London W1D 7ES
BO 0844 4124661
E enquiries@nimaxtheatres.com

LYRIC HAMMERSMITH T 0871 2211722 (T/BO)
Lyric Square, King Street, London W6 0QL
E enquiries@lyric.co.uk
W www.lyric.co.uk

NATIONAL T 020 7452 3333
South Bank, Upper Ground, London SE1 9PX
BO 020 7452 3000
W www.nationaltheatre.org.uk

NEW LONDON T 020 7242 9802
Drury Lane, London WC2B 5PW
BO 0844 4124654
E cuqui.rivera@reallyuseful.co.uk

NOEL COWARD T 020 7759 8011
Formerly Albery. A Delfont Mackintosh Theatre
St Martin's Lane, London WC2N 4AU
BO 0844 4825140

NOVELLO T 020 7759 9611
Formerly Strand
5 Aldwych, London WC2B 4LD
BO 0844 4825171

OLD VIC T 020 7928 2651
The Cut, London SE1 8NB
BO 0844 8717628
E ovtcadmin@oldvictheatre.com
W www.oldvictheatre.com

PALACE T 020 7434 0088
Shaftesbury Avenue, London W1D 5AY
BO 0844 7550016
W www.nimaxtheatres.com

PEACOCK T 020 7863 8268
For Administration see SADLER'S WELLS
Portugal Street, Kingsway, London WC2A 2HT
BO 0844 4124322
E info@sadlerswells.com
W www.sadlerswells.com

PHOENIX T 020 7438 9600
110 Charing Cross Road, London WC2H 0JP
BO 0844 8717615
E alicemiller@theambassadors.com

PICCADILLY T 020 7478 8800
Denman Street, London W1D 7DY
BO 020 7478 8805
E piccadillymanager@theambassadors.com

PLAYHOUSE T 020 7839 4292
Northumberland Avenue, London WC2N 5DE
BO 0844 8717631

PRINCE EDWARD T 020 7440 3021
28 Old Compton Street, London W1D 4HS
BO 0844 4825151
W www.delfontmackintosh.co.uk

PRINCE OF WALES T 020 7766 2100
Coventry Street, London W1D 6AS
BO 0844 4825115
E powmanagers@delmack.co.uk
W www.delfontmackintosh.co.uk

QUEEN'S T 020 7292 1350
Contact: Nicolas Shaw (Manager)
51 Shaftesbury Avenue
London W1D 6BA
BO 0844 4825160

REGENT'S PARK OPEN AIR T 0844 3753460
Inner Circle, Regent's Park, London NW1 4NU
BO 0844 8264242
W www.openairtheatre.com

RIVERSIDE STUDIOS T 020 8237 1000
Crisp Road, Hammersmith, London W6 9RL
BO 020 8237 1111
E info@riversidestudios.co.uk
W www.riversidestudios.co.uk

ROYAL COURT T 020 7565 5050
Sloane Square, London SW1W 8AS
BO 020 7565 5000
E info@royalcourttheatre.com
W www.royalcourttheatre.com

ROYAL OPERA HOUSE T 020 7240 1200
Bow Street, Covent Garden
London WC2E 9DD
BO 020 7304 4000

SADLER'S WELLS T 020 7863 8034
Rosebery Avenue, London EC1R 4TN
BO 0844 4124300
E info@sadlerswells.com
W www.sadlerswells.com

SAVOY T 020 7845 6050
Savoy Court, Strand
London WC2R 0ET
BO 0844 8717687
E savoytheatremanagement@theambassadors.com
W www.atgtickets.com

SHAFTESBURY T 020 7379 3345
Theatre of Comedy Company
210 Shaftesbury Avenue, London WC2H 8DP
BO 020 7379 5399
E info@shaftesburytheatre.com

SHAKESPEARE'S GLOBE T 020 7902 1400
21 New Globe Walk, Bankside, London SE1 9DT
BO 020 7401 9919
E info@shakespearesglobe.com
W www.shakespearesglobe.com

SHAW T 020 7666 9037
Contact: Artistic Director
100-110 Euston Road, London NW1 2AJ
BO 0844 2485075
E info@shaw-theatre.com
W www.shaw-theatre.com

SOHO T 020 7287 5060
21 Dean Street, London W1D 3NE
BO 020 7478 0100
E box1@sohotheatre.com
W www.sohotheatre.com

ST MARTIN'S T 020 7828 0600
West Street, London WC2H 9NZ
BO 0844 4991515
E enquiries@stmartinstheatre.co.uk
W www.the-mousetrap.co.uk

THEATRE ROYAL T 020 7930 8890
Haymarket, London SW1Y 4HT
BO 0845 4811870

TRICYCLE T 020 7372 6611
269 Kilburn High Road
London NW6 7JR
BO 020 7328 1000
E info@tricycle.co.uk
W www.tricycle.co.uk

VAUDEVILLE T 020 7632 9538
404 Strand, London WC2R 0NH
BO 0871 2970777

VICTORIA PALACE T 020 7828 0600
Victoria Street, London SW1E 5EA
BO 0844 2485000
E enquiries@victoriapalace.co.uk
W www.victoriapalace.co.uk

WYNDHAM'S T 020 7759 8077
Charing Cross Road, London WC2H 0DA
BO 0870 9500925

YOUNG VIC T 020 7922 2800
66 The Cut, London SE1 8LZ
BO 020 7922 2922
E info@youngvic.org
W www.youngvic.org

Jerwood Vanbrugh (183 seats)   **The Studio Theatre (200 seats)**
George Bernard Shaw (100 seats)   **The Club Theatre (45 seats)**
John Gielgud (70 seats)   **The Screen @ RADA (150 seats)**

www.rada.ac.uk/venues
+44 (0)20 7908 4822 | bookings@radaenterprises.org

ALBANY THE   BO 020 8692 4446
Douglas Way, Deptford, London SE8 4AG
E boxoffice@thealbany.org.uk   W www.thealbany.org.uk

ARCH 468 THEATRE STUDIO   T 07973 302908
Arch 468, 209A Coldharbour Lane, London SW9 8RU
E rebecca@arch468.com
W www.arch468.com

ARCOLA THEATRE   T 020 7503 1645
*Contact: Mehmet Ergen (Artistic Director), Leyla Nazli
(Executive Producer). Route: Victoria Line to Highbury &
Islington, then North London Line to Dalston Kingsland
(Main Line) - 5 min walk. Buses: 38 or 242 from West
End, 149 from London Bridge or 30, 67, 76, 243*
24 Ashwin Street, Dalston, London E8 3DL
BO 020 7503 1646
E info@arcolatheatre.com
W www.arcolatheatre.com

ARTSDEPOT   T 020 8369 5454
5 Nether Street, Tally Ho Corner
North Finchley, London N12 0GA
E info@artsdepot.co.uk
W www.artsdepot.co.uk

**BAC (BATTERSEA
ARTS CENTRE)**   BO 020 7223 2223
*Route: Victoria or Waterloo (Main Line) to Clapham
Junction then 5 min walk or Northern Line to Clapham
Common then 20 min walk*
Lavender Hill, London SW11 5TN
E mailbox@bac.org.uk
W www.bac.org.uk

BARONS COURT THEATRE   T 020 8932 4747
*'The Curtain's Up'. Route: Piccadilly or District Lines to
West Kensington or Barons Court*
28A Comeragh Road, West Kensington
London W14 9HR
E londontheatre@gmail.com
W www.offwestend.com

BATES, Tristan THEATRE   T 020 7632 8010
Contact: Ben Monks, Will Young (Creative Producers)
The Actors Centre, 1A Tower Street, London WC2H 9NP
BO 020 7240 6283
E tbt@tristanbatestheatre.co.uk
W www.tristanbatestheatre.co.uk

BECK THEATRE   T 020 8561 7506
*Route: Metropolitan Line to Uxbridge then buses 427 or
607, or Paddington (Main Line) to Hayes Harlington then
buses 90, H98 or 195 (10 min)*
Grange Road, Hayes, Middlesex UB3 2UE
BO 020 8561 8371
E enquiries@becktheatre.org.uk
W www.becktheatre.org.uk

BEDLAM THEATRE   BO 0131 225 9893
11B Bristo Place, Edinburgh EH1 1EZ
E info@bedlamtheatre.co.uk
W www.bedlamtheatre.co.uk

BIKE SHED THEATRE THE   T 01392 434169
162-163 Fore Street, Exeter EX4 3AT
E info@bikeshedtheatre.co.uk
W www.bikeshedtheatre.co.uk

BLACKHEATH HALLS   T 020 8318 9758
23 Lee Road, Blackheath, London SE3 9RQ
BO 020 8463 0100
E programming@blackheathhalls.com
W www.blackheathhalls.com

BLOOMSBURY THEATRE   T 020 7679 2777
Route: Tube to Euston, Euston Square or Warren Street
15 Gordon Street, Bloomsbury
London WC1H 0AH
BO 020 7388 8822
E admin@thebloomsbury.com
W www.thebloomsbury.com

BRENTWOOD THEATRE   T 01277 230833
*Contact: David Zelly (Production Manager). Route:
Liverpool Street (Main Line) to Shenfield, then 15 min walk*
15 Shenfield Road, Brentwood, Essex CM15 8AG
BO 01277 200305
E david@brentwood-theatre.org
W www.brentwood-theatre.org

BRIDEWELL THEATRE THE   T 020 7353 3331
*Route: Circle Line to St Paul's. City Thameslink Capital
Connect. 15 different bus routes*
St Bride Foundation, Bride Lane
Fleet Street, London EC4Y 8EQ
E info@sbf.org.uk
W www.bridewelltheatre.org

BROADWAY THE   T 020 8507 5610
Broadway, Barking IG11 7LS
BO 020 8507 5607
E admin@thebroadwaybarking.com
W www.thebroadwaybarking.com

**BROADWAY STUDIO
THEATRE THE**   T 020 8690 1000
*Contact: Martin Costello (Director).
Route: Charing Cross to Catford Bridge*
Catford, London SE6 4RU
BO 020 8690 0002
E martin@broadwaytheatre.org.uk
W www.broadwaytheatre.org.uk

**CALDER THEATRE
BOOKSHOP LTD**   T 020 7620 2900
*40 Seat Theatre Venue. Wide selection of plays on sale in
bookshop. Rehearsal space for hire*
51 The Cut, London SE1 8LF
E info@calderbook.com

CAMDEN PEOPLE'S THEATRE   T 020 7419 4841
*Route: Victoria or Northern Line to Euston or Warren
Street, Metropolitan or Circle Line to Euston Square
(2 min walk either way)*
58-60 Hampstead Road, London NW1 2PY
E admin@cptheatre.co.uk
W www.cptheatre.co.uk

CANAL CAFE THEATRE THE   T 020 7289 6056
Contact: Emma Taylor (Artistic Director)
The Bridge House, Delamere Terrace
Little Venice, London W2 6ND
BO 020 7289 6054
E mail@canalcafetheatre.com
W www.canalcafetheatre.com

CHARING CROSS THEATRE T 020 7930 5868
Formerly New Players Theatre
The Arches, Villiers Street
London WC2N 6NL
E info@charingcrosstheatre.co.uk
W www.charingcrosstheatre.co.uk

CHATS PALACE T 020 8533 0227
42-44 Brooksby's Walk, Hackney, London E9 6DF
E info@chatspalace.com
W www.chatspalace.co.uk

CHELSEA THEATRE T 020 7352 1967
Route: District or Circle Line to Sloane Square then short bus ride 11 or 22 down King's Road
World's End Place, King's Road, London SW10 0DR
E admin@chelseatheatre.org.uk
W www.chelseatheatre.org.uk

CHICKENSHED T 020 8351 6161
Contact: Mary Ward MBE (Artistic Director).
Route: Piccadilly Line to Oakwood, turn left outside tube & walk 8 min down Bramley Road or take 307 bus. Buses 298, 299, 699 or N19. Car parking available & easy access parking by reservation
Chase Side, Southgate, London N14 4PE
BO 020 8292 9222
E susanj@chickenshed.org.uk
W www.chickenshed.org.uk

CHRIST'S HOSPITAL THEATRE T 01403 247435
Contact: Melanie Bloor-Black (Director)
Horsham, West Sussex RH13 7LW
BO 01403 247434
E dps@christs-hospital.org.uk

CHURCHILL THE T 020 8290 8255
Contact: Chris Glover (General Manager)
High Street, Bromley, Kent BR1 1HA
BO 0844 8717620
W www.atgtickets.com/bromley

CLUB FOR ACTS & ACTORS THE T 020 7836 3172
Contact: Malcolm Knight (Concert Artistes Association).
Route: Piccadilly or Northern Line to Leicester Square then few mins walk
20 Bedford Street, London WC2E 9HP
E office@thecaa.org
W www.thecaa.org

COCKPIT THE T 020 7258 2925 (T/BO)
Contact: By e-mail (24/7)/Telephone (12-6pm).
Route: Tube to Marylebone/Edgware Road then short walk or bus 139 or 189 to Lisson Grove & 6, 8, 16, 18, 98, 332 or 414 to Edgware Road
Gateforth Street, Paddington, London NW8 8EH
E mail@thecockpit.org.uk
W www.thecockpit.org.uk

COLOUR HOUSE THEATRE THE T 020 8542 5511
Merton Abbey Mills, Watermill Way, London SW19 2RD
E info@colourhousetheatre.co.uk
W www.colourhousetheatre.co.uk

CORBETT THEATRE T 020 8508 5983
Route: Central Line (Epping Branch) to Debden then 6 min walk
East 15 Acting School, Hatfields
Rectory Lane, Loughton IG10 3RY
E east15@essex.ac.uk
W www.east15.ac.uk

COURTYARD THEATRE THE T 020 7729 2202 (T/BO)
Contact: June Abbott, Tim Gill (Joint Artistic Directors)
Bowling Green Walk, 40 Pitfield Street, London N1 6EU
E info@thecourtyard.org.uk
W www.thecourtyard.org.uk

CUSTARD FACTORY T 0121 224 7777
Gibb Street, Digbeth, Birmingham B9 4AA
E info@custardfactory.co.uk
W www.custardfactory.co.uk

DRILL HALL THE
See RADA: THE STUDIO THEATRE

EDINBURGH FESTIVAL FRINGE SOCIETY T 0131 226 0026
180 High Street, Edinburgh EH1 1QS
E admin@edfringe.com W www.edfringe.com

EDINBURGH UNIVERSITY THEATRE COMPANY
See BEDLAM THEATRE

EMBASSY THEATRE & STUDIOS T 020 7722 8183
Route: Jubilee Line to Swiss Cottage then 1 min walk
The Central School of Speech & Drama, 64 Eton Avenue
Swiss Cottage, London NW3 3HY
E enquiries@cssd.ac.uk W www.cssd.ac.uk

EPSOM PLAYHOUSE THE T 01372 742226
Contact: Elaine Teague (Assistant Manager).
Main Auditorium seats 450. Myers Studio seats 80
Ashley Avenue, Epsom, Surrey KT18 5AL
BO 01372 742555
E eteague@epsom-ewell.gov.uk
W www.epsomplayhouse.co.uk

ETCETERA THEATRE THE T 020 7482 4857
Hire Venue. In-house Productions
265 Camden High Street, London NW1 7BU
E etc@etceteratheatre.com
W www.etceteratheatre.com

FAIRFIELD HALLS T 020 8681 0821
Route: Victoria & London Bridge (Main Line) to East Croydon then 5 min walk
Ashcroft Theatre & Concert Hall, Park Lane
Croydon CR9 1DG
BO 020 8688 9291
E info@fairfield.co.uk W www.fairfield.co.uk

FINBOROUGH THEATRE T 020 7244 7439
Contact: Neil McPherson (Artistic Director).
Route: District or Piccadilly Line to Earls Court then 5 min walk. Buses 74, 328, C1, C3 then 3 min walk
118 Finborough Road, London SW10 9ED
BO 0844 8471652
E admin@finboroughtheatre.co.uk
W www.finboroughtheatre.co.uk

GATE THEATRE T 020 7229 5387
Route: Central, Circle or District Line to Notting Hill Gate (exit 3) then 1 min walk. Buses 23, 27, 28, 31, 52, 70, 94, 148, 328, 390, 452
11 Pembridge Road, Above Prince Albert Pub
Notting Hill, London W11 3HQ
BO 020 7229 0706
E boxoffice@gatetheatre.co.uk
W www.gatetheatre.co.uk

GREENWICH PLAYHOUSE T 020 8310 7276
Contact: Alice de Sousa
Head Office, 50 Openshaw Road, London SE2 0TE
BO 020 8858 9256
E boxoffice@galleontheatre.co.uk
W www.galleontheatre.co.uk

GREENWICH THEATRE T 020 8858 4447
Contact: James Haddrell (Executive Director).
Route: Jubilee Line (change Canary Wharf) then DLR to Greenwich Cutty Sark, 3 min walk or Charing Cross (Main Line) to Greenwich, 5 min walk
Crooms Hill, Greenwich, London SE10 8ES
BO 020 8858 7755
E info@greenwichtheatre.org.uk
W www.greenwichtheatre.org.uk

GUILDHALL SCHOOL OF MUSIC & DRAMA T 020 7628 2571
Route: Hammersmith & City, Circle or Metropolitan Line to Barbican or Moorgate (also served by Northern Line) then 5 min walk
Silk Street, Barbican, London EC2Y 8DT
E info@gsmd.ac.uk
W www.gsmd.ac.uk

HACKNEY EMPIRE THEATRE T 020 8510 4500
Route: North London Line to Hackney Central
291 Mare Street, Hackney, London E8 1EJ
BO 020 8985 2424
E info@hackneyempire.co.uk
W www.hackneyempire.com

HEN & CHICKENS THEATRE T 020 7704 2001
Route: Victoria Line or Main Line to Highbury & Islington directly opposite station
Unrestricted View
Above Hen & Chickens Theatre Bar
109 St Paul's Road, Islington, London N1 2NA
E henandchickens@aol.com
W www.henandchickens.com

ICA THEATRE T 020 7930 0493
No CVs. Venue only.
Route: Nearest stations Piccadilly & Charing Cross
The Mall, London SW1Y 5AH
BO 020 7930 3647
W www.ica.org.uk

IVY ARTS CENTRE THE BO 01483 444789
Stag Hill, Guildford GU2 7XH
E boxoffice@surrey.ac.uk
W www.gsauk.org

JACK STUDIO THEATRE THE T 020 8291 6354
410 Brockley Road, London SE4 2DH
E admin@brockleyjack.co.uk
W www.brockleyjack.co.uk

JACKSONS LANE T 020 8340 5226
269A Archway Road, London N6 5AA
E reception@jacksonslane.org.uk
W www.jacksonslane.org.uk

JERMYN STREET THEATRE T 020 7434 1443 (Admin)
Contact: Gene David Kirk (Artistic Director),
Penny Horner (General Manager)
16B Jermyn Street, London SW1Y 6ST
BO 020 7287 2875
E info@jermynstreettheatre.co.uk
W www.jermynstreettheatre.co.uk

KING'S HEAD THEATRE T 020 7226 8561
Contact: Adam Spreadbury-Maher (Artistic Director).
Route: Northern Line to Angel then 5 min walk. Approx halfway between Angel and Highbury & Islington tube stations
115 Upper Street, Islington, London N1 1QN
BO 020 7478 0160
E info@kingsheadtheatre.com
W www.kingsheadtheatre.com

KING'S LYNN CORN EXCHANGE T 01553 765565
Tuesday Market Place
King's Lynn, Norfolk PE30 1JW
BO 01553 764864
E entertainment_admin@west-norfolk.gov.uk
W www.kingslynncornexchange.co.uk

KOMEDIA T 01273 647101
Contact: Marina Kobler (Programmer)
44-47 Gardner Street, Brighton BN1 1UN
BO 01273 647100
E info@komedia.co.uk
W www.komedia.co.uk

LANDMARK ARTS CENTRE T 020 8977 7558
Ferry Road, Teddington, Middlesex TW11 9NN
E info@landmarkartscentre.org
W www.landmarkartscentre.org

LANDOR THEATRE THE T 020 7737 7276
Contact: Robert McWhir (Artistic Director),
Andrew Keates (Theatre Manager).
Route: Northern Line Clapham North then 2 min walk
70 Landor Road, London SW9 9PH
E info@landortheatre.co.uk
W www.landortheatre.co.uk

LEICESTER SQUARE THEATRE T 020 7534 1740
6 Leicester Place, London WC2H 7BX
BO 0844 8733433
E info@leicestersquaretheatre.com
W www.leicestersquaretheatre.com

LEIGHTON BUZZARD THEATRE T 0300 3008130
Lake Street, Leighton Buzzard, Bedfordshire LU7 1RX
BO 0300 3008125
E lbtboxoffice@centralbedfordshire.gov.uk
W www.leightonbuzzardtheatre.co.uk

LIBRARY THEATRE THE T 0114 273 4102
260 Seat Civic Theatre for Hire. Traditional 1930s Art Deco Style
Central Library, Tudor Square
Sheffield, South Yorkshire S1 1XZ
E philip.repper@sheffield.gov.uk
W www.sheffield.gov.uk/libraries/librarytheatre

LILIAN BAYLIS THEATRE T 020 7863 8065
For information see SADLER'S WELLS in Theatre: London section
Rosebery Avenue, London EC1R 4TN
BO 0844 8710090
E info@sadlerswells.com
W www.sadlerswells.com

LIVE THEATRE T 0191 261 2694
Broad Chare, Quayside, Newcastle upon Tyne NE1 3DQ
BO 0191 232 1232
E info@live.org.uk
W www.live.org.uk

LONDON THEATRE THE T 020 8694 1888
Lower Space, 443 New Cross Road
New Cross, London SE14 6TA
E thelondontheatre@live.co.uk
W www.thelondontheatre.com

LOST THEATRE T 020 7622 9208
208 Wandsworth Road, London SW8 2JU
E losttheatre@yahoo.co.uk
W www.losttheatre.co.uk

MADDERMARKET THEATRE T 01603 626560
Contact: Michael Lyas (General Manager)
St John's Alley, Norwich NR2 1DR
BO 01603 620917
E mmtheatre@btconnect.com
W www.maddermarket.co.uk

MENIER CHOCOLATE FACTORY T 020 7378 1712
53 Southwark Street, London SE1 1RU
BO 020 7378 1713
E office@menierchocolatefactory.com
W www.menierchocolatefactory.com

MILLFIELD ARTS CENTRE T 020 8887 7301
Route: Liverpool Street (Main Line) to Silver Street or tube to Turnpike Lane then bus 144 (15 min to Cambridge Roundabout)
Silver Street, London N18 1PJ
BO 020 8807 6680
E boxoffice@enfield.gov.uk
W www.millfieldartscentre.co.uk

NEW DIORAMA THEATRE THE   T 020 7916 5467
Hire Venue. Route: Circle & District Line to Great Portland Street then 1 min walk, or Victoria & Northern Line to Warren Street then 5 min walk
15-16 Triton Street, Regents Place, London NW1 3BF
W www.newdiorama.com

**NEW WIMBLEDON
THEATRE & STUDIO**   T 020 8545 7900
Route: Main Line or District Line to Wimbledon, then 3 min walk. Buses 57, 93, 155
The Broadway, Wimbledon, London SW19 1QG
BO 0844 8717646
W www.atgtickets.com/venue/new-wimbledon-theatre

NORTHBROOK THEATRE THE   BO 01903 606162
Contact: Theatre Co-ordinator
Northbrook College, Littlehampton Road
Worthing, West Sussex BN12 6NU
E box.office@nbcol.ac.uk
W www.northbrooktheatre.co.uk

NORWICH PUPPET THEATRE   T 01603 615564
St James, Whitefriars, Norwich NR3 1TN
BO 01603 629921
E info@puppettheatre.co.uk
W www.puppettheatre.co.uk

NOVELLO THEATRE THE   T 01344 620881
Redroofs Theatre Company. Route: Waterloo (Main Line) to Ascot then 1 mile from station
2 High Street, Sunninghill, Nr Ascot, Berkshire SL5 9NE

OLD RED LION THEATRE   T 020 7833 3053
Contact: Henry Filloux-Bennett, Nicholas Thompson (Artistic Directors). Route: Northern Line to Angel, then 1 min walk
418 St John Street, Islington, London EC1V 4NJ
BO 0844 4124307
E info@oldredliontheatre.co.uk

ORANGE TREE   T 020 8940 0141
*Contact: Sam Walters (Artistic Director).
Route: District Line, Waterloo (Main Line) or North London Line then virtually opposite station*
1 Clarence Street, Richmond TW9 2SA
BO 020 8940 3633
E admin@orangetreetheatre.co.uk

ORCHARD, DARTFORD THE   T 01322 220099
*Contact: Andrew Hill (Theatre Director).
Route: Charing Cross (Main Line) to Dartford*
Home Gardens, Dartford, Kent DA1 1ED
BO 01322 220000
E info@orchardtheatre.co.uk
W www.orchardtheatre.co.uk

OVAL HOUSE   T 020 7582 0080
Route: Northern Line to Oval then 1 min walk, or Victoria Line & Main Line to Vauxhall then 10 min walk
52-54 Kennington Oval, London SE11 5SW
BO 020 7582 7680
E info@ovalhouse.com   W www.ovalhouse.com

OVATION THEATRES LTD   T 020 8340 4256
Route: Northern Line to Highgate then 10 min walk. Buses 143, 210, 214, 271
Upstairs at the Gatehouse
Corner of Hampstead Lane/North Road
Highgate, London N6 4BD
BO 020 8340 3488
E events@ovationproductions.com
W www.upstairsatthegatehouse.com

PARK THEATRE
Route: 1 min walk from Finsbury Park via tube (Victoria/Piccadilly Lines), Main Line or bus
Clifton Terrace, Finsbury Park, London N4 3JP
E info@parktheatre.co.uk   W www.parktheatre.co.uk

PAVILION THEATRE   T 00 353 1 2312929
Marine Road, Dun Laoghaire, County Dublin, Ireland
E info@paviliontheatre.ie
W www.paviliontheatre.ie

PENTAMETERS   T 020 7435 3648
Route: Northern Line to Hampstead then 1 min walk. Buses 46, 268
(Theatre Entrance in Oriel Place)
28 Heath Street, London NW3 6TE
W www.pentameters.co.uk

PLACE THE   T 020 7121 1101
*Main London Venue for Contemporary Dance.
Route: Northern or Victoria Lines to Euston; Circle, Hammersmith & City, Metropolitan, Northern, Piccadilly or Victoria Lines to King's Cross St Pancras; Circle, Hammersmith & City or Metropolitan Lines to Euston Square; Piccadilly Line to Russell Square.
All within easy walking distance*
17 Duke's Road, London WC1H 9PY
BO 020 7121 1100
E theatre@theplace.org.uk
W www.theplace.org.uk

PLATFORM THEATRE
Central Saint Martins College of Arts & Design
University of the Arts London, Handyside Street
King's Cross, London N1C 4AA
E platformboxoffice@arts.ac.uk
W www.csm.arts.ac.uk/platform-theatre

PLEASANCE ISLINGTON   T 020 7619 6868
Contact: Anthony Alderson. Route: Piccadilly Line to Caledonian Road, turn left, walk 50 yds, turn left into North Road, 2 min walk. Buses 17, 91, 259, 393, N91
Carpenters Mews, North Road
(Off Caledonian Road), London N7 9EF
BO 020 7609 1800
E info@pleasance.co.uk
W www.pleasance.co.uk

POLKA THEATRE   T 020 8545 8323
Route: Waterloo (Main Line) or District Line to Wimbledon then 10 min walk. Northern Line to South Wimbledon then 10 min walk. Tram to Wimbledon, Buses 57, 93, 219, 493
240 The Broadway
Wimbledon SW19 1SB
BO 020 8543 4888
E stephen@polkatheatre.com
W www.polkatheatre.com

**PRINCESS THEATRE
HUNSTANTON**   T 01485 532252 (T/BO)
The Green, Hunstanton
Norfolk PE36 5AH
E admin@princesshunstanton.co.uk
W www.princesshunstanton.co.uk

PRINT ROOM THE   T 020 7221 6036
34 Hereford Road, Notting Hill
London W2 5AJ
E mail@the-print-room.org

PUTNEY ARTS THEATRE   T 020 8788 6943
Ravenna Road, Putney SW15 6AW
E info@putneyartstheatre.org.uk
W www.putneyartstheatre.org.uk

QUEEN'S THEATRE   T 01708 462362
*Contact: Bob Carlton (Artistic Director).
Route: Tube: District Line to Hornchurch. Train: Main Line to Romford or Gidea Park. Car: 15 miles from West End via A13, A1306 then A125, or A12 then A127*
Billet Lane, Hornchurch
Essex RM11 1QT
BO 01708 443333
E info@queens-theatre.co.uk
W www.queens-theatre.co.uk

QUESTORS THEATRE
EALING THE **T** 020 8567 0011
Route: Central or District Line to Ealing Broadway then
5 min walk. Buses 65, 83, 207, 427, 607, E2, E7, E8, E11
12 Mattock Lane
London W5 5BQ
BO 020 8567 5184
E jane@questors.org.uk
W www.questors.org.uk

RADA: THE CLUB THEATRE **T** 020 7908 4826
Malet Street, London WC1E 6ED
BO 020 7908 4800
E bookings@radaenterprises.org
W www.rada.ac.uk/venues

RADA: GBS THEATRE
(GEORGE BERNARD SHAW) **T** 020 7908 4826
Malet Street
London WC1E 6ED
BO 020 7908 4800
E bookings@radaenterprises.org
W www.rada.ac.uk/venues

RADA: GIELGUD, John
THEATRE **T** 020 7908 4826
Malet Street, London WC1E 6ED
BO 020 7908 4800
E bookings@radaenterprises.org
W www.rada.ac.uk/venues

RADA: JERWOOD
VANBRUGH THEATRE **T** 020 7908 4826
Malet Street, London WC1E 6ED
BO 020 7908 4800
E bookings@radaenterprises.org
W www.rada.ac.uk/venues

RADA: THE STUDIO
THEATRE **T** 020 7307 5060 (T/BO)
Formerly The Drill Hall
16 Chenies Street, London WC1E 7EX
E bookings@radaenterprises.org
W www.rada.ac.uk/venues

RED HEDGEHOG THE **T** 020 8348 8485 (Admin)
255-257 Archway Road
Highgate, London N6 5BS
BO 020 8348 5050
E theatre@theredhedgehog.co.uk
W www.theredhedgehog.co.uk

RED LADDER THEATRE
COMPANY LTD **T** 0113 245 5311
3 St Peter's Buildings
York Street, Leeds LS9 8AJ
E rod@redladder.co.uk
W www.redladder.co.uk

RICHMOND THEATRE **T** 020 8332 4500
Contact: Kate Wrightson (General Manager).
Route: 20 min from Waterloo (South West Trains) or
District Line to Richmond then 2 min walk
The Green, Richmond
Surrey TW9 1QJ
BO 0844 8717651
E richmondstagedoor@theambassadors.com
W www.atgtickets.com/richmond

RIDWARE THEATRE **T** 01889 504000
Contact: Alan & Margaret Williams. Venue only.
No resident performing company
Wheelwright's House
Pipe Ridware
Rugeley, Staffs WS15 3QL
E al@christmas-time.com
W www.ridwares.co.uk

RIVERSIDE STUDIOS **T** 020 8237 1000
Route: District, Piccadilly or Hammersmith & City Line to
Hammersmith then 5 min walk. Buses 9, 10, 27, 33, 72,
190, 209, 211, 266, 267, 283, 295, 391, 419
Crisp Road, London W6 9RL
BO 020 8237 1111
E info@riversidestudios.co.uk
W www.riversidestudios.co.uk

ROSE THEATRE, KINGSTON **T** 020 8546 6983
Contact: Stephen Unwin (Artistic Director),
Lisa Lepki (PA to Artistic Director)
24-26 High Street
Kingston upon Thames
Surrey KT1 1HL
E admin@rosetheatrekingston.org
W www.rosetheatrekingston.org

ROSEMARY BRANCH
THEATRE **T** 020 7704 6665
Route: Tube to Bank, Moorgate or Old Street (exit 5),
then 21, 76 or 141 bus to Baring Street, or 271 bus from
Highbury & Islington
2 Shepperton Road, London N1 3DT
E cecilia@rosemarybranch.co.uk
W www.rosemarybranch.co.uk

SAGE GATESHEAD THE **T** 0191 443 4661
St Mary's Square, Gateshead Quays
Gateshead NE8 2JR
F 0191 443 4551
E ticketoffice.mail@thesagegateshead.org
W www.thesagegateshead.org

SCOTTISH STORYTELLING
CENTRE **T** 0131 556 9579
Netherbow Theatre
43-45 High Street, Edinburgh EH1 1SR
E reception@scottishstorytellingcentre.com
W www.scottishstorytellingcentre.co.uk

SHAW THEATRE @ NOVOTEL
LONDON ST PANCRAS **T** 020 7666 9037
Contact: John-Jackson Almond (Artistic Director).
100-110 Euston Road, London NW1 2AJ
BO 0844 2485075
E info@shaw-theatre.com

SOUTH HILL PARK
ARTS CENTRE **T** 01344 484858
Route: Waterloo (Main Line) to Bracknell then 10 min bus
ride or taxi rank at station
Bracknell, Berkshire RG12 7PA
BO 01344 484123
E admin@southhillpark.org.uk
W www.southhillpark.org.uk

SOUTH LONDON THEATRE **T** 020 8670 3474
Route: Victoria or London Bridge (Main Line) to West
Norwood then 2 min walk, or Victoria Line to Brixton then
buses 2, 68, 196, 322
Bell Theatre & Prompt Corner
2A Norwood High Street
London SE27 9NS
E southlondontheatre@yahoo.co.uk
W www.southlondontheatre.co.uk

SOUTHWARK PLAYHOUSE **T** 020 7407 0234
Contact: Chris Smyrnios (Chief Executive).
Route: Trains to London Bridge, Jubilee/Northern Line
to London Bridge. Buses 47, 381, RV1, N47, N381. River
service to London Bridge City
Shipwright Yard
Corner of Tooley Street & Bermondsey Street
London SE1 2TF
E admin@southwarkplayhouse.co.uk
W www.southwarkplayhouse.co.uk

SPACE ARTS CENTRE THE T 020 7515 7799
269 Westferry Road, London E14 3RS
E info@space.org.uk
W www.space.org.uk

ST JOHN'S CHURCH T 020 7633 9819
Hosts Classical Concerts, Conferences, Large Meetings & Lectures
Waterloo Road
Southbank, London SE1 8TY
E bookings@stjohnswaterloo.org
W www.stjohnswaterloo.org

TABARD THEATRE T 020 8995 6035
Contact: Collin Hilton, Fred Perry (Artistic Directors), Simon Reilly (Theatre Manager)
2 Bath Road, London W4 1LW
E info@tabardtheatre.co.uk
W www.tabardtheatre.co.uk

THEATRE 503 T 020 7978 7040
Route: Victoria or Waterloo (Main Line) to Clapham Junction then 10 min walk, or buses 44, 319, 344, 345, or tube to South Kensington then buses 49 or 345 or tube to Sloane Square then bus 319
The Latchmere Pub
503 Battersea Park Road
London SW11 3BW
E info@theatre503.com
W www.theatre503.com

THEATRE ALIBI T/F 01392 217315
Emmanuel Hall, Emmanuel Road
Exeter EX4 1EJ
E info@theatrealibi.co.uk
W www.theatrealibi.co.uk

**THEATRE ROYAL
STRATFORD EAST** T 020 8534 7374
*Contact: Kerry Michael (Artistic Director).
Route: Central or Jubilee Lines, DLR, Overground or National Express trains to Stratford then 2 min walk*
Gerry Raffles Square
London E15 1BN
BO 020 8534 0310
E theatreroyal@stratfordeast.com
W www.stratfordeast.com

THEATRO TECHNIS T 020 7387 6617
*Contact: George Eugeniou (Artistic Director).
Route: Northern Line to Mornington Crescent then 3 min walk*
26 Crowndale Road, London NW1 1TT
E info@theatrotechnis.com
W www.theatrotechnis.com

TOBACCO FACTORY THEATRE T 0117 902 0345
Raleigh Road, Southville
Bristol BS3 1TF
E theatre@tobaccofactory.com
W www.tobaccofactorytheatre.com

TRICYCLE THEATRE T 020 7372 6611
Contact: Indhu Rubasingham (Artistic Director), Mary Lauder (General Manager). Route: Jubilee Line to Kilburn then 5 min walk or buses 16, 189, 32 pass the door, 98, 31, 206, 316, 332 pass nearby
269 Kilburn High Road
London NW6 7JR
BO 020 7328 1000
E admin@tricycle.co.uk
W www.tricycle.co.uk

TRON THEATRE T 0141 552 3748
63 Trongate, Glasgow G1 5HB
BO 0141 552 4267
E casting@tron.co.uk
W www.tron.co.uk

UNION THEATRE THE T 020 7261 9876
Contact: Sasha Regan (Artistic Director), Ben De Wynter (Associate Director), Steve Miller (Technical Director), Paul Flynn (All Casting Enquiries). Route: Jubilee Line to Southwark then 2 min walk
204 Union Street, Southwark
London SE1 0LX
E sasha@uniontheatre.freeserve.co.uk
W www.uniontheatre.biz

WAREHOUSE THEATRE T 020 8681 1257
Contact: Ted Craig (Artistic Director). Route: Adjacent to East Croydon (National Rail/Trams Interchange). Direct from Victoria (15 min), Clapham Junction (10 min) or by First Capital Connect from West Hampstead, Kentish Town, Kings Cross (25 min) & London Bridge (10 min)
Dingwall Road, Croydon CR0 2NF
BO 020 8680 4060
E ted@warehousetheatre.co.uk
W www.warehousetheatre.co.uk

WATERLOO EAST THEATRE T 020 7928 0060
Based at: Brad Street, London SE1 8TN
E info@waterlooeast.co.uk
W www.waterlooeast.co.uk

WATERLOO EAST THEATRE T 020 7928 0060
Admin: 3 Wooton Street
London SE1 8TG
E info@waterlooeast.co.uk
W www.waterlooeast.co.uk

WATERMANS T 020 8232 1019
40 High Street, Brentford TW8 0DS
BO 020 8232 1010
E info@watermans.org.uk
W www.watermans.org.uk

WESTRIDGE (OPEN CENTRE) T 01635 253322
Drawing Room Recitals
Star Lane, Highclere
Nr Newbury, Berkshire RG20 9PJ

WHITE BEAR THEATRE T 020 7793 9193
*Favours New Writing.
Route: Northern Line to Kennington (2 min walk)*
138 Kennington Park Road
London SE11 4DJ
E info@whitebeartheatre.co.uk
W www.whitebeartheatre.co.uk

WILTON'S MUSIC HALL T 020 7702 9555
Route: Tube: Under 10 min walk from Aldgate East (exit for Leman Street)/Tower Hill. DLR: Shadwell or Tower Gateway. Car: Follow the yellow AA signs to Wilton's Music Hall from the Highway, Aldgate or Tower Hill
Graces Alley
Off Ensign Street
London E1 8JB
W www.wiltons.org.uk

WIMBLEDON STUDIO THEATRE
See NEW WIMBLEDON THEATRE & STUDIO

WYCOMBE SWAN T 01494 514444
St Mary Street, High Wycombe
Buckinghamshire HP11 2XE
BO 01494 512000
E enquiries@wycombeswan.co.uk
W www.wycombeswan.co.uk

WYVERN THEATRE T 01793 535534
Theatre Square, Swindon
Wiltshire SN1 1QN
BO 01793 524481
E info@wyverntheatre.org.uk
W www.wyverntheatre.org.uk

ABERDEEN:
His Majesty's Theatre   T 0845 2708200
Rosemount Viaduct, Aberdeen AB25 1GL
BO 01224 641122
E hmtinfo@aberdeenperformingarts.com
W www.boxofficeaberdeen.com

ABERYSTWYTH:
Aberystwyth Arts Centre   T 01970 622882
Penglais, Aberystwyth, Ceredigion SY23 3DE
BO 01970 623232
E ggo@aber.ac.uk   W www.aber.ac.uk/artscentre

BACUP: Royal Court Theatre   BO 01706 874080
Rochdale Road, Bacup OL13 9NR
E vicechairman@brct.co   W www.brct.co

BASINGSTOKE:
The Haymarket Theatre   T 01256 819797
Wote Street, Basingstoke RG21 7NW
BO 01256 844244
E box.office@anvilarts.org.uk
W www.anvilarts.org.uk

BATH: Theatre Royal   T 01225 448815
Sawclose, Bath BA1 1ET
BO 01225 448844
E forename.surname@theatreroyal.org.uk
W www.theatreroyal.org.uk

BELFAST: Grand Opera House   T 028 9024 0411
Great Victoria Street, Belfast BT2 7HR
BO 028 9024 1919
E info@goh.co.uk
W www.goh.co.uk

BILLINGHAM: Forum Theatre   T 01642 551389
Town Centre, Billingham TS23 2LJ
E forumtheatre@btconnect.com
W www.forumtheatrebillingham.co.uk

BIRMINGHAM: Hippodrome   T 0870 7305555
Hurst Street, Birmingham B5 4TB
BO 0844 3385000
W www.birminghamhippodrome.com

BIRMINGHAM:
New Alexandra Theatre   T 0121 230 9070
Station Street, Birmingham B5 4DS
BO 0844 8713011
W www.atgtickets.com/birmingham

BLACKPOOL: Grand Theatre   T 01253 290111
33 Church Street, Blackpool FY1 1HT
BO 01253 290190
E admin@blackpoolgrand.co.uk
W www.blackpoolgrand.co.uk

BLACKPOOL: Opera House   T 01253 625252
Church Street, Blackpool FY1 1HW
BO 0844 8561111
W www.blackpoollive.com

BOURNEMOUTH:
Pavilion Theatre   T 01202 456400
Westover Road, Bournemouth BH1 2BU
BO 0844 5763000
W www.bic.co.uk

BRADFORD: Alhambra Theatre   T 01274 432375
Morley Street, Bradford BD7 1AJ
BO 01274 432000
E administration@oes.bradford.gov.uk
W www.bradford-theatres.co.uk

BRADFORD: Theatre in the Mill   T 01274 233185
University of Bradford, Shearbridge Road
Bradford BD7 1DP
BO 01274 233200
E theatre@bradford.ac.uk
W www.bradford.ac.uk/theatre

BRIGHTON:
Brighton Dome & Festivals Ltd   T 01273 700747
The Dome, Corn Exchange & Pavilion Theatres
12A Pavilion Buildings, Castle Square, Brighton BN1 1EE
BO 01273 709709
E info@brightondome.org
W www.brightondome.org

BRIGHTON:
Theatre Royal Brighton   T 01273 764400
New Road, Brighton BN1 1SD
BO 0844 8717650
W www.atgtickets.com/brighton

BRISTOL: Bristol Hippodrome   T 0117 302 3310
St Augustines Parade, Bristol BS1 4UZ
BO 0844 8713012
W www.atgtickets.com/bristol

BROXBOURNE:
Broxbourne Civic Hall   BO 01992 441946
High Street, Hoddesdon, Herts EN11 8BE
E civic.leisure@broxbourne.gov.uk
W www.broxbourne.gov.uk/whatson

BURY ST EDMUNDS:
Theatre Royal   T 01284 829944
Westgate Street, Bury St Edmunds IP33 1QR
BO 01284 769505
E admin@theatreroyal.org
W www.theatreroyal.org

BUXTON: Buxton Opera House &
Pavilion Arts Centre   T 01298 72050
Water Street, Buxton SK17 6XN
BO 0845 1272190
E admin@boh.org.uk
W www.buxtonoperahouse.org.uk

CAMBERLEY:
The Camberley Theatre   BO 01276 707600
Knoll Road, Camberley, Surrey GU15 3SY
E camberley.theatre@surreyheath.gov.uk
W www.camberleytheatre.biz

CAMBRIDGE: Cambridge Arts
Theatre Trust Ltd   T 01223 578904
6 St Edward's Passage, Cambridge CB2 3PJ
BO 01223 503333
E info@cambridgeartstheatre.com
W www.cambridgeartstheatre.com

CAMBRIDGE: Mumford Theatre   T 01223 417748
Anglia Ruskin University, East Road, Cambridge CB1 1PT
BO 0845 1962320
E mumford@anglia.ac.uk

CANTERBURY: Gulbenkian   BO 01227 769075
Theatre & Cinema
University of Kent, Canterbury CT2 7NB
E boxoffice@kent.ac.uk
W www.thegulbenkian.co.uk

CANTERBURY:
The Marlowe Theatre   BO 01227 787787
The Friars, Canterbury, Kent CT1 2AS
E info@marlowetheatre.com
W www.marlowetheatre.com

CARDIFF: New Theatre   T 029 2087 8787
Park Place, Cardiff CF10 3LN
BO 029 2087 8889
E ntmailings@cardiff.gov.uk
W www.newtheatrecardiff.co.uk

CARDIFF:
Wales Millennium Centre   T 029 2063 6400
Bute Place, Cardiff CF10 5AL
BO 029 2063 6464
E stagedoor@wmc.org.uk   W www.wmc.org.uk

CHELTENHAM:
Everyman Theatre　　　**T** 01242 512515
Regent Street, Cheltenham GL50 1HQ
BO 01242 572573
E admin@everymantheatre.org.uk
W www.everymantheatre.org.uk

CHICHESTER:
Festival Theatre　　　**T** 01243 784437
Oaklands Park, Chichester PO19 6AP
BO 01243 781312
E admin@cft.org.uk　　　**W** www.cft.org.uk

CRAWLEY: The Hawth　　　**T** 01293 552941
Hawth Avenue, Crawley, West Sussex RH10 6YZ
BO 01293 553636
E hawth@parkwoodtheatres.co.uk
W www.hawth.co.uk

CREWE: Lyceum Theatre　　　**T** 01270 686774
Heath Street, Crewe CW1 2DA
BO 01270 686777
E lyceum.theatre@cheshireeast.gov.uk

DARLINGTON: Civic Theatre　　　**T** 01325 387775
Parkgate, Darlington DL1 1RR
BO 01325 486555
E info@darlingtonarts.gov.uk
W www.darlingtonarts.co.uk

DERBY: Derby Theatre　　　**T** 01332 593900
15 Theatre Walk, St Peters Quarter, Derby DE1 2NF
E tickets@derbytheatre.co.uk
W www.derbytheatre.co.uk

DUBLIN: Gaiety Theatre　　　**T** 00 353 1 6795622
South King Street, Dublin 2, Ireland
BO 0818 719388
E info@gaietytheatre.com
W www.gaietytheatre.com

DUBLIN: Gate Theatre　　　**T** 00 353 1 8744368
1 Cavendish Row, Dublin 1, Ireland
BO 00 353 1 8744045
E info@gate-theatre.ie
W www.gate-theatre.ie

DUBLIN:
The Olympia Theatre　　　**T** 00 353 1 6725883
72 Dame Street, Dublin 2, Ireland
BO 00 353 1 6793323
E info@olympia.ie
W www.olympia.ie

EASTBOURNE:
Congress Theatre　　　**T** 01323 415500
Admin Office: Winter Garden, Compton Street
Eastbourne BN21 4BP
BO 01323 412000
E theatres@eastbourne.gov.uk
W www.eastbournetheatres.co.uk

EASTBOURNE:
Devonshire Park Theatre　　　**T** 01323 415500
Admin Office: Winter Garden, Compton Street
Eastbourne BN21 4BP
BO 01323 412000
E theatres@eastbourne.gov.uk
W www.eastbournetheatres.co.uk

EDINBURGH: King's Theatre　　　**T** 0131 662 1112
2 Leven Street, Edinburgh EH3 9LQ
BO 0131 529 6000
E empire@edtheatres.com
W www.edtheatres.com

EDINBURGH: Playhouse Theatre T 0131 524 3333
18-22 Greenside Place, Edinburgh EH1 3AA
BO 0844 8713014
E edinburghadministrators@theambassadors.com
W www.atgtickets.com/edinburgh

GLASGOW: King's Theatre　　　**T** 0141 240 1300
297 Bath Street, Glasgow G2 4JN
BO 0844 8717648
E glasgowstagedoor@theambassadors.com
W www.atgtickets.com

GLASGOW: Theatre Royal　　　**T** 0141 332 3321
282 Hope Street, Glasgow G2 3QA
BO 0844 8717647
W www.atgtickets.com/glasgow

GRAYS THURROCK:
Thameside Theatre　　　**T** 01375 413981
Orsett Road, Grays Thurrock RM17 5DX
BO 0845 3005264
E thameside.theatre@thurrock.gov.uk
W www.thurrock.gov.uk/theatre

HARLOW: Harlow Playhouse　　　**T** 01279 446760
Playhouse Square, Harlow CM20 1LS
BO 01279 431945
E playhouse@harlow.gov.uk
W www.playhouseharlow.com

HARROGATE:
Harrogate International Centre　　　**T** 01423 500500
Kings Road, Harrogate HG1 5LA
BO 0845 1308840
E sales@harrogateinternationalcentre.co.uk
W www.harrogateinternationalcentre.co.uk

HASTINGS: White Rock Theatre　　　**T** 01424 462283
White Rock, Hastings TN34 1JX
BO 01424 462288
E enquiries@whiterocktheatre.org.uk
W www.whiterocktheatre.org.uk

HAYES: Beck Theatre　　　**T** 020 8561 7506
Grange Road, Hayes, Middlesex UB3 2UE
BO 020 8561 8371
E enquiries@becktheatre.org.uk
W www.becktheatre.org.uk

HIGH WYCOMBE:
Wycombe Swan　　　**T** 01494 514444
St Mary Street, High Wycombe HP11 2XE
BO 01494 512000
E enquiries@wycombeswan.co.uk
W www.wycombeswan.co.uk

HUDDERSFIELD:
Lawrence Batley Theatre　　　**T** 01484 425282
Queen's Square, Queen Street, Huddersfield HD1 2SP
BO 01484 430528
E theatre@thelbt.org
W www.thelbt.org

HULL: Hull New Theatre　　　**T** 01482 613818
Kingston Square, Hull HU1 3HF
BO 01482 300300
E theatre.management@hullcc.gov.uk
W www.hullcc.gov.uk

HULL: Hull Truck Theatre　　　**T** 01482 224800
50 Ferensway, Hull HU2 8LB
BO 01482 323638
E admin@hulltruck.co.uk
W www.hulltruck.co.uk

ILFORD: Kenneth More Theatre T 020 8553 4464
Oakfield Road, Ilford IG1 1BT
BO 020 8553 4466
E kmtheatre@aol.com
W www.kmtheatre.co.uk

IPSWICH: Sir John Mills Theatre T 01473 218202
Eastern Angles Theatre Company
Gatacre Road, Ipswich IP1 2LQ
BO 01473 211498
E admin@easternangles.co.uk
W www.easternangles.co.uk

JERSEY: Jersey Opera House   T 01534 511100
Gloucester Street, St Helier
Jersey JE2 3QR
BO 01534 511115
E admin@jerseyoperahouse.co.uk
W www.jerseyoperahouse.co.uk

KINGSTON: Rose Theatre   T 020 8546 6983
24-26 High Street, Kingston Upon Thames
Surrey KT1 1HL
F 020 8546 8783
E admin@rosetheatrekingston.org
W www.rosetheatrekingston.org

KIRKCALDY:
Adam Smith Theatre   T 01592 583301
Bennochy Road, Kirkcaldy KY1 1ET
BO 01592 583302
E boxoffice.adamsmith@onfife.com

LEATHERHEAD:
The Leatherhead Theatre   T 01372 365130
7 Church Street, Leatherhead, Surrey KT22 8DN
BO 01372 365141
E info@the-theatre.org
W www.the-theatre.org

LEEDS:
City Varieties Music Hall   T 0113 391 7777
Swan Street, Leeds LS1 6LW
BO 0113 243 0808
E info@cityvarieties.co.uk
W www.cityvarieties.co.uk

LEEDS:
Grand Theatre & Opera House   T 0113 245 6014
46 New Briggate, Leeds LS1 6NZ
BO 0844 8482705
E boxoffice@leedsgrandtheatre.com
W www.leedsgrandtheatre.com

LICHFIELD: The Lichfield Garrick   T 01543 412110
Castle Dyke, Lichfield WS13 6HR
BO 01543 412121
E garrick@lichfieldgarrick.com
W www.lichfieldgarrick.com

LINCOLN: Theatre Royal   T 01522 519999
Clasketgate, Lincoln LN2 1JJ
E boxoffice@lincolntheatreroyal.com
W www.lincolntheatreroyal.com

LIVERPOOL: Empire Theatre   T 0151 702 7320
Lime Street, Liverpool L1 1JE
BO 0844 8713017
W www.atgtickets.com/liverpool

LLANDUDNO: Venue Cymru   T 01492 879771
Promenade, Llandudno, Conwy, North Wales LL30 1BB
BO 01492 872000
E info@venuecymru.co.uk
W www.venuecymru.co.uk

MALVERN: Malvern Theatres   T 01684 569256
Festival & Forum Theatres
Grange Road, Malvern WR14 3HB
BO 01684 892277
E post@malvern-theatres.co.uk
W www.malvern-theatres.co.uk

MANCHESTER:
O2 Apollo Manchester   T 0161 273 6921
Stockport Road, Ardwick Green, Manchester M12 6AP
BO 0844 4777677
E o2apollomanchester@livenation.com
W www.o2apollomanchester.co.uk

MANCHESTER: Opera House   T 0161 828 1700
Quay Street, Manchester M3 3HP
BO 0844 8713018
W www.palaceandoperahouse.org.uk

MANCHESTER: Palace Theatre   T 0161 245 6600
Oxford Street, Manchester M1 6FT
BO 0844 8713019
E manchesterstagedoor@theambassadors.com
W www.palaceandoperahouse.org.uk

MARGATE:
Theatre Royal Margate   T 01843 293397
Addington Street, Margate, Kent CT9 1PW
BO 0845 1301786
W www.theatreroyalmargate.com

MILTON KEYNES:
Milton Keynes Theatre   T 01908 547500
500 Marlborough Gate
Central Milton Keynes MK9 3NZ
BO 0844 8717652
W www.atgtickets.com/miltonkeynes

NEWARK: Palace Theatre   T 01636 655750
Appletongate, Newark NG24 1JY
BO 01636 655755
E carys.coultonjones@nsdc.info
W www.palacenewark.com

NEWCASTLE UPON TYNE: Northern Stage
(Theatrical Productions) Ltd   T 0191 242 7200
Barras Bridge
Newcastle upon Tyne NE1 7RH
BO 0191 230 5151
E info@northernstage.co.uk
W www.northernstage.co.uk

NEWCASTLE UPON TYNE:
Theatre Royal   T 0191 244 2500
100 Grey Street, Newcastle upon Tyne NE1 6BR
BO 0844 8112121
W www.theatreroyal.co.uk

NORTHAMPTON:
Royal & Derngate Theatres   T 01604 626222
19-21 Guildhall Road, Northampton NN1 1DP
BO 01604 624811
E steve.scrivens@royalandderngate.co.uk
W www.royalandderngate.co.uk

NORWICH:
Norwich Theatre Royal   T 01603 598500
Theatre Street, Norwich NR2 1RL
BO 01603 630000
W www.theatreroyalnorwich.co.uk

NOTTINGHAM: Royal Centre   T 0115 989 5500
Theatre Royal & Royal Concert Hall
Theatre Square
Nottingham NG1 5ND
BO 0115 989 5555
E enquiry@royalcentre-nottingham.co.uk
W www.royalcentre-nottingham.co.uk

OXFORD: New Theatre   T 01865 320760
George Street, Oxford OX1 2AG
BO 0844 8713020
E oxfordstagedoor@theambassadors.com

OXFORD: Oxford Playhouse   T 01865 305300
11-12 Beaumont Street, Oxford OX1 2LW
BO 01865 305305
E admin@oxfordplayhouse.com
W www.oxfordplayhouse.com

POOLE: Lighthouse,
Poole's Centre for the Arts   BO 0844 4068666
Kingland Road, Poole BH15 1UG
W www.lighthousepoole.co.uk

READING: The Hexagon   T 0118 937 2123
Queen's Walk, Reading RG1 7UA
BO 0118 960 6060
E boxoffice@readingarts.com
W www.readingarts.com

RICHMOND, N YORKS:
Georgian Theatre Royal   T 01748 823710
Victoria Road, Richmond, North Yorkshire DL10 4DW
BO 01748 825252
E admin@georgiantheatreroyal.co.uk
W www.georgiantheatreroyal.co.uk

RICHMOND, SURREY:
Richmond Theatre   T 020 8332 4500
The Green, Richmond, Surrey TW9 1QJ
BO 0844 8717651
E richmondstagedoor@theambassadors.com
W www.atgtickets.com/richmond

ROCHDALE:
Gracie Fields Theatre   T 01706 716689
Hudsons Walk, Rochdale
Lancashire OL11 5EF
E enquiries@graciefieldstheatre.com
W www.graciefieldstheatre.com

SHEFFIELD:
Sheffield Theatres Trust   T 0114 249 5999
Crucible, Lyceum & Crucible Studio
55 Norfolk Street, Sheffield S1 1DA
BO 0114 249 6000
E info@sheffieldtheatres.co.uk
W www.sheffieldtheatres.co.uk

SHERINGHAM:
The Little Theatre   T 01263 822117
2 Station Road, Sheringham
Norfolk NR26 8RE
BO 01263 822347
E enquiries@sheringhamlittletheatre.com
W www.sheringhamlittletheatre.com

SOMERSET: Warehouse Theatre   T 01460 57857
Brewery Lane, Ilminster, Somerset TA19 9AD
E annabowerman4@aol.com
W www.thewarehousetheatre.org.uk

SOUTHAMPTON:
The Mayflower Theatre   T 023 8071 1800
Empire Lane, Southampton SO15 1AP
BO 023 8071 1811
E info@mayflower.org.uk
W www.mayflower.org.uk

SOUTHEND: Southend Theatres   T 01702 390657
Cliffs Pavilion, Palace Theatre & Dixon Studio
Cliffs Pavilion, Station Road
Westcliff-on-Sea, Essex SS0 7RA
BO 01702 351135
E info@southendtheatres.org.uk
W www.southendtheatres.org.uk

ST ALBANS: Abbey Theatre   T 01727 847472
Holywell Hill, St Albans AL1 2DL
BO 01727 857861
E manager@abbeytheatre.org.uk
W www.abbeytheatre.org.uk

ST ALBANS: Alban Arena   T 01727 861078
Civic Centre, St Albans AL1 3LD
BO 01727 844488
E alban.arena@leisureconnection.co.uk
W www.alban-arena.co.uk

ST HELENS: Theatre Royal   T 01744 756333
Corporation Street, St Helens WA10 1LQ
BO 01744 756000
E info@sthelenstheatreroyal.co.uk
W www.sthelenstheatreroyal.com

STAFFORD:
Stafford Gatehouse Theatre   T 01785 253595
Eastgate Street, Stafford ST16 2LT
BO 01785 254653
E gatehouse@staffordbc.gov.uk
W www.staffordgatehousetheatre.co.uk

STEVENAGE:
Gordon Craig Theatre   T 01438 363200 (T/BO)
Stevenage Arts & Leisure Centre, Lytton Way
Stevenage SG1 1LZ
E gordoncraig@stevenage-leisure.co.uk
W www.gordon-craig.co.uk

SUNDERLAND:
Sunderland Empire   T 0191 566 1040 (Admin)
High Street West
Sunderland SR1 3EX
BO 0844 8713022
E sunderlandboxoffice@theambassadors.com
W www.atgtickets.com/sunderland

SWANAGE: Mowlem Theatre   BO 01929 422239
Shore Road, Swanage BH19 1DD
E mowlem.theatre@gmail.com

TAMWORTH: Assembly Rooms   T 01827 709619
Corporation Street
Tamworth B79 7DN
BO 01827 709618
E assemblyrooms@tamworth.gov.uk
W www.tamworthassemblyrooms.gov.uk

TEWKESBURY:
The Roses Theatre   T 01684 290734 (Admin)
Sun Street, Tewkesbury GL20 5NX
BO 01684 295074
E admin@rosestheatre.org
W www.rosestheatre.org

TORQUAY:
Babbacombe Theatre   BO 01803 328385
Babbacombe Downs, Torquay TQ1 3LU
E info@babbacombe-theatre.com
W www.babbacombe-theatre.com

TORQUAY: Princess Theatre   T 01803 206360
Torbay Road, Torquay TQ2 5EZ
BO 0844 8713023
E wendybennett@theambassadors.com
W www.atgtickets.com/torquay

TRURO: Hall For Cornwall   T 01872 321971
Black Quay, Truro, Cornwall TR1 2LL
BO 01872 262466
E admin@hallforcornwall.org.uk
W www.hallforcornwall.co.uk

WINCHESTER: Theatre Royal   T 01962 844600
21-23 Jewry Street, Winchester SO23 8SB
BO 01962 840440
E comms@theatreroyalwinchester.co.uk
W www.theatreroyalwinchester.co.uk

WORCESTER: Swan Theatre   T 01905 726969
The Moors, Worcester WR1 3ED
BO 01905 611427
E chris@worcesterlive.co.uk
W www.worcesterlive.co.uk

WORTHING: Connaught Theatre, Pavilion
Theatre & The Assembly Hall   T 01903 231799
Union Place, Worthing BN11 1LG
BO 01903 206206
E theatres@worthing.gov.uk
W www.worthingtheatres.co.uk

YEOVIL: Octagon Theatre   T 01935 845900
Hendford, Yeovil BA20 1UX
BO 01935 422884
E octagontheatre@southsomerset.gov.uk
W www.octagon-theatre.co.uk

YORK: Grand Opera House   T 01904 678700
Cumberland Street, York YO1 9SW
BO 0844 8713024
E yorkboxoffice@theambassadors.com
W www.atgtickets.com/york

AUTHENTIC PUNCH & JUDY   T/F 020 8300 3579
Contact: John Styles. Booths. Presentations. Puppets
42 Christchurch Road
Sidcup, Kent DA15 7HQ
W www.johnstylesentertainer.co.uk

BUCKLEY, Simon
Freelance Puppeteer
E simon@simonbuckley.co.uk
W www.simonbuckley.co.uk

COMPLETE WORKS THE   T 020 7377 0280
Contact: Phil Evans (Artistic Director)
The Old Truman Brewery
91 Brick Lane, London E1 6QL
F 020 7247 7405
E info@tcw.org.uk
W www.tcw.org.uk

**CORNELIUS & JONES
ORIGINAL PRODUCTIONS**   T/F 01908 612593
49 Carters Close, Sherington
Newport Pagnell
Buckinghamshire MK16 9NW
E admin@corneliusjones.com
W www.corneliusjones.com

**DNA PUPPETRY &
VISUAL THEATRE CO**   T 0161 408 1720
Hope Villa, 18 Woodland Avenue
Thornton Cleveleys, Lancashire FY5 4HB
E info@dynamicnewanimation.co.uk
W www.dynamicnewanimation.co.uk

INDIGO MOON THEATRE   T 07855 328552
35 Waltham Court, Beverley
East Yorkshire HU17 9JF
E info@indigomoontheatre.com
W www.indigomoontheatre.com

JACOLLY PUPPET THEATRE   T 01822 852346
Kirkella Road, Yelverton
West Devon PL20 6BB
E theatre@jacolly-puppets.co.uk
W www.jacolly-puppets.co.uk

LITTLE ANGEL THEATRE   T 020 7226 1787
14 Dagmar Passage
Cross Street, London N1 2DN
E info@littleangeltheatre.com
W www.littleangeltheatre.com

**MAJOR MUSTARD'S
TRAVELLING SHOW**   T 0121 426 4329
1 Carless Avenue
Harborne
Birmingham B17 9EG
E mm@majormustard.com

NORWICH PUPPET THEATRE   T 01603 615564
St James, Whitefriars
Norwich NR3 1TN
F 01603 617578
E info@puppettheatre.co.uk
W www.puppettheatre.co.uk

**PROFESSOR PATTEN'S
PUNCH & JUDY**   T 01707 873262
Magic. Puppetry
14 The Crest, Goffs Oak
Herts EN7 5NP
W www.dennispatten.co.uk

PUPPET THEATRE WALES   T 01446 790634
22 Starling Road
St Athan
Vale of Glamorgan CF62 4NJ
E info@puppettheatrewales.co.uk
W www.puppettheatrewales.co.uk

**TALK TO THE HAND
PRODUCTIONS**   T 020 7627 1052
Custom Characters Created & Performed
Studio 27B
Spaces Business Centre
15-17 Ingate Place
London SW8 3NS
T 07855 421454
E iestynmevans@hotmail.com
W www.talktothehandpuppets.com

TICKLISH ALLSORTS SHOW   T/F 01722 744949
57 Victoria Road, Wilton
Salisbury, Wiltshire SP2 0DZ
E garynunn@ntlworld.com
W www.ticklishallsorts.co.uk

TOPPER Chris PUPPETS   T 0151 424 8692
Puppets & Costume Characters. Created & Performed
75 Barrows Green Lane
Widnes, Cheshire WA8 3JH
E christopper@ntlworld.com
W www.christopperpuppets.co.uk

ALDEBURGH: Summer Theatre　**T** 01502 724462
July-August
The Jubilee Hall, Crabbe Street
Aldeburgh IP15 5BN
W www.southwoldtheatre.org

BELFAST: Lyric Theatre　**T** 028 9038 5685
Contact: Richard Croxford (Artistic Director), Clare Gault
(Theatre Administrator), Ciaran McAuley (Chief Executive),
Deirdre Ferguson (Finance Manager)
55 Ridgeway Street
Belfast BT9 5FB
E info@lyrictheatre.co.uk
W www.lyrictheatre.co.uk

BIRMINGHAM:
Birmingham Stage Company　**T** 0121 605 5116
Contact: Neal Foster (Actor/Manager)
The Old Rep Theatre
Station Street, Birmingham B5 4DY
BO 0800 3587070
E info@birminghamstage.com
W www.birminghamstage.com

BIRMINGHAM:
Birmingham Stage Company　**T** 020 7437 3391
Contact: Neal Foster (Actor/Manager),
Philip Compton (Executive Producer)
London Office:
Suite 228 The Linen Hall
162 Regent Street
London W1B 5TB
E info@birminghamstage.com
W www.birminghamstage.com

BIRMINGHAM:
Repertory Theatre　**T** 0121 245 2000
Contact: Roxana Silbert (Artistic Director),
Stuart Rogers (Executive Director)
St George's Court, 1 Albion Street
Birmingham B1 3AH
BO 0121 236 4455
E info@birmingham-rep.co.uk

BOLTON: Octagon Theatre　**T** 01204 529407
Contact: David Thacker (Artistic Director), Roddy Gauld
(Chief Executive), Lesley Etherington (Head of
Administration), Olly Seviour (Head of Production)
Howell Croft South, Bolton BL1 1SB
BO 01204 520661
E info@octagonbolton.co.uk
W www.octagonbolton.co.uk

BRISTOL:
Theatre Royal & Studio　**T** 0117 949 3993
Contact: Tom Morris (Artistic Director),
Emma Stenning (Executive Director)
Bristol Old Vic, King Street
Bristol BS1 4ED
BO 0117 987 7877
E admin@bristololdvic.org.uk
W www.bristololdvic.org.uk

CARDIFF: Sherman Cymru　**T** 029 2064 6901
Contact: Chris Ricketts (Director),
Margaret Jones (General Manager)
Senghennydd Road
Cardiff CF24 4YE
E artistic@shermancymru.co.uk

CHICHESTER:
Chichester Festival Theatre　**T** 01243 784437
Contact: Jonathan Church (Artistic Director), Alan Finch
(Executive Director), Janet Bakose (Theatre Manager)
Oaklands Park, Chichester
West Sussex PO19 6AP
BO 01243 781312
E admin@cft.org.uk
W www.cft.org.uk

CHICHESTER: Minerva Theatre at Chichester
Festival Theatre　**T** 01243 784437
Contact: Jonathan Church (Artistic Director), Alan Finch
(Executive Director), Janet Bakose (Theatre Manager)
Oaklands Park, Chichester
West Sussex PO19 6AP
BO 01243 781312
E admin@cft.org.uk
W www.cft.org.uk

COLCHESTER:
Mercury Theatre　**T** 01206 577006
Contact: Daniel Buckroyd (Artistic Director),
Theresa Veith (Executive Director)
Balkerne Gate, Colchester
Essex CO1 1PT
BO 01206 573948
E info@mercurytheatre.co.uk
W www.mercurytheatre.co.uk

COVENTRY: Belgrade
Main Stage & B2 Auditorium　**T** 024 7625 6431
Contact: Hamish Glen (Artistic Director/CEO),
Joanna Reid (Executive Director),
Nicola Young (Director of Communications)
Belgrade Square, Coventry
West Midlands CV1 1GS
BO 024 7655 3055
E admin@belgrade.co.uk
W www.belgrade.co.uk

DERBY: Derby LIVE　**BO** 01322 255800
Market Place, Derby DE1 3AH
E derbylive@derby.gov.uk
W www.derbylive.co.uk

DUBLIN: Abbey Theatre Amharclann na
Mainistreach　**T** 00 353 1 8872200
Contact: Fiach MacConghail (Director)
26 Lower Abbey Street, Dublin 1, Ireland
BO 00 353 1 8787222
E info@abbeytheatre.ie
W www.abbeytheatre.ie

DUNDEE:
Dundee Repertory Theatre　**T** 01382 227684
Contact: Ian Alexander (General Manager)
Tay Square, Dundee DD1 1PB
BO 01382 223530
E info@dundeereptheatre.co.uk
W www.dundeerep.co.uk

EDINBURGH:
Royal Lyceum Theatre Company　**T** 0131 248 4800
Contact: Mark Thomson (Artistic Director)
30B Grindlay Street, Edinburgh EH3 9AX
BO 0131 248 4848
E info@lyceum.org.uk
W www.lyceum.org.uk

EDINBURGH:
Traverse Theatre T 0131 228 3223 (Admin)
Contact: Orla O'Loughlin (Artistic Director), Linda Crooks (Executive Producer). New Writing. Own Productions. Touring & Visiting Companies
10 Cambridge Street, Edinburgh EH1 2ED
BO 0131 228 1404
E admin@traverse.co.uk
W www.traverse.co.uk

EXETER:
Exeter Northcott Theatre T 01392 223999
Contact: Kate Tyrrell (Chief Executive)
Stocker Road, Exeter
Devon EX4 4QB
BO 01392 493493
E info@exeternorthcott.co.uk
W www.exeternorthcott.co.uk

FRINTON:
Frinton Summer Theatre T 07905 589792
July-September
The McGrigor Hall, Fourth Avenue
Frinton-on-Sea, Essex CO13 9EB

GLASGOW: Citizens Theatre T 0141 429 5561
Contact: Dominic Hill (Artistic Director), Anna Stapleton (Administrative Director), Graham Sutherland (Head of Production)
Gorbals, Glasgow G5 9DS
BO 0141 429 0022
E info@citz.co.uk
W www.citz.co.uk

GUILDFORD:
Yvonne Arnaud Theatre T 01483 440077
Contact: James Barber (Director)
Millbrook, Guildford
Surrey GU1 3UX
BO 01483 440000
E yat@yvonne-arnaud.co.uk
W www.yvonne-arnaud.co.uk

HARROGATE:
Harrogate Theatre T 01423 502710
Contact: David Bown (Chief Executive). Mainly Co-productions. Touring & Visiting Companies
Oxford Street
Harrogate HG1 1QF
BO 01423 502116
E info@harrogatetheatre.co.uk
W www.harrogatetheatre.co.uk

HULL: Hull Truck Theatre T 01482 224800
Contact: Andrew Smaje (Chief Executive), Ian Archer (General Manager), Kate Denby (Producer), Philip Barnes (Finance Director), Nick Lane (Literary Manager)
50 Ferensway, Hull HU2 8LB
E admin@hulltruck.co.uk
W www.hulltruck.co.uk

IPSWICH:
The New Wolsey Theatre T 01473 295911
Contact: Peter Rowe (Artistic Director), Sarah Holmes (Chief Executive)
Civic Drive, Ipswich IP1 2AS
BO 01473 295900
E info@wolseytheatre.co.uk
W www.wolseytheatre.co.uk

KESWICK: Theatre by the Lake T 01768 772282
Contact: Ian Forrest (Artistic Director), Patric Gilchrist (Executive Director)
Lakeside, Keswick
Cumbria CA12 5DJ
BO 01768 774411
E enquiries@theatrebythelake.com
W www.theatrebythelake.com

LANCASTER: The Dukes T 01524 598505
Contact: Joe Sumsion (Director)
Moor Lane, Lancaster, Lancashire LA1 1QE
BO 01524 598500
E info@dukes-lancaster.org
W www.dukes-lancaster.org

LEEDS:
West Yorkshire Playhouse T 0113 213 7800
Contact: James Brining (Artistic Director/Chief Executive), Sheena Wrigley (Joint Chief Executive), Henrietta Duckworth (Producer)
Playhouse Square, Quarry Hil, Leeds LS2 7UP
W www.wyp.org.uk

LEICESTER: Curve T 0116 242 3560
Contact: Alex Smith (Assistant Producer), Paul Kerryson (Artistic Director), Fiona Allan (Chief Executive), Stella McCabe (Deputy Chief Executive), Iain Gillie (Executive Producer)
Rutland Street, Leicester LE1 1SB
E a.smith@curvetheatre.co.uk
W www.curveonline.co.uk

LIVERPOOL: Everyman &
Playhouse Theatres T 0151 708 3700
Contact: Gemma Bodinetz (Artistic Director), Deborah Aydon (Executive Director)
Everyman: 13 Hope Street, Liverpool L1 9BH
Playhouse: Williamson Square, Liverpool L1 1EL
BO 0151 709 4776
E info@everymanplayhouse.com
W www.everymanplayhouse.com

MANCHESTER:
Contact Theatre Company T 0161 274 0623
Contact: Baba Israel (Chief Executive/Artistic Director)
Oxford Road, Manchester M15 6JA
BO 0161 274 0600
E info@contact-theatre.org
W www.contact-theatre.org

MANCHESTER:
The Library Theatre Company T 0161 200 1536
Contact: Chris Honer (Artistic Director), Paul Clay (Executive Director)
Cornerhouse, 70 Oxford Street
Manchester M1 5NH
E admin@librarytheatre.com
W www.librarytheatre.com

MANCHESTER:
Royal Exchange Theatre T 0161 833 9333
Contact: Braham Murray, Gregory Hersov, Sarah Frankcom (Artistic Directors), Richard Morgan (Producer/Studio), Jerry Knight-Smith (Casting Director)
St Ann's Square
Manchester M2 7DH
BO 0161 833 9833
W www.royalexchange.co.uk

MILFORD HAVEN:
Torch Theatre T 01646 694192
Contact: Peter Doran (Artistic Director)
St Peter's Road, Milford Haven
Pembrokeshire SA73 2BU
BO 01646 695267
E info@torchtheatre.co.uk
W www.torchtheatre.co.uk

MOLD: Clwyd Theatr Cymru T 01352 756331
Repertoire. 4 Weekly. Also Touring
Mold, Flintshire
North Wales CH7 1YA
BO 0845 3303565
E admin@clwyd-theatr-cymru.co.uk
W www.clwyd-theatr-cymru.co.uk

MUSSELBURGH:
The Brunton Theatre T 0131 665 9900
Contact: Lesley Smith (General Manager). Annual Programme of Theatre, Dance, Music, Comedy & Children's Work
Ladywell Way
Musselburgh EH21 6AA
BO 0131 665 2240
W www.bruntontheatre.co.uk

NEWBURY: Watermill Theatre T 01635 45834
Contact: Hedda Beeby (Artistic & Executive Director), Clare Lindsay (General Manager). 4-8 Weekly. February-January
Bagnor, Nr Newbury
Berkshire RG20 8AE
BO 01635 46044
E admin@watermill.org.uk
W www.watermill.org.uk

NEWCASTLE-UNDER-LYME:
New Vic Theatre T 01782 717954
Contact: Theresa Heskins (Artistic Director), Fiona Wallace (Executive Director)
Etruria Road
Newcastle-under-Lyme
Staffordshire ST5 0JG
BO 01782 717962
E casting@newvictheatre.org.uk
W www.newvictheatre.org.uk

NEWCASTLE UPON TYNE: Northern Stage
(Theatrical Productions) Ltd T 0191 232 3366
Contact: Erica Whyman (Chief Executive)
Barras Bridge
Newcastle upon Tyne NE1 7RH
BO 0191 230 5151
E info@northernstage.co.uk
W www.northernstage.co.uk

NORTHAMPTON:
Royal & Derngate T 01604 626222
Contact: Martin Sutherland (Chief Executive), Laurie Sansom (Artistic Director), Dani Parr (Associate Director)
19-21 Guildhall Road
Northampton NN1 1DP
BO 01604 624811
E arts@royalandderngate.co.uk
W www.royalandderngate.co.uk

NOTTINGHAM:
Nottingham Playhouse T 0115 947 4361
Contact: Stephanie Sirr (Chief Executive), Giles Croft (Artistic Director), Andrew Breakwell (Director, Roundabout and Education)
Nottingham Playhouse Trust Ltd
Wellington Circus
Nottingham NG1 5AL
BO 0115 941 9419
E enquiry@nottinghamplayhouse.co.uk
W www.nottinghamplayhouse.co.uk

OLDHAM: Coliseum Theatre T 0161 624 1731
Contact: Kevin Shaw (Chief Executive). 3-4 Weekly
Fairbottom Street, Oldham
Lancashire OL1 3SW
BO 0161 624 2829
E mail@coliseum.org.uk
W www.coliseum.org.uk

PERTH: Perth Theatre T 01738 472700
Contact: Rachel O'Riordan (Artistic Director), Graeme Wallace (Head of Planning & Resources), Jane Spiers (Chief Executive). 2-3 Weekly
Horsecross Arts
185 High Street
Perth PH1 5UW
BO 01738 621031
E info@horsecross.co.uk
W www.horsecross.co.uk

PETERBOROUGH: Key Theatre T 01733 207237
Touring & Occasional Seasonal
Embankment Road
Peterborough
Cambridgeshire PE1 1EF
BO 01733 207239
E key.theatre@vivacity-peterborough.com

PITLOCHRY:
Pitlochry Festival Theatre T 01796 484600
Contact: John Durnin (Chief Executive/Artistic Director)
Pitlochry, Perthshire PH16 5DR
BO 01796 484626
E admin@pitlochryfestivaltheatre.org.uk
W www.pitlochryfestivaltheatre.org.uk

PLYMOUTH:
Theatre Royal & Drum Theatre T 01752 668282
Contact: Simon Stokes (Artistic Director), Adrian Vinken (Chief Executive)
Royal Parade, Plymouth
Devon PL1 2TR
BO 01752 267222
E info@theatreroyal.com
W www.theatreroyal.com

READING:
The Mill at Sonning Theatre T 0118 969 6039
Contact: Sally Hughes (Artistic Director), Ann Seymour (Assistant Administrator). 5-6 Weekly
Sonning Eye
Reading RG4 6TY
BO 0118 969 8000
W www.millatsonning.com

SALISBURY:
Playhouse & Salberg Studio   T 01722 320117
Contact: Gareth Machin (Artistic Director),
Michelle Carwardine-Palmer (Executive Director).
3-4 Weekly
Malthouse Lane
Salisbury, Wiltshire SP2 7RA
BO 01722 320333
E info@salisburyplayhouse.com
W www.salisburyplayhouse.com

SCARBOROUGH:
Stephen Joseph Theatre   T 01723 370540
Contact: Chris Monks (Artistic Director), Stephen Wood
(Executive Director). Repertoire/Repertory
Westborough, Scarborough
North Yorkshire YO11 1JW
BO 01723 370541
E enquiries@sjt.uk.com
W www.sjt.uk.com

SHEFFIELD: Crucible, Studio &
Lyceum Theatres   T 0114 249 5999
Contact: Dan Bates (Chief Executive)
55 Norfolk Street, Sheffield S1 1DA
BO 0114 249 6000
E info@sheffieldtheatres.co.uk
W www.sheffieldtheatres.co.uk

SHERINGHAM:
Sheringham Little Theatre   T 01263 822347
Contact: Debbie Thompson (Artistic Director)
2 Station Road, Sheringham, Norfolk NR26 8RE
E debbie@sheringhamlittletheatre.com
W www.sheringhamlittletheatre.com

SIDMOUTH:
Manor Pavilion Theatre   T 01395 579977
Weekly. June-September
Manor Road, Sidmouth, Devon EX10 8RP
W www.cvtheatre.co.uk

SOUTHAMPTON:
Nuffield Theatre   T 023 8031 5500
Contact: Patrick Sandford (Artistic Director),
Kate Anderson (Executive Director).
September-July. Tours
University Road, Southampton SO17 1TR
BO 023 8067 1771
E info@nuffieldtheatre.co.uk
W www.nuffieldtheatre.co.uk

SOUTHWOLD & ALDEBURGH:
Summer Theatre   T 01502 724462
Contact: The Jill Freud Company (Producer).
July-September
4 Foster Close, Southwold, Suffolk IP18 6LE
E enquiries@southwoldtheatre.org
W www.southwoldtheatre.org

ST ANDREWS:
Byre Theatre   T 01334 475000 (T/BO)
Contact: Jacqueline McKay (Chief Executive).
Not producing. Co-productions only
Abbey Street, St Andrews KY16 9LA
E enquiries@byretheatre.com
W www.byretheatre.com

STRATFORD-UPON-AVON: Royal Shakespeare
Company   T 0844 8001110 (T/BO)
Waterside, Stratford-upon-Avon
Warwickshire CV37 6BB
E info@rsc.org.uk
W www.rsc.org.uk

WATFORD:
Watford Palace Theatre   T 01923 235455
Contact: Brigid Larmour (Artistic Director/Chief
Executive), Mathew Russell (Executive Director)
20 Clarendon Road, Watford
Hertfordshire WD17 1JZ
BO 01923 225671
E enquiries@watfordpalacetheatre.co.uk
W www.watfordpalacetheatre.co.uk

WINDSOR: Theatre Royal   T 01753 863444
Contact: Simon Pearce (Director)
32 Thames Street, Windsor
Berkshire SL4 1PS
BO 01753 853888
E info@theatreroyalwindsor.co.uk
W www.theatreroyalwindsor.co.uk

WOKING: New Victoria Theatre,
The Ambassadors   T 01483 545999
Peacocks Centre, Woking GU21 6GQ
BO 0844 8717645
E wokingboxoffice@theambassadors.com
W www.atgtickets.com/woking

YORK: Theatre Royal   T 01904 658162
Contact: Damian Cruden (Artistic Director),
Liz Wilson (Chief Executive)
St Leonard's Place, York YO1 7HD
BO 01904 623568
E admin@yorktheatreroyal.co.uk
W www.yorktheatreroyal.co.uk

U →

Unions, Professional Guilds & Associations

Unions

What are performers' unions?

The unions listed in this section exist to protect and improve the rights, interests and working conditions of performers. They offer very important services to their members, such as advice on pay and conditions, help with contracts and negotiations, legal support and welfare advice. To join a performers' union there is usually a one-off joining fee and then an annual subscription fee calculated in relation to an individual's total yearly earnings.

Equity is the main actors' union in the UK. See www.equity.org.uk and their case study in this section for more details.

Do similar organisations exist for other sectors of the entertainment industry?

In addition to representation by trade unions, some skills also have professional bodies, guilds and associations which complement the work of trade unions. These include directors, producers, stage managers, designers and casting directors. These can also be found in the following listings.

What is the FIA?

The FIA (International Federation of Actors) www.fia-actors.com is an organisation which represents performers' trade unions, guilds and associations from all around the world. It tackles the same issues as individual actors' unions, but on an international rather than local level. Please see their case study in this section for further information.

I'm a professionally trained actor from overseas and I want to work in the UK. How do I get started?

If you are a national of a country in the European Economic Area (EEA) or Switzerland (excluding Bulgaria and Romania) you do not need to apply for permission from the Home Office In order to work as an actor in the UK. You will be able to look for and accept offers of work without needing a visa. Visit www.ukba.homeoffice.gov.uk/eucitizens/rightsandresponsibilites for details of your rights to enter, live in and work in the UK.

If you are from a country outside the EEA you will need to apply for a visa before you can work as an actor in the UK. You might want to visit www.bia.homeoffice.gov.uk/visas-immigration/working for full information.

You may also wish to join the UK's actors' union, Equity. For more information please visit their website www.equity.org.uk. If you can prove that you have relevant professional acting training and/or experience, you can also apply to join Spotlight to promote yourself to casting opportunities.

I am a UK resident and I want to work as an actor elsewhere in Europe. Where do I start?

A good starting point would be to contact the actors' union in the country in which you are hoping to work for information on their employment legislation. Contact details for performers' unions in Europe can be found in the following listings or obtained from the FIA www.fia-actors.com, who in most cases will be able to advise on what criteria you need to fulfil to be eligible for work.

As a UK national, you have the right to work in any country which is a member of the EEA without a work permit. You will be given the same employment rights as nationals of the country you are working in, but these rights will change according to the country you choose to work in and may not be the same as the UK.

For more general advice, the Foreign and Commonwealth Office (FCO) offers advice on living overseas and provides information on contacting the UK embassy in and relevant entry requirements for the country of your choice. Please see www.fco.gov.uk/en/travel-and-living-abroad for details. You could also visit Directgov's website www.direct.gov.uk/en/BritonsLivingAbroad for further useful guidance for British citizens living abroad.

You should also go further and start researching agents, casting directors, production companies and so on which are based in the country you wish to live and work in. Begin your search online and then decide whether to approach a person or company for further information once you have found out more about them. Learning the culture and becoming as fluent as possible in the language of your chosen country would be advisable, as this opens up a far wider range of job opportunities.

Unions

What are English Speaking Theatres?

English Speaking Theatres can provide British actors with an opportunity to work abroad in theatre. These companies vary greatly in terms of the plays they put on and the audiences they attract: they may aim to teach English to schoolchildren; help audiences develop an appreciation of English plays; or may exist simply because there is a demand for English speaking entertainment. Some are based in one venue while others tour round the country. Actors may be employed for an individual production or, especially if touring, for a series of plays. Performers interested in the possibility of working for this type of theatre company should refer to the 'Theatre: English Speaking in Europe' section for listings.

I am a UK resident and I want to work as an actor in the USA. Where do I start?

To work in America you will need a Green Card – a visa which entitles the holder to live and work there permanently as an immigrant – but you will not qualify for one unless you are sponsored by a prospective employer in the US or a relative who is a US citizen. Visit the US Embassy's website http://london.usembassy.gov/visas.html or alternatively visit the US Department of State's Bureau of Consular Affairs' website http://travel.state.gov/visa for information about the criteria you must meet and the fees you will have to pay. Relocation companies and legal services tailored to helping performers move to America can be found in the 'Accountants, Insurance & Law' section of Contacts.

Don't expect to be granted immediate entry to the USA. There is a limit to the number of people who can apply for immigrant status every year, so you could be on the waiting list for several years depending on the category of your application. You could enter the Green Card Lottery at www.greencard.co.uk for a chance to fast-track the processing of your application, although your visa will still have to be approved.

Finding employment from outside the USA will be difficult. You might want to try signing with an American talent agent to submit you for work, although there is huge competition for agents.

Try the Association of Talent Agents (ATA) www.agentassociation.com for US agent details. The most effective way to gain an American agent's interest would be to get a personal referral from an industry contact, such as a casting director or acting coach. You should also promote yourself as you would with Spotlight by signing up with casting directories such as www.breakdownservices.com

Acting employment in America is divided into union work and non-union work. The major actors' unions are AEA www.actorsequity.org and SAG-AFTRA www.sagaftra.org. As with any other union they protect and enhance the rights of their members and offer various services and benefits. You will only become eligible for membership once you have provided proof of a contract for a job which comes under a particular union's jurisdiction. Non-members can work on union jobs if a producer is willing to employ them. You can join more than one union, but once you have joined at least one you will be unable to accept any non-union work.

You may have to begin your career in America with non-union work, as experience or union membership in the UK does not make you eligible to join a union in the US. Work ungoverned by the unions could include student and independent films, small stage productions, commercials, voice-overs, extra work, and so on. You are unlikely to be paid well as non-union contracts are not governed by the minimum wages set by the unions, but you will be able to build on your CV and begin making yourself known in the US acting industry.

CASE STUDY

Phil Pemberton is the Campaigns & Publications Officer at Equity, the trade union for the UK entertainment industry. He works to provide a voice of authority for performers and the industry in general.

There are lots of good reasons to join a performers' union. The issues that impact most upon you as a performer will depend on your personal circumstances and your career, amongst other things, but the one thing that performers can be sure of is that Equity is the union that best represents your interests.

So, why should you join Equity? Here are ten good reasons to get you thinking…

1. Pay: Equity contracts set the minimum rates for employment throughout the entertainment industry and the provisions in our contracts protect members from exploitation and deliver minimum standards. The stronger we become, the more we push for improved deals. When members come together we can make real progress. In the last twelve months we've achieved a minimum wage of £500 in West End theatres.

2. Decent Treatment At Work: On everything from holiday entitlement to meal breaks and from health and safety protection to maximum working time, Equity has negotiated agreements across the industry to protect you from exploitation by unscrupulous employers and to increase awareness of best practice.

3. Equal Treatment: Regardless of your gender, your race or your sexuality, Equity works for equal opportunities across the entertainment industry and to end discrimination. Recent campaigns for greater opportunities for older women and for a media that is more representative of all sectors of the community have been high profile and continue to attract considerable support.

4. Protection: If your employers, managers or agents are treating you unfairly, Equity will be by your side to ensure that your rights are protected. Equity has a team of specialist organisers working full-time to represent your needs and we have strong legal support for when you need it.

5. Public Liability: For many performers, Equity's public liability insurance (which provides coverage of up to £10million) is an essential protection for their working lives and provides unbeatable value. If someone gets hurt during your act or if something gets damaged, then the knowledge that full insurance comes with your membership can help take the drama out of a crisis.

6. Compensation: If you are injured or get ill because of your working conditions our legal services can ensure you get proper compensation. We have specialist legal support and a 24 hour helpline if you need to make a personal injury claim.

7. Belonging: By becoming an Equity member you make a statement about your commitment to your vocation and your place within our industry. For almost 80 years Equity membership has been a symbol of unity in an industry where work is often transitory and geographically diverse. Your Equity card is a symbol of your professionalism.

8. Contribute: If you are serious about making a contribution to improving conditions for yourself and those you work with, the best way to help is to get involved in your union. In Equity our democratic structures mean your voice can be heard and that you can genuinely make a difference to your own working life and that of your fellow performers.

9. Influence: Equity is a major voice in the entertainment industry, contributing to public debate at local, regional, national and international levels. Our influence comes from the strength of our membership. Although we are not affiliated to any political party, we work with other entertainment unions to influence politicians and to protect your interests and the interests of the arts and media in general.

10. Pride: By being part of Equity you can be proud of your contribution to making your industry a safer and more rewarding place for everyone who works. Your membership makes our union stronger; your involvement gives your union greater influence. Working together we can make Equity a union we can all be proud of.

To find out more about Equity contact:
Guild House
Upper St Martin's Lane
London WC2H 9EG
T 020 7379 6000
E info@equity.org.uk
W www.equity.org.uk

Unions

CASE STUDY

The International Federation of Actors (FIA) is the umbrella organisation representing performers' unions, guilds and professional associations beyond national borders. Set up in 1952 by Equity and the French Actors' Union (SFA), it has spread to gather more than 100 affiliates in about 80 countries around the world. Together with its sister federation FIM (International Federation of Musicians) it is the only international trade body voicing the professional interests of performers at global level. It enjoys consultative status with the World Intellectual Property Organisation, the International Labour Organisation, UNESCO and the Council of Europe.

Increasingly, decisions are taken at supranational level that may have serious repercussions for the daily lives of hundreds of thousands of professional performers. Our remit at FIA is to anticipate change and ensure that performers' legitimate concerns are duly taken into account. Whether the focus is on intellectual property, core labour rights, cultural diversity, mobility, new media or any other issue that is relevant to them, we bring performers and their livelihoods right to the heart of the decision-making process. As other industrial players also actively foster their own interests at international level, our presence is essential to preserve an equitable level playing field for all. We work closely with other interested parties and their trade bodies across the industry to seek solutions to common problems, wherever possible, through dialogue and negotiation.

Our ability to speak with an authoritative voice relies on the collective strength of our members. To this aim, we relentlessly work to help performers around the world build knowledgeable and effective trade unions. Unions are a vital tool for performers as they secure them decent working conditions and a minimum safety net for them to make a living. They are resourceful contributors to the entertainment industry, as they structure dialogue, help prevent and solve conflicts, raise professional standards, promote excellence and campaign for the industry to continue to be successful and fairly reward its creative talent. Our committed work carries us to countries where our knowledge can truly make a difference and bring local performers hope for a better future. To this end, FIA is particularly active in

Africa, Latin America and Asia where we organise regular workshops and grow partnerships to reduce the divide between creative industries in developed and developing countries. We organise several regional meetings each year where unions in North America and in Europe can share experience, coordinate policies and respond to industrial developments.

We always strongly encourage performers to join and support their unions and offer our services to strengthen their network.

We are committed to raising professional standards in the industry and regularly publish researches, guidelines and basic advice for performers. With the cooperation of the International Labour Organisation, we recently completed a Health & Safety brief for performers working in live shows as well as in television and film production. We also released a collection of minimum terms of reference for dancers working in countries where there are no collective agreements in place as well as a pan-European study on gender portrayal in the entertainment industry.

We always strongly encourage performers to join and support their unions and offer our services to strengthen their network. We channel solidarity and expertise to our members and create mechanisms to extend assistance to performers when their work brings them far from their union's jurisdiction. Active membership in one of our affiliated unions gives performers privileged access to advice and counselling in many other countries where FIA affiliates are established.

FIA is the voice of performers in the world. By joining local unions, they can help us protect their interests more effectively beyond national borders. They can also help us make a real difference to many other fellow performers who still face very difficult conditions as they struggle to live by their creative work in less fortunate countries.

**To find out more about FIA contact:
31 rue de l'Hopital, Box 9
1000 Brussels, Belgium
T 00 32 2 2345653
F 00 32 2 2350861
E office@fia-actors.com
W www.fia-actors.com**

UNITED KINGDOM: BECTU - Broadcasting, Entertainment, Cinematograph & Theatre Union T 020 7346 0900
373-377 Clapham Road, London SW9 9BT
F 020 7346 0901
E info@bectu.org.uk
W www.bectu.org.uk

**UNITED KINGDOM:
CDG - Casting Directors' Guild**
Contact: Sophie Hallett
PO Box 64973, London SW20 2AW
E info@thecdg.co.uk
W www.thecdg.co.uk

**UNITED KINGDOM:
CPMA - Co-operative Personal Management Association** T 07876 641582
Contact: The Secretary
E cpmauk@yahoo.co.uk
W www.cpma.coop

**UNITED KINGDOM:
DGGB - Directors Guild of Great Britain** T 020 8871 1660
Studio 24, The Royal Victoria Patriotic Building
John Archer Way, London SW18 3SX
F 020 8870 3585
E info@dggb.org
W www.dggb.org

**UNITED KINGDOM:
EQUITY inc Variety Artistes' Federation** T 020 7379 6000
Guild House, Upper St Martin's Lane, London WC2H 9EG
E info@equity.org.uk
W www.equity.org.uk

**UNITED KINGDOM:
EQUITY inc Variety Artistes' Federation (Midlands)** T/F 024 7655 3612
Office 1, Steeple House
Percy Street, Coventry CV1 3BY
E tjohnson@midlands-equity.org.uk
W www.equity.org.uk

UNITED KINGDOM: EQUITY inc Variety Artistes' Federation (North West & Isle of Man) T 0161 244 5995
Express Networks, 1 George Leigh Street
Manchester M4 5DL
F 0161 244 5971
E info@manchester-equity.org.uk
W www.equity.org.uk

UNITED KINGDOM: EQUITY inc Variety Artistes' Federation (Scotland & Northern Ireland) T 0141 248 2472
114 Union Street, Glasgow G1 3QQ
F 0141 248 2473
E mcurren@equity.org.uk   W www.equity.org.uk

UNITED KINGDOM: EQUITY inc Variety Artistes' Federation (Wales & South West) T 029 2039 7971
Transport House, 1 Cathedral Road, Cardiff CF11 9SD
E info@cardiff-equity.org.uk
W www.equity.org.uk

**UNITED KINGDOM: FAA -
Film Artistes' Association** T 020 7346 0900
Amalgamated with BECTU
373-377 Clapham Road, London SW9 9BT
F 020 7346 0925
W www.bectu.org.uk

SOME THINGS ARE ONLY POSSIBLE WITH THE PROPER SUPPORT

www.equity.org.uk   ● info@equity.org.uk   ● 020 7379 6000

UNITED KINGDOM:
Musicians' Union T 020 7582 5566
60-62 Clapham Road, London SW9 0JJ
F 020 7582 9805
E info@themu.org
W www.themu.org

UNITED KINGDOM:
NAAA - North American
Actors Association T 07873 371891
Contact: By e-mail/Telephone only
E admin@naaa.org.uk
W www.naaa.org.uk

UNITED KINGDOM:
PMA - Personal Managers'
Association Ltd T 0845 6027191
E info@thepma.com W www.thepma.com

UNITED KINGDOM:
Writers' Guild of Great Britain T 020 7833 0777
40 Rosebery Avenue, London EC1R 4RX
E admin@writersguild.org.uk W www.writersguild.org.uk

BELGIUM:
ACV/TRANSCOM - Cultuur T 00 32 2 2890830
Galerij Agora, Grasmarkt 105 bus 40, 1000 Brussels
E info@acvcultuur.be W www.acvcultuur.be

BELGIUM: Centrale Générale
des Services Publics T 00 32 2 5085811
Place Fontainas 9-11, 1000 Brussels
F 00 32 2 5085902 W www.acod.be

BELGIUM: FIA - International
Federation of Actors T 00 32 2 2345653
31 rue de l'Hôpital, Box 9, 1000 Brussels
F 00 32 2 2350861
E office@fia-actors.com W www.fia-actors.com

DENMARK:
DAF - Dansk Artist Forbud T 00 45 33326677
Dronningensgade 68, 1420 Copenhagen K
F 00 45 33337330
E artisten@artisten.dk W www.artisten.dk

DENMARK:
Dansk Skuespillerforbund T 00 45 33242200
Tagensvej 85, 3. sal, 2200 København N
E dsf@skuespillerforbundet.dk
W www.skuespillerforbundet.dk

FINLAND: SNL -
Suomen Näyttelijäliitto T 00 353 9 25112135
Meritullinkatu 33, 00170 Helsinki
F 00 358 9 25112139
E toimisto@nayttelijaliitto.fi
W www.nayttelijaliitto.fi

FRANCE: Syndicat Français
des Artistes-Interprètes T 00 33 1 53250909
1 rue Janssen, 75019 Paris
F 00 33 1 53250901
E contact@sfa-cgt.fr
W www.sfa-cgt.fr

GERMANY: GDBA - Genossenschaft Deutscher
Bühnen-Angehöriger T 00 49 40 445185
Feldbrunnenstrasse 74, 20148 Hamburg
F 00 49 40 459352
E gdba@buehnengenossenschaft.de
W www.buehnengenossenschaft.de

GREECE: HAU -
Hellenic Actors' Union T 00 30 210 3833742
33 Kanigos, 106 82 Athens
F 00 30 210 3808651
E sei@sei.gr
W www.sei.gr

IRELAND:
IEG - Irish Equity Group T 00 353 1 8586403
SIPTU
Liberty Hall, Dublin 1
E equity@siptu.ie
W www.irishequity.ie

ITALY:
Sindicato Attori Italiano T 00 39 06 8417303
Via Ofanto 18, 00198 Rome
F 00 39 06 8546780
E sai@slc.cgil.it
W www.cgil.it/sai-slc

LUXEMBOURG: OGBL -
Onofhnagege Gewerkschaftbond
Letztbuerg T 00 352 64543777
60 bd. J.F. Kennedy, B.P. 149, L-4002 Esch/Alzette
E info@ogbl.lu W www.ogb-l.lu

NETHERLANDS: FNV -
Kunsten Informatie en Media T 00 31 20 3553636
Jan Tooropstraat 1, Postbus 9354, 1006 AJ Amsterdam
F 00 31 20 3553737
E algemeen@fnv-kiem.nl W www.fnv.nl/kiem

NORWAY: NSF -
Norsk Skuespillerforbund T 00 47 21027190
Welhavens Gate 1, 0166 Oslo
F 00 47 21027191
E nsf@skuespillerforbund.no
W www.skuespillerforbund.no

PORTUGAL: STE - Sindicato dos Trabalhadores
de Espectáculos T 00 351 21 8852728
Rua da Fé 23, 2ºPiso, 1150-149 Lisbon
F 00 351 21 8853787
E sind.trab.espect@mail.telepac.pt
W www.ste.com.sapo.pt

SPAIN:CC.OO. - Comisiones Obreras Servicios
a La Ciudadanaia Sector de Medios, Artes,
Cultura y Deporte T 00 34 91 5409295
Plaza Cristino Martos 4, 6A Planta, 28015 Madrid
F 00 34 91 5481613
E medios@fsc.ccoo.es W www.fsc.ccoo.es/medios

SPAIN: FAEE - Federación de
Artistas del Estado Español T 00 34 91 5222804
C/ Montera 34, 1ro Piso, 28013 Madrid
F 00 34 91 5226055
E federaciondeartistas@faee.es W www.faee.es

SWEDEN:
TF - Teaterförbundet T 00 46 8 4411300
Kaplansbacken 2A, Box 12 710, 112 94 Stockholm
F 00 46 8 6539507
E info@teaterforbundet.se W www.teaterforbundet.se

UNITED STATES OF AMERICA:
SAG-AFTRA T 001 323 954 1600
5757 Wilshire Boulevard, 7th Floor
Los Angeles, CA 90036
F 001 323 549 6095
E sagaftrainfo@sagaftra.org W www.sagaftra.org

UNITED STATES OF AMERICA:
SAG-AFTRA T 001 212 532 0800
260 Madison Avenue, New York, NY 10016-2401
F 001 212 532 2242
E sagaftrainfo@sagaftra.org
W www.sagaftra.org

UNITED STATES OF AMERICA:
SAG-AFTRA T 001 212 944 1030
360 Madison Avenue, 12th Floor, New York, NY 10017
F 001 212 944 6774
E sagaftrainfo@sagaftra.org W www.sagaftra.org

Index To Advertisers

Alphabetical Listing Of Advertisers

PHOTOGRAPHERS

PRODUCTION COMPANIES

PROPERTIES & TRADES

PUBLICATIONS & PUBLISHERS

REHEARSAL/AUDITION ROOMS/ CASTING SUITES

Index To Advertisers Contacts 2013

L

N →

Notes